British
Columbia
& the Canadian Rockies

**Yukon
Territory**
p243

**British
Columbia**
p107

Alberta
p42

dan Sainsbury

Contents

PGIAM /GETTY IMAGES ©

STEVERYMILL /GETTY IMAGES ©

ON THE ROAD

Contents

SPECIAL FEATURES

Welcome to BC & the Canadian Rockies

If you're searching for the promised land, there's a good chance you'll find it somewhere in the endless forests, inlet-punctuated coastline and meat-cleaver mountain ranges of Western Canada.

A Natural Show

Western Canada has historic sites, music venues and wonderful restaurants, but the real 'show' here isn't hidden away in a dark, dusty museum; it's paraded outside in a dramatically expansive landscape of mountains, lakes, plains, forests, rocky bluffs and storm-lashed beaches. You haven't fully experienced this spectacular corner of the planet until you've swum in a glacier-fed lake, run across an alpine meadow, followed in Indigenous footsteps across a remote mountain pass or watched a bear foraging for wild berries. Get in training!

Epic Adrenaline Rushes

West Coasters have been discovering ways to interact with the outdoors for decades, and there are countless operators that can help you do the same. Whistler morphs from skiing capital to mountain-biking bonanza. Banff and nearby national parks contain breathtaking trails. And Tofino is Canada's original 'surf city'. Recent years have added spine-tingling zip lines and *via ferrate* (fixed-protection climbing routes). Or you can do what the First Nations have been doing for thousands of years and hit the water in a canoe or kayak.

Urban Adventures

The wilderness is seductive but this region also offers sparkling city action. Alberta puts on a show with Edmonton's arts scene and Calgary's contemporary cowboy vibe, while British Columbia offers the best city-based shenanigans with two very different approaches. Provincial capital Victoria frames its increasingly cool scene with historic buildings, while Vancouver serves a full menu of ethnically diverse neighborhoods ripe for exploration. From slick Yaletown to cool Gastown to the West End's vibrant 'gayborhood', the 'City of Glass' is a place with many personalities.

First People

Responsible for more than 10,000 years of regional history, Western Canada's Indigenous culture is a complex story of creation beliefs, survival and diverse First Nations traditions. Piecing it together will take you from Haida Gwaii's towering totems to the chronicles of Vancouver's Museum of Anthropology. BC has 198 First Nations groups, nearly one-quarter of the Yukon's population claims Indigenous heritage, and Alberta is the heartland of the Blackfoot and Cree. Uncover their legends in galleries and cultural centers or listen to their stories in more than 30 languages.

Why I Love BC & the Canadian Rockies

By Brendan Sainsbury, Writer

I get my museum fixes in London and my musical pleasures in Cuba, but whenever I want an undiluted dose of the forest-covered, mountain-packed, wave-lashed 'natural world' in all its untainted glory, I don't have to stray too far from my front door in British Columbia. Four times the size of my native UK, BC (and the Rockies) is a place I love for its tolerance, diversity, optimism and big bold landscapes that fill me with a mixture of awe and exhilaration.

For more about our writers, see p320

Above: Yoho National Park (p220)

British Columbia & the Canadian Rockies

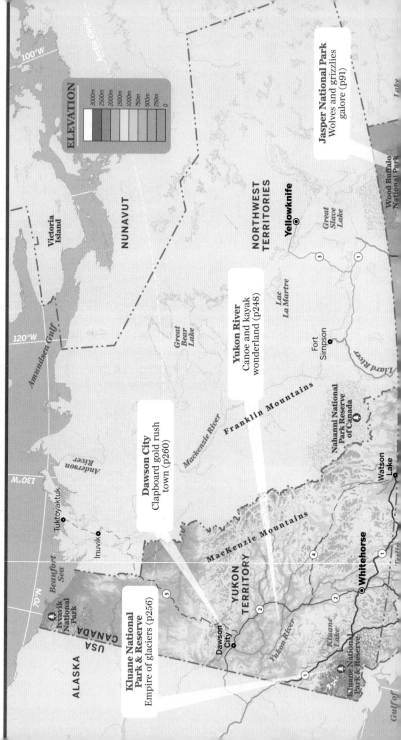

ELEVATION

3000m
2500m
2000m
1500m
1000m
750m
500m
250m
0

Kluane National Park & Reserve
Empire of glaciers (p256)

Dawson City
Clapboard gold rush town (p260)

Yukon River
Canoe and kayak wonderland (p248)

Jasper National Park
Wolves and grizzlies galore (p91)

ALASKA
USA
CANADA

Beaufort Sea

Tuktoyaktuk

Inuvik

Ivvavik National Park

Anderson River

Amundsen Gulf

Victoria Island

NUNAVUT

Great Bear Lake

Mackenzie River

MacKenzie Mountains

YUKON TERRITORY

Dawson City

Kluane Lake

Kluane National Park & Reserve

Whitehorse

Yukon River

Watson Lake

Nahanni National Park Reserve of Canada

Franklin Mountains

Fort Simpson

Lac La Martre

Liard River

NORTHWEST TERRITORIES

Great Slave Lake

Yellowknife

Wood Buffalo National Park

Arctic Circle

100°W
120°W
130°W
70°N

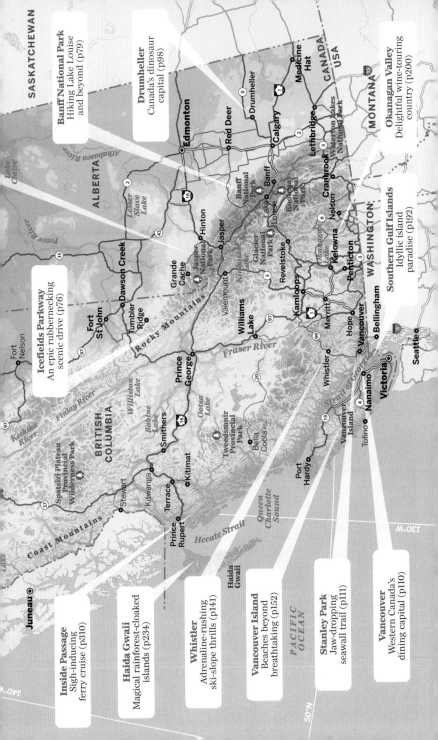

Banff National Park
Hiking Lake Louise and beyond (p79)

Drumheller
Canada's dinosaur capital (p98)

Okanagan Valley
Delightful wine-touring country (p200)

Southern Gulf Islands
Idyllic island paradise (p192)

Icefields Parkway
An epic rubbernecking scenic drive (p76)

Inside Passage
Sigh-inducing ferry cruise (p310)

Haida Gwaii
Magical rainforest-cloaked islands (p234)

Whistler
Adrenaline-rushing ski-slope thrills (p141)

Vancouver Island
Beaches beyond breathtaking (p152)

Stanley Park
Jaw-dropping seawall trail (p111)

Vancouver
Western Canada's dining capital (p110)

SASKATCHEWAN

ALBERTA

BRITISH COLUMBIA

CANADA
USA

MONTANA

WASHINGTON

Juneau

Seattle

PACIFIC OCEAN

50°N

140°W

130°W

Rocky Mountains

Coast Mountains

Fraser River

Strait of Georgia

Queen Charlotte Sound

Hecate Strait

Peace River

Athabasca River

British Columbia & the Canadian Rockies'
Top 17

1

Tofino

1 Even people with no eye for a picture can make photo art in Tofino (p178). The spectacular amalgamation of tempestuous ocean, brawny sea stacks, weathergnarled rainforest and velvety mountains is a sight to behold, especially when seen through the prism of one of those slow-burning West Coast sunsets. Add in a diminutive surf town that melds remarkably gently with its natural surroundings and you've got the makings of something very, very special. Wander deserted beaches, rent a longboard and go looking for whales or storms in the not-so-passive Pacific. Wonderful adventures await.

Lake Louise

2 No one should leave this mortal coil without first setting eyes on the robin-egg-blue waters of Lake Louise (p87) nestled bellow the icy hue of the Victoria Glacier and ringed by an impressive amphitheater of mountains. True, selfie sticks can often outnumber walking poles on the crowded lakeside promenade, but take a less obvious path to an alpine teahouse or through a valley of larch trees and you'll find that Homo sapiens soon get replaced by wilder company (bears if you're lucky). Welcome to Banff National Park's undisputed highlight.

MANUEL SULZER / GETTY IMAGES ©

LISSANDRA MELO / SHUTTERSTOCK ©

Skiing the Slopes at Whistler

3 Combining two mountains with a purpose-built but strikingly attractive alpine village that hosted the 2010 Winter Olympics, Whistler (p141) is the blueprint for all ski resorts. Want action? Snowboard over car-sized bumps on Whistler Bowl before hitting a boisterous pub at the gondola base. Want quiet? Go cross-country skiing in Callaghan Country and then sink into a giant Jacuzzi in a deluxe Creekside resort. Want cheap? Strap on snowshoes, fill up on cakes from Canada's best bakery and crash out in the nation's first capsule hotel. It's all here!

Stanley Park's Seawall Promenade

4 It sometimes takes awestruck visitors to remind Vancouverites they have Canada's finest urban park (p111) on their doorstep. But when you grow up alongside a 404-hectare temperate rainforest that's lined with multitudinous hiking and cycling trails, it's easy to think everyone is just as lucky. Stroll the park's 8.8km wave-licked, forest-backed seawall and you'll soon deplete your camera battery. But save some juice for the beady-eyed birdlife (especially the blue herons) around Lost Lagoon and a panoramic pyrotechnic sunset at Third Beach.

Wildlife Spotting in Jasper

5 Elk nose their way around the town's edge, nervous deer dart between the trees and seemingly giant bald eagles swoop high overhead. The dramatic mountain setting of Jasper National Park (p91) is enough to keep most camera-wielding visitors content, but the surfeit of wandering wildlife makes you feel like you're part of a 3D nature documentary. If you're lucky you might even spot the show's stars: grizzly bears snuffling for berries alongside the highway or, across the other side of a river, wolves silently tracking their next fresh-catch ungulate. Right: Bull elk

4

5

Dawson City

6 You're bouncing around for hours on some rickety old bus on the Klondike Hwy in the height of summer, not knowing whether it's three o'clock in the morning or afternoon, and suddenly you arrive in Dawson City (p260). Women in frilled skirts, straight out of a gambling hall, chat on wooden sidewalks, and a buzz of stories about gold can be heard everywhere. It's like stumbling into another world. Dawson City is small and remote, but also gloriously authentic, an ageing relic from a bygone era rather than a packaged theme park from the modern age.

Icefields Parkway

7 There are amazing road trips, then there's the Icefields Parkway (p76), a 230km-long ribbon of asphalt that parallels the Continental Dive between Lake Louise and Jasper, passing through some of Canada's most elemental landscapes en route. Giant mountains, mammoth moose, craning trees and gargantuan glaciers brood moodily from the sidelines. Most drive it, but riding it gives you more time to contemplate stop offs at cerulean Peyto Lake, powerful Athabasca Falls and the hikeable Athabasca Glacier, a frozen tributary of the colossal Columbia Icefield.

Paddling the Yukon River

8 Relive the days of craggy-faced gold prospectors by canoeing (or kayaking) from Whitehorse to Dawson City. Not for the faint-hearted and certainly not for the uninitiated, the 16-day Yukon River paddle (p248) will glide you past rough-and-tumble rocky landscapes lined with critter-packed forests. Keep your eyes on the water: you might feel like panning for gold if you spot something glittery. For a less intense taster, take a trip from Dawson City to Eagle City, Alaska: it's just three days.

Ferrying the Inside Passage

9 Relax in the golden sunlight on the outer deck of a BC Ferries' day-long sailing (p191) to Prince Rupert, an unusually gentle nautical odyssey guaranteed to slow heart rates to hibernation levels. With a soft breeze on your face, you can let the Inside Passage diorama roll past: sharp crags, tree-blanketed islands, red-capped light-houses and tiny shoreline settlements. Only the captain can stir you from the hypnotic relaxation with the announcement that a pod of breaching orcas is approaching.
Above: Cow Bay

ARTRAN / GETTY IMAGES ©

Dining in Vancouver

10 While a fancy dinner in Vancouver (p123) once meant rubbery steaks and baked potatoes, in more recent years this thriving metropolis has become one of Canada's foodie capitals. Start by trawling Granville Island Public Market for inspiration, grab lunch at one of the city's 100-plus food carts, then enjoy dinner at your pick of numerous top-notch restaurants. From shimmering seafood to authentic taquerias, Canada's best Asian cuisine and fresh-picked farm-to-table joints, the choice is only limited by your straining belt buckle.

Indigenous Culture in Haida Gwaii

11 Taking the ferry from Prince Rupert to this archipelago (p234) is like traveling to another country. Visit the Haida Heritage Centre and immerse yourself in the rich artistic culture of the people who have called this area home for thousands of years. You'll find intricately carved artworks, and current practitioners illustrate the resurgence of Haida culture. The magical Gwaii Haanas National Park Reserve offers mystical reminders of ancient communities.

Top right: Totem poles on Haida Gwaii

Wine Tasting in the Okanagan

12 Enjoying a winding trip around the bucolic, vine-striped hills of the Okanagan Valley (p200) region is the best way for any tipple-loving visitor to spend their time in Western Canada. There are dozens of wineries to tempt you, from legendary favorites such as Mission Hill Family Estate and Quails' Gate Winery to Summerhill Pyramid Winery, which ages its wine in a scaled-down replica of Egypt's Great Pyramid. One thing is certain: you won't go thirsty. Nominate a designated driver, and don't forget to dine: many winery tasting rooms are adjoined by excellent restaurants.

Hopping the Southern Gulf Islands

13 The islands (p192) off BC's southern mainland wink invitingly whenever you get close to the coast. But it's only when you take a short ferry trip that you realize how different life is here. Your body clock will readjust to island time and you'll feel deeply, and perhaps unexpectedly, tranquil. If you have time, visit more than one of these islands; each has a unique feel. Start with the Saturday Market on Salt Spring Island, then consider a kayak excursion around Mayne or exploring Galiano by bike.

Right: View from Galiano Island

DAVEMANTEL / GETTY IMAGES ©

Kluane National Park & Reserve

14 From the Alaska Hwy you get just a glimpse of the awesome beauty within the vast 22,015-sq-km Kluane National Park and Reserve (p256), one of the largest protected wilderness areas in the world. Hike for a day to the interior – or hop aboard a helicopter – and you'll witness an almost overwhelming, otherworldly landscape that has, not surprisingly, garnered Unesco World Heritage recognition. This is nature in all its grand, terrifying beauty.

Dino Digging in Drumheller

15 For kids (and adults) who are in that wide-eyed dinosaur phase, there's no better place on the planet than this desert-fringed Alberta town (p98). You'll find Canada's best dino museum here, which will indulge your child's insatiable need for facts, plus there's a chance to do a fossil dig and for photo ops with the world's biggest T rex (pictured) – a 26m-high fiberglass fella who looms over the town like Godzilla. Here, you're also in the heart of the Badlands, an eerie, evocative landscape where it's frighteningly easy to imagine giant roaming reptiles.

BIRDIMAGES / GETTY IMAGES ©

ICON SPORTSWIRE / GETTY IMAGES ©

Whale-watching in Victoria

16 While BC's compact capital city is lined with landmark historic buildings and has an excellent dining scene, you don't have to be a landlubber to have a great time here. Befitting its waterfront location, Victoria is a great spot to hop in a boat for a guided, ocean-sprayed visit (p158) with the region's orca population – if you're really lucky, you might even see a new calf or two. Either way, it's an unforgettable experience that will easily become a brag-worthy highlight of your trip to the West Coast.

Calgary Stampede

17 When you arrive at North America's best rodeo (p60), you'll be greeted by belt buckles the size of saucers and Stetson cowboy hats that could house small animals. But you'll soon be won over by this immersive introduction to cowboy culture; don your own hat and dive right in. Don't miss the buzzing midway fairground, the rootin'-tootin' live country music and the heart-stopping chuck-wagon races. When it comes to food, start with the barbecued steaks and then, if you're feeling adventurous, nibble on a prairie oyster or two.

Need to Know

For more information, see Survival Guide (p299)

Currency
Canadian dollar ($)

Language
English

Visas
Not required for visitors from the US, the Commonwealth and most of Western Europe for stays up to 180 days. Required by citizens of 130 other countries.

Money
ATMs widely available. Credit cards accepted in most hotels and restaurants.

Cell Phones
Local SIM cards can be used in unlocked European and Australian GSM cell phones. Other phones must be set to roaming.

Time
Pacific Time in most of BC and the Yukon (GMT/UTC minus eight hours); Mountain Time in Alberta (GMT/UTC minus seven hours)

When to Go

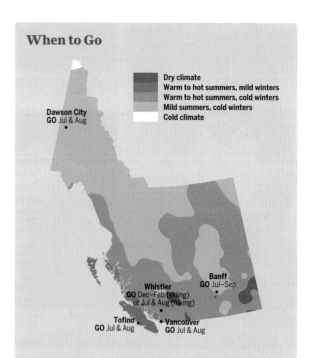

Dry climate
Warm to hot summers, mild winters
Warm to hot summers, cold winters
Mild summers, cold winters
Cold climate

Dawson City
GO Jul & Aug

Banff
GO Jul–Sep

Whistler
GO Dec–Feb (skiing)
or Jul & Aug (hiking)

Tofino
GO Jul & Aug

Vancouver
GO Jul & Aug

High Season
(Jun-Aug)

➡ Sunshine and warm weather prevail throughout the region.

➡ Accommodations prices reach a peak, sometimes 50% above low season.

➡ Festivals and farmers markets abound in communities large and small.

Shoulder
(Apr & May, Sep & Oct)

➡ Temperatures are cool but comfortable; rain is typical.

➡ Crowds and accommodations prices reduced.

➡ Hours for attractions outside cities are often reduced.

Low Season
(Nov–Mar)

➡ Snow and cold (below freezing) temperatures, especially in the north.

➡ The year's best hotel rates, except in ski resorts.

➡ Outside resorts and cities, visitor attractions may be closed.

Useful Websites

Hello BC (www.hellobc.com) The province's official Destination BC visitor website profiles regions and attractions and has an accommodations booking service.

Tourism Alberta (www.travel alberta.com) Official visitor site for the province, with download-able resources and accommodations listings.

Tourism Yukon (www.travel yukon.com) Official Yukon visitor site, packed with inspiring images and suggested experiences to help with planning a trip.

Lonely Planet (www.lonely planet.com/british-columbia) Destination information, hotel bookings, traveler forum and more.

Important Numbers

Dial all 10 digits when making local calls. Add 1 to the front of the number if the call is long-distance, even if it's within the same region (eg calling Whistler from Vancouver).

Country code	✆1
International access code	✆011
Emergency	✆911
Local directory assistance	✆411

Exchange Rates

Australia	A$1	$0.93
Euro zone	€1	$1.50
Japan	¥100	$1.23
NZ	NZ$1	$0.88
UK	UK£1	$1.70
US	US$1	$1.34

For current exchange rates, see www.xe.com.

Daily Costs

Budget: Less than $100

➡ Dorm bed: $30–45

➡ Campsite: $25–40

➡ Food court or street-food-vendor lunch: $8–10

➡ Transit day pass: $5–10

Midrange: $100–300

➡ En suite standard hotel room: $150–200

➡ Meal in midrange local restaurant (excluding drinks): $15–25

➡ Admission to top local attraction: $15–30

➡ Two drinks in local pub: $15–20

Top End: More than $300

➡ Boutique hotel or posh B&B: $250

➡ Three-course meal in good restaurant (excluding drinks): $75

➡ Car hire: up to $75 per day

➡ Ski day pass: $60–100

Opening Hours

The following standard opening hours apply throughout the region. Note that many attractions have reduced hours in the low season.

Banks 9am or 10am–5pm Monday to Friday; some open 9am to noon Saturday

Bars 11am–midnight or later; some only open from 5pm

Post offices 9am–5pm Monday to Friday; some open on Saturday

Restaurants breakfast 7am–11am, lunch 11:30am–2pm, dinner 5pm–9:30pm (8pm in rural areas)

Shops 10am–5pm or 6pm Monday to Saturday, noon–5pm Sunday; some (especially in malls) open to 8pm or 9pm Thursday and/or Friday

Supermarkets 9am–8pm; some open 24 hours

Arriving in BC & the Rockies

Vancouver International Airport SkyTrain's Canada Line runs to the city center ($8 to $10.75) every few minutes from 5:10am to 12:57am. Travel time around 25 minutes. Taxis to city-center hotels cost $35 to $45 (30 minutes).

Calgary International Airport Allied Airport Shuttles runs shuttle buses every 30 minutes from 8am to midnight ($15). Downtown-bound taxis cost around $40 (30 minutes).

Edmonton International Airport Sky Shuttle airport buses run to city hotels ($18), taking about 45 minutes to reach downtown. Taxis from the airport cost about $50.

Getting Around

Western Canada is vast with many transportation options, but car travel is the most popular way to move beyond the cities.

Car Good intercity highways encourage road trips. Vehicles are essential in far-flung areas.

Bus Good public transit in big cities; less comprehensive inter-city services provided by private operators across the region.

Train Efficient commuter rail transit in Vancouver, Calgary and Edmonton; limited VIA Rail and luxurious Rocky Mountaineer services in other regions.

Ferries Short- and long-haul routes serviced by BC Ferries along the western coastline.

For much more on **getting around**, see p309

If You Like...

Adrenaline Rushes

Whistler Canada's favorite ski resort is also packed with summer activities, from zip lining to white-water rafting. (p141)

Tofino Idyllic beaches and a spectacular wave-whipped waterfront make this Canada's top surfing spot. (p178)

Canmore Perfect for Rockies-region rock fans, the climbing here – including winter waterfall climbs – is superb. (p73)

Athabasca Glacier Avoid the too-easy bus tour and take a breathtaking guided hike on the icy surface, crampons included. (p76)

Mt Washington Vancouver Island's ski resort has recently installed a 2km-long zip line to lure in more summer visitors. (p184)

Wildlife-Watching

Jasper National Park Often stopping the traffic, the local elk – plus abundant deer, eagles and bears – make it perfectly clear who's in charge here. (p91)

Icefields Parkway Dramatic Rocky Mountains highway drive lined with jaw-dropping wildlife viewing. (p76)

Telegraph Cove Whale-watching operators prowl the seas around this favorite Vancouver Island departure point. (p189)

Khutzeymateen Grizzly Bear Sanctuary Around 50 of the salmon-snaffling furballs call the area around Prince Rupert home. (p233)

Northern Lights Wolf Centre A Yoho National Park refuge for the lupine critters, this is a great spot to learn all about wolves. (p218)

Historic Sites

Fort Langley National Historic Site The colonial outpost where BC was signed into existence offers a kid-friendly smorgasbord of activities and costumed 'residents.' (p137)

North Pacific Cannery National Historic Site You can feel the ghosts of canning workers past at this hulking wood-built former plant near Prince Rupert. (p233)

Head-Smashed-In Buffalo Jump With the region's most intriguing name, this fascinating indigenous interpretive center in Alberta recalls the local heritage. (p101)

Klondike National Historic Sites The gritty gold-rush days are on every street corner in Dawson City, where frontier buildings stud the area like shiny nuggets. (p261)

Barkerville Historic Town Stroll the streets of a pioneer town that once housed thousands of grubby frontiersmen, plus the occasional woman. (p230)

Diverse Food

Vancouver Canada's top dining scene is also its most diverse – from the best seafood to authentic Asian adventures. (p123)

Granville Island Public Market A stroll-worthy buffet of deli and bakery goods, and fresh fruit and vegetables. (p114)

Cowboy cuisine Alberta beef is second to none and Calgary is Canada's steak capital. (p62)

Salt Spring Saturday Market The biggest and best of hundreds of alfresco farmers and craft markets around the region. (p192)

Cowichan Bay Idyllic waterfront spot to sample goods from artisan cheese producers to gourmet farm-to-table restaurants. (p169)

Richmond A toss-up between Steveston's fish-and-chips and some of the best Chinese food outside China. (p135)

Arts & Culture

Audain Art Museum Whistler's sparkling art gallery would

be the pride of any European city. (p141)

Museum of Anthropology Best known for its spectacular array of northwest-coast indigenous art. (p115)

National Music Centre Calgary's music museum turns the spotlight on the sometimes overlooked heroes of Canadian music. (p58)

Vancouver Art Gallery This top museum has a keen eye for photoconceptualism and stages blockbuster visiting shows in summer. (p113)

Eastside Culture Crawl Vancouver's favorite grassroots art event is a wandering buffet of around 450 studios and galleries. (p121)

Art Gallery of Alberta Edmonton's fancy gallery is almost as striking as its mostly Canadian artworks. (p47)

Views to Savor

Maligne Lake This peak-ringed lake with its perfectly positioned island is a long-time muse for photographers and painters. (p91)

Lake Louise Glaciers, crags, tall trees and a robin-egg-blue lake make this one of the Rockies' signature viewpoints. (p87)

Stanley Park seawall Shoreline promenade where forest-covered mountains merge with shiny glass skyscrapers. (p111)

Tombstone Territorial Park The Yukon's rugged splendor, lined with sawtooth crags. (p266)

Tofino's beaches Always spectacular whether covered in mist, lashed by a storm or lit up at sunset. (p178)

Top: Ice climbing near Canmore (p73)

Bottom: North Pacific Cannery National Historic Site (p233)

Month by Month

January

It's peak ski season, with winter-wonderland views and temperatures below freezing in Alberta, the Yukon and much of BC; the south coast is warmer, with rain likely.

🍷 Winter Okanagan Wine Festival

BC's gable-roofed Sun Peaks Resort warms up with the winter Okanagan Wine Festival (www.the winefestivals.com), where ice wine is the major draw. Saturday night's progressive tasting crawl is essential.

⛷ Ice Magic Festival

Banff National Park's spectacular Lake Louise shoreline is the snow-swathed backdrop for this annual ice-carving event (www.banfflakelouise.com/area-events). Dress warmly and take lots of photos.

February

Spring may be in the air in southern BC, but winter dominates much of the region. Dressing for rain on the coast is advised, with thick coats (and hip flasks) suggested elsewhere.

🏃 Yukon Quest

This legendary 1600km dog-sled race zips from White-horse to Fairbanks, Alaska, through darkness and minus 50°C temperatures. It's a hardy celebration of the tough north. (p256)

⛷ Chinese New Year

This giant Vancouver celebration takes place in January or February, depending on the calendar each year, and it always includes plenty of color, great food and a large parade.

🍷 Vancouver International Wine Festival

Vancouver's oldest and finest wine party makes grape fans out of everyone in late February with its jam-packed, slightly tipsy galas and tasting events. (p121)

March

The ski season is winding up, though there are still plenty of great slopes to barrel down. Southern coastal cities and Vancouver Island are rainy.

April

Spring is budding across the region, but it's also a good time to bag deals on accommodations and snow gear in all the shoulder-season ski resorts.

⛷ World Ski & Snowboard Festival

One of the biggest festivals in Whistler, this hugely popular nine-day celebration includes dare-devil demonstrations, outdoor concerts and a smile-triggering party atmosphere. (p144)

May

Blossoms (and farmers markets) open up across the region, while bears are stirring from hibernation. Expect warmish sun in the south, and rain and late-season snow elsewhere.

🍷 Vancouver Craft Beer Week

Celebrating the region's well-established micro-brewing scene, Vancouver's top booze event showcases BC's best beer makers with tastings, parties and dinners. Arrive parched and drink deep. (p121)

June

Even in colder BC and Alberta areas the sun will be out, making this the time to consider donning your hiking boots and embracing the great outdoors.

☆ Bard on the Beach

This joyously West Coast approach to Shakespeare features up to four plays staged in a lovely tented complex on Vancouver's mountain-framed waterfront. Runs to September, but book ahead. (p131)

☆ Vancouver International Jazz Festival

Mammoth music celebration on stages around the city, including a generous helping of free outdoor shows. Book in advance for top-drawer acts. (p121)

July

It's summer and the living is easy for visitors who enjoy warming their skin under sunny skies. It's also

crowded, which means Banff and Jasper are super busy.

🎆 Canada Day Celebrations

Canada's version of July 4 in the US is the country's flag-waving annual birth-day party held on July 1. Expect celebrations across the region, with the biggest at downtown Vancouver's Canada Pl.

☆ Calgary Stampede

North America's biggest rodeo event is a rocking cavalcade of cowboy culture where everyone finds their inner wearer of Stetson cowboy hats. (p60)

August

Crowds (and hotel prices) are at their summer peak. Interior BC can be hot and humid, while the rest of the region is generally pleasantly warm and sunny.

☆ Edmonton International Fringe Theatre Festival

Canada's oldest and largest fringe fest lures thousands to Edmonton's Old Strathcona neighborhood for a multiday buffet of short but eclectic comic and dramatic performances. (p48)

🎆 Discovery Days

The pioneer-era streets of Dawson City are home to the Yukon's most popular annual event, a colorful weekend party of parades, games, races, and movie shows recalling the region's gold-rush heyday. (p263)

🎆 Pride Week

Canada's biggest and boldest pride event, this Vancouver party includes a massive mardi gras–style parade that draws thousands. Galas, fashion shows and saucy shenanigans keep things lively. (p121)

🏃 Crankworx

It's definitely summer in Whistler when the ski slopes become a bike park and this massive annual celebration of mountain-bike antics kicks off. (p144)

🎆 Vancouver Mural Festival

Taking over the backstreets of Mount Pleasant and beyond every August, this eye-popping street-art celebration has quickly become a city favorite. (p121)

September

A great month to visit: the crowds have departed, there are still stretches of sunny weather, and the colors are turning to fall's golden hues.

☆ Rifflandia

Victoria's coolest music festival lures local and visiting hipsters with dozens of live-music happenings at venues throughout the city. (p158)

☆ Vancouver International Film Festival

Starting at the end of September, this is the city's favorite movie-watching event. Book ahead for indie, international and documentary flicks. (p121)

October

Fall foliage is in full blaze but temperatures are cooling, while rain is returning to coastal communities.

🍷 Fall Okanagan Wine Festival

The Okanagan's annual wine fest (www.thewine festivals.com) sees numerous events including a Thanksgiving brunch and a 'wine awards' spread throughout the region's autumnal-hued rolling hills.

November

The ski season kicks off for some resorts while southern cities are unpacking their waterproofs.

🍴 Cornucopia

November in Whistler means this indulgent multi-day showcase of great food and wine. It's also a chance to dress up and schmooze at decadent parties. (p144)

December

The region is in festive mood. Temperatures are dropping and the snow is back in many areas.

✨ Santa Claus Parade

The best reason to stand outside in the Vancouver cold, this huge parade (https://vancouversanta clausparade.com) includes floats, marching bands and an appearance by jolly old Santa himself.

Top: Vancouver International Jazz Festival (p121)

Bottom: Yukon Quest (p256)

Itineraries

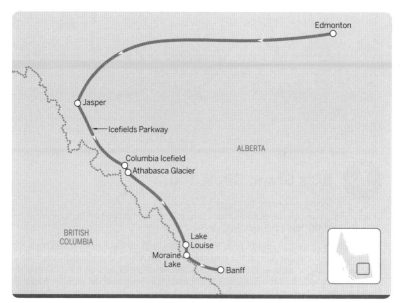

 Epic Rockies Roll

The Rockies are top of the list for most visitors to Canada. You can cover all the jaw-dropping highlights on this grand tour.

Start in gateway city **Edmonton**, spending a couple of days shopping, perusing museums and puttering around the Old Strathcona neighborhood. Then hit Hwy 16 westward for your first big drive: a half-day weave to **Jasper**. Check in for three nights, grab a beer at the Jasper Brewing Co and plan your wildlife-watching around the region's lakes and mountains. Next it's time to move on southwards via the **Icefields Parkway**, Canada's most scenic drive. It's shadowed by looming crags and studded with inquisitive bighorn sheep that peer at you from the clifftops. Stop en route at the **Columbia Icefield** and take a hike or truck tour on the **Athabasca Glacier**. After lunch at the nearby Columbia Icefield Discovery Centre, continue southwards to **Lake Louise** – take photos and wander the shoreline, saving time for a visit to the equally dazzling **Moraine Lake** a short drive away. Back in the car, you'll soon be in **Banff**. Treat yourself to a fancy hotel sleepover and spend the rest of your visit hiking flower-covered alpine trails and marveling at the epic World Heritage–listed landscapes.

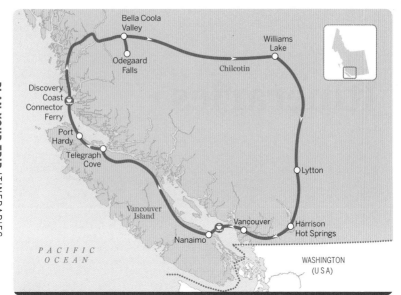

BC's Grand Circle Tour

2 WEEKS

There's much more to BC than its cities; take your time and head off the beaten path on this trip-of-a-lifetime circle odyssey.

Start your journey of discovery in **Vancouver**. Catch the BC Ferries vessel from West Vancouver's Horseshoe Bay for the short ride to **Nanaimo**, where you can sync into 'island time' and start to enjoy Vancouver Island's laid-back culture – it's distinctly more independent and small-town than the mainland. After spending the night in Nanaimo, head north on Hwy 19, taking an eastward detour to waterfront **Telegraph Cove**. Take a whale- or bear-watching tour here and check in for a night in one of Telegraph Cove Resort's restored cottages (book ahead in summer).

Continue north on Hwy 16 the next morning and check into **Port Hardy** for the night – if it's still daylight, consider an oceanfront hike. You'll have an early start to catch the **Discovery Coast Connector Ferry** the next morning (summer only), but it's well worth it for a languid all-day odyssey of coastline gazing with the ever-present promise of spotting eagles, whales, seals and more from the sun-dappled deck.

Arriving in tiny Bella Coola, which sits at the end of a long fjord, find yourself a rustic retreat for a few nights in the **Bella Coola Valley**. Spend your days exploring trails alongside huge old cedars and make the hike to pounding **Odegaard Falls**. Go for a river float and lose count of the grizzlies wandering the shores. When you leave, tackle the Hill, a thrill ride for drivers, and head east through the lonely **Chilcotin** area. Stop at the alpine waters of the little lakes along the way, or just take any little tributary road and lose civilization – what little there is – altogether. At **Williams Lake** say yee-ha to cowboy country.

Turn south on the Cariboo Hwy (Hwy 97), otherwise known as the Gold Rush Trail. The road follows the route of the first pioneers and gold seekers who settled in BC's unforgiving interior. From **Lytton**, head out white-water rafting on the Fraser and Thompson Rivers. After these chilly waters, warm up with a soak in **Harrison Hot Springs**. From here it's an easy drive on Hwy 1 back to Vancouver.

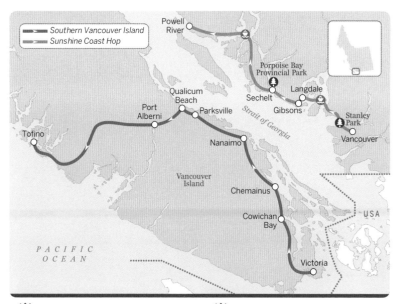

1 WEEK Southern Vancouver Island Jaunt

The BC capital is the perfect gateway for exploring the charms of Vancouver Island on a winding weave that links several inviting communities.

Start with two nights in capital city **Victoria**, giving yourself plenty of time to explore before departing northwards on day three via Hwy 1. Take your time weaving through the Malahat Mountain region, but allow time for a long lunch in the idyllic waterfront community of **Cowichan Bay**. It'll be hard to tear yourself away, but continue north to **Chemainus**, a former logging town now adorned with dozens of murals. It's not far to your sleepover in **Nanaimo**, the island's second city, where there are some decent restaurants and a popular museum. Next morning you'll be off to check out the friendly oceanfront communities of **Parksville** and **Qualicum Beach** – ideal for fans of beachcombing – before veering inland on Hwy 4 towards the dramatic west coast. **Port Alberni** is a handy lunch stop, but you'll likely be eager to thread through the winding mountain roads to **Tofino**. Spend several nights here soaking up BC's wild Pacific Ocean coastline.

4 DAYS Sunshine Coast Hop

It's hard to get lost on this easy escape from Vancouver; the area's only highway links all the main communities in a linear fashion. Drive on and enjoy a laid-back, island-like ambience.

Head north from **Vancouver** on Hwy 99 through **Stanley Park** and make for West Van's Horseshoe Bay ferry terminal. Take the Sunshine Coast vessel to **Langdale** and roll off onto Hwy 101, the region's main artery. After a few minutes you'll be in artist-studded **Gibsons**, an ideal lunch stop – try Persephone Brewing. Check into a local B&B, then take an early evening kayak tour on the glassy ocean. Rejoining Hwy 101 the next morning, continue on to **Sechelt** and consider a shoreline forest hike in **Porpoise Bay Provincial Park**. If you're lucky you'll also catch the summertime Farmers & Artisans Market, a great way to meet the locals. Stay in a waterfront B&B here, then hit the road early the next morning. You'll have a short ferry hop before arriving in **Powell River**. The area's top town, it combines old-school heritage and a funky young population. Stick around for a day or two of hiking and mountain biking, and be sure to toast your trip at Townsite Brewing.

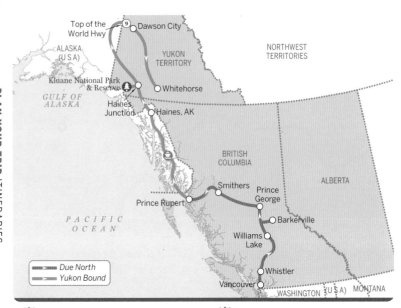

6 DAYS Due North

Southern BC lures the lion's share of visitors, but the north will always be calling your name. Dive in with this scenic weave.

From downtown **Vancouver**, drive through Stanley Park on Hwy 1 then join Hwy 99 northwards to **Whistler**. Spend the afternoon hiking or biking the summer trails and check into one of the resort's grand hotels; next morning continue north via Pemberton; keep your eyes peeled for towering Mt Currie. You're now in the heart of cowboy country, but it's probably too late to swap your car for a horse. After a five-hour drive, stop for two nights in a **Williams Lake** motel. Time your visit for the rodeo and you'll have a blast, or book a local white-water rafting tour. Next hit Hwy 97 towards Prince George – the heart of northern BC's logging country is about three hours away but stop off – via Hwy 26 – at **Barkerville**, an evocative recreation of an old pioneer town. After a **Prince George** layover, start early on the four-hour Yellowhead Hwy drive to **Smithers**, an artsy little town with cool sleepover options. Your final four-hour drive the next day delivers you eastward to **Prince Rupert**, northern BC's loveliest town.

2 WEEKS Yukon Bound

The best way to experience the north is to hop in a car and immerse yourself in some rugged Yukon-flavored wilderness.

Spend two days exploring **Prince Rupert** – the Museum of Northern BC and North Pacific Cannery are must sees – before rolling onto an Alaska Marine Highway ferry to Haines, AK. It's a two-day odyssey for which cruise ships charge a comparative arm and leg. Back on dry land, spend a night in **Haines, AK**. From here you'll be (almost) on the doorstep of one of the world's largest protected wildernesses. Around 250km away via the BC town of **Haines Junction**, **Kluane National Park & Reserve** is a vast World Heritage–listed realm of glaciers and mountains. Weave through the park and cross briefly again into Alaska to access the **Top of the World Hwy**. Continue on your merry way to **Dawson City**, Yukon's coolest old-school town. Stick around for two nights to enjoy the historic ambience, then head south on the Klondike Hwy for 538km to **Whitehorse**, the territory's capital. There are enough museums and galleries here to keep you occupied for another Yukon night.

Banff National Park (p79)

Plan Your Trip

National & Regional Parks

Canada-bound visitors often imagine towering sawtooth peaks, huge mirrored lakes and wildlife-packed forests, but what they're really imagining is British Columbia, the Rockies and the Yukon, home of the country's most awe-inspiring landscapes. From Unesco World Heritage sites to little-known expanses of wilderness, here's how to explore this region's awesome natural wonders.

Best Parks for...

Hiking

Pacific Rim National Park Reserve, Banff, Jasper and Waterton Lakes National Parks

Skiing

Banff National Park, Strathcona, Mt Seymour and Cypress Provincial Parks

Rock Climbing

Kootenay National Park, Stawamus Chief Provincial Park, Horne Lake Caves Provincial Park

Wildlife-Watching

Jasper, Banff, Wood Buffalo and Yoho National Parks

Kayaking

Gwaii Haanas and Gulf Islands National Park Reserves, Bowron Lake Provincial Park

World Heritage Sites

Banff, Jasper and Yoho National Parks, Dinosaur Provincial Park

National Historic Sites

Banff Park Museum, Head-Smashed-In Buffalo Jump, Gulf of Georgia Cannery

Where to Go

National Parks

These carefully protected parks of national and internationally recognized importance are the region's must-see attractions. They typically have excellent visitor centers and do all they can to maintain a successful balance between wilderness preservation and enabling tourist access.

Banff (p79) was designated Canada's first national park in 1885 and it remains its most popular, drawing in more than five million annual visitors. But its grand size means you can still escape into the backcountry and be wowed by its sheer-faced, glacier-cut peaks. It's often compared to its smaller sibling Jasper to the north. While Banff offers close proximity

to dramatic mountains lapped by ethere-ally blue lakes, Jasper (p91) is the region's center for watching incredible wildlife in its natural setting. And by wildlife, we mean the epic kind: bears, wolves, moose et al. That's not to say there isn't great mountain scenery in Jasper or wildlife aplenty in Banff, of course, but knowing this difference may help you choose between the two, if you have to.

High alpine adventure awaits around Rogers Pass in BC's Glacier National Park (p218), while the highlights of craggy and uncrowded Yoho National Park (p220) include spectacular glacier-fed lakes such as O'Hara and Emerald.

In BC's Kootenays region a multitude of microclimates are crammed into the comparatively tiny Kootenay National Park (p221), which straddles the border between BC and Alberta. Gateway town Radium Hot Springs is an ideal spot for a soak. Alternatively consider Mt Revelstoke National Park (p215), where you can hike wildlife-studded trails to the summit for views over the Selkirks.

Alberta is home to three other visually thrilling national parks: sublimely tranquil Waterton Lakes (p103), with its off-the-beaten-path location and network of alpine day hikes; giant Wood Buffalo, where the world's last free-roaming herd of wood bison hang out; and Elk Island (p54), a comparatively small park close to Edmonton that bristles with elk and plains bison.

The Yukon has two remote national parks: Vuntut and Ivvavik.

These are also national park reserves in BC and the Yukon. These are areas that have been earmarked as national parks, pending the settlement of indigenous land claims. They are managed in much the same way as national parks, with entry fees, visitor centers, and various environmental rules and regulations.

For more information on the region's national parks and national park reserves, visit the Parks Canada website (www.pc.gc.ca). Pick up a copy also of Lonely Planet's *Banff, Jasper & Glacier National Parks* guide.

Provincial & Territorial Parks

Alberta has more than 500 provincial parks and protected areas (see www.albertaparks.ca for listings), while BC is home to almost double that number (visit www.bcparks.ca for information). Among the highlights are Alberta's fossil-rich Dinosaur Provincial Park (p100), and Writing-on-Stone Provincial Park (p102) with its fascinating 3000-year-old aboriginal artworks.

The Yukon Territory's large parks (described in detail at www.env.gov.yk.ca) are called 'territorial parks.' These include the rugged, bird-studded **Herschel Island Territorial Park**, also known as Qikiqtaruk to the native people who still hold it sacred, and Tombstone Territorial Park (p266), a wild and windswept area of broad tundra-cloaked valleys and jaw-dropping hiking trails.

Alongside the region's provincial and territorial parks systems, there are hundreds of city parks and some of them are among Western Canada's must-see highlights. These include Calgary's Prince's Island Park (p58), and Vancouver's spectacular waterfront Stanley Park (p111), one of North America's finest urban green spaces.

CAIAIMAGE / JARUSHA BROWN / GETTY IMAGES ©

Yoho National Park (p220)

Need to Know
When (& How) to Go

Summer is the most popular time to visit Western Canada's parks, but that can mean rubbing shoulders with waves of tour groups at hot spots such as Banff, Jasper and Lake Louise. There are three ways to deal with this and ensure the magic of your visit. When you arrive at the

PARK TOUR OPERATORS

OPERATOR	ACTIVITIES	WHERE?	MORE INFORMATION
Athabasca Glacier Icewalks	guided glacier hikes	Columbia Icefield	www.icewalks.com
Brewster Travel	bus tours	Banff, Jasper and Columbia Icefield	www.banffjaspercollection.com
Cove Adventures	guided hikes to Cape Scott	North Vancouver Island	www.coveadventuretours.com
Discover Banff Tours	guided tours, including wildlife tours, of the region	Banff	www.bankfftours.com
Maple Leaf Adventures	multiday tours around Haida Gwaii (& beyond) on a vintage sailboat	Haida Gwaii	www.mapleleafadventures.com
Tonquin Valley Adventures	multiday horseback riding tours	Jasper	www.tonquinadventures.com
Up North Adventures	kayaking, guided bike trips & winter sports	Yukon	www.upnorthadventures.com
Yamnuska Mountain Adventures	guided rock climbing	Lake Louise	www.yamnuska.com

Kluane National Park & Reserve (p256)

aforementioned must-see spots, head off the beaten path and onto a less-trafficked trail. Secondly, add some less-visited national-park gems to your visit – Yoho and Glacier, for example, are great Rockies parks with far fewer visitors. Thirdly, consider visiting outside the peak summer period. Locals prefer late spring and early fall, at which times there are no crowds, the colors are more vibrant and the wildlife-watching – from post-hibernation bears to rutting elk and bighorn sheep – is often spectacular.

Fees

National parks charge for entry, and you'll need to display your pass in your car.

In large parks such as Banff and Jasper, passes are purchased at toll-booth-style barriers; in parks such as Vancouver Island's Pacific Rim National Park Reserve they're purchased at ticket machines or visitor centers. Daily fees go up to $9.80/free/19.60 per adult/child/family. If you're planning on visiting several parks over a number of days or weeks, the Parks Canada Discovery Pass is recommended. It costs $67.70/free/136.40 per adult/child/family and covers unlimited entry for 12 months to national parks and historic sites. The family passes include entry for groups of up to seven people (two adults only).

GREAT NATIONAL PARK HIKES

PARK	TRAIL	LENGTH (KM)	LEVEL
Banff	Lake Agnes	3.4	medium-hard
Jasper	Skyline Trail	45	medium
Pacific Rim	West Coast Trail	75	hard
Waterton Lakes	Carthew-Alderson Trail	19	medium
Yoho	Lake O'Hara Alpine Circuit	12	medium

Black bear, Jasper National Park (p91)

BC's and Alberta's provincial parks do not charge admission fees for day use. In addition, parking fees – which were first levied in 2002 – have been scrapped at most BC parks. Camping fees range from $5 to $25 per night.

The Yukon Parks system does not charge for entry to its parks.

Bears & Bugs

Wildlife attacks on humans in Canada's parks are rare, but you need to be aware that you are going to be encroaching on areas that some scarily large critters call home. While animals such as elk and deer may seem perfectly at ease with the cameras pointing their way in busy parks such as Banff and Jasper, Parks Canada works very hard to keep animals and humans from becoming too used to each other.

During spring and summer, black flies and mosquitoes blight the interior and northern reaches of BC, Alberta and the Yukon. The cumulative effect of scores of irritated, swollen bites can wreck your park trip. Bringing insect repellent is a necessity, as is camping in a tent with a zippered screen. In clearings, along shorelines or anywhere there's a breeze you should be safe from most bugs.

Driving Tips

Weather and driving conditions can change rapidly in the parks and wilderness areas of Western Canada. If you're driving in winter, expect snow. In addition, when you see an animal by the side of the road, the etiquette is to slow down and alert other drivers by using your hazard lights.

TOP FIVE PROVINCIAL PARKS

Try to weave in a visit to some of these parks. You won't regret it... and you'll have major bragging rights when you get back home.

➡ Bowron Lake Provincial Park (p230)

➡ Dinosaur Provincial Park (p100)

➡ Garibaldi Provincial Park (p139)

➡ Kokanee Glacier Provincial Park (p226)

➡ Strathcona Provincial Park (p187)

Plan Your Trip

Outdoor Activities

There's no deficiency of world-class hiking, mountain biking, skiing, kayaking, rafting and climbing in this region, and the experience will likely be one you'll brag about for years. Alternatively, rub shoulders with the friendly locals and watch someone else do all the work by taking in some popular spectator sports.

Top Short Hikes

Lake Louise, Banff (p87)
Stroll around the shore or hit the 1.6km uphill trail to the Big Beehive lookout for a grand panorama.

Stanley Park, Vancouver (p111)
A delightful tree-lined 8.8km seawall trail with ocean and mountain vistas.

Wild Pacific Trail. Ucluelet (p182)
Rain or shine, gale or breeze, this has to be Vancouver Island's best short coastal hike.

The Stawamus Chief Trail, Squamish (p140)
A short, steep 1.3km grunt up steps and smooth rock (with assisting cables) to the top of the legendary chief, with options to head higher.

Hiking

Hiking in this region ranges from a leisurely wander around Vancouver's salt-sprayed Stanley Park seawall to tramping across glaciers at the Columbia Icefield between Banff and Jasper. Whatever your fitness, a walk through nature is a must here.

On Vancouver Island, the spectacular Pacific Rim National Park Reserve offers some of nature's most dramatic vistas, with swaying old-growth rainforest fringing white-sand beaches. The park's signature West Coast Trail (p177) is a challenge, but it's one you'll never forget: rock-face ladders, stream crossings and wandering wildlife, plus the occasional passing whale, make it a rite of passage for serious hikers. It links to the lesser-known Juan de Fuca Marine Trail (p168) if you want to keep going. Atop Vancouver Island the remote North Coast Trail (p191) is equally dramatic but far less crowded – it's ideal if you like hiking without having other people around. You'll have a similar crowd-free ramble on the mainland's hidden gem, the Sunshine Coast Trail (p150).

In contrast, the Okanagan's Kettle Valley Rail Trail (p212) meanders over towering wooden trestle bridges in Myra Canyon. It offers hikers the perfect chance to explore this beautiful valley without having to worry about traffic or steep hills. It's also a popular bike route.

In the Rockies you'll find a hikers' paradise that will blow away even non-walkers. There are plenty of easy short walks at popular attractions such as the impossibly azure Lake Louise – turn your back on the tour-bus crowds and you'll suddenly feel at one with the vastness of nature. Banff is the hot spot for Rockies hikers and its best routes include Healy Pass near the BC border and the aptly named Paradise Valley near Lake Louise. Also consider migrating to the lesser-known (by the international crowd) Kananaskis Country, or the ample spaces of Jasper crowned by the multiday, above-the-tree-line Skyline Trail.

Those curious about doing a three- to four-day hike through a national historic site that spans two countries should check out the steep and difficult Chilkoot Trail, half in Alaska and half in the extreme northwest corner of BC. It's still lined with the detritus of those who desperately tried to seek their fortune during the gold rush. Further north in the Yukon, Kluane National Park and Reserve and Tombstone Territorial Park offer world-class challenges, as well as spectacles such as thousands of migrating caribou.

Cycling & Mountain Biking

Mountain biking is as huge as the mountains in BC and the Rockies. This is the birthplace of 'freeride,' which combines downhill and dirt jumping.

Home to some of BC's best technical trails, Rossland and its West Kootenay surroundings is a pedal-tastic hot spot. On the opposite side of the province, the village of Cumberland on Vancouver Island has a vast network of varied trails managed and maintained by a local non-profit (see www. cumberland.ca/mountain-biking) .You'll find a similar setup – and a burgeoning local scene – on Vancouver's North Shore. See www.nsmba.ca for more information on this area. The Sunshine Coast's Powell River is also worth checking out; see www. bikepowellriver.ca. Visit www.mountain bikingbc.ca for an introduction to the wider region.

Whistler has the province's best-organized mountain-bike park, with jumps, beams and bridges winding through 200km of maintained downhill trails. In summer the resort hosts the giant Crankworx festival (www.crankworx.com), a pedal-packed nirvana of contests, demos and live music.

Back in the urban sprawl, Victoria is one of Canada's best cycling cities, closely trailed by Vancouver, which has been carving out new citywide routes for cyclists in recent years. The city has also just introduced a public bike-share scheme.

In the Rockies region, Canmore and Banff are biking hot spots, with the latter offering a good combination of road and off-road options and plenty of wildlife-spotting opportunities. The two towns are linked by the paved (and well-used) Legacy trail and the quieter off-road Goat Creek trail.

If you're in the Yukon, there are more than 800km of trails extending from Whitehorse.

Skiing & Snowboarding

If you're staying in Vancouver, you can be on the slopes within 30 minutes' drive, while Whistler, one of North America's largest and best-equipped ski resorts, is just another hour away.

Many would argue that there's even better skiing to be found in BC's east, where

PEDAL-TASTIC NELSON

Free-riding pedalheads have plenty of favorite spots in British Columbia and the Rockies, but many also enjoy the bikey ambience of just hanging out in a cool community. In the heart of the Kootenay Rockies region, Nelson – which many locals will tell you is the coolest small town in BC – fits the bill perfectly. The historic downtown area is lined with funky hangouts (an after-ride Nelson Brewing beer is recommended), while the surrounding area is striped with great trails, from the epic downhill of Mountain Station to the winding Svoboda Road Trails in West Arm Provincial Park.

SKIING HOT SPOTS

BC has 13 major ski resorts and the Albertan Rockies half-a-dozen more. Here are some of the best:

Apex Mountain Resort (p206) Known for its plethora of double-black-diamond and technical runs (the drop is more than 600m), as well as gladed chutes and vast powdery bowls. Near Penticton.

Banff National Park ski resorts Three excellent mountain resorts, Ski Banff@ Norquay (p83), Sunshine Village (p83) and the Lake Louise Ski Area (p89), offer 250 runs of every description. Sunshine Village is the most popular. Lake Louise is the third largest in Canada.

Big White Ski Resort (p206) BC's highest ski resort features 119 runs and is excellent for downhill and backcountry skiing. The drop is 777m and you can night ski. Near Kelowna.

Cypress Mountain (p120) The most comprehensive of Vancouver's three sentinel skiing mountains, with 53 runs and 19km of cross-country trails.

Fernie Alpine Resort (p223) With 142 runs across five large bowls, there's plenty of virgin powder where you can leave your mark. Near the town of Fernie.

Grouse Mountain (p120) A short bus and gondola ride from Vancouver, Grouse is a favorite for night skiing and snowboarding.

Kicking Horse Mountain Resort (p218) Many of the runs here are rated advanced or expert. A gondola gives you a great vantage over the 1260m vertical of this relatively snow-heavy location. Near Golden.

Kimberley Alpine Resort (p224) A good all-round resort, especially if you like smaller ones with comparatively minimal nightlife. Near the town of Kimberley.

Mt Seymour (☑604-986-2261; www.mountseymour.com; 1700 Mt Seymour Rd, North Vancouver; adult/youth(13–18yr)/child $51/44/24; ☺9:30am-10pm Mon-Fri, from 8:30am Sat & Sun Dec-Apr) Some 1000m up, this North Shore provincial resort offers popular runs, including Brockton, Mystery Peak and Mushroom Junior Park. This is where most Vancouverites learn to ski. Near North Vancouver.

Mt Washington Alpine Resort (p184) Vancouver Island's main ski resort, with dozens of runs, plus cross-country trails and a snowshoe park. Near Comox.

Revelstoke Mountain Resort (p215) Opened in 2007, this resort has 40 runs with a focus on intermediate and advanced runs. Heli-skiing operators can take you out to track-free bowls across the ranges. Near Revelstoke.

Silver Star (p214) With 132 runs and a pioneer-town atmosphere, Silver Star has 12 lifts and a 760m vertical drop. Near Vernon.

Sun Peaks Resort (p200) BC's second-largest resort, with three mountains and more than 130 runs. Snowshoeing, dog sledding and Nordic skiing also available. Near Kamloops.

Whistler-Blackcomb (p143) This world-famous, dual-mountain paradise was the host resort for the 2010 Winter Olympic Games. Its lifts include the 4.4km-long gondola linking Mts Whistler and Blackcomb. Lists 37 lifts and more than 200 runs to keep the international crowds happy.

vast swaths of mountains – especially in the Kootenays – are annually covered by 10m or more of snow. This region now promotes the 'Powder Hwy,' a marketing moniker for a series of roads linking the major ski resorts.

Beating all-comers in the snowfall competition is the oft-overlooked Mt Washington Alpine Resort (p184) on Vancouver Island.

Elsewhere in the province, the Okanagan has resorts such as Sun Peaks (p200), Apex (p206) and Big White (p206), recording good snow year after year. Snowpack here ranges from 2m to more than 6m, depending on how close the resort is to the Pacific Ocean.

You'll slide through giant Gothic landscapes in the Rockies, especially at Sunshine Village (p83) in Banff National Park. For amazing cross-country skiing, head to Canmore, where the trails were part of the Canadian Winter Olympics held in Calgary in 1988, and Whistler's Olympic Park (p143), which hosted the 2010 Games.

For insights and resources covering the region and beyond, check the website of the Canadian Ski Council (www.skicanada.org).

Rock Climbing & Mountaineering

All those inviting crags you've spotted on your trip are an indication that Western Canada is a major climbing capital, ideal for both short rock routes and multiday alpine ascents.

Near Banff, the Rocky Mountain resort town of Canmore is an ideal first stop, no matter what your skill level. Climbing stores, the **Yamnuska Mountain Adventures** (☑403-678-4164; www.yamnuska. com; 50 Lincoln Park, Suite 200; ☻8:30am-5pm Mon-Sat) climbing school and thousands of limestone sport climbs within a 30-minute drive make this a one-stop shop for rock fans.

Further west, BC's Squamish 'Chief' is the highlight – home to many challenging routes – of a burgeoning local scene that includes dozens of area peaks. Tap the local scene via **Squamish Rock Guides** (☑604-892-7816; www.squamishrockguides.com; guided rock climbs half-day/day from $100/140).

If mountaineering is more your thing, the Rockies are, not surprisingly, a hot spot. On the border between BC and Alberta, Mt Assiniboine is the Matterhorn of Canada. Other western classics include Jasper's Mt Edith Cavell (p77), BC's Mt Robson, and Sir Donald in the Rockies. Closer to Vancouver, Garibaldi Peak in Garibaldi Provincial Park (p139) lures many city-based climbers for weekend jaunts.

If you need a guide, check in with the excellent Alpine Club of Canada (www.alpineclubofcanada.ca).

Diving

Justly famous for its superb, albeit chilly, conditions, BC features three of the top-ranked ocean dive spots in the world: Vancouver Island, the Sunshine Coast and the Gulf Islands. It's best to go in winter, when the plankton has decreased and visibility is at its best.

The water temperature drops to between 7°C and 10°C in winter; in summer, it may reach 15°C. Expect to see a full range of marine life, including oodles of crabs, from tiny hermits to intimidating kings. If you're lucky you may also encounter seals and sea lions, or bizarre creatures such as wolf eels and large Pacific octopuses.

Popular Vancouver Island dive areas include Port Hardy and Campbell River, but Nanaimo also lures many with its aquatic wildlife and its three sunk-to-order navy vessels that are now vibrant marine habitats.

For more information and operator listings for BC, see www.diveindustry association.com.

Water Sports

BC and beyond offers hundreds of opportunities for those who like messing about on the water. Lakes, rivers and coastline abound, just waiting for the dip of an oar. Major paddling spots usually have stations where you can rent kayaks, canoes and stand-up paddleboards.

Inland

The 116km Bowron Lake canoe circuit in Bowron Lake Provincial Park is one of the world's great canoe trips, covering 10 lakes with easy portages between each. Slightly less fabled – and less crowded – is another 100km-plus circuit in Wells Gray Provincial Park.

During the short Yukon summer, scores of paddlers from around the world head to the famed Yukon River and its tributaries, the route of the Klondike gold rush. You can still experience the stunning raw wilderness that the prospectors encountered, but from a modern canoe or kayak rather

WINDSURFING & KITEBOARDING

The breeze-licked tidal flats around Vancouver are popular with windsurfers. On many a day you'll see scores of colorful sails darting around the shallows like flocks of birds – it's a signature photo from the Kitsilano coastline. But further north, Squamish is the real center of the region's kiteboarding and windsurfing frenzy: an hour from Vancouver, its windwhipped Squamish Spit area is often studded with adrenaline-fueled locals. Stand-up paddleboarding is also taking off in the region: consider Deep Cove, on Vancouver's North Shore, for an introduction.

than a raft of lashed-together logs. Whitehorse is the center for guides and gear.

For shorter day paddles, Banff has several operators if you'd like to kayak the region's glassy, mountain-backed lakes.

For the ultimate adrenaline rush, try white-water rafting. Rugged canyons and seasonal melting snow make BC's rivers great for white-water action. You don't need to be experienced to have a go, as licensed commercial rafting operators offer guided tours for all abilities. Trips can last from three hours (average cost $100 per person) up to a couple of weeks. Popular areas include the Thompson River near Lytton, and the Kootenays – many consider the Kicking Horse River near Golden to be one of province's best raft trips. In the Yukon, Haines Junction is a good base, while in the Rockies the Jasper region has several popular operators offering trips on the grade II to III Athabasca and Sunwapta Rivers.

Coast

Although some people swear by their ocean-going canoes, the BC coast is truly the domain of kayaks. Since people first stretched skin over a frame and deployed a double paddle some 4000 years ago, these little crafts have been an excellent marriage of human and mode.

Options are as numerous as BC's endlessly crenulated coast and islands. The greatest concentration of outfitters is on Vancouver Island, which is one big paddling playground. The Broken Group Islands offer BC's best wilderness kayaking – they're revered for their remoteness and rugged natural beauty, and provide the opportunity to kayak to little islands and camp overnight.

It's always safest to kayak with other people. Someone in the group should know how to plot a course by navigational chart and compass, pilot in fog, read weather patterns, assess water hazards, interpret tide tables, handle boats in adverse conditions, and perform group and self-rescues. Always check weather forecasts before setting out, and don't expect your cell (mobile) phone to work.

If you have only a short time, you can rent a kayak for a few hours, or take an introductory lesson in pretty much any of Vancouver Island's coastal towns.

Urban paddlers can take in Vancouver's cityscape from the waters of False Creek (rentals available on Granville Island).

Horseback Riding

Surveying the region's spectacular scenery from between the perky ears of a trusty steed is highly recommended: feel free to bring a costume and release your inner Mountie. BC's Cariboo and Chilcotin regions have long been horseback-riding areas: you can stay on a ranch there or climb into the saddle for a tour. Alternatively, in the midst of the Great Bear Rainforest, there are plenty of trails to explore in the Bella Coola Valley. Saddling up in Banff or Jasper is one of the best ways to feel at one with the region, while Calgary is the home of the cowboy – drop by in summer for the spectacular Calgary Stampede (p60) rodeo fest, or check out your options on the region's cool Cowboy Trail (www.thecowboytrail.com).

Regions at a Glance

This region encompasses the adjoining provinces of British Columbia and Alberta, plus the less populated Yukon Territory, a remote northern wilderness next to Alaska. Incorporated are five national parks (Banff, Jasper, Yoho, Kootenay and Waterton) that make up Canada's World Heritage–listed Rocky Mountain Parks. Each offers spectacular outdoor vistas and once-in-a-lifetime experiences, but they also have distinctions you'll want to know about before planning your trip.

Southern coastal BC and the Rockies region attract the lion's share of visitors. Their biggest draws are Vancouver – cosmopolitan metropolis and gateway to Whistler, Victoria and wider Vancouver Island – and the iconic Banff and Jasper National Parks, which lure with wildlife-packed mountains. But if your idea of communing with nature means leaving the crowds behind, the vast and unremitting Yukon may be your promised land.

Alberta

Paleontology
Festivals
Indigenous Culture

Drumheller Dinosaurs

Only in Alberta can you witness a giant fiberglass T rex juxtaposed with a revered 'royal' museum containing Canada's largest collection of dinosaur fossils. Drive to Drumheller for the details.

On the Fringe

Edmonton might not be the world's hippest city, but it does host North America's largest fringe festival – 10 days of excitement, experimentation and eccentricity.

Head-Smashed-In Buffalo Jump

Along with its fantastic name, this Unesco World Heritage site harbors an excellent museum and interpretive center perched on the bluff of a sandstone cliff that details the culture and lifestyle of the Blackfoot people.

p42

British Columbia

Coastal Scenery
Food & Drink
Outdoor Activities

Ocean Vistas

The vast, multi-fjorded BC coastline defines a visit to this region, whether you're strolling the Stanley Park seawall, hiking Vancouver Island's rugged West Coast Trail or reclining on a BC Ferries deck and watching for passing orcas.

Locavores United

From Vancouver's top restaurant tables to produce-packed farmers markets throughout the province, BC's local bounty is a foodie's delight. Seafood is the way to go, preferably coupled with regional wine or craft beer.

Adrenaline Rush

From ski resorts large and small to life-enhancing hiking, mountain biking, kayaking and beyond, visitors will never run out of ways to challenge themselves in the great outdoors. Start small with a forest stroll and you'll be zip lining through the valleys in no time.

p107

Yukon Territory

Rich History
Raw Nature
Outdoor Activities

Gold Rush

The imprint of the 1898 Klondike gold rush is indelible here, especially on the clapboard streets of old Dawson City. You wouldn't be surprised to see a wily-faced geezer run down the main drag proclaiming his discovery – though if you do, it's probably time to stop drinking.

Spectacular Beauty

You won't have to jostle with the kind of crowds that flock to the Rockies at remote Kluane National Park and Reserve, and you'll be rewarded for your persistence with a vast, World Heritage–listed wonderland of glacier-sliced mountains. Humbling is the word.

Frontier Kayaking

Recreate the early days of gritty pioneer exploration by traveling the way they used to: by canoe or kayak along the Yukon River. Gold panning along the way is optional.

p243

On the Road

Alberta

POP 4,067,000

Best Places to Eat

➡ Corso 32 (p52)
➡ Market (p63)
➡ 49° North Pizza (p104)
➡ Trough (p75)

Best Places to Stay

➡ Deer Lodge (p90)
➡ Tekarra Lodge (p44)
➡ Mt Engadine Lodge (p72)
➡ Varscona (p50)

Why Go?

Alberta does lakes and mountains like Rome does cathedrals and chapels, but without the penance. For proof head west to Jasper and Banff, two of the world's oldest national parks; despite their wild and rugged terrain, they remain untrammeled and easily accessible. They're majestic, breathtaking, awesome. No one should leave without first laying eyes on Peyto Lake and the Columbia Icefield, nor before traveling east to the fossil-encrusted badlands around Drumheller, south to the Crypt Lake trail in Waterton Lakes National Park, and north to spot bison in the vast, empty northern parklands.

In the center of the province, the wheat blows and the cattle and pronghorn roam; here you'll find historic ranches, sacred native sights and the eerie, martian landscape of the hoodoos. Calgary has become unexpectedly cool, with top museums and cocktail bars, while Edmonton's fringe theater festival is the world's second largest.

When to Go
Edmonton

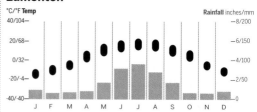

Jul Prime time for festivals, with Edmonton's Street Performers and the Calgary Stampede.

Jul–Sep Banff and Jasper's trails are snow-free, making a full range of hikes available.

Dec–Feb Winter-sports season in the Rocky Mountains.

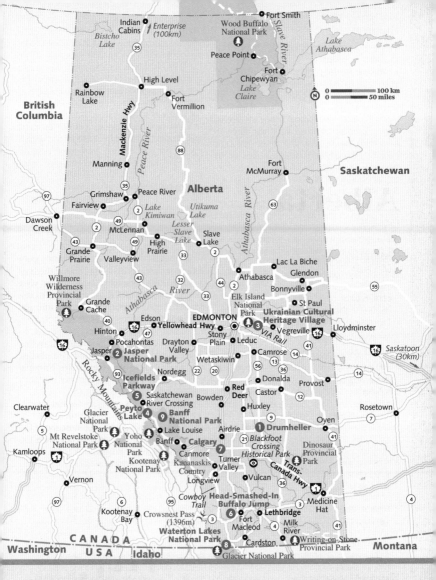

Alberta Highlights

1 **Royal Tyrrell Museum of Palaeontology** (p98) Exploring Jurassic remnants.

2 **Miette Hot Springs** (p91) Soaking amidst spectacular mountain peaks.

3 **Ukrainian Cultural Heritage Village** (p51) Stepping back in time to the days of new immigrants.

4 **Peyto Lake** (p77) Taking in its otherworldly emerald waters.

5 **Icefields Parkway** (p74) Driving between towering mountains and stunning vistas.

6 **Head-Smashed-In Buffalo Jump** (p101) Delving into the fascinating history of First Nations culture.

7 **National Music Centre** (p58) Learning about music at Calgary's newest museum.

8 **Waterton Lakes National Park** (p103) Exploring fairy-tale scenery by kayak.

9 **Lake Agnes Teahouse** (p90) Enjoying glacial-water tea high above bluer-than-blue Lake Louise. in Banff NP.

History

Things may have started off slowly in Alberta, but it's making up for lost time. Human habitation in the province dates back 7500 years: the indigenous peoples of the Blackfoot, Kainaiwa (Blood), Siksika, Peigan, Atsina (also called Gros Ventre), Cree, Tsuu T'ina (Sarcee) and Assiniboine tribes all settled here in prehistoric times, and their descendants still live here today. These nomadic peoples roamed the southern plains of the province in relative peace and harmony until the middle of the 17th century, when the first Europeans began to arrive.

With the arrival of the Europeans, Alberta began to change and evolve – the impact of these new arrivals was felt immediately. Trading cheap whiskey for buffalo skins set off the decline of both the buffalo and the traditional ways of the indigenous people. Within a generation, the indigenous peoples were restricted to reserves and the buffalo all but extinct.

In the 1820s, the Hudson's Bay Company set up shop in the area, and European settlers continued to trickle in. By 1870 the North West Mounted Police (NWMP) – the predecessor of the Royal Canadian Mounted Police (RCMP) – had built forts within the province to control the whiskey trade and maintain order. It was a good thing they did, because 10 years later the railroad reached Alberta and the trickle of settlers turned into a gush.

These new residents were mostly farmers, and farming became the basis of the economy for the next century. Vast reserves of oil and gas were discovered in the early 20th century, but it took time to develop them. At the conclusion of WWII there were 500 oil wells; by 1960, there were 10,000, by which time the petroleum business was the biggest in town. Nevertheless, in the 1980s and again in 2016, a serious dip in oil prices brought heavy recession – a stark reminder that natural resources can offer both boom and bust.

Thankfully, Albertans have strong civic pride, as shown by the rallying support following the 2013 floods in Calgary and the 2016 wildfires in Fort McMurray.

ALBERTA ITINERARIES

One Week

Spend the day in Calgary (p55) exploring the Glenbow Museum (p58) and the National Music Centre (p58), then grab a meal on trendy 17th Ave or wander through the artsy neighborhoods of Kensington and Inglewood. The next day, get into dino mode by taking a day trip to Drumheller (p98) and visiting the Royal Tyrrell Museum of Palaeontology (p98). Back in Calgary, head east to spot wild bison at Elk Island National Park (p54) and step back in time at the authentic Ukrainian Cultural Heritage Village (p51).

Wake early and head west. Have fresh bagels for breakfast in Canmore (p73) and then carry on to Banff National Park (p69) and check out the Whyte Museum of the Canadian Rockies (p79).

After a stay in Banff, follow the scenic Bow Valley Pkwy to Lake Louise (p87), finding time for the short, steep hike to the Lake Agnes Teahouse (p90) and a trip up the Lake Louise Gondola (p87) to spot grizzly bears. Head out on the spectacular Icefields Parkway (p76) to the Columbia Icefield (p77).

Roll into Jasper (p91) and check into Tekarra Lodge (p96) for some much-needed R & R. Drive out to Maligne Lake (p91), where a short hike might let you spot a bear or a moose. Carry on north to Miette Hot Springs (p91) for a fabulous soak amid mountain scenery. Escape the mountains and head to Edmonton, diving into the Old Strathcona neighborhood, and finishing your Alberta adventure with a gourmet meal at Corso 32 (p52).

The Complete Rockies

Follow the One Week itinerary, but before reaching Canmore, head south down Hwy 5, known as the Cowboy Trail (p68), to take in Bar U Ranch (☑403-395-3044; www.parks canada.gc.ca/baru; Hwy 22, Longview; adult $7.80; ☺10am-5pm mid-May–Sep). Continue south, detouring a bit to see Head-Smashed-In Buffalo Jump (p101) and then continuing to Waterton Lakes National Park (p103), experiencing this less-visited mountain paradise. Return north through Kananaskis Country (p), stopping for tea or an overnight stay at Mt Engadine Lodge (p72). Then carry on north to Canmore (p55).

Land & Climate

The prairies that cover the eastern and southern parts of Alberta give way to the towering Rocky Mountains that form the western edge of the province. That mountainous spine forms the iconic scenery for which Alberta is known.

Alberta is a sunny sort of place; any time of year you can expect the sun to be out. Winters can be cold, when the temperature can plummet to a bone-chilling -20°C (-4°F). Climate change has started to influence snowfall, with the cities receiving less and less every year.

Chinook winds often kick up in the winter months. These warm westerly winds blow in from the coast, deposit their moisture on the mountains and give Albertans a reprieve from the winter chill, sometimes increasing temperatures by as much as 20°C (36°F) in one day!

Summers tend to be hot and dry; the warmest months are July and August, when the temperature sits at a comfortable 25°C (77°F). The 'June Monsoon' is often rain-filled, while the cooler temperatures and fall colors of September are spectacular.

❶ Information

Travel Alberta (☑ 800-252-3782; www.travel alberta.com) Links to info on parks and visitor centers across the province.

❶ Getting There & Away

AIR

The two major airports are in Edmonton and Calgary, and there are daily flights to both from major hubs across the world. Carriers serving the province include Air Canada, American Airlines, British Airways, Delta, Horizon Air, KLM, United Airlines and WestJet.

BUS

Greyhound has ceased bus services in Alberta, but there is service via Red Arrow (https://red arrow.ca) to much of the province.

Moose Bus Adventures (☑ 604-297-0255; https://moosebus.travel) runs a variety of trips in western Canada. Tours start in Vancouver or Banff and along the way hit the highlights of the mountain parks and other Alberta must-sees. In winter it operates ski-focused tours that are a great option for car-less ski bums. Trips depart daily during the summer months and a few times per week in the winter season.

CAR & MOTORCYCLE

Alberta was designed with the automobile (and an unlimited supply of gas) in mind. There are high-quality, well-maintained highways and a

---

ALBERTA FAST FACTS

➡ Population: 4,067,175

➡ Area: 642,317 sq km

➡ Capital: Edmonton

➡ Quirky fact: A relative of the T-rex, the Albertosaurus was first discovered in the Horseshoe Canyon in 1884.

---

network of back roads to explore. Towns will for the most part have services, regardless of the population.

Be aware that in more remote areas, especially in the north, those services could be a large distance apart, and often you will be hours between cell service areas. Fill up your gas tank wherever possible and be prepared for possible emergencies with things like warm clothes and water.

TRAIN

Despite years of hard labor, countless work-related deaths and a reputation for being one of the great feats of 19th-century engineering, Alberta's contemporary rail network has been whittled down to just two regular passenger train services. **VIA Rail** (☑ 888-842-7245; www. viarail.ca) runs from Vancouver to Toronto two or three times per week, passing through Jasper and Edmonton in both directions. Edmonton to Vancouver costs $225 and takes 27 hours; Edmonton to Toronto costs $405 and takes 55 hours. The Toronto-bound train stops in Saskatoon, Saskatchewan; Winnipeg, Manitoba; and Sudbury Junction, Ontario. VIA Rail also operates the train from Jasper to Prince Rupert, BC ($117, 32 hours, three weekly).

Rocky Mountaineer (☑ 604-606-7200; www. rockymountaineer.com; 2/5/14/21 days from $1250/2010/4660/7580; ☉May-Oct) tours chug east from Vancouver through the Rockies via Kamloops to Jasper or Banff, or north from Vancouver to Jasper via Whistler and northern BC. These luxury trains have been transporting tourists on multiday journeys for a quarter century.

EDMONTON

☑ 780 / POP 932,000

Modern, spread out and frigidly cold for much of the year, Alberta's second-largest city and capital is a government town that you're more likely to read about in the business pages than the travel supplements. Edmonton is often a stopover en route to Jasper National Park, four hours' drive west, or explorations into the vast and empty landscape to the north.

Downtown has changed a lot in the past few years since Roger's Place was completed. Chic upscale shops and eateries sit in stark

Edmonton

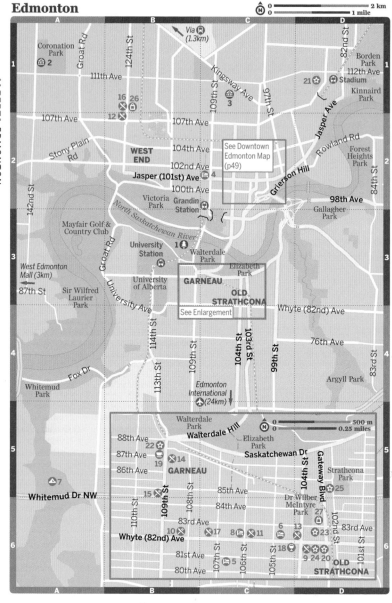

contrast to the homeless people outside. For the soul of the city, head south of the river to the university district and Whyte Ave, home to small theaters, diners and a spirited Friday-night mood. Edmonton also has a few decent museums, an annual fringe festival second only to Edinburgh's, and some top

nearby sights like the Ukrainian Cultural Village and Elk Island National Park.

History

The Cree and Blackfoot tribes can trace their ancestry in the Edmonton area for 5000

Edmonton

years. It wasn't until the late 18th century that Europeans first arrived in the area. A trade outpost was built by the Hudson's Bay Company in 1795, which was dubbed Fort Edmonton.

Trappers, traders and adventurers frequented the fort, but it wasn't until 1870, when the government purchased Fort Ed and opened up the area to pioneers, that Edmonton saw its first real growth in population. When the railway arrived in Calgary in 1891, growth really started to speed up.

Meanwhile, the indigenous tribes had been severely weakened by disease and the near extinction of their primary food source, the bison. Increasingly vulnerable, they signed away most of their land rights to the Canadian government in a series of treaties between 1871 and 1921 in return for money, reservation lands and hunting rights.

In the 1940s, WWII precipitated the construction of the Alaska Hwy, and the influx of workers further increased the population. Ukrainians and other Eastern European immigrants came to Edmonton in search of work and enriched the city.

Edmonton is again the hub for those looking to earn their fortune in the north. But it isn't gold or roads this time – it's oil.

In 2016, a terrifying forest fire raced through the Fort McMurray area, claiming no fatalities but burning hundreds of homes and thousands of acres. Edmonton was the main city to help out, offering temporary shelters and relocation, as well as food and supplies. That fire is history, but the threat remains, and tourists should heed fire warnings carefully.

◉ Sights

★ **Art Gallery of Alberta** GALLERY
(Map p49; ☑780-422-6223; www.youraga.ca; 2 Sir Winston Churchill Sq; adult/child $13.13/8.93; ⊙11am-5pm Tue-Sun, to 8pm Thu) With the opening of this maverick art gallery in 2010, Edmonton at last gained a modern signature building to counter the ubiquitous boxy skyscrapers with its giant glass-and-metal space helmet. Its collection comprises 6000 pieces of historical and contemporary art, many of which have a strong Canadian bias, that rotate through eight galleries. Numerous worthwhile temporary shows also pass through, and you'll find a shop, cafe and restaurant on-site.

Telus World of Science MUSEUM
(Map p46; ☑780-451-3344; www.telusworld ofscience.com; 11211 142nd St; adult/child $26/18; ⊙9am-5pm Oct-Apr, to 6pm May-Sep; 🖌) With an emphasis on interactive displays, this science museum has a million things to do, all under one roof, including a new planetarium. Fight crime with the latest technology, see what living on a spacecraft is all about, go on a dinosaur dig and explore what makes the human body tick. The center also includes an IMAX theater (extra cost) and an observatory with telescopes (no extra cost).

Ukrainian Museum of Canada MUSEUM
(Map p46; www.umcalberta.org; 10611 110th Ave; by donation; ⊙9:30am-4:30pm Mon-Fri May-Aug)

Given Edmonton's huge Ukrainian population and long history of immigration, this museum is surprisingly small. While it continues to search for bigger digs, it shows a tiny collection of traditional costumes, toys and artwork. The cultural center in the same building hosts pierogi suppers on the last Friday of each month (adult/child $17/6). Check its website (www.uocc-stjohn.ca) for details.

North Saskatchewan River Valley   PARK
(Map p46) Edmonton has more designated urban parkland than any other city in North America, most of it contained within an interconnected riverside green belt that effectively cuts the metropolis in half. The green zone is flecked with lakes, bridges, wild areas, golf courses, ravines, and approximately 160km worth of cycling and walking trails. It is easily accessed from downtown.

Royal Alberta Museum   MUSEUM
(Map p49; ☑ 780-453-9100; www.royalalberta museum.ca; 103A Ave; adult/child $19/10; ⊙ 10am-5pm Sep–mid-May, 10am-6pm mid-May–Sep, to 8pm Thu & Fri) Since getting its 'royal' prefix in 2005 when Queen Liz II dropped by, Edmonton's leading museum has a new downtown home, which opened in 2018. The new museum is the largest in western Canada, with an enormous collection of Alberta's natural and cultural history, featuring interactive exhibits and live animals.

Alberta Railway Museum   MUSEUM
(☑ 780-472-6229; www.albertarailwaymuseum. com; 24215 34th St; adult/child $10/5; ⊙ 10am-5pm Sat & Sun mid-May–Aug) This museum, on the northeast edge of the city, has a collection of more than 75 railcars, including steam and diesel locomotives and rolling stock, built and used between 1900 and 1950. On weekends, volunteers fire up some of the old engines, and you can hop on the diesel locomotives or the 1913 steam locomotive on holiday weekends.

Tours

Quirky free walking tours of downtown are offered in the summer months by students on vacation and employed by the Downtown Business Association. They leave weekdays at 1pm from the corner of 104th St and 101st Ave.

★ **Cobblestone Freeway**   CULTURAL
(☑ 780-436-7482; http://cobblestonefreeway.ca; day tours from $89) These tours have knowledgeable guides with strong links to the local Ukrainian community. You can experience traditional dance performances, authentic Ukrainian food and heritage sights, and neighboring Ukrainian communities. The tours can also get you to the city's must-see sights or as far afield as Jasper. Especially great at tailoring tours to travelers' interests; service is both personable and professional.

Edmonton Ghost Tours   WALKING
(www.edmontonghosttours.com; per person $15; ⊙ 9pm Mon-Thu Jul & Aug) Spooky walking tours led by storytellers recounting the ghostly history of Edmonton. Tours cover various neighborhoods; check the website to see where to meet. No booking is required; just turn up 15 minutes early.

Festivals & Events

**Edmonton International
Fringe Festival**   THEATER
(www.fringetheatre.ca; tickets $13-16; ⊙ mid-Aug) The ultimate Edmonton experience is an 11-day program of live alternative theater on outdoor stages, in the parks, and in small theaters and venues. It's second in size only to the Edinburgh Fringe Festival. Many shows are free and no ticket costs more than $16. There's no booking – you choose a theater and stand in line.

**International Street
Performers Festival**   THEATER
(www.edmontonstreetfest.com; ⊙ 2nd week Jul) Sometimes the best theater is outside. International performers perform alfresco in this busker bonanza. Performers are curated and most strut their stuff in Sir Winston Churchill Sq. Shows are by donation in the pass-the-hat fashion.

K-Days   CARNIVAL
(www.k-days.com; ⊙ late Jul) For years, Capital Ex (Klondike Days) was the big summer festival in Edmonton. Since 2012, it has been known as K-Days, with less focus on gold-rush history and more on contemporary fun. Big names in music grace two stages, the midway has adrenaline-charged rides and you'll still find a nugget's worth of olden-days fun.

Sleeping

While many hotels in the city bank on visitors traveling on an expense account, Edmonton has a decent range of independent accommodations, including some with some

Downtown Edmonton

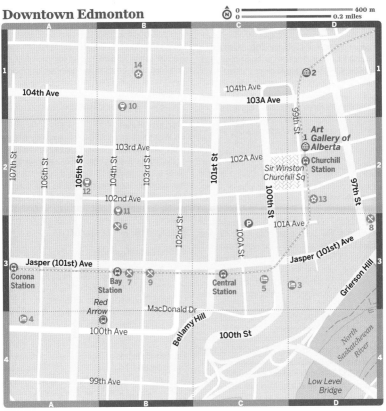

Downtown Edmonton

character. If you are in town mainly to visit the West Edmonton Mall, then staying in or near it is feasible, but the digs there are definitely leaning toward the touristy side of the spectrum.

HI Edmonton Hostel HOSTEL **$**
(Map p46; ☑780-988-6836; www.hihostels.ca; 10647 81st Ave; dm/d with shared bath $42/94,

d $109; P@🛜) In the heart of Old Strathcona, this busy hostel is a safe bet. Many of the rooms are a bit jam-packed with bunks and it feels somewhat like a converted old people's home (it used to be a convent), but renovations have brightened things up and produced a fantastic outdoor patio. The location and price are hard to beat.

DON'T MISS

FARMERS MARKET

Since it began in 1983, the **Old Strath-cona Farmers Market's** (Map p46; ☏780-439-1844; https://osfm.ca; 10310 83rd Ave, at 103rd St; ⏱noon-5pm Tue, 8am-3pm Sat Jul & Aug) motto has been 'We Make it! We Bake it! We Grow it! We Sell it!' Inside the city's old bus garage, it offers everything from organic food to arts and crafts, and hosts some 130 vendors. Everyone comes here on Saturday morning. You'd be wise to do the same.

Rainbow Valley
Campground & RV Park   CAMPGROUND $
(Map p46; ☏780-434-5531; www.rainbowvalley.com; Rainbow Valley Rd; tent/RV sites $39/45; ⏱May-Oct; 🅿) For an inner-city camping spot, this one is pretty good. It's in a good location to get to 'The Mall' and keep some distance from it at the same time. There are lots of trees, a playground, cookhouse, showers and wood-burning stoves. Rates are reduced out of peak season (ie late May and early September).

⭐**Union Bank Inn**   BOUTIQUE HOTEL $$
(Map p49; ☏780-423-3600; www.unionbankinn.com; 10053 Jasper Ave; r from $220; 🅿🕸@🛜) This posh boutique hotel on Jasper Ave, in a former bank building dating from 1910, is an upscale masterpiece. With just 40 rooms, the staff will be at your beck and call, and the in-room fireplaces make even Edmonton's frigid winters almost bearable. There's an equally fancy restaurant – Madison's Grill (p52) – on the ground floor.

⭐**Matrix**   BOUTIQUE HOTEL $$
(Map p49; ☏780-429-2861; www.matrixedmonton.com; 10640 100th Ave; r from $170; 🅿🕸🕸@🛜) Modern and slick, the lobby here could be James Bond's living room, complete with brushed aluminum panels, low leather furniture, and a large glassed-in fireplace. Rooms are similarly stylish with plenty of up-to-date gadgets. Service is stellar and genuine, breakfasts are mammoth, there's free wine and cheese in the evening, and a shuttle downtown. What more could you want?

⭐**Varscona**   BOUTIQUE HOTEL $$
(Map p46; ☏780-434-6111; www.varscona.com; 8208 106th St, cnr Whyte Ave; r incl breakfast from $180; 🅿🕸🕸@🛜) This charming hotel is elegant but not too hoity-toity, suggesting you can roll up in a tracksuit or a business suit – or some kind of combination of the two. Rooms have splashes of color and lots of comfort, and Edmonton's coolest neighborhood is on the doorstep. Parking, free breakfast, and evening wine and cheese sweeten the deal. Phone for discounts.

Metterra Hotel
on Whyte   BOUTIQUE HOTEL $$
(Map p46; ☏780-465-8150; www.metterra.com; 10454 Whyte Ave; r from $160; 🅿🕸🕸@🛜) Sleek and regularly updated, this small hotel has a prime location on Whyte Ave. Earthy tones, new mattresses and splashes of Indonesian art give rooms a luxurious feel. The friendly staff can fill you in on what's happening in the neighborhood.

Canterra Suites Hotel   HOTEL $$
(Map p46; ☏780-421-1212; www.canterrasuites.com; 11010 Jasper Ave; ste from $199; 🕸🕸🛜) Catering to traveling businesspeople, the Canterra has 40 large, comfortable suites equipped with modern kitchenettes. It's close to downtown and right next to a supermarket. Ideal for long- or short-term stays.

Fairmont Hotel
Macdonald   HOTEL $$$
(Map p49; ☏780-424-5181; www.fairmont.com; 10065 100th St; r from $259; 🅿🕸🕸🛜🏊) Stealing the best nook in town (as Fairmont always does), Edmonton's historic Fairmont Hotel exhibits the usual array of intricate stucco, Italian marble, ornate chandeliers and lush carpets. In the early 20th century it was one in a luxurious chain of railway hotels that dotted the cross-continental line from east to west. The top two floors were remodeled in 2019.

🍴 Eating

Edmonton's food scene reflects its multiculturalism and if you're willing to hunt around, you can get a quality meal at any price. The most varied and economical place to eat is on or around Whyte Ave, while the best downtown nexus is Jasper Ave or the rejuvenated warehouse district north of Jasper Ave on 104th St.

⭐**Duchess Bake Shop**   BAKERY, CAFE $
(Map p46; ☏780-488-4999; www.duchessbakeshop.com; 10720 124th St; baked goods from $2, breakfast & lunch $8-13; ⏱9am-7pm Tue-Fri, 10am-6pm Sat, to 5pm Sun) Duchess is a destination.

You'd cross town to eat here – barefoot in snow if necessary. Feeling like it dropped straight from France, complete with Louis XV–style chairs, the Duchess' French-press coffee and huge array of fresh baking leave you spoiled for choice. Mocha meringues, cream-cheese-and-leek croissants, and cherry basil eclairs are just the tip of the iceberg.

Duchess is also famous for its macarons. Try the salted caramel and you'll know why. Arrive early, before the queuing locals have stripped the cases bare. There's an affiliated provisions shop next door where you can pick up the cookbook, coffee and kits for baking at home.

★ **Block 1912** CAFE $
(Map p46; ☑780-433-6575; www.block1912.com; 10361 Whyte Ave; snacks $6.50-15; ⊘9am-11pm Sat-Thu, to midnight Fri) A regal attempt at a genuine Torinese coffee bar, this inviting place allows you to recline on European-style sofas and armchairs and enjoy your coffee, beer or wine beneath twinkly lights. Grab a snack or something more substantial like coffee-crusted steak or Thai chicken. Gelato comes in fab flavors like green apple or white-chocolate mousse and desserts are drool-worthy.

Remedy Cafe INDIAN $
(Map p49; ☑780-757-7720; http://remedycafe.ca; 10279 Jasper Ave; coffee & chai $3-5, mains $8-10; ⊘7:30-midnight Mon-Fri, from 8am Sat & Sun; 🛜)
The 'remedy' here is cheap, authentic Indian food served in an ultra-casual cafe – meaning you can use wi-fi with one hand and dip your naan in curry sauce with the other. Everyone raves about the chai and butter chicken, but there are also good cakes (vegans catered for) and excellent masala dosas (curried vegetables in a crisp pancake).

The larger, original **branch** (Map p46; ☑780-433-3096; 8631 109th St; coffee & chai $3-5, mains $8-17; ⊘7:30am-midnight Mon-Fri, from 8am Sat & Sun; 🛜) is in Garneau on the south side of the river.

Café Mosaics VEGETARIAN $
(Map p46; ☑780-433-9702; www.cafemosaics.com; 10844 Whyte Ave; mains $7-18; ⊘11am-9pm Mon-Thu, 10am-10pm Fri & Sat, 10am-9pm Sun; ☑🧒) 🍃 A Strathcona institution, this artsy, cool vegetarian-vegan haunt is a meat-free zone that has taken a page out of San Francisco's book: it makes vegetable dishes both interesting and tasty. Think earthy and clean, rather than hippy and crusty. As a litmus test, check the number of carnivores who take a day off meat to come here.

ALBERTA EDMONTON

EDMONTON'S UKRAINIAN COMMUNITIES

If you've been in Edmonton for any length of time, you may well be wondering, 'Why all the pierogies?'. Between the 19th and early 20th century, around 250,000 Ukrainians immigrated to Canada, settling in farming communities on the prairies where the landscape reminded them of the snowy steppes of home. Today the Ukrainian population in Canada is second only to that in Russia and Ukraine itself, and many famous Canadians trace their roots back to Ukraine, including Wayne Gretzky and Randy Bachman. The largest number of Ukrainian-Canadians live in and around Edmonton and, with nearly 11% of the city's population claiming Ukrainian heritage, the cultural influence extends far beyond pierogies.

It is difficult not to feel the presence of Ukrainians in Edmonton. There are stores and restaurants, dance groups and choirs, and domes decorating the skyline. The culture is very alive and very present. One of the most interesting ways to experience it is to explore the **Ukrainian Cultural Heritage Village** (☑780-662-3640; https://ukrainian village.ca; adult/child/family $15/10/40; ⊘10am-5pm May-Sep) with its character role players acting out what life in a rural Ukrainian-Canadian community would have been like. You can also check out other towns near the city, including **Vegreville**, with the world's largest Easter egg; **Mundare**, with a giant Ukrainian sausage; and **Glendon**, with the biggest – you guessed it – pierogi.

But today's Ukrainian-Canadian culture isn't just grandmas pushing pierogies; many young Edmontonians are full of Ukrainian pride. There are many Ukrainian specialty restaurants, and the churches often have special pierogi nights and sell bulk pierogies to take home for emergencies. To experience Ukrainian culture firsthand, check out Cobblestone Freeway (p48), which runs both city and regional tours.

Meat
RIBS **$$**

(Map p46; ☑ 587-520-6338; www.meatford inner.com; 8216 104th St; mains $16-28; ⊙ 5-10pm Mon-Thu, to 11pm Fri, 11am-11pm Sat, to 10pm Sun) Spicy fried chicken, pulled pork by the pound and beef brisket are why people pack into this tasty restaurant night after night. It's got decent beers on draft and a nice cocktail selection, but more than anything people come here for the (wait for it)...meat.

Tiramisu Bistro
ITALIAN **$$**

(Map p46; ☑ 780-452-3393; http://tiramisu bistro.ca; 10750 124th St; pastas $17-24; ⊙ 8am-9pm Mon-Thu, to 10pm Fri, 9am-10pm Sat, to 4pm Sun; ⊞) This bistro serves fresh salads, wraps, panini and pasta, but its risottos are the coup. Mornings bring breakfast pizzas and crepes with fillings like elk cherry sausage. It also has a kids' menu that assumes children like food beyond chicken strips. If you're ordering takeout, opt for the 'spaghetti cone,' which, like it sounds, is spaghetti you can hold in your hand.

Three Boars Eatery
TAPAS **$$**

(Map p46; ☑ 780-757-2600; www.threeboars.ca; 8424 109th St; small plates $16-24; ⊙ 5pm-midnight Tue-Thu, to 2am Fri & Sat, to 1am Sun) ⋒ Three Boars is part of the burgeoning farm-to-table food movement, using local suppliers to create gourmet food. It specializes in small plates, fine Edmonton microbrews on draft and divinely crafted cocktails. If you have an appetite for a large Alberta steak, this isn't your bag. If you're up for tasting a liver 'bomb' or smoked quail, it definitely is.

Blue Plate Diner
CAFE **$$**

(Map p49; ☑ 780-429-0740; www.blueplate diner.ca; 10145 104th St; mains $9-18; ⊙ 7:30am-9pm Mon-Thu, to 10pm Fri, 9am-10pm Sat, to 9pm Sun; ⊞) ⋒ In a redbrick building in Edmonton's warehouse district, this diner serves healthy food in hearty portions with vegetarian options. And there's style, too. Cool colored lighting and exposed brickwork mean you can eat locally grown veggies without feeling as if you've joined a hippie commune. The creative menu is well executed, there's an excellent kids' menu, and the desserts? Mmm...

Try the tofu stir-fry or steak sandwich and enjoy larger-than-average plates of crisp, locally grown vegetables. Alternatively, go for the enormous sticky buns, available weekends only, which the menu claims are 'larger than your head' (not quite, but they're big, trust us!).

Da-De-O
CAJUN **$$**

(Map p46; ☑ 780-433-0930; www.dadeo.ca; 10548a Whyte Ave; mains $15-30; ⊙ 11:30am-10pm Mon, Tue & Thu, to 11pm Fri & Sat, noon-9pm Sun) An unexpected summoning up of the Big Easy in the frozen north, this retro diner – complete with red vinyl chairs, chrome kitchen tables and a jukebox – whips up Cajun calamari, oysters, jambalaya and southern fried chicken. Plucked straight out of Louisiana legend are the spice-dusted sweet-potato fries and the ginormous po'boys (especially the blackened catfish). No minors allowed.

Tokyo Noodle Shop
JAPANESE **$$**

(Map p46; ☑ 780-430-0838; www.tokyonoodle shop.com; 10736 Whyte Ave; mains $11-27; ⊙ 11:30am-9:30pm Mon-Wed, to 10pm Thu, to 10:30pm Fri & Sat, 11:30am-9pm Sun) Great sushi and noodles by the gallon, plus bento boxes, rice bowls and all the tasty appetizers you'd expect in an authentic Japanese restaurant. Nothing fancy, but that's the point.

★ Corso 32
ITALIAN **$$$**

(Map p49; ☑ 780-421-4622; www.corso32.com; 10345 Jasper Ave; mains $31-36; ⊙ 5-10pm Sun-Thu, to 11pm Fri & Sat) Chef and owner, Daniel Costa, delivers the best of Italy. Classy, small and candlelit, with a narrow interior and minimalist decor, Corso 32's evolving menu features dishes with ingredients like homemade goat ricotta, rabbit and pancetta ragu or black truffle honey. The pasta is all handmade and the wine list is the best in Edmonton (if you're into Italian tipples).

Madison's Grill
FUSION **$$$**

(Map p49; ☑ 780-401-2222; www.unionbank inn.com/madisons-grill; 10053 Jasper Ave; mains $36-51; ⊙ 7am-10pm Mon-Fri, 8-11am & 5-10pm Sat, 8-11am & 5-9pm Sun) Located in the posh Union Bank Inn (p50), Madison's has no problem keeping up with the hotel's high standards of service and quality. Its delicate dishes are beautifully presented; try pork-cheek pierogi with Saskatoon berries, seared halibut with basil gnocchi, or fig- and brie-stuffed chicken roulade wrapped in prosciutto. The three-course meal with wine pairing for $105 is well worth it.

Hardware Grill
STEAK **$$$**

(Map p49; ☑ 780-423-0969; www.hardwaregrill. com; 9698 Jasper Ave; mains $32-50; ⊙ 5-9:30pm Mon-Thu, to 10pm Fri & Sat) A plush oasis in a converted brick building downtown, this restaurant is a comfortable, bustling place where you'll want to linger over the amazing wine list and original menu. Try crab-crusted salmon, crispy duck and waffle or bacon-wrapped elk, all with a side of mac 'n' cheese.

Drinking & Nightlife

The best nightlife scene has traditionally centered on or around Whyte Ave in Old Strathcona. Clubs open and close in a blink; bars tend to stay longer. Some bars host music and/or DJs.

★ **Baijiu**   COCKTAIL BAR
(Map p49; 780-421-7060; www.baijiuyeg.com; 10359 104 St NW; 5pm-midnight Tue-Thu, to 1am Fri & Sat) Baijiu is where anyone wanting great cocktails goes, but it's tough to describe the place exactly. First one thinks tiki, but it's not quite that. Then one thinks dance club, but it's not that either. The long bar, dim lights and talented bartenders are what make it great for drinks, but the food's good, too.

Yellowhead Brewery   GAY & LESBIAN
(Map p49; 780-423-3333; www.yellowhead brewery.com; 10229 105th St NW; 11am-9pm Thu-Sat, 10am & 1pm Sun brunch seatings) First things first. This isn't a pub per se. Nor is it gay per se. It's an all-welcome tasting room next door to a brewery where you can sup on Yellowhead's tasty offerings, which range from its flagship lager to a tasty and refreshing pale ale. It also serves small plates and offers brewery tours if you book in advance.

Cavern   WINE BAR
(Map p49; 780-455-1336; www.thecavern.ca; 10169 104th St NW; 11am-8pm Mon-Thu, to 11pm Fri & Sat) This industrial and candlelit small cafe is an underground bastion of good taste on in-vogue 104th St, particularly in the deli department (plates $6 to $22). You can browse the glass cabinet filled with divine cheese before you choose, and wash it down with a glass of wine. There are even instructions on how to make a great cheese board.

Transcend Coffee   COFFEE
(Map p46; 780-756-8882; www.transcend coffee.ca/garneau; 8708 109th St; coffee $4-6.50; 7am-9pm Mon-Fri, 8am-9pm Sat, 8am-6pm Sun;) In a city where cafes producing their own micro-roasted coffee beans are few, Transcend should be treated like gold dust. Expert baristas on first-name terms with their Guatemalan farmer-producers concoct cups of their own roasted coffee with

enough precision to satisfy a severely decaffeinated Seattleite. In a renovated theater, this spot is hip but not remotely pretentious.

Black Dog Freehouse   PUB
(Map p46; 780-439-1089; www.blackdog.ca; 10425 Whyte Ave; 2pm-2am) Insanely popular with all types, the Black Dog is essentially a pub with some hidden extras: a rooftop patio, known as the 'wooftop patio,' a traditional ground-floor bar (normally packed cheek by jowl on weekday nights), and a basement that features live music, DJs and occasional parties. The sum of the three parts has become a rollicking Edmonton institution.

☆ Entertainment

Theater! Don't leave Edmonton without trying some. *See* and *Vue* are free local alternative weekly papers with extensive arts and entertainment listings. For daily listings, see the entertainment section of the *Edmonton Journal* newspaper.

Garneau Theatre   CINEMA
(Map p46; 780-425-9212; www.metrocinema. org; 8712 109th St NW; adult/child $13/8) Edmonton's only surviving art deco–era cinema has operated under various guises since 1940, changing hands most recently in 2011. It's

WORTH A TRIP

ELK ISLAND NATIONAL PARK

In case you hadn't noticed, there are five national parks in Alberta, and three of them *aren't* Jasper or Banff. Overshadowed by the Gothic Rockies, tiny Elk Island National Park (☏780-922-5790; www.parkscanada.gc.ca/elkisland; adult/child/senior $7.80/free/6.80, campsites & RV sites $25.50, campfire permits $8.80; ☉ visitor center 8:30am-5:30pm, gates 24hr) attracts just 5% of Banff's annual visitor count despite its location only 50km east of Edmonton. Not that this detracts from its attractions. The park – the only one in Canada that is entirely fenced – contains the highest density of wild hoofed animals in the world after the Serengeti. If you come here, plan on seeing the 'big six' – plains bison, wood bison, mule deer, white-tailed deer, elk and the more elusive moose. It's also an official Dark Sky preserve, offering great night views for skywatchers.

The wood bison live entirely in the quieter southern portion of the park (which is cut in two by Hwy 16), while the plains bison inhabit the north. Most of the infrastructure lies in the north, too, around Astotin Lake. Here you'll find a campground, a nine-hole golf course (with a clubhouse containing a restaurant), a beach and a boat launch. Four of the park's 11 trails lead out from the lakeshore through trademark northern Albertan aspen parkland – a kind of natural intermingling of the prairies and the boreal forests.

Public transportation to the park is nonexistent. Car hire or a private tour are the best options.

---

filled with vintage decor, some original and some not, but who cares when you roll in for a *Trainspotting* matinee and the concession stand is selling beer?

Roxy Theatre THEATER
(Map p46; ☏780-453-2440; www.theatre network.ca; 8529 Gateway Blvd) This theater opened after Theatre Network's beloved 1940s Roxy theater burned down. Nevertheless, it keeps things eclectic, showing burlesque, live bands and comedy.

New Varscona Theatre THEATER
(Map p46; ☏780-433-3399; www.varscona theatre.com; 10329 83rd Ave; tickets from $15) There are only 176 precious seats at the Varscona, a cornerstone of the Old Strathcona theater district that puts on 350 performances annually of edgy plays, late-night comedy and morning kids' shows.

Blues on Whyte LIVE MUSIC
(Map p46; ☏780-439-9381; www.bluesonwhyte. com; 10329 Whyte Ave) This is the sort of place your mother warned you about: dirty, rough, but still somehow cool. It's a great place to check out some live music; blues and rock are the standards. The dance floor is small but hopping. There are also pool tables and a games room.

Princess Theatre CINEMA
(Map p46; ☏780-433-0728; www.princess theatre.ca; 10337 Whyte Ave; tickets adult/student

& child $11/8) The Princess is a grand old theater that defiantly sticks her middle finger up at the multiplexes that are dominant elsewhere. Dating from the pre-talkie days (1914), it screens mainstream, first-run, arthouse and classic films. Tickets for Mondays and weekend matinees are reduced ($6).

Citadel Theatre THEATER
(Map p49; ☏780-425-1820; www.citadeltheatre. com; 9828 101A Ave; tickets $35-115; ☉ Sep-May) Edmonton's foremost theater company, with a large indoor garden and multiple stages, is based right in downtown's Winston Churchill Sq. Expect glowing performances of Shakespeare and Stoppard, Dickens adaptations and the odd Sondheim musical.

Edmonton Oilers SPECTATOR SPORT
(Map p49; www.edmontonoilers.com; tickets from $41) To avoid any embarrassing situations, wise up on the Oilers before you arrive in Edmonton. The local National Hockey League (NHL) team dominated the game in the 1980s thanks to a certain player named Wayne Gretzky – aka 'The Great One' – but hasn't won much since. The season runs from October to April at the Roger's Place arena.

Edmonton Eskimos SPECTATOR SPORT
(Map p46; ☏780-448-3757; www.esks.com; tickets from $45) The Eskimos take part in the Canadian Football League (CFL) from July to October at Commonwealth Stadium (11000 Stadium Rd).

ℹ Information

Edmonton Tourism (☏ 780-401-7696; https://exploreedmonton.com) A website with lots of useful links and info.

International Currency Exchange (☏ 780-425-5426; www.ice-canada.ca; 101 St Pedway, Edmonton City Centre West, 2nd level; ⊙ 10am-5:25pm Mon-Fri, to 3:55pm Sat) Can exchange currencies and provide other tourist-related banking needs.

Royal Alexandra Hospital (☏ 780-477-4111; 10240 Kingsway Ave; ⊙ 24hr) Has a 24-hour trauma center. Located 1km north of the downtown core.

ℹ Getting There & Away

Edmonton International Airport (YEG; ☏ 780-890-8382; www.flyeia.com) is about 30km south of the city along the Calgary Trail, approximately a 45-minute drive from downtown.

Red Arrow (Map p49; www.redarrow.ca; 10014 104th St; ⊙ 5:30am-10pm Mon-Fri, from 7:30am Sat, from 8am Sun) buses stop downtown at the Holiday Inn Express and serve Calgary ($73, 3½ hours, six daily) and Fort McMurray ($90, six hours, three daily). The buses are well equipped, with wi-fi, sockets for your laptop, single or double seats, a free minibar and hot coffee.

All the major car-rental firms have offices at the airport and around town. **Driving Force** (www.thedrivingforce.com; 11025 184th St) will rent, lease or sell you a car. Check the website; it often has some good deals.

The **VIA Rail Station** (www.viarail.ca; 12360 121st St) is rather inconveniently situated 5km northwest of the city center near Edmonton City Centre Airport. The Canadian travels three times a week east to Saskatoon ($204, 10 hours), Winnipeg ($432, 25 hours) and Toronto ($937, 56 hours), and west to Jasper ($115, 6½ hours), Kamloops ($147, 19½ hours) and Vancouver ($313, 32 hours). At Jasper, you can connect to Prince George and Prince Rupert.

ℹ Getting Around

TO/FROM THE AIRPORT

Bus 747 leaves from outside the arrivals hall every 30 to 60 minutes and goes to Century Park ($5), the southernmost stop on Edmonton's Light Rail. From here regular trains connect to Strathcona and downtown.

Sky Shuttle Airport Service (☏ 780-465-8515; www.edmontonskyshuttle.com; adult/child $18/10) runs three different routes that service hotels in most areas of town, including downtown and the Strathcona area. The office is by carousel 12. Journey time is approximately 45 minutes. If you're looking for a lift to the airport, reserve at least 24 hours in advance.

Cab fare from the airport to downtown is about $50.

CAR & MOTORCYCLE

There is metered parking throughout the city, which is often free after 6pm. Most hotels in Old Strathcona offer complimentary parking to guests. Visitors can park their car for the day and explore the neighborhood easily on foot. Edmonton also has public parking lots, which cost about $17 per day or $1.50 per half-hour; after 6pm you can park for a flat fee.

PUBLIC TRANSPORTATION

City buses and a 16-stop Light Rail Transit (LRT) system cover most of the city. The fare is $3.50. Buses operate at 30-minute intervals between 5:30am and 1:30am. Check out the excellent transit planning resources at www.edmonton.ca. Daytime travel between Churchill and Grandin stations on the LRT is free.

Between mid-May and early September you can cross the High Level Bridge on a streetcar ($5 round-trip, every 30 minutes between 11am and 10pm). The vintage streetcars are a great way to travel to the Old Strathcona Market (103rd St at 94th Ave), where the line stops. Or go from Old Strathcona to the downtown stop, next to the Grandin LRT Station (109th St between 98th and 99th Aves).

TAXI

Two of the many taxi companies are **Yellow Cab** (☏ 780-462-3456; http://edmtaxi.com) and **Alberta Co-Op Taxi** (☏ 780-425-2525; http://co-optaxi.com). The fare from downtown to the West Edmonton Mall is about $25. Flag fall is $3.60, then it's 20¢ for every 150m. Most cab companies offer a flat rate to the airport calculated from your destination.

CALGARY

☏ 403 / POP 1,240,000

Calgary will surprise you with its beauty, cool eateries, nightlife beyond honky-tonk, and long, worthwhile to-do list. Calgarians aren't known for their modesty; it's their self-love and can-do attitude that got them through disastrous flooding in 2013 and, in 2016, saw them helping residents of wildfire-stricken Fort McMurray with unquestioning generosity. We mustn't forget – Calgary also hosted the highly successful 1988 Winter Olympics, elected North America's first Muslim mayor, and throws one of Canada's biggest festivals, the Calgary Stampede.

Calgary

KENSINGTON

NB Sunnyside
C-Train

11th St NW
10A St NW
10th St NW

9

Louise
Bridge

Memorial Dr
Peace
Bridge
Bow River

1st Ave SW
2nd Ave SW
3rd Ave SW

Eau Claire
Ave SW

5

13
25
6

4th Ave SW

5th Ave SW

14

DOWNTOWN

6th Ave SW
WB Downtown -
West Kerby
7th Ave SW
8th St SW
8th Ave SW
WB 7 St SW
EB 6 St SW
WB 4 St SW
WB 1
St SW
C-Train

3rd St SW

4

Pumphouse
Theatres (700m)

8th Ave SW
32
EB 3 St SW
Stephen Ave Walk
15

9th Ave SW

10th Ave SW
29

34

11th Ave SW
12th Ave SW
31

BELTLINE

12th St SW
11th St SW
10th St SW
9th St SW
8th St SW

12
13th Ave SW
17
14th Ave SW

6th St SW
5th St SW
4th St SW
2nd St SW
1st St SW

8
28

20
16

27
26
24 18
23 21

**DESIGN
DISTRICT**

10

15th Ave SW

16th Ave SW
17th Ave SW

**UPTOWN
17TH AVE**

18th Ave SW
18th Ave SW

19th Ave SW

7th St SW

19th Ave SW

20th Ave
SW
21st Ave
SW

**4TH ST -
MISSION
DISTRICT**

23rd Ave SW
19

24th Ave SW

Prospect Ave

Hillcrest Ave

25th Ave SW

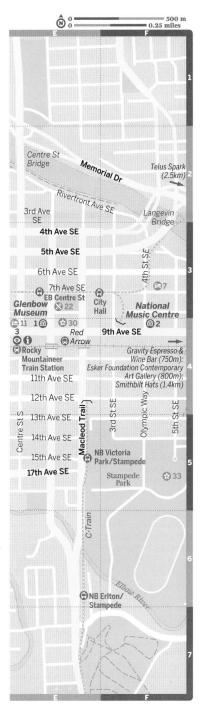

The city is waking up and smelling the single-origin home-roasted coffee, too, with top-notch craft bars, boutique shops, restaurants and entertainment venues exhibiting more color and experimentation. Long stretches of riverside jogging and even a lone surfing spot make for outdoor activities that other cities can't hold a candle to. The longer you stay, the more there is to surprise you.

History

From humble and relatively recent beginnings, Calgary has been transformed into a cosmopolitan modern city that has hosted an Olympics and continues to wield huge economic clout. Before the growth explosion, the Blackfoot people had called the area home for centuries. Eventually they were joined by the Sarcee and Stoney tribes on the banks of the Bow and Elbow Rivers.

In 1875 the North West Mounted Police (NWMP) built a fort and called it Fort Calgary after Calgary Bay on Scotland's Isle of Mull. The railroad followed a few years later and, buoyed by the promise of free land, settlers started the trek west to make Calgary their home. The Blackfoot, Sarcee and Stoney indigenous groups signed Treaty 7 with the British Crown in 1877, which ushered them into designated reservations and took away their wider land rights.

Long a center for ranching, the cowboy culture was set to become forever intertwined with the city. In the early 20th century, Calgary simmered along, growing slowly. Then, in the 1960s, everything changed. Overnight, ranching was seen as a thing of the past, and oil was the new favorite child. With the 'black gold' seeming to bubble up from the ground nearly everywhere in Alberta, Calgary became the natural choice of place to set up headquarters.

The population exploded, and the city began to grow at an alarming rate. As the price of oil continued to skyrocket, it was good times for the people of Cowtown. The 1970s boom stopped dead at the '80s bust. Things slowed and the city diversified.

The 21st century began with an even bigger boom. House prices have gone through the roof, there is almost zero unemployment and the economy is growing 40% faster than the rest of Canada. Not bad for a bunch of cowboys.

Calgary

◉ Sights

Calgary's downtown has the Glenbow Museum and the National Music Centre, but it's the surrounding neighborhoods that hold more allure. **Uptown 17th Avenue** has some of the top restaurants and bars and is a hive of activity in the evening. **Inglewood**, just east of downtown, is the city's hippest neighborhood, with antique shops, indie boutiques and some esoteric eating options. **Kensington**, north of the Bow River, has some good coffee bars and a tangible community spirit.

★ National Music Centre
MUSEUM

(☑403-543-5115; http://nmc.ca; 850 4th St SE; adult/child $18/11; ⊙10am-5pm May-Aug, Wed-Sun Sep-Apr) Looking like a whimsical copper castle, this fabulous new museum is entirely entertaining, taking you on a ride through Canada's musical history with rotating exhibits, cool artifacts (like the guitar Guess Who used to record 'American Woman') and interactive displays. Test your skill at the drums, electric guitar or in a sound-recording room and even create your own instruments. Don't miss the Body Phonic room or the solar-powered Skywalk with its repurposed pianos destroyed in the 2013 flood.

★ Glenbow Museum
MUSEUM

(☑403-777-5506; www.glenbow.org; 130 9th Ave SE; adult/child/family $18/11/45; ⊙9am-5pm Mon-Sat, noon-5pm Sun, closed Mon Oct-Jun) With an extensive permanent collection and an ever-changing array of traveling exhibitions, the impressive Glenbow has plenty for the history buff, art lover and pop-culture fiend to ponder. Temporary exhibits are often daring, covering contemporary art and culture. Permanent exhibits bring the past to life with strong historic personalities and lots of voice recordings. Hang out in a tipi, visit a trading post and walk through the railcar of a train.

Esker Foundation Contemporary Art Gallery
MUSEUM

(https://eskerfoundation.com; 1011 9th Ave SE, Inglewood; ⊙11am-6pm Sun, Tue & Wed, to 8pm Thu & Fri) **FREE** This small, private art gallery hosts fabulous temporary exhibitions in its beautiful 4th-floor location. Past exhibitions have considered everything from immigration to the Northwest Passage. Check the website for workshops and be sure to check out the very cool boardroom nest.

Prince's Island Park
PARK

For a little slice of Central Park in the heart of Cowtown, take the bridge over to this island, with grassy fields made for tossing Frisbees, plus bike paths and ample space to stretch out. During the summer months, you can catch a Shakespeare production in the park's natural grass amphitheater or check out the Folk Music Festival (p61) in July. You'll also find the upscale **River Island** restaurant here.

Watch yourself around the river. The water is cold and the current is strong and not suitable for swimming. The bridge to the island from downtown is at the north end of 3rd St SW, near the Eau Claire Market shopping area.

Heritage Park Historical Village
HISTORIC SITE

(☑ 403-268-8500; www.heritagepark.ca; 1900 Heritage Dr SW, at 14th St SW; adult/child $26.25/13.65; ☺ 10am-5pm daily May-Aug, Sat & Sun Sep & Oct; 🖶) Want to see what Calgary used to look like? Head down to this historical park (the largest in Canada!) where all the buildings are from 1915 or earlier. There are 10 hectares of recreated town to explore, with a fort, grain mill, church and school. Go for a hay ride, visit the antique midway or hop on a train. Costumed interpreters are on hand to answer any questions.

You can ride on the steam train, catch a trolley and even go for a spin on the SS *Moyie,* the resident stern-wheeler, as it churns around the Glenmore Reservoir. Heritage Park has always been a big hit with the kiddies and is a great place to soak up Western culture. To get there, take the C-Train to Heritage station, then bus 502. The park is 10km south of Calgary's downtown. It is a registered charity, so your money is going to a good cause.

Calgary Zoo
ZOO

(☑ 403-232-9300; www.calgaryzoo.com; 1300 Zoo Rd NE; adult/child $37/27; ☺ 9am-5pm; 🖶) More than 1000 animals from around the world, many in enclosures simulating their natural habitats, make Calgary's zoo one of the top rated in North America. The zoo's well-regarded conservation team study, reintroduce and protect endangered animals in Canada.

Besides the animals, the zoo has a **Botanical Garden**, with changing garden displays, a **tropical rainforest**, a good **butterfly enclosure** and the 6½-hectare **Prehistoric Park**, featuring fossil displays and life-size dinosaur replicas in natural settings. There's also a captive breeding program for whooping cranes. Picnic areas, concessions and cafes dot the zoo. During winter, when neither

you nor the animals will care to linger outdoors, the admission price is reduced. To get here, take the C-Train east to the Zoo stop.

Calgary Tower
NOTABLE BUILDING

(☑ 403-266-7171; www.calgarytower.com; 101 9th Ave SW; adult/youth $18/9; ☺ observation gallery 9am-9pm Sep-Jun, to 10pm Jul & Aug) This 1968 landmark tower is an iconic feature of the Calgary skyline, though it has now been usurped by numerous taller buildings and is in danger of being lost in a forest of skyscrapers. There is little doubt that the aesthetics of this once-proud concrete structure have passed into the realm of kitsch, but, love it or hate it, the slightly phallic 191m structure is a fixture of the downtown area.

Telus Spark
MUSEUM

(☑ 403-817-6800; www.sparkscience.ca; 220 St George's Dr NE; adult/child $26/19, plus $10 parking; ☺ 10am-5pm; 🖶) You'll wish science class was as fun as the Telus Spark. Kids get a big bang out of this user-friendly and very interactive science center. There is a giant dome, where light shows depicting the cosmos are projected, and a whole raft of other things to discover. Adults Only Nights (random Thursdays) let the 18-plus crowd experience the place without kids.

Contemporary Calgary
GALLERY

(☑ 403-770-1350; www.contemporarycalgary.com; 701 11th St SW; ☺ noon-6pm Wed-Sun) **FREE** This inspiring modern-art gallery has three floors of temporary exhibits that change every four months. The gallery is now in the former Centennial Planetarium in the southwest of Calgary, with displays of modern and contemporary art. The building itself is famous for its brutalist-style architecture.

Inglewood Bird Sanctuary
NATURE RESERVE

(☑ 311; 2425 9th Ave SE; ☺ grounds dawn-dusk, interpretive center 10am-4pm May-Sep, 10am-4pm Mon-Fri, noon-4pm Sat Oct-Apr) **FREE** Get the flock over here. With more than 260 bird species calling the sanctuary home, you're assured of meeting some feathered friends. It's a peaceful place, with walking paths and benches to observe the residents. Twenty-one species of mammal live here too, along with 347 plant species. The center has renovations in the works.

Fish Creek Provincial Park
PARK

(☑ 403-297-5293; www.albertaparks.ca; ☺ 8am-dusk) Cradling the southwest edge of Calgary, this huge park is a sanctuary of wilderness hidden within the city limits. Countless trails intertwine to form a labyrinth, to the delight of walkers, mountain bikers and the many animals who call the park home.

Calaway Park AMUSEMENT PARK
(☑ 403-240-3822; www.calawaypark.com; adult/family $42/130; ⊙ 10am-7pm Jul-early Sep, 11am-6pm Sat & Sun early Sep-early Oct, 10am-7pm Sat & Sun late May-Jun; ⊕) Children of all ages will enjoy Calaway Park, western Canada's largest outdoor family amusement park. It features 30 rides from wild to mild, live stage entertainment, 22 food vendors, 28 different carnival games, a trout-fishing pond and an interactive maze. Youngsters will love the fact that you can **camp** (☑ 403-249-7372; Hwy 1; tent/RV sites from $29/41; ⊙ mid-May–late Sep; ℗ 🛜) at the amusement park.

🏃 Activities & Tours

Eau Claire Rapid Rent CYCLING
(☑ 403-444-5845; Barclay Pde SW; bikes/rollerblades/helmet per day from $40/25/7; ⊙ 10am-6pm May-Sep) Rents out bikes, junior bikes, tandem bikes, child trailers and rollerblades. And rafts, if you happen to have a car and trailer.

Olympic Oval ICE SKATING
(☑ 403-220-7954; www.ucalgary.ca/oval; 288 Collegiate Blvd NW, University of Calgary; adult/child/family $7/5/18.50; ⊙ Aug–mid-Mar) Get the Olympic spirit at the University of Calgary, where you can go for a skate on Olympic Oval. Used for the speed-skating events at the Olympics, it offers public skating on the long track and has skates available to rent, as well as mandatory helmets. See the website for current schedules.

Canada Olympic Park ADVENTURE SPORTS
(☑ 403-247-5452; www.winsport.ca; 88 Canada Olympic Rd SW; mountain biking hill tickets/lessons $30/150; ⊙ 9am-9pm Mon-Fri, 10am-5pm Sat & Sun) In 1988 the Winter Olympics came to Canada for the first time. Calgary played host, and many of the events were contested at Canada Olympic Park. It's near the western edge of town along Hwy 1 – you can't miss the distinctive 70m and 90m ski jumps crowning the skyline.

Check out the **Sports Hall of Fame** (admission $12) and learn about some great Canadian athletes and the story of the Calgary games. If you're feeling more daring, go for a 60-second **bobsled ride** ($135) with a professional driver on a 120km/h Olympic course. It could be the most exhilarating and expensive minute of your life. Alternatively, you can take a trip along a **zip line** ($69) from the top of the ski jump. In winter you can go for a ski, or strap on a snowboard and hit the superpipe. Summer is for mountain biking, when you can ride the lift-serviced trails till your brakes wear out.

Calgary Walking Tours CULTURAL
(☑ 855-620-6520; www.calgarywalks.com; adult/under 3yr/youth $28/free/18) Join the two-hour Downtown City tour to learn about the architecture, history and culture of various buildings, sculptures, gardens and hidden nooks.

Legendary Tours CULTURAL
(☑ 403-285-8376; www.albertalegendarytours.com; tours from $126) These tours get you out to some of Alberta's lesser-known sites, including the Blackfoot Crossing Historical Park (p104) or a helicopter tour over the Columbia Icefield ($199), as well as to more common sites like Lake Louise.

✨ Festivals & Events

Calgary Stampede RODEO
(☑ ticket office 403-269-9822; www.calgarystampede.com; adult/child $18/9; ⊙ 2nd week Jul) Billed as the greatest outdoor show on earth, rodeos don't come much bigger than the Calgary Stampede. Daily shows feature bucking broncos, steer wrestling, chuckwagon races, a midway and a sensational grandstand show. Civic spirits soar, with free pancake breakfasts and a cowboy hat on every head in the city. All of this is strongly tempered by animal rights issues.

Each year, numerous animals are injured and several are put down. Humane societies and animal rights activists strongly oppose endangering animals for entertainment and money-making, and spotlight calf roping and chuckwagon races as two of the most dangerous activities at the Stampede. In 2019 three horses died.

Countering that grim reality is the fact that these same chuckwagon races often allow thoroughbred horses that would have been euthanized immediately after suffering injuries on the horse track to live on for years, even decades, doing what they love most: racing. The owners don't always like the term 'rescue' horse, but it's often true. So the Stampede is a complex, multifaceted issue and a personal one. If you do decide to go to the rodeo, be prepared for the possibility

CAR-LESS IN CALGARY

As the main operations center for Canada's oil industry, Calgary has a reputation for big, unsubtle automobiles plying endless low-rise suburbs on a network of busy highways. But, hidden from the ubiquitous petrol heads is a parallel universe of urban parkways (712km of 'em!) dedicated to walkers, cyclists and skaters, and many of them hug the banks of the city's two mighty rivers, the Bow and the Elbow. Even better, this non-car-traffic network is propped up by a cheap, efficient light-rail system: the C-Train carries a number of daily riders comparable to the Amsterdam metro. Yes, dear reader, Calgary without a car is not an impossible – or even unpleasant – experience.

Not surprisingly, the best trails hug the riverbanks. The Bow River through downtown and over into Prince's Island is eternally popular, with the pedestrian-only Peace Bridge providing a vital link. If you're feeling strong, you can follow the river path 20km south to Fish Creek Provincial Park and plenty more roadless action. Nose Creek Parkway is the main pedestrian artery to and from the north of the city, while the leafy Elbow River Pathway runs from Inglewood to Mission in the south.

Abutting the downtown Bow River Pathway is Eau Claire Rapid Rent, located next to the Eau Claire shopping center.

The city publishes an official *Calgary Pathways and Bikeways* map available from any local leisure center or downloadable from the City of Calgary website (www.calgary.ca). There's also a mobile app at www.calgary.ca/mobileapps.

of an injury to happen before your very eyes. There are lots of other entertainment options: rides, amusements and games. But the tradition has always been the rodeo.

If you do decide to visit Calgary during Stampede, book ahead for accommodations and prepare to pay premium prices: nearly every hotel will be full, and rates go through the roof.

Calgary Folk Music Festival   MUSIC
(www.calgaryfolkfest.com; ⊙ late Jul) Grassroots folk is celebrated at this annual four-day event featuring great live music on Prince's Island. Top-quality acts from around the globe make the trek to Cowtown. It's a mellow scene hanging out on the grass listening to the sounds of summer with what seems like 12,000 close friends. Tickets per day are around $85 or it's $195 for all four days.

Carifest   CARNIVAL
(☑ 403-836-1266; www.carifestcalgary.com; Shaw Millennium Park; ⊙ mid-Aug) The Caribbean comes alive right here in Calgary for two days in August. There's live music, food stalls and a parade full of Carnival-style outfits and merry-making.

🛏 Sleeping

★ HI Calgary City Centre   HOSTEL $
(☑ 403-269-8239; www.hihostels.ca/calgary; 520 7th Ave SE; dm/d from $61/162; @ 🛜) Clean, comfortable and pleasant, this helpful hostel is one of the only options for budget-minded travelers downtown, with fairly standard bunk rooms and a few doubles. It has a kitchen, laundry, pool table and internet facilities, as well as a patio with a barbecue. It's a popular crossroads for travelers and a good place to organize rides and share recommendations.

Compared to other hostels in the area, this is a tight ship, with little leeway for those who want to smoke (whatever herb that may be!), drink or be wild and crazy until 4am. It's open 24 hours, but quiet time is from 11pm to 7am, which means you'll actually be able to sleep. God forbid you're here trying to get work done, but if so, you'll find the days are almost library quiet and the common areas have lots of places to plug in sans distractions.

Calgary West Campground   CAMPGROUND $
(☑ 403-288-0411; www.calgarycampground.com; Hwy 1; tent/RV sites for 2 people $42/61, extra person $5; ⊙ mid-Apr–mid-Oct; 🅿 @ 🛜 🏊) Featuring terraced grounds with views across the city, this campground has sites with great facilities, including a heated outdoor pool, nature trails, mini-golf and free wi-fi. Situated west of downtown Calgary on the Trans-Canada Hwy (Hwy 1), it's a quick trip into the city.

★ Hotel Elan
BOUTIQUE HOTEL **$$**

(☎ 403-229-2040; www.hotelelan.ca; 1122 16th Ave SW; r weekday/weekend from $189/149; P❄@🖥) Stylish and modern, Hotel Elan is popular with business travelers. The 62 rooms are a splendid surprise, with heated bathroom floors and luxury linens among the creature comforts, along with rain shower heads and gourmet coffee pods. Away from downtown, it's an easy walk to the happening scene on 17th Ave.

★ Hotel Arts Kensington
BOUTIQUE HOTEL **$$**

(☎ 403-228-4442; www.hotelartskensington.com; 1126 Memorial Dr NW; r from $223; P⊖@🖥) Under new ownership and with a name change, this small inn has remained a great spot across the river. Impeccable service and rooms to match, plus soaker tubs, fireplaces, balconies, French doors and fine linens are all to be found. It's a short trip over the bridge to downtown and the hotel restaurant is top-notch.

Nuvo Hotel Suites
HOTEL **$$**

(☎ 403-452-6789; www.nuvohotel.com; 827 12th Ave SW; ste from $150; P⊖❄🖥🍽) Your hip home away from home, the Nuvo has large, stylish studio apartments with full kitchens, including washing machines, all for an excellent price in the Beltline neighborhood. Handy for downtown and Uptown 17th action. If you've got Fido or Rover along, this spot is pet friendly as well.

Centro Motel
MOTEL **$$**

(☎ 403-288-6658; www.centromotel.com; 4540 16th Ave NW; r incl breakfast from $114; P❄@🖥) A 'boutique motel' sounds like an oxymoron until you descend on the misleadingly named Centro (not in the center at all!), an old motel building that has been transformed with modern features. Rooms are comfy, almost chic, and come with bathrobes and walk-in spa showers. You'll find it 7km northwest of downtown on the Trans-Canada Hwy (Hwy 1, aka 16th Ave).

Hotel Alma
BOUTIQUE HOTEL **$$**

(☎ 403-220-3203; www.hotelalma.ca; 169 University Gate NW; r from $120, ste $180; ⊖🖥) Cleverly tucked away on the university campus, this fashionable boutique establishment has a definite hip vibe. Super-modern Euro-style rooms are small but cozy rather than cramped. The city suites have one bedroom and are lovely. Guests have a free breakfast, as well as access to on-campus facilities, including a fitness center and pool.

Hotel Arts
BOUTIQUE HOTEL **$$**

(☎ 403-266-4611; www.hotelarts.ca; 119 12th Ave SW; d $188-380; P⊖❄🖥🍽) This boutique hotel plays hard on the fact that it's not part of an international chain. Aimed at travelers with an aesthetic eye, there are hardwood floors, thread counts Egyptians would be envious of, and art on the walls that could be in a gallery. Standard king rooms are small but well designed with rain shower heads and blackout curtains.

★ Hotel Le Germain
BOUTIQUE HOTEL **$$$**

(☎ 403-264-8990; www.germaincalgary.com; 899 Centre St SW; d from $299; P⊖❄@🖥) 🐾 A posh boutique hotel to counteract the bland assortment of franchise inns that service downtown Calgary. Part of a small French-Canadian chain, the style verges on opulent. Rooms are elegant, while the 24-hour gym, in-room massage, complimentary newspapers and stylish lounge add luxury touches.

🍴 Eating

In Calgary, the restaurant scene is blossoming, with lots of options for great eats in all price ranges. Where solitary cows once roamed, vegetables and herbs now prosper, meaning that trusty old stalwart, Alberta beef, is no longer the only thing on the menu.

You'll find good eat streets in Kensington, Inglewood, Uptown 17th Ave and downtown on Stephen St.

★ Alforno Cafe & Bakery
CAFE **$**

(☎ 403-454-0308; www.alforno.ca; 222 7th St SW; mains $9-21; ⏱7am-9pm Mon-Fri, 8am-9pm Sat, 8am-5pm Sun) This ultra-modern, super-comfortable cafe is the kind of place you'll want to hang out all day. Bellinis, beer on tap, carafes of wine and excellent coffee won't discourage you from lingering, nor will magazines, comfy sofas or window seats. With pastas, flatbreads, salads, soups and panini, all homemade, it's difficult to leave room for the amazing cakes, tarts and biscuits.

The sweets category includes espresso shortbread with caramelized sugar and chocolate cream puffs. Breakfasts tempt with eggs Bennie, smashed avocado toast and a bacon breakfast sandwich.

★ 1886 Buffalo Cafe
BREAKFAST **$**

(☎ 403-269-9255; www.1886buffalocafe.com; 187 Barclay Pde SW; breakfast mains $9-19; ⏱6am-3pm Mon-Fri, from 7am Sat & Sun) This is a true salt-of-the-earth diner in the high-rise-dominated city center. Built in 1911 and the only surviving building from the lumber yard once here, the exterior's peeling clapboards sure make it look authentic. This is a ketchup on the table, unlimited coffee refills kind of place famous for its brunches, especially its huevos rancheros.

Myhre's Deli
DELI **$**

(☎ 403-244-6602; 1411 11th St SW; mains $11-14; ⏱ 11am-4pm, to 8pm Thu-Sun) Satisfying meat cravings for 15 years, this deli's mahogany interior and vintage signs are from the Palace of Eats, a Stephen Ave institution from 1918 to 1964. Well-filled smoked Montreal meat sandwiches are made fresh, and all-beef hot dogs, including the steamed Reuben dog with sauerkraut, are embellished with your choice of seven mustards. Everything is topped with a pickle.

Jelly Modern Doughnuts
BAKERY **$**

(☎ 403-453-2053; www.jellymoderndoughnuts. com; 1414 8th St SW; doughnuts $2.50-3; ⏱ 7am-6pm Mon-Fri, 9am-6pm Sat, to 5pm Sun) Bright pink and sugary-smelling, Jelly Modern has grabbed the initiative on weird doughnut flavors. The maple and bacon or bourbon vanilla varieties won't help ward off any impending heart attacks, but they'll make every other doughnut you've ever tasted seem positively bland by comparison.

Gravity Espresso & Wine Bar
CAFE **$**

(☎ 403-457-0697; www.cafegravity.com; 909 10th St SE; light lunches $7-12; ⏱ 8am-5pm Sun & Mon, to 10pm Tue-Thu, to midnight Fri & Sat) 🍷 This hybrid cafe-bar, which alters its personality depending on the clientele and the time of day, is a thoughtful, community-led business. The crux of the operation is the locally roasted Phil & Sebastian coffee beans, but that's just an overture for loads of other stuff, including live acoustic music, curry nights, home-baked snacks and fund-raisers.

Galaxie Diner
DINER **$**

(☎ 403-228-0001; www.galaxiediner.ca; 1413 11th St SW; mains $12-18; ⏱ 7am-3pm Mon-Fri, to 4pm Sat & Sun) Looking more authentic than themed, this classic, no-nonsense 1950s diner serves all-day breakfasts, burgers and milkshakes. Squeeze into a booth, grab a seat at the bar or (more likely) join the queue at the door. The Calgary Sandwich, a scrumptious mix of just about everything under the sun, is a popular favorite, as are the extra-thick, ample-sized, made-to-order milkshakes.

Without Papers
PIZZA **$$**

(☎ 403-457-1154; https://wopizza.ca; 1216 9th Ave SE, Inglewood; pizzas $17-22; ⏱ 11am-10pm Mon-Thu, to midnight Fri & Sat, noon-9pm Sun) These authentic pizzas are baked in an Italian pizza oven that was lowered through the ceiling (you can still see the hole!). The busy pizzeria's name is a nod to early Italian immigrants, while its pizzas and calzones are fresh and creative. The walls are covered in old movie posters and the tables are filled with happy pizza eaters.

Una
PIZZA **$$**

(☎ 403-453-1183; www.unapizzeria.com; 618 17th Ave SW; pizzas $17-24; ⏱ 11:30am-1am) There's often a line out the door but nobody seems to mind waiting – that's how good these thin-crust pizzas are. There's plenty of good house wine, too.

Ox Bar de Tapas
TAPAS **$$**

(☎ 403-457-1432; www.oxtapas.com; 528 17th Ave SW; tapas $5-18; ⏱ 5-11pm Sun, 4-10pm Tue-Thu, to midnight Fri & Sat) Recreating Spain in modern Calgary isn't an obvious go-to, but Ox Bar de Tapas has somehow managed it with colorful tiles and delicious tapas. Order piecemeal from a menu of Manchego cheese, tortilla (Spanish omelet) and cured *jamón serrano*.

★ Market
CANADIAN **$$$**

(☎ 403-474-4414; www.marketcalgary.ca; 718 17th Ave SW; mains lunch $19-26, dinner $18-42; ⏱ 11:30am-11pm) With an earthy yet futuristic feel, award-winning Market has gone a step further in the fresh-local trend. Not only does it bake its own bread, but it also butchers and cures meat, makes cheese and grows 16 varieties of heirloom seeds year-round. As if that weren't enough, it's then all whipped into meals that are scrumptious and entirely satisfying.

★ Teatro
ITALIAN **$$$**

(☎ 403-290-1012; www.teatro.ca; 200 8th Ave SE; mains lunch $19-40, dinner $30-60; ⏱ 11:30am-3pm Mon-Fri, 5-10pm Sun-Thu, to 11pm Fri & Sat) In a regal bank building next to the Epcor Centre for the Performing Arts, Teatro has an art nouveau touch with its marble bar top, swirling metalwork and high-backed curved sofas. Dishes are works of art and fuse Italian influences, French nouvelle cuisine and a bit of traditional Alberta. Service is friendly and impeccable.

JOSEPH HOLOIEN / SHUTTERSTOCK ©

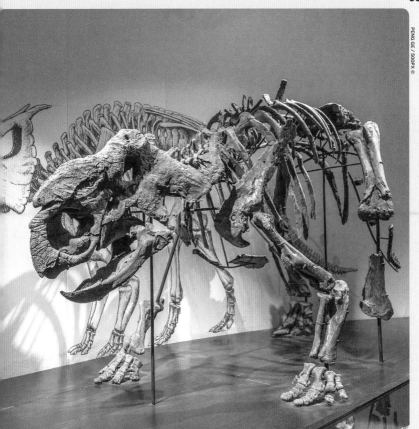

Ukrainian Cultural Heritage Village (p51)

Watching role-players acting out what life in a rural Ukrainian-Canadian community was like is an interesting way to experience Ukrainian culture.

Royal Tyrrell Museum of Palaeontology (p98)

One of the preeminent dinosaur museums on the planet, this museum was made even better by a $5.9 million expansion project completed in 2019.

Miette Hot Springs (p91)

More remote than Banff's historic springs, Miette Hot Springs are surrounded by peaks and are especially enjoyable when the fall snow is drifting down.

Icefields Parkway (p76)

This 230km highway winds through the pristine wilderness of the Canadian Rockies.

Mercato

ITALIAN $$$

(☎403-263-5535; www.mercatogourmet.com; 2224 4th St SW; mains $21-55; ⊗11:30am-9pm Sun-Wed, to 9:30pm Thu, to 10pm Fri & Sat, deli from 9am daily) Attached to an open-plan Italian market-deli that sells everything from coffee to salami, Mercato is one of those local restaurants that gets everything right. Decor, service, atmosphere, food and price all hit the spot in a modern but authentic take on la dolce vita in the endearing Mission neighborhood.

Blink

FUSION $$$

(☎403-263-5330; www.blinkcalgary.com; 111 8th Ave SW; mains $24-42; ⊗11am-2pm Mon-Fri, 5-10pm Mon-Sat) 🍴 It's true: you could miss this small oasis tucked along a busy street and that would be a shame. Inside this trendy gastro haven, an acclaimed chef oversees an ever-evolving menu of fine dishes like smoked ricotta ravioli with walnuts and truffle vinaigrette or grilled striploin with caramelized shallots and red-wine sauce. Food is fresh and, wherever possible, locally sourced.

Drinking & Nightlife

Craft cocktail, thy name is Calgary. Hit 17th Ave NW for a slew of martini lounges and crowded pubs, and 4th St SW for a lively after-work scene. There's even a password-protected speakeasy now. Other spots include Kensington Rd NW and Stephen Ave. Calgary's LGBTIQ+ scene is ever-improving; even the Stampede has a drag show now.

★ Betty Lou's Library

COCKTAIL BAR

(☎403-454-4774; www.bettylouslibrary.com; 908 17th Ave SW; ⊗5pm-12:30am Tue-Thu, to 2am Fri & Sat) Betty Lou's Library won't be for everyone, but if you like feeling like you've stepped back in time to Prohibition 1920s, then you'll get a kick out of coming here. The cocktails are superb; if you can't decide just ask one of the bartenders for a custom-crafted cup of yum. You'll need a password to enter, so call first.

The entrance is actually on 16th Ave, not 17th. Look for a red light, a bookshelf and a phone.

Note also that there are some house rules that are enforced – among them, no talking or making chitchat with other parties at the bar. That means this spot is best enjoyed with a friend or two, unless you like drinking alone.

★ Pr%f

COCKTAIL BAR

(☎403-246-2414; www.proofyyc.com; 1302 1st St SW; ⊗4pm-midnight Sun & Mon, to 1am Tue-Sat) No, that isn't a typo. Pr%f might be small but the bar is big enough to require a library ladder, and the drinks menu not only requires time, but also imagination. The menu itself is a beautiful thing to behold and the drinks look so stunning, you almost don't want to drink them. But you do. Trust us, you do.

Jusu

JUICE BAR

(☎403-452-2159; www.jusubar.com; 816 16th Ave SW; juice $7-12; ⊗9am-6pm) Cold-pressed juice is the latest craze in Calgary. Like a meal in a bottle, it can be found in trendy cafes or at this retail store. Some flavors are super-tasty, others more on the healthy side than flavorful, but you're sure to find something you like. At the end of each day, unused food is donated to local shelters.

Analog Coffee

COFFEE

(☎403-910-5959; www.analogcoffee.ca; 740 17th Ave SW; coffees $3-6; ⊗7am-10pm, to midnight Jul & Aug) The third-wave coffee scene is stirring in Calgary, led by companies like Fratello, which runs this narrow, overflowing hipsterish 17th Ave cafe. Beans of the day are displayed on a clipboard and there are rows of retro vinyl along the back wall. Teas are here, too, as are tasty desserts aplenty.

Barley Mill

PUB

(☎403-290-1500; www.barleymillcalgary.com; 201 Barclay Pde SW; ⊗11am-midnight, from 10am Sun) Built in a 1900s style, with the original distillery's lumber used for the top floor and an actual waterwheel churning outside, the Barley Mill draws crowds for its pub grub, long lineup of draft beers and a well-stocked bar. Two patios for when it's warm and a big stone fireplace for when it's not keep it busy in every season.

Twisted Element

GAY & LESBIAN

(☎403-802-0230; www.twistedelement.ca; 1006 11th Ave SW; ⊗9pm-2am Wed-Sun) Consistently voted the best queer dance venue by the local community, this club has weekly drag shows, karaoke nights and DJs spinning nightly.

☆ Entertainment

Calgary has a lively and varied entertainment scene, from comedy shows and improv theater to Shakespeare and indie films only a Canadian could love.

Ironwood Stage & Grill
LIVE MUSIC

(☑ 403-269-5581; www.ironwoodstage.ca; 1229 9th Ave SE, Inglewood; ☺ shows 8pm Sun-Thu, 9pm Fri & Sat) Cross over into the hip universe of Inglewood to find the grassroots of Calgary's music scene, here inside the Garry Theatre. Local bands alternate with bigger touring acts for nightly music in the welcoming, woody confines of Ironwood. Country and folk are the staples. Events are all ages.

Calgary Flames
SPECTATOR SPORT

(☑ 403-777-2177; http://flames.nhl.com) Arch-rival of the Edmonton Oilers, the Calgary Flames play ice hockey from October to April at the **Saddledome** (☑ 403-777-4646; Stampede Park). Make sure you wear red to the game and head down to 17th Ave afterward, or the 'Red Mile,' as they call it during play-offs.

Loose Moose Theatre Company
THEATER

(☑ 403-265-5682; www.loosemoose.com; 1235 26th Ave SE) Guaranteed to be a fun night out, Loose Moose has digs near the Inglewood neighborhood. It specializes in improv comedy and, at times, audience participation (you've been warned). You'll also find kids' theater.

Arts Commons
THEATER

(☑ 403-294-7455; https://artscommons.ca; 205 8th Ave SE) This is the hub for live theater in Calgary. With four theaters and one of the best concert halls in North America, you can see everything from ballet to Bollywood here.

Globe Cinema
CINEMA

(☑ 403-262-3309; www.globecinema.ca; 617 8th Ave SW; tickets $10; ☺ 6:30-9:30pm, matinees Sat & Sun) This art-house theater specializes in foreign films and Canadian cinema – both often hard to find in mainstream movie houses. Look for discounts on Tuesdays and matinees on the weekend.

Broken City Social Club
LIVE MUSIC

(☑ 403-262-9976; www.brokencity.ca; 613 11th Ave SW; ☺ 11am-2am) There's something on stage here most nights – everything from jazz jams to hip-hop, along with comedy and quiz nights. The rooftop patio is ace in the summer, and the small but well-curated menu keeps you happy whether you're after a steak sandwich or vegan cauliflower wings.

Calgary Stampeders
SPECTATOR SPORT

(☑ 403-289-0258; www.stampeders.com) The Calgary Stampeders, part of the Canadian Football League (CFL), play from July to September at **McMahon Stadium** (1817 Crowchild Trail NW) in the University District, 6km northwest of downtown.

Pumphouse Theatres
THEATER

(☑ 403-263-0079; http://pumphousetheatre.ca; 2140 Pumphouse Ave SW) Set in what used to be, you guessed it, the pumphouse, this theater company puts on avant-garde, edgy productions like *One Man Star Wars Trilogy*.

🔒 Shopping

Calgary has several hot shopping spots, but these districts are reasonably far apart. The Kensington area and 17th Ave SW have a good selection of interesting, fashionable clothing shops and funky trinket outlets. Stephen Ave Walk is a pedestrian mall with shops, bookstores and atmosphere. Inglewood is good for antiques, junk, apothecaries, and secondhand books and vinyl.

Tea Trader
TEA

(☑ 403-264-0728; www.teatrader.com; 1228a 9th Ave SE, Inglewood; ☺ 10am-5pm Tue-Sat, noon-4pm Sun) This wonderful shop is up a set of stairs and very easy to miss, but it's worth searching out for its lovely aroma wafting around the room, cheery, happy-to-help proprietors and wealth of tea options. Teas from all over the world line the shelves, as well as some local flavors. If you can't find what you're looking for, just ask!

Alberta Boot Co
SHOES

(☑ 403-263-4623; www.albertaboot.com; 50 50th Ave SE; ☺ 9am-6pm Mon-Sat) Visit the factory and store run by the province's only Western boot manufacturer and pick up a pair of your choice made of kangaroo, bullhide or boring old cowhide, or just breathe in the aroma of leather and tanning oil. Over 200 hours of labor go into each boot, and prices range from $385 to $2100 or more.

If the boots are too pricey, there are free coasters at the door made from leather scraps that make a nice souvenir.

Smithbilt Hats
HATS

(☑ 403-244-9131; https://smithbilthats.com; 1015 11th St SE; ☺ 9am-5pm Mon-Wed & Fri, to 7pm Thu, 10am-4pm Sat) Ever wondered how a cowboy hat is made? Here is your chance to find out. Smithbilt has been shaping hats in the traditional way since 1919 when you parked your horse out front. You can pick up one made of straw or beaver felt and priced accordingly, or just marvel at the artisans as they work, crafting, cutting and shaping.

Mountain Equipment Co-op SPORTS & OUTDOORS
(☑ 403-269-2420; www.mec.ca; 830 10th Ave SW; ⊘ 10am-9pm Mon-Fri, 9am-6pm Sat, 10am-5pm Sun) MEC is the place to get your outdoor kit sorted before heading into the hills. It's a Canadian institution with a huge selection of outdoor equipment, travel gear, active clothing and books.

ℹ Information

Rockyview General Hospital (☑ 403-943-3000; 7007 14th St SW; ⊘ 24hr) Emergency room open 24 hours.

Visit Calgary (www.visitcalgary.com; 101 9th Ave SW; ⊘ 8am-5pm) Operates a visitor center in the base of the Calgary Tower (p59). The staff can help you find accommodations. Information booths are also available at both the arrivals and departures levels of the airport.

ℹ Getting There & Away

AIR

Calgary International Airport (YYC; ☑ 403-735-1200; www.yyc.com; 2000 Airport Rd NE) is about 15km northeast of the center off Barlow Trail, a 25-minute drive away.

BUS

Luxurious **Red Arrow** (https://redarrow.ca; 205 9th Ave SE) buses run to Edmonton ($76,

3½ hours, six daily) and Lethbridge ($53, three hours, two daily).

Canmore and Banff ($72, 2¼ hours, eight daily) and Lake Louise ($99, 2½ hours, eight daily) are served by **Brewster Express** (☑ 403-762-6700; www.banffjaspercollection.com/brewster-express).

Red Arrow picks up downtown on the corner of 9th Ave SE and 1st Ave SE. Brewster Express buses pick up at various downtown hotels. Inquire when booking.

CAR & MOTORCYCLE

All the major car-rental firms are represented at the airport and downtown.

Alberta Motor Association (☑ 403-240-5300; https://ama.ab.ca; 4700 17th Ave SW)

CanaDream (☑ 888-480-9726, international calls 925-255-8383; www.canadream.com)

Cruise Canada (☑ 403-291-4963; www.cruisecanada.com)

ℹ Getting Around

TO/FROM THE AIRPORT

You can go between the airport and downtown on public transportation. From the airport, take bus 57 to the Whitehorn stop (northeast of the city center) and transfer to the C-Train; reverse that process coming from downtown. You can also take bus 300 from the city center all the way to the airport. Either way, the trip costs only $3.40, and takes between 45 minutes and an hour.

For transport to Banff or other places outside Calgary, the **Airporter Shuttle Express** (☑ 403-509-4799; www.airportshuttleexpress.com; from $85) and **Banff Airport Taxi** (☑ 403-720-5788;

> **WORTH A TRIP**
>
> ## TURNER VALLEY
>
> As you head south on the Cowboy Trail (Hwy 22), you'll pass through Turner Valley. At first glance it looks like many of the small towns in this region, but it's definitely worth stopping here to fill both your belly and your liquor cabinet.
>
> **Chuck Wagon Cafe** (☑ 403-933-0003; 105 Sunset Blvd; mains $9-20; ⊘ 8am-2:30pm Mon-Fri, to 3:30pm Sat & Sun) Housed in a tiny red barn, this legendary cafe feels much like the homestead kitchen it is – it draws hungry diners from miles around. The enormous, all-day breakfast of smoked hash, triple-A steak and eggs Benedict will have you shouting 'Yeehaw!' This is ranch cooking at its best.
>
> **Eau Claire Distillery** (☑ 403-933-5408; www.eauclairedistillery.ca; 113 Sunset Blvd SW; tasting $8.50, tasting & tour $15, cocktails $15; ⊘ 11am-5pm Sun-Thu, to 8pm Fri & Sat, tours noon, 2pm & 4pm) Next door to the cafe, this is the province's first craft distillery, using Alberta grain and custom-crafted German stills. Having taken over the town's original movie theater and built on the site of the neighboring brothel, this award-winning place pours tastings of gin and vodka that are infused with natural flavors like prickly pear and lemon, as well as single-malt whiskey. Take a tour and sit yourself down at the bar for a cocktail, or try the flight of 'Seven Deadly Gins.'

www.banffairporttaxi.com) are useful options. The Airporter Shuttle Express can also drop you in Calgary for around $85.

A taxi to the airport costs between about $40 and $55 from downtown.

CAR & MOTORCYCLE

Parking in downtown Calgary is an expensive nightmare – a policy designed to push people to use public transportation. Luckily, downtown hotels generally have garages. Private lots charge about $20 per day. There is also some metered parking, which accepts coins and credit cards. Outside the downtown core, parking is free and easy to find.

PUBLIC TRANSPORTATION

Calgary Transit (www.calgarytransit.com) is efficient and clean. Use the website's handy plan-your-trip section to find out how to get where you're going. You can choose from the Light Rapid Transit (LRT) rail system, aka the C-Train, and ordinary buses. One fare ($3.40) entitles you to transfer to other buses or C-Trains. The C-Train is free in the downtown area along 7th Ave between 10th St SW and 3rd St SE. If you're going further or need a transfer, buy your ticket from a machine on the C-Train platform. Most buses run at 15- to 30-minute intervals daily. There is no late-night service.

TAXI

For a cab, call **Checker Cabs** (☑ 403-299-9999; www.thecheckergroup.com) or **Calgary United Cabs** (☑ 403-777-1111; https://calgarycabs.ca).

BANFF & JASPER NATIONAL PARKS

With the Rocky Mountains stretched across them, Banff and Jasper National Parks are filled with dramatic, untamed wilderness. Rugged mountaintops scrape the skyline while enormous glaciers cling to their precipices. Glassy lakes flash emerald, turquoise and sapphire, filled by waterfalls tumbling down cliff faces and thundering through bottomless canyons. Deep forests blanket wide valleys and lofty alpine meadows explode with vibrant flowers. It's the scenery that you only expect to see on postcards, right here at your fingertips. And through it wander a cast of elusive wildlife characters such as bears, elk, moose, wolves and big-horn sheep.

Of the thousands of national parks scattered around the world today, Banff, created in 1885, is the third oldest and Canada's first, while adjacent Jasper was only 22 years

behind. Situated on the eastern side of the Canadian Rockies, the two bordering parks were designated Unesco World Heritage sites in 1984. In contrast to some of North America's more remote parks, they both support small towns that lure from two to five million visitors each year.

Despite the throngs who come for the parks' more famous sites, like Lake Louise and Miette Hot Springs, it's by no means difficult to escape to a more tranquil experience of this sublime wonderland. However you choose to experience the parks, be it through hiking, backcountry skiing, paddling or simply sitting at a lake's edge beneath towering, castle-like mountains, the intensity and scale of these parks will bowl over even the most seasoned traveler. The more you see, the more you'll come to appreciate these parks' magic – and the more you'll want to discover.

Kananaskis Country

☑ 403 / POP 1350

The area collectively known as Kananaskis Country (or K-Country to the locals) covers a vast area to the south and east of Banff National Park, comprising several side-by-side provincial parks and protected areas, including Peter Lougheed Provincial Park, Elbow Valley, Sheep Valley, Ghost River Wilderness Area and Don Getty Wildland Provincial Park.

While visitors and tourists make a bee-line for Banff's trails, many Albertans prefer to hike in K-Country, where the routes are quieter, the scenery is just as impressive and that all-important sense of wilderness is much easier to come by. It's less well known than Banff, but with a bit of research you'll find some fantastic hikes and trails, as well as plenty of sky-topping peaks, mountain lakes and outdoor pursuits. And with less traffic and no fencing, you are likely to encounter plenty of wildlife here.

🕴 Activities

★ **Peter Lougheed Provincial Park**   HIKING
(www.albertaparks.ca/peter-lougheed) Kananaski Country's quiet trails and backcountry offer superb hiking, especially around this 304-sq-km park on the west side of Kananaskis Valley, which includes the Upper and Lower Kananaskis lakes and the highest navigable vehicle pass in Canada. It's an excellent area

Banff National Park

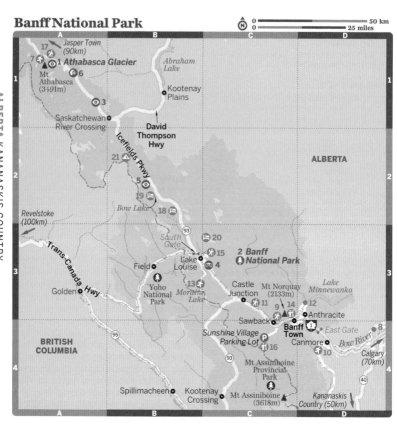

ALBERTA KANANASKIS COUNTRY

for wildlife spotting: watch for foxes, wolves, bears, lynx and coyotes.

This area is an important wildlife corridor and the valley has been subjected to very little development. Recommended half-day hikes include the 3km trail to **Boulton Creek** (one hour) and the loop hike to the natural bowl of Ptarmigan Cirque. Longer day routes include the 7.2km hike to **Mt Indefatigable** (four hours) and the 16km **Upper Kananaskis Lake Circuit** (five hours).

Trail leaflets and information on conditions are available from the park's **visitor center** (☎403-678-0760; www.albertaparks.ca/peter-lougheed; Kananaskis Lakes Trail; ☺9:30am-4:30pm Mon-Thu, to 5:30pm Fri-Sun Jul & Aug, 9:30am-4:30pm daily rest of year, closed mid-Mar–early May & mid-Oct–early Dec) near Kananaskis Lakes.

★ **King Creek Ridge**   HIKING
You have to be something of a masochist to tackle this 6.2km out-and-back trail, but

the views up top are beyond belief. Starting from the King Creek picnic area on the east side of Hwy 40, parallel the highway briefly north on a clear but unsignposted footpath to bypass a creek gully, then head northeast straight up into the hills.

Over the next 1.5km you'll gain about 500m as the trail climbs relentlessly up through a mix of forest and steep flowery meadows. After about 90 minutes your efforts are rewarded as you crest King Creek Ridge and wave after wave of knife-edged mountains unfolds to the east, with the entire Kananaskis Valley spread out below you to the north and south. Turn left (north) to continue along the ridgeline as long as you like. You'll reach the ridge's high point (2420m) about 3.1km into the hike. From here, retrace your steps down the mountain.

Ptarmigan Cirque   HIKING
This 5km, two-hour loop hike starts in the high country near Highwood Pass (at

Banff National Park

2206m, the highest paved pass in Canada; usually open from June to October) and just keeps getting higher. Park on the west side of Hwy 40 just south of the pass, then walk back north and cross east over the highway, following the signposted trail for Ptarmigan Cirque.

Kananaskis Outfitters ADVENTURE
(☑ 403-591-7000; www.kananaskisoutfitters.com; 1 Mt Sparrowhawk Cres, Kananaskis Village; bike/ski rental per day from $50/30; ☺9am-7pm Jul & Aug, shorter hours rest of year) This outfitter in Kananaskis Village rents out bikes, cross-country skis and fat bikes for winter rides. It also runs canoe tours in the summer on Barrier Lake and winter bike tours to the picturesquely frozen Troll Falls.

Kananaskis Nordic Spa SPA
(☑ 403-591-6800; www.knordicspa.com; 1 Centennial Dr, Kananaskis Village; day pass $85; ☺9am-9pm Sun-Thu, to 11pm Fri & Sat) K-Country's splashiest new attraction is this full-service spa with oodles of hot and cold pools, saunas, a steam cabin, an on-site bistro and a variety of massage treatments. A single pass grants all-day access to the grounds. It's first-come, first-served and you must be 18 or older to enter; prepare to join the waiting list during busy periods.

Nakiska SKIING
(www.skinakiska.com; Hwy 40; day pass adult/youth $90/68; ☺9am-4pm early Nov–mid-Apr) The K-Country's only ski resort was one of the main venues for the 1988 Winter Olympics.

It's still a popular place to hit the slopes, though the facilities and runs are much less developed than in nearby Banff. Shuttle buses run throughout winter from Canmore and Banff, making Nakiska a credible (and often quieter) alternative to the Big Three.

There are more than five dozen runs spread out over 413 hectares, with plenty of scope for off-piste riding on the slopes of Mt Allan. More than half of the runs are rated intermediate, so Nakiska is a good all-round resort for most mid-level skiers.

Snowboarders can tackle the challenging Najibska Rail Park. The resort also has some of the Rockies' only accessible areas for glade skiing.

Chinook Rafting RAFTING
(Map p70; ☑ 866-330-7238; www.chinookrafting.com; Hwy 1A; rafting adult/child from $97/62; ☺mid-May–mid-Sep) A great company for families, Chinook runs four-hour trips on Class II and III sections of the beautiful Kananaskis River. Kids must be five years or older to participate.

🛏 Sleeping & Eating

★ **Sundance Lodges** CAMPGROUND $
(☑ 403-591-7122; www.sundancelodges.com; Kananaskis Trail/Hwy 40; campsites $34, small tipis $70, large tipis or trappers' tents $94-99; ☺mid-May–Sep) For that authentic Canadian experience, try the hand-painted tipis and old-timey trappers' tents at this privately run campground. As you'd expect, facilities are basic – sleeping platforms and a kerosene lantern are about all you'll find inside

– so you'll need the usual camping gear, but kids are bound to lap up the John Muir vibe.

HI Kananaskis Wilderness Hostel HOSTEL **$**

(☑403-591-7333; www.hihostels.ca; 1 Ribbon Creek Rd, Kananaskis Village; dm/d $38/95; ☺reception 5-9pm, closed late Oct-late Nov & 2 weeks in Apr; P☎) The rustic exterior at this place just north of Kananaskis Village might fool you into thinking you'll be roughing it, but inside you'll find HI's most luxurious wilderness hostel, with indoor plumbing, propane-heated showers, shiny pine floors, plush sofas, a fire-lit lounge and a kingly kitchen. Four private rooms supplement the 14-bed dorms, and the region-savvy manager is very welcoming.

Mt Kidd RV Park CAMPGROUND **$**

(☑403-591-7700; www.mountkiddrv.com; 1 Mt Kidd Dr; RV sites without/with hookups $37/54; ☺year-round) Halfway along the Kananaskis Valley and handily placed for the facilities around Kananaskis Village, this place is the best option for trailer and RV campers, with full hookups and over 200 sites, plus comprehensive facilities, including tennis courts, a kids' wading pool, laundry, a basic grocery store and games rooms with ping pong, pool and foosball.

★ **Mt Engadine Lodge** LODGE **$$$**

(☑587-807-0570; www.mountengadine.com; 1 Mt Shark Rd; s/d/q $199/525/549, glamping tent $525, d/q cabin $499/599; P☎) You can't get much more rural – or more peaceful – than this remote mountain lodge decorated with antler chandeliers and antique skis and snowshoes. Lodge rooms and family suites with balcony and sitting room overlook unspoiled meadows and a natural salt lick frequented by moose. Surrounding the lodge are cozy cabins and glamping tents sleeping two to four.

Lodge rates include four hearty meals, including a build-your-own lunch, afternoon tea and a gourmet dinner whipped up by a five-star chef. Look for the Mt Shark Rd turnoff on the west side of the Smith Dorrien/Spray Trail Rd, about 30km northwest of the Kananaskis Lakes or 40km south of Canmore.

Moose Family Kitchen CAFE **$**

(☑403-591-7979; mains $5-11; ☺8am-10pm daily) Presided over by its delightful Japanese chef-owner, this no-nonsense cafe in the heart of Kananaskis Village serves an eclectic mix of bagels, sandwiches, panini, milkshakes, ramen, curry and teriyaki bowls. It's not fine dining, but it's all served with a smile, and it's one of the few budget options in K-Country.

★ **Mt Engadine**
Lodge Dining Room CANADIAN **$$**

(☑587-807-0570; www.mountengadine.com; Smith Dorrien/Spray Trail, Kananaskis; brunch/afternoon tea/dinner $25/17.50/55; ☺tea 2-5pm, dinner 7pm, brunch 10am-1pm Sun) It's worth detouring off the Smith Dorrien/Spray Trail for a bite at this charming backwoods lodge. Drop-ins are welcome for the daily afternoon tea, which features freshly baked goods, fancy cheeses, local meats and fresh fruit. With 24 hours' notice, day trippers can also enjoy the lodge's renowned multicourse family-style dinners (nightly) or the sumptuous Sunday brunch.

ℹ Information

Elbow Valley Visitor Centre (☑403-678-0760; www.albertaparks.ca; Hwy 66; ☺9am-12:30pm & 1:30-4:30pm Fri-Sun mid-May–mid-Oct) Just west of Bragg Creek.

Kananaskis Information Centre at Barrier Lake (☑403-678-0760; www.albertaparks.ca; Hwy 40; ☺9am-1pm & 1:30-6pm mid-Jun–early Sep, shorter hours rest of year) Located 6.5km south of the junction of Hwys 1 and 40.

Peter Lougheed Information Centre (p71) Near the junction of Hwys 40 and 742, north of Kananaskis Lakes.

ℹ Getting There & Away

Brewster Express (Map p80; ☑403-760-6934; www.banffjaspercollection.com/brewster-sightseeing; 100 Gopher St; ☺7am-9pm) runs buses between the Pomeroy Kananaskis Mountain Lodge in Kananaskis Village to Calgary's airport (adult/youth $72/36). You can also sometimes get a shuttle from the lodge to Nakoda Resort on Hwy 1, where you can meet up with Brewster buses to Banff or Jasper.

Navigating K-Country is much easier if you have your own wheels. There are two main roads through the area, which link up near the Kananaskis Lakes to form a convenient loop. The main Kananaskis Trail (Hwy 40) travels through the center of Kananaskis Valley from Barrier Lake, while the unpaved gravel Spray Lakes Trail (Hwy 742) heads northwest from the junction near Lower Kananaskis Lake all the way back to Canmore.

Be sure to double-check your policy if you're driving a rental; not all rental insurance will cover you on Hwy 742. Also be aware that there is virtually no cell-phone service along the route and no gas stations.

Canmore

📍 403 / POP 13,992

Canmore is Banff for locals, a former coal-mining town that reinvented itself as an outdoorsy hub during the 1988 Winter Olympics, when it hosted the cross-country skiing events. Spend time sitting in a downtown bar or cafe and you'll quickly intuit that most of the population lives here because they love it – and no wonder! The hiking, cycling, skiing and spiky mountain vistas are magnificent, and the rock climbing – Canmore acts as HQ for the Alpine Club of Canada – is world-class. Quieter, cheaper and more relaxed than Banff, Canmore makes a good launching pad for the national park or the more hidden pleasures of Kananaskis Country to the south.

While not officially part of Banff National Park, Canmore is a mere 24km southeast of Banff Town and 7km from the park's East Gate along Hwy 1.

◎ Sights & Actvities

Big Head   SCULPTURE

At the end of Main St, half-buried in gravel by the Bow River, sits the impressive sculpture known as the Big Head (for reasons that will quickly become obvious). Created by the artist Al Henderson, the sculpture was inspired by Canmore's name – the original town of Canmore in northwest Scotland was called *ceann mór*, a Gaelic word meaning 'great head' or 'chief.'

The sculpture has become a much-loved landmark, and the head's shiny pate is sometimes adorned to mark town festivities. It occasionally even gets its very own woolly toque in winter.

★ **Canmore Nordic Centre**   MOUNTAIN BIKING, SKIING

(📍403-678-2400; www.canmorenordiccentre.ca; Olympic Way; winter day-pass adult/youth/child $15/11.25/9, summer trail-use free; ⊙9am-5:30pm) Nestled at the foot of Mt Rundle on the way to the Spray Lakes Reservoir, this huge trail center was originally developed for the Nordic events of the 1988 Winter Olympics. It's now one of western Canada's best mountain-biking and cross-country skiing centers, with over 100km of trails developed by some of the nation's top trail designers.

There are graded routes to suit all abilities, from easy rides on wide dirt roads to technical single tracks and full-on downhills. You can bring your own bike, or hire one from Trail Sports (📍403-678-6764; www.trailsports.ab.ca; Canmore Nordic Centre, 2003 Olympic Way; bike per 2hr/day from $40/60, ski package per 2hr/day $25/30; ⊙9am-6pm), opposite the center's day lodge. If mountain biking is not your thing, most of the center's trails are also open to walkers, orienteerers and roller-skiers.

In winter, there are over 65km of ski trails – both machine-groomed and natural (ungroomed) – with 6.5km lit for night skiing.

Whatever the time of year, take precautions to avoid wildlife encounters, as the routes cross through areas of backcountry that form part of the Bow Valley Wildlife Corridor, and you might find that grizzlies, black bears and moose have decided to use the trails, too.

The center is a 4km drive from Canmore, just off Spray Lakes Rd. Cross the Bow River at the west edge of downtown, take Rundle Dr, continue south along Three Sisters Dr and follow signs to the Canmore Nordic Centre.

Gear Up   CYCLING

(📍403-678-1636; www.gearupsport.com; 1302 Bow Valley Trail; bike rental/ski rental per day from $50/20; ⊙9am-6pm; 🚲) This easy-to-navigate Canmore rental shop is handy on account of its position within freewheeling distance of the start of the Legacy Trail (p75). As well as trail bikes, they've got junior, full-suspension and trailers, climbing gear, paddleboards (including blow-ups for easy transportation) and both alpine and Nordic skis. Bikes come with a handy repair kit, plus helmet and lock.

Elevation Place   HEALTH & FITNESS

(📍403-678-8920; www.elevationplace.ca; 700 Railway Ave; adult/child pool only $8/5, full facility $16/8; ⊙9am-10pm Mon-Fri, to 9pm Sat & Sun; 🚲) Canmore's impressive sports center replicates many of the activities you can do outdoors, so if the weather's not cooperating, this is a fantastic place to escape the elements. The kid-friendly swimming pool is excellent, and the huge indoor climbing wall is an ideal place to get to grips with the basics before you tackle a real crag.

Snowy Owl Tours   DOG SLEDDING

(📍403-678-4369; www.snowyowltours.com; 829 10th St; 2hr tour 1-/2-person sled $425/475, 3- or 4-person sled $600) Dogsledding has been a traditional mode of travel in the Canadian

Rockies for centuries, and it's a wonderful way to see the wilderness. Snowy Owl offers sled trips ranging from two hours to two days on custom-built sleighs pulled by your own well-cared-for team of Siberian, Canadian and Alaskan huskies. The sledding season is usually from December to April.

On Top Mountaineering
CLIMBING

(☎ 403-678-2717; www.ontopmountaineering.com; 340 Canyon Close) This long-established, locally run outfit organizes outstanding outdoor adventures in the Rockies, including ice climbing, backpacking, classic peak ascents and five-day climbing courses. Other trips include trekking across glaciers from Bow Lake to Peyto Lake in summer and backcountry hut-to-hut skiing in winter. Alternatively, devise your own custom route with a private guide (from $520 per day for two people).

Canmore Cave Tours
ADVENTURE

(☎ 403-678-8819; www.canmorecavetours.com; 129 Bow Meadows Crescent, Unit 202) Buried deep beneath the Grotto Mountain near Canmore is a system of deep caves known as the **Rat's Nest**. Canmore Cave Tours runs guided trips into the maze of twisting passageways and claustrophobic caverns. Be prepared to get very wet and muddy, and brace yourself for chilly temperatures, as the caves stay at a constant 5°C (41°F) year-round.

🛏 Sleeping

⭐ Canmore
Clubhouse
HOSTEL $

(☎ 403-678-3200; www.alpineclubofcanada.ca; Indian Flats Rd; dm $45, d & tr $100; 🅿🐾) 🐾 Steeped in climbing history and mountain mystique, the Alpine Club of Canada's beautiful hostel sits on a rise 5km east of town, with stellar views of the Three Sisters through big picture windows. Dorms in the main building have access to a spacious guest kitchen and are supplemented by sweet, well-priced, three-person private rooms in the Boswell Cabin just uphill.

HI members and Alpine Club of Canada members get generous discounts. It's a great place to find climbing partners or just soak up the spirit of adventure. The Alpine Club, whose headquarters is located in the same building, sells bear spray and outdoor activity guides, offers classes in mountaineering and maintains several backcountry huts.

Canmore Downtown Hostel
HOSTEL $

(☎ 403-675-1000; www.canmoredowntownhostel.ca; 302 Old Canmore Rd; dm with shared/private bathroom $50/55, d/tr $185/216; 🐾) A welcome addition to Canmore, this bright modern hostel opened in 2019 and has already won a loyal following. Its location at the far end of a parking lot adjoining the Trans-Canada Highway doesn't immediately inspire confidence, but climb to the spacious 2nd floor common room, the teal-walled guest kitchen and the clean wood-clad dorms and things quickly improve.

A sister project to the Jasper Downtown Hostel (p94), this place has the same friendly, community-minded vibe, with $8 bear-spray rental, a notice board to help you find hiking partners and comfy seats for lounging. The microbrewery just across the parking lot doesn't hurt, and it's only a short walk to the shops and restaurants of downtown Canmore.

Bow River Campground
CAMPGROUND $

(☎ 403-673-2163; www.bowvalleycampgrounds.com; Hwy 1; tent/RV sites $28/40; ⊘May-Oct) The best option for camping close to Canmore is this riverside site 1.6km southeast along Hwy 1. It's sandwiched between the river and the highway, so it's not as peaceful as it could be, but it's pleasant enough if you can bag a spot by the water. New sites added in 2017 offer full electrical and water hook-ups for RVs.

Canadian Artisans
B&B $$

(☎ 403-678-4138; www.canadianartisans.ca; 1016 9th Ave; d $250; 🅿🐾) This quirky B&B is tucked away in the forest on the edge of Canmore. Two wooden suites are detached from the main house; they're comfortable, if not plush. The Treehouse Suite has picture windows, stained-glass door panels, a futuristic shower and a lovely vaulted roof. The Foresthouse is somewhat more cramped, with a whirlpool tub next to the queen-sized bed.

Windtower Lodge & Suites
HOTEL $$

(☎ 403-609-6600; www.windtower.ca; 160 Kananaskis Way; d/ste/2-room ste $199/319/509; 🅿@🐾) This modern, well-appointed hotel on a suburban backstreet is a good option if you're looking for a suite – both the one- and two-room options come with full kitchen, washing machine and dryer. Standard rooms are comfortable but small. Some rooms have fine views of the Three Sisters, and all have access to a fitness center and an outdoor hot tub.

LOCAL KNOWLEDGE

BANFF LEGACY TRAIL

It's not often that getting from point A to B involves dazzling scenery, the possibility of spotting a moose and a huge dose of mountain air. The Banff Legacy Trail (www. pc.gc.ca/en/pn-np/ab/banff/activ/cyclisme-biking/Heritage-Legacy) is a 26.8km paved route that connects cyclists, pedestrians and skaters with Canmore and Banff Town. Shadowing Hwy 1 and gaining 30m of elevation, the trail takes most pedalers two or three hours round-trip. For those not up to cycling/walking in both directions, Three Sisters Taxi (☑403-493-9990) offers a handy shuttle service between the trailheads to get you back to your starting point.

Banff and Canmore are linked by two additional trails, the rugged Rundle Riverside Trail (for experienced mountain bikers) and the easier Goat Creek Trail. Check with Parks Canada (www.pc.gc.ca) for current conditions.

Paintbox Lodge
B&B $$$

(☑403-609-0482; www.paintboxlodge.com; 629 10th St; r $275-399; P ☎) Run by ex-Olympic skiers Thomas Grandi and Sarah Renner, this B&B takes Canadian decor to a new level, right down to the tartan carpet. Its five unique suites offer a mix of country chic and luxury comfort. For maximum space ask for the Loft Suite, which sleeps four and features beamed ceilings, mountain-view balcony and sexy corner tub.

✖ Eating & Drinking

★ Communitea
CAFE $

(☑403-688-2233; www.thecommunitea.com; 1001 6th Ave; mains $12-15; ☺8am-7pm Jun-Sep, 9am-5pm Oct-May; ☎) ✈ Ethically aware and all organic, this community cafe exudes a warm, relaxed vibe and colorful modern aesthetic. Food is fresh and local, with noodles, rice bowls, smoked salmon and avocado toast, wraps, salads, and plenty of vegan, veggie and gluten-free options. Sip fresh-pressed juices, well-executed coffee and, of course, every type of tea you can conceive of.

Old School Bus
ICE CREAM $

(621 Main St; 1/2/3 scoops $4.25/5.75/7.25, kid's scoop $2.50; ☺11am-10pm) Permanently parked just off Main St, this converted school bus is *the* place for ice cream in Canmore. The chalkboard hawks a tempting spectrum of flavors, from white chocolate to blackberry to peanut butter, and the milkshakes are heavenly too. Cash only.

Rocky Mountain Flatbread
ITALIAN $$

(☑403-609-5508; www.rockymountainflatbread.ca; 838 10th St; pizza $14-31; ☺11:30am-9pm Sun-Thu, to 10pm Fri & Sat; ☑) ✈ In this outdoorsy town where you naturally end up craving pizza, Rocky Mountain Flatbread is a fabulous apparition. The thin-crusted flatbreads start simple with organic tomato sauce and Canadian mozzarella, but you can rev things up with additional ingredients like smoked bison, fig and Brie, or lemon chicken and apple.

Grizzly Paw
PUB FOOD $$

(☑403-678-9983; www.thegrizzlypaw.com; 622 Main St; mains $18-25; ☺11am-11pm Sun-Thu, to midnight Fri & Sat) ✈ Alberta's best microbrewery (offering seven year-round beers plus seasonal specials) is hiding in the mountains of Canmore. With beer and food pairings, big burgers, hand-crafted sodas and a view-filled patio, it's a popular spot. The purveyors of Beavertail Raspberry Ale and Grumpy Bear Honey Wheat also have a nearby brewery and microdistillery where tours and tasters are available.

★ Crazyweed Kitchen
INTERNATIONAL $$$

(☑403-609-2530; www.crazyweed.ca; 1600 Railway Ave; lunch mains $16-24, dinner mains $19-46; ☺11:30am-10pm Tue-Sun) This flashy bistro on the edge of town feels more big city than small town, with its sharp designer lines, funky artwork and globetrotting menu that takes in everything from wood-fired pizza, Malaysian noodles and Myanmar fish cakes to grass-fed Alberta rib eye. The tropical-themed cocktails lineup is equally inspired, with passion-fruit mojitos, grapefruit margaritas and tamarind whiskey sours.

★ Trough
CANADIAN $$$

(☑403-678-2820; www.thetrough.ca; 725 9th St; mains $34-46; ☺5:30-9pm Tue-Sun) Canmore's slinkiest bistro is a bit tucked away on 9th St, but worth discovering for a romantic night out. The mother-son team creates amazing dishes like Prince Edward

Island (PEI) mussels with house-smoked tomatoes, grilled Alberta lamb chops with rosemary-black pepper marinade, and BC halibut with mango and sweet peppers. With just nine tables, it's wise to book ahead.

★ **Tank 310** MICROBREWERY

(☑ 403-678-2487; www.thegrizzlypaw.com; 310 Old Canmore Rd; ⊙ 11am-9pm Thu & Sun, to 9:30pm Fri & Sat) Soaring ceilings and in-your-face views of Mt Rundle and the Three Sisters greet you at this cool gastropub launched by Grizzly Paw Brewing. Views aside, your attention will quickly shift to the beer. A full lineup of Grizzly Paw drafts, from Powder Hound Blonde to Evolution IPA, comes complemented by a solid menu of upscale pub grub.

❶ Information

Travel Alberta Canmore Visitor Information Centre (☑ 403-678-5277; www.travelalberta. com; 2801 Bow Valley Trail; ⊙ 9am-7pm May-Oct, to 5pm Nov-Apr; ☎) This regional visitor center with a free wi-fi lounge, just off the Trans-Canada Hwy northwest of town, focuses on the Canmore/Banff/Lake Louise area.

❶ Getting There & Away

Canmore is easily accessible from Banff Town (20 minutes) and Calgary (1¼ hours) via the Trans-Canada Highway (Hwy 1).

The **Banff Airporter** (☑ 403-762-3330; www. banffairporter.com; Coast Canmore Hotel, 511 Bow Valley Trail; Canmore to Calgary Airport adult/child $65/32.50) runs 11 buses daily between the Coast Canmore Hotel and Calgary Airport. **Brewster** (Map p80; ☑ 866-606-6700; www.banffjaspercollection.com/brewster-express; 100 Gopher St) offers slightly more expensive and less frequent connections to the airport and downtown Calgary ($72, six to nine daily).

Bus 3, operated by **Roam** (☑ 403-762-0606; www.roamtransit.com; Canmore to Banff adult/child $6/3), makes the 25-minute run between Canmore and Banff every 30 to 60 minutes. Buses stop downtown on 9th St near 7th Ave.

Icefields Parkway

☑ 403, 780

Nothing in North America compares to the Icefields Parkway. For much of its 230km length, this ribbon of highway winding through the heart of the Canadian Rockies is the lone sign of human influence in an otherwise pristine wilderness of jewel-hued glacial lakes, unbroken virgin forest and otherworldly mountain crags.

Much of the route followed by the parkway was established over the millennia by indigenous people and later adopted by 19th-century fur traders. An early road was built during the 1930s as a Depression-era work project, and the present highway was opened in the early 1960s.

Nowadays it's used almost entirely by tourists, aside from the occasional elk, coyote or bighorn meandering along its perimeter. It can get busy in July and August, particularly with large recreational vehicles. Many also tackle it on a bike – the roadway is wide and sprinkled with plenty of strategically spaced campgrounds, hostels and lodges.

◉ Sights & Activities

There are two types of sights here: static (lakes, glaciers and mountains) and moving (elk, bears, moose etc). If you don't see at least one wild animal (look out for the inevitable 'bear jams') you'll be very unlucky.

★ **Athabasca Glacier** GLACIER

(Map p70) The tongue of the Athabasca Glacier runs from the Columbia Icefield to within walking distance of the road opposite the Icefield Centre (p78). It can be visited on foot or in an Ice Explorer all-terrain vehicle. It has retreated about 2km since 1844, when it reached the rock moraine on the north side of the road. To reach its toe (bottom edge), walk from the Icefield Centre along the 1.8km Forefield Trail, then join the 1km Toe of the Glacier Trail.

You can also park at the start of the latter trail. While it is permitted to stand on a small roped section of the ice, do not attempt to cross the warning tape – many do, but the glacier is riddled with crevasses and there have been fatalities.

To walk safely on the Columbia Icefield, you'll need to enlist the help of **Athabasca Glacier Icewalks** (Map p70; ☑ 780-852-5595; www.icewalks.com; Icefield Centre, Icefields Pkwy; 3hr tour adult/child $110/60, 6hr tour $175/90; ⊙ late May–Sep), which supplies all the gear you'll need and a guide to show you the ropes. Its basic tour is three hours; there's a six-hour option for those wanting to venture further out on the glacier. Hikers must be at least seven years of age.

The other, far easier (and more popular) way to get on the glacier is via the **Columbia Icefield Adventure** (Map p70; www.banff

jaspercollection.com/attractions/columbia-icefield; adult/child $114/57; 9am-6pm Apr-Oct) tour. For many people this is the defining experience of their visit to the Canadian Rockies. The large hybrid bus-truck grinds a track onto the ice, where it stops to allow you to go for a 25-minute wander on the glacier. Dress warmly, wear good shoes and bring a water bottle to try some freshly melted glacial water. Tickets can be bought at the Icefield Centre or online; tours depart every 15 to 30 minutes.

Mt Edith Cavell   MOUNTAIN
(Map p92) Rising like a snowy sentinel over Jasper Town, Mt Edith Cavell (3363m) is one of the park's most distinctive and physically arresting peaks. What it lacks in height it makes up for in stark, ethereal beauty. Accessed via a winding, precipitous road that branches off the Icefields Pkwy 6km south of Jasper, the mountain is famous for its flower meadows and its wing-shaped Angel Glacier.

Athabasca Falls   WATERFALL
(Map p92) Despite being only 23m high, Athabasca Falls is Jasper's most dramatic and voluminous waterfall, a deafening combination of sound, spray and water. The thunderous Athabasca River has cut deeply into the soft limestone rock, carving potholes, canyons and water channels. Interpretive signs explain the basics of the local geology. Visitors crowd the large parking lot and short access trail. It's just west of the Icefields Pkwy, 30km south of Jasper Town, and at its most ferocious during summer.

Columbia Icefield   GLACIER
About halfway between Lake Louise village and Jasper Town, you'll glimpse the vast Columbia Icefield, covering an area the size of Vancouver and feeding eight glaciers. This remnant of the last ice age is up to 350m thick in places and stretches across the plateau between Mt Columbia (3747m) and Mt Athabasca (3491m). For serious hikers and climbers, this is also the only accessible area of the icefield. For information and conditions, visit Parks Canada (p79) at the Columbia Icefield Discovery Centre.

This is the largest icefield in the Rockies, feeding the North Saskatchewan, Columbia, Athabasca, Mackenzie and Fraser River systems with its meltwaters. The mountainous sides of this vast bowl of ice are some of the highest in the Rockies, with nine peaks higher than 3000m.

Peyto Lake   LAKE
(Map p70) You'll have already seen the indescribably vibrant blue color of Peyto Lake in a thousand publicity shots, but there's nothing like gazing at the real thing – especially since the viewing point for this lake is from a lofty vantage point several hundred feet above the water. The lake is best visited in early morning, between the time the sun first illuminates the water and the first tour bus arrives.

Weeping Wall   WATERFALL
(Map p70) This imposing rock wall towers above the east side of the Icefields Parkway, a few kilometers south of Sunwapta Pass and the Banff–Jasper border. In summer it's a sea of waterfalls, with tears of liquid pouring from the top, creating a veil of moisture. Come winter, the water freezes up solid to form an enormous sheet of ice. The vertical ice field is a popular playground for ice climbers, who travel from around the globe to test their mettle here.

Wilcox Ridge   HIKING
(Map p70) One of Jasper's most accessible high-country walks is the 9km out-and-back trail to Wilcox Ridge. Turn off the Icefields Pkwy 2km east of the Columbia Icefield Centre at Wilcox Campground. From the signposted trailhead, the path climbs rapidly above treeline, reaching a pair of red chairs after 30 minutes where you can sit and enjoy fine Athabasca Glacier views.

If you've had enough climbing, you can simply return from here to the parking lot. Otherwise continue ascending, gazing down over a river canyon on your left as you traverse wide-open meadows to reach Wilcox Pass (2370m) at the 3.2km mark. Here you'll turn left, following the undulating trail another 1.3km to reach the Wilcox Ridge viewpoint. Up top, dramatic, near-aerial views of the Athabasca Glacier unfold across the valley. To return to the parking lot simply retrace your steps downhill.

🛏 Sleeping & Eating

Waterfowl Lakes Campground   CAMPGROUND $
(Map p70; Icefields Pkwy; tent & RV sites $21.50; late Jun-early Sep) Tucked between two beautiful lakes about 60km north of Lake Louise, this campground just off the Icefields Pkwy has wooded sites and plenty of hiking opportunities. Facilities for the 116 first-come, first-served sites include flush toilets, hot water, BBQ shelters, food

ALBERTA ICEFIELDS PARKWAY

storage and interpretive programs, but no showers. Sites 1, 2, 4, 6 and 10 are all near the lakeshore.

HI Mt Edith Cavell
Wilderness Hostel
HOSTEL $

(Map p92; ☑ 780-852-3215; www.hihostels. ca; Cavell Rd; dm $38; ⊙ reception 5-8pm mid-Feb–mid-Oct) ✐ Secluded down a dead-end road near the base of Mt Edith Cavell and the Angel Glacier, this rustic place has wood-burning stoves in each of its two 16-bunk cabins and in the propane-lit kitchen-common room, where guests play cards and share stories of hikes to nearby Cavell Meadows and the remote Tonquin Valley (trailhead directly across the street).

HI Mosquito Creek
Wilderness Hostel
HOSTEL $

(Map p70; www.hihostels.ca; dm $38, private cabin for 2/3/4/5 people $95/115/135/155; ⊙ reception 5-10pm, closed Oct & Tue Nov-Apr) Tucked away under the trees beside a rushing creek, this charming 34-bed backcountry hostel was originally built to house German POWs during WWII. There's a rustic wood-fired sauna, a stove-lit lounge and a pocket-sized (propane-powered) kitchen where you can cook up communal grub. Two 12-bed dorms are supplemented by two private rooms sleeping up to five. No showers or electricity.

Num-Ti-Jah Lodge
INN $$$

(Map p70; ☑ 403-522-2167; www.num-ti-jah.com; d with mountain/lake view $375/425; ⊙ mid-May– mid-Oct; P 🛜) On the edge of Bow Lake, the historic Num-Ti-Jah Lodge is full to the brim with backcountry nostalgia. Built by pioneer Jimmy Simpson in 1923 (12 years before the highway), the carved-wood interior displays animal heads and photos from the golden age. The 16 rooms have big views, but show their age with worn furniture, dated decor and tiny bathrooms.

★ Elkhorn Dining Room
CANADIAN $$$

(Map p70; ☑ 403-522-2167; www.num-ti-jah.com; Icefields Pkwy; breakfast buffet cold/hot $14/22, dinner mains $30-50; ⊙ 8-10am & 6:30-9pm mid-May–mid-Oct) Rustic yet elegant, the Num-Ti-Jah's historic Elkhorn Dining Room lets you step back in time to Jimmy Simpson's original hunting lodge, complete with stone fireplace and majestic views. Dine on elk burgers or crispy steelhead trout beneath the watchful eye of moose, wolverines and other hunting trophies. Guests get seating priority; if you're staying elsewhere make sure you reserve ahead.

You'll also find the Bow Lake Cafe (mains $8 to $13; 9am to 5pm) where you can refuel with a sandwich, soup or baked goods from tall wooden stools.

ℹ️ Information

Columbia Icefield Discovery Centre (Icefields Pkwy) Situated on the Icefields Pkwy, close to the toe of the Athabasca Glacier, the green-roofed Icefield Centre is a bit of a zoo in the summer, with tour coaches cramming the car

---

CYCLING THE ICEFIELDS PARKWAY

With its ancient geology, landscape-altering glaciers, and lakes bluer than Picasso paintings from his blue period, the 230km-long Icefields Parkway is one of the world's most spectacular roads, and, by definition, one of the world's most spectacular bicycle rides – if your legs and lungs are up to it. Aside from the distance, there are several long uphill drags, occasional stiff headwinds and two major passes to contend with, namely Bow Summit (2088m) and Sunwapta Pass (2035m). Notwithstanding these issues, the route is highly popular in July and August (don't even think about doing it in the winter), with aspiring cyclists lapping up its bicycle-friendly features. No commercial trucks are allowed on the parkway, there's a generous shoulder throughout, two-wheeled company is virtually guaranteed, and accommodations along the route (campgrounds, hostels and the occasional lodge or hotel) are plentiful and strategically placed. There's a choice of six HI hostels and four lodge/motel accommodations en route. Book ahead. Basic provisions can be procured at Saskatchewan River Crossing, 83km north of Lake Louise.

Sturdy road bikes can be rented from Wilson Mountain Sports (☑ 403-522-3636; www.wmsll.com; Samson Mall, Lake Louise village; bike/ski rental per day from $39/25; ⊙ 8am-7pm) in Lake Louise village. Brewster (p86) buses can sometimes transport bicycles, but always check ahead. Backroads (☑ 510-527-1555; www.backroads.com; 5-day tour from $3449) runs a Canadian Rockies Bike Tour, a six-day organized trip that incorporates cycling along the parkway.

park. Decamp here to purchase tickets and board buses for the Snocoaches and Glacier Skywalk. You'll also find a hotel, cafeteria, restaurant, gift shop and Parks Canada information desk.

South Gate The entrance to the Parkway north of Lake Louise, where you can purchase your park pass and pick up a map and brochures.

❶ Getting There & Away

Brewster Express (☑ 877-625-4372; www.banffjaspercollection.com/brewster-express) has buses plying the parkway between Banff, Lake Louise and Jasper, with stops at Saskatchewan River Crossing, Columbia Icefield Discovery Centre and Sunwapta Falls.

If you're driving, start out with a full tank of gas. It's fairly pricey to fill up at Saskatchewan River Crossing, the only gas station in the 230km-long stretch between Lake Louise and Jasper.

Banff Town

☑ 403 / POP 7847

It seems hard to believe when you first lay eyes on Banff Town, but this overgrown village of less than 10,000 souls is the largest metropolis in the entire national park. Thankfully, Banff has largely avoided North America's notorious penchant for sprawl – though its few city blocks *do* manage to squeeze in a surprising amount of commercial hustle and bustle.

A resort town with boutique shops, nightclubs, museums and fancy restaurants may seem incongruous in this wild setting. But Banff is no ordinary town. It developed as a service center for the park that surrounds it. Today it brings in busloads of tourists keen to commune with shops as much as with nature; artists and writers are also drawn to the Rockies' unparalleled majesty. Whether you love or loathe Banff's cosmopolitan edge, wander 15 minutes in any direction and you're back in wild country, a primeval world of bears, elk and wolves.

◎ Sights

★**Banff National Park**　　　NATIONAL PARK
(Map p70; www.pc.gc.ca/banff; day pass adult/youth/family $9.80/free/19.60) Towering like giant castles in the sky, the mountains of Banff provide endless opportunities for wildlife-watching, hiking, boating, climbing, mountain biking, skiing or simply communing with nature. Rugged canyons compete for your attention with lush fields of alpine wildflowers, jewel-like blue-green lakes and dense emerald forests. Created in 1885 and ranging over 6641 sq km, Banff is the world's third-oldest national park – and was Canada's first.

★**Whyte Museum of the Canadian Rockies**　　　MUSEUM
(Map p80; ☑ 403-762-2291; www.whyte.org; 111 Bear St; adult/student/child $10/5/free; ◎ 10am-5pm) Founded by local artists Catharine and Peter Whyte, the century-old Whyte Museum is more than just a rainy-day option. It boasts a beautiful, ever-changing gallery displaying art from 1800 to the present, by regional, Canadian and international artists, many with a focus on the Rockies. Watch for work by the Group of Seven (aka the Algonquin School). There's also a permanent collection telling the story of Banff and the hardy men and women who forged a home among the mountains.

Upper Hot Springs Pool　　　HOT SPRINGS
(www.hotsprings.ca; Mountain Ave; adult/child/family $8.30/6.30/24.50; ◎ 9am-11pm mid-May–mid-Oct, 10am-10pm Sun-Thu, to 11pm Fri & Sat rest of year) Banff quite literally wouldn't be Banff if it weren't for its hot springs, which gush out from 2.5km beneath **Sulphur Mountain** at a constant temperature of between 32°C (90°F) and 46°C (114°F) – it was the springs that drew the first tourists to Banff. You can still sample the soothing mineral waters at the Upper Hot Springs Pool, near the Banff Gondola.

Fairmont Banff Springs　　　HISTORIC BUILDING
(www.fairmont.com/banffsprings; 405 Spray Ave) Looming up beside the Bow River, the Banff Springs is a local landmark in more ways than one. Originally built in 1888, and remodeled in 1928 to resemble a cross between a Scottish baronial castle and a European château, the turret-topped exterior conceals an eye-poppingly extravagant selection of ballrooms, lounges, dining rooms and balustraded staircases that would make William Randolph Hearst green with envy.

Cave & Basin National Historic Site　　　HISTORIC SITE
(☑ 403-762-1566; www.pc.gc.ca/en/lhn-nhs/ab/caveandbasin; 311 Cave Ave; adult/child $3.90/free; ◎ 9:30am-5pm mid-May–mid-Oct, 11am-5pm Wed-Sun rest of year) The Canadian National Park system was effectively born at these hot springs, discovered accidentally by three Canadian Pacific Railway employees on their

Banff Town

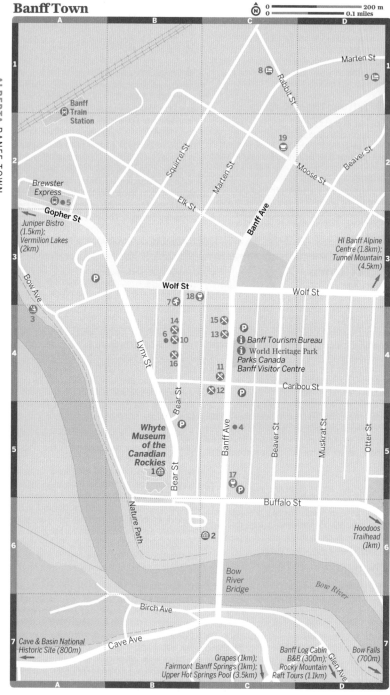

N
0   200 m
0   0.1 miles

Marten St

8

9

Banff
Train
Station

Brewster
Express

5

Gopher St

Juniper Bistro
(1.5km);
Vermilion Lakes
(2km)

Squirrel St

Elk St

Marten St

Rabbit St

Moose St

19

Banff Ave

Beaver St

HI Banff Alpine
Centre (1.8km);
Tunnel Mountain
(4.5km)

Bow Ave

3

Wolf St

Wolf St

7

18

15

14

6

10

13

Banff Tourism Bureau

World Heritage Park
Parks Canada
Banff Visitor Centre

16

11

12

Caribou St

Lynx St

Bear St

Whyte
Museum
of the
Canadian
Rockies

1

4

Banff Ave

Beaver St

Muskrat St

Otter St

17

Buffalo St

Nature Path

2

Hoodoos
Trailhead
(1km)

Bow
River
Bridge

Bow River

Birch Ave

Cave & Basin National
Historic Site (800m)

Cave Ave

Grapes (1km);
Fairmont Banff Springs (1km);
Upper Hot Springs Pool (3.5km)

Banff Log Cabin
B&B (300m);
Rocky Mountain
Raft Tours (1.1km)

Glen Ave

Bow Falls
(700m)

Banff Town

ALBERTA BANFF TOWN

of the Trans-Canada Hwy/Hwy 1 means that it's not as peaceful as it could be.

Banff Park Museum MUSEUM
(Map p80; ☎403-762-1558; www.pc.gc.ca/en/lhn-nhs/ab/banff; 91 Banff Ave; adult/child $3.90/free; ⊙9:30am-5pm Wed-Sun) Occupying the oldest surviving federal building in a Canadian National Park and dating from 1903, this museum is a national historic site. Its exhibits – a taxidermic collection of local animals, including grizzly and black bears, plus a tree carved with graffiti dating from 1841 – was curated by Norman Sanson, who ran the museum and Banff weather station until 1932. A number of the animals originally resided in a long-ago zoo that was briefly located behind the museum.

Activities

Canoeing & Kayaking
Despite a modern penchant for big cars, canoe travel is still very much a quintessential Canadian method of transportation. The best options near Banff Town are **Lake Minnewanka** and nearby **Two Jack Lake**, both to the northeast, or – closer to the town itself – the **Vermilion Lakes**. Unless you have your own canoe, you'll need to rent one; try **Banff Canoe Club** (Map p80; ☎403-762-5005; www.banffcanoeclub.com; cnr Wolf St & Bow Ave; canoe & kayak rental per 1st/additional hour $45/25, SUP/bike rental per hour $30/12; ⊙9am-9pm mid-Jun–Aug, reduced hours mid-May–mid-Jun & Sep).

Cycling
There are lots of riding options around Banff, both on the road and on selected trails. Popular routes around Banff Town include **Sundance** (7.4km round-trip) and **Spray River Loop** (12.5km); either is good for families. **Spray River & Goat Creek** (19km one way) and **Rundle Riverside** (14km one way) are both A-to-Bs with start/finish points near Canmore. The former is pretty straightforward; the latter is more challenging, with ups and downs and potential for thrills and spills.

Serious road cyclists should check out Hwy 1A (the Bow Valley Pkwy) between Banff and Lake Louise; the rolling hills and quiet road here are a roadie's dream. Parks Canada publishes the brochure *Mountain Biking & Cycling Guide – Banff National Park*, which describes trails and regulations. Pick it up at the Banff Visitor Centre (p86).

day off in 1883 (though known to indigenous peoples for 10,000 years). The springs quickly spurred a flurry of private businesses offering facilities for bathers to enjoy the then-trendy thermal treatments. To avert an environmental catastrophe, the government stepped in, declaring Banff Canada's first national park in order to preserve the springs.

Bow Falls WATERFALL
About 500m south of town, just before the junction with Spray River, the Bow River plunges into a churning melee of white water at Bow Falls. Though the drop is relatively small – just 9m at its highest point – Bow Falls is a dramatic sight, especially in spring following heavy snowmelt.

Vermilion Lakes NATURE RESERVE
West of town, this trio of tranquil lakes is a great place for **wildlife spotting**: elk, beavers, owls, bald eagles and ospreys can often be seen around the lakeshore, especially at dawn and dusk. A paved path – part of the **Legacy bike trail** – parallels the lakes' northern edge for 5.9km, but the proximity

Snowtips/Bactrax (Map p80; ☑ 403-762-8177; www.snowtips-bactrax.com; 225 Bear St; bike rental per hour/day from $10/35, cross-country/alpine ski rental per day from $20/40; ⊗ 8am-8pm Jun–mid-Oct, 7am-9pm rest of year) has a barn full of town and trail bikes to rent and will deliver them to your hotel.

Hiking

Hiking is Banff's key attraction and therefore the focus of many travelers who visit the area. The trails are easy to find, well signposted and maintained enough to be comfortable to walk on, yet rugged enough to provide a wilderness experience.

In general, the closer to Banff Town you are, the more people you can expect to see and the more developed the trail will be. But regardless of where in the park you go walking, you are assured to be rewarded for your efforts.

Before you head out, check at the Banff Visitor Centre (p86) for trail conditions and possible closures. Keep in mind that trails are often snow-covered much later into the summer season than you might expect, and trail closures due to bears are a possibility, especially in berry season (July to September).

One of the best hikes from the town center is the Bow River Falls & The Hoodoos Trail, which starts by the Bow River Bridge and tracks past the falls to the Hoodoos – weird-looking rock spires caused by wind and water erosion. The trail works its way around the back of Tunnel Mountain through forest and some river meadows (10.2km round-trip).

You can track the north shore of Lake Minnewanka for kilometers on a multi-use trail that is sometimes closed due to bear activity. The classic hike is to walk as far as the Aylmer Lookout, nearly 12km one way. Less taxing is the 5.6km round-trip hike to Stewart Canyon, where you can clamber down rocks and boulders to the Cascade River.

Some of the best multiday hikes start at the Sunshine Village parking lot (where skiers grab the gondola in winter). From here you can plan two- to four-day sorties up over Healy Pass and down to Egypt Lake, or else catch the gondola up to Sunshine Village, where you can cross the border into BC and head out across Sunshine Meadows into Mt Assiniboine Provincial Park.

The best backcountry experience is arguably the Sawback Trail, which travels from Banff up to Lake Louise the back way – it's over 74km, with six primitive campsites and three spectacular mountain passes.

Check out Lonely Planet's *Banff, Jasper & Glacier National Parks* guide for more details about more single-day and multiday hikes.

★ **Cory Pass Loop** HIKING
(Map p70) By the time you reach the midpoint of this adventurous 13km loop, you'll have a hard time believing you started from the Trans-Canada Hwy/Hwy 1. The trail's relentless 920m ascent into spectacular, wild high country culminates at Cory Pass (2350m), where you'll round the corner of Mt Edith and descend through a barren scree-covered landscape before looping back through dense forest.

★ **Johnston Canyon
& the Inkpots** HIKING
(Map p70; ♿) Aside from the Lake Louise shoreline, no place in Banff sees as much foot traffic as the wide, paved Johnston Canyon Trail. The crowds make total sense once you enter the canyon, where dramatic cliff faces vie for your attention with two gorgeous waterfalls. More intrepid hikers can climb to the Inkpots, colorful natural pools in a high mountain valley.

★ **Mt Assiniboine Trail** HIKING
Banff's most iconic backcountry hike is this three- to four-day, 55.7km odyssey to the pyramid-shaped peak of Mt Assiniboine, nicknamed the Matterhorn of the Rockies. Starting from the top of the Sunshine ski gondola, the trail takes in alpine meadows, rocky valleys, high mountain passes and a series of beautiful lakes en route to Assiniboine and the pristine Bryant Valley.

Horseback Riding

Banff's first European explorers – fur traders and railway engineers – penetrated the region primarily on horseback. You can recreate their pioneering spirit on guided rides with Banff Trail Riders (Map p80; ☑ 403-762-4551; www.horseback.com; 138 Banff Ave; guided rides per person $64-196), which will fit you out with a trusty steed and lead you on a one- to three-hour day trip or bring you into the backcountry for an overnight adventure at its Sundance Lodge. Instruction and guiding are included; a sore backside is more or less mandatory for beginners. Grin and bear it.

Skiing & Snowboarding

There are three ski areas in the national park, two of them in the vicinity of Banff Town. Large, snowy Sunshine Village is considered world-class. Tiny Norquay, a mere 5km from the center, is your half-day, family-friendly option.

Sunshine Village (Map p70; www.ski banff.com; day ski pass adult/youth $114/89) straddles the Alberta–BC border. Though slightly smaller than Lake Louise in terms of skiable terrain, it gets much bigger dumpings of snow, or 'Champagne powder' as Albertans like to call it (up to 9m annually). Aficionados laud Sunshine's advanced runs and lengthy ski season, which lingers until Victoria Day weekend in late May. A high-speed gondola whisks skiers up in 17 minutes to the village, which sports Banff's only ski-in hotel, the Sunshine Mountain Lodge.

Mt Norquay (Map p70; ☎ 403-762-4421; www.banffnorquay.com; Mt Norquay Rd; day ski pass adult/youth/child $89/68/35; ☺ 9am-4pm; ♿), a short distance uphill from downtown Banff, has a long history of entertaining Banff visitors. The smallest and least visited of the three local hills, this is a good place to body-swerve the major show-offs and hit the slopes for a succinct half-day.

Local buses shuttle riders from Banff hotels to both resorts (and Lake Louise) every 30 minutes during the season.

White-Water Rafting

The best rafting is outside the park (and province) on the **Kicking Horse River** in Yoho National Park, BC. There are Class IV rapids here, meaning big waves, swirling holes and a guaranteed soaking. Lesser rapids are found on the **Kananaskis River** and the Horseshoe Canyon section of the **Bow River**. The Bow River around Banff is better suited to mellower float trips.

Several rafting companies are located in the park, including Hydra River Guides (p84) and **Rocky Mountain Raft Tours** (☎ 403-762-3632; www.banffrafttours.com; Golf Course Loop Rd; ☺ mid-May–late Sep; ♿). Tour prices start around $60 for a one-hour float.

☞ Tours

Via Ferrata   OUTDOORS
(Map p70; ☎ 844-667-7829; www.banffnorquay.com/summer/via-ferrata; Mt Norquay; ☺ mid-Jun–mid-Oct) These fixed-protection climbing

---

THE MOUNTAIN MAN

Driving into Banff you might notice a distinctive face staring at you from the town-limits sign, sporting a jaunty hat, a drooping meerschaum pipe and a rather splendid handle-bar moustache. Meet 'Wild' Bill Peyto, one of the great characters of the Canadian Rockies and the original wild man of the mountains.

Born in Kent, England, in 1869, young William was the third eldest of a family of nine children. Having left the cramped environs of the Peyto household at 17, Bill set out to find his fortune in Canada, arriving in Halifax in 1887, where he initially found work as a railway laborer, part-time rancher and government employee. But it wasn't long before Bill found his true calling – as a mountain guide working for the packing and outfitting business owned by Tom Wilson.

Over the next decade he proved himself a skilled trapper, huntsman and alpinist, exploring Mistaya Valley and Peyto Lake, making the first successful ascent of Bow Summit in 1894 and notching up the first (failed) attempt at Mt Assiniboine the following year (he eventually scaled it in 1902). He even found time for some book-larnin', schooling himself in paleontology and geology using secondhand textbooks. Within a matter of years he had become one of the most skilled amateur naturalists in the Rockies.

He was also a notorious showman with an eye for a natty outfit. One of his clients, Norman Collie, painted a vivid picture of Wild Bill: 'Peyto assumes a wild and picturesque though somewhat tattered attire. A sombrero, with a rakish tilt to one side, a blue shirt set off by a white kerchief (which may have served civilization for napkin), and a buckskin coat with a fringe border add to his cowboy appearance. A heavy belt containing a row of cartridges, hunting knife and six-shooter as well as the restless activity of his wicked blue eyes, give him an air of bravado...'

You can still visit one of Bill's original log cabins on the grounds of the Whyte Museum in Banff, and his action-packed diary – which is appropriately titled *Ain't It Hell: Bill Peyto's Mountain Journal* – is available from the museum shop.

routes on Mt Norquay let your test your head for heights. Choose from the Explorer ($169, 2½ hours), the Ridgewalker ($219, four hours), the Skyline ($279, five hours) and the Summiteer ($349, six hours), which includes a three-wire suspension bridge to the top of Mt Norquay. Prices include full safety kit, accompanying guide and passage up the Norquay chairlift to the start point.

Hydra River Guides RAFTING
(Map p80; ☑ 403-762-4554; www.raftbanff.com; 211 Bear St; ⏲ 7:30am-9pm) This well-regarded company has been running rafting trips for over three decades. The most popular is the 20km Kicking Horse Classic ($149), with varied rapids (up to class IV) and a BBQ lunch; novices and families will appreciate the sedate Mild float trip (adult/child $79/59); for late risers there's the Last Waltz ($115), which doesn't get going until midafternoon.

Lake Minnewanka Cruises CRUISE
(Map p70; ☑ 866-606-6700; www.banffjasper collection.com/attractions/lake-minnewanka-cruise; Minnewanka Loop Dr; adult/child classic cruise $58/29, explorer cruise $81/41; ⏲ classic cruise hourly 10am-6pm late Jun–mid-Sep, noon-5pm mid-Sep–mid-Oct; explorer cruise 10am late Jun-early Sep) Hop on board the standard cruise across emerald-hued Lake Minnewanka, or opt for an extended 'explorer' cruise between snowy peaked mountains to the glacial pass of Devil's Gap, where you can catch a glimpse of the Prairies. Crew will fill you in on local geology and history.

🛏 Sleeping

Accommodations in Banff Town are generally expensive, especially in summer. Booking ahead is strongly recommended.

For listings of available accommodations, check the Banff Tourism Bureau (p86) and the Parks Canada Visitor Centre (p86).

Parks Canada operates several popular campgrounds. Sites at Tunnel Mountain and Two Jack – the two closest to town – should be reserved months in advance; others along the Bow Valley Parkway/Hwy 1A are first-come, first-served.

★ Samesun Banff HOSTEL $
(Map p80; ☑ 403-762-4499; www.banffhostel. com; 433 Banff Ave; dm incl breakfast from $65; P @ 🛜) Catering to a youthful international backpacker crowd, the welcoming Samesun offers a central Banff Ave location,

a full lineup of daily activities (hiking, cycling, canoeing, hot springs) and 112 dorm beds spread across modern, compact six- to 14-person rooms (some with fireplaces). A DIY breakfast is included, and the bustling on-site Beaver resto-bar keeps everyone happy with nightly drink specials.

Two Jack Lakeside CAMPGROUND $
(Minnewanka Loop Dr; tent & RV sites $27.40; ⏲ May-Oct; P) Right on Two Jack Lake, 11km northeast of town, Two Jack Lakeside is the most scenic of the Banff-area campgrounds, usually filling its 74 reservable sites months in advance. You can now also 'glamp' at Two Jack in one of 10 'oTENTiks' – fully serviced A-frame 'tents' with hot showers and electricity, sleeping up to six people for $120 per night.

HI Banff Alpine Centre HOSTEL $
(☑ 403-762-4123; www.hihostels.ca; 801 Hidden Ridge Way; dm from $55, d with shared/private bath from $177/214, private cabins from $238; P @ 🛜) Near the top of Tunnel Mountain, Banff's HI hostel is well away from the madness of Banff Ave. The classic mountain-lodge style buildings offer spick-and-span accommodations ranging from dorms to private doubles to cabins. Common areas are open and comfortable, with fireplaces, views and an on-site bar and restaurant. Public buses run by the front door, and passes are complimentary.

★ Buffaloberry B&B $$$
(Map p80; ☑ 403-762-3750; www.buffaloberry. com; 417 Marten St; r $465; P ❄ 🛜) Centrally located and surrounded by colorful flowering plants, this purpose-built B&B makes a cheerful, comfortable home base. The four individually decorated bedrooms are heavy on homey charm, and the underfloor heating and nightly turn-down treats keep the pamper factor high. With an ever-changing menu (think baked Camembert egg custard or 'triple B' – blueberry, buttermilk and buckwheat – pancakes), breakfasts are divine.

★ Fairmont Banff Springs HOTEL $$$
(☑ 403-762-2211; www.fairmont.com/banff-springs; 405 Spray Ave; r from $599; P ❄ @ 🛜 ♒) Rising like a Gaelic Balmoral above the trees at the base of Sulphur Mountain and visible from miles away, the Banff Springs is a wonder of early 1920s revivalist architecture and one of Canada's most iconic buildings. Wandering through its grand lobby and elegant

lounge, wine bar and restaurant, it's easy to forget that it's also a hotel.

Banff Log Cabin B&B
B&B $$$

(✆ 403-762-3516; www.banfflogcabin.ca; 222 Glen Cres; cabin incl breakfast $425; [P] [✿]) If having your own cozy cabin only steps from the rush of Bow River Falls sounds appealing, you'll love this B&B. Wedding planner/photographer owners Sharon and Malcolm ply guests with a comfy bed, prosecco and handmade local chocolates, tea kettles, an outdoor fire pit for roasting marshmallows and loaner bikes for the short ride across the pedestrian bridge into town.

 ## Eating

Wild Flour
CAFE $

(Map p80; ✆ 403-760-5074; www.wildflourbakery.ca; 211 Bear St; mains $5-10; ⊙7am-4pm; [✿][✿]) If you're searching for an inexpensive snack or a relatively guilt-free sugary treat, make a beeline for Banff's best bakery, where you'll find cheesecake, dark-chocolate torte and macaroons – along with breakfasts, delicious fresh-baked focaccia, well-stuffed sandwiches on homemade bread, and soups, all of it organic. Not surprisingly, the place gets busy – but outdoor courtyard seating helps alleviate the crush.

Evelyn's Coffee World
CAFE $

(Map p80; ✆ 403-762-0352; www.evelynscoffeebar.com; 215 Banff Ave; mains $6-10; ⊙7am-9pm, to 10pm Fri-Sun; [✿]) Pushing Starbucks onto the periphery, Evelyn's cranks out some of Banff's best coffee, along with wraps, pies and – best of all – its own selection of giant homemade cookies, the saviour of many an exhausted hiker.

★ Eddie Burger Bar
BURGERS $$

(Map p80; ✆ 403-762-2230; www.eddieburgerbar.ca; 6/137 Banff Ave; burgers $17-23; ⊙11am-2am, from 11:30am Oct-May) Not your average fast-food joint, Eddie's is devoted to building large, custom-made and crave-worthy burgers, from the usual classics to specialties like the elk burger with blueberry chutney. Add to this a hearty helping of poutine and an Oreo milkshake or a shaken Caesar (cocktail, not salad!) garnished with a chicken wing, and you're set – for the next week.

★ Bear Street Tavern
PUB FOOD $$

(Map p80; ✆ 403-762-2021; www.bearstreettavern.ca; 211 Bear St; mains $15-25; ⊙11:30am-late) This gastropub hits a double whammy: ingeniously flavored pizzas washed down with

locally brewed pints. Banffites head here in droves for a plate of pulled-pork nachos or a bison-and-onion pizza, accompanied by pitchers of hoppy ale. The patio overlooking Bison Courtyard is the best place to linger if the weather cooperates.

Block Kitchen & Bar
TAPAS $$

(Map p80; ✆ 403-985-2887; www.banffblock.com; 201 Banff Ave; tapas $9-28; ⊙11am-11pm; [✿]) This casual bar serves up tapas with heavy Asian and Mediterranean influences – or 'Mediterrasian,' as it calls it. The small but creative plates might not satisfy truly ravenous post-hiking appetites, but there are plenty of vegan and gluten-free options. The low-lit interior has a cool and quirky edge, while the breezy sidewalk terrace makes a pleasant perch in summertime.

Nourish
VEGETARIAN $$

(Map p80; ✆ 403-760-3933; www.nourishbistro.com; 211 Bear St; mains $18-26; ⊙11:30am-10:30pm Mon-Thu, 7:30-10:30am & 11:30am-10:30pm Fri-Sun; [✿]) Confronted by a strangely beautiful papier-mâché tree when you walk in the door, you instantly know this vegetarian bistro is not average. With locally sourced dishes like wild-mushroom ravioli, Moroccan cauliflower bites or 27-ingredient nachos with Canadian cheddar or vegan queso, Nourish has carved out a gourmet following in Banff. Dinner is served as shareable tapas and larger plates.

Juniper Bistro
BISTRO $$$

(✆ 403-763-6219; www.thejuniper.com/dining; 1 Juniper Way; breakfast & small plates from $14, mains $28-34; ⊙7am-11pm; [✿]) Spectacular mountain views combine with an innovative, locally sourced menu at Juniper's, a surprisingly good hotel restaurant on Banff's northern outskirts. Beyond breakfasts and dinners, the midafternoon 'Graze' menu is also enticing – think small plates of orange and cardamom-poached beets or bison carpaccio with juniper berry and pink peppercorn, all accompanied by fab cocktails and 'mocktails'. Vegetarian, vegan and gluten-free options abound.

Park
AMERICAN $$$

(Map p80; ✆ 403-762-5114; www.parkdistillery.com; 219 Banff Ave; mains $19-52; ⊙11am-10pm) Banff gets hip with a microdistillery to complement its microbrewery, plying spirits (gin, vodka and whiskey) and beer made from Alberta's foothills' grain. It all goes down perfectly with a mesquite beef hoagie, fish tacos or anything off the excellent appetizer menu. Cocktails are creative, fun and ever-changing.

Drinking & Nightlife

★ **Grapes** WINE BAR
(☑403-762-6860; www.fairont.com/banff-springs/dining/grapeswinebar; Fairmont Banff Springs, 405 Spray Ave; 5-9:30pm Sun-Thu, from 3pm Fri & Sat) Sporting original crown molding and dark wood paneling from its early days as a ladies' writing salon, this intimate wine bar in Banff's Fairmont makes an elegant spot for afternoon aperitifs. British Columbian Meritage and Ontario Riesling share the menu with international vintages, while tapas of house-cured meats, cheeses, pickled veggies and candied steelhead will tempt you to linger for dinner.

Whitebark Cafe COFFEE
(Map p80; ☑403-760-7298; www.whitebarkcafe.com; 401 Banff Ave; 6:30am-7pm) Early risers in need of their java fix should head straight to this sleek corner cafe attached to the Aspen Lodge. It's renowned among locals not only for its superb coffee, but also for its muffins, snacks and sandwiches. For an unconventional (and inexpensive) breakfast, check out its bacon-and-egg breakfast cup, a mini-meal encased in delicious flaky pastry.

Banff Ave Brewing Co MICROBREWERY
(Map p80; ☑403-762-1003; www.banffavebrewingco.ca; 110 Banff Ave; 11am-2am) Banff Ave's sprawling 2nd-floor beer hall bustles day and night, slinging a dozen craft brews created on the premises alongside a wide range of nibbles: buttered soft pretzels, bratwurst, burgers and the like. Late-night half-price pizza specials offer welcome relief to late-returning hikers and help keep things hopping into the wee hours.

St James's Gate Olde Irish Pub PUB
(Map p80; ☑403-762-9355; www.stjamesgate banff.com; 207 Wolf St; 11am-2am) Banff is a Celtic name, so it's hardly surprising to find an Irish pub here, and a rather good one at that. Check out the woodwork, crafted and shipped from the old country. Aside from stout on tap and a healthy selection of malts, there's classic pub grub, including an epic steak-and-Guinness pie.

ℹ Information

Banff Tourism Bureau (Map p80; ☑403-762-8421; www.banfflakelouise.com; 224 Banff Ave;

8am-8pm mid-May–Sep, 9am-5pm rest of year) Opposite the Parks Canada desks in the Banff Visitor Centre, this info desk provides advice on accommodations, activities and attractions.

Parks Canada Banff Visitor Centre (Map p80; ☑403-762-1550; www.pc.gc.ca/banff; 224 Banff Ave; 8am-8pm mid-May–Sep, 9am-5pm rest of year) The Parks Canada office provides park info and maps. This is where you can find current trail conditions and weather forecasts, and register for backcountry hiking and camping.

ℹ Getting There & Away

AIR

The nearest airport is Calgary International Airport (p68). Numerous year-round shuttle buses make the two-hour journey between the airport and Banff. Buses are less frequent in the spring and fall. Companies include **Banff Airporter** (☑403-762-3330; www.banffairporter.com; Banff to Calgary Airport adult/child $68/34), whose 11 daily buses can pick up and drop off passengers at virtually any Banff address, and the slightly more expensive Brewster Express, whose nine daily services (adult/child $72/36) also stop at most Banff hotels.

BUS

Brewster Express (☑403-221-8242; www.banffjaspercollection.com/brewster-express; 100 Gopher St; adult/child Banff to Calgary Airport $72/36, to Jasper $120/60, to Lake Louise $37/19) offers bus service from most Banff hotels to downtown Calgary ($72, 2½ hours), Jasper ($120, 4¾ hours) and Lake Louise ($37, one hour).

From late October through April, Jasper-based **SunDog Tour Company** (☑780-852-4056; www.sundogtours.com; 414 Connaught Dr, Jasper Town; 8am-5pm) also runs buses from Banff to Jasper ($79, four hours).

CAR & MOTORCYCLE

Several major car-rental companies have branches in Banff Town. During summer all vehicles might be reserved in advance, so call ahead. If you're flying into Calgary, reserving a car at the airport (where the fleets are huge) may yield a better deal than waiting to pick up a car when you reach Banff Town. In winter, all-weather tires or snow chains are often required; inquire locally about current road conditions.

ℹ Getting Around

Roam (☑403-762-0606; www.roamtransit.com; adult/child local routes $2/1, regional routes $6/3) Roam runs Banff's excellent public bus network. Five local routes serve Banff Town and its immediate surroundings: route

1 to Banff Hot Springs, 2 to Tunnel Mountain, 4 to Cave and Basin, 6 to Lake Minnewanka and 7 to the Banff Centre. Additional regional buses serve Canmore (route 3), Lake Louise (8X express and 8S scenic) and Johnston Canyon (route 9).

Banff Taxi (☑ 403-762-0000; www.banfftrans portation.com/banff-taxi-service.html) Taxi service for Banff and the surrounding area.

Lake Louise

☑ 403 / POP 1175

Considered by many to be the crown jewel of Banff National Park, Lake Louise is nearly impossible to describe without resorting to shameless clichés. Standing next to the serene, implausibly turquoise lake, Banff's wild grandeur feels (and is) tantalizingly close, with a surrounding amphitheater of finely chiseled mountains that hoist Victoria Glacier audaciously toward the heavens.

Famous for its teahouses, grizzly bears and hiking trails, Lake Louise is also renowned for its much-commented-on 'crowds,' plus the incongruous lump of towering concrete known as Chateau Lake Louise. But frankly, who cares? You don't come to Lake Louise to dodge other tourists. You come to share in one of the Rockies' most spectacular sights, one that has captured the imaginations of mountaineers, artists and visitors for more than a century.

Lake Louise 'village,' just off Trans-Canada Hwy/Hwy 1, is little more than an outdoor shopping mall, a gas station and a handful of hotels.

⊙ Sights

★**Moraine Lake**   LAKE
The spectacular, deep teal waters of Moraine Lake are one of Banff's iconic sights. The lake's rugged and remote setting in the **Valley of the Ten Peaks**, accessed via a narrow winding road, only add to its allure, Many visitors actually prefer Moraine Lake to the more famous Lake Louise – so many, in fact, that you'll have to be lucky or an early riser to get a parking spot here; the lot often fills up by 5:30am in peak season.

For many, the quintessential Moraine Lake experience is watching sunrise from the **Rockpile**, the famous viewpoint on the lake's northern shore. From the parking lot, it's a steep but short 10-minute climb to the best views.

There are also some excellent day hikes from the lake, or you can rent a boat at the

Moraine Lake Boathouse (Map p70; www. morainelake.com/day-visits; boat rental per hour $120; ⊘ 9am-5pm mid-Jun–mid-Sep, weather permitting) and paddle through the glacier-fed waters.

Moraine Lake Rd and its facilities are open from June to early October. In winter the access road is closed by snow.

★**Lake Louise**   LAKE
Named for Queen Victoria's fourth daughter (Princess Louise Caroline Alberta, who also lent her name to the province), the gob-smackingly gorgeous Lake Louise is a place that requires multiple viewings. Aside from the standard picture-postcard shot (blue sky, even bluer lake, glistening glacier), try visiting at six in the morning, at dusk in August, in the October rain or after a heavy winter storm.

Morant's Curve Viewpoint   VIEWPOINT
(Map p70) Evoking oohs, ahs and countless shutter clicks from every traveler who passes near, this pullover and viewpoint on the Bow Valley Pkwy/Hwy 1A sits at a scenic curve in the Bow River much favored by both the Canadian Pacific Railway and *National Geographic* photographer Nicholas Morant (1910–99), whose images helped publicize Banff during its early days as a national park.

Lake Louise Summer Gondola   CABLE CAR
(☑ 403-522-3555; www.lakelouisegondola.com; 1 Whitehorn Rd; adult/child $38/17; ⊘ 9am-4pm mid-May–mid-Jun, 8am-5:30pm mid-Jun–Jul, to 6pm Aug, to 5pm Sep–mid-Oct; ⊞) For a bird's-eye view of the Lake Louise area – and a good chance of spotting grizzly bears on the avalanche slopes – climb aboard the Lake Louise Gondola, which crawls up the side of **Whitehorn Mountain** via an open ski lift or enclosed gondola to a dizzying viewpoint 2088m above the valley floor. Look out for the imposing fang of 3544m-high **Mt Temple** piercing the skyline on the opposite side of the valley.

⚐ Activities

★**Lake Agnes & the Beehives**   HIKING
Two compelling attractions make this Lake Louise's most popular hike. First, the historic Lake Agnes Teahouse (p90), where hikers have been refueling since 1901, makes a supremely atmospheric spot to break for tea, sandwiches and baked goods at the 3.4km

Lake Louise Area

0 | 4 km
0 | 2 miles
N

Trans-Canada Hwy

93

Bow River

South Gate

Jasper (227km)

Lake Louise Ski Area (4km)

Icefields Pkwy

Gondola Base Terminal

HI Lake Louise Alpine Centre

Whitehorn Rd

Lake Louise Station Restaurant

Lake Louise Inn

Trailhead Cafe

Lake Louise Village

Mt St Piran (2649m)

Little Beehive

Fairmount Chateau Lake Louise

Deer Lodge

Louise Creek Trail

Lake Louise Teahouse

Lake Agnes

Mirror Lake

Paradise Lodge

Lake Louise Tent & RV Campground

Mt Niblock (2976m)

Big Beehive

Lake Louise Boathouse

Lake Louise Dr

Bow Valley Pkwy

1A

Mt Whyte (2983m)

Lake Louise

Fairview Rd

Banff (54km)

Trans-Canada Hwy

Mt Fairview (2744m)

Saddle Mountain (2433m)

Banff (52km)

Plain of Six Glaciers Teahouse

Plain of Six Glaciers

Mt Sheol (2779m)

Paradise Creek

Mt Aberdeen (3152m)

Paradise Valley

Banff National Park

Moraine Lake Rd (closed Oct–Jun)

The Mitre (2886m)

Lake Annette

Mt Lefroy (3423m)

Ringrose Peak (3278m)

Mt Temple (3453m)

Moraine Creek

Mt Hungabee (3490m)

Pinnacle Mountain (3067m)

Sentinel Pass

Larch Valley (2360m)

Eiffel Peak (3084m)

Moraine Lake Lodge

Wenkchemna Peaks (3170m)

Wenkchemna Pass

Eiffel Lake

Moraine Lake Boathouse

Mt Bell (2910m)

Yoho National Park

Mt Neptuak (3233m)

Valley of the Ten Peaks

Alberta

Moraine Lake

Consolation Lakes

Mt Tuzo (3245m)

Mt Bowlen (3072m)

Mt Fay (3235m)

Mt Babel (3101m)

Mt Deltaform (3424m)

Mt Tonsa (3054m)

Kootenay National Park

British Columbia

Mt Allen (3301m)

Mt Perren (3051m)

Mt Little (3088m)

mark. Second, the lake views from atop 2270m Big Beehive (the trail's ultimate destination) are phenomenal. Set off early to beat the crowds.

★ **Skoki Valley Trail** WALKING
(Map p70) The beautiful multiday hike into Skoki Valley is one of Banff's classic backcountry adventures. Starting from Temple Lodge at Lake Louise ski resort, the trail leads over Boulder Pass and Deception Pass, past numerous lakes and around Fossil Mountain to the rustic 1930s-vintage **Skoki Lodge** (Map p70; ☑ 403-522-3555; www.skoki. com; r per person incl 3 meals & afternoon tea $240-305) and **Merlin Meadows** wilderness campground. From here, various loop hikes fan out into the wilderness.

Plain of Six
Glaciers Trail HIKING
Combining magnificent lake and glacier perspectives with an afternoon tea break, this is one of Banff's most memorable hikes. Follow Lake Louise's western shore for 2km, then enter a long wooded valley flanked by crags popular with rock climbers and zigzag up to the historic Plain of Six Glaciers Teahouse (p90). A further 1km climb leads to impressive Victoria Glacier views.

Lake Louise
Ski Resort SKIING
(☑ 403-522-3555; www.skilouise.com; 1 Whitehorn Rd; day pass adult/youth $114/98; 👫) Lake Louise is the largest of Banff's 'Big Three' resorts (the other two being Sunshine and Norquay). It offers a humongous 1700 hectares of skiable land divided between 145 runs. It's great for families, with a good spread of beginner-rated (25%) runs on the Front Side/South Face (especially around the base area), along with plenty of intermediate-rated (45%) runs. The longest (8km) is on the Larch Face.

Lake Louise
Boathouse BOATING
(☑ 403-522-3511; www.fairmont.com/lake-louise/ promotions/canoeing; canoe rental per 30min/1hr $115/125; ⊙ 8am-8:30pm Jun-Sep, weather permitting) Hire a canoe from the Lake Louise Boathouse and paddle across the icy waters – you can dislodge yourself from at least some of the lakeside crowds, although you'll pay handsomely for the experience. Boats can carry three adults or two adults and two children. Life jackets are included.

Wild Water Adventures RAFTING
(☑ 403-522-2211; www.wildwater.com; 111 Lake Louise Dr; ⊙ 6am-8pm late May-early Oct) This operator will get you out on the Kicking Horse River rapids for everything from a gentle ride (adult/child $89/69) to the Maximum Horsepower trip ($169). Some trips will pick up from Lake Louise or Banff hotels; others require you to find your own way there (double-check when you book).

🛏 Sleeping

Lake Louise Tent & RV
Campground CAMPGROUND $
(www.reservation.pc.gc.ca; Lake Louise village; tent/RV sites $27.40/32.30; ⊙ tent park Jun-Sep, RV park year-round) Near the village, this efficient, wooded 395-site campground accommodates RVs on one side of the river and tents and soft-sided vehicles on the other, protected from bears behind an electric fence. Choose a site away from the railway tracks to enjoy views of Mt Temple in relative peace. Book online through the Parks Canada website.

HI Lake Louise Alpine Centre HOSTEL $
(☑ 403-522-2201; www.hihostels.ca; 203 Village Rd, Lake Louise village; dm/d $64/192; P) This is what a hostel should be – clean, friendly and full of interesting travelers – and the rustic, comfortable lodge-style buildings, with plenty of raw timber and stone, are fine examples of Canadian Rockies architecture. Dorm rooms are fairly standard and the small private rooms are a bit overpriced, but this is as close as you'll get to budget in Lake Louise.

★ **Moraine Lake Lodge** HOTEL $$$
(☑ 403-522-3733; www.morainelakelodge.com; 1 Moraine Lake Rd; r/cabin from $717/964; ⊙ Jun-Sep; P 🐾) 🍃 The experience here is intimate, personal and private, and the service is famously good. While billed as rustic (ie no TVs), the rooms and cabins offer mountain-inspired luxury with big picture windows, wood-burning or antique gas fireplaces, soaking tubs, feather comforters and balconies overlooking the lake. The fine-dining restaurant on-site wins equal plaudits. Canoe use is free for guests.

★ **Paradise Lodge**
& Bungalows CABIN $$$
(☑ 403-522-3595; www.paradiselodge.com; Lake Louise Dr; cabins $345-488, r in lodge $415-475; ⊙ mid-May–Sep) These cozy, lovingly restored

1930s log cabins along the Lake Louise road are only moments from the lakeshore. Each is unique, but expect comfy beds, kitchens or kitchenettes and claw-foot soaking tubs. Newer lodge rooms are hotel-style. Cheerful flowery grounds and tree-shaded lawns provide ample lounging opportunities. Kids will love the playground and miniature doghouse cabin for Beau the pooch.

★ **Deer Lodge** HOTEL **$$$**
(📞 403-410-7417; www.crmr.com; 109 Lake Louise Dr; r from $329; 🅿 📶) Tucked demurely behind Chateau Lake Louise, historic Deer Lodge dates from the 1920s and has managed to keep its genuine alpine feel intact. The rustic exterior and maze of corridors can't have changed much since the days of bobbed hair and F Scott Fitzgerald. Lodge rooms are fairly small but quaint, while spacious Heritage rooms have smart, boutique-like furnishings.

The beautifully restored lounge and log-cabin sitting room, especially with its stone fireplace ablaze, make time travel feel like a real possibility. Tranquility here is ensured – you won't find a TV anywhere.

✖️ Eating

★ **Lake Agnes Teahouse** TEAHOUSE **$**
(www.lakeagnesteahouse.com; lunch $7.50-15; ⏱ 8am-5pm early Jun-early Oct) The 3.4km hike from Lake Louise to Lake Agnes is among the area's most popular – surely because it ends here. This fabulously rustic alpine teahouse perched at 2135m (7005ft) seems to hang in the clouds beside the ethereal lake and its adjacent waterfall. Homemade soup, thick-cut sandwiches and lake-water tea help fuel the jaunt back down. Cash only. Expect queues.

Trailhead Café SANDWICHES **$**
(📞 403-522-2006; www.facebook.com/lakelouise AB; Samson Mall, Lake Louise village; sandwiches $6-10; ⏱ 7am-6pm) This is *the* place to come for breakfast or a takeout lunch. Wraps and sandwiches are made to order, the staff are well versed in the espresso machine, and the omelets, buttermilk pancakes and lox cream-cheese bagels will fuel you for the trail without breaking the bank. Expect a queue.

Plain of Six Glaciers Teahouse TEAHOUSE **$$**
(snacks & meals $9.50-25; ⏱ 9am-5pm mid-Jun–early Oct) Constructed in 1927 as a way

station for Swiss mountaineering guides leading clients up to the summit of Mt Victoria, this twin-level log chalet looks like something out of the pages of *Heidi*. Nestled in a quiet glade at 2100m, it dishes up homemade sandwiches, cakes, gourmet teas and hot chocolates to a steady stream of puffed-out hikers.

★ **Lake Louise Station Restaurant** CANADIAN **$$$**
(📞 403-522-2600; www.lakelouisestation.com; 200 Sentinel Rd, Lake Louise village; mains lunch $16-26, dinner $20-48; ⏱ 11:30am-4pm & 5-9pm Jun-Sep, noon-4pm & 5-8:30pm Wed-Sun May) Lake Louise's historic train station is the most atmospheric place in town to have a meal. Details like stacks of turn-of-the-century luggage, the stationmaster's desk and the original dining cars out back transport you back to 1910, when the elegant edifice was first built. Dig into maple-glazed salmon, Wiener schnitzel or slow-braised bison ribs and soak up the vintage vibe. Reservations recommended.

ℹ️ Information

Lake Louise Backcountry Trails Office
(📞 403-522-1264; Lake Louise Visitor Centre, Lake Louise village; ⏱ 8:30am-7pm Jun-Sep, 9am-5pm Oct-May) Parks Canada desk offering specialist advice on exploring the backcountry area around Lake Louise.

Lake Louise Tourism Bureau (📞 403-762-8421; www.banfflakelouise.com; Samson Mall, Lake Louise village; ⏱ 8:30am-7pm Jun-Sep, 9am-5pm Oct-May) Information on activities and accommodations in Lake Louise village.

Parks Canada Lake Louise Visitors Centre
(📞 403-522-3833; www.pc.gc.ca/en/pn-np/ ab/banff; Samson Mall, Lake Louise village; ⏱ 8:30am-7pm Jun-Sep, 9am-5pm Oct-May) Visit Parks Canada's newly renovated digs for national park info and to register for backcountry hikes.

ℹ️ Getting There & Away

Brewster (p76) runs bus services to Lake Louise from Calgary International Airport, Banff and Jasper; the bus terminal is a marked stop at Samson Mall.

For drivers, the quickest way to get to Lake Louise from Banff (55km, 40 minutes) is along the Trans-Canada Hwy/Hwy 1. Running parallel to the main highway, the Bow Valley Parkway is a slightly slower (one to 1¼ hours), but much more scenic alternative; as it isn't fenced, it's a great route for wildlife sightings.

Jasper Town & Around

☑ 780 / POP 4590

Arriving in Jasper Town, the first thing you may notice is how low-key it all feels. Yes, Jasper is the most important town for kilometers around, and sees nearly two million visitors each year. Yet it feels far removed from the traffic jams of Lake Louise and retains an agreeable humility that seems more reflective of its workaday railway town roots than of its modern status as a national park hub.

With only two main thoroughfares, Patricia St and Connaught Dr, holding the lion's share of businesses, you can easily explore Jasper on foot in half an hour. Sit on the lawn outside the early 20th-century log cabin at the heart of town, meditate on the murmur of the freight trains running by, and soak up the unhurried vibe. You really couldn't ask for a friendlier, more relaxing base for exploring the awe-inspiring wilderness that surrounds you.

◉ Sights

★ **Jasper National Park** NATIONAL PARK
(Map p92; www.pc.gc.ca/jasper; day pass adult/child/family $9.80/free/19.60) Wolves, elk, caribou, beaver and bear roam freely; glaciers stretch out between stark mountain peaks; waterfalls thunder over slopes; and valleys are wide and lush, with rivers charging turbulently through them – this is Jasper National Park, covering a diverse 11,228 sq km. Jasper is far from built up: while activities like hiking and mountain biking are well established and deservedly popular, it's still easy to experience the solitude and remoteness that abound in this park.

Some of the most popular natural wonders, like Miette Hot Springs and Maligne Canyon, are easily accessible, and many more attractions are just a short hike away. Keep a little spare time in your itinerary to take advantage of the many diversions you stumble upon – a sparkling lake to admire, a snowshoe tour to explore or a moose to watch ambling by. As the largest of Canada's Rocky Mountain parks, Jasper will quickly captivate you with its beauty and serenity.

★ **Miette Hot Springs** HOT SPRINGS
(Map p92; www.pc.gc.ca/hotsprings; Miette Rd; adult/child/family $7.05/5.15/20.35; ⊙9am-11pm mid-Jun–Aug, 10:30am-9pm May–mid-Jun & Sep–mid-Oct) More remote than Banff's historic springs, Miette Hot Springs ('discovered' in 1909) are 61km northeast of Jasper off Hwy 16, near the park's eastern boundary. The soothing waters, kept at a pleasant 37°C (98°F) to 40°C (104°F), are surrounded by peaks and are especially enjoyable when the fall snow is drifting down and steam envelops the crowd. Raining summer evenings also make for stunning, misty conditions.

Horseshoe Lake LAKE
(Map p92) This idyllic, blue-green horseshoe-shaped lake just off the Icefields Pkwy is missed by many visitors, making a stopover here all the more alluring. A choice spot for a bracing summer swim or a short stroll around the perimeter, the lake is surrounded by steep cliffs and is frequented by cliff divers. It's probably safer to watch than join in.

Maligne Lake LAKE
(Map p92) Almost 50km from Jasper at the end of a stunning road that bears its name, 22km-long Maligne Lake is the recipient of a lot of hype. It's the largest lake in the national park and there's no denying its appeal: the baby-blue water and a craning circle of rocky, photogenic peaks are a feast for the eyes.

Jasper Skytram CABLE CAR
(Map p92; ☑780-852-3093; www.jaspertramway.com; Whistlers Mountain Rd; adult/child/family $50/27/125; ⊙8am-9pm late Jun-Aug, 9am-8pm mid-May–late Jun, 10am-5pm late Mar–mid-May, Sep & Oct) If the average, boring views from Jasper just aren't blowing your hair back, go for a ride on this sightseeing gondola. The seven-minute journey (departures every nine minutes) zips up through various mountain life zones to the high barren slopes of the Whistlers. From the gondola's upper station a steep 1.25km hike leads to the mountain's true summit, where views stretch for 75km. Arrive early or late to avoid midday lines. There's a small restaurant and gift shop up top.

Pyramid Lake LAKE
(Map p92) Pyramid Lake is popular with canoers and kayakers in summer and ice-skaters in winter. From its eastern shore, a wooden pedestrian bridge leads out to Pyramid Island, a small nature preserve. At night, stargazers congregate on the bridge for unobstructed views of the heavens. It's roughly 7km northwest of Jasper Town.

Jasper National Park

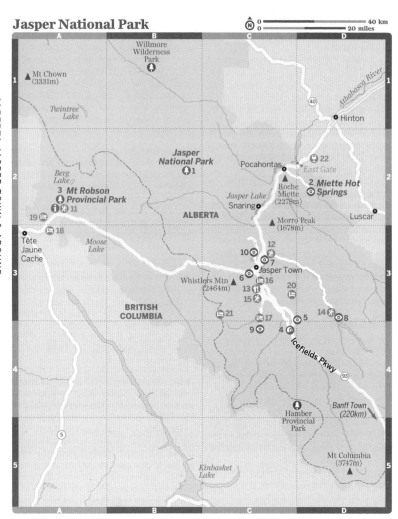

Lake Edith   LAKE

(Map p92) On the east side of the highway opposite Jasper town, Lake Edith is a popular summer getaway, ringed by cycling and hiking trails and frequented by kayakers and other boaters. It's equipped with picnic spots and a small beach area.

Jasper Planetarium   OBSERVATORY

(☎ 780-931-3275; www.jasperplanetarium.com; 1 Old Lodge Rd, Jasper Town; adult/child $29/15, incl telescope stargazing $59/25; ⊘ shows 3:30, 4:30, 7:45 & 8:45pm mid-Jun–mid-Sep, 7:45pm mid-Sep–Apr, 8:45pm May–mid-Jun, closed Nov & last week of Apr) Relocated to the Fairmont Jasper

Park Lodge on a year-round basis in 2019, Jasper's planetarium screens multiple shows daily in its 40-seat dome theater, whisking visitors off on a virtual tour of Jasper's Dark Sky Preserve. For an extra fee, you can also stargaze through the planetarium's giant telescope (billed as the largest in the Rockies).

🏃 Activities

Cycling

Jasper tops Banff for single-track mountain biking; in fact, it's one of the best places in Canada for the sport. Many rides are within striking distance of town. Flatter, on-road options include the long-distance

Jasper National Park

grunt along the Icefields Parkway. The holy grail for experienced off-road cyclists is the **Valley of the Five Lakes** – it's varied and scenic, with plenty of places where you can let it rip. For more information, get a copy of *Mountain Biking Guide, Jasper National Park* from the Jasper Information Centre (p97).

Vicious Cycle (☑780-852-1111; www.vicious canada.com; 630 Connaught Dr, Jasper Town; bike rental per hour/day from $8/32; ☺9am-6pm Sun-Thu, to 7pm Fri & Sat) and **The Bench Bike Shop** (☑780-852-7768; www.thebenchbikeshop. com; 606 Patricia St, Jasper Town; bike rental per hour/day from $10/30; ☺10am-6pm) can sort out bike rentals and offer additional trail tips.

Hiking

★ **Skyline Trail** HIKING
(Map p92) This 45.6km Canadian Rockies classic leads through awe-inspiringly rugged, wide-open high country along the crest of the Maligne Range. Most hikers allow two or three days to savor the expansive views, with overnight stops at a series of backcountry campsites or the rustic Shovel Pass Lodge (p96). A shuttle (p98) allows hikers to start at one trailhead and finish at the other.

★ **Tonquin Valley Trail** HIKING
(Map p92) For wilderness lovers, this 53.2km out-and-back into one of Jasper's most untouched lake valleys is the experience of a lifetime. Notorious for its mosquitoes and mud, it's not for the faint-hearted, but the access route through Maccarib Pass is highly scenic, while campgrounds and a

backcountry lodge offer accommodations with amazing views of Amethyst Lake and the sheer rock Ramparts.

★ **Maligne Canyon** HIKING
(Map p92) One of Jasper's most spectacular hikes is the easy amble through this steep, narrow gorge shaped by the torrential waters of the Maligne River. The canyon at its narrowest is only a few meters wide and drops a stomach-turning 50m beneath your feet. Crossed by six bridges, it's most easily accessed from the parking area on Maligne Lake Rd.

Horseback Riding
Tonquin Valley Backcountry Lodge (p96) runs incredible, fully guided summer pack trips into the roadless Tonquin Valley, including meals and accommodations at their backcountry lodge and complimentary use of boats on Amethyst Lake. For a more leisurely horseback experience, **Jasper Riding Stables** (☑780-852-7433; www.jasper stables.com; Stables Rd, Jasper Town; 1/2/3hr rides $52/95/135; ☺May–mid-Oct) offers enjoyable day rides lasting from one to three hours.

Skiing & Snowboarding
Jasper National Park's only downhill ski area is **Marmot Basin** (Map p92; www.ski marmot.com; Marmot Basin Rd; day pass adult/child $110/89), which lies 19km southwest of town off Hwy 93A. Though not legendary, the presence of 95 runs and the longest high-speed quad chairlift in the Canadian Rockies mean Marmot is no pushover – and

its relative isolation compared to the trio of ski areas in Banff means shorter lift lines.

On-site are some cross-country trails and a predictably expensive day lodge, but no overnight accommodations. Regular shuttles link to Jasper Town in season. Seriously cold weather can drift in suddenly off the mountains, so dress appropriately.

👉 Tours

Jasper Adventure Centre
OUTDOORS

(☑ 780-852-5595; www.jasperadventurecentre. com; 611 Patricia St, Jasper Town; ⊗ 8am-9pm late Jun-Aug, to 6pm May-late Jun & Sep–mid-Oct) Jasper's veteran guiding outfit runs numerous local tours, as well as some further afield to the Icefields and Lake Louise. One of their most popular trips is the three-hour Wildlife Discovery Tour (adult/child $69/35). In winter they share office space with Sun-Dog Tour Company (☑ 780-852-4056; www. sundogtours.com; 414 Connaught Dr, Jasper Town; ⊗ 8am-5pm), from where they organize dogsledding and ice walks in addition to their many year-round tours.

Jasper Walks & Talks
HIKING

(☑ 780-852-4994; www.walksntalks.com; 626 Connaught Dr, Jasper Town; walks per adult $65-90, per child $45-50) Longtime local resident and former Parks Canada guide Paula Beauchamp leads small groups on three- to six-hour tours with a focus on such local attractions as Maligne Canyon and Mt Edith Cavell Meadows. Bring a picnic lunch, good walking shoes, your camera and lots of questions for your very knowledgeable guide. Winter snowshoe adventures are also offered.

Maligne Lake Cruises
CRUISE

(Map p92; www.banffjaspercollection.com/attractions/maligne-lake-cruise; Maligne Lake; adult/child 90min cruise $79/40, 2hr cruise $114/57; ⊗ May-Sep) These interpretive boat tours take you to the far end of Maligne Lake, to iconic Spirit Island (which, it should be noted, is not actually an island). En route, the lake shimmers in beguiling shades of blue as guides fill you in on local history and geology. Nevertheless, the price does seem rather high for the service provided.

🛏 Sleeping

Accommodations in Jasper are generally cheaper than Banff, but that's not really saying much. The town's limited hotel and hostel rooms fill up quickly in summer, as do the cabins, bungalows and campgrounds in the surrounding countryside.

Jasper's 11 park campgrounds (four of which accept reservations) are open from mid-May to September or October, with one (Wapiti) staying open year-round. For information, visit the Parks Canada Jasper Information Centre (p97).

★ HI Jasper
HOSTEL $

(☑ 587-870-2395; www.hihostels.ca; 708 Sleepy Hollow Rd, Jasper Town; dm/d from $50/167; P @ ⟨wifi⟩) 🌿 Jasper's 157-bed HI hostel, opened two blocks from downtown in 2019 to replace the aging Whistlers Mountain facility, is a gem. The sprawling lower level houses a bevy of bright, welcoming common spaces – a guest kitchen and dining area complete with cozy booth seating, pool table, cafe, laundry facilities, free parking with EV charging stations, and more.

Upstairs, pairs of four-bed dorms share their own shower, toilet and sink area, while family rooms, private quads and wheelchair-accessible units are also available. There's excellent wi-fi throughout, along with individual reading lights and charging stations above each bed. A potential downside for light sleepers are the train tracks right outside the back windows.

Jasper Downtown Hostel
HOSTEL $

(☑ 780-852-2000; www.jasperdowntownhostel.ca; 400 Patricia St, Jasper Town; dm/d from $45/140; ⟨wifi⟩) With Jasper's town center smack on its doorstep, this former residence has been remodeled and expanded to create simple, modern two- to 10-bed dorms, many with en suite bathrooms, along with comfortable private rooms sleeping one to three. Upstairs rooms are brighter, with wooden floors, while common areas include a well-equipped kitchen, a spacious front patio and a simple lounge.

Athabasca Hotel
HOTEL $$

(☑ 780-852-3386; www.athabascahotel.com; 510 Patricia St, Jasper Town; r without/with bath $139/239, 1-/2-bedroom ste $395/425; P @ ⟨wifi⟩) Around since 1929, the Atha-B (as it's known) is the best budget hotel in town. A taxidermist's dream, with animal heads crowding the lobby, it has small, clean rooms with wooden and brass furnishings and thick, wine-colored carpets. Less expensive rooms share a bathroom. Dated but not worn, it feels like you're staying at Grandma's (if Grandma liked to hunt).

Jasper Town

Jasper Town

Activities, Courses & Tours
1	Jasper Adventure Centre	C3
2	Jasper Walks & Talks	C4
3	SunDog Tour Company	D2
4	The Bench Bike Shop	C3
5	Vicious Cycle	C4

Sleeping
6	Athabasca Hotel	C3
7	Jasper Downtown Hostel	D1

Eating
8	Coco's Cafe	C3
9	Olive Bistro	D1
10	Other Paw Bakery	D3
11	Patricia Street Deli	C3
12	Raven Bistro	C2
13	The Spice Joint	D3

Drinking & Nightlife
14	Jasper Brewing Co.	D3
15	SnowDome Coffee Bar	C3

Becker's Chalets　　　　CHALET **$$**
(Map p92; ☏780-852-3779; www.beckers chalets.com; Hwy 93; d/q chalet from $200/225; P✿) Just 6km south of Jasper Town and paces from the northern entrance to the Icefields Pwky, this complex of 118 chalets has something for everyone – from 33 cute 1930s-vintage 'heritage' cabins to a block of big modern four-plexes popular with families and European tour groups. Rates here are among Jasper's cheapest, even if it's a bit of a mob scene.

Shovel Pass Lodge　　　　LODGE **$$**
(Map p92; ☏780-852-4215; www.skylinetrail.com; per person incl meals $255; ☀late Jun–early Sep) Built in 1921 and rebuilt in 1991, the Shovel Pass Lodge is situated halfway along the emblematic Skyline Trail (p93). The seven guest cabins are basic, with log bed frames,

LOOK TO THE SKIES

Ten days in late October during the Dark Sky Festival (www.jasperdarksky.travel; ⊘late Oct) are filled with events celebrating space and the night sky. Hear talks by astronauts, astronomers and astrophotographers, listen to the symphony under the stars, see the aurora borealis reflected in a glacial lake and gaze through a telescope into the great beyond. There are some free events, but the big hitters sell out months in advance.

fresh linen, propane lights and hot water delivered daily. Two hearty meals and a packed lunch are includedd.

Miette Hot Springs Bungalows CABIN $$
(Map p92; ☑780-866-3750; www.miettebunga lows.com; Miette Hot Springs Rd; r/chalets/cabins from $135/165/235; ℙ) This low-key 'resort' at the hot springs is a collection of old fashioned but charming log cabins and motel rooms dating from 1938, and chalets from the 1970s. Cabins sleep up to six and have kitchenettes and stone fireplaces (some of the 17 motel rooms also have kitchenettes). The restaurant has reasonably priced standard meals. Bears regularly meander through the grounds.

★**Patricia Lake Bungalows** BUNGALOW $$$
(☑780-852-3560; www.patricialakebungalows. com; Patricia Lake Rd; bungalows $199-510) Reminiscent of an earlier era, this charming assemblage of bungalows sits placidly at the end of a dead-end road on the shores of lovely Patricia Lake, 5km north of Jasper Town. Owned by the same family for nearly half a century, it's the kind of place where you can truly leave the modern world behind.

★**Tekarra Lodge** HOTEL $$$
(☑780-852-3058; www.tekarralodge.com; Hwy 93A; lodge/cabins from $249/289; ⊘May-Oct; ℙ🛜🐾) In business since 1947, these cabins – some of the most atmospheric in the park – sit 1km south of town near the Athabasca River amid tall trees and splendid tranquility. Hardwood floors, wood-paneled walls plus stone fireplaces and kitchenettes inspire coziness. Family-friendly amenities abound, including an on-site playground, evening s'mores and songs by the campfire, bike rentals and a guest laundry.

★**Tonquin Valley Backcountry Lodge** LODGE $$$
(Map p92; ☑780-852-3909; www.tonquinvalley. com; per person incl meals summer/winter $325/185; ⊘mid-Feb–Mar & Jul–mid-Sep) These rustic cabins are located on Amethyst Lake, deep in Jasper's backcountry. Linen, a wood-burning stove, home-cooked meals and stunning views keep you cozy and you get use of a boat or canoe. There's a minimum two-night stay for hikers and skiers, or you can join a multiday horseback-riding trek to reach the lodge (five days from $2500).

🍴 Eating

★**Other Paw Bakery** CAFE $
(☑780-852-2253; www.bearspawbakery.com; 610 Connaught Dr, Jasper Town; mains $5-13; ⊘7am-6pm) An offshoot of the original Bear's Paw bakery around the corner, the Other Paw offers the same addictive mix of breads, pastries, muffins and coffee – while also serving up tasty sandwiches, salads, soups and well-stuffed wraps.

Patricia Street Deli SANDWICHES $
(☑780-852-4814; www.facebook.com/patricia streetdeli; 610 Patricia St, Jasper Town; sandwiches $9.50-12; ⊘10am-7pm) Come to the Patricia Street Deli hungry – really hungry. Homemade bread is made into generously filled sandwiches by people who are just as generous with their smiles and hiking tips. Choose from a huge list of fillings, including various pestos, chutneys, veggies and meat cuts. Join the queue and satiate your ravenous backcountry appetite.

Coco's Cafe CAFE $
(☑780-852-4550; www.cocoscafe.ca; 608b Patricia St, Jasper Town; mains $9-15; ⊘8am-4pm; 🌱) 🌱 If you're looking for breakfast, you can't go wrong at Coco's. There's not much room inside, but many are happy to cram in to plan hikes and trade bear sightings. There's plenty of locally sourced, vegan, veggie and celiac-friendly fare on the menu, while carnivores are kept happy with Montreal smoked meat, pulled pork and lox.

The Spice Joint JAMAICAN $
(☑780-852-3615; www.facebook.com/thespice joint; 614 Connaught Dr, Jasper Town; mains $12-16; ⊘10am-9pm) Since opening in 2018, this friendly snack shack decked out in red, yellow and green has brought a welcome dose of Caribbean flavor to Jasper's northern wilds. The menu revolves around Jamaican treats

like spicy jerk chicken, barbecued pork, Rasta greens and quinoa salad, all accompanied by fruit smoothies, ginger beer, rum, Red Stripe beer and Blue Mountain coffee.

Olive Bistro   MEDITERRANEAN **$$**
(☏780-852-5222; www.olivebistro.ca; Pyramid Lake Rd, Jasper Town; mains $14-35; ◷4-10pm May-Oct, 5-9pm Nov-Apr; 🍴) This casual restaurant with big booths has a classy menu. Main dishes such as slow-braised organic lamb shank, elk rigatoni or a vegan 'dragon bowl' come sandwiched between appetizers of white truffle scallops and indulgent desserts like a gourmet banana split. In summer, enjoy excellent cocktails during the 4pm to 6pm happy hour; in winter, there's live music twice monthly.

★**Maligne Canyon**
Wilderness Kitchen   BARBECUE **$$$**
(Map p92; ☏844-762-6713; www.banffjasper collection.com; Maligne Canyon Rd; lunch mains $16-26, dinner $55; ◷8am-10pm May-Sep, 9am-4pm Sun-Fri, to 10pm Sat Oct-Apr) The outdoor deck at the edge of gorgeous Maligne Canyon is temptation enough to dine at Jasper's newest restaurant. But the real clincher is the cornucopia of local meats, shown off to full advantage in the house special Maligne Canyon Platter: grilled venison sausage, smoked chicken, glazed baby back pork ribs, and barbecue Alberta beef brisket slow-cooked for 16 hours.

★**Raven Bistro**   MEDITERRANEAN **$$$**
(☏780-852-5151; www.theravenbistro.com; 504 Patricia St, Jasper Town; lunch mains $16-27, dinner mains $28-46; ◷11:30am-11pm; 🍴) This cozy, tastefully designed bistro offers vegetarian dishes, encourages shared plates and earns a loyal clientele with sublime offerings like Kaffir lime–coconut seafood pot or lamb shank glazed with fresh mint, horseradish, honey and Dijon mustard. Not in a lunch-dinner mood? Try the 'late riser' breakfast skillet, or come for happy hour (3pm to 5:30pm daily).

🍷 Drinking & Nightlife

★**SnowDome Coffee Bar**   COFFEE
(☏780-852-3852; http://snowdome.coffee; 607 Patricia St, Jasper Town; ◷7am-8pm; 📶) Some of Jasper's best damn coffee is – no joke! – served at this former Coin Clean Laundry, now reincarnated as a cafe-gallery-community hangout. Beyond the stellar espresso, SnowDome bakes killer muffins

(still oven-warm at opening time) and promotes good karma with its free mug basket and 'pay it forward' bulletin board where you can prepurchase coffee for an unsuspecting future customer.

Folding Mountain Taproom   MICROBREWERY
(Map p92; ☏780-817-6287; www.foldingmoun tain.com; 49321 Hwy 16, Jasper East; ◷11am-10pm) This up-and-coming microbrewery draws a boisterous mix of locals from nearby Hinton and travelers heading to or from the wilderness. Test the waters with a four-beer sampler (choose from Flash Flood IPA, Alpine Cranberry Sour or a dozen other brews on tap), then stick around for excellent burgers, salads and other pub grub. It's just 5km outside Jasper's eastern park gate.

Jasper Brewing Co   BREWERY
(☏780-852-4111; www.jasperbrewingco.ca; 624 Connaught Dr, Jasper Town; ◷11:30am-1am) 🍴 This brewpub was the first of its kind in a Canadian national park, using glacial water to make its fine ales, including the signature Rockhopper IPA and Jasper the Bear honey beer. It's a perennial favorite hangout for locals and tourists alike, with TVs and a good food menu.

ℹ Information

Parks Canada Jasper Information Centre
(☏780-852-6176; www.pc.gc.ca/jasper; 500 Connaught Dr, Jasper Town; ◷9am-7pm mid-May–early Oct, to 5pm rest of year) Parks Canada operates a well-staffed and helpful info desk in this wonderful midtown building – Jasper's oldest, dating from 1913. Directly adjacent are the local tourist information stand, plus an excellent gift shop.

Tourism Jasper (☏780-852-6236; www. jasper.travel; 500 Connaught Dr, Jasper Town; ◷9am-7pm mid-May–early Oct, to 5pm rest of year) Jasper's municipal tourist office, directly adjacent to the Parks Canada info center at the heart of town, offers a wealth of information about area activities and accommodations.

ℹ Getting There & Away

BUS
SunDog (p86) offers daily bus service year-round to Edmonton airport ($99, 5½ hours), along with winter service (late October through April) to Lake Louise ($69, four hours), Banff Town ($79, five hours) and Calgary airport ($135, seven hours).

From May through mid-October, **Brewster Express** (☏877-625-4372; www.banffjasper collection.com/brewster-express) runs its own daily express bus to Lake Louise ($97, 3½ hours), Banff ($120, 4¾ hours), Canmore ($144, 5¾ hours) and Calgary International Airport ($167, eight hours).

TRAIN

VIA Rail (☑ 888-842-7245; www.viarail.ca) offers tri-weekly train services west to Vancouver (from $148, 23½ hours) and bi-weekly services east to Toronto (from $367, 72 hours). In addition, there is a tri-weekly service to Prince Rupert, BC (from $156, 33 hours, with obligatory overnight stop in Prince George). Call or check in at the **train station** (607 Connaught Dr, Jasper Town) for exact schedule and fare details.

ⓘ Getting Around

Maligne Valley Hikers Express Shuttle (☑ 780-852-3331; www.maligneadventures. com; one way adult/child $35/17.50; ☺ late Jun-late Sep) Runs a daily 45-minute shuttle from Jasper Town to Maligne Lake, stopping en route at the North Skyline trailhead, then returning from Maligne Lake to Jasper at 10am.

Caribou Cabs (☑ 780-931-2334; www. facebook.com/cariboucabs) and **Jasper Taxi** (☑ 780-852-3600) offer dependable taxi service; call to arrange pickup. Ride-sharing services such as Uber and Lyft are not currently an option.

SOUTHERN ALBERTA

Alberta's national parks and cities grab most of the headlines, leaving the expansive south largely forgotten. This is true cowboy land, where the ghosts of herders like John Ware and the Sundance Kid are woven through the history of endless ranch land. It's often interrupted by deep, dramatic canyons carved in the last ice age, as well as towering hoodoos – funky, Dr Seuss–like rock sculptures. History abounds at Head-Smashed-In Buffalo Jump, and Writing-on-Stone and Dinosaur provincial parks, Unesco World Heritage areas that preserve the region's fascinating past.

Picture-perfect landscapes are plentiful here. The dusty badlands around Drumheller open up into wide open prairies that stretch east all the way to the Cyprus Hills of western Saskatchewan. To the west lies Waterton Lakes National Park, with some of the most spectacular scenery in the Rockies – utterly different from Banff and Jasper yet still under the radar of most visitors.

Drumheller

☑ 403 / POP 7982

As you approach Drumheller, the road dips down dramatically into the Red Deer Valley, looking like a big layered cake. This community was founded on coal but now thrives on another subterranean resource – dinosaur bones. A small town set amid Alberta's enigmatic badlands, it acts as the nexus of the so-called Dinosaur Trail. Paleontology is a serious business here (the nearby fantastic Royal Tyrrell Museum is as much research center as tourist site), and downtown the cartoon dino statues on most street corners add some color and character to an otherwise average town. Add in the museums in nearby East Coulee on the Hoodoo Drive and the ghosts of Wayne, and you're set.

The summers are hot, and the deep-cut river valley in which Drumheller sits provides a much-needed break to the monotony of the prairies. Hoodoos dominate this badlands landscape, which has featured in many a movie (mainly Westerns).

⊙ Sights & Activities

★ **Royal Tyrrell Museum of Palaeontology**   MUSEUM
(☑ 403-823-7707; www.tyrrellmuseum.com; 1500 North Dinosaur Trail, Midlands Provincial Park; adult/child/family $19/10/48; ☺ 9am-9pm mid-May–Aug, 10am-5pm Sep, 10am-5pm Tue-Sun Oct–mid-May; ⊞) This fantastic museum is one of the pre-eminent dinosaur museums on the planet, made even better by a $5.9 million expansion project completed in 2019. Even if you have no interest in dinos, you'll come out feeling like you missed your calling as a paleontologist. The exhibits are nothing short of mind-blowing. Unlike some other dinosaur exhibits, there's nothing dusty or musty about this super-modern place. Children will love the interactive displays.

Look for the skeleton of 'Hell-Boy,' a dinosaur discovered in 2005, and 'Black Beauty,' a 67-million-year-old *T rex* rearing its head into the sky. You can learn how the dinosaurs are extracted from the ground and even peer into the fossil lab.

There are also summertime opportunities to get among the badlands on a guided tour and discover your own dino treasures on a fossil search ($10) or a dinosaur dig ($15) – you'll feel like you've stepped right into your very own *Jurassic Park*.

Atlas Coal Mine
MINE

(☑403-822-2220;   https://atlascoalmine.ab.ca;
East Coulee; adult/family $12/35, tours $14-27;
☺9:45am-5pm Sep-Jun, to 6:30pm Jul & Aug)
Home to the last wooden tipple (a coal-loading structure) in Canada, Atlas Coal
Mine closed its production in 1959. Today
it's an engaging historic sight where you
can check out the original mine buildings
and chat with staff dressed as mine characters. Join an hourly tour to climb the tipple,
don a lamp and head down a tunnel – or to
learn about the darker, unmentionable side
of mining.

Rosedale Suspension Bridge
BRIDGE

(Hwy 56, Rosedale) This suspension bridge
isn't very long or particularly high, but it's
definitely not for the faint of heart. Made of
see-through wire mesh, it sways like a river
reed in the wind. The bridge was used by
miners from 1931 to 1957; on the far side
of the Red Deer river, you can see the now-
closed mines. Despite previous use of row-
boats and aerial cable cars, it was the bridge
that was considered dangerous due to high
winds and floods.

East Coulee School Museum
MUSEUM

(☑403-822-3970; http://ecsmuseum.ca; 359 2nd
Ave, East Coulee; $7; ☺10am-5pm May-Sep) This
original village school in art deco style dou-
bled in size to eight rooms during the coal
mining boom of the 1930s. Exhibits inside
detail the history of East Coulee (once bigger than Drumheller) and of the school itself. In the recreated classroom, peruse the
students' journals to get a sense of what life
was like back then, both for them and their
teachers.

World's Largest Dinosaur
LANDMARK

(60 1st Ave W; adult/family $4/10.50; ☺10am-
5:30pm; ☝) In a town filled with dinosaurs,
this *T rex* is the king of them all. Standing
26m high above a parking lot, it dominates
the Drumheller skyline (and is featured in
the *Guinness World Records*). It's worth
climbing the 106 steps to the top for the nov-
elty of standing in the dino's toothy jaws –
plus the views are mighty good. Ironically,
the dinosaur isn't technically very accurate:
at 46m long, it's about 4.5 times bigger than
its extinct counterpart.

Dinosaur Trail
& Hoodoo Drive
SCENIC DRIVE

Drumheller is on the Dinosaur Trail, a 48km
loop that runs northwest from town and
includes Hwys 837 and 838. The stunning
scenery is worth the drive – badlands and
river views await at every turn. The 25km
Hoodoo Drive starts about 18km southeast
of Drumheller on Hwy 10; it's usually done
as an out-and-back, with Wayne as the turn-
around point.

The Dinosaur Trail loop takes you past
Midland Provincial Park (no camping),
where you can take a self-guided hike, and
past the vast **Horsethief Canyon** and its picturesque views. Glide peacefully across the
Red Deer River on the free, cable-operated
Bleriot Ferry, which has been running since
1913; watch for beavers, which have a dam
here. This area is also frequented by moose,
lynx and cougars. On the west side of the valley, pause at **Orkney Viewpoint**, which overlooks the area's impressive canyons.

Along the Hoodoo Drive between Rosedale and Lehigh you'll find the best examples
of **hoodoos** – weird, eroded, mushroom-like
columns of sandstone rock – there's also an
interpretive trail.

This area was once the site of a prosperous coal-mining community; the historic
Atlas Coal Mine and East Coulee School Museum are both worth a stop. Take the side
trip on Hwy 10X (which includes 11 bridges within 6km) from Rosedale to the small
community of **Wayne** (population 27) with
its famous and supposedly haunted saloon.

🛏 Sleeping & Eating

★**Rosedeer Hotel**
HISTORIC HOTEL

(☑403-823-9189;   http://visitlastchancesaloon.
com; 555 Jewel St, Wayne; camping $20, rooms
$65-80; ℗) If you've wondered what it's like
to stay in a ghost town (or in what's ru-
mored to be a haunted hotel!), this is your
chance to find out. The Rosedeer is much
like it was in yesteryear: small rooms, simple furnishings and a rip-roaring Wild West
saloon downstairs. Don't come expecting
frills and fanciness, and reserve ahead (it
fills fast).

River Grove
Campground & Cabins
CAMPGROUND **$**

(☑403-823-6655; www.camprivergrove.com; 25
Poplar St; campsites/RV sites/cabins from
$38/47/104; ☺May-Sep; ℗☝) Right in town
and close to the big *T rex,* this shaded campground next to the river has lots of amenities, such as laundry machines and a big
playground for kids. There's even an arcade
for the surly teens among you.

Taste the Past B&B   B&B **$$**
(☑ 403-823-5889; www.bbcanada.com/taste; 281 2nd St W; s/d $130/150; P ❄ 🛜) This converted turn-of-the-century house has evolved into a cozy downtown B&B. All rooms have a private bathroom, and there is a communal living room that could have been airlifted straight from your Grandma's house. With only three rooms, a stay here feels more like visiting with friends.

⭐ **Café Olé**   CAFE **$**
(☑ 403-800-2090; www.facebook.com/cafeoledrum; 11 Railway Ave; sandwiches $8-13; ⏰ 8am-5pm Sun-Thu, to 7pm Fri & Sat; 🍽) This quiet, darkly lit cafe serves up soups, sandwiches, coffees, teas and desserts that would hold their own in New York City. Flavorful and fresh, mains pair perfectly with a London Fog chai or a fruit smoothie. The waitstaff are kind, helpful and attentive, though when busy things can be slow – but worth the wait, for sure.

⭐ **Last Chance Saloon**   BAR
(☑ 403-823-9189; www.visitlastchancesaloon.com; 555 Jewel St, Wayne; ⏰ 11am-11pm Mon-Sat, to 7pm Sun) Last Chance is the real thing – a Western saloon from 1913, complete with bear skins, old kerosene lamps, antique photos and bullet holes in the wall. Since its original heyday, Wayne's population has dwindled from 2500 to 27, many of whom you'll find in this lively, eclectic place. Meat pies, maple-bacon burgers and chicken dinners go well with the beer.

❶ Information

Tourist Information Center (☑ 403-823-1331; https://traveldrumheller.com; 60 1st Ave W; ⏰ 9am-9pm mid-May–Sep, 10am-5:30pm Oct–mid-May) Located by the feet of the giant *T rex*, with lots of maps and brochures on offer.

❶ Getting There & Away

Hammerhead Tours (☑ 403-590-6930; www.hammerheadtours.com) runs a full-day tour ($141) from Calgary to the Drumheller badlands and the Royal Tyrrell Museum.

There is currently no public transportation to Drumheller.

Dinosaur Provincial Park

In no other place on earth has such a large number of dinosaur bones been found in such a small area – over 40 species and 400 skeletons. Set where *The Lost World* meets *Little House on the Prairie*, **Dinosaur Provincial Park** (☑ 403-378-4342; www.dinosaurpark.ca; off Hwy 544; ⏰ 9am-5pm Sun-Thu, to 7pm Fri & Sat) **FREE** – a Unesco World Heritage site – comes at you without warning, deep in a chasm that opens before your feet from the grassy plain. A dehydrated fantasy landscape, there are hoodoos, colorful rock formations and dinosaurs aplenty.

The 81-sq-km park begs to be explored, with wildflowers, the odd rattler in the rocks and, if you're lucky, maybe even a *T rex*. This isn't just a tourist attraction but a hotbed for science: paleontologists have uncovered countless skeletons here, which now reside in many of the finest museums around the globe.

There are five short interpretive hiking trails to choose from and a driving loop runs through part of the park, giving you the chance to see a number of dinosaur skeletons in their death positions. To preserve the fossils, access to 70% of the park is restricted and may be seen only on guided hikes or **bus tours** (adult/child $20/10), which operate from late May to October. (The hikes and tours are popular, so be sure to reserve a place.)

The park's **Dinosaur Visitors Centre** (☑ 403-378-4342; http://albertaparks.ca; gallery admission adult/child $6/3; ⏰ 9am-5pm Sun-Thu, to 7pm Fri & Sat mid-May–Aug, shorter hours rest of year) is a field station of the Royal Tyrrell Museum (p98) in Drumheller and has a small, yet excellent, series of dino displays, as well as exhibits on the realities of paleontology.

In a hollow by a small creek sits the park's **Dinosaur Campground** (☑ 403-378-4342; https://albertaparks.ca; campsites/RV sites $26/33, comfort camping $105-130, reservation fee $12; ⏰ year-round; P). The ample tree cover is a welcome reprieve from the volcanic sun. Laundry facilities and hot showers are available, as are a small shop and cafe. This is a popular place, especially with the RV set, so phone ahead.

Though 75 million years ago dinosaurs cruised around a tropical landscape, it's now a hot and barren place – make sure you dress for the weather, with sunscreen and water at the ready. It's halfway between Calgary and Medicine Hat, and some 48km northeast of Brooks. From Hwy 1, take Secondary Hwy 873 to Hwy 544.

Head-Smashed-In Buffalo Jump

The story behind the place with the strangest name of any attraction in Alberta is one of ingenuity and resourcefulness – and is key to the First Nations' (and Canada's) cultural heritage. For thousands of years, the Blackfoot used the cliffs near the town of Fort Macleod to hunt bison. Head-Smashed-In Buffalo Jump (☑ 403-553-2731; https://headsmashedin.ca; Secondary Hwy 785; adult/child $15/10; ⊙10am-5pm) was a marvel of simple ingenuity. When the bison massed in the open prairie, braves from the tribe would gather and herd them toward the towering cliffs. As the animals got closer, they would be funneled to the edge and made to stampede over it to their doom, thus providing meat aplenty for the tribe. For the Blackfoot, the bison was sacred; to honor the fallen prey, every part of the animal was used.

The well-presented displays and films at the interpretive center built cleverly into the hillside are befitting of a Unesco World Heritage site, and it's definitely worth the excursion from Calgary or Lethbridge. You can walk along the cliff trail to the end of the drive land, the spot where the bison plummeted. The site, about 18km northwest of Fort Macleod and 16km west of Hwy 2, also has a cafe and a shop.

Lethbridge

☑ 403 / POP 92,700

In the heart of southern Alberta farming country sits the former coal-mining city of Lethbridge, divided by the distinctive coulees of the Oldman River. Though there isn't much to bring you to the city, copious parkland, decent dining, and a few good historical sites and museums will help you to easily fill a day. There are ample hiking opportunities in the Oldman River Valley, a 100m-deep coulee bisected by the proverbial Eiffel Tower of steel railway bridges, the largest of its kind in the world. The cottonwoods and pines below the bridge are a prime spot to see porcupines, the infamous North American rodent second only to the beaver in size.

The downtown area, like many North American downtowns, has made a good stab at preserving its not-so-ancient history. To the east, less inspiring Mayor Magrath Dr (Hwy 5) is a chain-store-infested main drag that could be Anywhere, North America.

◉ Sights & Activities

Alberta Birds of Prey Foundation ANIMAL SANCTUARY

(☑ 403-331-9520; www.burrowingowl.com; 2124 16th Ave, Coaldale; adult/child $12/8; ⊙9:30am-5pm mid-May–early Sep) This is a working rescue sanctuary that takes in raptors, owls and other birds of prey and – ideally – releases them promptly back into the wild. However, some animals that are non-releasable are used for trained demos, and the center allows kids and adults to get very close to birds they'd only see glimpses of otherwise. Owl on your shoulder, anyone?

Galt Museum & Archives MUSEUM

(☑ 403-320-3954; www.galtmuseum.com; 502 1st St; adult/child $6/3; ⊙10am-5pm Mon-Sat, to 9pm Thu, 1-5pm Sun) The story of Lethbridge is told at the Sir Alexander Galt Museum, encased in an old hospital building (1910) on the bluff high above the river. Interactive kid-oriented displays let you sit in a streetcar and watch historical footage. The view from the lobby out onto the coulee is great – and free.

Southern Alberta Art Gallery MUSEUM

(☑ 403-327-8770; www.saag.ca; 601 3rd Ave S; adult/child $5/free, Sun free; ⊙10am-5pm Tue-Sat, to 7pm Thu, 1-5pm Sun) With new temporary exhibits every three months, this small gallery focuses on contemporary art. Past exhibitions have included local artists as well as national and international ones, with everything from photography to installation art. The space itself is open and bright and the gift shop is ace.

Helen Schuler Nature Centre & Lethbridge Nature Reserve NATURE RESERVE

(☑ 403-320-3064; www.lethbridge.ca/nature; Indian Battle Rd; by donation; ⊙10am-4pm Tue-Sun Apr, May, Sep & Oct, 10am-6pm Jun-Aug, 1-4pm Tue-Sun Nov-Mar) Permanent displays tell the story of the river valley and coulee, while temporary exhibits focus on bats, bees and the like. Check out Taco Charlie, the tiger salamander, or wander upstairs and see the living roof – in summer, it's filled with blooms. The surrounding trails give you the opportunity to see long-eared and great horned owls and plenty of porcupines sleeping in the trees.

🛏️ Sleeping & Eating

Sandman Signature Lethbridge Lodge   HOTEL **$$**

(☑ 403-328-1123; www.sandmanhotels.com; 320 Scenic Dr S; r from $139; 🅿️ 😊 @ 🛜 🏊) Rooms here are clean and bright, if a little unmemorable; the atrium, on the other hand, is something else, making this a great deal. All of the rooms look down into the fake-foliage-filled tropical interior, complete with winding brick pathways, a kidney-shaped pool and water features.

Bread Milk & Honey   CAFE **$**

(☑ 403-381-8605; www.breadmilkhoney.ca; 427 5th St S; items $8-15; ⊙ 7am-5pm Mon-Fri, 9am-5pm Sat & Sun; 🛜) With excellent coffee and everything from oatmeal loaded with banana, cinnamon and almond to a bacon burrito, this is *the* place to come for breakfast. The interior is all exposed brick and wood; come and hang, get an avocado toast or a freshly baked scone, and enjoy the relaxed pace of a Lethbridge morn.

★ Telegraph Tap House   PUB FOOD **$$**

(☑ 403-942-4136; https://taphouse.pub; 310 6th Street S; mains $15-23; ⊙ 11am-11pm Mon-Thu, to 1am Fri, 9am-1am Sat, 9am-10:30pm Sun) So this is where cool Lethbridgians go. Park yourself at the bar with a craft brew and pulled-pork sliders or chili-cheese fries. Is the stack of antique suitcases left over from others who dared try the Baked Ultimate Poutine and didn't make it out the door?

★ Plum   COCKTAIL BAR

(☑ 403-394-1200; http://uncorkplum.com; 330 6th St; cocktails $9-12; ⊙ 11:30am-10pm, to midnight Fri & Sat) Lethbridge is not an elegant city, but Plum may make you rethink: it's got plush velour curtains, a marble bar with dim lighting and polished copper accents, dark wood and probably the tastiest cocktails you'll find for miles. The 'Baby Ben' is a big favorite, but all of the cocktails are delicious. And the bartenders are cheerful and fun.

It's also a tasty spot for dining. Don't be shy about coming for dinner or lunch.

ℹ️ Information

Chinook Country Tourist Association

(☑ 403-394-2403; https://tourismlethbridge. com; 2805 Scenic Dr S; ⊙ 9am-5pm Mon-Sat Oct-Apr, daily May-Sep) On the approach to Lethbridge from Hwy 5.

ℹ️ Getting There & Away

The **Lethbridge Airport** (☑ 403-329-4466; www.lethbridgeairport.ca; 417 Stubb Ross Rd), a short drive south on Hwy 5, is served by commuter affiliates of Air Canada. Six or seven flights per day go to Calgary.

Red Arrow (☑ 800-232-1958; www.redarrow. ca; 449 Mayor Magrath Dr S) buses connect once daily with Calgary ($53, three hours) and Fort Macleod ($36.50, 45 minutes).

Writing-on-Stone Provincial Park

Perhaps the best thing about this **park** (☑ 403-647-2364; www.albertaparks.ca; FREE) is that it really isn't on the way to anywhere. For those willing to get off the main thoroughfare, all efforts will be rewarded. It's named for the extensive carvings and paintings made by the Blackfoot on the sandstone cliffs along the banks of Milk River – more than 3000 years ago. There is an excellent, self-guided interpretive trail that takes you to some of the spectacular viewpoints and accessible pictographs and petroglyphs.

(You *must* stay on the trails to prevent damage to the hoodoos. Many visitors feel the need to add their own marks to the hoodoos – don't be one of them. Not only are you vandalizing a piece of history, you're also desecrating a sacred First Nations site.)

The best art is found in a restricted area (to protect it from vandalism), which you can visit only on a **guided tour** (10am, 2pm and 6pm daily in summer; adult/youth/child $19/11/7) with the park ranger. Other activities include canoeing and swimming in the river in summer and cross-country skiing in winter. Park wildlife is ample, and the visitor center, built in the shape of a traditional tipi, blends perfectly with the region's natural and cultural heritage. Beware: it can get exceedingly hot in the summer and you must have close-toed shoes. (This is rattlesnake country!)

The park's riverside **campground** has 67 sites, running water, showers and flush toilets. It's popular on weekends.

The park is southeast of Lethbridge and close to the US border; the Sweetgrass Hills of northern Montana are visible to the south. To get to the park, take Hwy 501 east for 42km from the town of Milk River, on Hwy 4.

Waterton Lakes National Park

Here flat prairies collide dramatically with the Rockies, with a sparkling lake and a hilltop castle that may make you wonder if you've fallen into a fairy tale. However, Waterton Lakes National Park (www.pc.gc.ca/waterton; per day family/adult/child $15.70/7.80/free) is little known to outside visitors, remaining a pocket of sublime tranquility. Visitor numbers took a hit after the 2017 Kenow Wildfire that burned over 19,000 hectares of the park, destroying infrastructure and damaging 80% of the trail network.

Established in 1895 and now part of a Unesco World Heritage site, Unesco Biosphere Reserve and International Peace Park (with the USA's Glacier National Park), this 525-sq-km reserve lies in Alberta's southwestern corner. The park is a sanctuary for numerous iconic animals – grizzlies, elk, deer and cougar – along with 800-odd wildflower species.

The town of Waterton, a low-key alpine village with a winter population of about 40, provides a marked contrast to larger, flashier Banff. Its 1920s-era Prince of Wales Hotel stands regally above town on the lakefront.

◉ Sights & Activities

Cameron Lake
LAKE

Backed by the sheer-sided slopes of Mt Custer, placid Cameron Lake is tucked tantalizingly beneath the Continental Divide at the three-way meeting point of Montana, Alberta and British Columbia. Poised at the end of the 16km Akamina Pkwy (currently closed due to fire damage), this is where day-trippers stop to picnic, hike and rent boats. From foam flowers to fireweed, copious wildflower species thrive here, while grizzly bears are known to frequent the lake's isolated southern shores.

Upper Waterton Lake
LAKE

Visible from all over town, this is the deepest lake in the Canadian Rockies, sinking to a murky 120m. One of the best vantage points is from the Prince of Wales Hotel, where a classic view is framed by an ethereal collection of Gothic mountains, including Mt Cleveland, Glacier National Park's highest peak. A more placid spot is Emerald Bay, famous for its turquoise waters and ever-popular with scuba divers.

Cameron Falls
WATERFALL

At the west end of Cameron Falls Dr (a short hop from the center of town) is this dramatically poised torrent of foaming water, notable among geologists for harboring the oldest exposed Precambrian rocks in the Canadian Rockies. Estimates suggest they are 1.5 billion years old, give or take the odd millennium. The lookout here is paved for wheelchair access and the falls are lit up at night.

Crypt Lake Trail
HIKING

Done in a day thanks to a water taxi with service to the trailhead, this thrilling obstacle-laden hike includes a climb up a ladder, a crawl through a narrow rocky tunnel and a sheer rock face with a cable for assistance, ending in gorgeous Crypt Lake. The ascent begins quickly and soon after you'll take in up-close views of waterfalls, mountains and lakes below. Allow enough time for your return trip down, as the boat is the only easy way back!

Waterton Shoreline Cruises
CRUISE

(☑ 403-859-2362; www.watertoncruise.com; adult/youth/child $53/26/18; ☺ May-Oct) Sail across the shimmering waters of Upper Waterton Lake to the far shore of Goat Haunt, Montana (USA). This family-owned business offers a scenic, 2¼-hour trip on the vintage MV *International* (1927), with lively commentary. Bring your passport: it docks in the USA for about 30 minutes (passengers weren't allowed to disembark during the 2019 summer season because of water and staffing shortages). July and August have four cruises daily (10am, 1pm, 4pm and 7pm).

Blakiston & Co Adventure Rentals
BOATING

(☑ 800-456-0772; www.blakistonandcompany.com; Crandell Mountain Lodge, 102 Mt View Rd; stand-up paddleboard rental per 1/4hr $30/85; ☺ Jun-Aug) Offers stand-up paddleboard (SUP), canoe and kayak (including ones with glass bottoms) rentals for Emerald Bay, the mostly calm patch of water across the street from the Crandell Mountain Lodge (from where this shop operates). E-bikes are also now available (one/two hours $35/50).

🛏 Sleeping & Eating

★ Northland Lodge
B&B $$

(☑ 403-859-2353; www.northlandlodgecanada.com; 408 Evergreen Ave; r $196-249; ☺ mid-May–mid-Oct; 🐾) On the edge of town within

WORTH A TRIP

BLACKFOOT CROSSING HISTORICAL PARK

Standing stoically in the center of a First Nations reserve, Blackfoot Historical Park (☎403-734-5171; www.blackfootcrossing.ca; Hwy 842; adult/child $15/10; ☉9am-6pm Jul & Aug, to 5pm Mon-Fri Mar-Jun, Sep & Oct, 10am-3pm Mon-Fri Nov-Feb) celebrates and embraces authentic Siksika (Blackfoot) culture and is entirely worth exploring.

The history of southern Alberta pre-1880 belongs to the Blackfoot confederacy, an amalgamation of the Peigan, Blood and Montana-based Blackfeet tribes. Blackfoot Crossing, long an important tribal nexus, was unique in that it was the only place where nomadic First Nations tribes built a semi-permanent settlement. It was here that the notorious Treaty 7 was signed by Chief Crowfoot in 1877, ceding land to the British crown and establishing the Siksika reservation. After a visit from Prince Charles in 1977, the idea for a historical site was hatched; after 30 years of planning, the park finally opened in 2007.

It's anchored by an architecturally stunning, ecofriendly main building that incorporates elements of tipis and feathered headdresses into its creative design. Within its walls lie a 100-seat theater showcasing cultural dances, a set of exhibits chronicling Blackfoot history and guided tours with local Siksika interpreters and storytellers. Outside, you can enjoy various trails, prairie viewpoints, and a tipi village where traditional crafts are practiced and taught.

To get here, head 100km east of Calgary on Hwy 1 and then 7km south on Hwy 842. The historical park hasn't yet made it onto the mainstream tourist track and remains curiously light on visitors.

earshot of gushing Cameron Falls is this cozy house that Louis Hill (the genius behind the Prince of Wales Hotel) built for himself. A B&B with a wide range of quaint rooms (some with shared bath) and a creaking staircase, it's steeped in character. The welcoming host's freshly baked breakfast is fabulous.

Crandell Mountain Lodge   HOTEL $$
(☎403-859-2288;   www.crandellmountainlodge.com; 102 Mt View Rd; r from $200; P🐾) With homemade cookies in the lobby, this 1940s lodge is doing a good impersonation of a Tudor cottage plucked from a quiet English village. The Crandell has old-fashioned rooms with quilts like Grandma used to make, fireplaces and a front deck facing Emerald Bay across the street. Service is very welcoming.

★Prince of
Wales Hotel   HISTORIC HOTEL $$$
(☎403-859-2231; www.princeofwaleswaterton.com; Prince of Wales Rd; r from $249; ☉May-Sep; P🐾) With a Hogwarts-like setting on a wind-buffeted bluff overlooking Upper Waterton Lake, the grand Prince of Wales blends Swiss-style architecture with the atmosphere of a Scottish castle. The old-world charms extend to serving staff in kilts and high tea in the main lounge – very civilized.

The large lake-facing windows frame the wilderness that awaits.

★Welch's Chocolates,
Ice Cream & Desserts   DESSERTS $
(cnr Windflower Ave & Cameron Falls Dr; desserts $3-12; ☉9am-10pm May-Oct) In a ranch-style house at the end of Windflower Ave, this family-run Waterton institution is filled with a Willy Wonka's worth of homemade chocolates, fudge and candy. It's also been dishing out ice cream, pies and pastries for 50 plus years, all scoffed down on the wraparound deck.

★49° North Pizza   PIZZA $$
(☎403-859-3000;   www.49degreesnorthpizza.com; 303 Windflower Ave; pizzas $12-30; ☉noon-9pm Mon-Fri, from 5pm Sat & Sun May-Sep) Seriously satisfying pizza with all of the expected renditions, plus some creative gourmet options such as bison and Saskatoon berries, as well as a choice of salads and a make-your-own 'power bowl' (brown rice with a bunch of vegetarian add-ons). Service is top-notch and there's a good beer selection; if the handful of tables and patio are full, you can get takeout.

ℹ Information

Parks Canada Visitor Centre (☎403-859-2378; www.pc.gc.ca/waterton; Fountain Ave;

⊙8am-6pm May-Sep) The central stop for information on everything from trail conditions to hotels (and the place to pay your park fee if the entrance isn't staffed or you arrive after hours). It's in a temporary stucture until a new large, contemporary-designed building opens in the spring of 2021.

My Waterton (www.mywaterton.ca) Waterton Lakes' Chamber of Commerce website with up-to-date visitor information, including a listing of monthly events.

❶ Getting There & Away

The park is open 24 hours a day, 365 days a year, although many amenities and a couple of park roads close in winter. Entry costs are family/adult/child $15.70/7.80/free per day ($11.75/5.80/free during the shoulder seasons). An annual Waterton pass costs $39.20 (adult). Park admission is free on Canada Day (July 1) and Parks Day (third Saturday in July). Passes, to be displayed on your vehicle's windshield, are valid until 4pm on the date of expiration.

If you enter the park when the booth is shut, get a pass early the next morning at the Parks Canada Visitor Centre. Upon entering, you'll receive a map of Waterton Lakes and Glacier National Parks, and the quarterly information-packed newspaper Waterton-Glacier Guide.

Waterton lies in Alberta's southwestern corner, 130km from Lethbridge and 156km from Calgary. The one road entrance into the park is in its northeastern corner, along Hwy 5. Most visitors coming from Glacier and the USA reach the junction with Hwy 5 via Hwy 6 (Chief Mountain International Hwy) from the southeast, after crossing at the **Chief Mountain border crossing** (Chief Mountain Hwy; ⊙7am-10pm Jun-Labour Day, 9am-6pm mid-May–late May & Labour Day-Sep 30). A passport, enhanced driver's license or NEXUS card is required for US and Canadian citizens; all others must present passports and fill out an I-94 or I-94W form (available for $6 at the border).

From Calgary, to the north, Hwy 2 shoots south toward Hwy 5 into the park. From the east, Hwy 5, through Cardston, heads west and then south into the park.

There is no public transportation from Canadian cities outside the park. **Pincher Creek Taxi** (☑403-632-9738) does provide service from the town of Pincher Creek to Waterton town for $75. The shuttle service that previously connected the Prince of Wales Hotel and Glacier Park Lodge in Montana is no longer offered.

Crowsnest Pass

West of Fort Macleod the Crowsnest Hwy (Hwy 3) heads through the prairies and into the Rocky Mountains to Crowsnest Pass (1396m) and the BC border. The Pass, as it's known, is a string of small communities just to the east of the BC border. Of note is the story of the town of Frank. In 1903 Frank was almost completely buried when 30 million cu meters (some 82 million tonnes' worth) of nearby Turtle Mountain collapsed and killed around 70 people. Some believe the coal mine dug into the base of the mountain was to blame. But the mining didn't stop; this black gold was the ticket to fortune for the entire region some hundred years ago. Eventually the demand for coal decreased, and after yet more cave-ins and fear of a second slide, the mines shut down for good.

★**Frank Slide**
Interpretive Centre   MUSEUM
(☑403-562-7388; www.frankslide.org; Hwy 3; adult/child $13/9; ⊙9am-6pm Jul & Aug, 10am-5pm Sep-Jun; ♿) This excellent museum overlooks the Crowsnest Valley and helps put a human face on the tragedy of the Frank landslide. Displays bring mining, the railroad and the early days of this area to life; kids will enjoy having things to pull, push and jump on, as well as puzzles and other interactive activities. There's also a fantastic film dramatizing the tragic events of 1903. Trails from the museum take you out over the slide site itself.

Most of the staff can trace their roots to the area and thus have a personal connection to the slide. You'll find it 1.5km off Hwy 3 and 27km east of the BC border.

NORTHERN ALBERTA

Despite the presence of its increasingly infamous oil sands, the top half of Alberta is little visited and even less known. Once you travel north of Edmonton, the population drops off to Siberian levels. The sense of remoteness here is almost eerie.

If it's solitude you seek, then this is paradise found. Endless stretches of pine forests seem to go on forever, nighttime brings aurora borealis displays that are better than any chemical hallucinogens, and it's here you can still see herds of wild bison roaming.

The Cree, Slavey and Dene were the first peoples to inhabit the region, and many of them still depend on fishing, hunting and trapping for survival. The northeast has virtually no roads and is dominated by Wood

Buffalo National Park, the Athabasca River and Lake Athabasca. The northwest is more accessible, with a network of highways connecting Alberta with northern BC and the NWT.

Peace River & Around

Heading northwest along Hwy 43 leads to the town of Dawson Creek, BC, and mile zero of the Alaska Hwy. Dawson is a whopping 590km from Edmonton, so it's a long way to go to check out this isolated section of northern Alberta. Along the way you'll pass through Grande Prairie, the base of operations for the local agricultural industry and home to chuckwagon-racing legend Kelly Sutherland.

Peace River is so named because the warring Cree and Beaver indigenous groups made peace along its banks. The town of Peace River sits at the confluence of the Heart, Peace and Smoky Rivers. West out of town, Hwy 2 leads to the Mackenzie Hwy.

Mackenzie Highway

The small town of Grimshaw is the official starting point of the Mackenzie Hwy (Hwy 35) north to the NWT. There's not much here except for the mile-zero sign and a few shops. The relatively flat and straight road is mostly paved, though there are stretches of loose gravel where the road is being reconstructed.

The mainly agricultural landscape between Grimshaw and Manning gives way to endless stretches of spruce and pine forest. Come prepared – this is frontier territory: services become fewer (and more expensive) as you head northward through the wilderness. Make sure you fill your tank any time you see a gas station from here on.

High Level, the last settlement of any size before the NWT border, is a timber-industry center. Workers often stay in its motels during the week. The only gas station between High Level and Enterprise (in the NWT) is at Indian Cabins.

Lake District

From St Paul, more than 200km northeast of Edmonton, to the NWT border lies Alberta's immense lake district. Fishing is popular (even in winter, when there is ice fishing), but many of the lakes, especially further north, have no road access and you have to fly in.

St Paul is the place to go if you are looking for little green people. Its flying-saucer landing pad – which is still awaiting its first customer – is open for business. It's billed as the world's largest, and only, UFO landing pad and UFO enthusiasts have been visiting ever since.

Highway 63 is the main route into the province's northeastern wilderness interior. The highway, with a few small settlements and campgrounds on the way, leads to Fort McMurray. The town itself isn't particularly interesting; non-oil workers who do visit come to see the aurora borealis.

Oil Sands Discovery Centre   MUSEUM
(☑780-743-7167;   http://history.alberta.ca/oil sands; 515 MacKenzie Blvd, Fort McMurray; adult/child/family $11/7/29; ☺9am-5pm mid-May–early Sep, 10am-4pm Tue-Sun early Sep–mid-May) The Athabasca Oil Sands are the world's largest single oil deposit – and Alberta's economic bread and butter. Interactive displays at this museum get you up close with their history and the technology behind how crude oil is extracted from them.

This area was devastated by a forest fire in 2016. On the way you'll still see acres and acres of charred woodland. Amazingly, nobody was burned, though people were displaced for months and some areas have yet to be rebuilt.

UFO Data Centre
& Tourist Information   GIFTS & SOUVENIRS
(☑780-645-6800, UFO hotline 888-733-8367; www.town.stpaul.ab.ca/UFO-Landing-Pad; 50th Ave, St Paul; ☺10am-6pm May-Sep) Next to the flying saucer landing pad, this information center has a space-themed gift shop and a book you can flip through to learn more about 137 recorded local sightings, along with images and accounts of local cattle mutilations, abductions and crop circles. There's also a UFO hotline for people to report new sightings.

British Columbia

Why Go?

Visitors to Canada's westernmost province should pack a long list of superlatives with them; the words 'wow,' 'amazing' and 'spectacular' will only go so far. Luckily, it's easy to wax lyrical about the mighty mountains, deep forests and dramatic coastlines that instantly lower heart rates to tranquil levels.

There's much more to British Columbia (BC) than nature-hugging dioramas, though. Cosmopolitan Vancouver fuses cuisines and cultures from Asia and beyond, while midsized cities such as Victoria and Kelowna have their own vibrant scenes. And it's hard to beat the welcoming, sometimes quirky character of smaller communities – from Cumberland to Powell River and Salt Spring – that are BC's beating heart.

Wherever you head, the great outdoors will always call: BC is unbeatable for life-enhancing skiing, kayaking and hiking experiences that can make this the trip of a lifetime.

Best Places to Eat

➡ Purebread (p145)

➡ Brasserie L'École (p162)

➡ Vij's (p129)

➡ St Lawrence Restaurant (p128)

Best Places to Stay

➡ Free Spirit Spheres (p174)

➡ Wickaninnish Inn (p180)

➡ Victorian Hotel (p122)

➡ Skwachàys Lodge (p122)

When to Go
Vancouver, BC

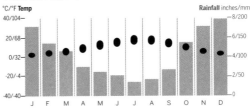

Dec–Mar Best powder action on the slopes of Whistler and Blackcomb mountains.

Jul & Aug Beaches, patios and a plethora of outdoor festivals in sun-dappled Vancouver.

Sep & Oct Dramatic surfing and early season storm-watching in beach-hugging Tofino.

British Columbia Highlights

1 **Stanley Park** (p111) Stretching your legs on the curvaceous 8.8km seawall stroll.

2 **Tofino** (p178) Surfing up a storm (or just watching a storm) on Vancouver Island's wild west coast.

3 **Okanagan Valley** (p200) Slurping some celebrated tipples on an ever-winding winery tour.

4 **Whistler** (p141) Skiing the Olympian slopes, then enjoying a warming après-ski beverage in the village.

5 **Gwaii Haanas National Park Reserve** (p235) Exploring the ancient and ethereal rainforest and kayaking the coastline for a bird's-eye view of the region.

6 **Salt Spring Island** (p192) Puttering around the lively Saturday Market and scoffing more than a few treats.

7 **Alert Bay** (p188) Walking the waterfront boardwalk and exploring evocative First Nations art and totem poles.

8 **Sea to Sky Gondola** (p139) Hopping on the gondola near Squamish for panoramic up-top views of Howe Sound and its mountainous cousins.

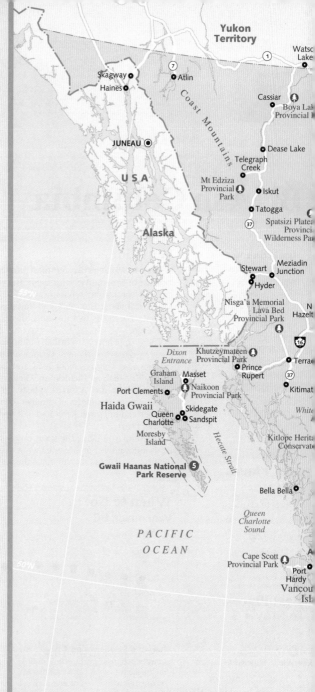

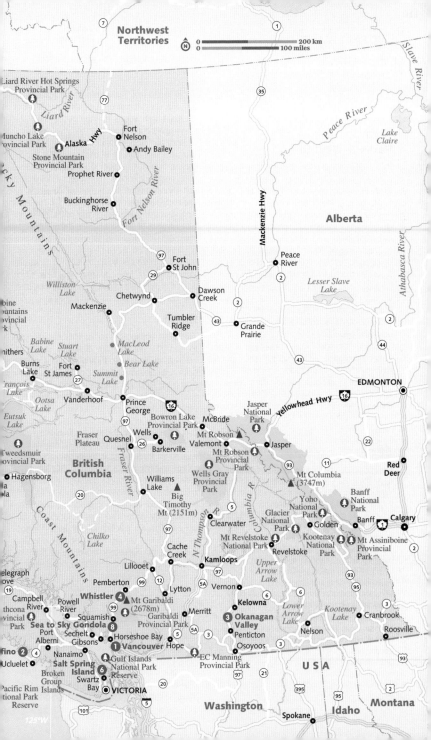

BC FAST FACTS

....

➡ Population: 4.7 million

➡ Area: 944,735 sq km

➡ Capital: Victoria

➡ Fact: BC is North America's third-largest film and TV production center.

Parks & Wildlife

BC's national parks include snowcapped Glacier and the Unesco World Heritage sites of Kootenay and Yoho. The newer Gulf Islands National Park Reserve protects a fragile coastal region. Visit the website of Parks Canada (www.pc.gc.ca) for information.

The region's 600+ provincial parks offer thousands of kilometers of hiking trails. Notables include Strathcona and remote Cape Scott, as well as the Cariboo's canoe-friendly Bowron Lake and the Kootenays' Matterhorn-like Mt Assiniboine. Check the website of BC Parks (www.bcparks.ca) for information.

Expect to spot some amazing wildlife. Land mammals – including elk, moose, wolves, grizzlies and black bears – will have most visitors scrambling for their cameras, and there are around 500 bird varieties, including blue herons and bald eagles galore. Ocean visitors should keep an eye out for orcas.

ⓘ Getting Around

The sheer size of BC can overwhelm some visitors: it's a scary-sounding 1508km drive from Vancouver to Prince Rupert, for example. While it's tempting to simply stick around Vancouver – the main point of entry for most BC-bound visitors – you won't really have experienced the province unless you head out of town.

Despite the distances, driving remains the most popular method of movement in BC. Plan your routes via the handy DriveBC website (www.drivebc.ca) and check out the dozens of services offered by the extensive BC Ferries (www.bcferries.com) system.

VIA Rail (www.viarail.com) operates two BC train services. One trundles across the north from Prince Rupert to Jasper (in Alberta). A second runs between Vancouver and Jasper (and on to Toronto).

VANCOUVER

📞 604, 778 / POP 631,500

Explorable neighborhoods, drink-and-dine delights and memorable cultural and outdoor activities framed by striking natural vistas – there's a superfluity of reasons to fall for this ocean-fringed metropolis. But there's much more to Vancouver than the downtown core.

Walk or hop public transit and within minutes you'll soon be hanging with the locals in one of the city's diverse and distinctive neighborhoods. Whether discovering the independent boutiques of Main St or the coffee shops of Commercial Dr, the red-brick bars of Gastown or the heritage-house beachfronts of Kitsilano, you'll find this city ideal for easy-access urban exploration. Just be sure to chat to the locals wherever you go: they might seem shy or aloof at first, but Vancouverites love talking up their town and offering their insider tips on stores, bars and restaurants you have to check out.

History

The First Nations lived in this area for up to 16,000 years before Spanish explorers arrived in the late 1500s. When Captain George Vancouver of the British Royal Navy sailed up to these shores in 1792, he met a couple of Spanish captains who informed him of their country's land claim (the beach they met on is now called Spanish Banks). But by the early 1800s, as European settlers began arriving, the British crown had gained an increasing stranglehold.

Fur trading and a feverish gold rush soon redefined the region as a resource-filled cornucopia. By the 1850s, thousands of fortune seekers had arrived, prompting the Brits to officially claim the area as a colony. Local entrepreneur John 'Gassy Jack' Deighton seized the initiative in 1867 by opening a bar on the forested shoreline of Burrard Inlet. This triggered a rash of development – nicknamed Gastown – that became the forerunner of modern-day Vancouver.

But not everything went to plan. While Vancouver rapidly reached a population of 1000, its buildings were almost completely destroyed in an 1886 blaze (quickly dubbed the Great Fire, even though it only lasted 20 minutes). A prompt rebuild followed and the new downtown core soon took shape. Buildings from this era still survive, as does Stanley Park. Originally the town's military reserve, it was opened as a public recreation area in 1888.

Relying on its port, the growing city became a hub of industry, importing thousands of immigrant workers to fuel economic development. The Chinatown built at this time is still one of the largest in North America. But WWI and the 1929 Wall Street crash brought deep depression and unemployment. The economy recovered during WWII, when shipbuilding and armaments manufacturing added to the traditional economic base of resource exploitation.

Growing steadily throughout the 1950s and 1960s, Vancouver added an NHL (National Hockey League) team and other accoutrements of a midsize North American city. Finally reflecting on its heritage, Gastown – by now a slum – was saved for gentrification in the 1970s, becoming a National Historic Site in 2010.

In 1986 the city hosted a highly successful World's Fair, sparking a wave of new development and adding the first of the mirrored skyscrapers that now define Vancouver's downtown core. A further economic lift arrived when the city staged the Olympic and Paralympic Winter Games in 2010, showcasing itself to a global audience of TV viewers. Recent years have seen a citywide tension between developer-driven house price surges and locals who say Vancouver's cost of living has risen too high. As the city grapples with its attempts to create sustainable growth, the next few years will be crucial.

◉ Sights

Few of Vancouver's main visitor attractions are downtown; the main museums are in Vanier Park and at the University of British Columbia (UBC). Other top sights and landmarks are in Stanley Park or Chinatown, while two major outdoor lures are on the North Shore. Luckily, most are easy to reach by car or transit hop from the city center.

◉ Downtown & West End

★**Stanley Park**   PARK
(Map p116; www.vancouver.ca/parks; West End; **P** ♿; ☐19) This magnificent 404-hectare park combines excellent attractions with a mystical natural aura. Don't miss a stroll or a cycle (rentals near the W Georgia St entrance) around the seawall: a kind of visual spa treatment fringed by a 150,000-tree temperate rainforest, it'll take you past the park's popular totem poles and alongside its shimmering oceanfront.

Lost Lagoon   LAKE
This rustic area near Stanley Park's entrance was originally part of Coal Harbour. But after a causeway was built in 1916, the new body of water was renamed, transforming itself into a freshwater lake a few years later. Today it's a **nature sanctuary** – keep your eyes peeled for beady-eyed herons – and its perimeter pathway is a favored stroll for nature-huggers.

The excellent **Stanley Park Nature House** (Map p116; ☎604-257-8544; www.stanleyparkecology.ca; north end of Alberni St, Lost Lagoon, Stanley Park; ⊙10am-5pm Tue-Sun Jul & Aug, 10am-4pm Sat & Sun Sep-Jun; ♿; ☐19) **FREE** provides exhibits and illumination on the park's wildlife, history and ecology. Ask about its fascinating park walks, covering everything from bird-watching strolls to artsy ambles around the park.

Stanley Park Seawall   WATERFRONT
(Stanley Park; ☐19) Built between 1917 and 1980, the 8.8km seawall trail is Vancouver's favorite outdoor hangout. Encircling the whole of Stanley Park, it offers spectacular waterfront, mountain-fringed vistas on one side and dense forest canopy on the other. You can walk the whole thing in around three blister-triggering hours or rent a bike from the Denman St operators near the park entrance to cover the route faster. But what's the rush? Slow down and slide into the natural side of life instead.

BEST SIGHTS
....

Stanley Park (p111) An oceanfront gem with seawall trails and visitor attractions.

Museum of Anthropology (p115) Vancouver's best cultural attraction, with exhibits from BC and beyond.

Science World (p115) Brilliant kid-friendly attraction under a landmark geodesic dome.

Capilano Suspension Bridge Park (p119) A leg-wobbling wooden walkway set in a forested park.

Vancouver Art Gallery (p113) Downtown art institution showcasing Canadian artists and blockbuster visiting exhibitions.

Vancouver

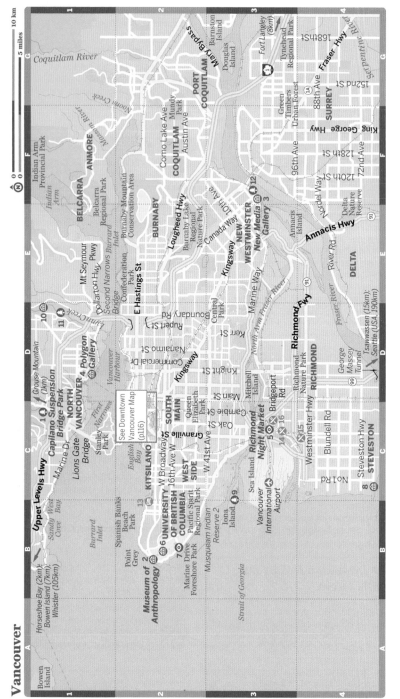

Vancouver

★ **Vancouver Art Gallery** GALLERY
(Map p116; ☑604-662-4700; www.vanartgallery.
bc.ca; 750 Hornby St, Downtown; adult/child
$24/6.50; ◷10am-5pm Wed-Mon, to 9pm Tue;
🚇5) Combining blockbuster international
shows with selections from its striking contemporary collection, the VAG is a magnet
for art fans. There are often three or four
different exhibitions on its public levels but
save time for the top-floor Emily Carr paintings, showcasing swirling nature-themed
works from BC's favorite historic artist.
Check ahead for FUSE ($29; ◷8pm-midnight),
a late-opening party with bars and live music. And if you're on a budget, consider the
by-donation entry after 5pm on Tuesdays
($10 suggested); expect a queue.

★ **Roedde House Museum** MUSEUM
(Map p116; ☑604-684-7040; www.roeddehouse.
org; 1415 Barclay St, West End; $5, Sun $8; ◷1-4pm
Tue-Fri & Sun; 🚇5) For a glimpse of what the
West End looked like before the apartment
blocks, visit this handsome 1893 Queen
Anne–style mansion, now a lovingly preserved museum. Designed by infamous ar-
chitect Francis Rattenbury, the yesteryear,
antique-studded rooms have a lived-in feel
while its guided tour (included with admission) tells you all about its middle-class
Roedde family residents. Look out for the
cylinder record player, 250-year-old grandfather clock and the taxidermied deer heads
that were hunted in Stanley Park in 1906.

Bill Reid Gallery of
Northwest Coast Art GALLERY
(Map p116; ☑604-682-3455; www.billreidgallery.
ca; 639 Hornby St, Downtown; adult/youth/child
$13/6/free; ◷10am-5pm May-Sep, 11am-5pm
Wed-Sun Oct-Apr; 🚇Burrard) Showcasing detailed carvings, paintings, jewelry and more
from Canada's most revered Haida artists
and others around the region, this open-
plan gallery occupies a handsome bi-level
hall. Bookended by a totem pole at one end
and a ceiling-mounted copper-lined canoe
at the other, explore the cabinets of intricate creations and the stories behind them,
including some breathtaking gold artifacts.
On the mezzanine level, you'll come face-
to-face with an 8.5m-long bronze of intertwined magical creatures, complete with
impressively long tongues.

Canada Place LANDMARK
(Map p116; ☑604-665-9000; www.canadaplace.
ca; 999 Canada Place Way, Downtown; 🅿♿;
🚇Waterfront; FREE) Vancouver's version of
the Sydney Opera House – judging by the
number of postcards it appears on – this
iconic landmark is shaped like sails jutting
into the sky over the harbor. Both a cruise-
ship terminal and a convention center, it's
also a stroll-worthy pier, providing photogenic views of the busy floatplane action
and looming North Shore mountains. Here
for Canada Day on July 1? This is the center
of the city's festivities, with displays, live music and fireworks.

Vancouver Aquarium AQUARIUM
(☑604-659-3400; www.vanaqua.org; 845 Avison
Way, Stanley Park; adult/child $38/21; ◷9:30am-
6pm Jul & Aug, 10am-5pm Sep-Jun; ♿; 🚌19)
Stanley Park's biggest draw is home to 9000
critters – including sharks, wolf eels and a
somewhat shy octopus. There's also a small,
walk-through rainforest area of birds, turtles
and a statue-still sloth. The aquarium keeps
captive whales and dolphins and organizes

animal encounters with these and its other creatures, which may concern some visitors.

◉ Gastown & Chinatown

★ **Vancouver Police Museum & Archives** MUSEUM
(Map p116; ☑604-665-3346; www.vancouver policemuseum.ca; 240 E Cordova St, Chinatown; adult/child $12/8; ⊙9am-5pm Tue-Sat; ☑3) Illuminating Vancouver's crime-and-vice-addled history, this quirky museum has had a recent makeover, uncovering the former coroner's courtroom (spot the elaborate cross-hatched ceiling) and sprucing up exhibits including a spine-chilling gallery of real-life cases (weapons included). The star attraction is the old autopsy room, complete with preserved slivers of human tissue; bullet-damaged brain slices are among them. Add a **Sins of the City** (www.sinsofthecity.ca; adult/student $18/14; ⊙Apr-Oct) area walking tour to learn all about Vancouver's salacious olden days; tours include museum entry.

★ **Dr Sun Yat-Sen Classical Chinese Garden & Park** GARDENS
(Map p116; ☑604-662-3207; www.vancouver chinesegarden.com; 578 Carrall St, Chinatown; adult/child $14/10; ⊙9:30am-7pm mid-Jun–Aug, 10am-6pm Sep & May–mid-Jun, 10am-4:30pm Oct-Apr; ⑤Stadium-Chinatown) A tranquil break from bustling Chinatown, this intimate 'garden of ease' reflects Taoist principles of balance and harmony. Entry includes an optional 45-minute guided tour, in which you'll learn about the symbolism behind the placement of the gnarled pine trees, winding covered pathways and ancient limestone formations. Look out for the colorful carp and lazy turtles in the jade-colored water.

Chinatown Millennium Gate LANDMARK
(Map p116; cnr W Pender & Taylor Sts, Chinatown; ⑤Stadium-Chinatown) Inaugurated in 2002, Chinatown's towering entrance is the landmark most visitors look for. Stand well back, since the decoration is mostly on its lofty upper reaches, an elaborately painted section topped with a terra-cotta-tiled roof. The characters inscribed on its eastern front implore you to 'Remember the past and look forward to the future.'

Steam Clock LANDMARK
(Map p116; cnr Water & Cambie Sts, Gastown; ⑤Waterfront) Halfway along Water St, this oddly popular tourist magnet lures the cameras with its tooting steam whistle. Built in

1977, the clock's mechanism is actually driven by electricity; only the pipes on top are steam fueled (reveal that to the patiently waiting tourists and you might cause a riot). It sounds every 15 minutes, and marks each hour with little whistling symphonies.

◉ Yaletown & Granville Island

★ **Granville Island Public Market** MARKET
(Map p116; ☑604-666-6655; www.granville island.com/public-market; Johnston St, Granville Island; ⊙9am-7pm; ☑50, ⛴miniferries) Granville Island's highlight is the covered Public Market, a multisensory smorgasbord of fish, cheese, fruit, teas and bakery treats (near-legendary Lee's Donuts included). Pick up some fixings for a picnic at nearby **Vanier Park** or hit the market's international food court (dine off-peak and you're more likely to snag a table). It's not all about food; there are often stands here hawking all manner of arts and crafts, from filigree jewelry to knitted baby hats.

Engine 374 Pavilion MUSEUM
(Map p116; www.roundhouse.ca; 181 Roundhouse Mews, Roundhouse Community Arts & Recreation Centre, Yaletown; ⊙10am-4pm, reduced hours off-season; ♿; ⑤Yaletown-Roundhouse) `FREE` May 23, 1887, was an auspicious date for Vancouver. That's when Engine 374 pulled the very first transcontinental passenger train into the fledgling city, symbolically linking the country and kick-starting the eventual metropolis. Retired in 1945, the engine was, after many years of neglect, restored and placed in this splendid pavilion. The friendly volunteers here will show you the best angle for snapping photos and share a few yesteryear railroading stories at the same time.

BC Sports Hall of Fame & Museum MUSEUM
(Map p116; ☑604-687-5520; www.bcsportshall offame.com; 777 Pacific Blvd, Gate A, BC Place Stadium, Yaletown; adult/child $15/12; ⊙10am-5pm; ♿; ⑤Stadium-Chinatown) Inside **BC Place Stadium** (☑604-669-2300; www.bcplace.com), this expertly curated attraction showcases top BC athletes, both amateur and professional, with an intriguing array of galleries crammed with fascinating memorabilia. There are medals, trophies and yesteryear sports uniforms on display (judging by the size of their shirts, hockey players were much smaller in the past), plus tonnes of hands-on activities to tire the kids out. Don't

miss the Indigenous Sport Gallery, covering everything from hockey to lacrosse to traditional indigenous games.

◉ Main Street

★ Science World
MUSEUM

(Map p116; ☑604-443-7440; www.science world.ca; 1455 Quebec St; adult/child $27.15/18.10; ◷10am-6pm Jul & Aug, reduced hours off-season; P🚗; ⓢMain St-Science World) Under Vancouver's favorite geodesic dome (OK, it's only one), this ever-popular science showcase has tonnes of hands-on galleries and a cool outdoor park crammed with rugged fun (yes, you *can* lift 2028kg). Inside, there are two floors of brilliant educational play, from plasma balls to whisper dishes. Check out the live critters in the Sara Stern Gallery, the bodily functions exhibits in the BodyWorks area, then fly over a city on the virtual-reality Birdly ride ($8 extra).

◉ Fairview & South Granville

★ VanDusen Botanical Garden
GARDENS

(☑604-257-8335; www.vandusengarden.org; 5251 Oak St; adult/child $11.25/5.50; ◷9am-8pm Jun-Aug, 9am-6pm Apr & Sep, 9am-7pm May, hours reduced Oct-Mar; P🚗; 🚌17) This highly popular green-thumbed oasis is a 22-hectare, 255,000-plant idyll that offers a strollable web of pathways weaving through specialized garden areas: the Rhododendron Walk blazes with color in spring, while the Korean Pavilion is a focal point for a fascinating Asian collection. Save time to get lost in the hedge maze and look out for the herons, owls and turtles that call the park and its ponds home. Informative guided tours are also offered here daily from April to October.

★ Bloedel Conservatory
GARDENS

(☑604-257-8584; www.vandusengarden.org; 4600 Cambie St, Queen Elizabeth Park; adult/child $6.75/3.30; ◷10am-5pm Jan-Mar, Nov & Dec, 10am-6pm Apr, Sep & Oct, 10am-8pm May-Aug; P🚗; 🚌15) Cresting the hill in Queen Elizabeth Park, this domed conservatory is a delightful rainy-day warm-up. At Vancouver's best-value paid attraction, you'll find tropical trees and plants bristling with hundreds of free-flying, bright-plumaged birds. Listen for the noisy resident parrots but also keep your eyes peeled for rainbow-hued Gouldian finches, shimmering African superb starlings and maybe even a dramatic Lady Amherst pheasant, snaking through the un-

dergrowth. Ask nicely and the attendants might even let you feed the smaller birds from a bowl.

◉ Kitsilano & University of British Columbia

★ Museum of Anthropology
MUSEUM

(MOA; Map p112; ☑604-822-5087; www.moa.ubc. ca; 6393 NW Marine Dr, UBC; adult/child $18/16; ◷10am-5pm Fri-Wed, 10am-9pm Thu, closed Mon Oct-May; P; 🚌99B-Line, then 68) Vancouver's best museum is studded with spectacular indigenous totem poles and breathtaking carvings – but it's also teeming with artifacts from cultures around the world, from intricate Swedish lace to bright Sri Lankan folk masks. Take one of the free daily tours (check ahead for times) for some context, but give yourself at least a couple of hours to explore on your own; it's easy to immerse yourself here. On a budget? Thursday evening entry is $10 (after 5pm).

Kitsilano Beach
BEACH

(cnr Cornwall Ave & Arbutus St, Kitsilano; 🚌2) Facing English Bay, Kits Beach is one of Vancouver's favorite summertime hangouts. The wide, sandy expanse attracts buff Frisbee tossers and giggling volleyball players, and those who just like to preen while catching the rays. The ocean is fine for a dip, though serious swimmers should consider the heated Kitsilano Pool (☑604-731-0011;

Downtown Vancouver

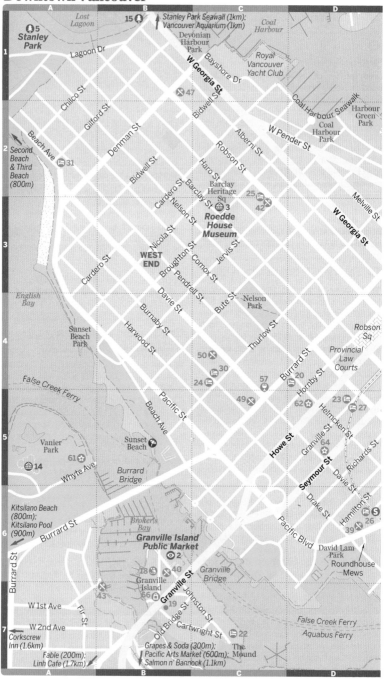

BRITISH COLUMBIA

Lost Lagoon

15

Stanley Park Seawall (1km); Vancouver Aquarium (1km)

Coal Harbour

5 Stanley Park

Devonian Harbour Park

Royal Vancouver Yacht Club

Lagoon Dr

W Georgia St

Bayshore Dr

Chilco St

Gilford St

47

Bidwell St

Alberni St

W Pender St

Coal Harbour Seawalk

Coal Harbour Park

Harbour Green Park

Second Beach & Third Beach (800m)

Beach Ave

31

Denman St

Bidwell St

Robson St

Haro St

Barclay St

Barclay Heritage Sq

Melville St

W Georgia St

Cardero St

Nelson St

25 42

3

Roedde House Museum

English Bay

Cardero St

Nicola St

Broughton St

Cornox St

Jervis St

WEST END

Pendrell St

Bute St

Nelson Park

Davie St

Robson Sq

Sunset Beach Park

Burnaby St

Harwood St

Thurlow St

Provincial Law Courts

False Creek Ferry

50

30

24

57

Burrard St

20

Hornby St

23 27

Pacific St

Beach Ave

49

62

Howe St

Granville St

64

Beach Ave

Vanier Park

61

14

Whyte Ave

Sunset Beach

Burrard Bridge

Helmcken St

Richards St

Seymour St

Davie St

Kitsilano Beach (800m); Kitsilano Pool (900m)

Burrard St

Broker's Bay

Drake St

Pacific Blvd

Hamilton St

26

39

David Lam Park

Roundhouse Mews

Granville Island Public Market

2

18 40

Granville Island

43

66

19

Granville Bridge

Johnston St

False Creek Ferry

Aquabus Ferry

Burrard St

Fir St

W 1st Ave

Old Bridge St

Cartwright St

22

W 2nd Ave

Corkscrew Inn (1.6km)

Fable (200m); Linh Cafe (1.7km)

Grapes & Soda (300m); Pacific Arts Market (600m); Salmon n' Bannock (1.1km)

The Mound

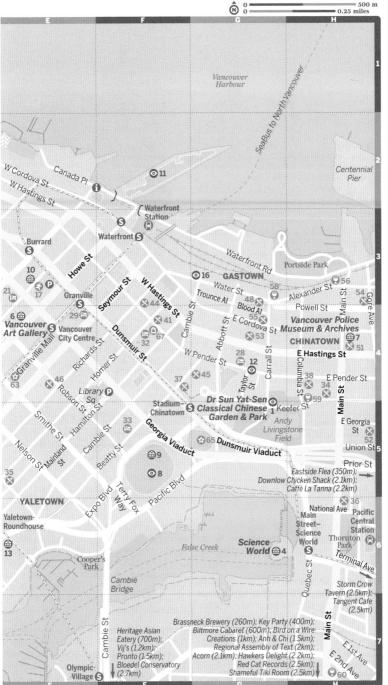

Vancouver Harbour

Centennial Pier

W Cordova St
W Hastings St
Canada Pl

11

Waterfront Station

Burrard

Waterfront

Waterfront Rd

Portside Park

16

GASTOWN

Water St

Trounce Al

Blood Al

E Cordova St

Alexander St

Powell St

5B

56

54

Gore Ave

Howe St

Seymour St

W Hastings St

Granville

10

21

17

6

Vancouver Art Gallery

Vancouver City Centre

29

44

41

32

67

Cambie St

Abbott St

48

55

53

Vancouver Police Museum & Archives

CHINATOWN

7

51

Granville Mall

63

Richards St

Homer St

46

Robson St

Library Sq

33

Dunsmuir St

W Pender St

28

12

37

45

Taylor St

Carrall St

Columbia St

Main St

E Hastings St

38

34

59

E Pender St

Smithe St

Hamilton St

Cambie St

Beatty St

Stadium-Chinatown

Georgia Viaduct

65

Dunsmuir Viaduct

Dr Sun Yat-Sen Classical Chinese Garden & Park

1

Keefer St

Andy Livingstone Field

E Georgia St

52

Union St

Nelson St

Mainland St

35

YALETOWN

Expo Blvd

Terry Fox Way

9

8

Pacific Blvd

Prior St

Eastside Flea (350m);
Downlow Chicken Shack (2.1km);
Caffè La Tanna (2.2km)

National Ave

Main Street–Science World

36

Pacific Central Station

Yaletown-Roundhouse

13

Cooper's Park

Cambie Bridge

False Creek

Science World

4

Quebec St

Thornton Park

Terminal Ave

Storm Crow Tavern (2.5km);
Tangent Cafe (2.5km)

Olympic Village

Cambie St

Heritage Asian Eatery (700m);
Vij's (1.2km);
Pronto (1.5km);
Bloedel Conservatory (2.7km)

Brassneck Brewery (260m); Key Party (400m);
Biltmore Cabaret (600m); Bird on a Wire
Creations (1km); Anh & Chi (1.5km);
Regional Assembly of Text (2km);
Acorn (2.1km); Hawkers Delight (2.2km);
Red Cat Records (2.5km);
Shameful Tiki Room (2.5km)

Main St

E 1st Ave

E 2nd Ave

60

0   500 m
0   0.25 miles

Downtown Vancouver

www.vancouverparks.ca; 2305 Cornwall Ave; adult/child $6.10/3.05; ☉ 7am-evening mid-Jun–Sep; ☉; ☐2), one of the world's largest outdoor salt-water pools.

Museum of Vancouver   MUSEUM
(MOV; Map p116; ☏604-736-4431; www.museum ofvancouver.ca; 1100 Chestnut St, Kitsilano; adult/child $20.50/9.75; ☉10am-5pm Sun-Wed, to 8pm Thu, to 9pm Fri & Sat; ☑; ☐2) The MOV serves up cool temporary exhibitions alongside in-depth permanent galleries of fascinating First Nations artifacts and evocative pioneer-era exhibits. But it really

comes to life in its vibrant 1950s pop culture and 1960s hippie counterculture sections, a reminder that Kitsilano was once the grass-smoking center of Vancouver's flower-power movement. Don't miss the shimmering gallery of vintage neon signs collected from around the city; it's a favorite with locals.

Beaty Biodiversity Museum   MUSEUM
(Map p112; ☏604-827-4955; www.beaty museum.ubc.ca; 2212 Main Mall, UBC; adult/child $14/10; ☉10am-5pm Tue-Sun; ☑; ☐99B-Line) A family-friendly museum showcasing a

two-million-item natural-history collection including birds, fossils and herbarium displays. The highlight is the 25m blue-whale skeleton, artfully displayed in the two-story entranceway. Don't miss the first display case, which is crammed with a beady-eyed menagerie of tooth-and-claw taxidermy. Consider visiting on the third Thursday of the month when entry is by donation after 5pm and the museum stays open until 8:30pm; there's often a special theme or live performance for these monthly Nocturnal events.

UBC Botanical Garden   GARDENS
(Map p112; ☎604-822-4208; www.botanicalgarden. ubc.ca; 6804 SW Marine Dr, UBC; adult/child $10/5; ☉10am-4:30pm; ⛟; ⛟99B-Line, then 68) You'll find a huge array of rhododendrons, a fascinating apothecary plot and a winter green space of off-season bloomers in this 28-hectare complex of themed gardens. Among the towering trees, look for northern flicker woodpeckers and chittering little Douglas squirrels. Also save time for the attraction's Greenheart TreeWalk (adult/child $23/10; ☉Apr-Oct; P⛟), which elevates visitors up to 23m above the forest floor on a 310m guided ecotour. The combined garden and Greenheart ticket costs adult/child $23/10.

HR MacMillan Space Centre   MUSEUM
(Map p116; ☎604-738-7827; www.spacecentre.ca; 1100 Chestnut St, Kitsilano; adult/child $19.50/14; ☉10am-5pm Jul & Aug, reduced hours off-season; P⛟; ⛟2) Focusing on the wonderful world of space, admission to this kid-favorite museum includes a gallery of hands-on exhibits (don't miss the Mars section where you can drive across the surface in a simulator) as well as a menu of live science demonstrations in the small theater and a cool 45-minute planetarium show upstairs. Check the daily schedule of shows and presentations online before you arrive. The Saturday-night planetarium performances are popular with locals and typically draw a more adult crowd.

◉ North Shore

★Capilano Suspension Bridge Park   PARK
(Map p112; ☎604-985-7474; www.capbridge. com; 3735 Capilano Rd, North Vancouver; adult/child $47/15; ☉8am-8pm May-Aug, reduced hours off-season; P⛟; ⛟236) As you inch gingerly across one of the world's longest (140m) and highest (70m) pedestrian suspension bridges, swaying gently over roiling Cap-

ilano Canyon, remember that its thick steel cables are firmly embedded in concrete. That should steady your feet – unless there are teenagers stamping across. Added park attractions include a glass-bottomed cliff-side walkway and an elevated canopy trail through the trees.

★Polygon Gallery   GALLERY
(Map p112; ☎604-986-1351; www.thepolygon.ca; 101 Carrie Cates Ct, North Vancouver; by donation; ☉10am-5pm Tue-Sun; ⛴Lonsdale Quay SeaBus) North Van's former Presentation House Gallery renamed itself and relocated to this dramatic, sawtooth-roofed waterfront landmark in 2017, providing greatly increased wall space for the multiple exhibitions staged here throughout the year. Photoconceptualism remains a focus but expect thought-provoking contemporary art installations and evocative Aboriginal exhibits as well. There are free 45-minute tours every Saturday at 2pm. On our visit, a new North Vancouver Museum was also under construction across the street.

Lynn Canyon Park   PARK
(Map p112; www.lynncanyon.ca; Park Rd, North Vancouver; ☉10am-5pm Jun-Sep, noon-4pm Oct-May; P⛟; ⛟228 then 227) FREE Amid a dense bristling of century-old trees, the main lure of this popular park is its Suspension Bridge, a free alternative to Capilano. Not quite as big as its tourist-magnet rival, it nevertheless provokes the same jelly-legged reaction as you sway over the river that tumbles 50m below – and it's always far less crowded. Hiking trails, swimming areas and picnic spots will keep you busy, while there's also a cafe to fuel up.

The park's Ecology Centre (☎604-990-3755; www.lynncanyonecologycentre.ca; 3663 Park

---

VANCOUVER FOR CHILDREN

Family-friendly Vancouver is stuffed with activities and attractions for kids, including Science World (p115), HR MacMillan Space Centre and the Vancouver Aquarium (p113). Keen to get them outdoors? Don't miss Stanley Park (p111) or Capilano Suspension Bridge Park. Several city festivals are also especially kid-friendly, while local transport experiences such as SeaBus and SkyTrain are highlights for many youngsters.

Rd, North Vancouver; by donation; ⊙10am-5pm Jun-Sep, 10am-5pm Mon-Fri & noon-4pm Sat & Sun Oct-May; 🚾; 🚌227) 🅿 houses interesting displays, including dioramas on the area's rich biodiversity. There are also some fascinating free history-themed walking tours in the park on Wednesdays and Thursdays in July and August; check www.nvma.ca/programs for details.

Mt Seymour Provincial Park   PARK
(www.bcparks.ca; 1700 Mt Seymour Rd, North Vancouver; ⊙dawn-dusk) **FREE** A popular rustic retreat from the downtown clamor, this huge, tree-lined park is suffused with summertime hiking trails that suit walkers of most abilities (the easiest path is the 2km Goldie Lake Trail). Many trails wind past lakes and centuries-old Douglas firs. This is also one of the city's main winter playgrounds.

🏃 Activities

Vancouver's variety of outdoorsy activities is a huge hook: you can ski in the morning and hit the beach in the afternoon; hike or bike scenic forests; paddleboard along the coastline; or kayak to your heart's content – and it will be content, with grand mountain views as your backdrop. There's also a full menu of spectator sports to catch here.

Ecomarine Paddlesport Centres   KAYAKING
(Map p116; 📞604-689-7575; www.ecomarine.com; 1668 Duranleau St, Granville Island; kayak/paddleboard rental per 2hr $39/30; ⊙10am-8pm mid-May–Aug, 10am-6pm Tue-Sun Sep–mid-May; 🚌50) Headquartered on Granville Island, the friendly folks at Ecomarine offer kayak (single and double) plus stand-up paddleboard (SUP) rentals, as well as popular guided tours, including the magical Urban Sunset Kayak ($79). Fancy exploring further? They also arrange multiday tours around some of BC's most magical marine regions.

★**Grouse Mountain**   SNOW SPORTS
(📞604-980-9311; www.grousemountain.com; 6400 Nancy Greene Way, North Vancouver; lift ticket adult/child $47/42; ⊙9am-10pm mid-Nov–mid-Apr; 🚾; 🚌236) Vancouver's favorite winter hangout, family-friendly Grouse offers four chairlifts plus 33 ski and snowboard runs (including night runs). Classes and lessons are available for beginners and beyond, and the area's forested snowshoe trails are magical. There are also a couple of dining options if you just want to relax and watch the snow with a hot chocolate in hand.

Cypress Mountain   SNOW SPORTS
(📞604-926-5612; www.cypressmountain.com; 6000 Cypress Bowl Rd, West Vancouver; lift ticket adult/youth/child $79/56/36; ⊙9am-10pm mid-Dec–Mar, to 4pm Apr; 🚾) Around 8km north of West Van via Hwy 99, Cypress Provincial Park (www.bcparks.ca; Cypress Bowl Rd, West Vancouver; ⊙dawn-dusk) **FREE** transforms into Cypress Mountain resort in winter, attracting well-insulated locals with its 53 runs, cross-country ski access and a family-friendly snow-tubing course. There are also 11km of snowshoe trails, with several guided tours available (the $59 chocolate fondue option is recommended).

🧭 Tours

★**Cycle City Tours**   CYCLING
(Map p116; 📞604-618-8626; www.cyclevancouver. com; 648 Hornby St, Downtown; tours from $65, bicycle rentals per hour/day $9.50/38; ⊙9am-6pm, reduced hours in winter; 🚇Burrard) Striped with bike lanes, Vancouver is a good city for two-wheeled exploring. But if you're not great at navigating, consider a guided tour with this popular operator. Its Grand Tour ($90) is a great city intro, while the Craft Beer Tour ($90) includes brunch and three breweries. Alternatively, go solo with a rental; there's a bike lane outside the store.

URBAN BIRDING

You don't have to go far to spot some beady-eyed locals in this city. Birding has become a popular pastime for many Vancouverites and if you're keen to join in the feather-fancying fun, consider spending an hour or two in Stanley Park (p111), Vanier Park, Pacific Spirit Park or Queen Elizabeth Park. Many city streets are also lined with established trees that are home to a surprisingly diverse array of beaked critters: on our West End exploration, we spotted hummingbirds, barred owls and northern flicker woodpeckers. Heading into adjoining Stanley Park, you might also see wrens, chickadees, downy woodpeckers, bald eagles, coots, ducks, cormorants and herons – which are also famous for nesting in a large and noisy heronry here every spring.

BRITISH COLUMBIA VANCOUVER

★ **Vancouver Foodie Tours**   TOURS
(📞604-295-8844; www.foodietours.ca; tours from $65) A popular culinary-themed city stroll operator running three tasty tours in Vancouver; choose between Best of Downtown, Gastronomic Gastown and Granville Island tours. Friendly red-coated guides lead you on belly-pleasing ventures with plenty to eat and drink; the trick is not to dine before you arrive.

Forbidden Vancouver   WALKING
(📞604-227-7570; www.forbiddenvancouver.ca; tours from $25) This quirky company offers highly entertaining tours, including a delve into Prohibition-era Vancouver, a Stanley Park 'secrets' tour and a combination chocolate-tasting and art-deco architecture walk. It also hosts regular behind-the-scenes tours of the infamous Penthouse nightclub as well as a recently added walk-and-talk around the city's LGBT+ history.

Sewell's Marina   BOATING
(📞604-921-3474; www.sewellsmarina.com; 6409 Bay St, Horseshoe Bay, West Vancouver; adult/child $93/60; ⊘8am-6pm Apr-Oct; 🚗; 🚌257) West Vancouver's Horseshoe Bay is the departure point for Sewell's two-hour Sea Safari boat tours. Orcas are always a highlight, but even if they're not around you'll almost certainly spot harbor seals lolling on the rocks and pretending to ignore you. Seabirds and bald eagles are also big stars of the show.

🎊 Festivals & Events

Vancouver International
Wine Festival   WINE
(www.vanwinefest.ca; 999 Canada Pl, Convention Centre West, Downtown; tickets from $40; ⊘late Feb) The city's oldest and best annual wine celebration, with a different regional focus every year.

Vancouver Craft Beer Week   BEER
(www.vancouvercraftbeerweek.com; event tickets from $15; ⊘late May) A showcase for BC's amazing craft-beer scene, with dozens of tasty events around the city.

Vancouver International
Jazz Festival   MUSIC
(www.coastaljazz.ca; ⊘Jun) City-wide cornucopia of superstar shows and free outdoor events from mid-June.

Vancouver Mural Festival   ART
(www.vanmuralfest.ca; Main St; ⊘Aug) Mostly radiating along Main St and its tributaries, this annual event transforms city walls with huge, eye-popping artworks.

Pride Week   LGBT
(www.vancouverpride.ca; West End; ⊘Aug) Parties, concerts and fashion shows, as well as the city's biggest annual street parade.

Pacific National Exhibition (PNE)   CULTURAL
(www.pne.ca; 2901 E Hastings St, Hastings Park; adult/under-13s $18/free; ⊘mid-Aug–Sep; 🚗; 🚌14) Family-friendly shows, music concerts and fairground fun (plus lots of calorific things to eat).

Vancouver International
Film Festival   FILM
(www.viff.org; ⊘late Sep) Popular two-week showcase of Canadian and international movies on screens throughout the city. Book ahead: tickets are hot items here.

Eastside Culture Crawl   ART
(www.culturecrawl.ca; ⊘mid-Nov) Vancouver's best visual-arts festival: a four-day gallery and studio open house with hundreds of participants.

🛏 Sleeping

Metro Vancouver is home to more than 23,000 hotel, B&B and hostel rooms, the majority in or around the downtown core. Airbnb also operates here, although a regulatory crackdown has reduced their number in recent years. Book far ahead for summer, unless you fancy sleeping rough in Stanley Park. Rates peak in July and August, but there are good spring and fall deals here (alongside increased rainy days).

🛏 Downtown & West End

Samesun Backpackers Lodge   HOSTEL $
(Map p116; 📞604-682-8226; www.samesun.com; 1018 Granville St, Downtown; dm/r incl breakfast from $62/180; @🛜; 🚌10) Vancouver's liveliest hostel is right on the city's nightlife strip. Ask for a back room if you fancy a few hours of sleep or head down to the on-site bar (provocatively called the Beaver) to hang out with the partying throng. Dorms, including some pod beds, are comfortably small, and there are also private rooms plus a large shared kitchen.

HI Vancouver Central   HOSTEL $
(Map p116; 📞604-685-5335; www.hihostels.ca/en/destinations/british-columbia/hi-vancouver-central; 1025 Granville St, Downtown; dm/r from

$60/120; ✸@⊛; ⊟10) On the Granville Strip, this warren-like hostel is more of a party joint than its **HI Downtown** (Map p116; ☏604-684-4565; www.hihostels.ca/en/destinations/british-columbia/hi-vancouver-downtown; 1114 Burnaby St, West End; dm/r from $62/135; @⊛; ⊟6) sibling. Some of the benefits of its past hotel incarnation remain, including air-conditioning and small rooms, some of which are now private, with the rest converted to dorms with up to four beds. There are dozens of two-bedded rooms (some en suite).

★Victorian Hotel   HOTEL $$

(Map p116; ☏604-681-6369; www.victorianhotel.ca; 514 Homer St, Downtown; d incl breakfast from $200; ⊜@⊛; Ⓢ Granville) The high-ceilinged rooms at this well-maintained heritage hotel combine glossy hardwood floors, a sprinkling of antiques, an occasional bay window and plenty of historical charm. The best rooms are in the extension, where raindrop showers, marble bathroom floors and flat-screen TVs add a slice of luxe. Rates include continental breakfast and rooms are provided with fans in summer.

★Sunset Inn & Suites   HOTEL $$

(Map p116; ☏604-688-2474; www.sunsetinn.com; 1111 Burnaby St, West End; d incl breakfast $225; P✸@⊛; ⊟6) A good-value cut above most of Vancouver's self-catering suite hotels, the popular Sunset Inn offers larger-than-average rooms with kitchens. Each has a balcony, and some – particularly those on south-facing higher floors – have partial views of English Bay. Rates include continental breakfast (with make-your-own waffles) and, rare for Vancouver, free parking. The attentive staff is among the best in the city.

Sylvia Hotel   HOTEL $$

(Map p116; ☏604-681-9321; www.sylviahotel.com; 1154 Gilford St, West End; d from $199; P@⊛⊛; ⊟5) This ivy-covered 1912 charmer enjoys a prime location overlooking English Bay. Generations of guests keep coming back – many requesting the same room every year – for a dollop of old-world ambience, plus a side order of first-name service. The rooms, some with older furnishings, have an array of comfortable configurations; the best are the large suites with kitchens and waterfront views.

Burrard Hotel   HOTEL $$

(Map p116; ☏604-681-2331; www.theburrard.com; 1100 Burrard St, Downtown; d from $240;

P✸⊛⊛; ⊟2) A groovy makeover a few years back transformed this 1950s downtown motel into a knowingly cool sleepover with a tongue-in-cheek retro feel (neon exterior sign included). Colorful, mostly compact rooms have been spruced up with modern flourishes and contemporary amenities such as refrigerators and flat-screen TVs. But not everything has changed; the hidden interior courtyard's towering palm trees echo yesteryear Vegas.

St Regis Hotel   BOUTIQUE HOTEL $$$

(Map p116; ☏604-681-1135; www.stregishotel.com; 602 Dunsmuir St, Downtown; d incl breakfast from $325; ✸@⊛; Ⓢ Granville) An elegant art-lined boutique sleepover in a 1913 heritage shell. Befitting its age, almost all the rooms seem to be a different size, and they exhibit a loungey élan with deco-esque furniture, earth-toned bedspreads, flat-screen TVs and multimedia hubs. Rates include value-added flourishes such as cooked breakfasts, access to the nearby gym and free long-distance and international phone calls.

Listel Hotel   BOUTIQUE HOTEL $$$

(Map p116; ☏604-684-8461; www.thelistelhotel.com; 1300 Robson St, West End; d from $340; P✸@⊛; ⊟5) ✐ A lounge-cool sleepover with famously friendly front-deskers. Rooms at the Listel have a relaxed West Coast feel and typically feature striking original artworks. But it's not all about looks; cool features include glass water bottles in the rooms, a daily wine reception (from 5pm) and the free use of loaner e-bikes if you want to explore nearby Stanley Park (p111).

Fairmont Hotel
Vancouver   HOTEL $$$

(Map p116; ☏604-684-3131; www.fairmont.com/hotel-vancouver; 900 W Georgia St, Downtown; d from $500; P✸@⊛⊛⊛; Ⓢ Vancouver City Centre) Opened in 1939 by visiting UK royals, this gargoyle-topped grand dame is a Vancouver historic landmark. Despite its vintage provenance, the hotel carefully balances comfort with elegance; the lobby is bedecked with crystal chandeliers but the rooms have an understated business-hotel feel. If you have the budget, check into the Gold Floor for a raft of pampering extras.

🛏 Gastown & Chinatown

★Skwachàys Lodge   BOUTIQUE HOTEL $$

(Map p116; ☏604-687-3589; www.skwachays.com; 29 W Pender St, Chinatown; d from $300;

✳ ⌃; S Stadium-Chinatown) The 18 small but elegantly designed rooms at this sparkling First Nations art hotel include the captivating Forest Spirits Suite, with floor-to-ceiling birch branches, and the sleek Longhouse Suite, with its illuminated metalwork frieze. Deluxe trappings, from plasma TVs to eco-friendly toiletries, are standard and there's an on-site gallery for purchasing one-of-a-kind artworks.

🛏 Yaletown & Granville Island

YWCA Hotel   HOTEL $
(Map p116; ☎604-895-5830; www.ywcahotel. com; 733 Beatty St, Yaletown; s/d/tr without bath $106/118/173; P ⇌ ✳ @ ⌃; S Stadium-Chinatown) A good-value, well-located option with nicely maintained (if spartan) rooms of the student-accommodations variety. There's a range of configurations, from singles to five-bed rooms, plus shared, semiprivate or private bathrooms. Each room has a TV and mini-refrigerator and there are TV lounges and communal kitchens too. Rates include access to the YWCA Health & Fitness Centre, a 15-minute walk away.

Opus Hotel   BOUTIQUE HOTEL $$$
(Map p116; ☎604-642-6787; www.opushotel. com; 322 Davie St, Yaletown; d $500; P ✳ ⌃ ✳; S Yaletown-Roundhouse) The 96-room Opus kick-started Vancouver's boutique-hotel scene and, with regular revamps, it's remained one of the city's top sleepover options. The designer rooms have contemporary-chic interiors with bold colors, mod furnishings and feng-shui bed placements, while many of the luxe bathrooms have clear windows overlooking the streets (visiting exhibitionists take note).

Granville Island Hotel   BOUTIQUE HOTEL $$$
(Map p116; ☎604-683-7373; www.granvilleisland hotel.com; 1253 Johnston St, Granville Island; d $400; P ✳ @ ⌃ ✳; 🚌50) This gracious boutique property hugs Granville Island's quiet southeastern tip, enjoying tranquil views across False Creek to Yaletown's mirrored towers. You'll be a stroll from the Public Market, with shopping and theater options on your doorstep. Rooms have a West Coast feel with some exposed-wood flourishes. There's also a rooftop Jacuzzi, while the on-site brewpub-restaurant has one of the city's best patios.

VANCOUVER'S BEST BLOGS
....

Miss 604 (www.miss604.com) Vancouver's leading blogger, covering local events and happenings.

Scout Magazine (www.scoutmagazine. ca) Trendy site profiling the city's food and drinks scene.

Bored in Vancouver (www.boredin vancouver.com) Alternative take on multiple scenes around the city.

Daily Hive Vancouver (www.dailyhive. com/vancouver) City news and lifestyle happenings.

🛏 Kitsilano & University of British Columbia

HI Vancouver Jericho Beach   HOSTEL $
(Map p112; ☎604-224-3208; www.hihostels.com; 1515 Discovery St, Kitsilano; dm/d $43/86; ☺May-Sep; P @ ⌃; 🚌4) One of Canada's largest hostels looks like a Victorian hospital but has a scenic near-the-beach location. Basic rooms make this the least palatial Vancouver HI hostel, but it has a large kitchen, bike rentals and a popular licenced cafe. Dorms are also larger here. Book ahead for the popular budget-hotel-style private rooms (with shared and private bathroom options).

Corkscrew Inn   B&B $$
(☎604-733-7276; www.corkscrewinn.com; 2735 W 2nd Ave, Kitsilano; d incl breakfast from $195; P ⌃; 🚌84) This flower-framed, gable-roofed property appears to have a drinking problem: it houses a little museum, available only to guests, that's lined with corkscrews and antique vineyard tools. Aside from the boozy paraphernalia, this immaculate century-old arts-and-crafts-style home has five wood-floored rooms (we like the art-deco room) and is a short walk from the beach. Sumptuous breakfast (with house-baked bread) included.

🍴 Eating

Vancouver has an eye-popping array of generally good-value dine-out options: authentic Asian restaurants, finger-licking brunch spots, fresh-catch seafood joints and a locally sourced farm-to-table scene are all on the menu here. You don't have to be a local to indulge: just follow your taste buds and dinner will become the most talked-about highlight of your Vancouver visit.

✗ Downtown & West End

★Molli Cafe
MEXICAN $

(Map p116; ☑604-336-6554; 1225 Burrard St, West End; tortas $10-13; ⊙8am-9pm Mon-Sat, 9am-8pm Sun; ☎; ☐2) It's easy to dismiss this unassuming cafe while strolling along Burrard, but that would be a huge mistake. Instead, nip inside and check out a menu of home-style Mexican dishes such as tacos, tortas, *mollete* open-faced sandwiches and the kind of fortifying soups your grandma used to make. All is lovingly prepared and served alongside a soundtrack of jaunty Mexican tunes.

Finch's
CAFE $

(Map p116; ☑604-899-4040; www.finchteahouse. com; 353 W Pender St, Downtown; mains $6-12; ⊙9am-5pm Mon-Fri, 11am-4pm Sat; ☑; ☐4) For a coveted seat at one of the dinged old tables, arrive off-peak at this sunny, super-friendly corner cafe, which combines creaky wooden floors and a junk-shop bric-a-brac aesthetic. Join hipsters and office workers who've been calling this their local for years and who come mainly for the freshly prepared baguette sandwiches (pear, blue Brie, prosciutto and roasted walnuts recommended).

Japadog
JAPANESE $

(Map p116; ☑604-569-1158; www.japadog.com; 530 Robson St, Downtown; mains $6-12; ⊙6:30am-10pm Mon-Fri, 7:30am-11pm Sat, 7:30am-9pm Sun; ☐10) You'll have spotted the lunchtime queues at the Japadog hotdog stands around town, but this was their first storefront, opening back in 2010. The ever-*genki* Japanese expats serve up a menu of lip-smacking wonder wieners – think turkey smokies with miso sauce and crunchy shrimp tempura dogs – but there are also irresistible fries (try the butter and *shoyu* version).

Kintaro Ramen Noodle
RAMEN $

(Map p116; ☑604-682-7568; 788 Denman St, West End; mains $6-10; ⊙11:30am-11pm; ☐5) One of Vancouver's oldest noodle shops, fancy-free Kintaro feels like a bustling ramen spot in backstreet Tokyo. Arrive off-peak to avoid queues and snag a counter seat to watch the steam-shrouded action. Miso ramen is recommended; a brimming bowl of sprouts, bamboo shoots and thick slices of barbecued pork. When you're done, walk off your noodle belly in Stanley Park.

★Indigo Age Cafe
VEGAN $$

(Map p116; ☑604-622-1797; www.indigoagecafe. com; 436 Richards St, Downtown; mains $15-20; ⊙11am-7pm Wed-Sun; ☎☑; ☐14) ✅ The kind of woodsy subterranean cave a health-minded hobbit would enjoy, this small vegan and raw-food restaurant has legions of local fans. Snag a table (peak-time reservations recommended) and dive into hearty, savor-worthy dishes from cabbage rolls to the colorful, best-selling Fresh Addiction Burger. Fancy a unique high tea? It offers a cool raw vegan version here; book ahead.

★Forage
CANADIAN $$

(Map p116; ☑604-661-1400; www.foragevancouver. com; 1300 Robson St, West End; mains $16-35; ⊙6:30-10am & 5-11pm Mon-Fri, 7am-2pm & 5-11pm Sat & Sun; ☎; ☐5) ✅ A popular farm-to-table eatery, this sustainability-focused restaurant is the perfect way to sample regional flavors. Brunch has become a firm local favorite (halibut eggs Benny recommended), and for dinner there's everything from bison steaks to slow-cooked salmon. Add a flight of BC craft beers, with top choices from the likes of Four Winds, Strange Fellows and more. Reservations recommended.

Jam Cafe
BREAKFAST $$

(Map p116; ☑778-379-1992; www.jamcafes.com; 556 Beatty St, Downtown; mains $9-17; ⊙8am-3pm; ☎☑; Ⓢ Stadium-Chinatown) The Vancouver outpost of Victoria's wildly popular breakfast and brunch superstar lures the city's longest queues, especially on weekends. Reservations are not accepted so you're well advised to dine off-peak and during the week. You'll find a white-walled room studded with Canadian knickknacks and a huge array of satisfying options, from chicken and biscuits to red-velvet pancakes.

Mumbai Local
INDIAN $$

(Map p116; ☑604-423-3281; www.mumbailocal. ca; 1148 Davie St, West End; mains $15-25; ⊙11am-10pm; ☎☑; ☐5) Seated alongside a striking Mumbai-themed mural, dive into some street-food snacks and dishes inspired by the home-style cuisine of this bustling Indian city. We loved the *chaat* sampler of crunchy savory treats plus the chickpea and potato patties in a bun, but don't miss the *dabba* combo of condiments, stew, dal, bread and rice served in a multilayer tiffin tin.

Chambar
EUROPEAN $$$

(Map p116; ☑604-879-7119; www.chambar.com; 568 Beatty St, Downtown; mains $28-36; ⊙8am-

11pm; **P**; **S** Stadium-Chinatown) This giant, brick-lined cave is a juggernaut of Vancouver's dining scene, serving an ever-changing all-day menu of sophisticated Belgian-esque dishes from morning waffles to excellent *moules frites* to a lip-smacking dinnertime lamb shank with figs and couscous. An impressive wine and cocktail list (try a blue-fig martini) is coupled with a great Belgian beer menu dripping with *tripels* and *lambics*.

✖ Gastown & Chinatown

★ Ovaltine Cafe
DINER **$**

(Map p116; ☑ 604-685-7021; www.facebook.com/ovaltinecafe; 251 E Hastings St, Chinatown; mains $7-10; ⊙ 6:30am-3pm Mon-Sat, 6:30am-2pm Sun; ⊟ 14) Like being inside Edward Hopper's *Nighthawks* diner painting, this time-capsule greasy spoon instantly transports you to the 1940s. Snag a booth alongside the hospital-green walls or, better yet, slide onto a tape-repaired spinning stool at the long counter. Truck-stop coffee is de rigueur here, alongside burgers, sandwiches and fried breakfasts that haven't changed in decades (yes, that's liver and onions on the menu).

Chinatown BBQ
CHINESE **$**

(Map p116; ☑ 604-428-2626; www.chinatownbbq.com; 130 E Pender St, Chinatown; mains $10-19; ⊙ 11am-8pm Tue-Sun; ⊟ 3) A modern-day version of this historic neighborhood's once-ubiquitous barbecue shops, this retro-feel eatery (vinyl booths, checkerboard floor and monochrome wall photos) serves simple, perfectly prepared platters of meat and rice plus more (we like the beef-brisket curry). Expect a soundtrack of traditional Chinese music and the thud of meat cleavers from the old dudes in the open kitchen.

Tacofino Taco Bar
MEXICAN **$**

(Map p116; ☑ 604-899-7907; www.tacofino.com; 15 W Cordova St, Gastown; tacos from $6; ⊙ 11:30am-10pm Sun-Wed, 11:30am-midnight Thu-Sat; 🛜📶; ⊟ 14) Food-truck favorite Tacofino made an instant splash with this huge, handsome dining room (think stylish geometric-patterned floors, hive-like lampshades and a tiny back patio). The simple menu focuses on a handful of taco options plus nachos, soups and a selection of beer, agave and tequila flights. Fish tacos are the top seller, but we love the super-tender lamb *birria* version.

Save on Meats
DINER **$**

(Map p116; ☑ 604-569-3568; www.saveonmeats.ca; 43 W Hastings St, Gastown; mains $6-15; ⊙ 11am-7pm Sun-Thu, 11am-11pm Fri & Sat; 🛜📶; ⊟ 14) A former old-school butcher shop that's been transformed into a popular hipster diner. Slide into a booth or hop on a swivel chair at the super-long counter and tuck into comfort dishes. They range from a good-value $6 all-day breakfast to the satisfying SOM burger, paired with a heaping tangle of 'haystack' fries. Add a BC-brewed Persephone beer to keep things lively.

Phnom Penh
VIETNAMESE, CAMBODIAN **$**

(Map p116; ☑ 604-682-5777; www.phnompenhrestaurant.ca; 244 E Georgia St, Chinatown; mains $8-18; ⊙ 10am-9pm Mon-Thu, 10am-10pm Fri-Sun; ⊟ 3) The dishes at this bustling, local-legend joint are split between Cambodian and Vietnamese soul-food classics. It's the highly addictive chicken wings and their lovely pepper sauce that keep regulars loyal. Once you've piled up the bones, dive back in for round two: papaya salad, butter beef and spring rolls show just how good a street-food-inspired Asian menu can be.

★ Campagnolo
ITALIAN **$$**

(Map p116; ☑ 604-484-6018; www.campagnolorestaurant.ca; 1020 Main St, Chinatown; mains $18-25; ⊙ 11:30am-2:30pm Mon-Fri, plus 5:30-10pm daily; 📶; ⊟ 3) Eyebrows were raised when this contemporary, rustic-style Italian restaurant opened in a hitherto sketchy part of town. But Campagnolo has lured locals and inspired a miniwave of other restaurants in the vicinity. Reserve ahead and dive into reinvented comfort dishes such as shrimp gnocchetti and a fennel sausage-topped pizza that may induce you to eat your body weight in thin-crust.

MeeT in Gastown
VEGAN **$$**

(Map p116; ☑ 604-696-1111; www.meeton main.com; 12 Water St, Gastown; mains $10-16; ⊙ 11am-11pm Sun-Thu, 11am-midnight Fri & Sat; 📶; **M** Waterfront) Serving great vegan comfort dishes without the rabbit-food approach, this wildly popular spot can be clamorously busy at times. But it's worth the wait for a wide-ranging array of herbivore- and carnivore-pleasing dishes, from rice bowls and mac 'n' cheese (made from vegan cashew 'cheese') to hearty burgers and poutine-like fries slathered in nut-based miso gravy (our recommendation).

AGUSTIN ESMORIS / SHUTTERSTOCK ©

1. Alert Bay (p188)
Home to the Namgis First Nation, there are lots of ways to experience Indigenous culture here.

2. Sea to Sky Gondola (p139)
Head to the top station of Squamish's spectacular gondola for stunning views.

3. Whistler (p141)
One of the world's largest, best-equipped and most popular ski resorts.

4. Salt Spring Island (p192)
The busiest and most developed of the Southern Gulf Islands.

Bao Bei CHINESE $$

(Map p116; 604-688-0876; www.bao-bei.ca; 163 Keefer St, Chinatown; small plates $6-23; 5:30pm-midnight Mon-Sat, 5:30-11pm Sun; 3) Reinterpreting a Chinatown heritage building with hipsteresque flourishes, this Chinese brasserie is a seductive dinner destination. Bringing a contemporary edge to Asian cuisine are tapas-sized, MSG-free dishes such as *shao bing* (stuffed Chinese flatbread), delectable dumplings and spicy-chicken steamed buns. There's also an enticing drinks menu guaranteed to make you linger, especially if you dive into the inventive cocktails.

Sai Woo ASIAN $$

(Map p116; 604-568-1117; www.saiwoo.ca; 158 E Pender, Chinatown; mains $13-23; 5pm-midnight Tue-Sat, 5-9pm Sun; 3) There's a film-set look to the exterior of this contemporary restaurant that resembles a replica of an old Hong Kong restaurant. But the long, slender interior is a candlelit cave with a lounge-like vibe. Expect a wide array of Asian dishes, from Szechuan spicy-beef noodles to Korean-style barbecued-pork pancakes, and consider the happy hour (5pm to 6pm) with half-price dumplings.

★**St Lawrence Restaurant** FRENCH $$$

(Map p116; 604-620-3800; www.stlawrencerestaurant.com; 269 Powell St, Railtown; mains $34-44; 5:30-10:30pm Tue-Sun; 4) Resembling a handsome wood-floored bistro that's been teleported straight from Montréal, this sparkling, country-chic dining room is a Railtown superstar. The Québecois approach carries over onto a small menu of elevated, perfectly prepared old-school mains such as trout in brown-butter sauce and the utterly delicious duck-leg confit with sausage. French-Canadian special-occasion dining at its finest.

✗ Yaletown & Granville Island

DD Mau VIETNAMESE $

(Map p116; 604-684-4446; www.ddmau.ca; 1239 Pacific Blvd, Yaletown; sandwiches $5-13; 11am-4pm Mon-Sat; ; S Yaletown-Roundhouse) At the forefront of Vancouver's love affair with Vietnamese banh mi sandwiches, this tiny, often-busy spot serves daily specials (always check these first) alongside five made-to-order regulars. Expect crisp baguette sandwiches (in large or half-order options) with diverse fillings including barbecue pork and

lemongrass chicken. Seating is extremely limited so aim for takeout or visit its larger Chinatown branch.

★**Go Fish** SEAFOOD $

(Map p116; 604-730-5040; 1505 W 1st Ave; mains $8-14; 11:30am-6pm Mon-Fri, noon-6pm Sat & Sun; 50) A short stroll westward along the seawall from the Granville Island entrance, this almost-too-popular seafood stand is one of the city's fave fish-and-chip joints, offering halibut, salmon and cod encased in crispy golden batter. The smashing fish tacos are also recommended, while changing daily specials – brought in by the nearby fishing boats – often include scallop burgers or ahi tuna sandwiches.

Edible Canada CANADIAN $$

(Map p116; 604-682-6681; www.ediblecanada.com; 1596 Johnston St, Granville Island; mains $12-35; 11am-8:30pm Mon-Fri, 9am-8:30pm Sat & Sun; 50) Granville Island's most popular bistro (book ahead) delivers a tempting menu of seasonal dishes. With ingredients from BC and across Canada, typical options include bison burgers, wild salmon or Québec-style duck poutine. Add a selection from the huge all-Canadian wine list (dominated by BC) or dive into a local beer flight that includes several Vancouver producers.

Blue Water Cafe SEAFOOD $$$

(Map p116; 604-688-8078; www.bluewatercafe.net; 1095 Hamilton St, Yaletown; mains $30-45; 5-11pm; S Yaletown-Roundhouse) Under celebrated executive chef Frank Pabst, this is one of Vancouver's best high-concept seafood restaurants. Gentle music fills the brick-lined, blue-hued interior, while top-notch char, sturgeon and butter-soft scallops grace the tables inside and on the patio. Not a seafood fan? There's also a small array of meaty 'principal plates' to sate your carnivorous appetite, including Kobe-style short ribs.

✗ Commercial Drive

★**Caffè La Tanna** ITALIAN $

(604-428-5462; www.caffelatana.ca; 635 Commercial Dr; mains $12-16; 8am-6pm; 20) Like a 1950s neighborhood cafe in Rome, this handsome little hidden gem looks like it's been here for decades. But it's a new addition to this quiet stretch of the Drive, luring delighted locals with its delicate housemade pastries and fresh pastas (watch the mesmerizing pasta production at the counter).

Check the daily special and peruse the shelves of Italian groceries, too.

Downlow Chicken Shack
CHICKEN $

(☑604-283-1385; www.dlchickenshack.ca; 905 Commercial Dr; mains $8-32; ⊙11am-9pm Tue-Sat, 11am-4:30pm Sun; 🐾; 🖵20) Spicy, deep-fried, southern-style chicken is the menu foundation at this bright and buzzing spot with its surprisingly happy grinning-bird logo. Choose from a variety of cuts, including wings, boneless thighs and the popular-but-messy chicken-breast sandwich, then add your heat level plus tasty sides. Aim for a summertime deck seat and don't miss their $2 Wing Wednesday deal.

Tangent Cafe
DINER $

(☑604-558-4641; www.tangentcafe.ca; 2095 Commercial Dr; mains $11-19; ⊙8am-3pm Mon & Tue, 8am-midnight Wed & Thu, 8am-1am Fri & Sat, 8am-10pm Sun; 🐾🖉; 🖵20) Lined with retro wood paneling, this warm and welcoming Drive hangout combines comfort-classic wraps and burgers with several Malaysian curries and some good vegetarian options. But breakfast, served until mid-afternoon, is when you're most likely to meet the locals. A great craft-beer menu (check the corner chalkboard) and regular live music (mostly jazz) also make this a popular nighttime haunt.

✖ Main Street

Hawkers Delight
ASIAN $

(☑604-709-8188; www.facebook.com/hawkers delightdeli; 4127 Main St; mains $5-13; ⊙noon-9pm Mon-Sat; 🖉; 🖵3) It's easy to miss this cash-only hole-in-the-wall, but it's worth retracing your steps for authentic Malaysian and Singaporean street food, made from scratch at this family-run favorite. Prices are temptingly low, so order to share – from spicy *mee pok* to noodle-heavy *mee goreng* and shrimp-packed *laksa*. Check the counter for addictive veggie fritters (just $1.45 for two).

★ Anh & Chi
VIETNAMESE $$

(☑604-878-8883; www.anhandchi.com; 3388 Main St; mains $16-25; ⊙11am-11pm; 🖉; 🖵3) You'll find warm and solicitous service at this delightful contemporary Vietnamese restaurant whose authentic, perfectly prepared dishes are a must for local foodies. Not sure what to order? Check out the menu's 'bucket list' dishes, including the highly recommended prawn-and-pork-packed crunchy crepe. Reservations are not accepted and waits here can be long; consider mid-afternoon weekday dining instead.

★ Acorn
VEGETARIAN $$

(☑604-566-9001; www.theacornrestaurant.ca; 3995 Main St; mains $18-22; ⊙5:30-10pm Mon-Thu, to 11pm Fri, 10am-2:30pm & 5:30-11pm Sat, to midnight Sun; 🖉; 🖵3) One of Vancouver's hottest vegetarian restaurants – hence the sometimes long wait for tables – the Acorn is ideal for those craving something more inventive than mung-bean soup. Consider seasonal, artfully presented treats such as beer-battered haloumi or vanilla-almond-beet cake and stick around at night: the bar serves until midnight if you need to pull up a stool and set the world to rights.

✖ Fairview & South Granville

★ Salmon n' Bannock
NORTHWESTERN US $$

(☑604-568-8971; www.facebook.com/salmonn bannockbistro; 1128 W Broadway, Fairview; mains $16-32; ⊙5-10pm Mon-Sat; 🖵9) Vancouver's only First Nations restaurant is an utterly delightful art-lined little bistro on an unassuming strip of Broadway shops. It's worth the easy bus trip, though, for fresh-made indigenous-influenced dishes made with local ingredients. The juicy salmon 'n' bannock burger has been a staple here for years but more elaborate, feast-like options include game sausages and bison pot roast.

Heritage Asian Eatery
ASIAN $$

(☑604-559-6058; www.eatheritage.ca; 382 W Broadway, Fairview; mains $12-18; ⊙11am-8pm; 🐾🖉; 🖵9) Bigger than its Pender St sibling, this bright, cafeteria-style spot serves a small, well-curated menu of comfort-food rice and noodle bowls. Serving top-notch dishes such as velvety pork belly and spicy lamb shank, it also offers a couple of flavor-hugging vegetarian options; go for the lip-smacking eggplant rice bowl. On your way out, add a warm egg-custard bun to your day.

★ Vij's
INDIAN $$$

(☑604-736-6664; www.vijs.ca; 3106 Cambie St, Cambie Village; mains $23-36; ⊙5:30-10pm; 🖉; 🖵15) Spicy aromas scent the air as you enter this warmly intimate dining space for Vancouver's finest Indian cuisine. Exemplary servers happily answer menu questions, while bringing over snacks and chai tea. There's a one-page array of tempting dishes but the trick is to order three or four to share

BRITISH COLUMBIA VANCOUVER

(mains are all available as small plates and orders come with rice and naan).

Kitsilano & University of British Columbia

Jamjar Canteen
LEBANESE $

(Map p112; ☏604-620-5320; www.jamjarcanteen.ca; 6035 University Blvd, UBC; mains $10-12; ⊙10:30am-10pm Mon-Fri, to 9pm Sat & Sun; 🛜 🖉; 🚍99B-Line) Visiting Canteen, a simplified version of the city's highly popular Jamjar Lebanese comfort-food restaurants, means choosing from four mains (lamb sausages or deep-fried cauliflower recommended) then adding the approach: rice bowl, salad bowl or wrap. Choices of olives, veggies, hummus and more are then requested before you can dive into your hearty lunch or dinner.

Fable Kitchen
CANADIAN $$

(☏604-732-1322; www.fablekitchen.ca; 1944 W 4th Ave, Kitsilano; mains $21-28; ⊙11am-2:30pm & 5:30-10pm Tue-Fri, 10am-2pm & 5-10pm Sat & Sun; 🚍4) One of Vancouver's favorite farm-to-table restaurants is a lovely rustic-chic room of exposed brick, wood beams and prominently displayed red rooster logos. But looks are just part of the appeal. Expect perfectly prepared bistro dishes showcasing local seasonal ingredients such as duck, pork and scallops. It's great gourmet comfort food with little pretension, hence the packed room most nights. Reservations recommended.

Linh Cafe
FRENCH, VIETNAMESE $$

(☏604-559-4668; www.linhcafe.com; 2836 W 4th Ave, Kitsilano; mains $14-45; ⊙11am-9pm Wed-Fri, 10am-9pm Sat & Sun; 🛜; 🚍4) Arrive off-peak (limited reservations are also available) at this chatty locals' favorite, a friendly, red-tabled restaurant serving French bistro classics and enticing Vietnamese specialties. You'll find everything from escargot to *steak frites* on the eclectic menu, but we recommend the deliciously brothy beef pho. On your way out, add a shiny little palmier pastry and a Vietnamese coffee to go.

Drinking & Nightlife

Vancouverites spend a lot of time drinking. And while BC has a tasty wine sector and is undergoing an artisanal distilling surge, it's the regional craft-beer scene that keeps many quaffers merry. For a night out with locally made libations as your side dish, join savvy city drinkers in the bars of Gastown, Main St and beyond.

★ Alibi Room
PUB

(Map p116; ☏604-623-3383; www.alibi.ca; 157 Alexander St, Gastown; ⊙5-11:30pm Mon-Thu, 5pm-12:30am Fri, 10am-12:30am Sat, 10am-11:30pm Sun; 🛜; 🚍4) Vancouver's best craft-beer tavern pours a near-legendary roster of 50-plus drafts, many from celebrated BC breweries including Four Winds, Yellow Dog and Dageraad. Hipsters and veteran-ale fans alike love the 'frat bat': choose your own four samples or ask to be surprised. Check the board for new guest casks and stick around for a gastropub dinner at one of the long communal tables.

Storm Crow Tavern
PUB

(☏604-566-9669; www.stormcrowtavern.com; 1305 Commercial Dr; ⊙11am-1am Mon-Sat, to midnight Sun; 🛜; 🚍20) Knowing the difference between Narnia and *Neverwhere* is not a prerequisite at this brilliant Commercial Dr nerd pub. But if you do, you'll certainly make new friends. With displays of *Doctor Who* figures and steampunk ray guns – plus TVs that might screen *Logan's Run* at any moment – dive into the craft beer and settle in for a fun evening.

Narrow Lounge
BAR

(Map p116; ☏778-737-5206; www.narrowlounge.com; 1898 Main St; ⊙5pm-1am Mon-Fri, to 2am Sat & Sun; 🚍3) Enter through the doorway on 3rd Ave – the red light tells you if it's open or not – then descend the graffiti-lined stairway into one of Vancouver's coolest small bars. Little bigger than a train carriage and lined with taxidermy and junk-shop pictures, it's an atmospheric nook where it always feels like 2am. In summer, try the hidden alfresco bar out back.

Grapes & Soda
WINE BAR

(☏604-336-2456; www.grapesandsoda.ca; 1541 W 6th Ave, South Granville; ⊙5:30-11pm Tue-Sat; 🚍10) A warm, small-table hangout that self-identifies as a 'natural wine bar' (there's a well-curated array of options from BC, Europe and beyond). This local favorite also serves excellent cocktails: from the countless bottles behind the small bar, they can seemingly concoct anything your taste buds desire, whether or not it's on the menu. Need help? Slide into a Scotch, ginger and walnut Cortejo.

★ Key Party
BAR

(www.keyparty.ca; 2303 Main St; ⊙5pm-1am Mon-Thu, to 2am Fri & Sat, to 1am Sun; 🚍3) Walk through the doorway of a fake storefront that looks like an accountancy office and you'll find yourself in a candlelit, boudoir-red speakeasy dominated by a dramatic mural of frolicking women and animals. Arrive early to avoid the queues, then fully explore the entertaining cocktail program (Kir Royale champagne jello shooters included).

Keefer Bar   COCKTAIL BAR
(Map p116; ☑604-688-1961; www.thekeeferbar.com; 135 Keefer St, Chinatown; ☺5pm-1am Sun-Thu, 5pm-2am Fri & Sat; ⓢStadium-Chinatown) This dark, narrow and atmospheric Chinatown bar has been claimed by local cocktail-loving coolsters since day one. Drop in for a full evening of liquid tasting and you'll have a blast. From perfectly prepared rosemary gimlets and tart blood moons to an excellent whiskey menu and some tasty tapas (we like the steam buns), it offers up a great night out.

★Brassneck Brewery   MICROBREWERY
(☑604-259-7686; www.brassneck.ca; 2148 Main St; ☺2-11pm Mon-Fri, noon-11pm Sat & Sun; ☐3) A beloved Vancouver microbrewery with a small, wood-lined tasting room. Peruse the ever-changing chalkboard of intriguing libations with names such as Pinky Promise, Silent Treatment and Faux Naive, or start with a delicious, highly accessible Passive Aggressive dry-hopped pale ale. It's often hard to find a seat here, so consider a weekday afternoon visit for a four-glass $8 tasting flight.

Shameful Tiki Room   BAR
(www.shamefultikiroom.com; 4362 Main St; ☺5pm-midnight Sun-Thu, to 1am Fri & Sat; ☐3) This windowless snug instantly transports you to a Polynesian beach. The lighting – including glowing puffer-fish lampshades – is permanently set to dusk and the walls are lined with tiki masks and rattan coverings under a straw-shrouded ceiling. But it's the drinks that rock; seriously well-crafted classics from zombies to blue Hawaiis to a four-person Volcano Bowl (don't forget to share it).

Guilt & Co   BAR
(Map p116; www.guiltandcompany.com; 1 Alexander St, Gastown; ☺7pm-late; ⓢWaterfront) This cavelike subterranean bar, beneath Gastown's brick-cobbled sidewalks, is also a brilliant venue to catch a tasty side dish of live music. Most shows are pay-what-you-can and can range from trumpet jazz to heartfelt singer-songwriters. Drinks-wise, there's a great cocktail list plus a small array of draft beers (and many more in cans and bottles).

Avoid weekends when there are often long queues.

Fountainhead Pub   GAY
(Map p116; ☑604-687-2222; www.fthdpub.com; 1025 Davie St, West End; ☺11am-midnight Mon-Thu & Sun, to 2am Fri & Sat; ☐6) The area's loudest and proudest gay neighborhood pub, this friendly joint is all about the patio, which spills onto Davie St like an overturned wine glass. Take part in the ongoing summer-evening pastime of ogling passersby or retreat to a quieter spot inside for a few lagers or a naughty cocktail: anyone for a Crispy Crotch or a Slippery Nipple?

☆ Entertainment

Live Music

★Commodore Ballroom   LIVE MUSIC
(Map p116; ☑604-739-4550; www.commodoreballroom.com; 868 Granville St, Downtown; tickets from $30; ☐10) Local bands know they've made it when they play Vancouver's best mid-sized venue, a restored art-deco ballroom that still has the city's bounciest dance floor – courtesy of tires placed under its floorboards. If you need a break from moshing, collapse at one of the tables lining the perimeter, catch your breath with a bottled brew and then plunge back in.

Biltmore Cabaret   LIVE MUSIC
(☑604-676-0541; www.biltmorecabaret.com; 2755 Prince Edward St; tickets from $15; ☐9) One of Vancouver's favorite alt venues, the intimate Biltmore is a firm fixture on the local indie scene. A low-ceilinged, good-vibe spot to mosh to local and touring musicians, it also has regular event nights; check the online calendar for upcoming happenings, including trivia nights and stand-up comedy shows.

Theater

★Arts Club Theatre Company   THEATER
(☑604-687-1644; www.artsclub.com; tickets from $29; ☺Sep-Jun) Vancouver's largest, most popular and most prolific theater company, the Arts Club stages shows at three venues around the city. A new artistic director has been appointed and is currently making her mark on the programming schedule.

★Bard on the Beach   PERFORMING ARTS
(Map p116; ☑604-739-0559; www.bardonthebeach.org; 1695 Whyte Ave, Vanier Park, Kitsilano; tickets from $24; ☺Jun-Sep; ♿; ☐2) Watching Shakespeare performed while the sun sets over the mountains beyond the tented main

stage is a Vancouver summertime highlight. There are usually three Shakespeare plays, plus one Bard-related work (*Rosencrantz and Guildenstern are Dead,* for example), to choose from during the season. Q&A talks are staged after some Tuesday performances; also opera, fireworks and wine-tasting special nights are held throughout the season.

Cinema

★ Cinematheque   CINEMA
(Map p116; ☑ 604-688-8202; www.thecinematheque.ca; 1131 Howe St, Downtown; tickets $12, double bills $16; ☐ 10) This beloved cinema operates like an ongoing film festival with a daily-changing program of movies. A $3 annual membership is required – organize it at the door – before you can skulk in the dark with other chin-stroking movie buffs who probably named their children (or pets) after Fellini and Bergman.

Vancity Theatre   CINEMA
(Map p116; ☑ 604-683-3456; www.viff.org; 1181 Seymour St, Downtown; tickets $13, double bills $20; ☐ 10) The state-of-the-art headquarters of the Vancouver International Film Festival (p121) screens a wide array of movies throughout the year in the kind of auditorium that cinephiles dream of: generous legroom, wide armrests and great sight lines from each of its 175 seats. It's a place where you can watch a four-hour subtitled epic about paint drying and still feel comfortable.

Sports

Vancouver Whitecaps   SOCCER
(Map p116; ☑ 604-669-9283; www.whitecapsfc.com; 777 Pacific Blvd, BC Place Stadium, Yaletown; tickets from $45; ⊙ Mar-Oct; ﹢; Ⓢ Stadium-Chinatown) Using BC Place Stadium (p114) as its home, Vancouver's professional soccer team plays in North America's top-tier Major League Soccer (MLS). Their on-field fortunes have ebbed and flowed since being promoted to the league in 2011, but they've been finding their feet (useful for soccer players) lately. Make time to buy a souvenir soccer shirt to impress everyone back home.

Vancouver Canucks   HOCKEY
(Map p116; ☑604-899-7400; www.nhl.com/canucks; 800 Griffiths Way, Rogers Arena, Downtown; tickets from $47; ⊙Sep-Apr; ⓈStadium-Chinatown) Recent years haven't been hugely successful for Vancouver's National Hockey League (NHL) team, which means it's sometimes easy to snag tickets to a game if you're simply visiting and want to see what 'ice hockey' (no

one calls it that here) is all about. You'll hear 'go Canucks, go!' booming from the seats and in local bars on game nights.

BC Lions   FOOTBALL
(Map p116; ☑ 604-589-7627; www.bclions.com; 777 Pacific Blvd, BC Place Stadium, Yaletown; tickets from $20; ⊙ Jun-Nov; ﹢; Ⓢ Stadium-Chinatown) Founded in 1954, the Lions are Vancouver's team in the Canadian Football League (CFL), which is arguably more exciting than its US counterpart, the NFL. The team has had some decent showings lately, but hasn't won the all-important Grey Cup since 2011. Tickets are easy to come by – unless the boys are laying into their arch enemies, the Calgary Stampeders.

🛍 Shopping

Vancouver's retail scene has developed dramatically in recent years. Hit Robson St's mainstream chains, then discover the hip, independent shops of Gastown, Main St and Commercial Dr. Granville Island is stuffed with artsy stores and studios, while South Granville and Kitsilano's 4th Ave serve up a wide range of tempting boutiques.

★Pacific Arts Market   ARTS & CRAFTS
(☑778-877-6449; www.pacificartsmarket.ca; 1448 W Broadway, South Granville; ⊙noon-5:30pm Tue & Wed, noon-7pm Thu & Fri, 11am-7pm Sat, 1-5pm Sun; ☐9) Head upstairs to this large, under-the-radar gallery space and you'll find a kaleidoscopic array of stands showcasing the work of 40+ Vancouver and BC artists. From paintings to jewelry and from fiber arts to handmade chocolate bars, it's the perfect spot to find authentic souvenirs to take back home. The artists change regularly and there's something for every budget here.

★Regional Assembly of Text   ARTS & CRAFTS
(☑ 604-877-2247; www.assemblyoftext.com; 3934 Main St; ⊙11am-6pm Mon-Sat, noon-5pm Sun; ☐3) This ironic antidote to the digital age lures ink-stained locals with its journals, handmade pencil boxes and T-shirts printed with typewriter motifs. Check out the tiny under-the-stairs gallery showcasing global zines and don't miss the monthly Letter Writing Club (7pm, first Thursday of every month), where you can hammer on vintage typewriters, crafting erudite missives to faraway loved ones.

Paper Hound   BOOKS
(Map p116; ☑ 604-428-1344; www.paperhound.ca; 344 W Pender St, Downtown; ⊙10am-7pm Sun-

Thu, to 8pm Fri & Sat; 🖳14) Proving the printed word is alive and kicking, this small but perfectly curated secondhand bookstore is a dog-eared favorite among locals. A perfect spot for browsing, you'll find tempting tomes (mostly used but some new) on everything from nature to poetry to chaos theory. Ask for recommendations; they really know their stuff here. Don't miss the bargain rack out front.

Red Cat Records MUSIC
(☑604-708-9422; www.redcat.ca; 4332 Main St; ⊙11am-7pm Mon-Thu, to 8pm Fri & Sat, to 6pm Sun; 🖳3) Arguably Vancouver's coolest record store and certainly the only one named after a much-missed cat... There's a brilliantly curated collection of new and used vinyl and CDs, and it's co-owned by musicians; ask them for tips on where to see great local acts such as Loscil and Nick Krgovich or peruse the huge list of shows in the window.

Kitsilano Farmers Market MARKET
(www.eatlocal.org; 2690 Larch St, Kitsilano Community Centre, Kitsilano; ⊙10am-2pm Sun May-Oct; 🖳9) 🍃 This seasonal farmers market is one of the city's most popular and is Kitsilano's best excuse to get out and hang with the locals. Arrive early for the best selection and you'll have the pick of freshly plucked local fruit and veg, such as sweet strawberries or spectacularly flavorful heirloom tomatoes. You'll likely never want to shop in a mainstream supermarket again.

Eastside Flea MARKET
(www.eastsideflea.com; 550 Malkin Ave, Eastside Studios; $3-5; ⊙11am-5pm Sat & Sun, once or twice a month; 🖳22) A size upgrade from its previous venue has delivered a cavernous market hall of hip arts and crafts-isans hawking everything from handmade chocolate bars to intricate jewelry and a humungous array of cool-ass vintage clothing. Give yourself plenty of time to hang out here; there's a pool table and retro arcade machines plus food trucks and a long bar serving local craft beer.

Bird on a Wire Creations ARTS & CRAFTS
(☑604-874-7415; www.birdonawirecreations.com; 2535 Main St; ⊙10am-6pm Mon-Sat, 11am-5pm Sun; 🖳3) Specializing in BC artisans, there's an eminently browsable and surprisingly diverse array of tasteful handmade goodies at this ever-friendly store. Your credit cards will start to sweat as you move among the cute jewelry, artsy T-shirts, ceramic tea tankards and fiber arts kids' toys (that adults want, too). But it's not just for show; there are regular craft classes here too.

⭐**Karen Cooper Gallery** ART
(Map p116; ☑604-559-5112; www.karencooper gallery.com; 1506 Duranleau St, Granville Island; ⊙10am-6pm, reduced hours in winter; 🖳50) You'll feel like you've entered a tranquil forest clearing when you open the door of this delightful nature-themed photography gallery. Cooper's striking work focuses on BC's jaw-dropping wild beauty, from coniferous trees to grizzly bears. Take your time and don't be surprised if you fall in love with a handsome image of a bald eagle perched on a mountain tree.

ℹ Information

MEDICAL SERVICES

Shoppers Drug Mart (☑604-669-2424; 1125 Davie St, West End; ⊙24hr; 🖳6) Pharmacy chain.

Ultima Medicentre (☑604-683-8138; 1055 Dunsmuir St, Downtown; ⊙8am-5pm Mon-Fri; ⑤Burrard) Full range of walk-in clinic medical services. Appointments not essential.

Vancouver General Hospital (☑604-875-4111; www.vch.ca; 855 W 12th Ave, Fairview; Ⓜ Broadway-City Hall)

MONEY

Vancouver Bullion & Currency Exchange (☑604-685-1008; www.vbce.ca; 800 W Pender St, Downtown; ⊙8:30am-5pm Mon-Fri; ⑤Granville) Aside from the banks, try Vancouver Bullion & Currency Exchange for currency exchange. It often has a wider range of currencies and competitive rates.

TOURIST INFORMATION

Tourism Vancouver Visitor Centre (Map p116; ☑604-683-2000; www.tourism vancouver.com; 200 Burrard St, Downtown; ⊙9am-5pm; ⑤Waterfront) A large repository of resources for visitors, with a staff of helpful advisers ready to assist in planning your trip in the city and around the area. Services and info available include free maps, visitor guides, accommodation and tour bookings, plus a host of glossy brochures on the city and the wider BC region.

ℹ Getting There & Away

AIR

Canada's second-busiest airport, **Vancouver International Airport** (YVR; Map p112; ☑604-207-7077; www.yvr.ca; 3211 Grant McConachie Way, Richmond; 🚐) is 13km south of downtown in the city of Richmond. There are two main terminals – international (including flights to the US) and domestic – just a short indoor stroll apart. A third (and much smaller) South Terminal is located a quick drive away; free shuttle-bus links are provided. This terminal services floatplanes, helicopters and smaller aircraft traveling to small communities in BC and beyond. In addition, short-hop **floatplane** (www.harbourair.com) and **heli-copter services** (www.helijet.com) to and from Vancouver Island and beyond also depart from the city's downtown waterfront, near Canada Place. Baggage carts are free (no deposit required) and there is also free wi-fi.

BOAT

BC Ferries (☑ 250-386-3431; www.bcferries. com) services arrive at Tsawwassen, an hour south of Vancouver, and at Horseshoe Bay, 30 minutes from downtown in West Vancouver. The company operates one of the world's largest ferry networks, including some spectacular routes throughout the province.

Main services to Tsawwassen arrive from Vancouver Island's Swartz Bay, near Victoria, and Duke Point, near Nanaimo. Services also arrive from the Southern Gulf Islands.

Services to Horseshoe Bay arrive from Nanaimo's Departure Bay. Services also arrive here from Bowen Island and from Langdale on the Sunshine Coast.

To depart Tsawwassen via transit, take bus 620 (adult/child $5.70/3.90) to Bridgeport Station in Richmond and transfer to the Canada Line. It takes about an hour to reach downtown.

From Horseshoe Bay to downtown, take bus 257 (adult/child $4.20/2.90), which is faster than bus 250. It takes about 40 minutes.

BUS

Intercity nontransit buses trundle into Vancouver's neon-signed **Pacific Central Station** (1150 Station St, Chinatown; Ⓢ Main St-Science World). Almost all Greyhound bus services (www.greyhound.com) into Vancouver have been cancelled in recent years; the only remaining route is from Seattle (from $20, four hours). **BC Connector** (www.bcconnector.com) operates bus services from Kelowna, Kamloops and Whistler as well as Victoria (via BC Ferries). Cross-border services from **Bolt Bus** (www.boltbus.com) and **Quick Shuttle** (www.quickcoach.com) also arrive here.

CAR & MOTORCYCLE

If you've rented a car in the US and are driving it into Canada, bring a copy of the rental agreement to save any possible hassles with border officials.

Gas is generally cheaper in the US, so be sure to fill up before you cross into Canada.

TRAIN

Pacific Central Station is the city's main terminus for long-distance trains from across Canada on **VIA Rail** (www.viarail.com), and from Seattle (just south of the border) and beyond on **Amtrak** (www.amtrak.com).

The Main St-Science World SkyTrain station is just across the street for connections to downtown and beyond.

There are car-rental desks in the station and cabs are also available just outside the building.

❶ Getting Around

TO/FROM THE AIRPORT

Taxi

➡ Follow the signs from inside the airport terminal to the cab stand just outside. A system of zone fares operates from YVR; your fare will typically be between $20 and $45 (most downtown Vancouver destinations cost $35). Confirm your fare with the driver before you set off.

➡ Rates do not include tips; 15% is the norm.

➡ Limo-car services are also available close to the main taxi stand. Expect to pay around $20 more for your ride to the city if you want to arrive in style.

Train

SkyTrain's 16-station **Canada Line** (see the route maps at www.translink.ca) operates a rapid-transit train service from the airport to downtown. Trains run every few minutes from early morning until after midnight and take around 25 minutes to reach downtown's Waterfront Station. The airport station is located just outside, between the domestic and international terminals. Follow the signs from inside either terminal and buy your ticket from the platform vending machines. These accept cash and credit cards – look for green-jacketed Canada Line staff if you're bleary-eyed and need assistance after your long-haul flight. Fares from the airport cost between $8 and $10.75, depending on your destination and the time of day.

BICYCLE

➡ Vancouver is a relatively good cycling city, with more than 300km of designated routes crisscrossing the region.

➡ Cyclists can take their bikes for free on SkyTrains, SeaBuses and transit buses, which are all now fitted with bike racks. Cyclists are required by law to wear helmets.

➡ There are dedicated bike lanes in the city, and locals and visitors alike can use **Mobi** (☑ 778-655-1800; www.mobibikes.ca), a public bike-share scheme.

➡ Download free cycle route maps from the TransLink website (www.translink.ca) or plan your route using https://vancouver.bikeroute planner.com.

➡ If you're traveling sans bike, you can also rent wheels from businesses around the city, especially on Denman St near Stanley Park – home of Vancouver's most popular scenic cycling route.

CAR & MOTORCYCLE

For sightseeing in the city, you'll be fine without a car (the city center is especially easy to explore on foot and transit routes are extensive). For visits that incorporate the wider region's mountains and communities, however, a vehicle makes life much simpler: the further you travel from downtown, the more limited your transit options become. There are car-rental desks in Pacific Central Station.

PUBLIC TRANSPORTATION

Bus

Vancouver's **TransLink** (www.translink.ca) bus network is extensive. All vehicles are equipped with bike racks and all are wheelchair accessible. Exact change (or more) is required; buses use fare machines and change is not given. Fares cost adult/child $3/1.95 and are valid for up to 90 minutes of transfer travel. While Vancouver's transit system covers three geographic fare zones, all bus trips are regarded as one-zone fares.

Bus services operate from early morning to after midnight in central areas. There is also an additional 12-route NightBus system that runs from 2am. Look for NightBus signs at designated stops.

Seabus

The iconic SeaBus shuttle is part of the TransLink transit system (regular transit fares apply) and it operates throughout the day, taking around 15 minutes to cross Burrard Inlet between Waterfront Station and North Vancouver's Lonsdale Quay. At Lonsdale you can then connect to buses servicing North Vancouver and West Vancouver; this is where you pick up bus 236 to both Capilano Suspension Bridge and Grouse Mountain.

SeaBus services leave from Waterfront Station between 6:16am and 1:22am, Monday to Saturday (8:16am to 11:16pm on Sunday). Vessels are wheelchair accessible and bike-friendly.

Tickets must be purchased from vending machines on either side of the route before boarding. The machines take credit and debit cards, and also give change up to $20 for cash transactions.

SkyTrain

TransLink's SkyTrain rapid-transit network is a great way to move around the region, especially beyond the city center. A new route to the University of BC campus is expected to open in the coming years.

Compass tickets for SkyTrain trips can be purchased from station vending machines (change is given; machines also accept debit and credit cards) prior to boarding.

SkyTrain journeys cost $3 to $5.75 (plus $5 more if you're traveling from the airport), depending on how far you are journeying.

TAXI

At the time of research, Vancouver was in the process of paving the way for ride-hailing schemes such as Uber and Lyft. Until then, try the following long-established taxi companies:

Black Top & Checker Cabs (☑604-731-1111; www.btccabs.ca; ☎)

Vancouver Taxi (☑604-871-1111; www.vancouvertaxi.cab)

Yellow Cab (☑604-681-1111; www.yellowcabonline.com; ☎)

LOWER MAINLAND

Stretching from coastal Horseshoe Bay as far inland as the verdant Fraser Valley, this region encompasses the towns and suburbs within an hour or two of downtown Vancouver, including those communities immediately adjoining the city that together are known as Metro Vancouver. Ideal for day trips, the area is striped with forested coastal parks, wildlife sanctuaries and an increasing number of wineries.

The snow-capped dome-shaped mountain dominating the skyline to the south is Mt Baker (3286m), an active volcano just across the border in the US.

Richmond & Steveston

The region's modern-day Chinatown is easy to reach via Canada Line SkyTrain from Vancouver, making for an easy half-day excursion. There are two distinctly different experiences to be had here. Richmond proper is a utilitarian grid of Asian shopping malls, car parks and (with a bit of delving) some of the best Asian restaurants outside Asia. A little to the south, waterfront Steveston village is second only to Fort Langley in its historical significance, harboring two museums, an afternoon's worth of blustery dyke walks and legendary fish-and-chips.

◉ Sights

★**Richmond Night Market**   MARKET
(Map p112; ☑604-244-8448; www.richmondnightmarket.com; 8351 River Rd, Richmond; adult/child $5/free; ☉7pm-midnight Fri-Sun mid-May–mid-Oct; ⓢBridgeport) Arguably Richmond's biggest lure is this atmospheric, always

busy, Asian-flavored night market that has grown from humble beginnings in 2000 to become the largest night market in North America. Beyond the predictable (but fun) trinket stalls and fairground attractions, the complex is best known for its abundance of steam-billowing food stalls that ply everything from *poke* bowls to fried octopus. The live entertainment is equally diverse with punk rock alternating with martial-arts displays.

Gulf of Georgia Cannery
MUSEUM

(Map p112; ☑604-664-9009; www.gulfofgeorgia cannery.org; 12138 4th Ave, Steventon; adult/child $12/free; ☺10am-5pm; 🚻; 🚌401, 🚇Richmond-Brighouse) British Columbia's best 'industrial museum' illuminates the sights and sounds of the region's bygone era of labor-intensive fish processing. Most of the machinery remains and there's an evocative focus on the people who used to work here; you'll hear recorded testimonies from old employees percolating through the air like ghosts, bringing to life the days they spent immersed in entrails as thousands of cans rolled down the production line. Take one of the excellent, free, volunteer-led tours for the full story.

Britannia Shipyard
MUSEUM

(☑640-718-8038; www.britanniashipyard.ca; 5180 Westwater Dr, Steventon; ☺10am-5pm, from noon Oct-Apr; 🚌402, 🚇Richmond-Brighouse) **FREE** A riverfront complex of historic sheds housing dusty tools, boats and reminders of the region's maritime past, this is one of the most evocative, fancy-free historic sites in the region. Check out the preserved Murakami House, where a large Japanese family lived before being unceremoniously interned during the war. Interpretive boards tell the story; well-versed volunteers fill in the gaps.

Iona Beach Regional Park
PARK

(Map p112; ☑604-224-5739; 900 Ferguson Rd, Richmond; ☺dawn-dusk) This long, slender sand-and-grass isthmus at the mouth of the Fraser River, which can be reached by car or bike, is one of the region's best birding destinations. Look out for migrating avian critters (snow geese included) plus 'locals' such as kinglets, hummingbirds, bald eagles and many more. Turtles also call this park home and you'll have great shoreline views to point your camera at, especially from the 4km-long Iona Jetty.

Eating

President Plaza Food Court
FOOD HALL **$**

(Map p112; ☑604-270-8677; 8181 Cambie Rd, Richmond; mains $5-8; ☺10am-7pm; 🚇Aberdeen) Richmond's bustling shopping-mall food courts echo the hawker stands found in many Asian cities, and one of the most authentic is this upstairs hidden gem that's lined with independent vendors. Order a few plates to share and you'll soon be diving into savory pancakes, silken-tofu soup and chewy Beijing donut bread.

Shibuyatei
RAMEN **$**

(Map p112; ☑778-297-1777; 2971 Sexsmith Rd, Richmond; mains $7-14; ☺11:30am-2pm & 5-9pm Thu-Tue; 🚇Bridgeport) Inauspiciously located next to a car wash a couple of long-jumps from Bridgeport station, this unadorned hole-in-the-wall serves sushi but it's really all about great ramen bowls (with no MSG) and Japanese curries, served with chicken or pork *katsu* (deep-fried). It's a one-man operation so avoid peak times if you don't want to wait too long.

Pajo's
SEAFOOD **$**

(Map p112; ☑604-272-1588; www.pajos.com; The Wharf, Steventon; mains $12-20; ☺11am-8pm, reduced hours off-season; 🚌401, 🚇Richmond-Brighouse) This weather-dependent floating fish shack nestled amid the fishing boats offers a three-way choice of salmon, cod and halibut to have with your chips. They also offer burgers, but seriously you didn't come here for that! If it's raining, try Dave's, a bricks-and-mortar place in Moncton St around the corner.

★ Shanghai River Restaurant
CHINESE **$$**

(Map p112; ☑604-233-8885; www.shanghai riverrestaurant.com; 7381 Westminster Hwy, Richmond; mains $10-22; ☺11am-3pm & 5:30-10pm; 🚇Richmond-Brighouse) Dining at Shanghai River is like attending a jam-packed Asian-style banquet brimming with an array of food. Fried eel arrive in hot stone bowls, whole fish adorn overstuffed plates, while smaller dishes of crispy pot stickers, prawns with candied walnuts, Szechuan smoked duck and soup dumplings fly by.

ℹ Information

Tourism Richmond Visitor Centre (Map p112; ☑604-271-8280; www.tourismrichmond.com; 3811 Moncton St, Steventon; ☺9:30am-6pm Jul & Aug, 9:30am-5pm Mon-Sat, noon-4pm Sun Sep-Jun; 🚌401, 🚇Richmond-Brighouse)

Super-helpful spot inside old Steveston post office with a small affiliated museum.

ℹ Getting There & Away

TransLink's (www.translink.ca) Canada Line SkyTrains trundle in from Vancouver every few minutes throughout the day. The service splits at Bridgeport station, with some trains heading to the airport and others winding further into Richmond; make sure you're on the right one. Transit buses (including those to Steveston) connect to the Canada Line at Bridgeport and other stations.

New Westminster

POP 76,000

A short SkyTrain ride from downtown Vancouver, 'New West' is one of BC's most historic communities – in theory, at least. It was briefly the capital of the new Colony of British Columbia in 1859. Its star faded during much of the last century, but recent years have seen attempts at revival. A small but succinct museum catalogs its brief moment in the limelight while (in the same building) an inventive media gallery deftly snaps you back to the 21st century.

◉ Sights

★ New Media Gallery
GALLERY
(Map p112; ☏604-875-1865; www.newmediagallery.ca; 777 Columbia St, Anvil Centre; ⊙10am-5pm Tue-Sun, to 8pm Thu; ⑤New Westminster) FREE With the right curators and a foresighted arts community, it's amazing what you can do with 200 sq meters of space. This small gallery in New West's super-modern Anvil Centre puts together what are, arguably, the most cutting-edge exhibitions on the Lower Mainland. The bent is unashamedly modern – we're talking 21st-century art that lights up, talks back and interacts with the observer rather than traditional two-dimensional paintings. All visitors receive a free tour explaining more about what they're seeing.

Westminster Pier Park
PARK
(Map p112; ☏604-521-3711; www.newwestcity.ca/parks-and-recreation/parks; 1 Sixth St; ⑤Columbia) Sandwiched between railway tracks and the mighty Fraser River, this linear boardwalk park is an excellent New West addition. Join the locals for a breezy promenade stroll and check out the public art, water-facing seats (heron-sightings are common) and stepped wall of screen-printed photos detailing the city's past. There's also a seasonal concession stand serving ice-cream and more.

New Westminster Museum & Archives
MUSEUM
(Map p112; ☏604-527-4640; www.anvilcentre.com; 777 Columbia St, Anvil Centre; ⊙10am-5pm, to 8pm Thu; ⑤New Westminster) FREE On the 3rd floor of the swish Anvil Centre, this well-presented small museum illuminates New West's tumultuous history, from its First Nations origins and later pioneer era to its shiny postwar boom and slow economic decline. Look for the mailbox-red stagecoach that carried VIPs around the region and make time to peruse the evocative, wall-mounted photos of the yesteryear city.

✕ Eating

Re-Up BBQ
BARBECUE $
(Map p112; ☏604-553-3997; www.reupbbq.com; 810 Quayside Dr, River Market; mains $9-14; ⊙10am-7pm; ⑤New Westminster) A one-time pioneer of the Vancouver food-truck scene now touring its own permanent eatery, this is the place to sink your choppers into heaping servings of ribs, brisket and pulled pork. Arrive hungry and save room for housemade 'slaw and beans plus a refreshing southern sweet tea.

★ El Santo
MEXICAN $$
(Map p112; ☏604-553-1849; www.elsanto.ca; 680 Columbia St; mains $16-30; ⊙11:30am-10pm, to

---

WORTH A TRIP

WHERE BC BEGAN

Located 40km east of Vancouver, the historic village of Fort Langley is where BC's colonial story began. The original **fort** (☏604-513-4777; www.parkscanada.gc.ca/fortlangley; adult/child $8/4; ⊙10am-5pm; ⸕; ⬚562), built in 1827 and now a National Historic Site, predated the founding of Vancouver by well over half a century, and it was from here that, in 1858, James Douglas announced the province's creation. The fort is well worth a visit: with its preserved buildings and costumer interpreters, it's a popular attraction for families. Today, Fort Langley is a pretty little village within the wider Langley township, but with its tree-lined avenues and boutique shops it harbors its own distinct character and atmosphere. It's a rewarding day or half-day trip from central Vancouver.

11pm Fri & Sat; ⑤ New Wesminster) Way more sophisticated than your typical nachos 'n' burritos Mexican restaurant, El Santo is the mark of a trend in New West's culinary renaissance. Presenting menu items in Spanish with English translations, it offers a minimalist take on Latino favorites using BC ingredients – such as Fraser valley chicken with a Mexican mole rub and BC perch with a mezcal-chipotle glaze.

Bruncheria Cafe BREAKFAST **$$**
(Map p112; ☑604-544-0018; 656 Columbia St; mains $15-22; ☺7:30am-3:30pm; 📶📇; ⑤ New Westminster) Offering healthy artisan breakfasts in a comfy interior encased in one of New West's older heritage buildings. The cafe is a spirited new venture and includes some more unusual early morning offerings such as yogurt, granola and fruit served in a coconut shell.

ℹ Information

Tourism New Westminster (Map p112; ☑604-526-1905; www.tourismnewwest
minster.com; 777 Columbia St, Anvil Centre; ☺10am-5pm Mon-Sat, to 4pm Oct-May)

ℹ Getting There & Away

Frequent TransLink (www.translink.ca) SkyTrain services from downtown Vancouver take about 25 minutes to whisk you to New West. It's a two-zone fare ($4.20).

BOWEN ISLAND

POP 3600

One of the best days out you can have from Vancouver – it's just a 20-minute boat hop from Horseshoe Bay, but it feels a million miles from downtown – Bowen is like British Columbia in miniature. Time slows down a notch here in yoga retreats, boutique apothecaries and the handsome heritage buildings of the cozy harbor, appropriately called Snug Cove.

Bowen Island Sea Kayaking KAYAKING
(☑604-947-9266; www.bowenislandkayaking.com; Bowen Island Marina, Snug Cove; rentals/tours from $52/$82; ☺10am-6pm Apr-Oct) Handily tucked along the boardwalk jetty just steps from the ferry dock, this congenial operation is a one-stop shop if you're looking to kayak or paddleboard around the area. Rentals are popular, of course, but they also offer guided tours – we love the all-day Pasley Island tour ($185).

Bowen Island Tours TOURS
(☑604-812-5041; www.bowenislandtours.com; adult/child from $25/12) A series of tour options run by a friendly Bowen guide. The best of the bunch is the history-themed weave that regales participants with stories of the old steamship resort days. Your friendly guide also has plenty of suggestions for the rest of your visit on Bowen.

Doc Morgan's Restaurant & Pub BISTRO **$$**
(☑604-947-0808; www.docmorgans.ca; 437 Bowen Island Trunk Rd; mains $16-23; ☺11:30am-9pm, to 10pm Sat & Sun) Doc's wood-paneled yesteryear interior is an ideal rainy day hangout, while the outdoor deck is perfect for languid sunny day-dining perusing the maritime action in Snug Cove. Service is exemplary, delivering a typical pub menu with a few less predictable flourishes. Start with a healthy salad and then tear up the diet-sheet for sticky toffee pudding.

ℹ Information

Visitors Center (☑604-200-2399; www.tourism
bowenisland.com; 432 Cardena Rd; ☺9am-4pm mid-May–Sep) Drop into the visitors center, just steps from the ferry dock, for insider tips.

ℹ Getting There & Away

Take a TransLink (www.translink.ca) transit bus from downtown Vancouver – the 257 express bus is best – and you'll be at the Horseshoe Bay BC Ferries (www.bcferries.com) terminal in around 40 minutes. Ferry services depart from here to Bowen Island's Snug Cove throughout the day (adult/child/car $11/5/30, 20 minutes).

SEA TO SKY HIGHWAY

Otherwise known as Hwy 99, this unforgettably spectacular cliffside roadway links a string of communities between West Vancouver and Lillooet and is the main route to Squamish and Whistler from Metro Vancouver. If you can take your eyes off the collage of mountains and sea, the winding road has several worthwhile stops, especially if you're in the market for hiking, climbing, mining history or – at the opposite end of the spectrum – imbibing small-batch alcoholic beverages.

Squamish & Around

Watch out Whistler, Squamish is awakening. A one-time coffee stop on the way to

BC's famous skiing capital, this small former logging town has become a destination in its own right in the last 10 years. Climbers from around the world converge on the town to tackle the intimidating rock-walls of the Chief, while kitesurfers brave the stiff winds of Howe Sound, and hikers enjoy the steep network of paths that stretch between Shannon Falls and the top of the cable-car station.

Beware: 30-minute coffee stops can easily morph into seven-day adventure frenzies.

◉ Sights

★ Sea to Sky Gondola   CABLE CAR
(☑604-892-2551; www.seatoskygondola.com; 36800 Hwy 99, Squamish; adult/child $42/14; ⊙10am-6pm May-Oct, reduced hours Nov-Apr) On a warm summer's evening, with a 7.5km ascent under your belt and a pint of craft beer on the table in front of you, there are few better places in Canada than the top station of Squamish's spectacular gondola. The glorious glass-and-wood Summit Lodge is a triumph of environmentally congruous Northwest architecture while the views – Howe Sound on one side and the 100m-long Sky Pilot suspension bridge on the other – are unforgettable.

For an active day out, hike up from Shannon Falls on the Sea to Summit Trail and take the gondola down afterwards (down-only gondola tickets cost $15). There is a whole network of additional trails heading out from the Summit Lodge – some easy, others forging further up the mountain. You can also enjoy the wobbly suspension bridge, several viewing platforms and the lodge restaurant with its alfresco deck where the hills are alive with the sound of (live) music in the summer.

★ Garibaldi Provincial Park   PARK
(www.env.gov.bc.ca/bcparks/explore/parkpgs/garibaldi; Hwy 99) This 1950-sq-km park is justly renowned for hiking trails colored by diverse flora, abundant wildlife and panoramic vistas. Summer hikers seem magnetically drawn here but the trails also double as cross-country ski routes in winter. There are five main trail areas – directions to each are marked by the blue-and-white signs you'll see off Hwy 99. Among the park's most popular trails, the Cheakamus Lake hike (3km) is relatively easy, with minimal elevation.

The Elfin Lakes trail (11km) is a lovely, relatively easy day hike. The Garibaldi Lake hike (9km) is an outstanding introduction to 'Beautiful BC' wilderness, fusing scenic alpine meadows and breathtaking mountain vistas.

Britannia Mine Museum   MUSEUM
(☑604-896-2260; www.britanniaminemuseum.ca; Hwy 99, Britannia Beach; adult/child $30/19; ⊙9am-5pm; ⊕) Once the British Empire's largest copper mine, this giant and superbly restored industrial museum is just 10 minutes before Squamish on Hwy 99. The rattling underground train tour is highly recommended (included with entry) and there are plenty of kid-friendly exhibits, including hands-on gold panning. You'll never moan about your boss again as you discover just how grim it was to work a *real* job back in the day. Save time for the gift shop and a sparkly pyrite souvenir.

Shannon Falls Provincial Park   WATERFALL
(www.bcparks.ca; Hwy 99, Squamish) About 4km before you reach Squamish, you'll hear the pounding waters of Shannon Falls Provincial Park. Pull into the parking lot and stroll the short trail to BC's third-highest waterfall, where water cascades down a 335m drop. A few picnic tables make this a lovely spot for an alfresco lunch.

Stawamus Chief
Provincial Park   PARK
(www.bcparks.ca; Hwy 99, Squamish) On the way into Squamish from Vancouver, you'll see a sheer, 652m-high granite rock face looming ahead. Attracting hardy climbers the world over, it's called the 'Chief' and it's the highlight of Stawamus Chief Provincial Park. You don't have to gear up to experience the summit's vistas: there are hiking routes up the back for anyone who wants to have a go. Consider Squamish Rock Guides (p37) for climbing assistance or lessons.

West Coast Railway
Heritage Park   MUSEUM
(☑604-898-9336; www.wcra.org; 39645 Government Rd, Squamish; adult/child $25/15; ⊙10am-3pm; ⊕) Train nuts should continue just past central Squamish to this large, mostly alfresco museum that's lined with clapboard buildings and several historic locomotives and carriages – including BC's legendary Royal Hudson steam engine, housed in the purpose-built Roundhouse. There's also an old walk-through mail train and an erstwhile stationmaster's house. Check ahead for kid-friendly special events, particularly during Christmas and school holidays.

BRITISH COLUMBIA SQUAMISH & AROUND

BRITISH COLUMBIA SQUAMISH & AROUND

HIKING AROUND SQUAMISH

The installation of the Sea to Sky gondola in 2014 massively improved Squamish's hiking potential. A new trail now winds its way up to the spectacular summit station perched 885m above Howe Sound from where several other trails crisscross above the treeline. Meanwhile, glowering to the north sits the moodily magnificent Stawamus Chief.

🏃 Activities

★ Sea to Sky Trail   HIKING

A 7.5km trail that climbs from Shannon Falls to the top of the Sea to Sky Gondola (p139), this relatively new path is rated 'intermediate' save for a couple of steeper sections where cables and ropes are provided for assistance. Pack plenty of water and snacks for the ascent and enjoy a drink and canteen-style meal at the summit lodge.

Stawamus Chief Trail   HIKING

A short, but steep climb up the side of Squamish's sentinel mountain so beloved by rock climbers. The path provides access to all three of the Chief's summits (between 1.3km and 3.4km one-way) and is rated 'hard' due to its unrelenting steepness and scrambling sections. Hand supports are provided near the top.

Sea to Sky Air   TOURS

(☑ 604-898-1975; www.seatoskyair.ca; Squamish Airport; from $96; ⊙ 9am-5pm Apr-Sep, 9am-4pm Wed-Sun Oct-Mar) Running a series of small airplane tours from the town's forest-fringed little airport, the friendly folk here will soon have you snapping photos over snow-peaked valleys and glittering glacier-fed lakes. But the best option is the Introductory Flight Experience ($249), where you'll start with a runway plane inspection, shimmy up into the sky alongside the pilot and then take the controls.

Squamish Spit   KITESURFING

(www.squamishwindsports.com; per day $20) A popular kiteboarding (and windsurfing) hot spot between May and October. The Squamish Windsports Society manages the spit's launching and landing facility; see their website for weather and water conditions as well as information about access to the spit.

🛏 Sleeping & Eating

Alice Lake Provincial Park   CAMPGROUND $

(www.discovercamping.ca; Hwy 99, Brackendale; campsites $43) This large, family-friendly campground, 13km north of Squamish, has more than 100 sites. There are two shower buildings with flush toilets, and campers often indulge in swimming, hiking and biking (rentals available). Consider an interpretive ranger tour through the woods (July and August only). Reserve far ahead; this is one of BC's most popular campgrounds.

Sunwolf   CABIN $$

(☑ 604-898-1537; www.sunwolf.net; 70002 Squamish Valley Rd, Brackendale; cabin from $130; ⊛🐾) This idyllic place – a former logging resort – has a clutch of 12 comfortable, well-maintained cabins along a forested riverbank. The owners also run year-round rafting and eagle-viewing trips (adult/child $119/79).

The well-loved on-site cafe, Fergie's has partially reopened since sustaining fire damage. It traditionally serves potent coffee and fortifying breakfasts.

The resort is near Brackendale, 14km north of Squamish.

Howe Sound Inn   INN $$

(☑ 604-892-2603; www.howesoundinn.com; 37801 Cleveland Ave, Squamish; d $145; 🐾) Quality rustic is the approach at this comfortable inn, where the rooms are warm and inviting with plenty of wooden furnishings. Recover from your climbing escapades in the property's popular sauna – or just head to the downstairs **brewpub** (☑ 778-654-3358; mains $15-26; ⊙ 11am-midnight, to 1am Fri, from 8am Sat & Sun), which serves some of BC's best housemade beers. Inn guests can request free brewery tours.

Even if you're not staying, it's worth stopping in at the restaurant here for great pub grub with a gourmet twist.

Galileo Coffee Company   CAFE $

(☑ 604-896-0272; www.galileocoffee.com; 173 Hwy 99, Britannia Beach; baked goods from $4; ⊙ 6am-2pm, from 7am Sat & Sun; 🐾) Lovable small-batch coffee roaster that's commandeered a clapboard house next to Hwy 99 that once belonged to the Britannia Mine manager. The sweet snacks are everyone's favorite carb-load and the coffee is essential rocket fuel to help you up the Chief.

Backcountry Brewing   BREWERY

(☑ 604-567-2739; www.backcountrybrewing.com; 405/1201 Commercial Way, Squamsih; ⊙ noon-

11pm, to midnight Fri, from 11am Sat & Sun) One of the newest micro-businesses to populate the commercial district north of Squamish, this brewery is equipped with a large tasting room designed (in their own words) with the feel of a 1970s ski cabin. There's also a full-blown kitchen dispatching that finest of beer accompaniments, pizza ($15 to $20). Beer-wise, you'd be unwise to miss the punchy Widowmaker IPA.

ℹ Information

Squamish Adventure Centre (☏ 604-815-5084; www.explioresquamish.com; 38551 Loggers Lane, Squamish; ⊙ 8am-6pm mid-May–mid-Sep, reduced hours rest of year; ☎) One of several astoundingly good visitor centers in southern BC, this gracefully curvaceous building beside Hwy 99 is part museum, part cafe and part information portal. You can spend half a morning here, perusing maps, browsing the outdoor museum or sipping coffee inside.

ℹ Getting There & Away

Skylynx (www.yvrskylynx.com) buses connect with Vancouver airport ($55, two hours, eight daily)

The comfortable **Squamish Connector** (☏ 604-802-2119; www.squamishconnector.com) minibus shuttle heads north to Whistler ($25, one hour) and south to Vancouver ($25, one hour) twice daily. It stops outside the Squamish Adventure Centre.

WHISTLER

POP 11,800

Named for the furry marmots that populate the area and whistle like deflating balloons, this gabled alpine village and 2010 Olympics venue is one of the world's largest, best-equipped and most popular ski resorts. Colonizing two mountains – Whistler and Blackcomb – and lying a mere 90 minutes north of Vancouver, the Village, which dates from the late 1970s, is a poster child for attractive design with nary an ugly building or piece of litter to pierce the natural beauty. Skiing may be Whistler's raison d'être, but these days summer visitors with their BMXs and SUPs outnumber their ski-season equivalents. Adding more diversity, the resort has recently developed an art scene worthy of a small European city. The caveat? Whistler is busy (2.3 million visitors a year) and expensive. For a quieter, more economical experi-ence, be selective with your dates and don't follow the herd.

◉ Sights

★ **Audain Art Museum** · · · · · · · · · · · GALLERY
(☏ 604-962-0413; www.audainartmuseum.com; 4350 Blackcomb Way; adult/child $18/free; ⊙ 10am-5pm, to 9pm Fri, closed Tue) The opening of the Audain in 2016 elevated Whistler from 'world-class ski resort' to 'world-class ski resort with serious art credentials'. With two-dozen works by iconic painter Emily Carr, a priceless collection of indigenous masks, and sparkling photoconceptualist images by Jeff Wall, Rodney Graham et al, this is no rainy-day filler. BC artists take center stage. Alongside Carr you'll spot material from the 'Group of Seven' modernists, plus works by contemporary First Nations artists including Robert Davidson.

Peak 2 Peak Gondola · · · · · · · · · · CABLE CAR
(☏ 604-967-8950; www.whistlerblackcomb.com/discover/360-experience; 4545 Blackcomb Way; adult/child $63/32; ⊙ 10am-5pm) Built to link the area's two main mountaintops, the world's second-longest free-span gondola eases passengers along a lofty and ethereally peaceful 4.4km ride that takes around 11 minutes to complete. En route, you can gaze down on forest, crags, skiers and bears – especially if you snag one of the two glass-bottomed cars. The gondola's completion in 2008 effectively joined Whistler and Blackcomb into one giant ski area, making it one of the world's largest.

Squamish Lil'wat Cultural Centre · · · · MUSEUM
(☏ 604-964-0990; www.slcc.ca; 4584 Blackcomb Way; adult/child $18/5; ⊙ 10am-5pm daily Apr-Oct, Tue-Sun Nov-Mar) This handsome, wood-beamed facility showcases two quite different First Nations groups – the Lil'wat and the Squamish – who have inhabited this region for eons. Take a tour for the vital context behind the museumlike exhibits and keep your eyes open for on-site artist demonstrations during the summer, when there are also Tuesday-night barbecue dinners. There's also an on-site cafe serving bannock tacos.

Whistler Museum & Archives · · · · · · MUSEUM
(☏ 604-932-2019; www.whistlermuseum.org; 4333 Main St; suggested donation $5; ⊙ 11am-5pm, to 9pm Thu) Tucked into an anonymous green shed behind the library building, this great little museum traces Whistler's development

Whistler

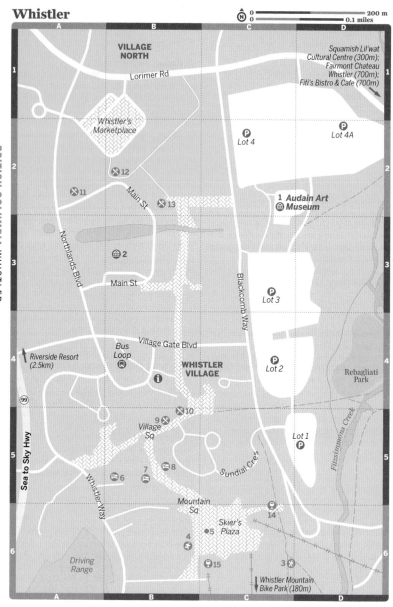

0   200 m
0   0.1 miles

VILLAGE NORTH

Squamish Lil'wat
Cultural Centre (300m);
Fairmont Chateau
Whistler (700m);
Fifi's Bistro & Cafe (700m)

Lorimer Rd

Whistler's
Marketplace

P
Lot 4

P
Lot 4A

12

11

Main St

13

1 **Audain Art
Museum**

2

Main St

Blackcomb Way

P
Lot 3

Village Gate Blvd

Bus
Loop

**WHISTLER
VILLAGE**

P
Lot 2

Rebagliati
Park

Riverside Resort
(2.5km)

99

10

9

Village
Sq

Sundial Cres

Lot 1
P

Fitzsimmons Creek

7

8

6

Mountain
Sq

Skier's
Plaza

14

4

5

15

3

Driving
Range

Whistler Mountain
Bike Park (180m)

Sea to Sky Hwy

Northlands Blvd

Whistler Way

BRITISH COLUMBIA WHISTLER

from 1970s hippy hangout to 21st-century resort. The story is as compelling as it is short, speckled with interesting exhibits such as the original 1965 ski-lift gondola and a 2010 Olympic torch. Don't leave without digesting the story of the infamous 1973 'Toad Hall' photo.

Cloudraker Skybridge   BRIDGE
The newest attraction on Whistler Mountain is this 130m-long suspension bridge with a see-through base that connects the top of Whistler Peak with the Raven's Eye viewing platform on the West Ridge. Opened in summer 2018, the bridge is accessed by

Whistler

hiking downhill for 15 minutes from the Roundhouse Lodge and then taking the Peak Empress chairlift to the top of Whistler Mountain. If you are a vertigo sufferer, bear in mind that both chairlift and suspension bridge are mildly exposed.

Entrance is included with the Peak 2 Peak Gondola (p141) ticket.

⚡ Activities

★ **Whistler-Blackcomb** SNOW SPORTS
(📞604-967-8950; www.whistlerblackcomb.com; day pass adult/child $178/89) Comprising 37 lifts and crisscrossed with over 200 runs, the Whistler-Blackcomb sister mountains, physically linked by the resort's mammoth 4.4km Peak 2 Peak Gondola (p141) are, indisputably, one of the largest and best ski areas in North America. The variety and quality of the facilities here is staggering and regular upgrades have maintained the resort's Olympian edge.

More than half the resort's runs are aimed at intermediate-level skiers, and the season typically runs from late November to April on Whistler and November to June on Blackcomb – December to February is the peak for both.

You can beat the crowds with an early-morning Fresh Tracks ticket ($23.95), available in advance at the Whistler Village gondola. Coupled with your regular lift ticket, it gets you an extra hour on the slopes (boarding from 7:15pm) and the ticket includes a buffet breakfast at the Roundhouse Lodge up top.

Snowboarders should also check out the freestyle terrain parks, mostly located on Blackcomb, including the Snow Cross and the Big Easy Terrain Garden. There's also the popular Habitat Terrain Park on Whistler.

Whistler Olympic Park SNOW SPORTS
(📞604-964-0060; www.whistlersportlegacies.com; 5 Callaghan Valley Rd; trail pass skiing/snowshoeing $28/17; ⊙9am-4:30pm mid-Dec–late Mar) Just 25km southwest of the village via Hwy 99, the pristine, snow-swathed Callaghan Valley hosted several 2010 Olympic Nordic events. There are essentially two cross-country skiing areas here: the Whistler Olympic Park (where you can sample the Nordic and biathlon courses) and Ski Callaghan, which predates it. One pass covers both.

A modern, rarely overcrowded day lodge at the end of the road rents skis and snowshoes and has an economical cafe. There are 90km of trails leading out from the lodge plus around 40km of snowshoe trails. Several are pet-friendly. For an altogether more unique experience, it is possible to partake in biathlon lessons ($99, weekends only) at the nearby Olympic shooting range and race circuit.

A shuttle bus from Whistler Village ($10 round-trip) serves the park with one drop-off and two pickups per day in season. Book via the website.

**Whistler Mountain
Bike Park** MOUNTAIN BIKING
(📞604-967-8950; http://bike.whistlerblackcomb. com; half-day lift ticket adult/child $59/32; ⊙May-Oct) Colonizing the melted ski slopes in summer and accessed via lifts at the village's south end, this park offers barreling downhill runs and an orgy of jumps and bridges twisting through well-maintained forested trails. Luckily, you don't have to be a bike courier to stand the knee-buckling pace: easier routes are marked in green, while blue intermediate trails and black-diamond advanced paths are also offered. BYO bike, or hire from **Summit Sport** (📞604-932-9225;

BRITISH COLUMBIA WHISTLER

www.summitsport.com; 4293 Mountain Sq; downhill/trail per day $150/80; ⊙ 9am-8:30pm).

Outside the park area, regional trails include Comfortably Numb (a tough 26km with steep climbs and bridges), A River Runs Through It (suitable for all skill levels, it has teeter-totters and log obstacles) and the gentle Valley Trail (an easy 14km loop that encircles the village and its lake, meadow and mountain chateau surroundings, and is recommended for first-timers).

Singing Pass Trail
HIKING

Your best bet for a challenging multi-terrain hike departing directly from Whistler village is the 11.5km (one-way) Singing Pass trail which takes you up above the tree line and subsequently offers a couple of continuation hikes for those with energy to burn.

One extension carries on to beautiful Russet Lake (an extra 3km one-way), another undulates over the so-called 'musical bumps' to the Roundhouse Lodge (21km from the village) close to the top of Whistler Mountain. From here you can catch the gondola back down.

Ziptrek Ecotours
ADVENTURE SPORTS

(☑ 604-935-0001; www.ziptrek.com; 4280 Mountain Sq, Carleton Lodge; adult/child from $119/99; 🚶) Not content with having one of the world's longest gondolas, Whistler opened North America's longest zip line in 2016, the super-scary Sasquatch (open June to September) – a 2.2km-long catapult between Whistler and Blackcomb Mountains where it's possible to attain speeds of up to 100km/h. They also have several less dramatic zip lines, some aimed at kids, plus a great canopy walking tour ($49).

Wedge Rafting
RAFTING

(☑ 604-932-7171; www.wedgerafting.com; 4293 Mountain Sq; tours adult/child from $119/79; 🚶) A great way to wet your pants and still have fun, Wedge offers three white-water rafting tours around the region, including the kid-friendly Cheakamus River excursion.

🎊 Festivals & Events

Winterpride
LGBT

(www.whistlerpride.com; ⊙ Jan) A week of gay-friendly snow action and late-night partying.

World Ski & Snowboard Festival
SPORTS

(www.wssf.com; ⊙ Apr) A multi-day showcase of pro ski and snowboard competitions, plus partying.

Crankworx
SPORTS

(www.crankworx.com; ⊙ Aug) An adrenaline-filled celebration of bike stunts, speed contests and mud-splattered shenanigans.

Cornucopia
FOOD & DRINK

(www.whistlercornucopia.com; ⊙ Nov) Bacchanalian food and wine fest crammed with parties.

🛏 Sleeping

Accommodation in Whistler is expensive but of a high quality (even the HI hostel is plush). Most hotels offer deluxe rooms with kitchenettes, fireplaces and balconies. Many are also equipped with sofa beds and hot tubs and are classified as studios or suites. The bigger hotels have gyms, spas, outdoor pools and hot tubs. Parking, if available, costs up to $40 extra. Breakfast is seldom included in room rates.

HI Whistler Hostel
HOSTEL $

(☑ 604-962-0025; www.hihostels.ca/whistler; 1035 Legacy Way; dm/r $43/120; @ 🛜) Built as athletes' accommodation for the 2010 Winter Olympics, this sparkling hostel is 7km south of the village, near Function Junction. Transit buses to/from town stop right outside. Book ahead for private rooms (with private baths and TVs) or save by staying in a small dorm. Eschewing the sometimes institutionalized HI hostel feel, this one has IKEA-style furnishings, art-lined walls and a licensed cafe.

There's also a great TV room for rainy-day hunkering. If it's fine, hit the nearby biking and hiking trails or barbecue on one of the two mountain-view decks.

Pangea Pod Hotel
HOTEL $$

(☑ 604-962-1011; www.pangeapod.com; 4333 Sunrise Alley; pods from $140; ❄ 🛜) Posing as a smarter, more private version of a hostel, Canada's first capsule hotel is based on the Japanese model, offering bed-sized 'pods' equipped with double futons, privacy curtains, individual air-con units, reading lights, lockers and mirrors. Colorfully tiled showers, powder rooms and loos are shared, but kept scrupulously clean.

Add in a happening bar/restaurant, ample gear storage and young, helpful staff and you've got a rare Whistler bargain bang in the center of the village.

Riverside Resort
CAMPGROUND, CABIN $$

(☑ 604-905-5533; www.parkbridge.com/en-ca/rv-cottages/riverside-resort; 8018 Mons Rd; camp-

CROSS-COUNTRY SKIING AROUND WHISTLER

Whistler has 120km of cross-country skiing trails spread over two areas: Lost Lake Park, a short walk from the Village, and the interlinked Olympic Park–Callaghan Country network, 25km by road to the west. Both areas offer groomed trails appropriate for classic and skate skiing and are graded easy (green) to advanced (black). Lost Lake is a pretty but relatively benign area with placid vistas and 30km of trails that partially utilize the snowed-in Chateau Whistler golf course. The Olympic Park has more technical terrain including the Nordic and Biathlon Olympic courses. The adjacent Callaghan Valley has a wilder flavor, including an opportunity to ski to the backcountry Journeyman Lodge, where you can dine and/or spend the night.

sites/yurts/cabins $43/130/235; 🕾😮) Just a few minutes past Whistler on Hwy 99, this facility-packed, family-friendly campground and RV park has elevated itself in recent years by adding cozy cabin and yurt options. The yurts come with basic furnishings, electricity and bedding provided, and are especially recommended. The resort's on-site Riverside Junction Cafe serves great breakfasts. Yurts and cabins have a two-night minimum stay.

Crystal Lodge & Suites HOTEL **$$**
(🖉604-932-2221; www.crystal-lodge.com; 4154 Village Green; d/ste from $160/210; 🌢🕾😮) Not all rooms are created equal at the Crystal, forged from the fusion of two quite different hotel towers. Cheaper rooms in the South Tower are standard style – baths and fridges are the highlight – but those in the Lodge Wing match the handsome rock-and-beam lobby, complete with small balconies. Both share excellent proximity to restaurants and ski lifts.

Adara Hotel BOUTIQUE HOTEL **$$**
(🖉604-905-4009; www.adarahotel.com; 4122 Village Green; r from $219; 🕾😮) Unlike all those lodges now claiming to be boutique hotels, the sophisticated and blissfully affordable Adara is the real deal. With warm wood furnishings studded with orange exclamation marks, the rooms offer spa-like baths, cool aesthetics and 'floating' fireplaces that look like TVs. Boutique extras include fresh cookies and in-room boot dryers. Prices dip significantly in shoulder season.

★**Nita Lake Lodge** BOUTIQUE HOTEL **$$$**
(🖉604-966-5700; www.nitalakelodge.com; 2135 Lake Placid Rd; d $289; 🕾😮) Adjoining the handsome Creekside railway station, this chic timber-framed lodge offers 'suites' rather than mere rooms, the smallest of which is an ample 45 sq meters. Hugging the lakeside, the swankier suites feature individual patios, rock fireplaces and baths with heated floors and large tubs; some also have handy kitchens.

Creekside's ski lifts are a walkable few minutes away and there's an on-site spa. The hotel also has an excellent West Coast restaurant and a free shuttle to whisk you to the village if you'd prefer to dine further afield. Check the website for weekday bargains.

Fairmont Chateau Whistler HOTEL **$$$**
(🖉604-938-8000; www.fairmont.com/whistler; 4599 Chateau Blvd; d $480; 🌢🕾😮) Enjoying ski-in, gondola-out privileges at the foot of Blackcomb Mountain, the Fairmont is like a 'village' within *the* Village. Chateau-esque in nature and grand in scale, it's not nearly as old as other Canadian landmark hotels, although the huge campus includes designer shops, a spa, gym, pools (it's plural here!) and a sprawling bar worthy of a baronial castle.

🍴 Eating

★**Purebread** BAKERY **$**
(🖉604-962-1182; www.purebread.ca; 4338 Main St; baked goods $3-6; ⊙8am-6pm) Imagine the best bakery you've ever visited, elevate the quality by the power of 10 and you might just get Purebread. Founded as a pin-prick-sized business in Whistler's Function Junction business park in 2010, this slice of baking heaven has since expanded to fill this larger cafe in the central village.

It's hard to overstate the ambrosial perfection of the melt-in-your-mouth scones, wonderfully stodgy cakes and doorstep-sized sandwiches. Rather like a Whistler 'black diamond,' it will remain etched in your memory long after you leave.

La Cantina
Urban Taco Bar MEXICAN **$**
(🖉604-962-9950; www.tacoslacantina.ca; 4340 Lorimer Rd; mains $8-14; ⊙11:30am-9pm; 🏷) A busy corner eatery where you order at the

WORTH A TRIP

DETOUR TO COWBOY COUNTRY

If you're craving an alternative to tourist-heavy Whistler Village (but you don't want to head into the wilderness like Grizzly Adams on a day out), head for Pemberton – the next community north along Hwy 99. Founded as a farming and cowboy town, it still has a distant-outpost feel, with enough to keep you occupied for a half-day. The 99 Pemberton Commuter transit bus runs here from Whistler ($4.50, 30 minutes, four times daily), but a car will enable you to explore much more effectively. Plan ahead via www.tourism pemberton.com.

Start with coffee and a giant cinnamon bun at the woodsy little **Blackbird Bakery** (☑604-894-6226; www.blackbirdbread.com; 7424 Frontier St; baked goods & sandwiches $3-8; ☑6am-8pm, from 7am Sun) in the former train station, then walk over to **Pemberton Museum** (☑604-894-5504; www.pembertonmuseum.org; 7455 Prospect St; by donation; ☑10am-5pm May-Oct) for the lowdown on how this quirky little town started. Ask them about the Pemberton mascot, a neckerchief-wearing potato dressed like a cowboy.

Next, head over to **Pemberton Distillery** (☑604-894-0222; www.pembertondistillery. ca; 1954 Venture Pl; ☑noon-5pm Wed & Thu, to 6pm Fri & Sat Jun-early Sep, reduced hours rest of year). A pioneer of BC's latter-day artisan booze movement, it has tours and a tasting room. And while it started with silky potato vodka, it has expanded production to include top-selling gin and a seductive whiskey and wild-honey liqueur. Next – with designated driver at the wheel – trundle 20 minutes out of town and uphill to **Joffre Lakes**. There's a lovely two-hour hike from the trailhead here or you can just snap some glacier photos from the parking lot.

Finally, when dinner beckons, weave back into town and find a table at the rustic, red-walled **Pony** (☑604-894-5700; www.theponyrestaurant.ca; 1392 Portage Rd; mains $22-38; ☑6:30am-late; ☑). The town's main dining hangout, it serves an elevated comfort-food menu (pizzas recommended) and some choice BC craft beers.

counter and then grab a perch (the high stools down the side usually have some empty spots), aim for a selection of $3 tacos or dive into a bulging burrito if you're really hungry. This place gets jam-packed at peak times so consider a takeout rather than resorting to fisticuffs to find a seat.

★**Hunter Gather**   CANADIAN **$$**
(☑604-966-2372; www.huntergatherwhistler.com; 4368 Main St; mains $15-29; ☑noon-10pm) A noisy but cheerful emporium of local food, this new place has quickly become known for its smoked meats (the 'hunter' part) and local veg (the 'gather' part). Relish the beef brisket (smoked for 18 hours) and the golden-brown Pemberton potatoes, pan-fried to a state of crispy deliciousness. Punters must order and pay up-front and then grab a pew.

The scene inside is all action, from the busy open-to-view kitchen to tipsy diners sharing backcountry stories over long wooden tables. Good selection of craft beers too.

Bar Oso   SPANISH **$$**
(☑604-962-4540; www.baroso.ca; 4222 Village Sq; small plates $9-27; ☑11:30am-late) Affiliated

with Araxi a couple of doors away, Bar Oso takes a casual Spanish approach to dining creating small *pintxos* (Basque tapas) and *raciones* (shared plates) that dabble in Mediterranean flavors. You can load up the cured hams on the charcuterie board or go full-on Spanish with the *tortilla patata* (Spanish omelet).

Red Door Bistro   FRENCH **$$$**
(☑604-962-6262; www.reddoorbistro.ca; 2129 Lake Placid Rd; mains $26-43; ☑5-10pm) As soon as you know you're coming to Whistler, call for a reservation at this hot little Creekside eatery, largely a local residents' domain. Taking a French-bistro approach to fine, mostly West Coast ingredients means juniper-rubbed elk with mint pesto, or a seafood bouillabaisse – the menu is a changeable feast (check the blackboard). Food presentation is artistic and the service is spot on.

Araxi Restaurant & Bar   CANADIAN **$$$**
(☑604-932-4540; www.araxi.com; 4222 Village Sq; mains $28-48; ☑from 5pm) Whistler's best gourmet restaurant, Araxi cooks up an inventive and exquisite Pacific Northwest menu and has charming and courteous ser-

vice. Try the diver-caught scallops and enjoy a bottle or two from the 15,000-bottle wine selection, but allow space for dessert: an artisanal cheese plate or the dreamy hazelnut panna cotta...or both.

Drinking & Nightlife

Garibaldi Lift Company PUB

(☑604-905-2220; 4165 Springs Lane; ⊙11am-1am) The closest bar to the slopes. You can smell the sweat of the skiers (or mountain bikers) hurtling past the patio at this cavernous bar that's known by every local as the GLC. The furnishings have the scuffs and dings of a well-worn pub, and the best time to come is when DJs or bands turn the place into a clubbish mosh pit.

Dubh Linn Gate PUB

(☑604-905-4047; www.dubhlinngate.com; 4320 Sundial Cres; ⊙8am-1am, from 7am Sat & Sun) Arguably the best pub at the bottom of the Whistler Village gondola (after all, it's Irish), this dark-wood-lined joint would feel just like an authentic Galway watering hole if not for the alfresco firepits and dudes wielding snowboards. Tuck yourself into a shady corner table inside and revive yourself with a stout – there's Guinness as well as Murphy's.

ⓘ Information

Whistler Visitors Centre (☑604-935-3357; www.whistler.com; 4230 Gateway Dr; ⊙8am-8pm Sun-Wed, to 10pm Thu-Sat Jun-Aug, reduced hours Sep-May) Flyer-lined visitor center with friendly staff right next to the bus station.

Check out Whistler Insider Blog (www.whistler.com/blog) for more info.

ⓘ Getting There & Away

While most visitors arrive by car from Vancouver via Hwy 99, there are several economical buses from Vancouver, including the following:

Skylynx (www.yvrskylynx.com) Seven services a day between Vancouver Airport and Whistler Village (from $58.50, three hours). Buses are modern with seat belts, toilets and wi-fi, and drivers are congenial and safe. En route, the bus stops at the Hyatt Hotel in Downtown Vancouver and, by request, at Whistler Creekside. Book online.

Snowbus (www.snowbus.com) Two buses a day from YVR Airport ($40) via Vancouver's Hyatt Hotel to Whistler, including a dawn service that gets you to the slopes before 8am. Winter only.

Buses pull into the village's outdoor **Bus Loop** next to the Whistler Visitors Centre.

SUNSHINE COAST

Fringing the forested coastline for 139km from Langdale in the south to Lund in the north, the Sunshine Coast – separated from the Lower Mainland by the Coast Mountains and the Strait of Georgia – has an independent, island-like mentality that belies the fact it's just a short hop by ferry or plane from Metro Vancouver. Hwy 101 handily strings together the key communities of Gibsons, Roberts Creek, Sechelt and Powell River, making this an easy and leisurely region to explore. Popular with hikers, kayakers and mountain bikers, it also has a small-scale arts scene.

Gibsons

POP 4600

If you're arriving on the Sunshine Coast via BC Ferries from Horseshoe Bay, your first port of call after docking in Langdale and driving or busing into town will be the pretty waterfront strip called Gibsons Landing. A rainbow of painted wooden buildings overlooking the marina, its streets are lined with browsable boutiques and eclectic eateries while its wharf is a summer-hugging promenade for languid boat watching.

Transformation is coming to the Gibsons Landing waterfront in the form of a controversial new harbor complex consisting of a hotel, luxury condos and a conference center. Despite initial approval, the project stalled in 2018 due to environmental concerns and has yet to reach fruition. Drop in to the **visitor center** (☑604-886-2374; www.gibsonsvisitorinfo.com; 417 Marine Dr; ⊙10am-4pm Wed-Sun) for the latest news.

◉ Sights & Activities

Gibsons Public Art Gallery GALLERY

(☑604-886-0531; www.gpag.ca; 431 Marine Dr; ⊙11am-4pm Jun-Aug, Thu-Mon only Sep-May) **FREE** A delightful little gallery with a firm focus on showcasing Sunshine Coast works, from painting to sculpture and fiber art. The diverse roster of shows changes every month – opening nights are a good time to meet creative Gibsonites – and this is also a great spot to buy locally produced artworks at reasonable prices. If you're here in August, check out the town's Art Stroll event, which includes this and other galleries and stores.

BRITISH COLUMBIA GIBSONS

Sunshine Kayaking

KAYAKING

(☑604-886-9760; www.sunshinekayaking.com; Molly's Lane; rentals per 2/24hr $49/98; ⊙9am-7pm) Expanding over the years from its kayak-renting early days, these friendly folks now also offer diving, SUP and even fishing charters. But it's the guided kayaking tours that many visitors aim for – book ahead for one of the monthly Full Moon Tours, an unforgettable way to experience the tranquil beauty of the West Coast. Call ahead for reservations.

Talaysay Tours

TOURS

(☑604-628-8555; www.talaysay.com; Porpoise Bay Provincial Park; tours $199; ⊙May-Sep) For a First Nations take on the Salish Sea and the Pacific Northwest region, take a boat trip around the islands and channels of Howe Sound. Four-hour boat trips depart from Gibsons and are led by an indigenous guide who points out the flora, fauna and fascinating cultural history of the area.

🛏 Sleeping & Eating

Arcturus Retreat Bed & Breakfast

B&B $$

(☑604-886-1940; www.arcturusretreat.ca; 160 Pike Rd; d from $160; 🛜) Well located just up the hill from the Langdale ferry dock, this is one of the most convenient places to stay in Gibsons – no car required (they'll pick you up from the ferry). The homely quarters and warm welcome add to the appeal and the owners are also full of suggestions for what to do on the Sunshine Coast.

Bonniebrook Lodge

HOTEL $$

(☑604-886-2887; www.bonniebrook.com; 1532 Ocean Beach Esplanade; d from $249; 🛜) A handsome, wood-built retreat constructed in 1929 but luxuriously updated, this historic charmer occupies a tranquil waterfront stretch that feels like a million miles from any city. All the rooms are delightfully sumptuous with fireplaces and hot tubs, but if you pay extra for one of the two top-floor penthouse suites, you'll have your own balcony overlooking the ocean.

Smitty's Oyster House

SEAFOOD $$

(☑604-886-4665; www.smittysoysterhouse.com; 643 School Rd Wharf; mains $18-29; ⊙noon-late Tue-Sat, to 8pm Sun, reduced hours in winter) The best spot for seafood in Gibsons (especially if you snag a seat at the communal long table alongside the marina boardwalk), Smitty's sparked a renaissance in local dining when it opened a few years back. It's as popular as ever, especially on summer evenings when

this is the perfect place to scoff a pile of fresh-shucked bivalves.

Drift Cafe & Bistro

BISTRO $$$

(☑604-886-5858; www.drift-gibsons.ca; 546 Gibsons Way; mains $19-28; ⊙10am-2pm & 5-9pm Fri-Tue) Residing in a cute little cottage no larger than a two-car garage, Drift (formerly Nova Kitchen) continues to impress, serving everything from egg-and-bacon breakfasts to sweet seared scallops with bacon risotto. On warm days, the deck overlooking the water practically doubles the restaurant's size and is a great spot to enjoy a Persephone beer with your gourmet grub.

★Persephone Brewing Company

BREWERY

(☑778-462-3007; www.persephonebrewing.com; 1053 Stewart Rd; ⊙10am-9pm late May-early Sep, 11am-7pm early Sep-late May) Welcome to one of Canada's only farm-to-barrel microbreweries. Among numerous sustainable practices, Persephone grows its own hops at an on-site 11-acre farm and harvests them specifically for its home-brewed beer. Try them in a pint of crisp Coast Life Lager in the brewery's big red barn of a tasting room or add a sample to your four-taster flight.

Hops are only half of it. Persephone also grow apples for cider and vegetables for food. The veg are served out of a sleek silver food truck either spread over crispy pizzas or hidden in well-stuffed tacos. All in all, this is an idyllic spot to imbibe, located five minutes from the ferry terminal, with picnic tables, a gabled barn and rows of hops blowing in the breeze. Tours are offered on Sundays. Kids are welcome (for homemade lemonade).

❶ Getting There & Away

BC Ferries (www.bcferries.com) services arrive at Langdale, 6km northeast of Gibsons, from West Vancouver's Horseshoe Bay (passenger/vehicle $14/46, 40 minutes, nine daily).

Sunshine Coast Regional Transit System (www.busonline.ca) buses arrive in Gibsons from the Langdale ferry terminal and other Sunshine Coast communities (one-way/day pass $2/5).

Roberts Creek

Just off Hwy 101 via Roberts Creek Rd, the funky 'downtown' here looks like a little hobbit community, if hobbits had gone through a hippie phase. Poke around the wood-built, shack-like stores and eateries and then wander downhill to the beach, checking out the huge, ever-changing Community Mandala painted on the ground.

Sleeping & Eating

Up the Creek Backpackers B&B HOSTEL $
(604-837-5943; www.upthecreek.ca; 1261 Roberts Creek Rd; dm/r $28/84;) Run by a round-the-world cyclist, Up the Creek has incorporated all the best facets of a classic hostel: a place where you can relax but still meet people and feel at home. Take your pick from small dorms, private rooms aimed at couples and families, a back-garden cabin and a tent pitch in the grounds ($15).

They'll even rent you a two-person tent if you've left yours at home ($28). The small shared kitchen is well equipped and there's an active eco approach including rigorous recycling.

Cyclists are welcomed and public transport users actively encouraged. They offer free loaner bikes (helmets included) if you fancy exploring Roberts Creek's network of quiet lanes and cycling trails on your own.

Shades of Jade Inn & Spa B&B $$
(604-885-3211; www.shadesofjade.ca; 1489 Henderson Rd; d from $199;) Aimed at tranquility-craving adults, this luxe two-unit B&B – with its Asian–West Coast decor – couldn't be more relaxing. Each spacious room (including the Tall Cedars Suite with its secluded deck) is equipped with a kitchen and steam shower while there's an outdoor hot tub plus on-site spa treatments to provide you with multiple reasons to never leave.

Gumboot Cafe CAFE $
(www.thegumbootcafe.com; 1057 Roberts Creek Rd; mains $7-11; 7am-5pm, from 8am Sat & Sun;) A cool, wood-floored hangout that's ideal for eavesdropping on local gossip – or just perusing the ever-changing art lining the walls. Either way, drop by for coffee and a breakfast fuel-up (the Italian baked eggs work wonders) or arrange to be here for lunch when bulging sandwiches jostle for attention with thin crust pizzas (look for the daily special).

Regular live music is on the creative side – think psychedelic folk and ukulele jams.

Gumboot Restaurant CANADIAN $$
(604-885-4216; www.gumbootrestaurant.com; 1041 Roberts Creek Rd; mains $14-27; 10am-8:30pm Mon-Thu, 9am-9pm Fri & Sat, 9am-8:30pm

SUNSHINE COAST GALLERY CRAWL

Pick up the free *Purple Banner* flyer at area visitor centers for the location of dozens of studios and galleries throughout the region. Many are open for drop-in visitors (especially in summer) – look out for the purple flags along the road on your travels – and they're a great way to meet the locals and find unique souvenirs. For further information, see www.suncoastarts.com. Also, if you're here in October, don't miss the three-day **Sunshine Coast Art Crawl** (www.sunshinecoastartcrawl.com), a party-like showcase of local studios, galleries and events.

Sun;) Talk about a West Coast classic! This delightful bistro (with gorgeous garden patio) combines an old-school welcome with a lovingly prepared menu backed up by Sunshine Coast beers and Vancouver Island wines. Eye-catching dishes include curried pierogi (dumplings), boo-tine (like poutine, but with gnocchi rather than fries) and the Korean-style chicken wings.

Getting There & Away

Regular Sunshine Coast Regional Transit System (www.busonline.ca) buses run from the ferry terminal at Langdale into Roberts Creek and beyond ($2).

Sechelt
POP 10,000

Not quite as alluring as Gibsons, Roberts Creek or Powell River, Sechelt is nevertheless a good stop-off on your Sunshine Coast jaunt: there are several places to fuel up (both your car and your body) plus access to some cool outdoor activities – kayaking and off-road cycling are particularly well represented.

Sights & Activities

Porpoise Bay Provincial Park PARK
(www.env.gov.bc.ca/bcparks/explore/parkpgs/porpoise; Hwy 101) A forest-backed oceanfront park popular with families, campers and kayakers venturing out into Sechelt Inlet, visiting tree-huggers will also enjoy communing with the towering Douglas fir and western hemlock that call this place home.

Looking for a hike? Head to Angus Creek where abundant birds hang around the estuary as if they own the place.

Pedals & Paddles
KAYAKING

(☑604-885-6440; www.pedalspaddles.com; 7425 Sechelt Inlet Rd; rentals per 2/24hr $34/80) Kayak rentals (and guided kayak tours) are the mainstay of this popular operation but if you're here in July and August – and your looking for something less strenuous – try their zodiac tours that will zip you around the natural sights and sounds of the inlet.

Sechelt Farmers & Artisans Market
MARKET

(Cowrie St; ☉9am-2:30pm Sat Easter-Sep) Combining fresh local produce (look out for seasonal BC peaches and cherries) with cool arts and crafts, this market is Sechelt's liveliest community hub – especially during its mid-summer peak. Food trucks and food stands add to the appeal.

🛏 Sleeping & Eating

Beachside by the Bay
B&B $$

(☑604-741-0771; www.beachsidebythebay.com; 5005 Sunshine Coast Hwy; d from $212; 🛜) This tranquil property comprises two spacious suites and a cottage where communing with the ocean is guaranteed. There's a three-night minimum stay in July and August, but that will give you plenty of time to experience the alfresco hot tub, watch the sunset (and passing eagles) or prepare your own dinner using your private kitchen or barbecue.

DON'T MISS

THE OTHER WEST COAST TRAIL

Vancouver Island's West Coast Trail is so popular it's hard not to run into other hikers en route. But the Sunshine Coast offers its own under-the-radar version that many West Coasters have only just started discovering. Running from Sarah Point to Saltery Bay, the 180km-long Sunshine Coast Trail is a wilderness paradise of ancient forests, eagle-dotted waterfronts and snowcapped vistas. Unlike the West Coast Trail, this one is free and reservations are not required – there are also 15 free-use sleeping huts dotted along the route. For more information, visit www.sunshinecoasttrail.com.

★ Painted Boat Resort Spa & Marina
RESORT $$$

(☑604-883-2122; www.paintedboat.com; 12849 Lagoon Rd; d from $440; 🛜🏊) A boutique waterfront resort where the spacious villa accommodations look like a West Coast dream home. One- and two-bedroom units hug the waterfront showing off decor that's top-of-the-line contemporary. Rooms include kitchens, and there's a deluxe on-site spa with its own garden and an outdoor infinity pool, plus kayak rental at the marina.

★ Basted Baker
CAFE $

(☑604-885-1368; www.bastedbaker.com; 5685 Cowrie St; $9-14; ☉8am-4pm Mon-Fri, 9am-3pm Sun; 🛜🍴) Sechelt's best dining option is a slightly out of the ordinary bakery that retains the ambience of a casual bistro and specializes in biscuit sandwiches. With an unlimited appetite, you could effectively stay here all day, demolishing eggs benny, salad bowls and individually tailored quiches. And did we mention the perfectly confected coffee and the gloriously sticky cinnamon buns?

Biscuit-wise, we're talking American-style – fresh, crumbly creations that resemble giant scones and require a small stick to hold savory fillings (such as smoked salmon and poached egg) in place. Hash browns make perfect bedfellows.

❶ Getting There & Away

Regular Sunshine Coast Regional Transit System (www.busonline.ca) buses arrive in Sechelt from the Langdale ferry terminal and other Sunshine Coast communities ($2).

Harbour Air (☑604-885-2111; www.harbour air.com) flies floatplanes from downtown Vancouver to Sechelt twice a day ($118, 20 minutes).

Powell River

POP 13,100

The last significant settlement as you head north on the Sunshine Coast retains an idiosyncratic end-of-the-road flavor. Surrounded by mossy rainforest and lapped by the sheltered waters of Malaspina Strait, Powell River's prettiness is tempered by the presence of a smoke-belching paper factory and a harbor full of permanently barking sea lions. On the waterfront, a fleet of 10 concrete ships dating from the 1940s acts as an improvised breakwater. Anyone familiar with the offbeat, surreal world of 1990s TV series *Twin Peaks* will feel instantly at home.

There are two main hubs in Powell River: the 'new town' (Westview) where you disembark from the ferry and the best restaurants are located, and the Powell River Historic District consisting of a small assemblage of heritage buildings gathered incongruously around the paper mill and embellished by a brewpub and Canada's oldest continuously operating cinema. It's 5km between the two.

Activities

Pick up a free walking-tour flyer from the visitor centre and wander the Townsite's heritage buildings, including many carefully restored arts-and-crafts constructions. Highlights include **Dr Henderson's House** (6211 Walnut Ave) and the lovely **Patricia Theatre** (604-483-9345; www.patriciatheatre. com; 5848 Ash Ave), Canada's oldest continually operating cinema.

Powell River Sea Kayak   KAYAKING
(604-483-2160; www.bcseakayak.com; 10676 Crowther Rd; rental per 3/8hr $50/65) Arguably the best way to view the natural splendors of this region is from the water. And if you've already done the ferry, it's time for some quality kayak time. Book a rental via these guys and explore around Cortes Island, Savary Island or up to Lund. Or let someone else do the navigating on a guided tour.

Dive deeper into the wilderness by staying at their Cabana Desolation Eco Resort. The company is based in end-of-the-road Lund, 27km north of Powell River.

Sleeping & Eating

Old Courthouse Inn   HOTEL $$
(604-483-4000; www.oldcourthouseinn.ca; 6243 Walnut St; s/d from $119/139; 🛜) A wonderful slice of yesteryear or an old-fashioned over-cluttered inn, depending on your penchant for antiques, this mock-Tudor hotel keeps one foot in the past, reliving its glory days as the town courthouse. The eight rooms retain the feel of the 1940s, but with modern amenities (wi-fi, TVs) thrown in, and a generous hot breakfast is included in the on-site cafe.

Base Camp   CAFE $
(604-485-5826; www.basecamp-coffee.com; 4548 Marine Dr; mains $8-16; 🕖7am-5pm; 🛜) The town's quintessential community coffee hangout has, no doubt, served as base camp for many energetic Sunshine Coast excursions judging by the breakfasts – be it the maple granola parfait or the curried tofu scramble. The communal tables are great for eavesdropping and the large local map on the wall will help get you oriented while you enjoy the java.

Costa del Sol   MEXICAN $
(604-485-2227; www.costadelsollatincuisine. com; 4578 Marine Ave; mains $10-16; 🕚11:30am-late Wed-Mon; 🚲) Arriving off-peak is the best way to avoid the crush and maybe even snag a table at this bright-painted former police station with a striking Emiliano Zapata mural within. The menu is Latin with a strong Mexican bent (gourmet tacos are the mainstays) though there's a nod to Louisiana in the jam-packed jambalaya bowl.

Coastal Cookery   BISTRO $$
(604-485-5568; www.coastalcookery.com; 4553 Marine Ave; mains $12-28; 🕚11:30am-late) This casual dining favorite has the town's best patio plus a great menu of tweaked classics and seasonal specials – with a strong focus on BC ingredients. If Salt Spring mussels are on the menu, order them immediately or just dive headfirst into the chicken-and-waffle sandwich (especially if you have a marathon to run).

★**Townsite Brewing**   BREWERY
(604-483-2111; www.townsitebrewing.com; 5824 Ash Ave; 🕚11am-9pm) An elder statesman of BC's craft-beer scene (which means it's more than five years old), this brilliant, Belgian-focused brewery occupies a heritage post office building. Take a free 3pm tour on Saturdays or sidle up to the tasting bar for a sip or three of Tinhat, Zunga or the only-available-here Suncoast Pale Ale. A four-glass tasting flight costs $8.

Information

Visitors Centre (604-485-4701; www.powell river.info; 4670 Joyce Ave; 🕘9am-6pm Jul & Aug, to 5pm Mon-Sat Sep-Jun) Close to Powell River's main shopping mall.

Getting There & Away

Pacific Coastal Airlines (www.pacificcoastal. com) flies into Powell River from the South Terminal of Vancouver International Airport between three and five times daily (from $145, 35 minutes).

If you're driving here from the lower Sunshine Coast, you'll hop the BC Ferries (www.bcferries. com) service between Earls Cove and Saltery Bay en route (passenger/vehicle $14/45, 50 minutes, up to seven daily). From there, it's a 40-minute drive to Powell River. The company also operates

Vancouver Island

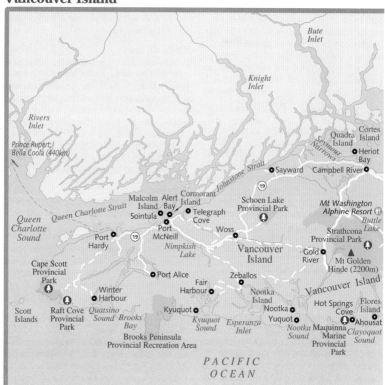

Powell River services to and from Texada Island (passenger/vehicle $10/23, 35 minutes, up to nine daily) and Vancouver Island's Comox (passenger/vehicle $14/42, 90 minutes, up to five daily). Powell River's ferry terminal is in Westview.

VANCOUVER ISLAND

Vancouver Island is studded with colorful, quirky communities, many founded on logging or fishing and featuring the word 'Port' in their names.

Locals are a friendly bunch, proud of their region and its distinct differences. The island is the largest populated landmass between western North America and New Zealand – around 500km long and 100km wide – and hosts a broad range of attractions, experiences and activities that feel many miles from the bustle of mainland Vancouver.

While the history-wrapped BC capital Victoria is the arrival point for many, it shouldn't be the only place you visit here. (And, to make a good impression, don't mistakenly refer to the place as 'Victoria Island.') Food and wine fans will love the Cowichan Valley farm region; outdoor-activity enthusiasts shouldn't miss the surf-loving, wild West Coast radiating from Tofino; and visitors venturing north will find an uncrowded region of independent communities fringed by rugged wilderness.

ℹ Information

For an introduction to the island, contact **Tourism Vancouver Island** (☑250-754-3500; www.van couverisland.travel) for listings and resources.

Victoria

☑250 / POP 88,000

Double-decker buses, afternoon tea, homes that look like castles, and pubs with names such as the Sticky Wicket and the Penny Farthing... Victoria has long traded on its British

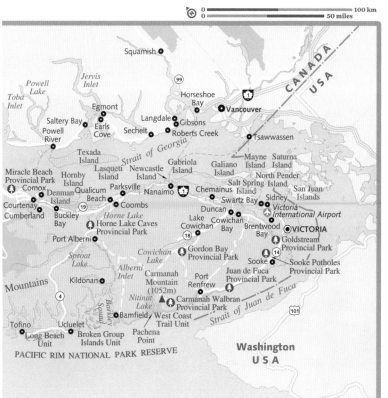

affiliations. But while the fish-and-chips remain first class and cricket games still enliven Beacon Hill Park, the days when Victoria was more British than Britain are long gone. In Victoria 2.0, the food culture embraces fusion, the beer leans toward craft brews and the abundance of bicycles seems to have more in common with Holland than England.

Compared to the glassy skyscrapers of Vancouver, Victoria is more laid-back and low-rise. On balmy summer days, a distinct holiday atmosphere takes over as people pile off the ferries to escape the mayhem of the mainland and forget work. Sure, Victoria might have become trendier and more sophisticated in recent years but, in pace and essence, it remains comfortably old-fashioned.

◉ Sights

★ **Royal BC Museum** MUSEUM
(Map p156; ☑ 250-356-7226; www.royalbcmuseum.bc.ca; 675 Belleville St; adult/child $17/11, incl IMAX $26.95/21.25; ⊙ 10am-5pm daily, to 10pm Fri & Sat mid-May–Sep; 🐾; 🚌 70) Arguably the finest museum in British Columbia and carrier of a 'royal' prefix since 1987, Victoria's flagship sight mixes the cream of BC's provincial exhibits with a revolving lineup of world-class temporary exhibitions. Adding value is an IMAX Theatre (☑ 250-480-4887; www.imaxvictoria.com; tickets $11.95) and a small park replete with indigenous and early pioneer history. Permanent fixtures inside the museum are split into natural history (2nd floor) and human history (3rd floor). Both focus almost exclusively on BC.

The natural history section beautifully recreates some of BC's classic ecosystems, peppered with a selection of taxidermied animals. Highlights include hyper-realistic sea lions and a life-size woolly mammoth with meter-long fur.

The human history section illuminates BC's First Nations with a recreated Kwakwaka'wakw clanhouse and a sonic exhibit that greets you in 34 different indigenous

Victoria

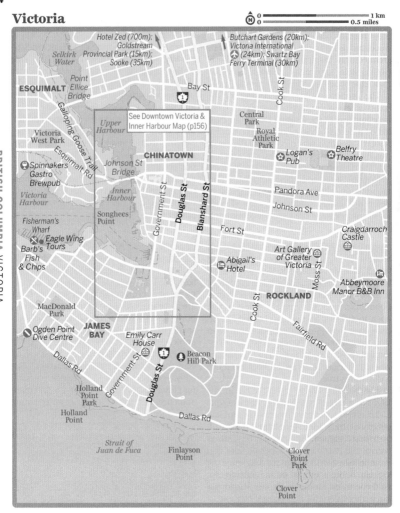

languages. Further on, you'll encounter a diorama of an early-20th-century BC street complete with a cinema showing Charlie Chaplin movies.

In adjacent **Thunderbird Park**, behind a line of weathered totem poles, lie two of the province's oldest buildings. The small log cabin **St Ann's Schoolhouse** dates from 1844 when it served as a fur trading post. Next door, the **Helmcken House** is the former home of fur-trade-era doctor, John Helmcken.

★**Craigdarroch Castle**   MUSEUM
(☎250-592-5323; www.thecastle.ca; 1050 Joan Cres; adult/child $14.60/5.10; ⊗9am-7pm mid-Jun–early Sep, 10am-4:30pm early Sep–mid-Jun; P; 🚌14) More ostentatious country mansion than fortified castle, Craigdarroch, with its turrets, stained-glass windows and palatial interior, looks like it might have been teleported over from the Scottish Highlands. Beautifully preserved by a local historical society, the interior is filled with rich period detail and notable for its spectacular wood-paneled staircase that ascends from the entry vestibule. You'll need at least an hour to admire the four floors of rooms, including a dining room, smoking room, billiard room and dance hall.

Surrounded today by an attractive assemblage of lesser mansions in a Victoria suburb, Craigdarroch once stood on 28 acres of woodland. Built in the late 1880s, it drew its architectural inspiration from a medieval Gothic style known as 'Scottish Baronial', then experiencing a Victorian revival.

The property is also interesting for the complex family dramas that once played out here courtesy of the feuding Dunsmuir clan, led by a Scottish coal-mining baron named Robert Dunsmuir who died before the house was finished. One room is dedicated to telling the Dunsmuir story: the family lived here until 1908 and their squabbles over money and inheritance became legendary. Before you leave, climb the tower's 87 steps for distant views of the Olympic Mountains.

Parliament Buildings   HISTORIC BUILDING
(Map p156; ☑ 250-387-3046; www.leg.bc.ca; 501 Belleville St; ⊙ tours 9am-5pm mid-May–Aug, from 8:30am Mon-Fri Sep–mid-May; ☑ 70) **FREE** This dramatically handsome confection of turrets, domes and stained glass is British Columbia's working legislature and is also open to visitors. You can go behind the facade on a free 45-minute guided tour then stop for lunch at the 'secret' politicians' restaurant (p162) inside. Return in the evening when the elegant exterior is illuminated like a Christmas tree.

The buildings were constructed in the 1890s in a mix of renaissance, Romanesque and classical styles after the government had outgrown the original legislature, the less illustriously named 'Birdcages.' The current ceremonial entrance has a mosaic floor and is embellished with Italian marble, while the graceful dome is topped on the outside by a gold-encrusted statue of George Vancouver (an early explorer of BC's coastal regions).

Miniature World   MUSEUM
(Map p156; ☑ 250-385-9731; www.miniature world.com; 649 Humboldt St; adult/child $16/8; ⊙ 9am-9pm mid-May–mid-Sep, to 5pm mid-Sep– mid-May; ☑; ☑ 70) Tucked along the side of the Fairmont Empress Hotel, this huge collection of skillfully crafted models depicting important battles, historic towns and popular stories is far more fascinating than it sounds. Lined with dozens of diminutive diorama scenes, divided into themes ranging from Camelot to space and from fairyland to Olde England, it has plenty of push-button action, several trundling trains and the chance to see yourself on a miniature movie-theater screen. An immaculately maintained reminder of innocent yesteryear attractions.

Victoria Bug Zoo   ZOO
(Map p156; ☑ 250-384-2847; www.victoria bugzoo.com; 631 Courtney St; adult/child $12/8; ⊙ 10am-5pm Mon-Fri, to 6pm Sat & Sun, reduced hours Sep-May; ☑; ☑ 70) It's not big, nor are its resident critters (although some of them are alarmingly colossal by insect standards); however, this diminutive indoor 'zoo' is a small marvel thanks to the enthusiasm and knowledge of its guides. Atlas beetles, dragon-headed crickets and thorny devils are all explained, admired and – on occasion – lifted out of their tanks to be handed around for closer inspection. Children are the main audience, but this is a hugely entertaining and educational experience on any level.

Beacon Hill Park   PARK
(www.victoria.ca/EN/main/residents/parks/beacon hill.html; Douglas St; P ☑; ☑ 3) Fringed by crashing ocean, this waterfront park is ideal for feeling the breeze in your hair – check out the windswept trees along the cliff top. You'll also find a gigantic totem pole, Victorian

BRITISH COLUMBIA VICTORIA

CYCLING AROUND VICTORIA

Victoria is a progressive city when it comes to cycling and its biking infrastructure has improved by leaps and bounds in recent years. In 2017, the first proper downtown bike lane (with its own traffic lights and signage) was laid on Pandora St. The plan is to have another 32km of separated bike lanes in place by 2022.

The bike-friendliness dates from the 1990s when two regional hiking-biking trails were developed to connect Victoria with the surrounding countryside. The 55km Galloping Goose Trail runs along an old railway line to Sooke and beyond, while the 33km Lochside Regional Trail connects downtown Victoria with the Swartz Bay Ferry Terminal. Both trails allow cyclists to pedal unmolested by traffic right into the heart of the city. They share a southern nexus on the downtown side of the Johnson St Bridge, recently equipped with a designated bike lane.

Downtown Victoria & Inner Harbour

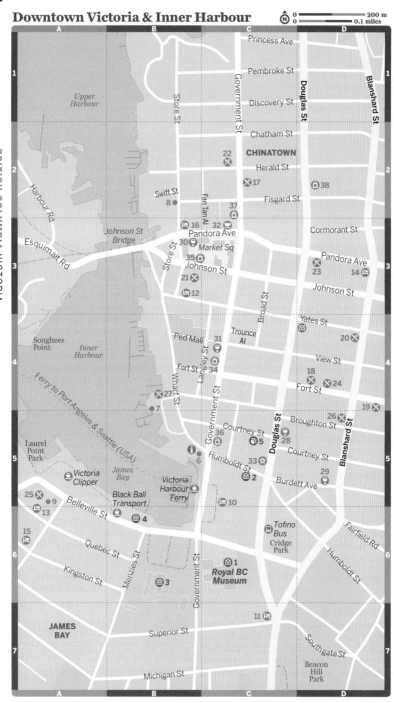

Downtown Victoria & Inner Harbour

BRITISH COLUMBIA VICTORIA

cricket pitch and a marker for Mile 0 of Hwy 1, alongside a statue of the Canadian legend Terry Fox, who ran across the country in 1980 for cancer research. If you're here with kids, consider the popular children's farm (www.beaconhillchildrensfarm.ca) as well.

Robert Bateman Centre   GALLERY
(Map p156; ☏ 250-940-3630; www.bateman centre.org; 470 Belleville St; adult/child $10/6; ⊙10am-5pm daily, to 9pm Fri & Sat Jun-Aug; 📵70) Colonizing part of the Inner Harbour's landmark Steamship Terminal building, this gallery showcases the photo-realistic work of Canada's most celebrated nature painter, the eponymous Bateman, along with a revolving roster of works by other artists. Start with the five-minute intro movie, then check out the dozens of achingly beautiful paintings showing animals in their natural surroundings in BC and beyond.

Emily Carr House   MUSEUM
(☏ 250-383-5843; www.emilycarr.com; 207 Government St; adult/child $6.75/4.50; ⊙11am-4pm Tue-Sat May-Sep; 🅿; 📵3) The birthplace of BC's best-known painter, this bright-yellow gingerbread-style house has plenty of period rooms, plus displays on the artist's life and career. There are changing displays of local contemporary works, but head to the Art Gallery of Greater Victoria if you want to see more of Carr's paintings. On your visit here, look out for the friendly house cats.

Art Gallery of Greater Victoria   GALLERY
(☏ 250-384-4171; www.aggv.ca; 1040 Moss St; adult/child $13/2.50; ⊙10am-5pm Tue, Wed, Fri & Sat, to 9pm Thu, noon-5pm Sun; 📵14) Granted, it's not the Louvre, or even Vancouver Art Gallery for that matter, but this east-of-downtown art nook does harbor one of Canada's best Emily Carr collections. Aside from the Victoria-born painter's swirling nature canvases, you'll find an immersive display of Asian art and changing temporary exhibitions. Check online for events, including lectures and frequent guided tours. Admission is by donation on the first Tuesday of every month.

🏃 Activities

★ Galloping Goose Trail   CYCLING
Victoria's best-loved trail follows the grade of an old railway line and is named for an erstwhile train carriage that rattled through these parts in the early 20th century. As a result, the trail is flat, passable on a hybrid bike, and flecked with remnants of

Vancouver Island's pioneering railroad history, including several trestles and a smattering of explanatory boards.

The first 13km is on concrete and relatively urban. Further west, the trail becomes increasingly rural, with pastoral sections interspersing with woodland and regular glimpses of water (both bays and lakes).

Lochside Regional Trail
CYCLING

A semi-rural hiking-biking trail linking Victoria's downtown core with the main ferry terminal 33km to the north, the Lochside bisects pastoral fields, woodland and quiet suburbs. It's pancake-flat, family-friendly and well-utilized by both tourists and locals, particularly in the summer. The trail – a mixture of gravel, concrete and quiet roads – is marked with kilometer posts.

Ocean River Sports
KAYAKING

(Map p156; ☑ 250-381-4233; www.oceanriver.com; 1630 Store St; rentals per 2hr $40, tours from $79; ⊙10am-5pm Mon-Sat, from 11am Sun) Offers kayak rentals and organizes popular kayak day tours in the area (including evening options). Harbor tours cast off from the dock behind the shop. Stand-up paddling and multiday tours are also available.

Ogden Point Dive Centre
DIVING

(☑ 250-380-9119; www.divevictoria.com; 199 Dallas Rd; ⊙9am-6pm) Shore-diving is available from Ogden Point a few minutes from the Inner Harbour. This local outfit offers two-day Discover Scuba courses for $189 including instruction and one ocean dive.

👉 Tours

⭐ Pedaler
CYCLING

(Map p156; ☑ 778-265-7433; www.thepedaler. ca; 321 Belleville St; tours from $50, rentals per day $30; ⊙9am-6pm, reduced hours Nov–mid-Mar) Pedaler offers bike rentals and several guided two-wheeled tours around the city, including the 'Hoppy Hour Ride' with its craft-beer-sampling focus. Get kitted out with a sturdy hybrid at the office in the 'olde' Huntingdon Manor building and go explore the Galloping Goose Trail (p157). Helmets, locks and rain ponchos are thrown in.

Eagle Wing Tours
WHALE-WATCHING

(☑ 250-384-8008; www.eaglewingtours.ca; 12 Erie St, Fisherman's Wharf; adult/child from $115/75; ⊙Mar-Oct) Popular and long-established operator of whale-watching boat tours.

Harbour Air
SCENIC FLIGHTS

(Map p156; ☑ 250-384-2215; www.harbourair.com; 950 Wharf St; tours from $119) For a bird's-eye Victoria view, these floatplane tours from the Inner Harbour are fab, especially when they dive-bomb the water on landing.

Architectural Institute of BC
WALKING

(Map p156; ☑ ext 325 604-683-8588; www.aibc.ca; tours $10; ⊙10am & 1pm Tue-Sun Jul & Aug) The institute puts on three great-value history- and building-themed walking tours, covering Chinatown, the James Bay residential district and the little-touched-upon history of the now demolished Fort Victoria. All tours start at the downtown visitor center (p165).

Hike Victoria
HIKING

(☑ 250-889-3008; www.hikevictoria.com; tours $65-86) Guided nature hikes (with pickup from your hotel) on the outskirts of Victoria. Distances range from 1km to 5.5km, with a focus on taking great photos.

🎊 Festivals & Events

Victoria Day Parade
PARADE

(www.gvfs.ca; ⊙mid-May) Street fiesta, with dancers, marching bands and 50,000-plus spectators. It usually starts on the corner of Douglas and Finlayson Sts and runs down Douglas St to the intersection with Courtenay St.

Victoria Ska & Reggae Fest
MUSIC

(www.victoriaskafest.ca; ⊙mid-Jun) The largest music festival of its kind in Canada.

Victoria Fringe Theatre Festival
THEATER

(www.victoriafringe.com; ⊙late Aug) Two weeks of quirky short plays and stand-up performances throughout the city.

Victoria International Buskers Festival
PERFORMING ARTS

(⊙early Sep) Five days of street-performing action from local and international artists in Bastion and Market Sqs.

Rifflandia
MUSIC

(www.rifflandia.com; ⊙Sep) Victoria's coolest music festival sees indie bands playing around the city.

🛏 Sleeping

From heritage B&Bs to cool boutiques and swanky high-end options, Victoria is stuffed with accommodations for all budgets. Off-season sees great deals. Tourism

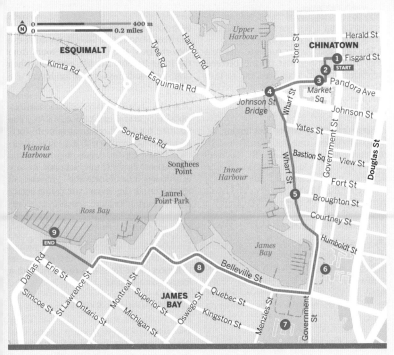

Walking Tour
Chinatown & the Inner Harbour

START CHINATOWN GATE
END FISHERMAN'S WHARF
LENGTH 2KM; 1½ HOURS

Victoria's Chinatown might not be as large, but it's the second-oldest Chinese neighborhood in North America after San Francisco.

A handsome **1 gate** near the corner of Government and Fisgard Sts marks its entrance. Beyond, lies Fisgard, the most ostensibly Chinese of the quarter's compact streets.

Leading off it on the south side is **2 Fan Tan Alley**, a narrow passageway connecting with Pandora Ave. Once a muddle of opium dens and gambling clubs, today it's home to used record stores and trinket shops.

3 Pandora Ave was the first street in Victoria to have a separated bike lane. Cross the road, before turning right and strolling past vintage clothes shops and a couple of pubs.

The bridge right in front of you as you approach the water is the new **4 Johnson St Bridge**, a bascule (lifting) bridge that was completely remodeled in 2018. It now has dedicated pedestrian and bike lanes and is the de facto starting point for the Lochside and Galloping Goose interurban trails.

Turn left into Wharf St and look out for a small **5 monument** overlooking the harbor near the junction of Broughton St. This is where Fort Victoria once stood, a fur trading post built in 1843.

Curve on round to the Inner Harbour dominated by the palatial **6 Fairmont Empress Hotel** (p161) built in 1908 on former mudflats. If you're feeling thirsty (and rich), pop inside for afternoon tea.

At right-angles to the Empress and looking equally regal is BC's **7 Parliament building** (p155). Follow Belleville St west past a string of harborside accommodations including the Queen Anne–style **8 Huntingdon Manor Hotel** (p160), fronted by one of Victoria's oldest heritage buildings.

The main road kinks inland and dips deeper into the quiet James Bay neighborhood, before emerging at **9 Fisherman's Wharf** (www.fishermanswharfvictoria.com) where the homes float, and fish-and-chips are de rigueur.

LOCAL KNOWLEDGE

THE BEST OF VICTORIA

Place to Sleep Abigail's Hotel (p161)

Place for Dinner Brasserie L'École (p162)

Place to Drink Drake (p163)

Place for Breakfast Jam Cafe (p162)

Place for Afternoon Tea Pendray Tea House (p162)

Victoria's **room-reservation service** (☑ 800-663-3883, 250-953-2033; www.tourism victoria.com/hotels) can show you what's available. Keep in mind that most downtown accommodations also charge for parking.

★ Ocean Island Inn
HOSTEL $

(Map p156; ☑ 250-385-1789; www.oceanisland. com; 791 Pandora Ave; dm/d from $36/56; @ 🛜; 🖵70) The kind of hostel that'll make you want to become a backpacker (again), the Ocean is a fabulous blitz of sharp color accents, global travel memorabilia and more handy extras than a deluxe five-star hotel. Bank on free breakfast (including waffles!), free dinner, a free nightly drink, free bag storage (handy for the West Coast Trail) and free friendly advice.

Funky rooms are a available in single-sex and mixed dorms, micro doubles and queens with private bathrooms, plus there's a shared modern kitchen and plenty of common space to mingle and swap travel escapades.

The same owners also have private, self-catering suites across town in a James Bay character house from $135; see www. oisuites.com for information.

HI Victoria Hostel
HOSTEL $

(Map p156; ☑250-385-4511; www.hihostels.ca/ victoria; 516 Yates St; dm/d $33/80; @🛜; 🖵70) This quiet downtown hostel in a high-ceilinged heritage building has two large single-sex dorms (sleeping 44 guests, no less), three small mixed dorms and a couple of private rooms. There's a games room and a book-lined reading area, but you're also in the heart of the action if you want to do your own thing. Free breakfast, tea and coffee included.

Hotel Zed
MOTEL $$

(☑250-388-4345; www.hotelzed.com; 3110 Douglas St; d from $209; P🛜⚽👟; 🖵70) If you like an accommodations that – in its own words – likes to 'rebel against the ordinary' then you'll love the Zed, an eccentric motel that has been given a tongue-in-cheek retro makeover, complete with rainbow paintwork and free VW-van rides to downtown (a 20-minute walk away). The rooms are also fun: 1970s phones, bathroom comic books and brightly painted walls.

Abbeymoore Manor B&B Inn
B&B $$$

(☑250-370-1470; www.abbeymoore.com; 1470 Rockland Ave; d from $239; P@🛜; 🖵14) A Victoria B&B worthy of Queen Victoria, the Abbeymoore has a decidedly posh address and was designed in the arts-and-crafts style in 1912. Seven deluxe rooms mix period details with satisfying modern touches in a way that is grand rather than kitschy. Hot breakfasts are equally creative and you're never far from a complimentary coffee and cookie.

Swans Suite Hotel
BOUTIQUE HOTEL $$

(Map p156; ☑250-361-3310; www.swanshotel.com; 506 Pandora Ave; ste $195; 🛜👟; 🖵70) This former brick-built warehouse has been transformed into an art-lined boutique hotel. Most rooms are spacious loft suites where you climb upstairs to bed down in a gabled nook, and each is decorated with a comfy combination of wood beams, rustic-chic furniture and deep leather sofas. The full kitchens are handy but there's also a brewpub downstairs for liquid sustenance.

Huntingdon Manor Hotel
HOTEL $$

(Map p156; ☑250-381-3456; www.huntingdon manor.com; 330 Quebec St; r from $195; P✳@🛜👟; 🖵30) The noticeably 'olde' white clapboard edifice along the harbor hides a comfortable, well-priced hotel that mixes stiff wood-paneling with large, modern rooms. Book online and you'll get a hot breakfast included in the rate. There's a traditional tearoom on-site (in one of Victoria's oldest structures) should you get the afternoon munchies. Staff are extra-courteous.

Helm's Inn
HOTEL $$

(Map p156; ☑250-385-5767; www.helmsinn.com; 600 Douglas St; d from $140; P@🛜; 🖵70) One of downtown's best-value hotels, this three-building, motel-style property has 42 surprisingly large rooms, all with handy kitchen facilities (either full kitchens or refrigerators and microwaves). Family-run for three decades, it also has a coin laundry, cookies in the lobby and a communal seating nook around a fireplace. It's sandwiched between the Royal BC Museum and Beacon Hill Park.

★ **Abigail's Hotel**　　　　　B&B **$$$**
(☑ 250-388-5363; www.abigailshotel.com; 906 McClure St; d from $249; **P**@🛜; 🖵7) A boutique hotel with the ambience of a B&B, the historic, regal and faintly English Abigail's is Victoria's most Victorian accommodations despite the fact it was only built in 1930 with a mock Tudor facade. Near-perfect rooms come with heavy drapes, shapely furniture and marble bathrooms. In the morning, you can swan downstairs for a spectacular breakfast.

Complimentary afternoon appetizers are also laid on and guests have the run of a country-mansion-style library and lounge with a crackling fireplace. No guests under 13 years of age.

Fairmont Empress Hotel　　　HOTEL **$$$**
(Map p156; ☑250-384-8111; www.fairmont.com/empress-victoria; 721 Government St; d from $340; **P**✳@🛜🐾; 🖵70) One of the most famous hotels in Canada, the Empress was built in 1908 in French-chateau-esque style. There have been numerous renovations and a who's-who of famous guests, from movie stars to royalty, prancing through in the years since. Modern-day guests can still expect classic decor and effortlessly solicitous service.

It's as much a historic monument as an accommodations option, so expect plenty of company (read: tourists) in the grandiose communal areas.

Oswego Hotel　　　　BOUTIQUE HOTEL **$$$**
(Map p156; ☑250-294-7500; www.oswegohotelvictoria.com; 500 Oswego St; d $265; **P**🛜🐾; 🖵30) Well hidden on a residential side street a short stroll from the Inner Harbour, this contemporary boutique sleepover is an in-the-know favorite. Suite rooms have granite floors, cedar beams and, in most units, small balconies. All have kitchens (with dishwashers) and deep baths, making them more like apartments than hotel rooms. Cleverly, the smaller studio rooms have space-saving high-end Murphy beds.

✖ **Eating**

Crust Bakery　　　　　　　BAKERY **$**
(Map p156; ☑250-978-2253; www.crustbakery.ca; 730 Fort St; baked goods $3-6; ⊙8am-5:30pm; 🖵14) There are several bakeries on this stretch of Fort St, but the Crust jumps out at you first. Maybe it's the deliciousness of the

aromas, or the delicate presentation, or the rich buttery-ness of the croissants, savory pastries and sweet tartlets with flavors like chocolate mousse and crème brûlée.

La Taqueria　　　　　　　MEXICAN **$**
(Map p156; ☑778-265-6255; www.lataqueria.com; 766 Fort St; tacos up to $3; ⊙11am-8:30pm Mon-Sat, noon-6pm Sun; ✍; 🖵14) A huge, aquamarine-painted satellite of Vancouver's popular and authentic Mexican joint, this ultra-friendly spot specializes in offering a wide array of soft-taco options (choose four for $10.50, less for vegetarian), including different specials every day. Quesadillas are also available and you can wash everything down with margaritas, Mexican beer or mezcal – or all three.

Red Fish Blue Fish　　　　SEAFOOD **$**
(Map p156; ☑250-298-6877; www.redfish-bluefish.com; 1006 Wharf St; mains $6-18; ⊙11am-7pm Mar-Oct; 🖵70) 🐾 On the waterfront boardwalk at the foot of Broughton St, this freight-container takeout shack serves fresh-made, finger-licking sustainable seafood. Highlights include jerk fish poutine, amazing chowder and tempura-battered oysters (you can also get traditional fish-and-chips, of course). Expanded new seating has added to the appeal but watch out for hovering gull mobsters as you try to eat.

Foo Asian Street Food　　　　ASIAN **$**
(Map p156; ☑250-383-3111; www.foofood.ca; 769 Yates St; mains $14-15; ⊙11:30am-10pm Mon-Sat, to 9pm Sun; **P**; 🖵70) Like a food truck that grew roots in a car park, this local-fave shack focuses on quickly rendered dishes inspired by Asian hawker stalls. Grab a perch inside or out, check the specials board and dive into fresh-cooked, good-value options, from saag paneer to papaya salad. Beer-wise, there's a love for local brews from the likes of Hoyne and Driftwood.

John's Place　　　　　　DINER **$**
(Map p156; ☑250-389-0711; www.johnsplace.ca; 723 Pandora Ave; mains $9-17; ⊙7am-3pm Mon-Fri, from 8am Sat & Sun; 🛜✍; 🖵70) This friendly, diner-style hangout is lined with memorabilia (complete with obligatory jukebox), while its enormous menu is a cut above standard diner fare. Start off with a basket of addictive housemade bread then load up on generous pasta dishes, piled-high salad mains or pancakes that come with a stupendous cream-cheese-and-syrup dip.

★ Jam Cafe
BREAKFAST **$$**

(Map p156; ☑778-440-4489; http://jamcafes.com; 542 Herald St; breakfast $13-17; ☺8am-3pm; ☎🖉; 🚍70) No need to conduct an opinion poll: the perennial lines in the street outside Jam suggest that this is the best breakfast spot in Victoria. The reasons? Tasteful vintage decor (if you'll excuse them the moose's head); fast, discreet service; and the kind of creative breakfast dishes that you'd never have the energy or ingenuity to cook yourself.

Jam classics include the 'cracker jack' (a banana-and-nutella brioche sandwich), the 'three pigs' (sausages fried in pancake batter) and the naan burrito (eggs, goat's cheese, avocado and spices). It's first-come, first-served, so join the line.

Fishhook
SEAFOOD **$$**

(Map p156; ☑250-477-0470; www.fishhookvic.com; 805 Fort St; mains $13-24; ☺11am-9pm; 🚍14) 🖉 Don't miss the smoky, coconutty chowder at this tiny Indian- and French-influenced seafood restaurant, but make sure you add a tartine open-faced sandwich: it's the house specialty. If you still have room (and you're reluctant to give up your place at the communal table), split a seafood biryani platter with your dining partner. Focused on local and sustainable fish.

Pendray Tea House
TEAHOUSE **$$**

(Map p156; ☑250-388-3892; www.pendrayinnandteahouse.com; 309 Belleville St; afternoon tea $24; ☺11am-2pm Mon-Sat, to 7pm Sun; 🚍30) A decorous little tearoom in one of Victoria's oldest houses in front of the Huntingdon Manor hotel where you can get the full monty – 'high tea' – with all the trimmings for $54, or a lighter version for $24. Reservations recommended.

Pink Bicycle
BURGERS **$$**

(Map p156; ☑250-384-1008; www.pinkbicycleburger.com; 1008 Blanshard St; mains $13-17; ☺11:30am-9pm Mon-Sat; ☎; 🚍14) A long way from the greasy patties of yore, the Pink Bicycle (named for the machine that has pride of place in the window) deals in gourmet burgers served in sesame-seed buns and filled idiosyncratically with seared ahi tuna or free-range bison with smoked cheddar. The diminutive interior shimmers with candlelight at night adding nuance to the framed art-nouveau prints.

Barb's Fish & Chips
FISH & CHIPS **$$**

(☑250-384-6515; www.barbsfishandchips.com; 1 Dallas Rd, Fisherman's Wharf; meals $10-23; ☺11am-dusk mid-Mar–Oct; 🚍30) With its British antecedents and proximity to the sea, Victoria knows how to fry up fine fish-and-chips and this Fisherman's Wharf institution, in business for more than 30 years, is a good place to start taste-testing. Enjoy the batter-fried goodness alongside the bobbing boats with beady-eyed gulls for company.

Legislative Dining Room
CANADIAN **$$**

(Map p156; ☑250-387-3959; www.leg.bc.ca; 501 Belleville St, Parliament Buildings; mains $9-18; ☺8am-3pm Mon-Thu, to 2pm Fri; 🚍70) One of Victoria's best-kept dining secrets, the Parliament Buildings (p155) have their own subsidized, old-school restaurant where both MLAs and the public can drop by for a silver-service menu of regional dishes, ranging from salmon salads to velvety steaks and a BC-only wine list. Entry is via the security desk just inside the building's main entrance; photo ID is required.

★ Il Terrazzo
ITALIAN **$$$**

(Map p156; ☑250-361-0028; www.ilterrazzo.com; 555 Johnson St; mains $21-44; ☺11:30am-3pm & 5pm-late Mon-Fri, 5pm-late Sat & Sun; 🚍24) Authentic Italian flavors melded with a laid-back Victoria spirit make a devastatingly good combo. If you don't believe us, come to Il Terrazzo, a restaurant that's as much about its atmosphere and service as it is about its Italian-inspired, locally nurtured food. Aside from the usual suspects (seafood linguine, margherita pizza), there is a handful of more unusual renditions.

★ Brasserie L'École
FRENCH **$$$**

(Map p156; ☑250-475-6260; www.lecole.ca; 1715 Government St; mains $20-50; ☺5:30-10pm Tue-Thu, to 11pm Fri & Sat; 🚍70) *Bonsoir!* You may have just arrived at the best restaurant in Victoria, a small but wonderfully elegant bistro discreetly furnished in *la mode français,* but without any of the infamous Parisian pretension. Service is warm and impeccable, and the renditions of classic French dishes are exquisitely executed. *Moules frites* (mussels and fries), duck confit and superb Bordeaux wines all hit the spot.

The restaurant operates on a first-come, first-served basis and there's often a line when it opens at 5:30pm. Join it!

Drinking & Nightlife

Victoria is one of BC's best beer towns; look out for local craft brews at pubs around the city. There is also a good smattering of traditional pubs, some of which wouldn't look out of place in England.

★ **Drake** BAR
(Map p156; ☑250-590-9075; www.drakeeatery. com; 517 Pandora Ave; ⊙11:30am-midnight; 🛜; 🚐70) Victoria's best tap house, this red-brick hangout has more than 30 amazing craft drafts, typically including revered BC producers Townsite, Driftwood and Four Winds. Arrive on a rainy afternoon and you'll find yourself still here several hours later. Food-wise, the smoked tuna club is a top seller but the cheese and meat boards are ideal for grazing.

★ **Garrick's Head Pub** PUB
(Map p156; ☑250-384-6835; www.garrickshead. com; 66 Bastion Sq; ⊙11am-late; 🚐70) A great spot to dive into BC's brilliant craft-beer scene. Pull up a seat at the long bar with its 55-plus taps – a comprehensive menu of beers from Driftwood, Phillips, Hoyne and beyond. There are always 10 rotating lines with intriguing tipples (ask for samples) plus a comfort-grub menu of burgers and such to line your boozy stomach.

Habit Coffee COFFEE
(Map p156; ☑250-294-1127; www.habitcoffee.com; 552 Pandora Ave; ⊙7am-6pm Mon-Fri, from 8am Sat & Sun; 🛜; 🚐70) 🚲 If you like your coffee ethically sourced and sustainably produced, hit Habit, where the potent brews and simple snacks are made with practically zero waste and the staff use bicycles to transport goods between two Victoria locations.

Clive's Classic Lounge LOUNGE
(Map p156; ☑250-361-5684; www.clivesclassic lounge.com; 740 Burdett Ave; ⊙5pm-midnight Sun-Thu, to 1am Fri & Sat; 🚐70) Tucked into the lobby level of the Chateau Victoria Hotel, this is the best spot in town for perfectly prepared cocktails. Completely lacking the snobbishness of most big-city cocktail haunts, this ever-cozy spot is totally dedicated to its mixed-drinks menu, which means timeless classic cocktails, as well as cool fusion tipples that are a revelation.

Spinnakers Gastro Brewpub PUB
(☑250-386-2739; www.spinnakers.com; 308 Catherine St; ⊙11am-11pm; 🛜; 🚐15) One of Canada's first craft brewers, this wood-floored smasher is a short hop from downtown via Victoria Harbour Ferry (p165). Sail in for copper-colored Nut Brown Ale or the lip-smacking Lion's Head Cascadia Dark Ale, and check out the daily casks to see what's on special. Save room to eat: the menu here is true gourmet gastropub grub.

Big Bad John's PUB
(Map p156; ☑250-383-7137; www.strathcona hotel.com; 919 Douglas St; ⊙noon-2am; 🚐70) Easily missed from the outside, this dark little hillbilly-themed bar feels like you've stepped into the backwoods. But rather than some dodgy banjo players with mismatched ears, you'll find good-time locals enjoying the cave-like ambience of peanut-shell-covered floors and a ceiling dotted with old bras. A good spot to say you've been to, at least once.

AFFTERNOON TEA

Victoria may have jumped on the third-wave-coffee bandwagon in recent years, but the city still harbors a devout love for afternoon tea, a habit it inherited from its orange-pekoe-swilling British founders. For every trendy cafe full of hipsters ordering avocado on toast, there exists at least one refined tearoom with walls the color of clotted cream and patrons sipping daintily from china teacups as if they've just stepped out of an episode of *Downton Abbey*.

The cathedral of afternoon tea in Victoria (and possibly all Canada) is the Fairmont Empress Hotel, where a full spread, served in the elegant lobby-lounge to a tinkling piano accompaniment, goes for a weighty $82 per person. Your substantial investment will be rewarded by three-tier trays loaded up with finger sandwiches, homemade pastries, fresh scones (with obligatory Devon-style clotted cream), and optional flutes of champagne. Make sure you cancel any dinner plans.

For those not in the market for pricey afternoon indulgences, tea needn't always be so expansive or expensive. Numerous tearooms and cafes around Victoria offer more modest versions of the repast, sometimes referred to as 'cream tea' (ie a pot of tea with an accompaniment of scones, jam and cream).

WORTH A TRIP

KINSOL TRESTLE

Standing as a testament to 20th-century railroad engineering, the Kinsol Trestle emerges out of Vancouver Island's misty forest like a giant Meccano set made from wood. Welcome to one of the largest timber trestles in the world.

Built between 1911 and 1920, and named after the local King Solomon mines, the Kinsol once carried log-dragging locomotives across the deeply cut Koksilah River. With changing patterns in industry, the last train crossed the trestle in 1979 and the wooden railway bridge was subsequently left to rot. A concerted community campaign between 2007 and 2011 raised the funds to refurbish and reopen the trestle as a multiuse path.

Today, it is possible to experience this glorious structure by walking or cycling along a trail that starts from a car park a kilometer from its southern end (take the Shawnigan Lake road west for 10km from Hwy 1 just north of Mill Bay). Signs at the site explain the history and engineering behind the structure while, on the trestle's north side, a steep path winds down to the river.

The Kinsol is approximately 50 minutes' drive from Victoria heading north and easily done as a day trip.

☆ Entertainment

Check the weekly freebie *Monday Magazine* for the lowdown on local happenings. Entertainment resources online include **Live Victoria** (www.livevictoria.com) and **Play in Victoria** (www.playinvictoria.net).

Vic Theatre   CINEMA
(Map p156; ☑ 250-389-0440; www.thevic.ca; 808 Douglas St; 🚌70) Screening art-house and festival movies in the heart of downtown, the Vic charges a $2 membership alongside your ticket admission.

Belfry Theatre   THEATER
(☑ 250-385-6815; www.belfry.bc.ca; 1291 Gladstone Ave; 🚌22) The celebrated Belfry Theatre showcases contemporary plays in its lovely former church-building venue, a 20-minute stroll from downtown.

Logan's Pub   LIVE MUSIC
(☑ 250-360-2711; www.loganspub.com; 1821 Cook St; ⊙3pm-1am Mon-Fri, from 10am Sat, 10am-midnight Sun; 🚌6) This no-nonsense pub looks like nothing special from the outside, but since 1997 the Logan has been the hotbed of Victoria's alt-rock scene. Come here to see bands with names like Alcoholic White Trash and Acid Mothers Temple. Fridays and Saturdays are best. Check the online calendar to see what's coming up. It's a 10-minute walk from downtown.

🛍 Shopping

While Government St is a souvenir-shopping magnet, those looking for more original purchases should head to the Johnson St stretch between Store and Government Sts, which is lined with cool independent stores.

★ Munro's Books   BOOKS
(Map p156; ☑ 250-382-2464; www.munrobooks. com; 1108 Government St; ⊙9am-6pm Mon-Wed, to 9pm Thu-Sat, 9:30am-6pm Sun; 🚌70) The name is no coincidence. Victoria's cathedral to reading was established in 1963 by Nobel-prize-winning Canadian author Alice Munro and her husband Jim. Encased in a heritage building on the city's famous Government St, it's an obligatory pilgrimage for bibliophiles with its high ceilings, wide array of local-interest tomes and well-read staff, some of whom have worked here for decades.

Regional Assembly of Text   STATIONERY
(Map p156; ☑ 778-265-6067; www.assemblyof text.com; 560 Johnson St; ⊙11am-6pm Mon-Sat, noon-5pm Sun; 🚌70) This branch of Vancouver's charming hipster stationery store is socked into a quirky space resembling a hotel lobby from 1968. You'll find the same clever greeting cards and cool journals, plus the best Victoria postcards ever. Add the button-making table, typewriter stations and a *Mister Mitten* chapbook purchase and you'll be beaming brighter than a shiny new paper clip.

Victoria Public Market   MARKET
(Map p156; ☑ 778-433-2787; www.victoriapublic market.com; 1701 Douglas St; ⊙10am-6pm Mon-Sat, 11am-5pm Sun; 🚌4) At this indoor market lined with artisan food businesses, tempting deli counters and food-court dining, you'll find everything from chocolate to cheese to

challenge your diet. Check the website for upcoming events, too.

Rogers' Chocolates FOOD
(Map p156; ☑ 250-881-8771; www.rogerschoc olates.com; 913 Government St; ☺ 9:30am-7pm; ♿ 70) This charming, museum-like confectioner serves the best ice-cream bars, but repeat offenders usually spend their time hitting the 20-flavor-strong menu of rich Victoria Creams (soft-centered chocolates), one of which is usually enough to substitute for lunch. Varieties range from peppermint to seasonal specialties and they're good souvenirs, if you don't eat them all before you get home (which you will).

Silk Road TEA
(Map p156; ☑ 250-704-2688; https://silkroad teastore.com; 1624 Government St; ☺ 10am-5:30pm Mon-Sat, 11am-5pm Sun; ♿ 70) A pilgrimage spot for fans of regular and exotic teas, where you can pick up all manner of leafy paraphernalia. Alternatively, sidle up to the tasting bar to quaff some adventurous brews. There's also a small on-site spa, where you can indulge in oil treatments and aromatherapy.

ⓘ Information

Downtown Medical Centre (☑ 250-380-2210; 622 Courtney St; ☺ 8:30am-5pm Mon-Fri; ♿ 70) Handy walk-in clinic.

Main Post Office (Map p156; 709 Yates St; ☺ 9am-5pm Mon-Fri; ♿ 70) Near the corner of Yates and Douglas Sts.

Tourism Victoria Visitor Centre (Map p156; ☑ 250-953-2033; www.tourismvictoria.com; 812 Wharf St; ☺ 8:30am-8:30pm mid-May–Aug, 9am-5pm Sep–mid-May; ♿ 70) Tons of brochures, plenty of staff, ample help.

ⓘ Getting There & Away

AIR

Victoria International Airport (☑ 250-953-7500; www.victoriaairport.com) is 26km north of the city via Hwy 17. Frequent **Air Canada** (www.aircanada.com) flights arrive from Vancouver ($193, 25 minutes) and Calgary ($285, 1¾ hours). **WestJet** (www.westjet.com) offers similar services. **Alaska Airlines** (www.alaskaair.com) links to Seattle (US$246, 45 minutes) five times a week.

YYJ Airport Shuttle (☑ 778-351-4995; www.yyjairportshuttle.com) buses run between the airport and downtown Victoria ($25, 30 minutes). In contrast, a taxi to downtown costs around $50.

Harbour Air (☑ 250-384-2215; www.harbour air.com; 950 Wharf St) flies into the Inner Harbour from downtown Vancouver ($242, 30 minutes) throughout the day. Similar **Helijet** (www.helijet.com) helicopter services arrive from Vancouver ($245, 35 minutes).

BOAT

BC Ferries (☑ 250-386-3431; www.bcferries. com) Runs large car ferries from mainland Tsawwassen (adult/vehicle $17.20/57.50, 1½ hours) to Swartz Bay, 33km north of Victoria via Hwy 17. Services run eight to 12 times a day. There are additional ferry services from Swartz Bay to and from the Southern Gulf Islands.

Black Ball Transport (Map p156; ☑ 250-386-2202; www.cohoferry.com; 430 Belleville St) Car ferries operate from the Inner Harbour to and from Port Angeles in the US (adult/child/vehicle US$18.50/9.25/65.50, 1½ hours, up to four daily).

Victoria Clipper (Map p156; ☑ 250-382-8100; www.clippervacations.com) Has a dock in the Inner Harbour from where it runs a passenger-only catamaran to and from Seattle (adult/child US$124/74, three hours, up to two daily).

BUS

With Greyhound no longer serving Vancouver Island, the best transportation company is **Tofino Bus** (Map p156; ☑ 250-725-2871; www.tofino bus.com), which runs three daily services via Nanaimo ($33, two hours) to all points north as far as Campbell River ($65, 5¼ hours) with bus 1 carrying on to Port Hardy ($115, nine hours). A separate service runs to and from Tofino ($75, 6½ hours, one daily) via Port Alberni ($60, 4½ hours, two daily).

Frequent **BC Ferries Connector** (☑ 778-265-9474; www.bcfconnector.com) services, via the ferry, arrive from Vancouver (from $49.50, 3½ hours) and Vancouver International Airport ($58, four hours).

ⓘ Getting Around

BICYCLE

Victoria is a great cycling capital, with routes crisscrossing the city and beyond. Check the website of the **Greater Victoria Cycling Coalition** (www. gvcc.bc.ca) for local resources. Bike rentals are offered by **Cycle BC Rentals** (☑ 250-380-2453; www.cyclebc.ca; 685 Humboldt St; per hour/day $8/28; ☺ 10am-4pm; ♿ 1) or Pedaler (p158).

BOAT

Victoria Harbour Ferry (Map p156; ☑ 250-708-0201; www.victoriaharbourferry.com; fares from $7; ☺ Mar-Oct) calls in at over a dozen docks around the Inner Harbour and beyond with its colorful armada of little boats.

BUS

Victoria Regional Transit (www.bctransit.com/victoria) buses (single fare/day pass $2.50/5) cover a wide area from Sidney to Sooke, with some routes served by modern-day double-deckers. Children under five travel free.

Buses 70 and 72 link downtown with the Swartz Bay Ferry Terminal. Bus 75 goes to Butchart Gardens. Bus 61 goes to Sooke.

TAXI

BlueBird Cabs (☑ 250-382-2222; www.taxicab.com)

Yellow Cab (☑ 250-381-2222; www.yellowcabvictoria.com)

Southern Vancouver Island

Not far from Victoria's madding crowds, Southern Vancouver Island is a laid-back region of quirky little towns that are never far from tree-lined cycle routes, waterfront hiking trails and rocky outcrops bristling with gnarled Garry oaks. The wildlife here is abundant and you'll likely spot bald eagles swooping overhead, sea otters cavorting on the beaches and perhaps the occasional orca sliding silently by just off the coast.

Saanich Peninsula & Around

Home to Vancouver Island's main airport and busiest ferry terminal, this peninsula north of Victoria has plenty to offer day-trippers looking to escape from the city. Pencil in time for Canada's finest botanical gardens and the bookshop bonanza of seaside Sidney.

SIDNEY

Seafront Sidney is a pleasant afternoon diversion with a walkable waterfront and enough bookstores to satisfy a far larger city. Located at the Saanich Peninsula's northern end, it's a popular retirement community.

◉ Sights & Actvities

Shaw Centre for the Salish Sea　　AQUARIUM
(☑ 250-665-7511; www.salishseacentre.org; 9811 Seaport Pl; adult/child $17.50/12; ◉ 10am-4:30pm; ☑) Sidney's kid-luring highlight, this aquarium is accessed through a dramatic Disney-style entrance that makes you think you're descending below the waves. Then you'll step into a gallery of aquatic exhibits, including alien-like jellyfish, a large touch tank with purple starfish and an octopus

that likes to unscrew a glass jar to snag its fresh crab dinner.

Sidney Whale Watching　　WHALE-WATCHING
(☑ 250-656-7599; www.sidneywhalewatching.com; 2537 Beacon Ave; adult/child $129/95; ◉ Mar-Oct) With luck on your side, you could spot orcas and gray whales (minkes and fin whales are also possible) on a salt-licked boat jaunt with this outfit. If not, there are usually seals and seabirds aplenty to crane your neck toward. Boats zigzag through the Southern Gulf Island and San Juan Island archipelagos searching for the best whale foraging grounds.

The company also rents out kayaks and stand-up paddleboards for $60 per day.

⛺ Sleeping & Eating

Sidney Pier Hotel & Spa　　HOTEL $$
(☑ 250-655-9445; www.sidneypier.com; 9805 Seaport Pl; d/ste $245/275; @ �索 ☎) This swish waterfront property fuses West Coast lounge cool with beach pastel colors and is a worthy alternative to staying in Victoria. Many rooms have shoreline views, and each has local artworks lining the walls. A spa and large gym add value, plus you're steps from a rather good micro-distillery. There's also an on-site deli-cafe and West Coast–themed restaurant.

Beacon Cafe　　CAFE $
(☑ 778-426-3663; 2505 Beacon Ave; snacks $6-11; ◉ 8am-4pm) A steadfastly local corner cafe with a few regal touches. The chairs owe a nod to the elegant 'Louis Quinze' epoch while the mantlepiece pays ceramic homage to the British royal family with Jubilee mugs and royal wedding plates. Pastries and sandwiches abound, but the place is best enjoyed for its hot smoothies (including apple-pie flavor) and all-day high tea.

Sabhai Thai　　THAI $$
(☑ 250-655-4085; www.sabhai.ca; 2493 Beacon Ave; mains $11-19; ◉ 11:30am-2pm & 4:30-9pm Mon-Sat, 4:30-9pm Sun) A cozy locals' favorite with a bonus patio and a good line in authentic curry dishes and pad Thai. The lunch combos ($11 to $13) are good value and include rice and spring rolls.

⌂ Shopping

Sidney is an official 'booktown,' one of only two in Canada. At least half-a-dozen bookstores lie on or around Beacon Ave and all are locally owned.

★ Haunted Books   BOOKS

(📞 250-656-8805; 9807 3rd St; ⊙10am-5pm) An agreeably Dickensian bookstore stuffed to the rafters with random busts, faded old maps, a grandfather clock and piles of dusty old tomes. Despite its name, Haunted's eclectic book collection extends way beyond ghost stories. It's by far the most atmospheric of Sidney's half-dozen book nooks – and the oldest.

Tanner's Books   BOOKS

(📞 250-656-2345; www.tannersbooks.com; 2436 Beacon Ave; ⊙8am-8pm Mon-Sat, to 6pm Sun; 🔲) You can easily spend a leisurely afternoon perusing the selection at this cavernous corner bookstore with its large array of magazines and comprehensive travel-book section. Tanner's also organizes evening book readings, typically at the Red Brick Cafe across the street – check the bookstore's website for listings.

Beacon Books   BOOKS

(📞 250-655-4447; 2372 Beacon Ave; ⊙10am-5pm Mon-Sat, 11am-4pm Sun) A multi-room town-center bookstore piled high with used books, all guarded by a house cat that may or may not let you stroke her (probably not). Look out for the collection of vintage postcards, then send one home, pretending you're vacationing in 1942.

🛈 Information

Visitor Center (📞 250-665-7362; www.sidney. ca; 2281 Beacon Ave; ⊙9am-5pm, reduced hours Nov-Mar) Comprehensive coverage of the whole Saanich Peninsula.

🛈 Getting There & Away

It takes around an hour to get here by **Victoria Regional Transit System** (📞 250-382-6161; www.bctransit.com/victoria) bus from Victoria ($2.50, bus 70 or 72). Buses carry on to the **Swartz Bay BC Ferries Terminal** (📞 250-386-3431; www.bcferries.com), 6km to the north, and to Victoria International Airport (p165), 5km to the west.

BRENTWOOD BAY

This countryside swath a 30-minute drive from Victoria has some attractions of its own. You can cycle across it on the urban-to-rural Lochside Regional Trail, upgrade your book collection in seaside Sidney and admire one of the finest gardens in Canada – and one of BC's most popular visitor attractions – at Butchart Gardens.

★ Butchart Gardens   GARDENS

(📞 250-652-5256; www.butchartgardens.com; 800 Benvenuto Ave; adult/teen/child $33.80/16.90/3; ⊙8:45am-10pm Jun-Aug, reduced hours Sep-May; 🚌75) Far more than just another pretty flower arrangement, Butchart is a national historic site and a triumph of early-20th-century gardening aesthetics. With its well-tended blooms, ornate fountains and diverse international flavor (from Japanese to Italian), it's hard to imagine that this land was once an abandoned limestone quarry. Tour buses roll in relentlessly throughout the summer, but the gardens with their undulating topography are big enough to absorb the melee.

Food outlets and gift shops crowd the entrance, including the **Dining Room Restaurant**, which serves a smashing afternoon tea.

Butchart is open year-round, although summer is, arguably, the best (and busiest) season to visit: there are Saturday-night fireworks in July and August. The Christmas-lights season from early December to early January is another highlight.

The gardens were the brainchild of Jennie Butchart, whose husband founded the limestone quarry. She began planting and landscaping over the old quarry in 1912. Expanded and manicured throughout the course of a century, the site now counts over one million blooms to cater for its one million annual visitors. Passed down through several generations, the gardens are still owned by the Butchart family.

Victoria Butterfly Gardens   GARDENS

(📞 250-652-3822; www.butterflygardens.com; 1461 Benvenuto Ave; adult/child $16.50/6.50; ⊙10am-4pm mid-Mar–Sep, to 3pm Oct–mid-Mar) These gardens offer a kaleidoscope of thousands of fluttering critters, from around 50 species, in a free-flying environment. As well as watching them flit about and land on your head, you can learn about ecosystem lifecycles, and eyeball exotic fish, plants and birds. Look out for Spike, the long-beaked puna ibis, who struts around the garden trails as if he owns the place.

Sooke & Around

Only a 45-minute drive from Victoria, Sooke is the gateway to some of South Vancouver Island's best wilderness areas, but still has enough facilities to offer choice and comfort. You can cycle to the town from Victoria on the Galloping Goose Trail or catch a metro bus along Hwy 14. Twisted Garry oaks and unkempt hedgerows signal your arrival in a more rural domain.

◎ Sights & Activities

Sooke Region Museum   MUSEUM
(☑ 250-642-6351; www.sookeregionmuseum.com; 2070 Phillips Rd; ⊙ 9am-5pm Tue-Sun) **FREE**
This jam-packed community museum is like a 100-year-old attic turned inside-out. It illuminates the area's rugged pioneer days with dioramas, glass cases, clothing and old newspapers. Check out Moss Cottage in the museum grounds – built in 1869, it's the oldest residence west of Victoria – and the Douglas fir cut-out that's older than 1200 years. The museum shares the same building and hours as the visitor center.

Sooke Potholes Provincial Park   PARK
(☑ 250-474-1336; www.bcparks.ca; Sooke River Rd)
This relaxed park has been a favorite natural hangout among locals for generations. With the potholes (natural rock pools) carved into the river base during the last ice age, it's ideal for summertime swimming and tube-floating. It's 5km drive from Hwy 14 along River Rd, or even better, a short ride on the Galloping Goose Trail (p157).

Juan de Fuca Marine Trail   HIKING
Rivaling the West Coast Trail as a must-do trek, the 47km Juan de Fuca Marine Trail is located in Juan de Fuca Provincial Park

(☑ 250-474-1336;   www.env.gov.bc.ca/bcparks/explore/parkpgs/juan_de_fuca; Hwy 14) and takes around four days to complete, though you don't have to do the whole thing. Some sections are often muddy and difficult to hike, while bear sightings and swift weather changes are not uncommon.

From east to west, the trailhead access points are China Beach, Sombrio Beach, Parkinson Creek and Botanical Beach. The most difficult stretch is between Bear Beach and China Beach.

The route has several basic backcountry campsites and you can pay your camping fee ($10 per adult) at any of the trailheads. The most popular spot to pitch your tent is the more salubrious, family-friendly China Beach Campground, which has pit toilets and cold-water taps but no showers. There's a waterfall at the western end of the beach and booking ahead in summer is essential.

Booking ahead is also required on the West Coast Trail Express minibus that runs between Victoria, the trailheads and Port Renfrew.

Adrena LINE   ZIP-LINING
(☑ 250-642-1933; www.adrenalinezip.com; 5128 Sooke Rd; adult/child from $89/70; ⊙ 9am-5pm Mar-Oct) If you're craving some thrills, find your inner screamer on a forested zip-line tour. The full-moon zips are the most fun but book ahead since they run irregularly, depending on the lunar schedule. If you

---

VANCOUVER ISLAND BOOZE TRAIL

Vancouver Island's blossoming local-food movement has spread to booze, with wineries, breweries, cideries and distilleries popping up across the region, giving visitors plenty of reason to appoint a designated driver. But unless you know where to go, many of these artisanal operators can be hard to find. Here are some thirst-slaking recommendations for visitors.

In the Comox Valley, Cumberland Brewing (p185) is one of the island's tastiest new beer makers – don't miss the Red Tape Pale Ale. A weave around the Cowichan region delivers you to Cherry Point Vineyards (☑ 250-743-1272; www.cherrypointvineyards. com; 840 Cherry Point Rd, Cobble Hill; ⊙ 10am-5pm), with its lip-smacking blackberry port; Averill Creek (☑ 250-709-9986; www.averillcreek.ca; 6552 North Rd, Duncan; tastings $5; ⊙ 11am-5pm Mar-Dec), with its patio views and lovely pinot noirs; and the rustic-chic Merridale Estate Cidery (☑ 250-743-4293; www.merridalecider.com; 1230 Merridale Rd, Cobble Hill; ⊙ 11am-5pm, reduced hours Oct-Mar), an inviting apple-cider producer that also makes brandy and has a great patio bistro.

Further south in Saanich – just a short drive from Victoria – organic apples are also on the tasting menu at Sea Cider (☑ 250-544-4824; www.seacider.ca; 2487 Mt St Michael Rd, Saanichton; ⊙ 11am-4pm). Booze of a stronger hue is the approach at Sidney's Victoria Distillers (☑ 250-544-8218; www.victoriadistillers.com; 9891 Seaport Pl; tours $7; ⊙ noon-5pm Wed & Thu, to 6pm Fri-Sun), where the lovely Oaken Gin is recommended. Both offer tours and tastings.

don't have your own transport, Adrena can also shuttle you to and from Victoria for an extra $20.

🛏 Sleeping & Eating

China Beach Campground   CAMPGROUND $
(☑519-826-6850, 800-689-9025; www.discover camping.ca; campsites $20; ⊙mid-May–mid-Sep) A popular forested campground with vehicle-accessible sites – the only one in Juan de Fuca Provincial Park. It's not far from the waterfront.

Sooke Harbour House   HOTEL $$$
(☑250-642-3421; www.sookeharbourhouse. com; 1528 Whiffen Spit Rd; d from $329; 🛜🐾) Whether you opt for the Emily Carr or the Blue Heron, each of the 28 guest rooms here has a decadent tub or steam shower, while most also have wood-burning fireplaces, balconies and expansive sea views. Expect a decanter of blackberry port to be waiting in your room when you arrive; try not to drink it all in one go.

Stick in the Mud Cafe   CAFE $
(☑250-642-5635; www.stickinthemud.ca; 6715 Eustace Rd; snacks $5-10; ⊙6am-5pm Mon-Fri, from 7:30am Sat & Sun) Fortify yourself with an 'eggamajig' (a tangy egg-filled English muffin) before hitting the Galloping Goose Trail (p157) – it'll carry you an extra few miles. For more energy add a smoothie. The cafe is hidden behind a boring strip mall and embellished by a colorful alfresco mural.

ⓘ Getting There & Away

Victoria Regional Transit System (☑250-382-6161; www.bctransit.com/victoria; $2.50) Bus 61 goes direct from the city to Sooke.

PORT RENFREW

Conveniently nestled between the Juan de Fuca and West Coast Trails, delightfully remote Port Renfrew is a great access point for either route. There are several places to rest your weary head and fuel up with non-gourmet grub.

🛏 Sleeping & Eating

Wild Renfrew   HOTEL, CABIN $$
(☑250-647-5541; www.wildrenfrew.com; 17310 Parkinson Rd; d/cabins from $139/199; 🛜🐾) With woodland cabins and lodge rooms recently upgraded, there are many ways to unplug from the city and sink into the retreat-like feel of the rainforest here. The luxury wood seaside cottages are best and each includes a

kitchen for preparing your alfresco balcony breakfast in the morning – there's also a pub nearby if you're feeling lazy.

Coastal Kitchen Cafe   CAFE $
(☑250-647-5545; 17245 Parkinson Rd; mains $8-19; ⊙8am-4pm May-Sep) For a respite from campground pasta, this laid-back, locally loved hangout serves food to satisfy a post–West Coast Trail appetite with BC craft beers to wash it down. The menu highlight? Avocado toast with poached egg and smoked salmon.

Renfrew Pub   PUB
(☑250-647-5541; 17310 Parkinson Rd; ⊙11:30-8pm Sun-Fri, to 9pm Sat) Summer drinking here is all about snagging a spot on the patio alongside the wharf. On lazy days, it's hard to peel yourself away from the shimmering shoreline views, especially if you've a round or two of BC craft ale. Pure joy, especially if you've just emerged from a hike on the West Coast Trail. The food's good too.

ⓘ Getting There & Away

It's hard to miss Port Renfrew if you're driving around Vancouver Island: it's located at the western end of Hwy 14.

West Coast Trail Express (☑888-999-2288, 250-477-8700; www.trailbus.com) shuttle-bus services arrive at the West Coast Trail trailhead at Port Renfrew from Sooke ($50), Victoria ($55) and Nanaimo ($125). The bus runs daily from mid-May to late September. Book ahead.

Cowichan Valley

A swift drive northwest of Victoria on Hwy 1, the mild, almost Mediterranean climate of the Cowichan Valley has helped it develop as the island's major farming region. There's also a growing number of vineyards, cider-makers and even a tea farm.

Cowichan Bay

'Cow Bay' to the locals, the region's most attractive pit stop is a colorful string of wooden buildings perched over a mountain-framed ocean inlet. It's well worth an afternoon of your time, although it might take that long to find parking on a busy summer day.

Maritime Centre   MUSEUM
(☑250-746-4955; www.classicboats.org; 1761 Cowichan Bay Rd; suggested donation $5; ⊙9am-4pm Wed-Sun) A lovely pier-length attraction aimed at anyone with more than a passing

interest in salty history, this folksy facility is lined with intricate models, seafaring displays and usually at least one or two locals working on some kind of boat-building or repairing project. It's all wonderfully sprawling and random.

True Grain Bread   FOOD
(☑ 250-746-7664; www.truegrain.ca; 1725 Cowichan Bay Rd; ⊘ 8am-6pm, closed Mon Nov-Feb) Adding the welcome aroma of baking bread to the oily harbor smells, True Grain is part of a three-shop island chain. From sourdough to raisin, the bread is all handcrafted, organic and milled on-site (from BC-farmed grain). Homemade crackers and cookies will add to your picnic hamper – if it's not already too weighed-down with the chocolate buns.

Masthead Restaurant   NORTHWESTERN US $$$
(☑ 250-748-3714; www.themastheadrestaurant.com; 1705 Cowichan Bay Rd; mains $22-54; ⊘ 5-10pm) The patio deck of this charming, 1863 heritage-building restaurant is a fine place for a splurge, and the $37 three-course BC-sourced tasting menu is surprisingly good value. Seasonal ingredients form the approach here and there are also some good Cowichan Valley wines to try if you're feeling boozily adventurous.

❶ Getting There & Away

Driving the island's main Hwy 1 thoroughfare, take the Cowichan Bay Rd turnoff (it's about 45 minutes away from Victoria). This leads right into the village. Parking is challenging here in summer so arrive early to find a roadside spot.

Tofino Bus (www.tofinobus.com) stops at the Koksilah Transit Exchange on Hwy 1, 2.5km from the waterfront community. Four buses a day head north to Nanaimo ($25, 1¼ hours) and south to Victoria ($20, 50 minutes). Reserve in advance.

Chemainus

POP 3900

After its last big sawmill shut down in 1983, tiny Chemainus became the model for BC communities dealing with declining natural-resource jobs. Instead of submitting to a slow death, town officials commissioned a giant wall-mural depicting local history. More than 45 artworks were later added and street art, along with an excellent local theater, remains the mainstay of Chemainus' modern tourism industry.

Stroll the Chemainus streets (expect a permanent aroma of fresh-cut logs from the small sawmill nearby) on a mural hunt and you'll pass artsy boutiques and tempting ice-cream shops, some housed in heritage buildings and others in attractive faux-historic piles. In the evening, the surprisingly large **Chemainus Theatre** (www.chemainustheatrefestival.ca; 9737 Chemainus Rd; tickets from $25) stages professional productions, mostly popular plays and musicals, to keep you occupied.

Chemainus is more a place for a quick bite than a protracted dinner. Its best spot for a repast is the **Willow Street Cafe** (☑ 250-246-2434; www.willowstreetcafe.com; 9749 Willow St; mains $12-15; ⊘ 8am-5pm; ☏).

Check in at the **visitor center** (☑ 250-246-3944; www.visitchemainus.ca; 9799 Waterwheel Cres; ⊘ 9:30am-5pm mid-Jun–Aug, reduced hours in winter) for mural maps and further information, plus the little community museum in the same building.

❶ Getting There & Away

Chemainus is an hour's drive north from Victoria via Hwy 1; look for the exit after you pass through Duncan.

Tofino Bus (www.tofinobus.com) calls in at least three times daily on its way between Victoria ($25, one hour) and Nanaimo ($20, one hour). Reserve ahead. The bus stops on Hwy 1, 2.5km from the town center.

Nanaimo

☑ 250 / POP 90,000

Vancouver Island's 'second metropolis,' Nanaimo will never have the allure of tourist-magnet Victoria, but the Harbour City has undergone some quiet upgrades since the 1990s. It's seen the emergence, especially on Commercial St, of some good shops and eateries, plus a popular museum. With dedicated ferry services from the mainland, the city is also a handy hub for exploring the rest of the island.

◉ Sights & Activities

Nanaimo Museum   MUSEUM
(☑ 250-753-1821; www.nanaimomuseum.ca; 100 Museum Way; adult/child $2/75¢; ⊘ 10am-5pm daily, closed Sun Sep–mid-May) This popular museum just off the Commercial St main drag showcases the region's heritage, from First Nations to colonial, maritime, sporting and beyond. Highlights of the eclectic collec-

Nanaimo

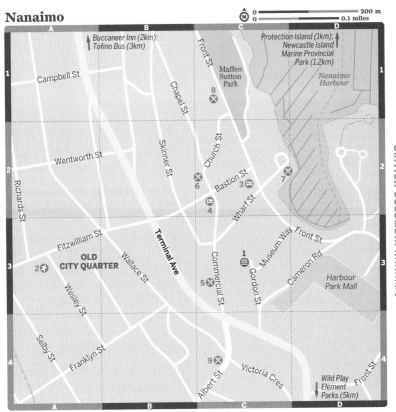

Nanaimo

tion include exhibits on the local sweet treat, Nanaimo bars (p172), and bathtub racing – plus a carved golden beaver from an 1890s tugboat. Ask at the front desk about the museum's guided walking-tour program as well

as summertime entry to the nearby **Bastion**, an 1853 wooden tower fortification.

**Newcastle Island
Marine Provincial Park**   PARK
(www.newcastleisland.ca) 🌿 Nanaimo's rustic outdoor getaway (also known as Saysutshun in the indigenous language) offers 22km of **hiking** and **biking** trails, plus beaches and wildlife-spotting. Traditional Coast Salish land, it was the site of shipyards and coal mines before becoming a popular summer excursion for locals in the 1930s when a tea pavilion was added. Accessed by a 10-minute ferry hop from the harbor (adult/child return $8/5), the island has a seasonal eatery and regular First Nations dancing displays.

Wild Play Element Parks   AMUSEMENT PARK
(📞250-716-7874; www.wildplay.com; 35 Nanaimo River Rd; ⏰10am-6pm mid-May–Sep, reduced hours Oct–mid-May; 👶) The perfect spot to tire your kids out, this tree-lined adventure playground is packed with adrenaline-pumping fun, from

THE NANAIMO BAR

The town's culinary gift to the world is a small three-layered slab of wafer topped with cream and icing that's intensely sweet and heavy on calories. While there are numerous varieties, classic Nanaimo bars usually combine coconut, vanilla custard and chocolate flavors to dramatic effect.

The bar's exact origins are subject to conjecture. There are at least 100 different recipes and, while the ingredients vary, the sweet slabs all adhere to one central premise: no baking is required. The City of Nanaimo has come up with a 34-stop 'Nanaimo Trail' where you can enjoy the bar in myriad weird manifestations including in a cocktail at **Modern Cafe** (☑250-754-5022; www.themoderncafe.ca; 221 Commercial St; mains $15-30; ⊙8am-late) or deep-fried in batter at **Pirate Chips** (☑250-753-2447; www.piratechips.ca; 75 Front St; mains $10-21; ⊙11am-8pm Tue-Thu & Sun, to 9pm Fri & Sat).

bungee jumping to scream-triggering ziplining. Along with its fun obstacle courses, there's plenty of additional action to keep the whole family occupied, from woodsy walking trails to busy volleyball courts. Bring a picnic and come for at least half a day.

Board Game House AMUSEMENT PARK
(☑250- 703-1669; www.bghouse.ca; 411B Fitzwilliam St; adult/child $5/2.50; ⊙noon-10pm Tue-Thu, to 11pm Fri, 11am-11pm Sat, 11am-7pm Sun; ⚐) Proving computers haven't completely killed off Dungeons & Dragons, this new venture in Nanaimo's Old City Quarter is a cafe, store and activity center where you can sit down and play retro board games over a sandwich and (highly recommended) milkshake. Ideal for drizzly, drippy autumn afternoons (of which Nanaimo has many).

🛏 Sleeping

Painted Turtle Guesthouse HOSTEL $
(☑250-753-4432; www.paintedturtle.ca; 121 Bastion St; dm/r $38/79; @⚐) Vancouver Island does well with hostels and this superbly located Nanaimo venture is an ideal overnighter if you're heading to Tofino, Victoria or up north. HI-affiliated, the hostel has small dorms along with 10 hotel-style private rooms (there are also two family rooms). Hardwood floors and IKEA-style furnishings line a large and welcoming kitchen-lounge combo.

Buccaneer Inn MOTEL $$
(☑250-753-1246; www.buccaneerinn.com; 1577 Stewart Ave; d/ste from $99/169; P⚐) This friendly, family-run motel has a gleaming white exterior that makes it hard to pass by. It's worth staying in as the neat-and-tidy approach is carried over into the maritime-themed rooms, most of which have kitchen facilities. Splurge on a spacious suite

and you'll have a fireplace, full kitchen and flat-screen TV. It's handy for the Departure Bay ferry terminal.

Coast Bastion Hotel HOTEL $$
(☑250-753-6601; www.coasthotels.com; 11 Bastion St; d from $185; ❀@⚐❄) Downtown's best hotel has an unbeatable location overlooking the harbor, with most guests enjoying sparkling waterfront views – when it's not foggy. Rooms have been well refurbished with a lounge-modern élan in recent years. Bank on wall-mounted flat-screens and, in most rooms, small refrigerators. The lobby restaurant-bar is a popular hangout and there's a spa if you want to chillax.

🍴 Eating & Drinking

★ **Gabriel's Gourmet Cafe** INTERNATIONAL $
(☑250-714-0271; www.gabrielscafe.ca; 39 Commercial St; mains $10-15; ⊙8am-7pm; ⚐▨) ✎ Place your order upfront, grab a table (made from reused bowling-alley wood) and wait for the magic to appear. Gabriel's out-of-the-ordinary renditions of familiar dishes – wraps, soups, bowls and breakfasts – are made by people on first-name terms with their local farmer. Vegans and vegetarians are well catered for and there's some sidewalk seating if it's too busy indoors.

The attention to detail is equal to the attention to ethical sourcing. Try the spoon-licking-good Malaysian-peanut-sauce chicken rice bowl or the quinoa-and-chickpea fritter with hummus. It's hard to believe that this busy hub was run out of a wheel-less food truck until relatively recently.

Vault Cafe CAFE $
(☑778-441-2950; 499 Wallace St; mains $13-16; ⊙7am-10pm Mon & Tue, to midnight Wed-Fri, 8am-midnight Sat, 9am-4pm Sun; ⚐) This old bank building reborn in bright pink might

have floated over from bohemian Paris in the age of Joyce and Hemingway. There's plenty to gaze at inside, from the romantic lamps to the elegant sofas to the Toulouse-Lautrec style prints. Good coffee, bagels and regular live music are the icing on top.

Penny's Palapa   MEXICAN $$
(☑250-753-2150; www.pennyspalapa.com; 10 Wharf St, Dock H; mains $9-19; ⊙11am-8pm May-Sep; ☑) This flower-and-flag-bedecked floating hut and patio in the harbor is lovely for an alfresco meal among the jostling boats. The inventive, well-priced menu of Mexican delights includes seasonal seafood specials (the signature halibut tacos are great) plus some good vegan options. The dining area fills rapidly on balmy summer evenings. When it comes to drinks, it's all about the margaritas.

★ Crow and Gate   PUB
(☑250-722-3731; www.crowandgate.ca; 2313 Yellow Point Rd, Cedra; ⊙11am-11pm) Taking you back to dear ole Blighty (England) is this out-of-town Brit-style pub with a dark, wood-beam interior and a wonderfully stodgy menu of housemade pies, Scotch eggs and bangers and mash. Providing a beery backup is a formidable lineup of foamy drafts including Guinness and English-style (but BC-brewed) Blue Buck Ale.

It's 13km from town, but insanely popular, especially in the summer when you can sit in the idyllic country garden and quaff to your heart's content. No minors.

ℹ Information

Nanaimo Visitor Centre (☑250-751-1556; www.tourismnanaimo.com; 2450 Northfield Rd; ⊙9am-6pm Apr-Sep, reduced hours Oct-Mar) The main visitor center is 6km northwest of the city center, but there's also a smaller booth overlooking the harbor that gives out information in the summer.

ℹ Getting There & Away

AIR
Nanaimo Airport (YCD; ☑250-924-2157; www.nanaimoairport.com) is 18km south of town via Hwy 1. Frequent **Air Canada** (www.aircanada.com) and **WestJet** (www.westjet.com) flights arrive here from Vancouver (from $175, 25 minutes) throughout the day. There are also a couple of flights to and from Calgary ($220, 1½ hours).

Frequent and convenient **Harbour Air** (☑250-714-0900; www.harbourair.com) floatplane

services arrive in the inner harbor from downtown Vancouver ($110, 20 minutes).

BOAT
Nanaimo has two different ferry terminals located 19km apart by road.

BC Ferries (☑250-386-3431; www.bcferries.com) from Tsawwassen (passenger/vehicle $17.20/57.50, two hours) arrive at Duke Point, 14km south of Nanaimo. Services from West Vancouver's Horseshoe Bay (passenger/vehicle $17.20/57.50, 95 minutes) arrive at Departure Bay, 3km north of the city center via Hwy 1.

BUS
Tofino Bus (☑866-986-3466; www.tofinobus.com) serves all points north, west and south, including Campbell River ($42, 2½ hours, three daily), Tofino ($53, four hours, two daily) and Victoria ($32, 2¼ hours, three daily). Services pick up at Woodgrove Mall and the Departure Bay ferry terminal.

ℹ Getting Around

Downtown Nanaimo, around the harbor, is highly walkable, but after that the city spreads out and a car or strong biking legs are required. Be aware that taxis are expensive here.

Nanaimo Airporter (www.nanaimoairporter.com; from $26) Provides door-to-door service to downtown from both ferry terminals, as well as handy airport drop-off and pickup.

Nanaimo Regional Transit (www.bctransit.com; single trip/day pass $2.50/6.25) Buses stop along Gordon St, west of Harbour Park Mall. Bus 2 goes to the Departure Bay ferry terminal. No city buses run to Duke Point.

Parksville & Qualicum

Qualicum Beach is not without its rebellious spirit, despite having the oldest demographic in Canada (average age: 60). Strict planning laws mean there are no big shops or restaurant franchises in this small seaside settlement, with its handsome timber-framed houses and strong community vibe.

Anchored by a historic hotel where John Wayne once laid his Stetson, Qualicum is known for its golf courses, long pebbly beach and pastoral surroundings that produce high-quality Qualicum cheeses (sold in supermarkets throughout southern BC). Otherwise, this is primarily a place to chill out, sip tea in manicured gardens and plan sorties to nearby caves and provincial parks.

Parksville, 15 minutes south of Qualicum, has the best of the area's beaches and is hence a little busier and more popular with families.

◉ Sights

Morningstar Farm   FARM
(☑ 250-954-3931; www.morningstarfarm.ca; 403 Lowrys Rd; ⊙ 9am-5pm; 🖪) **FREE** Check out the region's 'locavore' credentials at this delightful and highly welcoming working farmstead. Let your kids run wild – most will quickly fall in love with the rabbits – then hunt down some samples from the on-site Little Qualicum Cheeseworks and Mooberry Winery: the 'Bleu Claire' cheese is recommended, along with a bottle of velvety blueberry wine to go.

The farm is located roughly halfway between Parksville and Qualicum Beach.

Coombs Old Country Market   MARKET
(☑ 250-248-6272; www.oldcountrymarket.com; 2326 Alberni Hwy, Coombs; ⊙ 9am-6pm Feb-Dec) The mother of all pit stops, this wood-framed and turf-roofed food and crafts menagerie is stuffed with bakery and produce delectables. It attracts huge numbers of visitors on summer days, when cameras are pointed at the grassy roof where a herd of goats spends the season. Nip inside for giant ice-cream cones, heaping pizzas and the deli makings of a great picnic. Need a souvenir? Grab a Billy Gruff chocolate bar.

Save some time to explore the attendant store and attractions clustered around the site, from clothing emporiums to an Italian trattoria.

Milner Gardens & Woodland   GARDENS
(☑ 250-752-6153; www2.viu.ca/milnergardens; 2179 W Island Hwy, Qualicum Beach; adult/youth/child $12/7/free; ⊙ 10am-5pm mid-Apr–Aug, reduced hours Feb-Apr, Sep-Oct, closed Nov-Jan) This idyllic outdoor attraction combines rambling forest trails shaded by centuries-old trees with flower-packed gardens planted with magnificent trilliums and rhododendrons. Meander down to the 1930s **tearoom** on a bluff overlooking the water. Then tuck into tea and scones ($13.50) on the porch and drink in views of the bird-lined shore and snowcapped peaks shimmering on the horizon.

Horne Lake Caves
& Outdoor Centre   PARK
(☑ 250-248-7829; www.hornelake.com; tours from $27; ⊙ 9am-5pm) BC's best spelunking, a 45-minute drive from Parksville. Some caves are open to the public for self-exploration, though the excellent guided tours are recommended, ranging from family-friendly to

extreme; book ahead for these. To get there, take Hwy 19 toward Courtenay, then take exit 75 and proceed for 12km on the gravel road; if you get lost en route give the outdoor center a call.

🛏 Sleeping & Eating

★ Crown Mansion   BOUTIQUE HOTEL **$$**
(☑ 250-752-5776; www.crownmansion.com; 292 E Crescent Rd, Qualicum Beach; d from $179; 🅿 🛜) The effortlessly regal Crown Mansion is easily worthy of its name. Dating from 1914, this country hotel mixes modern comforts with handsome historical features: check out the elaborate wooden fireplace complete with family crest. The suite rooms on the ground floor of a newer wing are the best deal with their humongous bathrooms (with heated floors) and four-poster beds.

Famous past guests include American actors John Wayne and Rita Hayworth, as well as the King of Siam. Complimentary continental breakfast is served in a music room complete with bay window near the entrance.

Blue Willow Guest House   B&B **$$**
(☑ 250-752-9052; www.bluewillowguesthouse.com; 524 Quatna Rd, Qualicum Beach; d from $155) A surprisingly spacious, delightfully tranquil Victorian-style cottage, this lovely B&B has a book-lined lounge, exposed beams and a fragrant country garden. The two rooms and one self-contained suite are lined with antiques and each is extremely homey. The attention to detail carries over to the gourmet breakfast: served in the conservatory, it's accompanied by finger-licking home-baked treats.

★ Free Spirit Spheres   CABIN **$$$**
(☑ 250-757-9445; www.freespiritspheres.com; 420 Horne Lake Rd, Qualicum Beach; spheres from $314) When it comes to extravagantly unconventional accommodations, these three wooden spheres, handmade by owner-inventor Tom Chudleigh and suspended like giant eyes within the forest canopy, score 10 out of 10. Compact two- to three-person spheres have pull-down beds, built-in cabinets and mini-libraries rather than TVs and are a perfect way to commune with BC's giant trees.

Named 'Eve' (the smallest and most basic), 'Eryn' and 'Melody,' each sphere is reached by a wooden spiral staircase with an outhouse situated at the bottom (oh, those nighttime walks!). There's also a ground-level facilities block with a surprisingly deluxe sauna, BBQ and hotel-quality showers.

The spheres are located 18km northwest of Qualicum Beach, but are well hidden in the forest and hard to find. Book ahead and ask for directions.

Tom is in the process of building another sphere and moving the whole project to another site. Check online for updates.

Bistro 694   CANADIAN $$$
([✓] 250-752-0301; www.bistro694.com; 694 Memorial Ave, Qualicum Beach; mains $22-32; ☺4-9pm Thu-Sun) Any local will tell you to cancel your other dinner plans and head straight here. You'll find an intimate, candlelit dining room little bigger than a train carriage and a big-city menu fusing top-notch regional ingredients with knowing international nods. It's worth taking the seafood route, especially if the Balinese prawn curry or highly addictive seafood crepes are available.

ⓘ Information

For more information on the area, visit www. parksvillequalicumbeach.com.

ⓘ Getting There & Away

Tofino Bus services arrive in Parksville from Victoria ($42, 3½ hours, four daily) and Nanaimo ($19, 30 minutes, four daily), among other destinations.

Port Alberni

[✓] 250 / POP 18,000
With resource jobs declining, Alberni – located on Hwy 4 between the island's east and west coasts – has been dipping its toe into tourism in recent years. And while the downtown core is a little run-down, there are some good historical attractions and outdoor activities to consider before you drive on through.

◎ Sights & Acivities

Cathedral Grove   PARK
(www.bcparks.ca; MacMillan Provincial Park; [P]) This spiritual home of tree-huggers is the mystical highlight of **MacMillan Provincial Park**. Located between Parksville and Port Alberni, it's often overrun with summer visitors – try not to knock them down as they scamper across the highway in front of you. Short accessible trails on either side of the road wind through a dense canopy of vegetation, offering glimpses of some of BC's oldest trees, including centuries-old Douglas firs more than 3m in diameter. Only huggable in groups.

Alberni Valley Museum   MUSEUM
([✓] 250-723-2181; www.alberniheritage.com; 4255 Wallace St; by donation; ☺10am-5pm Tue-Sat, to 8pm Thu) Don't be put off by the unassuming concrete exterior: this is one of Vancouver Island's best community museums. Studded with fascinating First Nations displays – plus an eclectic array of vintage exhibits ranging from bottle caps to dresses and old-school toys – it's worth an hour of anyone's time.

History buffs should also hop aboard the summertime **Alberni Pacific Railway steam train** (www.alberniheritage.com/ alberni-pacific-railway), likewise operated by the Alberni Valley Heritage Network, for a trundle to McLean Mill; it's a National Historic Site.

MV Frances Barkley   CRUISE
([✓] 250-723-8313; www.ladyrosemarine.com; 5425 Argyle St; round-trip Bamfield/Ucluelet $84/88) This historic boat service is a vital link for the region's remote communities, ferrying freight, supplies and passengers between Alberni and Bamfield thrice weekly. In summer, with its route extended to Ucluelet and the utterly beautiful Broken Group Islands, it lures kayakers and mountain bikers – as well as those who just fancy an idyllic day cruise up Barkley Sound.

Port Alberni–Bamfield takes 4½ hours one-way. The summer run to the Broken Group Islands and Ucluelet takes three and five hours respectively. The company also runs a lodge on the Broken Group Islands that can be booked through the website.

Batstar Adventure Tours   KAYAKING
([✓] 250-724-2050; www.batstar.com; 6360 Springfield Rd) If you're unsure about exploring the beautiful but undeniably remote Broken Group Islands by kayak on your own, this outfit can sort you out. From long-weekend jaunts to multiday odysseys of the life-changing variety, all the details, including food and accommodations, are taken care of on these guided adventures.

🛏 Sleeping & Eating

Hummingbird Guesthouse   B&B $$
([✓] 250-720-2111; www.hummingbirdguesthouse. com; 5769 River Rd; ste from $150; ☎) With four large suites and a huge deck with its own

LOCAL KNOWLEDGE

THE DOPE ON POT RULES

Canada became the second country in the world to legalize non-medicinal marijuana in October 2018. Federal law allows public possession of up to 30g of marijuana, but its consumption is generally limited to places where cigarette smoking is permitted. The product can either be bought from licensed private or government-run stores, or purchased from registered online vendors. Private individuals are legally permitted to grow up to four marijuana plants.

The legal age for marijuana consumption is 19 in BC and the Yukon and 18 in Alberta. Driving under the influence of the drug and transporting it across international boundaries is illegal.

Some cities have local bylaws concerning the drug's use. For example, in Calgary it is illegal to consume marijuana in public places. Wise up before you travel to avoid getting caught out.

hot tub, this modern B&B has a home-away-from-home feel. There's a shared kitchen on each of the two floors and each suite has satellite TV; one has its own sauna. For families, there's a teen-friendly game room out back. Hummingbirds in the garden are laid on free of charge.

Mountain View Bakery & Deli　　　BAKERY $
(☑ 250-724-1813; 4561 Gertrude St; snacks $4-10; ⊘ 7:30am-6pm Tue-Sat) If you're making a transportation connection in Port Alberni, pray you have time to dash across the road to this traditional bakery with a huge selection of pies, samosas, wraps, sandwiches, pastries, brownies, cheesecakes, muffins, buns and...there goes your bus!

Bare Bones Fish & Chips　　　FISH & CHIPS $$
(☑ 250-720-0900; 4824 Johnston Rd; mains $9-21; ⊘ 11:30am-7:30pm Sun-Thu, to 8pm Fri & Sat) Occupying a decommissioned wooden church, this smashing fry-joint serves cod, salmon and halibut in three different styles (beer-battered recommended), adding a tangle of delicious chips and the restaurant's own lemon-dill dip. Arrive off-peak to avoid the rush (this place is a true local favorite) and add a prawn side dish if you're still hungry (you won't be).

ⓘ Information

For more on what to do in the region, visit www.albernivalleytourism.com.

ⓘ Getting There & Away

Tofino Bus (☑ 866-986-3466; www.tofinobus.com; 4541 Margaret St) services arrive here from Victoria ($60, 4½ hours, two daily) and Tofino ($36, 2½ hours, two daily), among other places.

Pacific Rim National Park Reserve

Dramatic, wave-whipped beaches and brooding, mist-licked forests make the Pacific Rim National Park Reserve a must-see for anyone interested in encountering BC's raw West Coast wilderness. The 500-sq-km park comprises the northern Long Beach Unit, between Tofino and Ucluelet; the Broken Group Islands Unit in Barkley Sound; and, to the south, the ever-popular West Coast Trail Unit. If you're stopping in the park, you'll need to pay and display a pass, available from the visitor center or from the yellow dispensers dotted along the highway.

Long Beach Unit

Attracting the lion's share of park visitors, Long Beach Unit is easily accessible by car along the Pacific Rim Hwy, or you can walk or cycle in from Tofino and Ucluelet. Wide sandy beaches, untamed surf, lots of beach-combing nooks, plus a living museum of dense, old-growth rainforest, are the main reasons for the summer tourist clamor. Cox Bay Beach alone is an ideal hangout for surfers and families. Seabirds, sand dollars and purple-and-orange starfish abound.

For an introduction to the area's natural history and First Nations heritage, visit the Kwisitis Visitor Centre (Wick Rd; ⊘ 10am-5pm May-Oct, Fri-Sun only Mar, Apr, Nov & Dec) FREE overlooking Wickaninnish Beach. If you're suddenly inspired to plunge in for a stroll, try one of the following walking trails, keeping your eyes peeled for bald eagles and giant banana slugs. Safety precautions apply: tread carefully over slippery surfaces and never turn your back on the mischievous surf.

Long Beach Great scenery along the sandy shore (1.2km; easy).

Rainforest Trail Two interpretive loops through old-growth forest (1km; moderate).

Schooner Trail Passes through old- and second-growth forests with beach access (1km; moderate).

Shorepine Bog Loops around a moss-layered bog (800m; easy and wheelchair-accessible).

West Coast Trail Unit

The 75km West Coast Trail is BC's best-known hiking route. It's also one of the toughest, not for the uninitiated. There are two things you'll need to know before tackling it: it might hurt and you'll want to do it again next year.

The trail winds along the wave-lapped rainforest shoreline between trailhead information centers at Pachena Bay, 5km south of Bamfield on the north end, and Gordon River, 5km north of Port Renfrew on the southern tip. The entire stretch takes between five and seven days to complete. Alternatively, a midpoint entrance at Nitinat Lake, operated by the Ditidaht First Nation (⌨250-745-3999; www.westcoasttrail.com), can cut your visit to a two- or three-day adventure. Check the website for packages.

Open from May to the end of September, access to the route is limited to 75 overnight backpackers each day and reservations (⌨519-826-5391, 877-737-3783; www.reservation. pc.gc.ca; nonrefundable reservation fee $11) are required. Book as far ahead as you can – reservations open in January each year. All overnighters must pay a trail-user fee ($127.50), plus a per-person reservation fee ($24.50) and the price of the short ferry crossings along the length of the route. All overnighters must attend a detailed orientation session before departing. If you don't have a reservation on the day you arrive, your name can be added to a standby list for any remaining spots (don't count on this, though, especially during the summer peak).

If you don't want to go the whole hog (you wimp), you can do a day hike or hike half the trail from Pachena Bay, considered the easier end of the route. Overnight hikers who only hike this end of the trail can exit from Nitinat Lake. Day hikers are exempt from the pricey trail-user fee, but they need to get a day-use permit at one of the trailheads.

West Coast Trail walkers must be able to manage rough, slippery terrain, stream crossings and adverse, suddenly changing weather. There are more than 100 little, and some not-so-little, bridges and 70 ladders. Be prepared to treat or boil all water and cook on a lightweight camping stove; you'll be bringing in all your own food. Hikers can rest their weary muscles at any of the basic campsites along the route, most of which have solar-composting outhouses. It's recommended that you set out from a trailhead at least five hours before sundown to ensure you reach a campsite before nightfall – stumbling around in the dark is the prime cause of accidents on this route.

West Coast Trail Express (p178) runs a handy shuttle service to and from the trailheads. Book ahead.

Broken Groups Islands Unit

Comprising some 300 islands and rocks scattered across 80 sq km around the entrance to Barkley Sound, this serene natural wilderness is beloved of visiting kayakers – especially those who enjoy close-up views of whales, porpoises and multitudinous birdlife. Compasses are required for navigating here, unless you fancy paddling to Hawaii.

If you're up for a trek, Lady Rose Marine Services (p178) will ship you and your kayak from Port Alberni to its Sechart Lodge three hours away in Barkley Sound. The lodge rents kayaks if you'd rather travel light and it also offers accommodations (single/double $211/357, including meals).

From there, popular paddle destinations include Gibraltar Island, one hour away, with its sheltered campground and explorable beaches and tidal pools. Willis Island (1½ hours from Sechart) is also popular. It has a campground and, at low tide, you can walk to the surrounding islands. Remote Benson Island (four hours from Sechart) has a campground, grazing deer and a blowhole.

Camping fees are $9.80 per night, payable at Sechart or to the boat-based staff who patrol the region – they can collect additional fees from you if you decide to stay longer. The campgrounds are predictably basic and have solar composting toilets, but you must carry out all your garbage. Bring your own drinking water since island creeks are often dry in summer.

BRITISH COLUMBIA PACIFIC RIM NATIONAL PARK RESERVE

ℹ Information

Pacific Rim Visitors Centre (☑ 250-726-4600; www.pacificrimvisitor.ca; 2791 Pacific Rim Hwy, Ucuelet; ⊙10am-4:30pm Tue-Sat) At the junction of Hwy 4 and the Tofino–Ucluelet road, 8km north of Ucluelet and 32km south of Tofino.

ℹ Getting There & Away

West Coast Trail Express (☑ 250-477-8700; www.trailbus.com) shuttle-bus services arrive at West Coast Trail Unit trailheads at Bamfield and Port Renfrew from Victoria ($55 to $110) and Nanaimo ($125). The bus runs daily from mid-May to late September. Book ahead.

The kayakers paradise of the Broken Group Islands Unit can be accessed by boat via **Lady Rose Marine Services** (☑ 250-723-8313; www. ladyrosemarine.com) from Port Alberni and Ucluelet.

The Long Beach Unit can be accessed from Tofino and Ucluelet on foot, by bicycle or by car.

Tofino

☑ 250 / POP 1950

Christened 'Tuff City' by its early inhabitants due to its isolation and heavy reliance on logging, 21st-century Tofino remains a diminutive end-of-the-road town bordered by rugged wilderness on one side and the raging Pacific on the other. Although less than 2000 Tofitians live here permanently, the population swells tenfold in the summer when visitors from far and wide arrive for whale-watching, kayaking, fishing and – best of all – surfing.

Tofino is the undisputed surfing capital of Canada and the annual inundation of wave-riding surf bums gives the place a laid-back, modern-hippie flavor. Eschewing international chains and restaurant franchises, the town supports a burgeoning farm-to-table food movement and counts on a strong history of environmental activism.

◎ Sights

Meares Island   PARK

Visible across Clayoquot Sound and accessible via kayak or water taxi from the Tofino waterfront, Meares Island was the site of the key 1984 Clayoquot Sound anti-logging protest that kicked off the region's latter-day environmental movement. As a result, it preserves some geriatric trees including a 1500-year-old red cedar, called the 'Hanging Garden,' that would have been a sapling not long after the Roman Empire fell. There are two hiking trails on Meares.

The **Big Tree Trail** is a 4.2km loop, some of it on boardwalk, that takes in the Hanging Garden and other impressively large trees. The **Lone Cone Trail** is a steep scramble to the top of the distinctive crinkled mountain visible from Tofino. It's 7km round-trip with 730m of ascent. The trails start in different places. A water taxi costs $25 for the Big Tree and $40 for the Lone Cone.

Ahousat   PARK

(www.wildsidetrail.com; trail fee $25) Situated on remote Flores Island and accessed by tour boat or kayak, Ahousat is the mystical location of the spectacular **Wild Side Heritage Trail**, a moderately difficult path that traverses 11km of forests, beaches and headlands between Ahousat and Cow Bay. There's a natural warm spring on the island and it's also home to a First Nations band. A popular destination for kayakers, camping (no facilities) is allowed.

There's a twice-daily water taxi in the summer to Flores Island ($20, 30 minutes). At a push the 22km round-trip hike can be done in a long nine-hour day.

**Tofino Botanical
Gardens**   GARDENS

(☑ 250-725-1220; www.tbgf.org; 1084 Pacific Rim Hwy; 3-days adult/child $12/free; ⊙8am-dusk) Explore what coastal temperate rainforests are all about by checking out the frog pond, forest boardwalk, native plants and educational workshops at this smashing, bird-packed attraction. New sculptures have been added to the garden in recent years, many by local artists. Pick up a field guide from the front desk to illuminate your self-guided exploration.There's a $1 discount on admission if you arrive car-free.

**Maquinna Marine
Provincial Park**   HOT SPRINGS

(www.bcparks.ca) One of the most popular day trips from Tofino, the highlight here is **Hot Spring Cove**. Tranquility-minded trekkers travel to the park by Zodiac boat or seaplane, watching for whales and other sea critters en route. From the boat landing, 2km of boardwalks lead to the natural hot pools.

Eagle Aerie Gallery   GALLERY

(☑ 250-725-3235; www.royhenryvickers.com; 350 Campbell St; ⊙10am-5pm) **FREE** Showcasing the work of First Nations artist Roy Henry Vickers, this dramatic, longhouse-style building is a downtown landmark. Inside you'll find beautifully presented paintings and carvings (most of them for sale) as well as occasional opportunities to meet the man himself.

Activities

★ Tonquin Trail   HIKING

If you're freshly arrived in Tofino and want to know what makes this place so special, head down First St and join the undulating gravel trail to Tonquin Beach (1.2km one-way) where a magical parting of the trees reveals a rock-punctuated swath of sand known for its life-affirming sunsets.

If you can drag yourself away from the natural light show, the trail leads further south along the coast to Third Beach and Middle Beach with several peek-a-boo lookouts on the way.

Ocean Outfitters   BOATING

(☏ 250-725-2866; www.oceanoutfitters.bc.ca; 368 Main St; adult/child $109/89) The largest of the local water-excursion operators (judging by its slick office, which also contains a coffee bar), Ocean Outfitters offers the popular Tofino tour triumvirate of whale-watching, bear-viewing and hot-springs treks. It also runs water taxis to Meares Island as well as multiday kayaking excursions up Tofino Inlet.

Pacific Surf School   SURFING

(www.pacificsurfschool.com; 430 Campbell St; board rental 6/24hr $20/25) Offers rentals, camps and lessons for beginners and board rental for old hands.

T'ashii Paddle School   CANOEING

(☏ 250-266-3787; www.tofinopaddle.com; 1258 Pacific Rim Hwy; tours from $65) Tour the regional waters in a canoe (you'll be doing the paddling) with a First Nations guide who provides an evocative interpretive narration. Walking tours also available.

Tofino Sea Kayaking   KAYAKING

(☏ 250-725-4222; www.tofinoseakayaking.com; 320 Main St; tours from $69) Evocative guided paddles around Clayoquot Sound, over to Meares Island and further up the coast. The outfit offers rentals ($50 per day) for go-it-aloners and multiday excursions with camping for adventurers.

🛌 Sleeping

Whalers on the Point Guesthouse   HOSTEL $

(☏ 250-725-3443; www.hihostels.ca; 81 West St; dm/r $59/169; 🖥) Close to the action, but with a secluded waterfront location, this excellent HI hostel is a comfy, wood-lined retreat. Dorms are mercifully small (the female-only one has the best waterfront views) and there are some highly sought-after private rooms. Facilities include a BBQ patio, games room and a wet sauna. Reservations are essential in summer.

Ocean Village Beach Resort   CABIN $$

(☏ 250-725-3755; www.oceanvillageresort.com; 555 Hellesen Dr; ste from $239; 🅿🖥♿🐾) This immaculate beachside resort of bee-hive-shaped cedar cabins – hence the woodsy aroma when you step in the door – is a family favorite with a Scandinavian look. All units face the nearby shoreline and have handy kitchens. If your kids tire of the beach, there's an indoor saltwater pool and lots of board games to keep them occupied.

Ecolodge   HOSTEL $$

(☏ 250-725-1220; www.tbgf.org; 1084 Pacific Rim Hwy; r incl breakfast from $159; 🅿@🖥) 🌿 This quiet, wood-built education center on the grounds of the botanical gardens is popular with families and groups for its selection of rooms, large kitchen and on-site laundry. There's a bunk room that's around $45 per

---

STORMING TOFINO

Started as a clever marketing ploy to lure off-season visitors, storm-watching has become a popular reason to visit the island's wild West Coast between November and March. View spectacularly crashing winter waves, then scamper back inside for hot chocolate with a face freckled by sea salt. There are usually good off-peak accommodations deals during storm-watching season and many hotels can supply you with loaner 'Tofino tuxedos,' otherwise known as waterproof gear. The best spots to catch a few crashing spectacles are Cox Bay, Chesterman Beach, Long Beach, Second Bay and Wickaninnish Beach. Just remember not to get too close or turn your back on the waves: these gigantic swells can have you in the water within seconds.

person per night in summer for groups of four. Rates include garden entry.

Tofino Resort & Marina
HOTEL $$

(☑1-855-615-7592; www.tofinoresortandmarina. com; 634 Campbell St; r from $159; ☎) All mod cons greet you at this updated small resort with an affiliated bar and restaurant overlooking the marina. Even the viewless rooms have king-sized beds, snazzy bathrooms (with sensor-activated lights), and blown-up aerial photos of Tofino's coastline accented on one wall.

★ Wickaninnish Inn
HOTEL $$$

(☑250-725-3100; www.wickinn.com; Chesterman Beach; d $360-840; P ☎ 🐾) 🍴 Cornering the market in luxury winter storm-watching packages, 'the Wick' is worth a stay any time of year. Embodying nature with its recycled-wood furnishings, natural stone tiles and the ambience of a place grown rather than constructed, the sumptuous guest rooms have push-button TVs that rise out of the furniture, two-person hot tubs, gas fireplaces, floor-to-ceiling windows and wave-whipped balconies.

A litany of deluxe extras includes raincoats and umbrellas for outside, bathrobes and slippers if you're staying indoors, a fitness center, a gourmet restaurant and 42 different room types. Despite the obvious lure for romantics, the Wick is also proactively child-friendly and pet-friendly.

Wildpod
CABIN $$$

(☑250-725-2020; www.wildpod.ca; 174 West St; d $295-375; P ☎) Luxury 'glamping' comes to Tofino in the shape of these six yurt-like pods made out of PVC that sit perched on the waterside at Grice Point in full view of passing whales. The individually themed pods (named sand, rock, wave, wood, nest and leaf) all have mega-comfortable beds, deluxe toiletries, propane fireplaces and mini-kitchenettes and sit on raised cedar decks.

🍴 Eating & Drinking

Shed
CANADIAN $

(☑250-725-7433; www.shedtofino.com; 461 Campbell St; mains $11-16; ☺8:30am-10pm; 🍴) True, it's a shed of sorts, albeit a very nice one with candles, an open kitchen, lovely wood furnishings – and quite decent food: count on quick-fire burgers, salads and creative 'bowls' headlined by the standout Pachamama bowl, a deft melange of squash, kale, ricotta and brussels sprouts. Coming in a worthy runner-up is the tuna *poke* bowl.

Rhino Coffee House
CAFE $

(☑250-725-2558; www.rhinocoffeehouse.com; 430 Campbell St; doughnuts $2-4; ☺7:30am-4pm; ☎) In outdoor-orientated Tofino, it's easy to justify a doughnut for breakfast, and the best place in Tofino to procure one is at Rhino. Toss a coin to decide whether you'll opt for the cinnamon-beer flavor or the less boozy sour cream.

Sobo
CANADIAN $$

(☑250-725-2341; www.sobo.ca; 311 Neill St; mains $17-36; ☺11:30am-9pm) It's hard not to love a restaurant whose name is short for 'sophisticated bohemian,' a label that might have

---

DON'T MISS

TOFINO'S INDIE SHOPPING MALL

Most shopping malls host a predictable gaggle of well-known brands housed in functional boxy buildings that look like they were designed by an eighth-grade technical-drawing student. Not so in Tofino where the timber-framed **Beaches Shopping Centre** looks as if it grew organically out of the forest and is home to a sweet consortium of independent homegrown businesses. Located 4km south of Tofino proper, you could easily spend a happy half-day here imbibing java at **Tofitian** (www.tofitian.com; 1180 Pacific Rim Hwy; snacks $3-8; ☺7am-4pm Apr-Oct, to 3pm Nov-Mar; ☎) or gobbling sweets and ice cream at **Chocolate Tofino** (☑250-725-2526; www.chocolatetofino.com; ice cream $4-8; ☺10am-9pm Jun-Aug, reduced hours Sep-May) just around the corner (salted caramels recommended). When lunch beckons, join the line or call your order in at **Tacofino** (☑250-726-8288; www.tacofino.com; mains $11-12; ☺11am-7pm, reduced hours Nov-Mar), or avoid queuing completely by heading to **Wildside Grill** (☑250-725-9453; www.wildsidegrill.com; mains $13-15; ☺9am-9pm, reduced hours Sep-May) for panko-fried fish. With its proximity to Tofino's surf beaches, the shopping center is also a good place to rent a board, or a bicycle, before continuing on your merry way.

been invented with Tofino in mind. Once a humble food truck, Sobo is now an ultra-contemporary bricks-and-mortar bistro with floor-to-ceiling windows. The salads are exceptional and the pizzas (especially the exotic mushroom) aren't far behind.

The menu's showstopper, though, is the broiled oysters with miso mayonnaise.

Shelter CANADIAN $$
(☏ 250-725-3353; www.shelterrestaurant.com; 601 Campbell St; mains $12-32; ⊙ 11am-midnight) This low-ceilinged designer 'shed' has kept expanding over the years, but has never lost its welcoming locals' hangout feel. The perfect spot to grab lunch (fish tacos and a patio seat will do nicely), Shelter becomes an intimate dinner venue every evening, when the menu ratchets up. *Steak-frites* and the 'Tofino surf' bowl (salmon, chicken and veg) call loudly.

⭐ **Wolf in the Fog** CANADIAN $$$
(☏ 250-725-9653; www.wolfinthefog.com; 150 Fourth St; mains $21-45; ⊙ 10am-late, dinner from 5pm) Reserve ahead for your table at this sparkling regional- and seasonal-focused restaurant that earned a spot on the Canada's 100 Best Restaurants list in 2018. The menu is split into single and sharing plates. The latter is headlined by whole crab served with a vegetable pot-pie and creamed spinach; it's $80, but arguably worth the investment.

The bar is open for coffee and a light menu during the day, but head upstairs for dinner from 5pm.

Tofino Brewing Company BREWERY
(☏ 250-725-2899; www.tofinobrewingco.com; 681 Industrial Way; ⊙ 11am-10pm) Slip into this recently renovated tasting room in an industrial park and enjoy a $7 'flight' of taster suds amid the polished beer vats and au naturel pine furnishings. For a true beach-to-table experience ask for the kelp stout made using locally foraged Pacific seaweed.

Like at all good tasting rooms, there are no TVs or obnoxious jukeboxes to distract you, just the light chatter of people enjoying their beer.

ℹ Information

Tourism Tofino Visitor Centre (☏ 250-725-3414; www.tourismtofino.com; 1426 Pacific Rim Hwy; ⊙ 9am-8pm Jun-Aug, reduced hours Sep-May) This visitor center (with handy washrooms) 6.5km south of town has detailed information on area accommodations, hiking

trails and hot surf spots. There's also a kiosk in the town center in summer that dispenses advice to out-of-towners.

ℹ Getting There & Away

Pacific Coastal Airlines (☏ 800-663-2872; www.pacificcoastal.com) Flights arrive at **Tofino–Long Beach Airport** (☏ 250-725-3751; www.tofinoairport.com) from Vancouver ($145, 40 minutes, one daily).

Tofino Bus (www.tofinobus.com; 346 Campbell St) runs one bus per day to and from Ucluelet ($18, 40 minutes), Port Alberni ($36, 2½ hours), Nanaimo ($51, three to four hours), Victoria ($75, 6½ hours) and Vancouver ($61, 7¼ hours) via the Nanaimo–Horseshoe Bay ferry.

ℹ Getting Around

Cycling is popular in Tofino. You can cycle to most of the beaches (and along them too) via the MUP (multiuse path), a 7km paved bike trail that leads south from town as far as Cox Bay. There are plans to extend the trail as far as Ucluelet, hopefully by 2020. Bike rental is around $35 per day and the roads are mostly flat. **Tofino Bike Co** (☏ 250-266-7655; www.tofinobike.com; 1180 Pacific Rim Hwy, Beaches Shopping Centre; full-day rental $35; ⊙ 10am-5pm) can set you up.

From June to September, there's a free shuttle running hourly between 8am and 10pm to and from town and the visitor center.

Ucluelet

☏ 250 / POP 1700

Both the cousin of Tofino and the antidote to it, Ucluelet ('Ukee' to its friends) is situated on a similarly spectacular slice of Pacific Coast 40km to the south. But while Tofino is trendy, tourist-focused and challenging on the credit card, Ukee is blue-collar, less manicured and more down-to-earth.

Still largely undiscovered by the international set, 95% of whom head directly to Tofino, Ukee has plenty of fans, most of them loyal islanders who dig the sleepy rhythms, cheap motels and reliable snack shacks. And, lest we forget, those iconic surf beaches are still a short drive or bike ride away.

◉ Sights & Activities

Ucluelet Aquarium AQUARIUM
(☏ 250-726-2782; www.ucluaquarium.org; Main St Waterfront Promenade; adult/child $15/8; ⊙ 10am-5pm mid-Mar–Nov; ⊕) ✎ This excellent catch-and-release facility on the waterfront focuses on illuminating the marine critters found in the region's local

waters, which can mean anything from alien-looking sea cucumbers to a squirming, and frankly mesmerizing, Pacific octopus or two. But it's the enthusiasm of the young staff that sets this place apart, along with the ability to educate on issues of conservation without browbeating. A great kid-friendly facility – expect to walk away with renewed excitement about the wonders of ocean wildlife.

★ **Wild Pacific Trail**   HIKING
(www.wildpacifictrail.com) Where the temperate rainforest comes down to kiss the ocean, the citizens of Ukee have built a magnificent 10km trail that can be equally spectacular in both the sun and (stormy) rain. It starts with a 2.6km loop that winds past a 1915 Amphitrite lighthouse and progresses northwest as far as the Ancient Cedars loop and the Rocky Bluffs beyond.

The trail is well signposted and fastidiously mapped. To complete the whole 10km you'll need to take a couple of interconnecting paths along quiet roads calling in at several attractive beaches on the way. Various information boards provide background on the area's history and nature, and the path is dotted with benches, lookouts and so-called 'artist's loops' equipped with viewing platforms. Pack your easel.

Check the website for the latest news on the trail, included the summertime guided-walk program.

Subtidal Adventures   WILDLIFE
(☑ 250-726-7336;   www.subtidaladventures.com; 1950 Peninsula Rd; adult/child $109/89) A long-established local company offering open-to-the-elements Zodiac boat tours that show off the regional wildlife scene, with options including a summer favorite that often includes sightings of bears, several types of whales, lots of seabirds and maybe a sea otter (if you're lucky).

Majestic
Ocean Kayaking   KAYAKING
(☑ 250-726-2868; www.oceankayaking.com; 1167 Helen Rd; tours from $79) Majestic Ocean Kayaking leads day trips around the area. The easiest and shortest trips stick to Ucluelet's sheltered harbor. Highly recommended are the single-day and multiday trips south into Barkley Sound, and the Broken Group Islands, an archipelago of 100-plus islands that's part of Pacific Rim National Park.

🛏 Sleeping

C&N Backpackers   HOSTEL $
(☑ 250-726-7416; www.cnnbackpackers.com; 2081 Peninsula Rd; dm/r $39/90; ☺ Apr-Oct; @ 🖤) Take your shoes off at the door and slide into this large timber hostel, where the gigantic back garden is the best place to hang (in a hammock) on lazy evenings. A spacious downstairs kitchen and up-to-date bathrooms with parquet floors add to the appeal, while the dorms are joined by three sought-after private rooms.

Surfs Inn Guesthouse   CABIN, HOSTEL $$
(☑ 250-726-4426; www.surfsinn.ca; 1874 Peninsula Rd; ste/2-/3-/4-bedroom cottages $129/199/250/300; P 🖤) Hidden from the road behind vegetation, this funky collection of brightly painted houses and cottages hosts four choices of lovely accommodations, ranging from a loft suite to a four-bedroom house. All have kitchens or kitchenettes and three of them have outdoor BBQs and decks. The town and its supermarket is a short hop away on foot.

West Coast Motel   MOTEL $$
(☑ 250-726-7732; www.westcoastmotel.com; 279 Hemlock St; d from $99; P 🖤 ☒) The best motel in town juxtaposes its standard rooms (refrigerator, coffee machine, TV) with free access to the town's main fitness center, with which it shares a building. There's also a pool and sauna and friendly service to boot.

★ **Black Rock Oceanfront Resort**   HOTEL $$$
(☑ 250-726-4800; www.blackrockresort.com; 596 Marine Dr; studios/1-/2-bedroom ste from $345/450/700; P 🖤 ☒) Ucluelet's fanciest hotel feels like a transplant from Tofino. Set dramatically on the Pacific waterfront and painted the same gray hue as the rocks, it curves around the jagged shoreline seemingly oblivious to the stormy surf. On offer are kitchen-equipped suites wrapped in contemporary West Coast wood-and-stone and deluxe bathrooms the size of entire Vancouver apartments.

Many rooms have great views of the choppy surf and, just in case yours doesn't, there's a vista-hugging **restaurant** specializing in regional nosh. The lobby-level bar is shaped like a rolling wave.

🍴 Eating

★ **Zoe's Bakery & Cafe**   BAKERY $
(☑ 250-726-2253; www.zoesbakeryandcafe.com; 250 Main St; sandwiches $8-10; ☺ 7am-5pm, re-

duced hours Nov-Mar) Ukee has about three places to refuel your car and at least another three to refuel your brain and legs while sating your sugar addiction, including the reliable Zoe's where the coffee goes down like maple syrup with bread-pudding egg bakes and cinnamon buns topped with generous dollops of icing.

Ravenlady
SEAFOOD $$
(www.ravenlady.ca; 1801 Bay St; mains $15-18; ☺noon-2pm & 5-8pm Fri-Tue) The sole exponent of Ucluelet's food-truck scene is far superior to many bricks-and-mortar seafood restaurants. Specializing in fresh-shucked regional oysters, there are also gourmet delights from seared-tuna tacos to baguette po'boys stuffed to the gills with albacore tuna or panko-fried oysters. The truck is named after a magnificent stainless-steel sculpture vaguely reminiscent of Botticelli's *Venus* that stands beside it.

Frankie's Resto-Bar
BARBECUE $$
(☎250-726-2225; www.frankiesrestobar.com; 1576 Imperial Lane; mains $15-25; ☺5-9:30pm) Not a lot else has changed at the establishment formerly known as Hanks, still a fount of carnivorous comfort grub where the key word is 'pork.' The menu offers ample opportunities to face-plant into generous portions of pork belly, pork mac 'n' cheese, pulled pork and good old sausages. A week's worth of calories in a single, highly satisfying sitting.

Norwoods
CANADIAN $$$
(☎250-726-7001; www.norwoods.ca; 1714 Peninsula Rd; mains $28-48; ☺5-10pm) Showing how far Ucluelet's dining scene has elevated itself in recent years, this lovely candlelit room would easily be at home in Tofino. The ever-changing menu focuses on seasonal regional ingredients; think halibut and duck breast. All are prepared with a sophisticated international approach, plus there's a full menu of BC (and beyond) wines, many offered by the glass.

ⓘ Information

Ucluelet Visitor Centre (www.ucluelet.ca; 1604 Peninsula Rd; ☺9am-5pm Jun-Aug, 9:30am-4:30pm Mon-Fri Sep-May) To learn a few good reasons to stick around in Ukee, including a dining scene that finally has some great options, make for the downtown visitor center.

ⓘ Getting There & Away

Tofino Bus (www.tofinobus.com) Buses to Port Alberni, Nanaimo, Victoria and Tofino leave from outside Murray's Grocery Store.

Denman & Hornby Islands

The main Northern Gulf Islands, Denman and Hornby share laid-back attitudes, artistic flair and some tranquil outdoor activities. You'll arrive by ferry at Denman first from Buckley Bay on Vancouver Island, then hop from Denman across to Hornby. Stop at Denman Village, near the first ferry dock, and pick up a free map and attractions guide for both islands.

Denman has three provincial parks: **Fillongley**, with easy hiking and beachcombing; **Boyle Point**, with a beautiful lighthouse walk; and **Sandy Island**.

Among Hornby's provincial parks, **Tribune Bay** features a long sandy beach with safe swimming, while **Helliwell** has notable hiking and **Ford's Cove** offers the chance to dive with sharks. Hiking and mountain-biking trails crisscross large **Mt Geoffrey Regional Park**.

Denman Hornby Canoes & Kayaks
KAYAKING
(☎250-335-0079; www.denmanpaddling.ca; 4005 East Rd, Denman Island; ☺half-day rental/tour from $50/120) The perfect way to explore the idyllic waters around and between the two islands. You can rent kayaks or stand-up paddleboards from this family-run operator based in a water-side house on Denman's eastern shore. The outfit also hosts guided tours, aimed at paddlers of all skill levels. The staff are happy to customize tours.

🛏 Sleeping & Eating

Blue Owl
B&B $$
(☎250-335-3440; www.blueowldenman.ca; 8850 Owl Cres, Denman Island; s/d $125/140; 🛜🐾) An idyllically rustic retreat for those craving an escape from city life, this woodsy little cottage is a short walk from the ocean. Loaner bikes are freely available if you fancy exploring (there's a swimmable lake nearby), but you might want to just cozy up in your room (or in the sauna!). There's a two-night minimum stay.

Sea Breeze Lodge
HOTEL $$
(☎250-335-2321; www.seabreezelodge.com; 5205 Fowler Rd, Hornby Island; adult/child $215/100) This 12-acre retreat, with 16 cottages

overlooking the ocean, is a popular island fixture. Rooms are comfortable rather than palatial, though some have fireplaces and full kitchens. You can swim, kayak and fish or just flop lazily around in the oceanside hot tub. Rates are per person.

Thatch Pub & Restaurant   PUB FOOD $
(☑ 250-335-0136; www.thatchpub.ca; 4325 Shingle Spit Rd, Hornby Island; mains $12-18; ⊙ 11:30am-9pm Jul & Aug; reduced hours Sep-Jun) Hornby Island's only pub is also its most reliable place for a bite. It's open year-round, through only three nights a week in the off-season. The food's a cheerful mix of sandwiches, tacos, burgers and flatbreads with a roast-beef buffet on Fridays. Beer-wise, it serves Cumberland Brewing's Forest Fog on tap.

ℹ Information

For more information on the islands, check out www.visitdenmanisland.ca and www.hornby island.com.

ℹ Getting There & Away

BC Ferries (☑ 250-386-3431; www.bcferries. com) Hourly services travel between Denman and Buckley Bay or Hornby Island (passenger/vehicle $8.90/20.65, 10 minutes).

Comox Valley

This region of rolling mountains, alpine meadows and colorful communities, comprises the towns of Comox and Courtenay as well as the hipster-favorite village of Cumberland. It's a good outdoor-adventure base and a hotbed for mountain biking, with Mt Washington as its activity highlight.

◎ Sights & Activities

**Courtenay and District
Museum & Palaeontology Centre**   MUSEUM
(☑ 250-334-0686; www.courtenaymuseum.ca; 207 4th St, Courtenay; by donation; ⊙ 10am-5pm Mon-Sat, noon-4pm Sun, closed Mon & Sun in winter; ⊞) With its life-size replica of an elasmosaur (a prehistoric marine reptile first discovered in the area), this excellent small museum also houses pioneer and First Nations exhibits. Pick up a dino-themed chocolate bar from the gift shop: the perfect edible souvenir.

Cumberland Museum   MUSEUM
(☑ 250-336-2445; www.cumberlandmuseum. ca; 2680 Dunsmuir Ave, Cumberland; adult/child $5/4; ⊙ 10am-5pm Jun-Aug, closed Mon Sep-May)

A wonderfully quirky museum located on a row of false-fronted buildings that looks like a Dodge City movie set, with evocative exhibits on the area's pioneer past and its Japanese and Chinese communities. There's also a walk-through mine tunnel that offers a glimpse of just how tough the job would have been (the frightening iron lung exhibited upstairs does the same).

Dodge City Cycles   CYCLING
(☑ 250-336-2200; www.dodgecitycycles.com; 2705 Dunsmuir Ave, Cumberland; bike rentals per 2/24hr $50/120; ⊙ 9am-6pm Mon-Sat, 10am-2:30pm Sun) Mega-friendly and informative bike shop with rentals and insider tips on the local terrain. It sells comprehensive color-coded bike-trail maps for $6.95. From the front door, it's practically one pedal-turn to a nirvana of singletrack.

Mt Washington Alpine Resort   OUTDOORS
(☑ 250-338-1386; www.mountwashington.ca; winter lift ticket adult/child $95/52) The island's only major ski area is something of a local secret cherished by the type of crowd-avoiding skier who doesn't care for the busy conveyor belt of Whistler. It's less than one-third the size of Whistler, but can claim higher snowfall (up to 10m in a season) and lower prices by nearly half.

🛏 Sleeping

★ **Riding Fool Hostel**   HOSTEL $
(☑ 250-336-8250; www.ridingfool.com; 2705 Dunsmuir Ave, Cumberland; dm/r $32/68; @ 🗟) One of BC's finest hostels colonizes a restored Cumberland heritage building with its rustic wooden interiors, large kitchen and lounge areas and, along with small dorms, the kind of immaculate family and private rooms often found in midrange hotels. Bicycle rentals are available from the excellent Dodge City Cycles out front.

**Old House Village
Hotel & Spa**   HOTEL $$
(☑ 250-703-0202; www.oldhousevillage.com; 1730 Riverside Lane, Courtenay; d $179; 🗟 ▣) There's nothing particularly old about this high-quality modern hotel with slick rooms, slick service and a steamy year-round outdoor pool. Raising the bar is an on-site spa, an expansive basement gym and thoughtful little extras such as free cookies in a glass jar by reception next to a fancy coffee machine. Rooms have a gleaming, straight-out-of-the-catalog look.

Eating & Drinking

Cooks Restaurant   FAST FOOD $
(☑ 250-400-4222; www.cooksrestaurant.ca; 3273 3rd St, Cumberland; mains $9-12; ☺ noon-8pm Tue-Sat) In a town that trades on its outdoor affiliations, there's always a place for guilty-pleasure eating indulgences which, in the case of this new snack shack, means burgers. The ultra-simple menu narrows things down to a three-way choice between fried-chicken sandwiches, grilled-cheese sandwiches and the default burgers. It's all unashamedly uncomplicated and old-school with everything made from scratch.

Waverley Hotel Pub   BURGERS $$
(☑ 250-336-8322; www.waverleyhotel.ca; 2692 Dunsmuir Ave, Cumberland; mains $13-18; ☺ 10:30am-10pm Sun, from 11am Mon & Tue, 11am-late Wed-Sat; 🐕 ✍) Hit this historic, antler-studded saloon for a pub-grub dinner while you flick through a copy of glossy local magazine *CV Collective*. There are a dozen or so craft drafts to keep you company, while the menu covers all tastes from avowed carnivores (elk burgers) to strict vegetarians (quinoa salad). The honey teriyaki chicken wings have a fanatical following.

Locals Restaurant   CANADIAN $$$
(☑ 250-338-6493; www.localscomoxvalley.com; 1760 Riverside Lane, Courtenay; mains $30-38; ☺ 11am-9pm; ✍) ✎ 'Locally produced' is a mantra you hear a lot on Vancouver Island and it's taken particularly seriously at this attractive, if pricey, wooden restaurant on the river just south of Courtenay's town center. A checklist on the back of the menu highlights the nearby farms and vineyards that have contributed to the creative dishes.

Cumberland Brewing   BREWERY
(☑ 250-400-2739; www.cumberlandbrewing.com; 2732 Dunsmuir Ave, Cumberland; ☺ noon-9pm Sun, Tue & Wed, to 10pm Thu-Sat) A microbrewery that's mastered the neighborhood-pub vibe, this tasty spot combines a woodsy little tasting room with a larger outdoor seating area striped with communal tables. Dive into a tasting flight of four beers; make sure it includes the Red Tape Pale Ale.

Information

Vancouver Island Visitors Centre (☑ 885-400-2882; www.discovercomoxvalley.com; 3607 Small Rd, Cumberland; ☺ 9am-5pm) Super-slick visitor center with mega-helpful staff, museum-worthy exhibits and

surgery-clean toilets. It's 2km northeast of Cumberland, just off Hwy 19.

Getting There & Away

If you're flying in from the mainland, **Pacific Coastal Airlines** (☑ 604-273-8666; www.pacificcoastal.com) services arrive at **Comox Valley Airport** (☑ 250-890-0829; www.comoxairport.com) from Vancouver's South Terminal ($125, 35 minutes, two to three daily).

BC Ferries (www.bcferries.com) runs services between Comox and Powell River (passenger/car $13.50/42.20, 1½ hours, four daily) on the Sunshine Coast.

The area's three main communities are linked by easy-to-explore highway routes, while **Tofino Bus** (☑ 250-725-2871; www.tofinobus.com; 2663 Kilpatrick Ave, Courtenay) services trundle into Courtenay at least twice a day from towns across the island, including Port Hardy ($62, five hours, one daily) and Nanaimo ($38, 1½ hours, three daily).

Campbell River

☑ 250 / POP 35,400
Southerners will tell you this marks the end of civilization on Vancouver Island, but Campbell River is a handy drop-off point for wilderness tourism in Strathcona Provincial Park. While the town's core isn't the island's prettiest, it benefits from a sheltered waterside location (Quadra Island lies across the strait) and an impressively proactive Rotary Club that has initiated numerous rejuvenation projects. These include a Maritime Heritage Centre and a spectacular suspension bridge in nearby Elk Falls Provincial Park.

Campbell River used to dub itself the 'Salmon Capital of the World' and though the industry has diminished in the 21st century, fishing remains entrenched in the town's heritage. You can even rent a rod and try your luck fishing from the pier.

Sights

Museum at Campbell River   MUSEUM
(☑ 250-287-3103; www.crmuseum.ca; 470 Island Hwy; adult/child $8/5; ☺ 10am-5pm mid-May–Sep, from noon Tue-Sun Oct–mid-May) This fascinating museum is worth an hour of anyone's time. Its diverse collection showcases indigenous masks, an 1890s pioneer cabin and video footage of the world's largest artificial, non-nuclear blast (an underwater mountain in Seymour Narrows that caused dozens of shipwrecks before it was blown apart in a controlled explosion in 1958). In summer,

ask about the museum's daylong, history-themed boat cruises around the area.

Maritime Heritage Centre
MUSEUM

(☑250-286-3161; www.maritimeheritagecentre.ca; 621 Island Way; adult/child $7/3.50; ☉10am-4pm Mon-Fri) A labor of love for the local Rotary Club, this small museum anchored by a restored Seine fishing boat stands as a testament to Campbell River's salmon-fishing heritage. Volunteer guides walk you around the exhibits (boat included), imparting fascinating snippets of fishing history in the process. The restored Seine vessel once featured on Canada's $5 bill.

Elk Falls Provincial Park
STATE PARK

(www.env.gov.bc.ca/bcparks/explore/parkpgs/elk_falls; Hwy 28) This small but nature-packed provincial park was given fresh impetus for visitors with the building of a new center-piece, a 60m-long suspension bridge over the Campbell River just east of the gushing torrent of Elk Falls. The green pocket is barely 5km from the city center and well endowed with trails, a campground and a salmon hatchery. The suspension bridge was conceived and partially funded by Campbell River's proactive Rotary Club.

🛏 Sleeping & Eating

Heron's Landing Hotel
HOTEL $$

(☑250-923-2848; www.heronslandinghotel.com; 492 S Island Hwy; d from $130; @☎🐾) Superior motel-style accommodations with renovated rooms, including large loft suites ideal for families. Rates include breakfast but rooms also have their own kitchens if you want to cook up your own eggs-and-bacon special. There are also handy coin-operated laundry facilities on-site. Some rooms have water-facing balconies.

Dick's Fish & Chips
FISH & CHIPS $$

(☑250-287-3336; www.dicksfishandchips.com; 660 Island Hwy; mains $12-18; ☉11am-dusk) A steamy-windowed fish-and-chips shop, this restaurant a short walk from Discover Pier is often busy, so consider an off-peak visit. Alongside the usual golden-battered meals, you'll find popular salmon, oyster and halibut burgers, as well as housemade mushy peas that some Vancouver Islanders just can't live without.

FoggDukkers Coffee
COFFEE

(907 S Island Hwy; ☉6am-7pm) A wonderfully disheveled beach shack that doubles as an ultra-friendly coffee bar. Inside there are humorous signposts, a jumble of seats and a wood-fire stove usually commandeered by a bevy of gossiping locals. On warmer evenings you can adjourn outside with your coffee and cookies to a firepit overlooking the beach.

ℹ Information

Campbell River Visitor Centre (1235 Shoppers Row; ☉9am-5pm Tue-Sun) Staff here will fill you in on what to do in Campbell River and around the nearby region.

ℹ Getting There & Away

Campbell River Transit (☑250-287-7433; www.bctransit.com; fare $2) Operates buses throughout the area.

Pacific Coastal Airlines (☑604-273-8666; www.pacificcoastal.com) Operates flights from Vancouver YVR airport's South Terminal ($145, 45 minutes, up to five daily).

Tofino Bus (☑250-725-2871; www.tofinobus.com) All Island Express buses roll in from Port Hardy, Nanaimo and Victoria at least once daily, stopping next to the Coast Discovery Inn.

THE TYEE CLUB

Anyone can have a go at fishing in Campbell River – just rent a rod, hang it over the Discovery Pier and wait for something to bite. But to become a member of the prestigious Tyee Club, you'll need a little extra skill – or luck. Founded in 1924, the club only admits fishers who have reeled in a prized Chinook 'tyee' salmon weighing 30lb or more using light tackle from a non-motorized rowing boat.

It's not an easy proposition. An average season sees only around 40 to 50 tyees caught and, for every success, there are many disappointments. Hollywood actor and avid fisher John Wayne famously never achieved the honor despite many enthusiastic attempts. If the legendary Duke's failure doesn't deter you, the tyee season runs from mid-July to mid-September. See www.tyeeclub.org for more details.

QUADRA ISLAND HOP

For a day out with a difference, take your bike on the 10-minute BC Ferries (p173) trip from Campbell River to rustic **Quadra Island**. There's an extensive network of trails across the island; maps are sold in local stores. Many of the forested trails are former logging routes, and the local community has spent a lot of time building and maintaining the trails for mountain bikers of all skill levels. If you don't have your wheels, you can rent a bike on the island or in Campbell River. For more information on visiting the island, see www.quadraisland.ca.

Quadra's fascinating **Nuyumbalees Cultural Centre** (www.nuyumbalees.com; 34 Weway Rd; adult/child $10/5; ⊙10am-5pm May-Sep) illuminates the heritage and traditions of the local Kwakwaka'wakw First Nations people, showcasing carvings and artifacts and staging traditional dance performances. But if you just want to chill out with the locals, head to **Spirit Sq**, where performers entertain in summer.

If you decide to stick around for dinner, head for the waterfront pub or restaurant at the handsome **Heriot Bay Inn & Marina** (☑250-285-3322; www.heriotbayinn.com; Heriot Bay; d/cabins from $109/229; ᴘ☎) where, if you have a few too many drinks, you might also choose to stay the night. The hotel has motel-style rooms and charming rustic cabins.

Strathcona Provincial Park

Centered on Mt Golden Hinde (2200m), the island's highest point, **Strathcona Provincial Park** (☑250-474-1336; www.env.gov.bc.ca/bcparks/explore/parkpgs/strath) is a magnificent pristine wilderness crisscrossed with enticing trail systems. Give yourself plenty of time and you'll soon be communing with waterfalls, alpine meadows, glacial lakes and mountain crags.

There are two main areas: Butte Lake, accessible from Campbell River, and the Forbidden Plateau, a network of trails close to the Mt Washington Ski Resort, a short drive west of Courtenay.

On arrival at the park's main entrance, get your bearings at **Strathcona Park Lodge & Outdoor Education Centre**. It's a one-stop shop for park activities, including kayaking, zip-lining, guided treks and rock climbing. All-in adventure packages are available, some aimed specifically at families. Head to the **Whale Room** or **Myrna's** for a yummy fuel-up before you get too active.

Notable park hiking trails include **Paradise Meadows Loop** (2.2km), an easy amble in a delicate wildflower and evergreen ecosystem, and **Mt Becher** (5km), with its great views over the Comox Valley and mountain-lined Strait of Georgia. Around Buttle Lake, easier walks include **Lady Falls** (900m) and the trail along **Karst Creek** (2km), which winds past sinkholes, streams and tumbling waterfalls.

The park's **lodge** (☑250-286-3122; www.strathconaparklodge.com/escape/accommodation; 41040 Gold River Hwy; r/cabins from $139/250; ☎) offers good accommodations, ranging from rooms in the main building to secluded timber-framed cottages. If you're a true back-to-nature fan, there are five campsites available in the park. Consider pitching your tent at **Buttle Lake Campground** (☑519-826-6850, 800-689-9025; www.discovercamping.ca; campsites $20; ⊙Apr-Oct); the swimming area and playground alone make it a great choice for families.

There are a couple of good dining options in the Strathcona Park Lodge just outside the park or you can cook your own grub at your campsite spot or self-catering cabin.

ⓘ Getting There & Away

If you're driving around the island, you'll reach the park via Hwy 28 from Campbell River. To access the Forbidden Plateau area, take the Mt Washington ski resort road just north of Courtenay (exit number 13 of Hwy 19).

Public transport is limited. A ski shuttle runs daily December to April from Comox/Courtenay to the Mt Washington ski resort. Another bus serves Victoria (www.mtwskibus.com).

North Vancouver Island

In this remote region of outstanding natural beauty, the infrastructure is best described as rudimentary. Like anything north of Campbell River, it's what islanders call the real 'north.' With its light scattering of people and wild islet-buffered coastline battling rough, temperamental seas, the area is faintly reminiscent of the Scottish Highlands, but with more trees. (Indeed several local landmarks are named after Scots – including the most northwesterly point, Cape Scott.) Trees are big business in these parts. The north island is known for its logging, indigenous culture and glaring lack of paved roads. The only notable settlements – Port Hardy and Port McNeill – are little more than large villages.

Port McNeill

Barreling down the hill almost into the harbor, Port McNeill is a useful pit stop for those heading to Port Hardy or craving a coffee before boarding the ferry to delightful (and highly recommended) Alert Bay.

Check out the **museum** (351 Shelley Cres; donations accepted; ⊙ 10am-5pm Jul-Sep, 1-4pm Sat & Sun Oct-Jun) for the region's backstory and don't miss the **World's Biggest Burl** as you stroll toward the entrance. A giant warty outgrowth from a huge tree, it's the best selfie opportunity in the area.

🛏 Sleeping & Eating

Black Bear Resort   MOTEL $$
(✆ 250-956-4900; www.port-mcneill-accommodation.com; 1812 Campbell Way; d/cabin incl breakfast from $162/212; @🛜🏊) More a superior motel than a resort, this hillside spot overlooks the town and is conveniently located across from the town's shops and restaurants. Standard rooms are small but clean and include microwaves and refrigerators; full-kitchen units are also available, as are a string of roadside cabins. Big bonus: there's an indoor pool, small gym and sauna.

Archipelagos Bistro   MEDITERRANEAN $$
(✆ 250-956-4553; 1703 Broughton Blvd; mains $14-37; ⊙ 5-8pm Sun, Mon, Wed & Thu, to 9pm Fri & Sat) Granted, it's not a bistro in the European sense, but that doesn't stop Archipelagos being a welcome new addition to Port McNeill's limited dining scene. Skip the burgers and opt instead for the Mediterranean-influenced 'planks' (cheese, smoked meat or vegetable boards) and the best risottos north of Victoria.

ℹ Information

Visitor Center (✆ 250-956-3881; www.townportmcneill.bc.ca; 1594 Beach Dr; ⊙ 8:30am-5:30pm May-Sep, reduced hours in winter) Super-helpful office on the waterfront.

ℹ Getting There & Away

Tofino Bus (✆ 250-287-7151; www.tofinobus.com) Buses stop next to the Alert Bay ferry terminal.

Alert Bay

One of the region's best days out is just a 45-minute ferry ride from Port McNeill. Located on Cormorant Island and radiating from the ferry dock along easily strolled waterfront boardwalks, Alert Bay's brightly painted shacks and houses-on-piles are highly photogenic – even the ones that are crumbling into the briny sea. Home to the Namgis First Nation, there are lots of ways to experience indigenous culture here, plus some cozy spots to eat or sleep. Expect eagles and ravens to be whirling overhead.

◎ Sights & Activities

⭐**U'mista Cultural Centre**   MUSEUM
(✆ 250-974-5403; www.umista.ca; 1 Front St; adult/child $12/5; ⊙ 9am-5pm Tue-Sat Sep-Jun, daily Jul & Aug) This must-see longhouse-like facility proudly displays dozens of culturally priceless Kwakwaka'wakw artifacts confiscated when potlatch ceremonies were outlawed in Canada, and distributed to museums and collections around the world. The cultural center has been slowly negotiating their return and the main gallery here is a wonderful manifestation of their efforts (and ongoing work). The mask collection is especially haunting. Summer programs include book readings and cedar-bark-weaving demonstrations, while the on-site gift shop brims with ethically sourced First Nations art.

Namgis Big House   PERFORMING ARTS
(cnr Wood St & Hill St; ⊙ Thu-Sat Jul & Aug) This traditional clan house hosts dance performances by Alert Bay's local Namgis community in summer. Ask at the visitor center for performance times and current ticket prices. Head up Park St from the waterfront to find the house, which is next to a soccer field and behind a gigantic (if dilapidated) totem pole.

Ecological Park   PARK
A big draw on tiny Cormorant Island, this hidden nature park consists of a small marsh guarded by a clutch of starkly beautiful dead trees (most of them still standing) that eerily resemble totem poles. Nature trails wind through the sodden grounds, some of them

on boardwalks. It's a mystical spot that is faintly redolent of Florida's everglades.

Seasmoke Whale Watching   WHALE-WATCHING
(☑ 250-974-5225; www.seasmokewhalewatching.com; 69 Fir St; adult/child $119/99; ☉ tours mid-Jun–Sep) Killer whales, humpbacks and even minke whales can be part of the mix during these seasonal sailboat tours from Alert Bay. A relaxing way to experience the region (expect abundant marine birds en route), the 3½-hour tours also keep an eye out for eagles, seals and anything else that is interesting and moves.

🛏 Sleeping & Eating

Seine Boat Inn   INN $$
(☑ 877-334-9465; www.seineboatinn.com; 60 Fir St; r from $135; 🛜) Named for a local fishing style utilizing weighted nets, the Seine sits on a forest of pilings above the water in an attractive dockside building. The cabin-sized rooms with rich wood finishes and water views make you feel as if you're sleeping in a docked ship, although the potted plants and trellis-covered decks quickly remind you you're on terra firma.

Alert Bay Cabins   CABIN $$
(☑ 604-974-5457; www.alertbaycabins.net; 390 Poplar Rd; cabins $145-200) A clutch of well-maintained cabins, each with kitchen or kitchenette, this is a great retreat-like option if you want to get away from it all. Cabins accommodate four to six people. Call ahead and the staff will even pick you up from the ferry (otherwise it's a 2.5km walk).

Pass 'n Thyme   BISTRO $$
(☑ 250-974-2670; 4 Maple Rd; mains $13-21; ☉ 11am-8pm Tue-Thu & Sat, to 9pm Fri) Head up the ramp alongside and aim for a picture-window table overlooking shimmering, boat-bobbling Broughton Strait. You'll soon be diving into some excellent grilled halibut and chips alongside everyone else who was on the ferry (this is one of Alert Bay's few eateries). Burgers, wraps and made-from-scratch soups round out the menu. The deep-fried ice-cream tops it off.

🛈 Information

Visitor Center (☑ 250-974-5024; www.alertbay.ca; 118 Fir St; ☉ 9am-5pm Mon-Fri Jun, Sep & Oct, daily Jul & Aug) One of the friendliest visitor centers around. Head here first when you arrive (turn right along the boardwalk from the ferry) and ask for tips on what to see and do. The staff will point you toward the island's top totem-pole spots and also give you some handy hints on where to eat.

🛈 Getting There & Away

BC Ferries (☑ 250-386-3431; www.bcferries.com) Services arrive in Alert Bay from Port McNeill (adult/vehicle $12.35/28.40, 45 minutes, up to six daily).

Telegraph Cove

Built as a one-shack telegraph station, this former fishing village and cannery has since expanded into one of the north's main visitor lures. Its pioneer-outpost feel is enhanced by the dozens of brightly painted wooden buildings perched around the marina on stilts. Be aware, although the permanent population consists of around 20 people, it can get very crowded with summer day-trippers.

⊙ Sights & Activities

Whale Interpretive Centre   MUSEUM
(☑ 250-928-3129; www.killerwhalecentre.org; adult/child $5/3; ☉ 9:30am-5:30pm mid-May–Oct) This unique, beautifully rustic barn-like museum is bristling with hands-on artifacts and artfully displayed skeletons of cougars and sea otters, but the main hooks are the many whale skeletons, mostly hanging from the ceiling. Minke, grey, fin and pygmy are part of the menagerie but give yourself plenty of time to peruse everything carefully.

Tide Rip Grizzly Tours   BOATING
(☑ 250-339-5320; www.tiderip.com; tours $320-370; ☉ May-Sep) For a magical all-day boat tour to commune with the region's Knight Inlet grizzly bears, book ahead with this popular Telegraph Cove operator. Knight Inlet is on the BC mainland as grizzlies don't traditionally live on Vancouver Island (although the occasional bear has been known to swim across).

North Island Kayaks   KAYAKING
(☑ 250-928-3114; www.kayakbc.ca; Lagoon Rd; 2hr trip from $65) Wildlife-watching kayak trips with guides are offered from June to September, ranging from two-hour family jaunts to eight-day excursions in search of humpback whales, sea lions and First Nations culture.

🛏 Sleeping & Eating

Telegraph Cove Resort   RESORT $$
(☑ 250-928-3131; www.telegraphcoveresort.com; campsites/cabins/r from $38/150/220) The

dominant business in Telegraph Cove, this well-established heritage resort provides accommodations in forested tent spaces as well as a string of rustic, highly popular cabins on stilts overlooking the marina. A new 24-room lodge built from local wood to resemble the nearby Whale Interpretive Centre (p189) manages to look fabulous without spoiling the fishing-village ambience.

Killer Whale Cafe
BISTRO $$

(☑250-928-3155; www.telegraphcoveresort.com/ dining; mains $14-20; ◎11am-11pm mid-May– mid-October) Part of the sprawling Telegraph Cove Resort (p189), Killer Whale Cafe is the cove's best eatery – the salmon, mussel and prawn linguine is recommended. Aim for a window seat in this creaky-floored heritage building so you can gaze over the marina. There's usually a salmon barbecue fired up outside in the summer.

❶ Getting There & Away

Telegraph Cove is a winding but well-signposted turnoff drive from Hwy 19. There is no scheduled public transport. Car-less travelers should hop on the **Tofino Bus** (www.tofinobus.com) to Port McNeill and take a taxi from there (approximately $40 one-way). **Waivin Flags Taxi** (☑250-230-7655; www.waivinflags.com) offers a reliable service.

Port Hardy

☑250 / POP 4000

The last semblance of settlement heading north on Vancouver Island, Port Hardy is little more than a large village, but it has a strong First Nations culture and acts as a hub for those keen to explore the north's many rugged outdoor experiences. It's named somewhat bizarrely for Horatio Nelson's flag captain at the Battle of Trafalgar.

◉ Sights & Activities

Storey Beach
BEACH

If you haven't got time to hit the epic beaches of Cape Scott, decamp to this closer-to-town option mixing urban comforts (picnic tables and parking) with typical north island ruggedness (expect occasional wildlife visits in summer). It's particularly good at low tide. For a day trip, pack a picnic and walk in from Port Hardy via the **Fort Rupert Trail**.

North Island Lanes
BOWLING

(☑250-949-6307; 7210 Market St; per game incl shoes $6; ◎1-3pm Tue, 5-9:30pm Wed-Sun, 5-10pm Fri & Sat) With old-school bowling alleys tumbling like knocked-over pins across BC, this immaculately preserved six-lane hangout is a must-see even if you don't want to play. The yellow-painted walls and retro-cool backlights make it like a living 1970s museum. But rather than being a mothballed old exhibit, it's also one of the friendliest and liveliest evening hangouts in town.

Nakwakto
Rapids Tours
BOATING

(☑250-230-3574; www.nakwaktorapidstours.com; 154 Tsulquate Reserve; adult/child $195/135; ◎by appointment) There's more to this four-hour boat tour than experiencing the roiling waters of 'the world's fastest tidal surge.' Your First Nations guides will also provide a rich interpretive narration as well as taking you to some of the region's most remote areas. You'll feel like you're a million miles away from the big city. Check the website for trip dates.

🛏 Sleeping & Eating

North Coast Trail
Backpackers Hostel
HOSTEL $

(☑250-949-9441; www.northcoasthostel.com; 8635 Granville St; dm/r $32/69; @🛜) This well-used, well-loved hostel is a warren of small and larger dorms, overseen by friendly owners with plenty of tips for exploring the region. The hostel's hub is a large rec room and, while the kitchen is small, the adjoining mural-painted cafe can keep you well fueled. Small, simple private rooms are available and traveling families are also welcomed.

★ Kwa'lilas Hotel
HOTEL $$

(☑855-949-8525; www.kwalilashotel.ca; 9040 Granville St; r from $182; 🅿❄🛜) A beautiful manifestation of Kwakwaka'wakw culture, this new-ish cedar-wood hotel is rich with indigenous art. The modern, uncluttered look extends to the rooms, which are clean, bright and decorated with indigenous motifs. Value-for-money extras include air-con (unusual in these parts), an on-site pub and cafe, a tribal gift shop and great service.

Cafe Guido
CAFE $

(☑250-949-9808; www.cafeguido.com; 7135 Market St; mains $6-9; ◎7am-6pm Mon-Fri, from 8am Sat, 8am-5pm Sun; 🛜) This three-pronged business (craft shop upstairs, bookstore below decks) is Port Hardy's local hub, dispatching the best coffee north of Campbell River and serving flaky scones that you'll have to visit Tofino to emulate. Backing it all up are grilled pesto-flatbread sandwiches and service that is at once laid-back and efficient.

Sporty Bar & Grill
PUB FOOD $$

(☎ 250-949-7811; www.sportybar.ca; 8700 Hastings St; mains $11-24; ⊙ 11:30am-11pm; 🐾) Great service and pub grub push this regular-looking neighborhood bar to the top of the Port Hardy dine-out tree. Sporty's (as everyone calls it) offers hearty burgers, pizzas and fish-and-chips – and also a great-value Cobb salad ($14) that's well worth face-planting into. Beer-wise, eschew the Lucky Lager (the north's traditional favorite) and go for Victoria-brewed Hermann's Dark Lager.

❶ Information

Port Hardy Visitor Information Centre
(☎ 250-949-7622; www.visitporthardy.com; 7250 Market St; ⊙ 9am-6pm Jun-Sep, 8am-4pm Mon-Fri Oct-May) Lined with flyers and staffed by locals who can help you plan your visit in town and beyond, this should be your first port of call in Port Hardy. The staff are especially adept with area hiking tips.

❶ Getting There & Away

BC Ferries (☎ 250-386-3431; www.bcferries.com) Ferries arrive from mainland Prince Rupert (passenger/vehicle $175/399, 16 hours) via the scenically splendid Inside Passage. The ferry terminal is 10km by road from the town center at Bear Cove.

Pacific Coastal Airlines (www.pacificcoastal.com) Services arrive from Vancouver's South Terminal ($265, 65 minutes, two to three daily).

Tofino Bus (☎ 250-725-2871; www.tofinobus.com) Currently the only bus service connecting Port Hardy to the rest of Vancouver Island. Office is underneath the Pier Side Landing (8600 Granville St).

Cape Scott Provincial Park

This should be your number-one destination if you really want to experience the raw, ravishing beauty of BC, especially its unkempt shorelines, breeze-licked rainforests and lonely sandy bays animated with tumbling waves and beady-eyed seabirds. The nature-hugging trailhead of this remote park on the island's crenulated northern tip is more than 550km from Victoria.

Hike the park's well-maintained 2.5km San Josef Bay Trail and you'll pass from the shady confines of the trees right onto one of the best beaches in BC, a windswept expanse of roiling water, forested crags and the kind of age-old caves that could easily harbor lost smugglers. You can camp right here on the beach or just admire the passing ospreys before plunging back into the trees.

From the same parking lot, a trail leads 23km to Cape Scott. You can make a day hike out of the first 3km as far as Eric Lake.

If you really like a challenge, consider the 59km North Coast Trail, which typically takes between five and eight days. The trail is basically an extension of the Cape Scott Trail, but is usually done east to west finishing at the San Josef Bay trailhead parking lot.

One of the area's shortest trails (2km), in adjoining Raft Cove Provincial Park (www.env.gov.bc.ca/bcparks/explore/parkpgs/raft_cove), brings you to the wide, crescent beach and the beautiful lagoons of Raft Cove. You're likely to have the entire 1.3km expanse to yourself, although the locals also like to surf here – it's their secret, so don't tell anyone.

Cove Adventures
HIKING

(☎ 250-230-4575; www.coveadventuretours.com; 8640 Granville St; adult/child $195/145) If you don't fancy driving the rutted road to Cape Scott, join a tour with this excellent company that runs daily minibuses from Port Hardy between May and mid-October. The staff will take you along the San Josef Bay Trail and beyond and furnish you with stories of First Nations inhabitants and early Danish settlers. Expect to see wildlife.

❶ Information

For additional information on visiting Cape Scott Provincial Park and the North Coast Trail, visit www.capescottpark.com.

❶ Getting There & Away

It's 70km of rough gravel road between Port Hardy and Cape Scott Provincial Park. Throw in logging trucks and inclement weather and the going can be tough. Be prepared.

If you're aiming to tackle the North Coast Trail, take an early morning **Cape Scott Water Taxi** (☎ 250-949-6541; www.capescottwatertaxi.ca; 6555 Port Hardy Bay Rd) service to Shushartie Bay, and after your hike, hop the **North Coast Trail Shuttle** (☎ 250-949-6541; www.northcoasttrailshuttle.com) minibus back to Port Hardy. Book ahead for both services. The boat/bus costs $100/80 per person.

SOUTHERN GULF ISLANDS

Stressed Vancouverites love escaping into the restorative arms of these laid-back islands, strung like a shimmering necklace between the mainland and Vancouver Island. Formerly colonized by hippies and US draft dodgers, Salt Spring, Galiano, Mayne, Saturna, and North and South Pender deliver on their promise of rustic, sigh-triggering getaways. For more visitor information, see www.sgislands.com.

Salt Spring Island

POP 10,500

The busiest and most developed of the Southern Gulf Islands, Salt Spring has a reputation for palatial vacation homes, but it's also lined with artist studios and artisan food-and-drink producers who welcome visitors. Well worth a long weekend visit, the heart of the community is Ganges, home of Salt Spring's awesome summer market.

👁 Sights & Actvities

⭐ **Saturday Market** MARKET
(www.saltspringmarket.com; Centennial Park, Ganges; ⊙9am-4pm Sat Apr-Oct) At the best market in British Columbia, the gigantic cornucopia of produce, edible goodies and locally made artworks lures everyone like a magnet on summer Saturdays. Arrive in the morning; it can be oppressively jam-packed at times. Alternatively, join the locals at the smaller, produce-only Tuesday market. Everything at both markets is made, baked or grown on the island.

Salt Spring Island Cheese FARM
(☑250-653-2300; www.saltspringcheese.com; 285 Reynolds Rd; ⊙11am-5pm, to 4pm Oct-Apr; 👪) A family-friendly farmstead with a strollable garden, wandering chickens and a winery-like tasting room and shop, this quintessential Salt Spring spot produces goat- and sheep-milk chèvres, feta and Camembert styles; the soft goat-cheese rounds in several flavors (the peppercorn one packs a punch) are the farm's specialty. You can watch the handmade production through special windows but look out for the farm's gamboling goats.

Ruckle Provincial Park PARK
(www.bcparks.ca) A pocket of ragged shoreline and gnarly arbutus forest on Salt Spring's southeastern rump contains around 16km of trails and the oldest active farm in BC. Yeo Point is an ideal pit stop.

Salt Spring Adventure Co KAYAKING
(☑250-537-2764; www.saltspringadventures.com; 125 Rainbow Rd, Ganges; rentals/tours from $40/65; ⊙9am-6pm May-Sep) When it's time to hit the water, touch base with this well-established local operator. They can kit you out for a bobbling kayak tour around Ganges Harbour, but they also serve the SUP crowd. Bike rentals and half-day whale-watching tours ($130) are also on the menu.

🛏 Sleeping & Eating

Wisteria Guest House B&B $$
(☑250-537-5899; www.wisteriaguesthouse.com; 268 Park Dr; d/cottage from $120/180; 🐾) This home-away-from-home B&B has brightly painted guest rooms in the main building, some with shared baths. There is also a pair of private-entrance studios and a small cottage with a compact kitchen – the immaculate studio 1 is our favorite. Breakfast is served in the large communal lounge, surrounded by a rambling, flower-strewn garden. A two-night minimum stay sometimes applies; check ahead.

⭐ **Hastings House Hotel** HOTEL $$$
(☑800-661-9255; www.hastingshouse.com; 160 Upper Ganges Rd, Ganges; d from $485; 🐾) This smashing rustic-chic hotel with 17 rooms is just up the hill from the main Ganges action, but it feels like staying in a country cottage estate in England – indeed it was built by an Englishman in 1939 to resemble his historic Sussex home. The immaculate grounds are strewn with locally made artworks and the waterfront views are like a pastoral watercolor.

Cottages on Salt Spring Island COTTAGE $$$
(☑250-931-7258; www.cottagesonsaltspring.com; 315 Robinson Rd; cottages from $300; P🐾👪) A small 'village' of deluxe cottages spread over lakeside grounds 3km northeast of Ganges. The semi-detached cottage units have huge modern interiors (most have three levels) with king-size beds, full kitchens and spectacular bathrooms equipped with tubs and separate showers. There are four different cottage configurations with the largest measuring 150 sq meters. All have two bedrooms.

Buzzy's Luncheonette JEWISH $
(☑250-222-8650; 122 Fulford-Ganges Rd; sandwiches $8-12; ⊙11am-4pm Mon-Sat) It's

🛏 Sleeping & Eating

Woods on Pender   CABIN **$$**

(☎ 250-629-3353; www.woodsonpender.com; 4709 Canal Rd, North Pender; d/cabin/caravan from $130/220/275; 🚳🏊) With lodge rooms and rustic cabins also available, the stars here are the six self-catering Airstream caravans, each with its own barbecue-equipped deck. The tree-lined site also includes hot tubs, outdoor games and a restaurant serving farm-to-table food. There's a three-night minimum stay in summer.

Poet's Cove Resort & Spa   HOTEL **$$$**

(☎ 250-629-2100; www.poetscove.com; 9801 Spalding Rd, South Pender; d from $350; P🚳🏊) This luxurious harbor-front lodge has arts-and-crafts-accented rooms plus larger cabins and villas curved around a gorgeous marina. The elegant lobby sets the tone and it's backed up by a range of other activities including swimming pools (two of them), basketball nets, a tennis court, kayak rentals, a gym and a full-treatment spa, complete with that all-important steam cave.

Jo's Place   CANADIAN **$$**

(☎ 250-629-6033; www.josplacepender.com; 4605 Bedwell Harbour Rd, North Pender; mains $15-24; ⊗ 8am-2pm, plus 5-8pm Fri-Sun) It's worth making Jo's your first stop after the ferry, so good is the food, service and ambience, especially if you're in the mood for brunch when the eclectic menu parades bubble and squeak, and pear and Gorgonzola omelets.

ℹ Getting There & Away

BC Ferries (www.bcferries.com) Frequent services arrive from Tsawwassen (adult/child/car $18/9/67), Swartz Bay (adult/child/car $12/6/36) and other islands.

Seair Seaplanes (☎ 604-273-8900; www.seairseaplanes.com) Services arrive on North Pender from Vancouver International Airport ($125, three daily).

Galiano Island

POP 1150

With the most ecological diversity of the Southern Gulf Islands, this skinny landmass – named after a 1790s Spanish explorer – offers activities for marine enthusiasts and landlubbers alike.

The Sturdies Bay ferry end is busier than the rest of the island (with restaurants and shops to match) while the island becomes ever more forested and tranquil as you drive away from the dock.

🏃 Activities

Once you've got your bearings – that is, driven off the ferry – head for Montague Harbour Marine Provincial Park for trails to beaches, meadows and a cliff carved by glaciers. In contrast, Bodega Ridge Provincial Park is renowned for eagle and cormorant birdlife plus spectacular vistas.

You can hike up the island's highest hill, Mt Galiano, from a trailhead on the Georgeson Bay Rd.

The protected waters of Trincomali Channel and the more chaotic waters of Active Pass satisfy paddlers of all skill levels. **Galiano Kayaks** (☎ 250-539-2442; www.seakayak.ca; 3451 Montague Rd; per 2hr/day from $35/60, tours from $60) can help with rentals and guided tours.

🛏 Sleeping & Eating

⭐**Galiano Inn**   HOTEL **$$**

(☎ 250-539-3388; www.galianoinn.com; 134 Madrona Dr; d from $249; 🚳🏊) The island's most deluxe accommodations occupies a small unobtrusive collection of buildings right next to the ferry dock, complete with spa, manicured lawns and the casual-gourmet **Atrevida Restaurant** (mains $22-32; ⊗ 6-9pm Jun-Sep, reduced hours Oct-May). All rooms face the placid water and the one-bedroom villas positively spoil you with multi-jet showers, wine coolers and outdoor patios furnished with hot tubs, barbecues and wood-burning fireplaces.

Bodega Ridge   CABIN **$$$**

(☎ 250-539-2677; www.bodegaridge.com; 120 Manastee Rd; cabins $300; 🚳) Those craving a nature retreat will love this tranquil woodland clutch of seven cedar cabins at the quieter end of Galiano. It's a also a great base for hiking the island's tree-lined backcountry. Each cabin has a full kitchen.

Sturdies Bay Bakery   CAFE **$**

(☎ 250-539-2004; 2450 Sturdies Bay Rd; mains $6-12; ⊗ 7am-3pm Mon-Thu, to 5pm Fri-Sun; 🚳) For your first taste of Galiano (both literally and figuratively), take the first left off the ferry and hit this cafe-bakery for meat pies, apple turnovers and cake-like scones washed down with island-roasted coffee. Popular with locals and visitors alike.

BRITISH COLUMBIA GALIANO ISLAND

❶ Information

Drop into the **visitors info booth** (www.galiano island.com; 2590 Sturdies Bay Rd; ⊙10am-5pm Mon-Sat Jun-Aug, reduced hours Sep-May) before you leave the ferry area. Nearby **Galiano Island Books** (☑250-539-3340; www.galiano islandbooks.com; 76 Mardona Dr; ⊙10am-5pm) also has friendly staff who can point you in the right direction.

❶ Getting There & Away

BC Ferries (www.bcferries.com) Frequent services arrive at the Sturdies Bay dock from Tsawwassen (adult/child/car $18/9/67, 55 minutes), Swartz Bay (adult/child/car $12/6/36, 1¼ hours) and other islands.

Seair Seaplanes (p195) has flights from Vancouver International Airport arrive at Montague Harbour ($119, two daily).

Saturna Island

POP 350

Tranquil, tiny Saturna is a natural retreat remote enough to deter casual visitors. Almost half the island, laced with curving bays, stunning rock bluffs and towering arbutus trees, is part of the Gulf Islands National Park Reserve and the only crowds you'll see are feral goats that call this area home. If you've had enough of civilization, this is the place to be.

On the north side of the island, Winter Cove has a white-sand beach that's popular for swimming, boating and fishing. Great for a hike is Mt Warburton Pike (497m), where you'll spot wild goats, soaring eagles and restorative panoramic views of the surrounding islands: focus your binoculars and you might spy a whale or two sailing quietly along the coast.

If you're here on Canada Day (July 1), join the locals at the annual **Lamb Barbecue** (www.saturnalambbarbeque.com; adult/child $25/12; ⊙Jul 1). It's the biggest party on the island.

Alongside campsites and B&Bs, you'll find a small selection of additional sleeping options. Aim for **Saturna Lodge** (☑250-539-2254; www.saturna.ca; 130 Payne Rd; d $159-199; ⌨), a peaceful respite surrounded by a tree-fringed garden.

Saturna only has two regular places to eat: a cafe in a grocery store and a dockside pub. There's also a restaurant in the Saturna Lodge open Thursday to Saturdays for dinner; book ahead.

❶ Information

Visit the Saturna Island Tourism Association website (www.saturnatourism.com) for more information.

❶ Getting There & Away

BC Ferries (www.bcferries.com) Services dock at Lyall Harbour on the west of the island from Tsawwassen (adult/child/car $18/9/67), Swartz Bay (adult/child/car $12/6/36) and other islands.

Seair Seaplane (p195) services arrive at Lyall Harbour from Vancouver International Airport ($125, three daily).

Mayne Island

POP 1100

One of the smaller and quieter Gulf Islands, Mayne wasn't always so soporific. In the 1850s, gold-seeking miners made camp here on their way to the Cariboo in the BC interior. These days the biggest racket is probably the sound of a folksy guitarist strumming at the summer farmers market.

Measuring 21 sq km, Mayne is conveniently compact (you can circumnavigate it on foot in half a day) but ideal for crowd-escaping travelers who are happy with life's simple pleasures – a good bakery, a tasteful small resort and perfect kayaking waters off Bennett Bay.

For further visitor information, see www.mayneislandchamber.ca.

◉ Sights & Actvities

The heritage Agricultural Hall in Miners Bay hosts a summer Farmers Market of local crafts and produce. Elsewhere, the south shore's Dinner Bay Park has a lovely sandy beach, as well as an immaculate Japanese Garden.

Japanese Garden   GARDENS
(Dinner Point Rd, Dinner Bay Community Park) **FREE** This immaculate Japanese Garden was built by locals to commemorate the island's early-20th-century Japanese residents, most of whom were interred in BC's interior during WWII. With its pond, stone lanterns, trees and large bell, it's a meditative place even by easygoing Mayne standards.

Kayaking Gulf Islands   KAYAKING
(☑250-539-0864; www.bennettbaykayaking.com; 494 Arbutus Dr; kayak rentals/tours from $39/66; ⊙Apr-Oct) This popular operator rents kayaks and SUPs, and many visitors also go for their

guided tours. We recommend the Sea Lion Tour, which offers plenty of opportunities to view the lolling marine critters on rocks.

🛏 Sleeping & Eating

Mayne Island Resort HOTEL **$$**
(☑ 250-539-3122; www.mayneislandresort.com; 494 Arbutus Dr; d/villa $159/299; 🐾 🐦 🐕) Superbly inviting option with lots of deluxe flourishes, there are cottages and inn rooms to choose from here. You'll also find a **restaurant** (www.bennettbaybistro.com; mains $15-28; ⊙ 11:30am-8:30pm), on-site spa and beach proximity at this top-notch hotel.

Fairview Farm B&B B&B **$$**
(☑ 250-539-5582; www.fairviewonmayne.net; 601 Bell Bay Rd; d $135-150) A delightful escape from the city, this yellow clapboard Victorian heritage house once stood in downtown Vancouver but was floated over to Mayne Island in 1980. The two lovely guest rooms will make you feel like you're immersed in a rustic idyll, and are backed up by heaping home-cooked breakfasts. Wildlife roam the surroundings and the beach is just steps away.

Sunny Mayne Bakery Cafe CAFE **$**
(☑ 250-539-2323; www.sunnymaynebakery.com; 472 Village Bay Rd; mains $4-10; ⊙ 6am-6pm) All Mayne visitors should make a beeline for the island's most reliable eating joint (open year-round with earlier closing in the winter), a source of immense muffins, custom cakes, homemade pizzas and thick soups.

ℹ Getting There & Away

BC Ferries (www.bcferries.com) Frequent services arrive at Village Bay from Tsawwassen (adult/child/car $18/9/67), Swartz Bay (adult/child/car $12/6/36) and other islands.

Seair Seaplanes (p195) Flights arrive from Vancouver International Airport at Miners Bay ($125, two daily).

FRASER & THOMPSON VALLEYS

Those looking for an inland escape from Vancouver can shoot east on Hwy 1 through the fertile plains of the Fraser River valley. Mostly people just whiz past this farmland, and you should too, unless you have a hankering to see a turnip in the rough. That said, Harrison Hot Springs makes a pleasant stop.

From Hope, if you're heading to Kamloops you have a choice. Take the faster, more direct route on Hwy 5, or the old Hwy 1. If you decide on the latter, the Fraser Canyon will thrill with stunning river-gorge beauty and the Thompson River looks little changed in decades.

EC Manning Provincial Park

This 708-sq-km **provincial park** (www.env. gov.bc.ca/bcparks; 🅿), 30km southeast of Hope, is a hint of bigger – much bigger – things to come as you head east, away from the farmlands of the Lower Mainland, towards the Rocky Mountains. It packs in a lot: dry valleys, dark mountainous forests; roiling rivers and alpine meadows. The park makes a good pause along Hwy 3, but don't expect solitude, as there are scores of folk from the burgs west seeking the same thing.

⊙ Sights & Activities

Manning is a four-seasons playground. Manning Park Resort has winter sports. In summer, boat rentals are available on Lightning Lake, and you can enjoy the alpine splendor on day hikes.

The following walks are easily reached from Hwy 3.

Dry Ridge Trail Crosses from the dry interior into an alpine climate; excellent views and wildflowers (3km round-trip, one hour).

Canyon Nature Trail Nice loop trail with a river crossing on a bridge (2km, 45 minutes).

Lightning Lake Loop The perfect intro: a level loop around this central lake (9km, two hours). Look for critters in the evening.

🛏 Sleeping

Lightning Lake Campground CAMPGROUND **$**
(☑ reservations 800-689-9025; www.discovercamping.ca; tent & RV sites $35; 🅿) A popular campground that accepts advance reservations.

Manning Park Resort RESORT **$$**
(☑ 800-330-3321; www.manningpark.com; 7500 Hwy 3; dm/r from $35/120; 🅿 🐾 🐦 🐕) Sprawling Manning Park Resort has the only indoor accommodations in the park, with lodges and cabins, plus a variety of eating options,

Fraser & Thompson Valleys

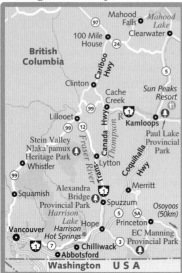

and a grocery and liquor store. There are hot tubs, requisite after a day of downhill skiing and snowboarding (adult/child day pass $57/37). The resort also boasts 100km of groomed trails for cross-country skiing and snowshoeing.

❶ Information

EC Manning Provincial Park Visitor Center
(☑604-668-5953; Hwy 3; ☉9am-6pm mid-Jun–mid-Sep) The park's visitor center is 30km inside the western boundary. It has detailed hiking descriptions, and a relief model of the park and nearby beaver ponds.

Fraser River Canyon

At the height of the Fraser River Gold Rush of 1858, it is said that the now-tiny town of Yale reached a population of 30,000, making it the largest city north of San Francisco and west of Chicago. It's certainly hard to believe these days as although the signs read Hwy 1, you feel like you're in a backwater of Canada as you head north from Hope to Cache Creek, 85km west of Kamloops. The first road was completed in 1926 and the present highway dates from the 1960s. The road shadows the swiftly flowing Fraser River through the eponymous canyon and, as you'd expect, white-water rafting is huge here. Grand scenery and several good provincial parks make this a winning trip.

◉ Sights & Actvities

Alexandra Bridge
Provincial Park   HISTORIC SITE
(www.env.gov.bc.ca/bcparks; off Hwy 1; ℗) Alexandra Bridge Provincial Park, 2km north of Spuzzum, makes for a scenic stop, where you can picnic while gazing up at the old bridge's historic 1926 span.

Fraser River
Raft Expeditions   RAFTING
(☑604-863-2336; www.fraserraft.com; 30950 Hwy 1, Yale; day trips from $179) This rafting outfit based in Yale covers all the main waterways in the area.

Lytton

☑250, 778 / POP 260

At the confluence of the Fraser and Thompson rivers, the area around Lytton has been inhabited by the Nlaka'pamux people for over 10,000 years. They call it Kumsheen, meaning 'river meeting.' It was originally known as 'The Forks' to Europeans, then renamed Lytton at the height of the gold rush in 1858 after Sir Edward Bulwer-Lytton, Britain's Secretary of State and the writer who coined the saying 'the pen is mightier than the sword.'

These days Lytton is a small but interesting town with a number of historic buildings and the surprising reputation as being the hottest spot in Canada during summer heat waves. The free Lytton Ferry connects First Nation communities on the west side of the river with Lytton township, while there is also pedestrian access via a walkway on the Canadian National Railway bridge crossing the river.

◉ Sights & Activities

Stein Valley Nlaka'pamux
Heritage Park   PARK
(www.env.gov.bc.ca/bcparks; Stein Valley Rd; ℗) This ecologically diverse park is co-managed by BC Parks and the Lytton First Nation. It offers some excellent long-distance hiking through dry valleys and snow-clad peaks amid one of the best-preserved watersheds in lower BC. The main trail head is on the west side of the Fraser River by Lytton, accessed via the free Lytton Ferry. After disembarking the ferry, follow the road to the right

for 5km to Stein Valley Rd. Vehicles are not allowed in the park.

Kumsheen Rafting Resort RAFTING
(☎800-663-6667; www.kumsheen.com; Hwy 1, 5km east of Lytton; half-/full-day rafting from $139/189) Offers a variety of half- and full-day rafting trips on the Thompson, Fraser and Nicola rivers and has two-day packages. It also offers funky accommodations such as canvas cabins and tipis.

🛏 Sleeping & Eating

Totem Motel MOTEL $
(☎250-455-2321; www.totemmotellytton.com; 320 Fraser St; r from $85; ⊜❄🛜) This cute place a block back from Lytton's main street is based in a 1912 building that was originally the town's post office until the 1950s. The lodge has three self-contained units, while there are 12 cottage-style units with kitchen and bathroom. In a good spot overlooking the Fraser River.

Klowa Art Café CAFE $
(☎778-765-4450; www.klowa.ca; 350 Main St; snacks from $3; ⊗8am-5pm Mon-Fri, from 10am Sat & Sun) Lovely family-run place on Lytton's main street combining local art, knitwear and a cafe in a cheerful atmosphere. Great coffee, cookies and baked goods.

ⓘ Information

Lytton Visitor Info Centre (☎250-455-2523; www.lytton.ca; 400 Fraser St; ⊗9am-5pm mid-May–mid-Sep) All you need to know, with maps and brochures, is here at the friendly visitor center.

Kamloops

☎250, 778 / POP 90,300
If you've opted to follow Hwy 1 from Vancouver east to the Rockies and Banff, Kamloops makes a useful break in the journey. Motels abound, and there's a walkable heritage center. Historically, the Shuswap First Nation found the area's many rivers and lakes useful for transportation and salmon fishing. Traders set up camp for fur hunting in 1811.

The focus of the downtown area is tree-lined Victoria St, which is a lively place on sunny days; very busy train tracks separate the wide Thompson River from downtown. Franchises and malls line the highlands along Hwy 1.

◉ Sights

Kamloops Art Gallery GALLERY
(☎250-377-2400; www.kag.bc.ca; 465 Victoria St; adult/child $5/3; ⊗10am-5pm Mon-Sat Mon, Tue, Fri & Sat, to 8pm Wed & Thu) Suitably loft-like in feel, this gallery, which shares the civic building with the town library, has an emphasis on contemporary Western and indigenous works by regional artists.

Kamloops Museum & Archives MUSEUM
(☎250-828-3576; www.kamloops.ca/museum; cnr Seymour St & 2nd Ave; adult/child $3/1; ⊗9:30am-4:30pm Tue-Sat; 🖐) Kamloops Museum is in a vintage building and has a fitting collection of historic photographs. Come here for the scoop on river-namesake David Thompson, and an entire floor dedicated to exhibits for kids.

Riverside Park PARK
A short stroll from the center of town and sitting, as its name suggests, on the banks of the Thomson River, lovely Riverside Park is a source of pride for locals. Lots going on here, with walking trails, sports facilities and 'music in the park' held nightly during summer.

Kamloops Heritage Railway HISTORIC SITE
(☎250-374-2141; www.kamrail.com; 510 Lorne St; 🅿) Across the train tracks from downtown, the Kamloops Heritage Railway runs steam-engine-powered excursions. Check the website for a variety of trips throughout the year.

🛏 Sleeping & Eating

★Plaza Hotel HOTEL $$
(☎877-977-5292, 250-377-8075; www.theplazahotel.ca; 405 Victoria St; r from $99; 🅿⊜❄🛜) In a town of bland modernity as far as lodgings go, the Plaza reeks of character. This 67-room, six-story classic has changed little on the outside since its opening in 1928. Rooms are nicely redone in a chic heritage style, though, and the included breakfast is excellent. Use of the nearby YMCA's pool and gym is included too.

South Thompson Inn Guest Ranch LODGE $$
(☎250-573-3777; www.stigr.com; 3438 Shuswap Rd E; r from $180; 🅿⊜❄🛜🏊) Some 20km east of town off Shuswap Rd on the north side of the South Thompson River, this luxe waterfront lodge is set amid rolling grasslands. Its 58 rooms are spread between the

wood-framed main building, a small manor house and some converted stables. Plenty of things to do and the Rivershore Golf Links are right next door.

Scott's Inn MOTEL **$$**
(☑ 250-372-8221; www.scottsinnkamloops.ca; 551 11th Ave; r from $118; P ⊕ ✳ @ 🛜 🐾) Unlike many of its competitors, Scott's is close to the center and very well run. The 51 rooms are nicely furnished for a motel, and extras include an indoor pool, hot tub, cafe and rooftop sundeck.

Art We Are CAFE **$**
(☑ 250-828-7998; www.theartweare.com; 246 Victoria St; mains from $8; ⊙ 9am-9pm Mon-Sat; 🛜 🐾) Tea joint, local artist venue, hangout, bakery and more – this funky cafe is a great place to let some Kamloops hours slip by. The organic menu changes daily. Saturday night has live rock or blues.

★ **Noble Pig** PUB FOOD **$$**
(☑ 778-471-5999; www.thenoblepig.ca; 650 Victoria St; mains from $14; ⊙ 11:30am-11pm Mon-Wed, to midnight Thu-Sat, 3-10pm Sun) This slick microbrewery has a rotating lineup of its own beers (its excellent IPA is always on tap) plus other top BC brews. The food is equally good and includes salads, burgers, pizza and various specials. The inside is warm and welcoming; in summer you can't beat the huge patio.

Brownstone Restaurant CANADIAN **$$$**
(☑ 250-851-9939; www.brownstone-restaurant. com; 118 Victoria St; mains from $22; ⊙ 5-11pm) Top-notch dining at its own historic site, the atmospheric 1904 Canadian Bank of Commerce building, said to have once been the workplace of poet Robert Service. The menu, excellently prepared and presented with attention to detail, features innovative dishes such as bacon-wrapped elk meatloaf ($29).

❶ Information

Kamloops Visitors Center (☑ 250-374-3377, 800-662-1994; www.tourismkamloops.com; 1290 W Hwy 1, exit 368; ⊙ 8am-6pm; 🛜) Just off Hwy 1, overlooking town.

❶ Getting There & Away

VIA Rail (www.viarail.ca) serves Kamloops North Station with tri-weekly services from Vancouver (9½ hours) to Jasper, AB (another 9½ hours) and beyond.

Rider Express (www.riderexpress.ca) runs buses connecting Vancouver, Kamloops, Cal-

gary and places in-between, with a bus in each direction daily.

Ebus (www.myebus.ca) runs buses connecting Vancouver, Kamloops and Kelowna.

Adventure Charters (www.adventurecharters. ca) has buses south to Hope and Surrey, and north to Williams Lake and Prince George.

Sun Peaks

The hills looming northeast of Kamloops are home to the **Sun Peaks Resort** (☑ 800-807-3257; www.sunpeaksresort.com; 1280 Alpine Rd; lift tickets adult/child $115/58, mountain biking $56/34). This ever-growing resort, proudly the second-largest ski area in Canada, boasts 135 ski runs (including some 8km-long powder trails), eight lifts and a pleasant base-area village. In summer, lifts provide access to more than two dozen mountain-bike trails.

Sun Peaks has many lodges, B&Bs and luxury condos.

The resort area has several eateries for all budgets.

❶ Getting There & Away

Sun Peaks is 50km northeast of Kamloops via Hwy 5. In winter there are shuttles from Kamloops ($20).

OKANAGAN VALLEY

It's hard to know which harvest is growing faster in this fertile and beautiful valley midway between Vancouver and Alberta: tourists or fruit. The 180km-long Okanagan Valley is home to orchards of peaches and apricots, and scores of excellent wineries whose vines spread across the terraced hills, soaking up some of Canada's sunniest weather. The valley has provided a summer escape for generations of Canadians, who frolic in the string of lakes linking the Okanagan's towns.

Osoyoos, near the US border, is almost arid, but things become greener heading north. Central Kelowna is a fast-growing city that's a heady mix of lakeside beauty and fun.

In July and August the entire valley is as overburdened as a grapevine before harvest; the best times to visit are late spring and early fall, when the crowds lessen. Snowy winters also make nearby Big White resort an attraction for skiers and snowboarders.

Osoyoos

📍 250, 778 / POP 5100

Once-modest Osoyoos has embraced an up-scale future. The town takes its name from the First Nations word *soyoos,* which means 'sand bar across'; even if the translation is a bit rough, the definition is not: much of the town is indeed on a narrow spit of land that divides Osoyoos Lake. It is ringed with beaches, and the waters irrigate the lush farms, orchards and vineyards that line Hwy 97 going north out of town.

Nature's bounty aside, this is the arid end of the Okanagan Valley and locals like to say that the town marks the northern end of Mexico's Sonoran Desert; much of the town is done up in a style that loses something across borders. From the cactus-speckled sands to the town's cheesy faux-tile-and-stucco architecture, it's a big change from the BC image of pine trees and mountains found in both directions on Hwy 3.

👁 Sights & Activities

Osoyoos Lake is one of the warmest in the country. That, together with Osoyoos' sandy beaches, means great swimming, a huge relief when the summer temp hits 42°C (108°F). Many lakeside motels and camp-grounds hire out kayaks, canoes and small boats.

Osoyoos Desert Centre   PARK
(📞250-495-2470; www.desert.org; 14580 146 Ave, off Hwy 97; adult/child $8/6; ⏰9:30am-4:30pm mid-May–mid-Sep, shorter hours mid-Sep–mid-May; 🅿) Hear the rattle of a snake and the songs of birds at the Osoyoos Desert Centre, 3km north of town, where interpretive kiosks along raised boardwalks meander through the dry land. The nonprofit center offers 90-minute guided tours. Special gardens focus on delights such as delicate wildflowers.

Nk'Mip Desert & Heritage Centre   MUSEUM
(📞250-495-7901; www.nkmipdesert.com; 1000 Rancher Creek Rd; adult/child $12/8; ⏰9:30am-4:30pm May-Sep, shorter hours Oct-Apr; 🅿) Part of a First Nations empire, the Nk'Mip Desert & Heritage Centre features cultural demon-strations and tours of the arid ecology. Located off 45th St north of Hwy 3, it also has a desert golf course, the noted winery Nk'Mip Cellars, a resort and more.

Orchard Hill Estate Cidery   CIDERY
(📞778-437-2335; www.orchardhillcidery.com; 3480 Fruitvale Way; ⏰10am-5pm) FREE All wined out? Stop on the side of Hwy 97 at this family roadside place for a free tasting of their excellent cider. Our pick: the Red Roof Apple Cider ($12.50 a bottle).

🛏 Sleeping & Eating

Nk'Mip Campground & RV Resort   CAMPGROUND $
(📞250-495-7279; www.campingosoyoos.com; 8000 45th St; tent/RV sites from $35/48; 🅿🐾📶) Choose from more than 300 sites at this year-round lakeside resort off Hwy 3. There is a good campground store.

★Watermark Beach Resort   RESORT $$
(📞250-495-5500; www.watermarkbeachresort.com; 15 Park Pl; r from $150; 🅿🐾❄📶🏊) A top spot right on the water in Osoyoos, perfect for couples and families. Facilities include a heated outdoor swimming pool, hot tubs, spa, restaurants and access to a gorgeous beach right out front. It also has two-bedroom townhouses.

Walnut Beach Resort   RESORT $$
(📞250-495-5400; www.walnutbeachresort.com; 4200 Lakeshore Dr; r from $150; 🅿🐾📶🏊) This large resort is an upscale addition to the east shore of the southern half of the lake. There are 112 large suites (some with two bedrooms) and a vast terrace surround-ing a pool.

Jojo's Café   CAFE $
(📞250-495-6652; www.jojoscafe.ca; 8316 Main St; pastries from $1.50; ⏰7am-4pm) Definitely the most happening spot in the morning in Osoyoos. Battle the locals for an inside table or grab a seat out on the sidewalk after or-dering a set breakfast (from $5.95), or just settle for a muffin and coffee. Jojo's exudes a cool vibe and everyone knows it.

ℹ Information

Osoyoos Visitors Center (📞250-495-5070; www.destinationosoyoos.com; cnr Hwys 3 & 97; ⏰9am-6pm; 📶) This large center has info, maps and books.

Oliver

📍 250, 778 / POP 4920

Oliver has emerged as a hub of excellent wineries and other natural bounty and is,

OKANAGAN VALLEY WINERIES

The abundance of sunshine, fertile soil and cool winters have allowed the local wine industry to thrive. Kelowna and the region in the valley's north are known for whites, such as Pinot Grigio. South, near Penticton and Oliver, reds are the stars, especially ever-popular Merlot.

A majority of the more than 120 wineries are close to Hwy 97, which makes tasting a breeze. Most offer tours and all will gladly sell you a bottle or 20; in fact, many of the best wines are only sold at the cellar door. Some wineries feature excellent cafes and bistros that offer fine views and complex regional fare to complement what's in the glass.

Festivals

Okanagan seasonal **wine festivals** (www.thewinefestivals.com) are major events, especially the one in fall.

The usual dates are fall (early October), winter (mid-January), spring (early May) and summer (early August). Events take place at wineries across the valley.

Information

Good sources of information on Okanagan Valley wines include the **BC Wine Information Centre** in Penticton's visitor center (p207) and the Okanagan Wine & Orchard Museum (p209) in Kelowna. *John Schreiner's Okanagan Wine Tour Guide* is an authoritative guidebook.

Tours

Numerous companies allow you to do the sipping while they do the driving.

Club Wine Tours (☎ 250-762-9951; www.clubwinetours.com; 1152 Sunset Dr, Kelowna; tours from $75) The 'signature' tour includes four wineries and lunch in a vineyard.

Distinctly Kelowna Tours (p209) Offers winery tours by valley region; many include stops for lunch.

Visiting the Wineries

Wine tastings at those wineries open to visitors vary greatly. Some places have just a couple of wines on offer; others offer dozens of vintages. Some tasting rooms are glorified sales areas; others have magnificent views of the vineyards, valley and lakes. Some charge; others are free.

Among the dozens of options, the following (listed north to south) are recommended. Summerhill Pyramid and Cedar Creek Estate are south of Kelowna along the lake's east shore. The rest of the wineries can be reached via Hwy 97.

Sandhill Wines (☎ 250-979-4211; www.sandhillwines.ca; 1125 Richter St; ⊙ 10am-6pm; P) Formerly known as Calona Vineyards, Sandhill Wines was the Okanagan's first winery when it kicked off production in 1932. Its architecturally striking tasting room is an atmospheric spot to try its ever-popular, melon-note Pinot Blanc.

Summerhill Pyramid Winery (☎ 250-764-8000; www.summerhill.bc.ca; 4870 Chute Lake Rd; ⊙ 9am-6pm; P) In the hills along the lake's eastern shore is one of the Okanagan's most colorful wineries. Summerhill Pyramid Winery combines a traditional tasting room with a huge pyramid where every Summerhill wine is aged in barrels. The winery's **Summerhill Pyramid Bistro** (mains from $15; ⊙ 11am-11pm) 🍃 offers locally sourced dishes; the wines are organic.

CedarCreek Estate Winery (☎ 778-738-1020; www.cedarcreek.bc.ca; 5445 Lakeshore Rd; ⊙ 10am-7pm Jul & Aug, 11am-5pm Sep-Jun; P) Known for excellent tours, its Riesling and its Ehrenfelser, a refreshing fruity white wine. Its **Home Block at CedarCreek** (☎ 250-980-4663; mains from $24; ⊙ 10am-9pm Jun–mid-Sep) has the kind of view that makes you want to eat here twice.

Quails' Gate Winery (☎250-769-4451; www.quailsgate.com; 3303 Boucherie Rd, West Kelowna; ☺10am-8pm; P) A small winery with a huge reputation; it's known for its Pinot Noir, Chardonnay and Chenin Blanc. The **Old Vines Restaurant** (☎250-769-2500; mains from $23; ☺11am-10pm) is among the best.

Mission Hill Family Estate (☎250-768-6400; www.missionhillwinery.com; 1730 Mission Hill Rd, West Kelowna; ☺10am-7pm; P) As if it were a Tuscan hill town, this winery's architecture wows. Go for a taste of one of the blended reds (try the Bordeaux) or the excellent Syrah. Terrace (p208) is one of the valley's best restaurants and sources fine foods locally; book ahead.

Haywire Winery at Okanagan Crush Pad (☎250-494-4445; www.okanagancrushpad.com; 16576 Fosbery Rd, Summerland; ☺11am-5pm; P) Ages many of its wines in concrete tanks, reviving a centuries-old practice that largely died out when the industry shifted to stainless steel. Tastings range across more than 20 varieties from the multiple labels produced here.

Hester Creek (☎250-498-4435; www.hestercreek.com; 877 Road 8; ☺10am-7pm; P) Has a sweeping location and a great new tasting room and is known for its reds, especially its richly flavored Cabernet Franc. Terrafina at Hester Creek by RauDZ (p205) has a Med accent.

Inniskillin (☎866-455-0559; www.inniskillin.com; 7857 Tucelnuit Dr; ☺10am-5pm; P) BC's first producer of Zinfandel is also home to the elixirs known as ice wines, which are harvested when the grapes are frozen on the vine; go for the golden-hued Riesling.

Road 13 (☎250-498-8330; www.road13vineyards.com; 799 Ponderosa Rd; ☺10am-5:30pm; P) Its very drinkable reds (Pinot Noir) and whites (Chenin Blanc) win plaudits. The no-frills vibe extends to its picnic tables with gorgeous views and the motto 'It's all about dirt.' The attractive lounge has views of the grapes.

Rust Wine Co (☎250-498-3276; www.rustwine.com; 4444 Golden Mile Dr; ☺10:30am-7pm; P) Recently rebranded, these guys produce excellent whites, reds and rosé, though it's best known for the Zinfandel. Breathtaking views in the valley overlook the Black Sage Bench to the east and Osoyoos to the south.

Black Hills Estate (☎250-498-0666; www.blackhillswinery.com; 4190 Black Sage Rd; guided tastings from $10; ☺10am-6pm; P) The tasting room here is an arresting vision of glass and metal, with deeply shaded patios for sunset tippling. Besides vintages such as Viognier, there are many blends, including Alibi, a blend of Sauvignon Blanc and Semillon.

Church & State Wines (☎250-498-2700; www.churchandstatewines.com; 4516 Ryegrass Rd; ☺11am-6pm; P) Making a big splash at its Coyote Bowl vineyards, especially with its full-bodied, luscious Syrahs. Also home to the Lost Inhibitions label, which produces popularly priced wines with names such as Chill the F*uck Out and I Freakin' Love You.

Burrowing Owl Estate Winery (☎250-498-0620; www.burrowingowlwine.ca; 500 Burrowing Owl Pl; ☺10am-6pm mid-Fed–mid-Dec; P) 🌿 Wine with an eco-accent that includes organic farm techniques; try the Syrah. Other award-winners include the Cabernet Franc and Meritage. This Golden Mile landmark includes a hotel and the excellent **Sonora Room** (mains from $24; ☺11:30am-9pm) restaurant.

LaStella Winery (☎250-495-8180; www.lastella.ca; 8123 148 Ave; ☺11am-5pm; P) A beautiful vision of Italy rises up near Osoyoos Lake. Terra-cotta roof tiles and floors and granite touches combine for one of the valley's most beautiful wineries. The Cabernet Sauvignon–based Maestoso is highly regarded.

BRITISH COLUMBIA

Okanagan Valley

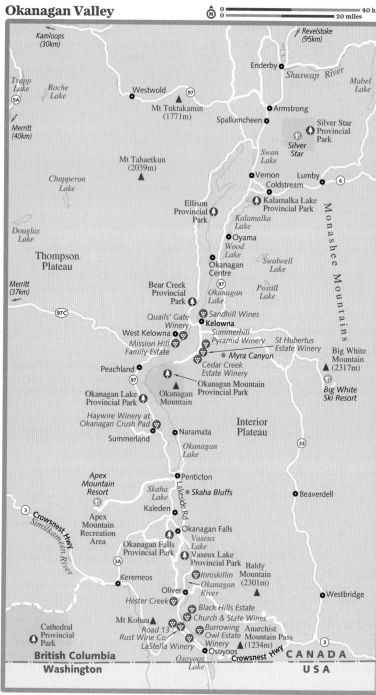

N
0 — 40 km
0 — 20 miles

Kamloops
(30km)

Revelstoke
(95km)

Enderby

Shuswap River

Trapp
Lake

Roche
Lake

Westwold

97

Armstrong

Mabel
Lake

5A

Mt Tuktakamin
(1771m)

Spallumcheen

Silver Star
Provincial
Park

Merritt
(40km)

Silver
Star

BRITISH COLUMBIA

Mt Tahaetkun
(2039m)

Chapperon
Lake

Vernon
Coldstream

Lumby

6

Douglas
Lake

Ellison
Provincial
Park

Kalamalka Lake
Provincial Park

Kalamalka
Lake

Thompson
Plateau

Oyama

Wood
Lake

Merritt
(37km)

97C

Bear Creek
Provincial
Park

Okanagan
Lake

Okanagan
Centre

Swalwell
Lake

Postill
Lake

Monashee Mountains

Quails' Gate
Winery

Sandhill Wines

Kelowna

West Kelowna

Mission Hill
Family Estate

Summerhill
Pyramid Winery

St Hubertus
Estate Winery

Peachland

Cedar Creek
Estate Winery

Myra Canyon

Big White
Mountain
(2317m)

97

Okanagan Lake
Provincial Park

Okanagan
Mountain

Okanagan Mountain
Provincial Park

Big White
Ski Resort

Haywire Winery at
Okanagan Crush Pad

Summerland

Naramata

Interior
Plateau

Okanagan
Lake

33

Apex
Mountain
Resort

Penticton

Skaha
Lake

Lakeside Rd

Skaha Bluffs

Beaverdell

3

Crowsnest Hwy

Kaleden

Apex
Mountain
Recreation
Area

Okanagan Falls

Vaseux
Lake

3A

Okanagan Falls
Provincial Park

Vaseux Lake
Provincial Park

Keremeos

Inniskillin

Okanagan
River

Baldy
Mountain
(2301m)

Westbridge

Oliver

Hester Creek

Black Hills Estate

Cathedral
Provincial
Park

Mt Kobau

Church & State Wines

Road 13
Rust Wine Co
LaStella Winery

Burrowing
Owl Estate
Winery

Anarchist
Mountain Pass
(1234m)

3

British Columbia

Osoyoos

Crowsnest Hwy

C A N A D A

Washington

Osoyoos
Lake

U S A

without doubt, a very cheeky little town. The Tourism Association has managed to trademark the slogan 'Wine Capital of Canada', much to the chagrin of its rivals, and you'll find signboards claiming such at the entry to town. They've also laid claim to the website www.winecapitalofcanada. com and it will be interesting to see what comes next.

Over the 20km drive between Oliver and Osoyoos, Hwy 97 plunges through orchard after orchard laden with lush fruits, earning it the moniker 'The Golden Mile.' Roadside stands display the ripe bounty and many places will let you pick your own. This little town enjoys life with a twinkle in its eye.

🛏 Sleeping & Eating

Mount View Motel   MOTEL $
(☎250-498-3446; www.mountviewmotel.com; 5856 Main St; r from $80; P⊖❄🛜) Close to the center of town, seven units sunbathe around a flower-bedecked vintage motor court. All have kitchens – and corkscrews. The decor features new wood floors and a contemporary style.

★Burrowing Owl
Guest House   BOUTIQUE HOTEL $$$
(☎250-498-0620; www.burrowingowlwine.ca; 500 Burrowing Owl Pl, off Black Sage Rd; r from $170; P⊖❄🛜🏊) One of the Okanagan's best wineries (p203) has 10 rooms with patios facing southwest over the vineyards. There's a big pool, a hot tub, king-size beds and corporate Mission-style decor. The Sonora Room (p203) is noted for its fusion cuisine. It's 13km south of Oliver, off Hwy 97.

Villa at Hester Creek   INN $$$
(☎250-498-4435; www.hestercreek.com/visit/ villa; 877 Road 8; r from $200; P⊖❄🛜) One of the valley's top wineries, Hester Creek (p203) has six suites in a Mediterranean-style villa with a sweeping view over the vineyards. The trappings are plush, with fireplaces, soaking tubs and more. On-site Terrafina serves excellent Tuscan-accented fare using foods from the region.

Medici's Gelateria   GELATO $
(☎250-498-2228; 522 Fairview Rd; treats from $3; ⊙10am-5pm) Frozen delights so good you'll worship them – appropriate, given the setting in an old church. Also serves good coffee, plus soups, panini and more, all made with local produce. It's just west of Hwy 97.

★Terrafina at Hester
Creek by RauDZ   ITALIAN $$$
(☎250-498-2229; www.terrafinabyraudz.com; 887 Road 8; mains from $23; ⊙11:30am-9pm) This intimate Tuscan-style restaurant at Hester Creek Estate Winery (p203) is run by the creative minds behind RauDZ Regional Table (p211) in Kelowna. Its outdoor terrace is one of the valley's finest.

ℹ Information

Oliver Visitor Center (☎778-439-2363; www. winecapitalofcanada.com; 6431 Station St; ⊙10am-4pm) Located in the old train station near the center of town. It has affable staff, excellent regional info, and walking and biking maps.

Vaseux Lake

About 10km north of Oliver on Hwy 97, nature reasserts itself at this lake – an azure gem, framed by sheer granite cliffs.

If you're not in a hurry, the small roads on the east side of Skaha Lake between Okanagan Falls and Penticton are much more interesting for their wineries and views than Hwy 97.

Vaseux Lake Provincial Park   PARK
(www.env.gov.bc.ca/bcparks; Hwy 97) This lakeside park has a 300m boardwalk for viewing oodles of birds, bighorn sheep, mountain goats and some of the 14 species of bat. You can also hike to the Bighorn National Wildlife Area and the Vaseux Lake National Migratory Bird Sanctuary, which has more than 160 bird species.

Penticton

☎250, 778 / POP 37,035

Penticton combines the idle pleasures of a beach resort with its own edgy vibe. It's long been a final stop in life for Canadian retirees, which adds a certain spin to its Salish-derived name Pen-Tak-Tin, meaning 'place to stay forever.' The town today is growing fast, along with the rest of the Okanagan Valley.

Penticton makes a good base for your valley pleasures. There are plenty of activities and diversions to fill your days, even if you don't travel further afield. Ditch Hwy 97, which runs west of the center, for Main St and the attractively walkable downtown area, which extends about 10 blocks southward from the picture-perfect lakefront;

avert your eyes from the long stretch of strip malls and high-rise condos further south.

⊙ Sights

Okanagan Beach boasts about 1.3km of sand, with average summer water temperatures of about 22°C (72°F). If things are jammed, quieter shores are often found at 1.5km-long **Skaha Beach** on Skaha Lake, south of the center.

★ SS Sicamous

Heritage Park HISTORIC SITE
(☑250-492-0403; www.sssicamous.ca; 1099 Lakeshore Dr W; adult/child $6/3; ⊙10am-5:30pm Fri-Mon) Back when the best way to get around inland BC was by boat, the SS *Sicamous* hauled passengers and freight on Okanagan Lake from 1914 to 1936. Now the boat has been restored and permanently moored; a tour is an evocative self-guided ramble.

Skaha Bluffs

Provincial Park PARK
(www.env.gov.bc.ca/bcparks; Smythe Dr; ⊙Mar-Nov) Propelled by the dry weather and compact gneiss rock, climbers from all over the world come to this park to enjoy climbing on more than 400 bolted routes. For comprehensive info on the bluffs, which are off Lakeside Rd on the east side of Skaha Lake, visit www.offtracktravel.ca/climbing-skaha-bluffs-guide. A climbing area trails map is on the BC Parks website.

Penticton Museum MUSEUM
(☑250-490-2451; www.pentictonmuseum.com; 785 Main St; by donation; ⊙10am-5pm Tue-Sat) Inside the library, the Penticton Museum has delightfully eclectic displays, including the de rigueur natural-history exhibit with stuffed animals and birds, and everything you'd want to know about the juicy fruits of the **Peach Festival** (www.peachfest.com; ⊙early Aug).

🏃 Activities

★ Coyote Cruises WATER SPORTS
(☑250-492-2115; www.coyotecruises.ca; 215 Riverside Dr; rentals & shuttle $18; ⊙11am-4pm mid-Jun–Sep) Coyote Cruises rents out inner-tubes (single, double, quad or for a party of 10) that you can float in 7km down the Okanagan River Channel to Skaha Lake. It then buses you back to the start near Okanagan Lake. If you have your own floatable, it's $5 for the bus ride.

Apex Mountain Resort SKIING
(☑250-292-8222, condition report 250-487-4848; www.apexresort.com; off Green Mountain Rd; lift tickets adult/child $87/54) One of Canada's best small ski resorts is 37km west of Penticton. It has more than 68 downhill runs for all ability levels, but the mountain is known for its plethora of double-black-diamond and technical runs; the drop is more than 600m. It is usually quieter than nearby **Big White** (☑250-765-8888, snow report 250-765-7669; www.bigwhite.com; off Hwy 33; 1-day lift pass adult/child $105/64).

Freedom the Bike Shop CYCLING
(☑250-493-0686; www.freedombikeshop.com; 533 Main St; bicycle rental per day from $45; ⊙9:30am-5:30pm Mon-Sat) Rents bikes and offers a wealth of information. Can arrange transport to/from the Kettle Valley Rail Trail (p212).

🛏 Sleeping

Penticton Lakeside Resort HOTEL $$
(☑250-493-8221; www.pentictonlakesideresort.com; 21 Lakeshore Dr W; r from $150; 🅿❄❋ 🌐🏊) Plush Penticton Lakeside Resort & Conference Centre, lakefront and at the foot of Main St, may be described by some as a six-floor monstrosity. Indoor pool, hot tub, restaurants, panoramic views and, undoubtedly, the top location in town – though it might just feel a tad sterile.

ON YER BIKE

Long dry days and rolling hills add up to perfect conditions for mountain biking. Get to popular rides by heading east out of town, toward Naramata. Follow signs to the city dump and **Campbell's Mountain**, where you'll find a singletrack and dual-slalom course, both of which aren't too technical. Once you get there, the riding is mostly on the right-hand side, but once you pass the cattle guard, it opens up and you can ride anywhere.

Cyclists can try the route through Naramata and onto the Kettle Valley Rail Trail (p212). Other good options include the small, winery-lined roads south of town and east of Skaha Lake.

Bowmont Motel
MOTEL **$$**

(☑250-490-0231; www.bowmontmotel.com; 80 Riverside Dr; r from $87; **P ⊜ ✳ 🛜 🏊**) Look past the dubious faux-Southwestern facade and you'll find an excellent indie motel near the lake. The 45 rooms are immaculate and all share terraces or balconies. Each has a full kitchen, there is a gas barbecue near the pool and off-season room rates plummet.

Crooked Tree Guest Suites
B&B **$$**

(☑250-490-8022; www.crooked-tree.com; 1278 Spiller Rd; ste from $195; **P ⊜ ✳ 🛜**) Okanagan Lake glistens below from this mountainside retreat, 9km east of downtown Penticton. The three large apartments have multiple decks amid this woodsy aerie and are well stocked with luxuries. Minimum stay is two nights.

🍴 Eating & Drinking

⭐Burger 55
BURGERS **$**

(☑778-476-5559; www.burger55.com; 52 Front St; mains from $9; ⊙11am-7pm Sun-Thu, to 8pm Fri & Sat) Best burger in Canada? It's your fault if it isn't, as you have myriad ways to customize at this downtown restaurant. Seven kinds of buns, 10 kinds of cheese, and toppings include roasted garlic and *pico de gallo* plus more. Sides, such as fries, are equally excellent. There's a fine patio and a good beer list.

⭐Penticton Farmers Market
MARKET **$**

(☑250-493-8540; www.pentictonfarmersmarket. org; 100 Main St; ⊙8:30am-1pm Sat May-Oct) Penticton definitely has its share of good eats. The farmers market, based at Gyro Park on Main St, has large numbers of local organic producers.

Bench Market
CAFE **$**

(☑250-492-2222; www.thebenchmarket.com; 368 Vancouver Ave; meals from $9; ⊙7am-4pm Mon-Fri, from 8am Sat & Sun) Always buzzing – and not just because of the excellent organic coffee – this neighborhood fave is consistently busy. The patio is where locals meet and exchange gossip. Egg dishes star at breakfast; lunch is about sandwiches and salads. Great baked goods and other deli items are sold through the day.

Il Vecchio Deli
DELI **$**

(☑250-492-7610; 317 Robinson St; sandwiches from $6; ⊙9am-5pm Mon-Sat) The smell that greets you as you enter confirms your choice. The best lunch sandwiches in town can be consumed at a couple of tables in

---

ℹ️ FRUIT-A-PALOOZA

Roadside stands and farms where you can buy and even pick your own fruit line Hwy 97 between Osoyoos and Penticton. Major Okanagan Valley crops and their harvest times are as follows.

Cherries Mid-June to late July

Apricots Mid-July to mid-August

Peaches Mid-July to mid-September

Pears Mid-August to late September

Apples Early September to late October

Table Grapes Early September to late October

---

this atmospheric deli, but will taste better on a picnic. Choices are many; we like the sandwich with garlic salami and marinated eggplant.

⭐Dream Cafe
FUSION **$$**

(☑250-490-9012; www.thedreamcafe.ca; 67 Front St; mains from $12; ⊙6-11pm daily, 11am-2pm Sat & Sun; 🎵) The heady aroma of spices hits as you enter this pillow-bedecked, upscale-yet-funky bistro. Asian and Indian flavors mix on the menu, which has numerous veggie options. There's live acoustic music by touring pros on many nights; tables outside hum all summer long.

⭐Bad Tattoo Brewing
MICROBREWERY

(☑250-493-8686; www.facebook.com/badtattoo brewing; 169 Estabrook Ave; ⊙11am-10pm Sun-Thu, to 11pm Fri & Sat) There's a 'born to be bad' attitude going on here along with some great beer. Get a flight of five brews ($10) then go for what you like. Locals are refilling growlers, while the pizzas are good if you're here for something solid. The Los Muertos Cerveza Negra, a dark lager brew, gets raves reviews.

ℹ️ Information

Penticton & Wine Country Visitor Centre (☑250-276-2170; www.visitpenticton.com; 888 Westminster Ave W; ⊙9am-5pm; 🛜) Has a full range of info on area activities and wine.

ℹ️ Getting There & Away

Penticton Regional Airport (CYYF) is 3km south of town and has daily flights to Vancouver and Calgary with Air Canada (www.aircanada.com) and Westjet (www.westjet.com).

Penticton is on Hwy 97, 63km south of Kelowna and 62km north of Osoyoos. You'll want your own wheels.

Penticton to Kelowna

Lakeside resort town Summerland, 18km north of Penticton on Hwy 97, features some fine 19th-century heritage buildings on the hillside above the ever-widening and busy highway. There are some good wineries here, too.

Hugging the lake below Hwy 97, some 25km south of Kelowna, the little town of Peachland is good for a quick, breezy stroll along the water amid parks and interesting shops. Try not to lose your lunch on Canada's highest zip line.

Between Peachland and Kelowna, urban sprawl becomes unavoidable, especially through the billboard-lined nightmare of West Kelowna (aka Westbank).

🏃 Activities

Kettle Valley Steam Railway RAIL
(📞877-494-8424; www.kettlevalleyrail.org; 18404 Bathville Rd, Summerland; adult/child $25/16; ⊗May-Oct) The Kettle Valley Steam Railway is an operating, 16km remnant of the famous tracks. Ride behind an old steam locomotive in open-air cars and enjoy orchard views.

Zipzone Peachland ADVENTURE SPORTS
(📞855-947-9663; www.zipzone.ca; 5875 Brenda Mines Rd, Peachland; adult/child from $114/84; ⊗9:30am-6pm May-Oct) Zoom along Canada's highest freestyle zip lines here, where you can sail high over Deep Creek Canyon.

🛏 Sleeping & Eating

A View of the Lake B&B $$
(📞250-769-7854; www.aviewofthelake.com; 1877 Horizon Dr, West Kelowna; r from $130; 🅿🐕❄🛜) Set on the west side of Okanagan Lake, this B&B offers privacy and magnificent views. Book the Grandview Suite for a lake vista that extends even to the air-jet bathtub. Rooms are peaceful, beds are comfy and the three-course breakfast on the deck is gourmet.

★Peach Pitt MARKET $
(📞778-516-7003; cnr Hwy 97 & Jones Flat Rd, Summerland; treats from $3; ⊗9am-6pm May-Oct) Amid oodles of competition, this roadside stand on Hwy 97 on the north side of Summerland stands out. The owners have an orchard right behind the market. They also

have deals with some of the valley's best producers (the $3 tub of raspberries will have you checking local real-estate prices) and they create wonderful baked goods.

★Terrace Restaurant MODERN AMERICAN $$$
(📞250-768-6467; www.missionhillwinery.com; 1730 Mission Hill Rd, Mission Hill Family Estate, West Kelowna; mains from $25; ⊗noon-8:30pm Jun-Oct) A suitably impressive restaurant to go with a very impressive winery. Terrace (yes, there are views) exemplifies farm-to-table with its fresh and inventive menu.

Kelowna

📞250, 778 / POP 127,380

A kayaker paddles past scores of new tract houses on a hillside: it's an iconic image for ever-growing Kelowna, the unofficial 'capital' of the Okanagan and the sprawling center of all that's good and not-so-good with the region.

Entering from the north, the ever-lengthening urban sprawl of tree-lined Hwy 97/Harvey Ave seems to go on forever. Once past the ceaseless waves of chains and strip malls, the downtown is a welcome respite. Museums, culture, nightlife and the park-lined lakefront feature. You can spend a day strolling here. About 2km south of the center is Pandosy Village, a charming and upscale lakeside enclave.

◉ Sights

The focal point of the city's shoreline, the immaculate downtown Kelowna City Park (waterfront) is home to manicured gardens, water features and Hot Sands Beach (Waterfront Park), where the water is a respite from the hot summer air.

Restaurants and pubs take advantage of the uninterrupted views of the lake and forested shore opposite. North of the marina, Waterfront Park (lakefront) has a variegated shoreline and a popular open-air stage.

Among the many outdoor statues near the lake, look for the one of the Ogopogo (Kelowna City Park), the lake's mythical – and hokey – monster. More prosaic is Bear (Water St), a huge, lacy confection in metal. The visitor center has a lavish public art guide.

Be sure to pick up the Cultural District walking-tour brochures at the visitor center (p212) and visit www.kelownamuseums.ca for exhibitions info.

BRITISH COLUMBIA PENTICTON TO KELOWNA

BC Tree Fruits Cidery & Tasting Bar   WINERY

(☑250-979-2629; www.bctreefruitscider.com; 880 Vaughan Ave; tasting $5; ☺11am-5pm) The cidery division of BC Tree Fruits, a 400-family BC cooperative, is booming. Head to the Cidery & Tasting Bar, next to its fruit and vegetable market (☑250-763-8872; www.bctree.com; 826 Vaughan Ave; prices by the kg; ☺9am-5pm Mon-Sat) on Vaughan St to try innovative ciders such as Apple & Hops, Pears & Peaches and Rosé. Locals bring refillable growlers (glass jars) and buy by the liter, though visitors can purchase by the can.

Carmelis Goat Cheese Artisan   FARM

(☑250-764-9033; www.carmelisgoatcheese.com; 170 Timberline Rd; ☺10am-6pm May-Sep, 11am-5pm Mar, Apr & Oct; P ☉) FREE At Carmelis you can sample soft-ripened cheeses with names such as Moonlight and Heavenly, or the hard-ripened Smoked Carmel or Goat-gonzola. For those with a milder palate, there are supersoft unripened versions, such as feta and yogurt cheese. And then there's the delectable goat's-milk gelato!

Okanagan Wine & Orchard Museum   MUSEUM

(☑778-478-0325; www.kelownamuseums.ca; 1304 Ellis St; by donation; ☺10am-5pm Mon-Sat, 11am-4pm Sun) Located in the historic Laurel Packing House, the Okanagan Wine & Orchard Museum recounts the Okanagan Valley from its ranchland past, grazed by cows, to its present, grazed by tourists. The old fruit-packing-crate labels are works of art.

Okanagan Lavender Farm   FARM

(☑250-764-7795; www.okanaganlavender.com; 4380 Takla Rd; tours $5-15; ☺10am-5pm, tours 10:15am, 11:30am & 2:30pm Jun-Aug; P ☉) Visiting Okanagan Lavender Farm is a heady experience. Rows and rows of more than 60 types of lavender waft in the breeze against a backdrop of the Okanagan Lake. Enjoy a guided or self-guided tour of the aromatic acres, and pop into the shop for everything from bath products to lavender lemonade. The farm is 9km south of the center.

🏃 Activities

The balmy weather makes Kelowna ideal for fresh-air fun, whether on the lake or in the surrounding hills.

You'll find great hiking and mountain-biking opportunities all around town. The 17km Mission Creek Greenway is a meandering, wooded path following creek along the south edge of town. The western half is a wide and easy expanse, but to the east the route becomes sinuous as it climbs into the hills.

Knox Mountain, which sits at the northern end of the city, is another good place to hike or ride. Populated with bobcats and snakes, the 235-hectare park has well-maintained trails and rewards visitors with excellent views from the top.

Cycling on the Kettle Valley Rail Trail (p212) and amid the vineyards is hugely popular.

Okanagan Rent A Boat   BOATING

(☑250-862-2469; www.lakefrontsports.com; 1350b Water St, Delta Grand Okanagan Resort; kayak rental per 2hr $40; ☺May-Sep) Rent speedboats (starting at $259 per hour), Jet Skis, kayaks, wakeboards, pedal boats and much more from this seasonal booth on the lakefront.

Myra Canyon Bike Rentals   CYCLING

(☑250-878-8763; www.myracanyonrental.com; Myra Canyon; bicycle rental per half-day adult/child from $39/30, bike tours from $70; ☺9am-5:30pm mid-May–mid-Oct) Offers bike rentals and tours in the Myra Canyon.

Distinctly Kelowna Tours   WINE

(☑250-979-1211; www.distinctlykelownawinetours.ca; 875 Wardlaw Ave, Kelowna; tours from $100) Offers winery tours by valley region; many include stops for lunch.

DON'T MISS

SCENIC DRIVE TO NARAMATA

On all but the busiest summer weekends, you can escape many of Penticton's mobs by taking the road less traveled, 18km north from town along the east shore of Okanagan Lake. The route through the Naramata Bench (www.naramatabench.com) is lined with countless wineries, as well as farms producing organic lavender and the like. This is a good route for cycling and at several points you can access the Kettle Valley Rail Trail (p212). There are numerous places to hike, picnic, bird-watch or do whatever else occurs to you in beautiful and often secluded surroundings. Naramata itself is a cute little village.

Kelowna

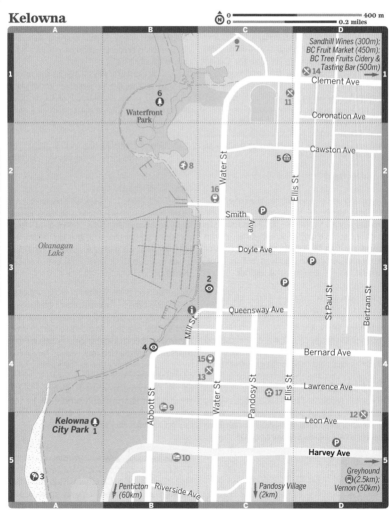

🛏 Sleeping

★**Hotel Zed**　　　　　　　MOTEL **$$**
(📞250-763-7771; www.hotelzed.com; 1627 Abbott St; r from $90; 🅿️👜❄️🛜🏊) An old Travelodge has been reborn as this funky throwback to a 1960s that never existed. The rooms come in many shapes and sizes; all are in cheery colors. Extras such as free bike rentals, Ping-Pong, hot tub, comic books in the bathrooms and much more are way cool. It's perfectly located downtown, across from City Park (p208).

★**Hotel Eldorado**　　　　　HOTEL **$$**
(📞250-763-7500;　　www.hoteleldoradokelowna. com; 500 Cook Rd; r from $180; 🅿️👜❄️🛜🏊) This historic lakeshore retreat, south of Pandosy Village, has 19 heritage rooms where you can bask in antique-filled luxury. A modern, low-key wing has 30 more rooms and six opulent waterfront suites. It's classy, artful and funky all at once. Definitely the choice spot for a luxurious getaway.

Lakeshore Bed & Breakfast　　B&B **$$**
(📞250-764-4375; www.lakeshorebb.ca; 4186 Lakeshore Rd; r from $115; 🅿️👜❄️🛜) This bright, two-room B&B has a prime lakefront loca-

Kelowna

Top Sights
1 Kelowna City Park ... A5

Sights
2 Bear Statue ... C3
3 Hot Sands Beach ... A5
4 Ogopogo Statue ... B4
5 Okanagan Wine & Orchard Museum ... C2
6 Waterfront Park ... B1

Activities, Courses & Tours
7 Club Wine Tours ... C1
8 Okanagan Rent A Boat ... B2

Sleeping
9 Hotel Zed ... B4
10 Samesun Kelowna ... B5

Eating
11 BNA Brewing Co & Eatery ... C1
12 Little Hobo Soup & Sandwich Shop ... D5
13 RauDZ Regional Table ... C4
14 Train Station Pub ... D1

Drinking & Nightlife
15 Micro Bar & Bites ... C4
16 Tree Brewing Beer Institute ... C2

Entertainment
17 Blue Gator Bar & Grill ... C4

tion, 6km south of the center, complete with its own tiny strip of sand. The larger of the two rooms is a real deal, with broad water views and a private outdoor sitting area. Furnishings are modern and upscale.

Samesun Kelowna HOSTEL $$
(250-763-9814; www.samesun.com; 245 Harvey Ave; dm/r from $57/140;) Near the center and the lake, this purpose-built hostel has 88 dorm beds in four- and eight-bed dorms, plus private rooms. There is a hot tub; activities include various group outings.

Eating

Little Hobo Soup & Sandwich Shop CAFE $
(778-478-0411; www.facebook.com/littlehobo kelowna; 596 Leon Ave; mains from $7; 8am-2pm Mon-Fri) This unadorned sandwich shop is hugely popular and for good reason: the food is excellent. Custom sandwiches are good, but the daily specials really shine (meatloaf, pasta, pierogi etc) and the variety of soups is simply superb.

Kelowna Farmers Market MARKET $
(250-878-5029; www.kelownafarmersand craftersmarket.com; cnr Springfield Rd & Dilworth Dr; 8am-1pm Wed & Sat Apr-Oct) The farmers market has more than 150 vendors, including many with prepared foods. Local artisans also display their wares. It's east of downtown near the Orchard Park Shopping Centre, off Hwy 97.

★ **BNA Brewing Co & Eatery** CANADIAN $$
(236-420-0025; www.bnabrewing.com; 1250 Ellis St; mains from $14; 4pm-late) While the beer tasting room is open from midday to 6pm daily, dining kicks in from 4pm at this welcoming spot in a historic building. There's a good line of tapas-like plates for sharing, as well as a wide range of main courses. If you've come for the beer, try the Don't Lose Your Dinosaur IPA.

★ **RauDZ Regional Table** FUSION $$
(250-868-8805; www.raudz.com; 1560 Water St; mains from $17; 5-10pm) Noted chef Rod Butters has defined the farm-to-table movement with his casual bistro that's a temple to Okanagan produce and wine. The dining room is as airy and open as the kitchen. The seasonal menu takes global inspiration for its Mediterranean-infused dishes, which are good for sharing, and serves steaks and seafood. Suppliers include locally renowned Carmelis goat's cheese.

★ **Train Station Pub** PUB FOOD $$
(778-484-5558; www.thetrainstationpub.com; 1177 Ellis St; mains from $12; 9:30am-late) The long-disused 1926 Canadian National train station has been reborn as an upscale pub with an excellent selection of beers. The usual pub-food standards show color and flair; enjoy the wide terrace on balmy days.

Drinking & Nightlife

★ **Tree Brewing Beer Institute** BREWERY
(778-484-0306; www.treebrewingbeerinstitute.com; 1346 Water St; 11am-11pm) These guys feature tank to tap craft beer, including experimental brews in an unfiltered state. Intriguing stuff if you like checking out new tastes. There are seven tanks on the go with an array of lagers, Kölsch, ales and various IPAs, while there are pizzas and sandwiches to choose from too.

Micro Bar & Bites PUB

(☑778-484-3500; www.microkelowna.com; 1500 Water St; ⊙2pm-midnight) This great small bar just off Bernard Ave is hard to leave. Craft beers, local wines and fine cocktails are served. Small bites are fresh and inventive, good for sharing – or for lunch. Gather at the beautiful wood-block bar or at a sidewalk table.

Blue Gator Bar & Grill LIVE MUSIC

(☑250-860-1529; www.bluegator.net; 441 Lawrence Ave; ⊙10am-6pm Mon-Wed, to late Thu-Sat) Head for blues, rock, acoustic jam and more at the valley's sweaty dive for live music and cold beer.

ℹ Information

Tourism Kelowna (☑250-861-1515; www.tourismkelowna.com; 238 Queensway Ave; ⊙8:30am-8:30pm) In an impressive facility on the waterfront; excellent source for free maps and tour info.

ℹ Getting There & Away

Kelowna International Airport (☑250-807-4300; www.kelownaairport.com; 5533 Airport Way, off Hwy 97) The airport is 20km north of the center on Hwy 97 and handles over 70 flights daily to a growing number of destinations.

Ebus (www.myebus.ca) runs buses connecting Vancouver, Kamloops and Kelowna.

Vernon

☑250, 778 / POP 40,100

The Okanagan glitz is reaching north to Vernon, though winters have more of the traditional inland BC bite here and there are fewer wineries. The orchard-scented valley is surrounded by three lakes – Kalamalka, Okanagan and Swan – that attract funseekers all summer long.

Downtown life is found along busy 30th Ave, known as Main St. Confusingly, 30th Ave is intersected by 30th St in the middle of downtown, so mind your streets and avenues.

◉ Sights & Activities

★ **Planet Bee Honey Farm & Meadery** FARM

(☑250-542-8088; www.planetbee.com; 5011 Bella Vista Rd; ⊙8am-6pm; P) **FREE** At Planet Bee you can learn all the sweet secrets of the golden nectar, taste 25 different honeys

---

DON'T MISS

KETTLE VALLEY RAIL TRAIL

The famous **Kettle Valley Rail Trail** vies with wine-drinking and peach-picking as the attraction of choice for the region's visitors – smart ones do all three.

Once stretching 525km in curving, meandering length, the railway was built so that silver ore could be transported from the southern Kootenays to Vancouver. Finished in 1916, it remains one of the most expensive railways ever built, on a per-kilometer basis. It was entirely shut by 1989, but it wasn't long before its easy grades (never more than 2.2%) and dozens of bridges were incorporated into the **Trans Canada Trail (TCT)**.

Of the entire Kettle Valley Rail Trail, the most spectacular stretch is close to Kelowna. The 24km section through the **Myra Canyon** has fantastic views of the sinuous canyon from **18 trestles** that span the gorge for the cliff-hugging path. That you can enjoy the route at all is something of a miracle, as 12 of the wooden trestles were destroyed by fire in 2003. All have been rebuilt; much credit goes to the **Myra Canyon Trestle Restoration Society** (www.myra-trestles.com), the website of which has downloadable maps and info. The broad views sweep down to Kelowna and the lake, more than 900m below. You can see alpine meadows reclaiming the fire-cleared landscape.

To reach the area closest to the most spectacular trestles from Kelowna, follow Harvey Ave (Hwy 97) east to Gordon Dr. Turn south and then go east 2.6km on KLO Rd and then join McCulloch Rd for 7.4km after the junction. Look for the Myra Forest Service Rd; turn south and make a winding 8.7km climb on a car-friendly gravel road to the parking lot. It's about a 40-minute drive from Kelowna's center.

Myra Canyon is just part of an overall 174km network of trails in the Okanagan that follows the old railway through tunnels, past Naramata and as far south as Penticton and beyond. You can easily access the trail at many points, or book hiking and cycling tours. Myra Canyon Bike Rentals (p209) offers bike rentals and tours at the main trailhead.

and see a working hive up close. Even better, taste the selection of delicious meads, a wine made from honey. Follow 30th Ave west from downtown for 3km.

Davison Orchards FARM
(📞 250-549-3266; www.davisonorchards.ca; 3111 Davison Rd; ⊙8am-8pm Apr-Oct; P👶) FREE Has tractor rides, homemade ice cream, fresh apple juice, a cafe, winsome barnyard animals and more. Great for the family, but definitely on the beaten path. Follow 30th Ave west from downtown for 3km.

Kalamalka Lake Provincial Park PARK
(www.env.gov.bc.ca/bcparks; off Hwy 6; P) The beautiful 9-sq-km Kalamalka Lake Provincial Park lies south of town on the eastern side of the warm, shallow lake. The park offers great swimming at Jade and Kalamalka Beaches, good fishing and a network of mountain-biking and hiking trails. Innerspace Watersports operates a seasonal booth in the park.

Innerspace Watersports WATER SPORTS
(📞 250-549-2040; www.innerspacewatersports. com; 3006 32nd St; canoe rental per hour $25; ⊙10am-5:30pm Mon-Sat) Offers canoe and stand-up paddleboard rentals at Kalamalka Lake Provincial Park. Its full-service store in town has scuba gear. Park location is open mid-June to August.

🛏 Sleeping & Eating

Ellison Provincial Park CAMPGROUND $
(📞 info 250-494-6500, reservations 800-689-9025; www.discovercamping.ca; Okanagan Landing Rd; tent & RV sites $32; ⊙Apr-Oct; P) Some 16km southwest of Vernon, this is a great tree-shaded, 219-acre place near the lake. The 71 campsites fill up early, so reserve in advance.

Beaver Lake Mountain Resort LODGE $$
(📞 250-762-2225; www.beaverlakeresort.com; 6350 Beaver Lake Rd; tent & RV sites from $37, cabins from $100; P😊@🛜) Set high in the hills east of Hwy 97, about midway between Vernon and Kelowna, this postcard-perfect lakeside resort has a range of rustic log cabins and some more luxurious cabins that sleep up to six people.

Tiki Village Motor Inn MOTEL $$
(📞 250-503-5566; www.tikivillagevernon.com; 2408 34th St; r from $109; P😊✳🛜🏊) An ode to the glory days of decorative concrete blocks, the Tiki has suitably expansive plant-

ings and 30 rooms with a vaguely Polynesian minimalist theme. All rooms have a fridge; some have a kitchenette.

⭐**Naked Pig Kitchen** BARBECUE $$
(📞 778-475-5475; www.nakedpig.ca; 2933 30th Ave; mains from $13; ⊙11am-9pm) It doesn't get much better than this if you're into smokehouse BBQ. This is slow craft-style cooking using local produce and the Naked Pig's own tasty BBQ sauces. It's not all about meat though, with the veggie burger a menu favorite and the Naked Pig boasting its own line of coffee, the Naked Pig Roast.

Bamboo Beach Fusion Grille FUSION $$
(📞 250-542-7701; www.bamboobeach.ca; 3313 30th Ave; mains from $13; ⊙11:30am-2pm & 5-8pm Tue-Fri, 5-8.30pm Sat; 🍴) Flavors from across Asia season popular local foods at this sprightly restaurant. Look for Japanese, Korean and Thai influences in the halibut curry, fish-and-chips and much more. The curry soba noodles show the talent of the Japanese-trained chef.

ℹ Information

Vernon Visitor Center (📞 250-542-1415; www. tourismvernon.com; 3004 39th Ave; ⊙9am-6pm; 🛜) North of the town center.

ℹ Getting There & Away

Ebus (www.myebus.ca) Links Vernon with Kamloops and Kelowna, with connections to Vancouver.

Vernon Regional Transit System (📞 250-545-7221; www.transitbc.com; fares from $2) Buses leave from the Downtown Exchange bus stop at the corner of 31st Ave and 30th St. For Kalamalka Lake, catch bus 1; for Okanagan Lake, bus 7.

North of Vernon

Just north of Vernon, beautiful Hwy 97 heads northwest to Kamloops via tree-clad valleys punctuated by lakes. Armstrong, 23km north of Vernon, is a cute little village. Attractions are few in this area, which is more notable for its major highway connections.

Silver Star (p214) is one of the region's top ski resorts, 24km northeast of Vernon.

💿 Sights & Activities

Historic O'Keefe Ranch HISTORIC SITE
(📞 250-542-7868; www.okeeferanch.ca; 9380 Hwy 97N; adult/child $13.50/8.50; ⊙10am-5pm

May, Jun & Sep, to 6pm Jul & Aug) Home to the O'Keefe family between 1867 and 1977, the O'Keefe Ranch retains its original log cabin, and has lots of live displays of old ranching techniques. Before orchards – and later grapes – covered the valley, ranching as portrayed here was the typical way of life. The ranch is 12km north of Vernon, 4km after Hwy 97 splits from Hwy 97A, which continues northeast to Sicamous and Hwy 1.

Silver Star SKIING
(☑250-542-0224; www.skisilverstar.com; 123 Shortt St, Silver Star Mountain; 1-day lift ticket adult/child $95/50) Silver Star, 24km northeast of Vernon and 75km from Kelowna, is extremely popular with skiers and snowboarders in winter. In summer the lifts haul mountain bikers and hikers up to the lofty green vistas. Lots of lodges and hotels, cafes, restaurants and pubs. Shuttles come via Vernon from Kelowna and Kelowna Airport.

Shuswap Region

Rorschach-test-like **Shuswap Lake** anchors a somewhat bland but pleasing region of green, wooded hills, some farms and two small towns, **Sicamous** and **Salmon Arm**. The former has a lakefront park that's good for picnics, just northwest of Hwy 1.

The entire area is home to several lake-based provincial parks and is a popular destination for families looking for outdoor fun. Many explore the sinuous lakes via houseboats.

Roderick Haig-Brown Provincial Park PARK
(www.env.gov.bc.ca/bcparks; off Hwy 1, Saquilax) The main attraction here is the annual spawning of sockeye salmon. The 10.59-sq-km park protects both sides of the Adams River between Shuswap Lake and Adams Lake, a natural bottleneck for the bright-red sockeye when they run upriver every October. The fish population peaks every four years, when as many as four million salmon crowd the Adams' shallow riverbed.

Fruit World FRUIT STALL $
(☑250-836-5555; 1330 Maier Rd, Sicamous; ⊗9am-6pm) Fruit from all over, plus vegetables, preserves, honey, olive oil and all sorts of good stuff, just over the road from D Dutchmen Dairy.

D Dutchmen Dairy ICE CREAM $
(☑250-836-4304; www.dutchmendairy.ca; 1321 Maier Rd, Sicamous; treats from $3; ⊗8am-9pm

Jun-Sep) Meet the cows, then lick the ice cream at this offbeat dairy close to Hwy 1. There are 40 flavors of ice cream and traditional frozen treats to choose from.

THE KOOTENAYS & THE ROCKIES

You can't help sighing as you ponder the plethora of snow-covered peaks in BC's Kootenay region. Deep river valleys cleaved by white-water rivers, impossibly sheer rock faces, alpine meadows and a sawtooth of white-dappled mountains stretching across the horizon inspire awe, action and contemplation.

Coming from the west, the mountain majesty builds as if choreographed. The roughly parallel ranges of the Monashees and the Selkirks striate the West Kootenays, with the Arrow Lakes adding texture. Appealing towns such as Revelstoke and Nelson nestle against the mountains and are outdoor fun centers year-round. The East Kootenays cover the Purcell Mountains region below Golden, taking in Radium Hot Springs and delightful Fernie.

BC's Rocky Mountains national parks (Mt Revelstoke, Glacier, Yoho and Kootenay) don't have the profile of Banff and Jasper over the border, but for many that's an advantage: each has its own spectacular qualities, often relatively unexploited by Banff-bound hordes.

Revelstoke

☑250, 778 / POP 7950
Gateway to serious mountains, Revelstoke doesn't need to toot its own horn – the ceaseless procession of trains through the center does that. Built as an important point on the Canadian Pacific Transcontinental Railroad that first linked eastern and western Canada, Revelstoke echoes not just with whistles but with history. The compact center is lined with heritage buildings, yet it's more than a museum piece. There's a vibrant local arts community, and most locals take full advantage of the boundless opportunities for hiking, kayaking and, most of all, skiing.

It's more than worth a long pause as you pass on Hwy 1, which bypasses the town center to the northeast. The main streets include 1st St and Mackenzie Ave.

⊙ Sights

Grizzly Plaza, between Mackenzie and Orton Aves, is a pedestrian precinct and the heart of downtown, where free live-music performances take place every evening in July and August.

While outdoor activities are Revelstoke's real drawcard, a stroll of the center and a moment spent at the museums is a must. Pick up the *Public Art* and *Heritage* walking-tour brochures at the visitor center (p218).

★ Mt Revelstoke
National Park   PARK
(www.pc.gc.ca/revelstoke; off Hwy 1; adult/child incl Glacier National Park $7.80/free) Grand in beauty if not in size, this 260-sq-km national park, just northeast of its namesake town, is a vision of peaks and valleys – many all but untrodden.

There are several good **hiking trails** from the summit. To overnight in the wild, you must have a Wilderness Pass camping permit ($10, in addition to your park pass), available from **Parks Canada Revelstoke Office** (☑250-837-7500; www.pc.gc.ca; 301 3rd St; ⊙8am-4:30pm Mon-Fri) or Rogers Pass Centre (p218) inside Glacier National Park (p218).

★ Jones Distilling   DISTILLERY
(www.jonesdistilling.com; 616 3 St W; ⊙noon-6pm Thu-Sun) In what was the 1914-built brick Mountain View School building, over the road from the Columbia River, Jones Distillery is making a name with its award-winning Revelstoke Gin Series and Mr Jones Vodka. Focusing on local ingredients and Revelstoke enthusiasm, the rewards are coming. Book tastings and tours through the Canadian Gin Guild (www.canadianginguild.com).

Revelstoke
Railway Museum   MUSEUM
(☑250-837-6060; www.railwaymuseum.com; 719 Track St W; adult/child $10/5; ⊙9am-5pm May-Sep, shorter hours Oct-Apr; [P]) In an attractive building across the tracks from the town center, Revelstoke Railway Museum contains restored steam locomotives, including one of the largest steam engines ever used on Canadian Pacific Railway (CPR) lines. Photographs and artifacts document the construction of the CPR, which was instrumental – actually, essential – in linking eastern and western Canada.

🏃 Activities

Sandwiched between the vast but relatively unknown Selkirk and Monashee mountain ranges, Revelstoke draws serious snow buffs looking for vast landscapes of crowd-free powder. It's where North America's first ski jump was built, in 1915.

For **cross-country skiing**, head to the 22km of groomed trails at Mt MacPherson Ski Area, 7km south of town on Hwy 23; see www.revelstokenordic.org for information.

All that white snow turns into white water come spring and **rafting** is big here. **Mountain biking** is also huge; pick up trail maps from the visitor center (p218).

Revelstoke Mountain Resort   SKIING
(☑866-373-4754; www.revelstokemountainresort.com; Camozzi Rd; 1-day lift ticket adult/child $88/30) Just 6km southeast of town, the Revelstoke Mountain Resort has ambitions to become the biggest ski resort this side of the Alps. It has seemingly endless virgin slopes and 65 runs. In one run you can ski both 700m of bowl and 700m of trees. At 1713m, the vertical drop is the greatest in North America.

Apex Rafting Co   RAFTING
(☑250-837-6376; www.apexrafting.com; 112 1st St E; adult/child $124/99; ⊙Jun-Aug; 📷) Runs kid-friendly two-hour guided trips on the Illecillewaet River in spring and summer.

Wandering Wheels   CYCLING
(☑250-814-7609; www.wanderingwheels.ca; 120 MacKenzie Ave; lessons per hour from $35, tours from $60; ⊙Jun-Oct) Offers bike shuttle services, lessons, heli-bike and tours.

🛏 Sleeping

Revelstoke Backpacker Hostel   HOSTEL $
(☑250-837-4050; www.revyhostel.com; 400 2nd St W; dm/r from $35/65; [P]⊙🛜) Ramble though the numerous rooms online for this perennial backpacker favorite. The dorms are popular so book ahead. It has bike and ski storage, plus summer barbecues, free passes to the town's aquatic center and free resort shuttle in winter.

★ Regent Hotel   HOTEL $$
(☑250-837-2107; www.regenthotel.ca; 112 1st St E; r from $110; [P]⊙❄🛜♨) The poshest place in the center is not lavish, but it is comfy. The 42 modern rooms bear no traces of the hotel's 1914 roots and exterior. The restaurant and lounge are justifiably popular. Many

The Kootenays & The Rockies

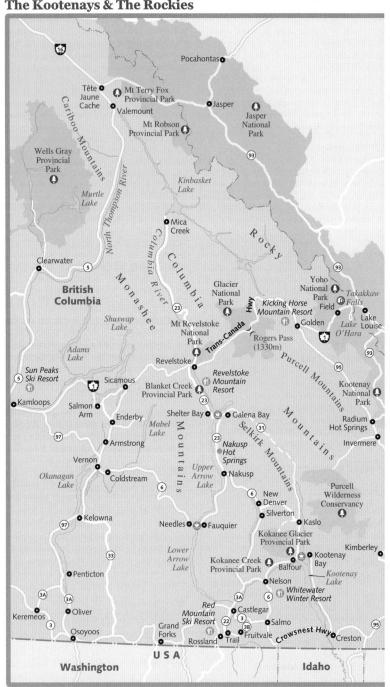

guests bob the night away in the outdoor hot tub.

Swiss Chalet Motel MOTEL **$$**

(☑877-837-4650; www.swisschaletmotel.com; 1101 West Victoria Rd; r from $96; ⓟ🐾❄🛜) Rooms may be small, but they're clean and comfy at this place on the main road, a 10-minute walk from the center of Revelstoke. Perks include a complimentary breakfast, tickets to the aquatic center, guest laundry and a free shuttle service during ski season to Revelstoke Mountain Resort (p215).

Courthouse Inn B&B **$$**

(☑250-837-3369; www.courthouseinnrevelstoke. com; 312 Kootenay St; r from $129; ⓟ🐾❄🛜) A posh 10-room B&B close to the center. Extras include a lavish breakfast, boot and glove driers for winter and lots of personal service. You can't beat the quiet location; rooms have no TV or phone.

✖ Eating & Drinking

★ **Modern Bakeshop & Café** CAFE **$**

(☑250-837-6886; www.themodernbakeshopand cafe.com; 212 Mackenzie Ave; mains from $6; ⊙6:30am-5pm Mon-Sat; 🛜) Try a croque monsieur (grilled ham-and-cheese sandwich) or an elaborate pastry for a taste of Europe at this cute art-deco cafe. Many items, such as the muffins, are made with organic ingredients. Discover the baked 'boofy uptrack bar' for a treat. Nice seating outside.

Taco Club MEXICAN **$**

(☑250-837-0988; www.thetacoclub.ca; 206 MacKenzie Ave; mains from $6; ⊙11am-10pm) Once Revelstoke's favorite food truck, Taco Club has now laid down some roots in a vintage building downtown. Tacos and burritos are excellent, and all the usual suspects for sides are available. Enjoy the outside seating on long summer evenings.

Old School Eatery CANADIAN **$$**

(☑250-814-4144; www.oldschooleatery.ca; 616 3 St W; dinner mains from $14; ⊙11am-9pm Tue-Fri, from 9am Sat & Sun) Sharing the old Mountain View School building of 1914 with Jones Distilling (p215), the Old School Eatery is becoming a favorite in Revelstoke, particularly for brunch in the weekends. With what they describe as 'sophisticated comfort food', you'll find top dinner options too, such as Creole pork chop ($28) and Moroccan lamb chops ($32), all in an old school room.

★ **Mt Begbie Brewing** MICROBREWERY
(☑250-837-2756; www.mt-begbie.com; 2155 Oak Dr; ⊙11:30am-9pm Mon-Sat, tours at 4pm) Head out just east of town to Mt Begbie's new tasting area and store to try the popular local brews. The Powerhouse Pale Ale and the Brave Liver, a seasonal winter Scottish pale ale (at 6.5%), should put a smile on your face. There's decent food plus both indoor and outdoor seating.

❶ Information

Revelstoke Visitor Center (☑250-837-5345; www.seerevelstoke.com; 301 Victoria Rd; ⊙8:30am-7pm) Excellent source for hiking and mountain-biking info and maps.

❶ Getting There & Away

Riders Express (www.riderexpress.ca) runs buses connecting Vancouver, Kamloops and Calgary, with a bus stopping daily in Revelstoke and Golden in both directions.

Revelstoke to Golden

Keep your eyes on the road or, better yet, let someone else drive as you traverse the Trans-Canada Hwy (Hwy 1) for 148km between Revelstoke and Golden. Stunning mountain peaks follow one after another as you go.

Glacier National Park PARK
(www.pc.gc.ca; adult/child incl Mt Revelstoke National Park $8/4) To be accurate, this 1350-sq-km park should be called '430 Glaciers National Park'. The annual snowfall can be as much as 23m, and due to the sheer mountain slopes, this is one of the world's most active avalanche areas. For this reason, skiing, caving and mountaineering are regulated; you must register with park wardens before venturing into the backcountry. Check the weather and get an avalanche report. **Rogers Pass** ranks as one of the world's most beautiful mountain passes.

Be sure to pause at the **Hemlock Grove Trail**, 54km east of Revelstoke, where a 400m boardwalk winds through an ancient hemlock rainforest.

Glacier National Park has good camping options at **Illecillewaet Campground** (www.pc.gc.ca; Rogers Pass, off Hwy 1; tent & RV sites from $16; ⊙late Jun–early Oct) and **Loop Brook Campground** (www.pc.gc.ca; Rogers Pass, off Hwy 1; tent & RV sites from $16; ⊙Jul–late Sep), both on the Revelstoke side of Rogers Pass. Sites are available on a first-come, first-served basis. Otherwise, you'll need to stay in either Revelstoke or Golden.

Rogers Pass Centre (☑250-814-5233; off Hwy 1; ⊙8am-7pm mid-Jun–early Sep, shorter hours mid-Sep–mid-Jun) displays Canadian Pacific Railway (CPR) dioramas, 72km east of Revelstoke and 76km west of Golden. It show films about Glacier National Park, organizes guided walks in summer and has an excellent bookstore run by the Friends of Mt Revelstoke and Glacier.

Golden
☑250, 778 / POP 3700

Golden is well situated for national-park explorations – there are six nearby. White-water rafting excitement lies even closer, where the Kicking Horse River converges with the Columbia.

Don't just breeze past the strip of franchised yuck on Hwy 1: you'll miss the tidy town center down by the tumbling Kicking Horse River.

◉ Sights & Activities

Golden is the center for **white-water rafting** trips on the turbulent and chilly Kicking Horse River. Along with the powerful grade III and IV rapids, the breathtaking scenery along the sheer walls of the Kicking Horse Valley makes this rafting experience one of North America's best.

Northern Lights Wolf Centre PARK
(☑250-344-6798; www.northernlightswildlife.com; 1745 Short Rd; adult/child $12/6; ⊙9am-7pm Jul & Aug, 10am-6pm May, Jun & Sep, noon-5pm Oct-Apr; P) This small wildlife center houses a small pack of gray wolves and wolf-husky crosses, all born and bred in captivity. Visits include an introduction to the resident wolves – although most of the viewing is done through wire-frame pens.

★ **Alpine Rafting** RAFTING
(☑250-344-6521; www.alpinerafting.com; 1509 Lafontaine Rd; raft trips from $89; ⊙Jun-Sep; ♿) Offers several good family rafting options, including a white-water run for kids aged four years and over, right up to the more extreme class IV 'Kicking Horse Challenge.'

Kicking Horse
Mountain Resort SKIING, MOUNTAIN BIKING
(☑250-439-5425; www.kickinghorseresort.com; Kicking Horse Trail; 1-day lift ticket adult/child winter

$94/38, summer $42/21) Some 60% of the 120 ski runs at Kicking Horse Mountain Resort are rated advanced or expert. With a 1260m (4133ft) vertical drop and a snowy position between the Rockies and the Purcells, the resort's popularity grows each year. It's renowned for its summer mountain biking, which includes the longest cycling descent in Canada.

🛏 Sleeping

⭐ **Dreamcatcher Hostel** HOSTEL $
(☑ 250-439-1090; www.dreamcatcherhostel.com; 528 9th Ave N; dm/r from $32/90; 🅿 😊 🛜) Run by two veteran travelers, this centrally located hostel has everything a budget traveler could hope for. There are three dorm rooms, five private rooms, as well as a vast kitchen and a comfy common room with a stone fireplace. Outside there's a garden and a barbecue.

Kicking Horse Canyon B&B GUESTHOUSE $$
(☑ 250-899-0840; www.kickinghorsecanyonbb.com; 644 Lapp Rd; d from $120; 🅿 😊 🛜) Hidden away among the hills to the east of Golden, this endearingly offbeat B&B takes you into the bosom of the family the minute you cross the threshold. Run by genial host Jeannie Cook and her husband, Jerry, it's a real alpine home-away-from-home, surrounded by private grassy grounds with views across the mountains.

Chancellor Peak Chalets LODGE $$$
(☑ 250-344-7038; www.chancellorpeakchalets.com; 2924 Kicking Horse Rd; cabins from $289; 🅿 😊 ❄ 🛜) The 11 log chalets at this riverside retreat have two levels and sleep up to six. The chalets have soaker tubs, full kitchens and all the nature you can breathe in. The chalets are 25km southeast of Golden, just outside Yoho National Park.

🍴 Eating & Drinking

⭐ **Bacchus Books & Cafe** CAFE $
(☑ 250-344-5600; www.bacchusbooks.ca; 409 9th Ave N; mains from $8; 😊 9am-5:30pm) This bohemian hideaway at the end of 8th St is a favorite haunt for Golden's artsy crowd. Browse for books (new and secondhand) in the downstairs bookstore, then head upstairs to find a table for tea among the higgledy-piggledy shelves. Sandwiches, salads and cakes are made on the premises, and the coffee is as good as you'll find in Golden.

ⓘ AVALANCHE WARNING

The Kootenays are the heart of avalanche country. Such events kill more people in BC each year than any other natural phenomenon – the annual toll is stubbornly high.

Avalanches can occur at any time, even on terrain that seems relatively flat. Roughly half the people caught in one don't survive. It's vital that people venturing out onto the snow ask about conditions first; if an area is closed, don't go there. Whether you're backcountry ski touring or simply hiking in the alpine region, you'll want to rent a homing beacon; most outdoors shops can supply one.

In Revelstoke, **Avalanche Canada** (☑ 250-837-2141; www.avalanche.ca) tracks avalanche reports and offers forecasts for BC and the Canadian Rockies. It has a vital website and a phone app.

⭐ **Island Restaurant** INTERNATIONAL $$
(☑ 250-344-2400; www.islandrestaurant.ca; 101 10th Ave; dinner mains from $14; 😊 9am-9pm) On a small river island in the middle of Kicking Horse River in the center of Golden, this place features a flower-embellished riverside patio and international dishes and drinks. The food wears many hats, from a Jamaican-jerk chicken sandwich to Thai Thursdays and full-on Mexican nights on Mondays and Tuesdays.

Wolf Den PUB FOOD $$
(☑ 250-344-9863; www.thewolfsdengolden.ca; 1105 9th St; dinner mains from $14; 😊 4-10pm) An excellent pub with live music on Sundays. It's hugely popular with locals, who love the burgers and hearty fare, which are way above average. The beer menu includes some of BC's best on tap. It's just south of the river from downtown.

⭐ **Whitetooth Brewing Company** MICROBREWERY
(☑ 250-344-2838; www.whitetoothbrewing.com; 623 8th Ave N; 😊 2-10pm) Golden's microbrewery features tank-to-tap brews and a marvelous sunny patio for those long summer evenings. Whitetooth is a hit with locals who come to fill their growlers and relax on the patio. We like the Icefields Belgian-inspired pale ale.

ℹ Information

Golden Visitor Information Centre (☏250-439-7290; www.tourismgolden.com; 1000 Hwy 1; ◷9am-7pm Jun-Sep) In a purpose-built building on Hwy 1 and Hwy 95 into town from the southeast.

ℹ Getting There & Away

Riders Express (www.riderexpress.ca) Runs buses connecting Vancouver, Kamloops and Calgary, with a bus stopping daily in Revelstoke and Golden in both directions.

Yoho National Park

The surging waters of glacier-fed, ice-blue Kicking Horse River that plow through a valley of the same name are an apt image for dramatic Yoho National Park. This spectacular park is home to looming peaks, pounding waterfalls, glacial lakes and patches of pretty meadows.

◉ Sights & Activities

★**Yoho National Park**   NATIONAL PARK
(☏250-343-6783; www.pc.gc.ca; off Hwy 1; adult/child $10/5) Although the smallest (1310 sq km) of the four national parks in the Rockies, Yoho is a diamond in the (very) rough. This wilderness is the real deal; it's some of the continent's least tarnished.

East of Field on Hwy 1 is the Takakkaw Falls road, open from late June to early October. At 255m, Takakkaw Falls is one of the highest waterfalls in Canada. From here the **Iceline Trail**, a 20km hiking loop, passes many glaciers and spectacular scenery.

Near the south gate of the park, you can reach pretty **Wapta Falls** along a 2.4km trail. The easy walk takes about 45 minutes each way.

Don't miss the surging waters at Natural Bridge, which you can admire on the short drive from Hwy 1 near Field to iconic Emerald Lake.

★**Burgess Shale
Fossil Beds**   NATIONAL PARK
This World Heritage site protects the amazing Cambrian-age fossil beds on Mt Stephen and Mt Field. These 515-million-year-old fossils preserve the remains of marine creatures that were some of the earliest forms of life on earth. You can only get to the fossil beds by guided hikes, which are led by naturalists from the Burgess Shale Geoscience Foundation. Reservations are essential.

**Kicking Horse Pass
& Spiral Tunnels**   VIEWPOINT
The historic Kicking Horse Pass between Banff and Yoho National Parks is one of the most important passes in the Canadian Rockies. It was discovered in 1858 by the Palliser Expedition, which was tasked with discovering a possible route across the Rockies for the Canadian Pacific Railway. Accessible 8km east of Field from the westbound lanes of Hwy 1, the viewing area is often closed and the view obscured by vegetation.

Takakkaw Falls   WATERFALL
A thundering torrent of water tumbles from its source in the nearby Daly Glacier over a sheer cliff face for 255m (836ft), making it the second-highest waterfall in Canada. At the end of the road, a trail leads for around 800m (half a mile) from the Takakkaw parking lot to the base of the falls. The road is open from late June to early October.

Emerald Lake   LAKE
For most visitors, this vividly colored lake is Yoho's most unmissable sight. Ringed by forest and silhouetted by impressive mountains, including the iconic profile of **Mt Burgess** to the southeast, it's a truly beautiful – if incredibly busy – spot. Escape the mobs in a rental canoe. The lake road is signed off Hwy 1 just to the southwest of Field and continues for 10km (6.2 miles) to the lake shore.

🛏 Sleeping

**Kicking Horse
Campground**   CAMPGROUND $
(www.reservation.pc.gc.ca; Yoho Valley Rd; tent & RV sites $27.40; ◷May 23–Oct 14; 🅿🛜) This is probably the most popular campground in Yoho. It's in a nice forested location, with plenty of space between the 88 sites, and there are showers. Riverside sites (especially 68 to 74) are the pick of the bunch.

HI-Yoho National Park   HOSTEL $
(Whiskey Jack Hostel; ☏403-670-7580; www.hihostels.ca; Yoho Valley Rd; dm from $28; ◷Jun 29–Sep 23) Yoho National Park's Takakkaw Falls are so close you can see them from the hostel's timber deck. Three nine-bed dorms and a basic kitchen comprise the rudimentary facilities; it's usually booked out in summer.

Lake O'Hara

Perched high in the mountains, Lake O'Hara is an encapsulation of the Rockies region, and worth the significant hassle to reach it.

Compact wooded hillsides, alpine meadows, snow-covered passes, mountain vistas and glaciers wrap around the stunning lake. A day trip is rewarding, but if you stay overnight in the backcountry you'll be able to access many hiking trails – some quite difficult, and all quite spectacular. The Alpine Circuit (12km) has a bit of everything.

🛌 Sleeping

Lake O'Hara Campground CAMPGROUND $
(📞 reservations 250-343-6433; www.pc.gc.ca; Yoho National Park; tent sites $10, reservation fee $12; ☺ mid-Jun–Sep) Reserve three months in advance to snare one of 30 campsites. Available spots are often taken in the first hour that reservation phone lines are open (from 8am Mountain time). If you don't have advance reservations, three to five campsites are set aside for 'standby' users; call at 8am the day before you wish to stay.

★ Lake O'Hara Lodge LODGE $$$
(📞 250-343-6418; www.lakeohara.com; Yoho National Park; s/d from $500/665, cabins $940; ☺ Jan-Apr & Jun-Oct; ⊜🖢) 🍴 Leaving guests slack-jawed for more than 90 years, the lodge is the only place to stay at the lake if you're not traveling with a tent. It's luxurious in a rustic way, and its environmental practices are lauded. Food comes from BC producers and is excellent. Minimum stay is two nights.

ℹ Getting There & Away

To reach the lake, take the **shuttle bus** (📞 reservations 877-737-3783; www.pc.gc.ca; adult/child return $15/8, reservation fee $12; ☺ mid-Jun–Sep) from the Lake O'Hara parking lot, 15km east of Field on Hwy 1. A quota system governs bus access to the lake. Given the lake's popularity, reservations are basically mandatory, unless you want to walk. That said, if you don't have advance reservations, six day-use seats on the bus are set aside for 'standby' users. Call at 8am the day before and think 'lucky.'

You can freely walk the 11km from the parking area, but no bikes are allowed. The area around Lake O'Hara usually remains covered with snow or else stays very muddy until mid-July.

Field

Right off Hwy 1, this historic railroad town is worth a stop for its dramatic overlook of the river and quaint yet unfussy atmosphere. Many buildings date from the early days of the railways, when the town was the Canadian Pacific Railway's headquarters for exploration and, later, for strategic planning, when engineers were working on the problem of moving trains over Kicking Horse Pass.

Burgess Shale
Geoscience Foundation HIKING
(📞 800-343-3006; www.burgess-shale.bc.ca; 201 Kicking Horse Ave; tours adult/child from $94.50/65; ☺ 9am-4pm Tue-Sat mid-Jun–mid-Sep) The only way to visit the amazing 515-million-year-old Burgess Shale fossil beds is on a hike led by the Burgess Shale Geoscience Foundation. Book online and follow instructions for the morning meeting location. There are two core hikes, one to Walcott Quarry and another to the adjacent fossil fields on Mt Stephen.

Both are strenuous full-day trips with plenty of elevation gain, so you'll need to be fit and wear proper footwear.

Fireweed Hostel HOSTEL $
(📞 250-343-6999; www.fireweedhostel.com; 313 Stephen Ave; dm/r from $30/80; ⊜🖢) This four-room hostel in Field is a real find, beautifully finished in rustic pine. Dorms are small but smart; each room has two pine bunk beds and a shared bath off the hallway, and all have full use of a kitchen and sitting room.

★ Truffle Pigs Lodge HOTEL $$
(📞 250-343-6303; www.trufflepigs.com; 100 Centre St; r from $120; ☺ Jun-Sep; 🅿⊜❄🖢) Field's only hotel is a timber building with heritage charm. The 14 rooms are fairly simply decked out, though. Some have small kitchens. The owners run the town's well-known restaurant, **Truffle Pigs bistro** (mains from $12; ☺ 8am-9pm; 🖢) 🍴, in the same attractive building.

ℹ Information

Yoho National Park Information Centre
(📞 250-343-6783; www.pc.gc.ca; off Hwy 1; ☺ 9am-7pm May-Oct) Pick up maps and trail descriptions. Rangers can advise on itineraries and conditions. Alberta Tourism staffs a desk here in summer and Friends of Yoho maintains a book shop.

Kootenay National Park

Kootenay is the the only national park in Canada with both glaciers and cacti. From Radium Hot Springs you can create a fine driving loop through Kootenay into Alberta's Banff National Park, then back into BC at Golden through Yoho National Park; many of the top sights are easily reached by car.

The very remote Mt Assiniboine Provincial Park offers true adventurers a remarkable wilderness experience.

◉ Sights

Kootenay National Park   NATIONAL PARK
(📞250-347-9505; www.pc.gc.ca/kootenay; Hwy 93; adult/child $9.80/free, tent/RV sites $21.50/38.20; ☉camping May-Oct) Shaped like a lightning bolt, 1406-sq-km Kootenay National Park is centered on a long, wide, tree-covered valley shadowed by cold, gray peaks. It has a more moderate climate than other Rocky Mountains parks and, in the southern regions especially, summers can be hot and dry, which is a factor in the frequent fires.

The interpretive **Fireweed Trails** (500m or 2km) loop through the surrounding forest at the north end of Hwy 93. Panels explain how nature is recovering from a 1968 fire. Some 7km further on, **Marble Canyon** has a pounding creek flowing through a nascent forest. Another 3km south on the main road you'll find the easy 2km trail through forest to ocher pools known as the **Paint Pots**. Panels describe both the mining history of this rusty earth and its importance to Indigenous people.

Learn how the park's appearance has changed over time at the **Kootenay Valley Viewpoint**, where informative panels vie with the view. Just 3km south, **Olive Lake** makes a perfect picnic or rest stop. A 500m lakeside interpretive trail describes some of the visitors who've come before you.

Mt Assiniboine
Provincial Park   PARK
(www.env.gov.bc.ca/bcparks) Between Kootenay and Banff National Parks lies this lesser-known and smaller (39-sq-km) provincial park, part of the Rockies' Unesco World Heritage site. The pointed peak of Mt Assiniboine (3618m), often referred to as Canada's Matterhorn, and its near neighbors have become a magnet for experienced rock climbers and mountaineers. Backcountry hikers revel in its meadows and glaciers.

The park's main focus is crystal-clear **Lake Magog**, which is reachable on a 27km trek from Banff National Park or by helicopter. At the lake, there's a lodge, camping and huts.

🛏 Sleeping

★**Kootenay Park Lodge**   CABIN $$
(📞403-762-9196;   www.kootenayparklodge.com; Hwy 93, Vermilion Crossing, Kootenay National Park; d cabins from $125; ☉mid-May–late Sep; P🐾❄🛜) The pick of the few places to stay inside the park, this lodge has a range of cute log cabins complete with verandah, fridge and hot plates. Think rustic charm. There is a restaurant open June 1 through mid-September, a general store selling coffee and snacks, and for those who can't do without it, spotty wi-fi.

Assiniboine Lodge   LODGE $$$
(📞403-678-2883;   www.assiniboinelodge.com; Mt Assiniboine Provincial Park; r per person $350, shared & private cabin per person from $350; ☉Feb, Mar & Jun-Oct; 🛜) The only lodge in Assiniboine is also the oldest ski lodge in the Canadian Rockies, surrounded by mountain meadows and gloriously backed by Mt Assiniboine. Rustic rooms sleep one or two people (solo travelers usually must share), plus there are shared (three to five people) or private cabins. Rates include meals and hiking-guide service. Helicopter transport is $175 each way.

❶ Information

The main **Kootenay National Park visitor center** (📞250-347-9331; www.radiumhot springs.com; 7556 Main St E; ☉visitor center 9am-5pm year-round, Parks Canada May-Oct, later in summer; 🛜) is in Radium Hot Springs. It has excellent resources for hikers.

Radium Hot Springs

Lying just outside the southwest corner of Kootenay National Park, Radium Hot Springs is a major gateway to the entire Rocky Mountains national park area.

Radium boasts a large resident population of bighorn sheep, which often wander through town, but the big attraction is the namesake hot springs, 3km northeast of town.

There's a definite German-Austrian vibe here with accommodations such as Motel Tyrol, Alpen Motel, Motel Bavaria, restaurants like the Old Salzburg and Helna Stube, and even an Edelweiss St.

Radium Hot Springs   HOT SPRINGS
(📞250-347-9485;   www.pc.gc.ca/hotsprings; off Hwy 93; adult/child $7.30/4.95; ☉9am-11pm) The large hot springs pools have just been mod-

ernized and can get very busy in summer. The water comes from the ground at 44°C, enters the first pool at 39°C and hits the cooler one at 29°C. It's 3km northeast of the township, inside the park gate, with plenty of parking.

Radium Park Lodge MOTEL $
(☑778-527-4857; www.radiumparklodge.com; 4873 Stanley St; r from $79; ⓟ➾❄🌐♨) Clean and comfortable motel rooms at Radium Hot Springs, near the entrance to the parks. Continental breakfast is included and there's plenty of parking a couple of blocks back from the highway.

Inn on Canyon GUESTHOUSE $$
(☑250-347-9392; www.villagecountryinn.bc.ca; 7557 Canyon Ave; r from $109; ⓟ➾🌐) A cute gabled house just off the main drag. Its rooms are sparkling clean and decked out in country fashion.

Big Horn Cafe CAFE $
(☑403-861-2978; www.bighorncafe.net; 7527 Main St; snacks from $3; ⊙6am-4:30pm; 🌐) An ideal road-trip breaker where you can refuel with coffee and a cinnamon bun or something more savory.

Radium Hot Springs to Fernie

South from Radium Hot Springs, Hwy 93/95 follows the wide Columbia River valley between the Purcell and Rocky Mountains. It's not especially interesting, unless you're into the area's industry (ski-resort construction), agriculture (golf courses) or wild game (condo buyers).

South of Skookumchuck on Hwy 93/95, the road forks. Go left on Hwy 95 and you'll come to **Fort Steele Heritage Town** (☑250-426-7342; www.fortsteele.ca; 9851 Hwy 93/95; adult/youth $18/12; ⊙10am-5pm mid-Jun–Aug, shorter hours winter).

From Fort Steele, it's 95km to Fernie along Hwys 93 and 3.

Fernie

☑250 / POP 5250
Surrounded by mountains on four sides – that's the sheer granite Lizard Range you see looking west – Fernie defines cool. Once devoted solely to lumber and coal, the town has used its sensational setting to branch out. Skiers love the 8m-plus of dry powder

that annually blankets the runs seen from town. In summer, this same dramatic setting lures scores of hikers and mountain bikers.

Despite the town's discovery by pleasure seekers, it still retains a down-to-earth, vintage-brick vibe, best felt in the cafes, bars, shops and galleries along Victoria (2nd) Ave in the historic center, three blocks south of Hwy 3 (7th Ave).

⊙ Sights & Activities

Fernie Museum MUSEUM
(☑250-423-7016; www.ferniemuseum.com; 491 2nd Ave; adult/child $5/free; ⊙10am-5:30pm) Impressively housed in a 1909 bank building, the Fernie Museum has engaging displays and is an excellent source of info about the town and region. Experience the fires, floods, booms and busts that have shaped the town.

Mt Fernie Provincial Park PARK
(☑250-422-3003; www.env.gov.bc.ca/bcparks; Mt Fernie Park Rd, off Hwy 3) Mountain biking is popular at Mt Fernie Provincial Park, just 3km south of town. It also offers hikes for all skills and interests, plus camping.

★**Fernie Alpine Resort** SKIING
(☑250-423-4655; www.skifernie.com; 5339 Ski Area Rd; 1-day pass adult/child $94/38) In fall, all eyes turn to the mountains for more than just their beauty: they're looking for snow. A five-minute drive from downtown, fast-growing Fernie Alpine Resort boasts 142 runs, five bowls and almost endless dumps of powder. Most hotels run shuttles here daily.

Guide's Hut CYCLING
(☑250-423-3650; www.theguideshut.ca; 671 2 Ave; guiding per hour $30; ⊙10am-6pm) Raise your mountain-biking game with expert coaching and instruction, and let them show you the far reaches of the Elk Valley.

Mountain High River Adventures RAFTING
(☑250-423-5008; www.raftfernie.com; 2001 6th Ave; trips adult/child from $140/100; ⊙8am-6pm May-Sep) The Elk River is a classic white-water river, with three grade IV rapids and 11 grade III rapids. In addition to rafting, Mountain High offers kayaking, floats, rentals and more on the surging waters. Its new Adventure Centre is at Fernie RV Resort.

❶ CHECK YOUR WATCH

It is a constant source of confusion that the East Kootenays lie in the Mountain time zone, along with Alberta, unlike the rest of BC, which falls within the Pacific time zone. West on Hwy 1 from Golden, the time changes at the east gate of Glacier National Park. Going west on Hwy 3, the time changes between Cranbrook and Creston. Mountain time is one hour later than Pacific time.

🛏 Sleeping

HI Raging Elk Hostel   HOSTEL $
(☑ 250-423-6811; www.ragingelk.com; 892 6th Ave; dm/r from $30/85; 🅿🖥🤶) Wide decks allow plenty of inspirational mountain-gazing at this well-run central hostel. Raging Elk has good advice for those hoping to mix time on the slopes or trails with seasonal work. The pub (open 4pm to midnight) is a hoot (and offers cheap beer).

★ Park Place Lodge   HOTEL $$
(☑ 250-423-6871; www.parkplacelodge.com; 742 Hwy 3; r from $130; 🅿🖥❄🤶🏊) The nicest lodging close to the center, Park Place offers 64 comfortable rooms with fridge and microwave, and access to an indoor pool and hot tub. Some have balcony and views.

Snow Valley Lodging   MOTEL $$
(☑ 877-696-7669; www.snowvalleymotel.com; 1041 7th Ave/Hwy 3; r from $99; 🅿🖥❄🤶) Great value in the middle of town. There are rooms, 'tiny homes' and suites that you can pick online and book direct. Throw in complimentary laundry facilities, bike use, BBQ area and hot tub and you have a great place to stay in Fernie.

🍴 Eating & Drinking

Blue Toque Diner   CAFE $
(☑ 250-423-4637; www.bluetoquediner.com; 601 1st Ave; mains from $12; ⊙9am-2:30pm Thu-Mon; 🅿) Part of the Arts Station community gallery, this is *the* place for breakfast. The menu features lots of seasonal and organic vegetarian specials.

★ Nevados Tapas & Tequila   LATIN AMERICAN $$
(☑ 250-423-5566; www.nevados.ca; 531 2 Ave; tapas from $4.50; ⊙5-10pm) The hottest spot in Fernie, Nevados is invitingly dark inside with century-old exposed-brick walls and a lovely outside terrace for long summer eve-nings. It's all on here, with a two-page tequila menu, local craft beers and a delightful selection of Latin tapas and full meals. Try the pork *arepa*, street food from Venezuela.

★ Yamagoya   JAPANESE $$
(☑ 250-430-0090; www.yamagoya.ca; 741 7th Ave/Hwy 3; small dishes from $4, mains from $11; ⊙5-10pm) As compact as a California roll, this gem of a sushi place serves a wide range of classics, from sashimi to tempura. The miso soup is good, especially after a day of skiing. In addition to sake, there's a great beer selection. Also has outdoor seating.

Fernie Distillers   DISTILLERY
(www.ferniedistillers.com; 531 1st Ave; ⊙4-10pm Wed-Sun, from 2pm Sat & Sun) Fernie's distillery sits next to the old station building and produces small-batch (200 bottles per batch) hand-crafted gin and vodka. Turn up, view the stills, chat with the owners, sip the product and enjoy an extremely convivial laid-back atmosphere. The Prospector Gin and No 9 Mine Vodka are great, but don't forget to ask about the 'seasonal spirit'.

❶ Information

Visitor Center (☑ 250-423-6868; www.ferniechamber.com; 102 Commerce Rd; ⊙9am-5pm Mon-Fri) Located east of town off Hwy 3, just past the Elk River crossing.

Kimberley
🎵 250, 778 / POP 7425
When big-time mining left Kimberley in 1973, a plan was hatched to transform the little mountain village at 1113m altitude into the Bavarian City of the Rockies. The center became a pedestrian zone named the Platzl; locals were encouraged to prance about in lederhosen and dirndl; and sausage was added to many a menu. Now, more than three decades later, that shtick is long-gone, though the city still claims to have the largest freestanding cuckoo clock in Canada. There's still a bit of fake half-timbering here and there, but for the most part Kimberley is a diverse place that makes a worthwhile detour off Hwy 95 between Cranbrook and Radium Hot Springs.

Kimberley Alpine Resort   SKIING
(☑ 250-427-4881; www.skikimberley.com; 301 N Star Blvd; 1-day lift pass adult/child $75/30) In winter this popular resort has more than 700 hectares of skiable terrain, including

80 runs, and mild weather. Lots going on in summer including hiking, mountain biking, golf, canoeing, kayaking, rafting and fly-fishing.

Kimberley's Underground Mining Railway   RAIL
(☑ 250-427-7365; www.kimberleysunderground miningrailway.ca; Gerry Sorensen Way; adult/child $25/10; ☉ tours 11am, 1pm & 3pm May-Sep, trains to resort 10am Sat & Sun) Take a ride on Kimberley's Underground Mining Railway, where the tiny train putters through the steep-walled Mark Creek Valley toward some sweeping mountain vistas.

ℹ️ Information
Kimberley Visitor Centre (☑ 778-481-1891; www.tourismkimberley.com; 270 Kimberley Ave; ☉ 10am-5pm daily Jul & Aug, closed Sun Sep-Jun) The visitor centre has everything you need to know.

Cranbrook
☑ 250, 778 / POP 19,250
The region's main center, 31km southeast of Kimberley, Cranbrook is a modest crossroads. Hwy 3/95 bisects the town and is lined with a charmless array of strip malls.

⭐ Cranbrook History Centre   MUSEUM
(☑ 250-489-3918; www.cranbrookhistorycentre.com; 57 Van Horne St S, Hwy 3/95; adult/child $5/3; ☉ 10am-5pm Tue-Sun) The one great reason for stopping in Cranbrook? This museum, which includes the **Canadian Museum of Rail Travel**. It has some fine examples of classic Canadian trains, including the luxurious 1929 edition of the Trans-Canada Limited, a legendary train that ran from Montréal to Vancouver.

Lazy Bear Lodge   MOTEL $
(☑ 250-426-6086; www.lazybear.ca; 621 Cranbrook Street N; r from $75; P ☕ ❄ ☎) Unlike most of the chain places along Hwy 95, locally owned Lazy Bear has been catering to visitors for nigh on 50 years. Nothing fancy, but its motel-type rooms are clean and affordable, plus there's a nice outdoor pool.

⭐ Fire Hall Kitchen & Tap   GASTROPUB $$
(☑ 778-520-0911; www.irehallcbk.ca; 37 11 Ave St; dinner mains from $12; ☉ 8am-10pm Sun-Thu, to midnight Fri & Sat) Top BC craft beers (20 on tap!) and great food all day in what used to be Cranbrook's fire station. Rooftop and streetside seating, plus a beautifully reno-vated interior, make this an extremely atmospheric place to eat and drink.

Cranbrook to Rossland
Hwy 3 twists and turns its way 300km from Cranbrook to Osoyoos at the south end of the Okanagan Valley. Along the way it hugs the hills close to the US border and passes eight border crossings.

Creston, 123km west of Cranbrook, is known for its many orchards and as the home of Columbia Brewing Co's Kokanee True Ale. Hwy 3A heads north from here for a scenic 80km to the free **Kootenay Lake Ferry**, which connects to Nelson. This is a fun and scenic journey.

Some 85km west of Creston, **Salmo** is notable mostly as the junction with Hwy 6, which runs north for a bland 40km to Nelson. The Crowsnest Hwy splits 10km to the west. Hwy 3 bumps north through **Castlegar**, which has the closest large airport to Nelson and a very large pulp mill. Hwy 3B dips down through cute cafe-filled town **Fruitvale** and industrial **Trail**.

🛏️ Sleeping & Eating
Valley View Motel   MOTEL $
(☑ 250-428-2336; www.valleyviewmotel.info; 216 Valley View Dr, Creston; r from $75; P ☕ ❄ ☎) In motel-ville Creston, this is your best bet. On a view-splayed hillside, it's clean, comfortable and quiet.

Retro Cafe   FRENCH $
(☑ 250-428-2726; www.retrocafe.ca; 1431 NW Blvd, Creston; mains from $8; ☉ 7am-4pm Mon-Fri, to 3pm Sat) A French mirage in Creston, 'retro' will probably be the last thing on your mind as you scour the hand-scrawled blackboard and tuck into *très délicieux* crepes.

Rossland
☑ 250, 778 / POP 3730
Rossland is a world apart. High in the Southern Monashee Mountains (1023m), this old mining village is one of Canada's best places for **mountain biking**. A long history of mining has left the hills crisscrossed with old trails and abandoned rail lines, all of which are perfect for riding.

Free-riding is all the rage as the ridgelines are easily accessed and there are lots of rocky paths for plunging downhill. The **Seven Summits & Dewdney Trail** is a 35.8km singletrack along the crest of the Rossland Range. The **Kootenay Columbia Trails Society** (www.kcts.ca) has good maps online.

Red Mountain Ski Resort
SKIING

(☑250-362-7384, snow report 250-362-5500; www.redresort.com; Hwy 3B; 1-day lift pass adult/child $96/48) Red Mountain Ski Resort draws mountain bikers in summer and plenty of ski enthusiasts in winter. Red, as it's called, includes the 1590m-high Red Mountain, the 2075m-high Granite Mountain and the 2048m-high Grey Mountain, for a total of 1670 hectares of challenging, powdery terrain and 110 runs. Plenty going on with heli-, cat-, cross-country and backcountry skiing too.

Flying Steamshovel
Gastropub & Inn
INN $

(☑250-362-7323; www.theflyingsteamshovel. com; 2003 2 Ave; r from $80; ☺☜) Lots going on here at the Flying Steamshovel, from the main street in Rossland. Great location, comfortable rooms, free parking – and if you're into craft beer, 14 different brews on tap. The restaurant offers a huge variety from its *poke* bowl to yellow coconut curry to the John Candy burger. Check the website for live concert listings.

❶ Information

Rossland Visitor Centre (☑250-362-7722; www.rosslandmuseum.ca; 1100 Hwy 3B, Rossland Museum; ☺11am-5pm May-Sep) Located in the Rossland Museum building, at the junction of Hwy 22 (coming from the US border) and Hwy 3B.

Nelson

☑250,778 / POP 10,660

Nelson is an excellent reason to visit the Kootenays and should feature on any itinerary in the region. Tidy brick buildings climb the side of a hill overlooking the west arm of deep-blue Kootenay Lake, and the waterfront is lined with parks and beaches. The thriving cafe, culture and nightlife scene is a bonus. However, what really propels Nelson is its personality: a funky mix of hippies, creative types and rugged individualists. You can find all these along Baker St, the pedestrian-friendly main drag where wafts of patchouli mingle with hints of fresh-roasted coffee.

Born as a mining town in the late 1800s, Nelson embarked on a decades-long heritage-preservation project in 1977. Today there are more than 350 carefully preserved and restored period buildings. The town is also an excellent base for hiking, skiing and kayaking the nearby lakes and hills.

◉ Sights

Almost a third of Nelson's **historic buildings** have been restored to their high- and late-Victorian architectural splendor. Pick up the superb *Heritage Walking Tour* from the visitor center (p228). It gives details of more than 30 buildings in the center and offers a good lesson in Victorian architecture.

Lakeside Park
PARK

(Lakeside Dr; ℗) By the iconic Nelson Bridge, Lakeside Park is a flower-filled, shady park and a beach, and has a great summer cafe.

Touchstones Nelson
Museum of Art & History
MUSEUM

(☑250-352-9813; www.touchstonesnelson.ca; 502 Vernon St; adult/child $8/6; ☺10am-5pm Mon-Wed, Fri & Sat, to 8pm Thu, to 4pm Sun Jun-Aug, closed Mon Sep-May) An enormous renovation transformed what was once a baronial old city hall (1902) into Touchstones Nelson, a museum of local history and art. Every month brings new exhibitions, many of which celebrate local artists. The history displays are engaging and interactive, banishing images of musty piles of poorly labeled artifacts.

🏃 Activities

⭐**Kokanee Glacier**
Provincial Park
HIKING

(www.env.gov.bc.ca/bcparks; Kokanee Glacier Rd) This park boasts 85km of some of the area's most superb hiking trails. The fantastic summer-only 2.5km (two-hour) round-trip hike to **Kokanee Lake** on a well-marked trail can be continued to the treeless, boulder-strewn expanse around the glacier. Turn off Hwy 3A 20.5km northeast of Nelson, then head another 16km on Kokanee Glacier Rd.

Whitewater Winter Resort
SKIING

(☑250-354-4944, snow report 250-352-7669; www.skiwhitewater.com; off Hwy 6; 1-day lift ticket adult/child $76/38) Known for its heavy powdery snowfall, this laid-back resort 12km south of Nelson off Hwy 6 has small-town charm. Lifts are few, but so are the crowds, who enjoy a drop of 623m on 81 runs. There are 11 groomed Nordic trails.

Sacred Ride

MOUNTAIN BIKING

(📞 250-354-3831; www.sacredride.ca; 213 Baker St; bicycle rental per day from $45; ⊘ 9am-5:30pm Mon-Sat) The Sacred Ride has a wide variety of rentals. Also sells *Your Ticket to Ride,* an extensive trail map.

ROAM

KAYAKING

(Rivers, Oceans & Mountains; 📞 250-354-2056; www.roamshop.com; 639 Baker St; kayak rental per day $40; ⊘ 8am-7pm Mon-Sat, to 5pm Sun) ROAM sells and rents gear and offers advice. Book **Kootenay Kayak Company** (📞 250-505-4549; www.kootenaykayak.com; kayak rentals per day $40-50, tours from $55) tours here.

Streetcar 23

RAIL

(📞 250-352-7672; www.nelsonstreetcar.org; Waterfront Pathway; adult/child $3/2; ⊘ 11am-4:30pm mid-May–mid-Nov) One of the town's originals, streetcar 23 follows a 2km track from Lakeside Park to the wharf at the foot of Hall St.

🛏 Sleeping

⭐ **Dancing Bear Inn**

HOSTEL $

(📞 250-352-7573; www.dancingbearinn.com; 171 Baker St; dm/r from $29/59; P 🐶 🛜) 🖋 The brilliant management here offers advice and smooths the stay of guests in the 14 shared and private rooms, all of which share baths. There's a gourmet kitchen, library, patio and laundry.

⭐ **Adventure Hotel**

HOTEL $$

(📞 250-352-7211; www.adventurehotel.ca; 616 Vernon St; r from $95; P 🐶 ❄ 🛜) Rooms come in three flavors at this well-located, slick, renovated hotel: budget (tiny, two bunk beds, shower down the hall), economy (full private bath) and deluxe (a choice of beds). Common areas include a lounge, patio, gym and rooftop sauna. The building also features the hotel's Uptown Sports Bar, Louie's Steakhouse and Empire Coffee café.

Hume Hotel & Spa

HOTEL $$

(📞 250-352-5331; www.humehotel.com; 422 Vernon St; r incl breakfast from $120; P 🐶 ❄ 🛜) This 1898 classic hotel maintains its period grandeur. The 43 rooms vary greatly in shape and size; ask for the huge corner rooms with views of the hills and lake. Rates include a delicious breakfast. It has several appealing nightlife venues.

Victoria Falls Guest House

INN $$

(📞 250-551-3663; www.victoriafallsguesthouse.com; 213 Victoria St; r from $95; P 🐶 🛜) The wide porch wraps right around this festive, yellow, renovated Victorian. The five suites have sitting areas and cooking facilities. Decor ranges from cozy antiques to family-friendly bunk beds. There is a barbecue.

🍴 Eating & Drinking

Cottonwood Community Market

MARKET $

(www.ecosociety.ca; 199 Carbonate St, Cottonwood Falls Park; ⊘ 9:30am-3pm Sat mid-May–Oct) 🖋 Close to downtown and next to the surging Cottonwood waterfall, this market encapsulates Nelson. There's great organic produce; fine baked goods, many with heretofore-unheard-of grains; and various craft items with artistic roots in tie-dyeing. A second event is the **Downtown Market** (Hall St; ⊘ 9:30am-3pm Wed mid-Jun–Sep).

Full Circle Cafe

DINER $

(📞 250-354-4458; www.facebook.com/fullcircle cafe; 402 Baker S; mains from $8; ⊘ 6:30am-2:30pm) A downtown diner beloved for its omelets, the Full Circle will have you doing just that as you return for skillfully made breakfast classics, such as eggs Benedict. It gets popular on weekends, so prepare for a wait.

⭐ Jackson's Hole & Grill

CANADIAN $$

(📞 250-354-1919; www.jacksonsgrill.ca; 524 Vernon St; dinner mains from $14; ⊘ 11:30am-9pm Sun-Tue, to 10pm Wed & Thu, to midnight Fri & Sat) In a historic building that has been around since 1897, this place is both lively and friendly. Used as Dixie's Café in the Steve Martin and Darryl Hannah Hollywood classic *Roxanne* in 1986, Jackson's serves soups, salads, sandwiches, wraps, burgers and pastas. Plenty to choose from in a very convivial atmosphere.

⭐ All Seasons Cafe

FUSION $$$

(📞 250-352-0101; www.allseasonscafe.com; 620 Herridge Lane; mains from $22; ⊘ 5-10pm) Sitting on the patio here beneath little lights twinkling in the huge maple above you is a Nelson highlight; in winter, candles inside provide the same romantic flair. The eclectic menu changes with the seasons but always celebrates BC foods. Presentations are artful; service is gracious.

★**Backroads Brewing Company** MICROBREWERY
(☑778-463-3361; www.backroadsbrewing.com; 460 Baker St; ☺noon-10pm Mon-Thu, to 11pm Fri & Sat, to 8pm Sun) Nelson's local brews from tank to tap on Baker St. Small-batch, hand-crafted ales and lagers such as the El Dorado Golden Ale and Navigator Irish Red keep the locals coming back for more. Limited food apart from bar snacks, but that's not what you're here for, right?

Royal on Baker BAR
(☑250-354-7014; www.royalgrillnelson.com; 330 Baker St; ☺5pm-2am) This gritty old pub on Baker gets some of the region's best music acts. It has a whole section of tables outside on the street and serves decent pub food.

Oso Negro Café CAFE
(☑250-532-7761; www.osonegrocoffee.com; 604 Ward St; ☺7am-6pm; ☎) This local favorite corner cafe roasts its own coffee in 20 blends. Outside there are tables in a garden that burbles with water features amid statues. Enjoy baked goods and other snacks.

ℹ Information

Discover Nelson Visitor Centre (☑250-352-3433; www.discovernelson.com; 90 Baker St; ☺8:30am-6pm daily May-Oct, to 5pm Mon-Fri Nov-Apr) Housed in the beautifully restored train station, it offers excellent brochures detailing driving and walking tours, plus has an excellent cafe.

ℹ Getting There & Away

West Kootenay Regional Airport (www.wkrairport.ca; Hwy 3A) The closest major airport to Nelson is 42km southwest at Castlegar.

West Kootenay Transit System (☑855-993-3100; www.bctransit.com; fares $2) The main stop is at the corner of Ward and Baker Sts.

Nelson to Revelstoke

Heading north from Nelson to Revelstoke, there are two options, both scenic. Hwy 6 heads west for 16km before turning north at South Slocan. The road eventually runs alongside pretty Slocan Lake for about 30km before reaching New Denver, 97km from Nelson.

The most interesting route is north and east from Nelson on Hwy 3A. Head 34km northeast to Balfour, where the free **Kootenay Lake Ferry** (☑250-229-4215; www2.gov.bc.ca/gov/content/transportation/passenger-travel) connects to Kootenay Bay. The ferry's worthwhile for its long lake vistas of blue mountains rising sharply from the water. From Kootenay Bay, Hwy 3A heads 80km south to Creston. Continuing north from the ferry at Balfour, the road becomes Hwy 31 and follows the lake 34km to Kaslo, passing cute towns. West from Kaslo to New Denver on Rte 31A is spectacular. North of there you pass Nakusp village and another free ferry before reaching Revelstoke. This is a great all-day trip.

Kaslo

A cute little town, Kaslo is an underrated gem with a beautiful lakeside setting.

SS Moyie HISTORIC SITE
(☑250-353-2525; www.klhs.bc.ca; 324 Front St; adult/child $12/5; ☺10am-5pm mid-May–mid-Oct) Don't miss the restored 1898 lake steamer SS *Moyie*. It also has tourist info on the myriad ways to kayak and canoe the sparkling-blue waters.

Kaslo Hotel & Pub HOTEL **$$**
(☑250-353-7714; www.kaslohotel.com; 430 Front St; r from $125; ☻❄☎) This appealing three-story downtown veteran (1896) has lake views and a good pub. Rooms have balcony and porch.

New Denver

Wild mountain streams are just some of the spectacular highlights on Hwy 31A, which goes up and over some rugged hills west of Kaslo. At the end of this twisting 47km road, you reach New Denver, which seems about five years away from ghost-town status. But that's not necessarily bad, as this historic little gem slumbers away peacefully right on the clear waters of Slocan Lake. The equally sleepy old mining town of Silverton is just south.

Silvery Slocan Museum MUSEUM
(☑250-358-2201; www.newdenver.ca/silvery-slocan-museum; 202 6th Ave; by donation; ☺9am-5pm daily Jul & Aug, Sat & Sun only Sep-Jun) Housed in the 1897 Bank of Montreal

building, this museum features well-done displays from the booming mining days, a tiny vault and an untouched tin ceiling. It also has visitor info.

Nakusp

📍 250, 778 / POP 1570

Situated right on Upper Arrow Lake, Nakusp was forever changed by BC's orgy of dam building in the 1950s and 1960s. The water level here was raised and the town was relocated to its current spot, which is why it has a 1960s-era look. It has some attractive cafes and a tiny museum.

Nakusp Hot Springs HOT SPRINGS
(📞 250-265-4528; www.nakusphotsprings.com; 8500 Hot Springs Rd; adult/child $10.50/9.50; ⊙9:30am-9:30pm) These hot springs, 12km northeast of Nakusp off Hwy 23, feel a bit artificial after receiving a revamp. However, you'll forget this as you soak away your cares amid an amphitheater of trees.

CARIBOO CHILCOTIN COAST

This vast and beautiful region covers a huge swath of BC north of Whistler. It comprises three very distinct areas. The Cariboo region includes numerous ranches, and terrain that's little changed from the 1850s, when the 'Gold Rush Trail' passed through from Lillooet to Barkerville.

Populated with more moose than people, the Chilcotin lies to the west of Hwy 97, the region's north–south spine. Its mostly wild, rolling landscape has a few ranches and some indigenous villages. Traveling west along Hwy 20 from Williams Lake leads you to the Bella Coola Valley, a spectacular bear-and-wildlife-filled inlet along the coast.

Much of the region can be reached via Hwy 97, enabling you to build a circle itinerary to other parts of BC via Prince George in the north.

ⓘ Getting There & Away

Adventure Charter (www.adventurecharters.ca/) runs buses north from Kamloops to Williams Lake and on to Prince George.

Hwy 97 forms the spine of the region; it's a good-quality road that continues to be improved.

Williams Lake to Prince George

Cattle and lumber have shaped Williams Lake as the hub for the region. At 205km north of the junction of Hwys 1 and 97 at Cache Creek, this small town is a busy three-way crossroads.

Dead-end Hwy 20 heads 450km west to coastal Bella Coola; Hwy 97 heads south to Cache Creek and north for 124km to Quesnel. There's not much character on the highways in Williams Lake. Head west on Oliver St into the old part of town to escape the chain stores, restaurants and hotels.

From Quesnel, Hwy 26 leads east to the area's main attractions, Barkerville Historic Park and Bowron Lake Provincial Park. North from Quesnel, it's 116km on Hwy 97 to Prince George.

Lakeside Motel MOTEL $$
(📞 250-392-4181; www.lakesidemotelwilliamslake.net; 1505 Cariboo Hwy; r from $90; 🅿😊❄🛜) A good option if you like avoiding rather charmless chain hotels, Lakeside Motel is like its name suggests, beside the lake. The rooms are basic, but they have patios and there's plenty of grass outside. Rooms have microwave, refrigerator and flat-screen TV, and guests can use the laundry facilities, BBQ and picnic area.

New World Coffee & Tea House CAFE $
(📞 778-412-5282; www.newworldcoffee.ca; 72 Oliver St, Wiliams Lake; mains from $8; ⊙8am-5pm Mon-Fri, 9:30am-4pm Sat) In the town center, this sprightly cafe has a bakery and excellent coffee. Get a sandwich to go, or eat in to enjoy the menu of soups, salads, hot specials and more. Look for the yellow street frontage and enjoy the outdoor seating.

ⓘ Information

Williams Lake Visitor Centre (📞250-392-5025; www.williamslake.ca; 1660 Broadway S, off Hwy 97; ⊙9am-6pm) In a massive log building as you come into town from the south, this place has excellent regional info. In the same building you'll find the Museum of the Cariboo Chilcotin (entry by donation).

Barkerville & Around

In 1862 Billy Barker, previously of Cornwall, struck gold deep in the Cariboo. Barkerville soon sprung up, populated by the usual fly-by-night crowds of prostitutes, dupes, tricksters and just plain prospectors. Today it's a compelling attraction, a time capsule of the Old West.

Barkerville lies 82km east of Quesnel along Hwy 26. Historic **Cottonwood House**, a parklike area, makes an atmospheric stop on the way. Nearby **Wells**, which you'll pass through on Hwy 26, has a top eating option.

Barkerville Historic Town   HISTORIC SITE
(🖉888-994-3332; www.barkerville.ca; Hwy 26; adult/child $16/6; ☺8am-8pm mid-Jun–Aug, 8:30am-4pm mid-May–mid-Jun & Sep) You can visit more than 125 restored heritage buildings in Barkerville Historic Town, which also has shops, cafes and a couple of B&Bs. In summer, people dressed in period garb roam through town and, if you can tune out the crowds, it feels more authentic than forced. At other times of the year, you can wander the town for free, but don't expect to find much open.

★**Bear's Paw Cafe**   CAFE $
(🖉250-994-3538; www.thebearspawcafe.com; Hwy 26, Wells; lunch mains from $10; ☺9am-8pm Thu-Tue) If some of the clientele are a tad wiffy, it's because this is the spot that outdoors types head straight to when dropping back into civilization. The cafe boasts freshly made foods, locally roasted espresso and treats to die for, while right outside there's a food truck (June to September) on the patio.

ⓘ Information

Wells Visitor Centre (🖉250-994-2323; www.wells.ca/tourism/visitor-information-centre; 11900 Hwy 26, Wells; ☺9am-5pm May-Sep) Has regional info.

Bowron Lake

The place heaven-bound canoeists go when they die, Bowron Lake Provincial Park is a fantasyland of 10 lakes surrounded by snow-capped peaks.

★**Bowron Lake Provincial Park**   PARK
(www.env.gov.bc.ca/bcparks; off Hwy 26; ☺May-Sep; 🅿) Forming a natural circle with sections of the Isaac, Cariboo and Bowron Rivers, the park's 116km canoe circuit (permits $30 to $60) is one of the world's finest. There are eight portages, with the longest (2km) over well-defined trails. The park website has maps, and details everything

you'll need to know for planning your trip, including mandatory reservations, which sometimes book up in advance. Campsites cost $18. Check out Bowron Lake Canoe Rentals (www.bowronlakecanoe.com).

The whole canoe circuit takes between six and 10 days, and you'll need to be completely self-sufficient. September is a good time to visit, both for the bold colors of changing leaves and the lack of summer crowds.

Wells Gray Provincial Park

Plunging 141m onto rocks below, **Helmcken Falls** may only be Canada's fourth-highest waterfall but it is one of the undiscovered facets of Wells Gray Provincial Park, itself an underappreciated gem. **Clearwater**, 123km north of Kamloops on Hwy 5, is the town near the park entrance and has everything you'll need for a visit.

◎ Sights & Activities

Wells Gray Provincial Park   PARK
(www.env.gov.bc.ca/bcparks; Wells Gray Rd) BC's fourth-largest park is bounded by the Clearwater River and its tributaries, which define the park's boundaries. Highlights for visitors include five major lakes, two large river systems, scores of waterfalls such as **Helmcken Falls** and most every kind of BC land-based wildlife. Many hiking trails and sights, such as Helmcken Falls, are accessible off the main park road, which ends at **Clearwater Lake**.

You'll find opportunities for **hiking**, **cross-country skiing** and **horseback riding** along more than 20 trails of varying lengths. Rustic backcountry campgrounds dot the area around four of the lakes.

Clearwater Lake Tours   OUTDOORS
(🖉250-674-2121; www.clearwaterlaketours.com; canoe/kayak rental per day from $60) Rents canoes and kayaks, leads tours of the park and runs taxi-boats to Azure Lake and Rainbow Falls. Based at Osprey Cafe at Clearwater Lake, the only cafe and the only wi-fi in the park.

🛏 Sleeping & Eating

Wells Grey Provincial Park Campgrounds   CAMPGROUND $
(🖉800-689-9025; www.discovercamping.ca; Wells Grey Provincial Park; campsites from $20; 🅿) There are three vehicle-accessible yet

simple campgrounds in the park. Woodsy **Pyramid Campground** is close to Helmcken Falls. There's also plenty of **backcountry camping** ($5).

★ Lake House   B&B $$

(☑ 250-674-5198; www.thelakehouseclearwater. com; 309 Harby Rd; r from $195; P ➔ ❄ ☎) This lovely B&B sits right on the edge of Dutch Lake and features three exquisite rooms in a large log house, handmade rustic wooden furniture, an attractive common lounge area and a delicious breakfast. Guests have complimentary use of canoes, paddleboards and a rowboat from the Lake House's private jetty. All rooms have a private terrace overlooking the lake.

★ Hop 'N' Hog Tap & Smokehouse   CANADIAN $$

(☑ 250-674-3654; www.canadiansmokehouse. com; 424 Clearwater Valley Rd, Clearwater; mains from $20; ☺ 5-9:30pm May-Oct) One for the hard-core carnivores among us, Hop 'N' Hog specializes in smoked meats and sausages and has 10 rotating taps of BC craft beer. The smoked beef brisket ($26.50) is a doozy, while herbivores are not forgotten with the smoked vegetarian platter ($25). Wine and liquor options abound.

ℹ️ Information

Clearwater Wells Gray Park Visitors Centre
(☑ 250-674-3334; www.wellsgraypark.info; 416 Eden Rd, off Hwy 5, Clearwater; ☺ 9am-7pm May-Oct; ☎) Has full park and regional info.

Chilcotin & Highway 20

Meandering over the lonely hills west of the Chilcotin, Hwy 20 runs 450km from Williams Lake to the Bella Coola Valley. You'll come across a few indigenous villages, as well as gravel roads that lead off to the odd provincial park and deserted lake.

Long spoken about by drivers in hushed and concerned tones, Hwy 20 has received steady improvement and is now more than 90% paved. However, the unpaved section remains a doozy: **The Hill** is a 30km stretch of gravel 386km west of Williams Lake. It descends 1524m from Heckman's Pass to the valley, which is nearly at sea level, through a series of sharp switchbacks and 11% grades. But by taking your time and using low gear, you'll actually enjoy the stunning views. It's safe for all vehicles – visitors in rented SUVs will be humbled when a local in a Ford beater zips past.

★ Eagle's Nest Resort   LODGE $$

(☑ 250-742-3707; www.eaglesnest-resort.com; Anahim Lake; r from $100; P ➔ ☎) At Anahim Lake, 320km west of Williams Lake and 130km east of Bella Coola, this small resort lodge has a variety of rooms, cabins and a cottage. Enjoy birds and wildlife, meals in the lakeside dining room, and the outdoor hot tub, or rent a boat or canoe.

KiNiKiNiK Restaurant & Store   CANADIAN $$

(☑ 250-394-6000; www.pasturetoplate.ca; 9391 Hwy 20, Redstone; mains from $12; ☺ 10am-5pm Jun-Sep) This is a good stop on the long Hwy 20 drive, 145km west of Williams Lake and 305km east of Bella Coola, featuring a sod roof, restaurant and cabin accommodation. KiNiKiNiK uses organic ingredients and meats for sausages, salads and sandwiches. Rooms, available year-round, run from $120; you'll want to book ahead.

Bella Coola Valley

The verdant Bella Coola Valley is at the heart of Great Bear Rainforest, a lush land of huge stands of trees, surging white water and lots of bears. It's a spiritual place: Nuxalk First Nation artists are active here and, for many creative types from elsewhere, this is literally the end of the road. The valley lies west of the dry expanses of the Chilcotin.

The valley stretches 53km to the shores of the **North Bentinck Arm**, a deep, glacier-fed fjord that runs 40km inland from the Pacific Ocean. The two main towns, **Bella Coola** on the water and **Hagensborg** 15km east, almost seem as one, with most places of interest in or between the two.

🔘 Sights & Activities

Tweedsmuir Provincial Park   PARK
(www.env.gov.bc.ca/bcparks; off Hwy 20) Spanning the Chilcotin and the east end of the valley, the southern portion of Tweedsmuir Provincial Park is the second-largest provincial park in BC. It's a seemingly barely charted place, perfect for challenging backcountry adventures. Day hikes off Hwy 20 in the valley follow trails into lush and untouched coastal rainforest. Campsites $20.

Kynoch Adventures   ADVENTURE, WILDLIFE
(☑ 250-982-2298; https://kynoch-adventures. business.site; 1896 Hwy 20, Hagensborg)

Specializes in critter-spotting trips down local rivers and wilderness hikes. Highly recommended float trips to spot the valley's renowned **grizzly bear** population run from late August into October ($150 per person).

🛏 Sleeping & Eating

Rip Rap Campsite
CAMPGROUND $

(☑ 250-982-2752; www.riprapcamp.com; 1854 Hwy 20, Hagensborg; campsites/cabins from $22/75; ☺ May-Oct; P ☎) A much-lauded campground, Rip Rap has plenty of services and a great viewing deck overlooking the river, 15km east of Bella Coola village. Four cabins, two with private toilet and shower, two with shared facilities.

★ Bella Coola Mountain Lodge
INN $$

(☑ 250-982-2298; www.bcmountainlodge.com; 1900 Hwy 20, Hagensborg; r from $140; P ☺ @ ☎) ℐ The rooms, many with kitchen facilities, are huge and there's an excellent espresso bar at this lodge 15km east of Bella Coola village. The owners also run Kynoch Adventures (p231), which offers river tours and wilderness hikes.

Bella Coola Valley Restaurant
CANADIAN $$

(☑ 250-799-0045; MacKenzie St, Bella Coola; dinner mains from $14; ☺ 7am-8pm) It's simple and unfussy, but you won't go hungry in the village of Bella Coola. Choose from sandwiches and Valley favorites such as fish-and-chips ($12.95) for lunch, or pastas and steak for dinner.

ℹ Information

Bella Coola Valley Tourism (☑ 250-799-5202; https://bellacoola.ca; 442 MacKenzie St, Bella Coola; ☺ 10am-6pm Jun-Sep) Oodles of info and advice (get the trail guide).

ℹ Getting There & Away

BC Ferries (☑ 888-223-3779; www.bcferries. com) runs direct ferries connecting Port Hardy to Bella Coola, but to get to Prince Rupert from Bella Coola requires a transfer in Bella Bella, a small Inside Passage town – a major inconvenience. Schedules allow a trip every few days in summer (much less often in winter).

There are no buses along Hwy 20 from Williams Lake, but you can get to Bella Coola by charter plane. **Pacific Coastal Airlines** (☑ 800-663-2872; www.pacificcoastal.com) has daily one-hour flights from Vancouver.

NORTHERN BRITISH COLUMBIA

Northern British Columbia is where you'll truly feel that you've crossed that ethereal border into some place different. Nowhere else are the rich cultures of Canada's indigenous people so keenly felt, from the Haida on Haida Gwaii to the Tsimshian on the mainland. Nowhere else does land so exude mystery, whether it's the storm-shrouded coast and islands or the silent majesty of glaciers carving passages through entire mountain ranges. And nowhere else is so alive with fabled fauna, from orcas to moose to grizzlies.

It's also a region of promise. Highways such as the fabled Alaska or the awe-inspiring Stewart-Cassiar encourage adventure, discovery or even a new life. Here, your

---

GREAT BEAR RAINFOREST

It's the last major tract of coastal temperate rainforest left on the planet. The Great Bear Rainforest is a wild region of islands, fjords and towering peaks. Covering 64,000 sq km (7% of British Columbia), it stretches south from Alaska along the BC coast and Haida Gwaii to roughly Campbell River on Vancouver Island (which isn't itself part of the forest). The forests and waters are remarkably rich in life: whales, salmon, eagles, elk, otters and more thrive. Remote river valleys are lined with forests of old Sitka spruce, Pacific silver fir and various cedars that are often 100m tall and 1500 years old.

In 2016, BC's provincial government announced that 85% of the Great Bear Rainforest region would be permanently protected from industrial logging. For an introduction to the continuing campaign to save this area, head to www.savethegreatbear.org.

From Bella Coola you can arrange boat trips and treks to magical places in the Great Bear, including hidden rivers where you might see a rare **Kermode bear**, a white-furred offshoot of the black bear known in tribal legend as the 'spirit bear' and the namesake of the rainforest.

place next to nature will never be in doubt; you'll revel in your own insignificance.

Prince Rupert

📍 250, 778 / POP 12,220

People are always 'discovering' Prince Rupert, and realizing what a find it is. This intriguing town with a gorgeous harbor is not just a transportation hub for ferries heading south to Vancouver Island, west to Haida Gwaii and north to Alaska: it's a destination in its own right. It has two excellent museums, fine restaurants and a culture that draws much from its indigenous heritage. It may rain 220 days a year, but that doesn't stop the drip-dry locals enjoying activities in the misty mountains and waterways.

Prince Rupert's economic driver is its deep, ice-free anchorage and port. International freighters use the container port year-round and an increasing number of cruise ships turn up in summer. Plentiful salmon drew dozens of canneries to the coast in the 1800s, while Prince Rupert once enjoyed the title of 'halibut capital of the world'.

◉ Sights & Activities

A short walk from the center, Cow Bay is a delightful place for a stroll. The eponymous spotted decor is everywhere, but somehow avoids seeming clichéd. There are shops, cafes and a good view of the waterfront, especially from the docks at the Atlin Terminal.

You'll see totem poles all around town; two flank the statue of Charlie Hays beside City Hall on 3rd Ave. Also watch around town for more than 30 huge murals adorning buildings. Noted artist Jeff King paints history and nature.

Among the many local walks, a good place to start is the Butze Rapids Trail, a 4.5km loop beginning 6km south of town. It has interpretive signs.

Further afield, Khutzeymateen Grizzly Bear Sanctuary is a natural area home to more than 50 of the giants; it can be visited through Prince Rupert Adventure Tours.

★ North Pacific Cannery
National Historic Site   HISTORIC SITE
(📞 250-628-3538; www.northpacificcannery.ca; 1889 Skeena Dr; adult/child $12/8; ⊙10am-5pm daily Jul & Aug, Tue-Sun May, Jun & Sep) Explore the history of fishing and canning along the Skeena River. This fascinating all-wood complex was used from 1889 to 1968; exhib-

its document the miserable conditions of the workers, and tours cover the industrial process or cannery life. Prince Rupert Transit has bus service to the site. Situated about 20km south of Prince Rupert, near the town of Port Edward.

★ Museum of Northern BC   MUSEUM
(📞 250-624-3207; www.museumofnorthernbc. com; 100 1st Ave W; adult/child $6/2; ⊙9am-5pm daily Jun-Aug, Tue-Sat Sep-May) Residing in a building styled after an indigenous longhouse, this museum is a must-see. It shows how local civilizations enjoyed sustainable cultures that lasted for thousands of years. The displays include a wealth of excellent Haida, Gitksan and Tsimshian art and plenty of info on totem poles. The bookstore is excellent.

★ Prince Rupert
Adventure Tours   WILDLIFE
(📞 250-627-9166; www.adventuretours.net; 205 Cow Bay Rd; bear tours $290, whale tours $145) Excellent boat tours include Khutzeymateen grizzly-watching trips (from mid-May to early August) and whale tours (August and September). Trips can last many hours as you track the region's rich wildlife.

🛏 Sleeping

Black Rooster Inn & Apartments   INN $
(📞 250-627-5337; www.blackrooster.ca; 501 6th Ave W; r from $85; 🅿❄🐾🛜) This bright and friendly renovated house just 400m up the hill from the center has a patio and an appealing common room. Rooms range from spartan singles to large apartments.

Cow Bay Pioneer Guesthouse   HOSTEL $
(📞 250-624-2334; www.pioneerprincerupert.com; 167 3rd Ave E; dm/r from $30/70; 🅿❄🛜) Located between Cow Bay and downtown, bright blue Pioneer Guesthouse has spotless, compact rooms accented with vibrant colors. Besides the mixed dorms there are two rooms with en suite and a two-bedroom master suite. There's a small kitchen and barbecue facilities out back.

★ Eagle Bluff B&B   B&B $$
(📞 250-627-4955; www.eaglebluff.ca; 201 Cow Bay Rd; r from $95; ❄🐾🛜) In an ideal location on Cow Bay, this pier-side B&B is in a heritage building that has a striking red-and-white paint job. Inside, the seven rooms have harbor views – some quite spectacular; two share baths.

★ **Crest Hotel**   HOTEL **$$**

(☑ 250-624-6771; www.cresthotel.bc.ca; 222 1st Ave W; r from $130; P ⊜ ❄ 🛜) Prince Rupert's premier hotel has harbor-view rooms that are worth every penny, right down to the built-in bay-window seats with loaner binoculars. Avoid the smallish rooms overlooking the parking lot. Suites are opulent.

🍴 Eating & Drinking

Cowpuccino's   CAFE **$**

(☑ 250-627-1395; 25 Cow Bay Rd; coffee from $2.50; ⊙ 7am-9pm, to 6pm Sat & Sun; 🛜) This woodsy local cafe will make you forget the rain with its coffee and fine selection of baked goods (great cookies) and sandwiches. Good for picnics or eating in.

★ **Dolly's Fish Market**   SEAFOOD **$$**

(☑ 250-624-6090; www.dollysfishmarket.com; 7 Cow Bay Rd; chowder from $4.95; ⊙ 11am-9pm) It's hard to miss bright red Dolly's as you wander around Cow Bay. This is seafood country and you can't go wrong with Dolly's legendary chowders, in three different sizes ($4.95 to $10.95), cream or tomato base, or go for the superb Boston clam chowder. Lots of other options too, such as oysters, prawns and classic fish-and-chips.

★ **Charley's Lounge**   PUB FOOD **$$**

(☑ 250-624-6771; www.cresthotel.bc.ca; 222 1st Ave W, Crest Hotel; mains from $14; ⊙ noon-10pm) Locals flock to trade gossip while gazing out over the harbor from the heated patio. The food matches the view: the pub menu features some of Rupert's best seafood.

Fukasaku   JAPANESE **$$**

(☑ 250-627-7874; www.fukasaku.ca; 215 Cow Bay Rd, Atlin Terminal; mains from $15; ⊙ noon-2pm & 5-8:30pm Tue-Sat) 🌿 This excellent sushi place has a menu crafted with certified sustainability in mind. Enjoy uberfresh seafood in rolls, sashimi, *donburi* etc. The dining area is properly minimalist.

★ **Wheelhouse Brewing Company**   MICROBREWERY

(☑ 250-624-2739; www.wheelhousebrewing.com; 217 1 Ave E; ⊙ 4pm-late Wed-Fri, from noon Sat, to 9pm Sun) This rollicking little brewpub is the project of three buddies who are knocking out some of Northern BC's best microbrews. You can find their beer all over town, but here at home base they serve fresh beer right from the taps. Strictly a drinking spot with minimal snacks.

ℹ Information

Prince Rupert Visitor Center (☑ 250-624-5637; www.visitprincerupert.com; 215 Cow Bay Rd, Atlin Terminal; ⊙ 9am-6pm) Has regional info.

ℹ Getting There & Away

AIR

Prince Rupert Airport (☑ 250-624-6274; www.ypr.ca) is located on Digby Island, across the harbor from town. The trip involves a bus and ferry; pickup is at the Prince Rupert Hotel about two hours before flight time. Confirm all the details with your airline or the airport. Call 250-622-2222 for up-to-date details.

Air Canada (www.aircanada.com) flies to Vancouver.

BOAT

BC Ferries (☑ 250-386-3431; www.bcferries. com) Sails the Inside Passage run to Port Hardy, hailed for its amazing scenery. There are three services per week in summer and one per week in winter. There is also service to Haida Gwaii.

BUS

BC Bus North (☑ 1-844-564-7494; www.bcbus. ca) runs twice per week return along Hwy 16 connecting Prince George, Smithers and Prince Rupert.

TRAIN

VIA Rail (www.viarail.ca) operates tri-weekly services to Prince George (12½ hours) and, after an overnight stop, on to Jasper, AB (another 7½ hours).

Haida Gwaii

Haida Gwaii forms a dagger-shaped archipelago of some 450 islands lying 80km west of the BC coast, and offers a magical trip for those who make the effort. The number-one attraction here is remote Gwaii Haanas National Park, which makes up the bottom third of the archipelago. Attention has long focused on the many unique species of flora and fauna to the extent that 'Canada's Galápagos' is a popular moniker. But each year it becomes more apparent that the real soul of the islands is the Haida culture itself.

Haida reverence for the environment is protecting the last stands of superb old-growth rainforests, where the spruce and cedars are some of the world's largest. Amid this sparsely populated, wild and rainy place are bald eagles, bears and much more wildlife. Offshore in marine-protected waters, sea lions, whales and orcas abound, and once-rare right whales and sea otters have been spotted.

◉ Sights

★ Gwaii Haanas National Park Reserve, National Marine Conservation Area Reserve & Haida Heritage Site   NATIONAL PARK

(☑ 250-559-8818; www.pc.gc.ca/en/pn-np/bc/gwaiihaanas) This huge Unesco World Heritage site encompasses Moresby and 137 smaller islands at its southern end. It combines a time-capsule look at abandoned Haida villages with hot springs, amazing natural beauty and some of the continents best kayaking. A visit demands advance planning as the number of visitors entering the park each day is limited. The easiest way is to take a guided trip with a licensed operator; access to the park is by boat or floatplane only.

Archaeological finds have documented more than 500 ancient Haida sites, including villages and burial caves throughout the islands. The most famous village is **SGang Gwaay** (Ninstints) on Anthony Island, where rows of weathered totem poles stare eerily out to sea. Other major sights include the ancient village of **Skedans**, on Louise Island, and **Hotspring Island**, whose natural hot springs are back on after being disrupted by earthquakes in 2012. The sites are protected by Haida Gwaii caretakers, who live on the islands in summer.

In 2013 the magnificent **Gwaii Haanas Legacy Pole** was raised at Windy Bay, the first new pole in the protected area in 130 years.

The easiest way to get into the park is with a tour company. Parks Canada (p237) has a lists of licensed operators on its website. Many operators can also set you up with rental kayaks (average per day/week $60/300) and gear for independent travel.

To visit independently, you must make a reservation, pay a visitor use fee (adult $20 per day, child free) and attend a 90-minute orientation. The number of daily reservations is limited, so plan well in advance, especially for the busiest period of July to mid-August. Details of the requirements are on the excellent Parks Canada website, which has links to the essential annual trip planner. The Parks Canada office is next to the Haida Heritage Centre at Kay Llnagaay.

★ Haida Heritage Centre at Kay Llnagaay   MUSEUM

(☑ 250-559-7885; www.haidaheritagecentre.com; Second Beach Rd. Hwy 16, Skidegate; adult/child $16/5; ⊙ 9am-5pm Jul & Aug, reduced hours Sep-Jun) One of the top attractions in the north is this marvelous cultural center. With exhibits on history, wildlife and culture, it would be enough reason to visit the islands just by itself. The rich traditions of the Haida are fully explored in galleries, programs and work areas, where contemporary artists create works such as the totem poles lining the shore. Look for the remarkable model of Skidegate before colonial times.

Crystal Cabin   GALLERY

(☑ 250-557-4383; www.crystalcabingallery.com; 778a Richardson Rd, Tlell; ⊙ 9am-6pm May-Sep, reduced hours Oct-Apr) The works of 20 Haida artists are featured at the jewelry workshop of April and Sarah Dutheil, second-generation artisans and sisters who were taught by their father, local legend and authority on island geology, Dutes. April has written on Haida Gwaii agate collecting and is happy to explain Dutes' Tlell Stone Circle, which is just outside the cabin. There are many forms of art here, including carvings from argillite, a local rock that can only be carved by Haida artisans.

Naikoon Provincial Park   PARK

(☑ 250-626-5115; www.env.gov.bc.ca/bcparks; off Hwy 16) Much of the island's northeastern side is devoted to the beautiful 726-sq-km Naikoon Provincial Park, which combines sand dunes and low sphagnum bogs, surrounded by stunted and gnarled lodgepole pine, and red and yellow cedar. The starkly beautiful **beaches** on the north coast feature strong winds, pounding surf and flotsam from across the Pacific. They can be reached via the stunning 26km-long Tow Hill Rd, east of Masset.

Wooden steps and a boardwalk make visiting the **Tow Hill Lookout** and **Blow Hole** near the end of Tow Hill Rd easy. Allow about one hour for a looping walk with many steps. A 21km loop trail traverses a good bit of the park to/from **Fife Beach** at the end of the road. The park has campsites ($18).

⚡ Activities

Away from the park, Haida Gwaii has myriad other natural places to explore on land and sea.

★**Golden Spruce Trail**　　　　WALKING
Just south of Port Clements, this is an excellent short walk (30 minutes return) through moss-covered forest featuring huge red cedar and Sitka spruce to the Yakoun River. Across the river is where the legendary Golden Spruce used to stand. To get to the trailhead, carry on through Port Clements on Bayview Dr, then for 3.5km on the gravel road.

★**Moresby Explorers**　　　　ADVENTURE
(☑250-637-2215, 800-806-7633; www.moresbyexplorers.com; 365 Beach Rd, Sandspit; day tours from $250) Offers one-day Zodiac tours, including the Louise Island trip that takes in the town of Skedans and its important totem poles, as well as much longer trips (the four-day trip is highly recommended). Also rents kayaks and gear, and provides logistics.

Haida Style Expeditions　　　　CULTURAL
(☑250-637-1151; www.haidastyle.com; Second Beach Rd/Hwy 16, Skidegate; tours per person from $250; ☺Apr-Sep) Buzz through the Gwaii Haanas National Park Reserve (p235) in a large inflatable boat. This Haida-run outfit runs four different day tours (eight to 12 hours) that together take in the most important sights in the park.

🛏 Sleeping

★**Premier Creek Lodging**　　　　INN $
(☑888-322-3388, 250-559-8415; www.haidagwaii.net/premier; 3101 Oceanview Dr, QCC; s/d from $45/75; P❈✳🛜) Dating from 1910, this is the top place to stay in the town of Queen Charlotte. The lodge has 14 rooms that range from tiny but great-value singles to spacious rooms with views, kitchen and porch.

Agate Beach Campground　　　　CAMPGROUND $
(☑250-557-4390; www.env.gov.bc.ca/bcparks; Tow Hill Rd, North Shore, Naikoon Provincial Park; tent & RV sites $18; P) This stunning, wind-whipped campground is right on the beach on the north shore. Frolic on the sand, hunt for its namesake rocks and see if you can snare some flotsam.

★**Cacilia's B&B**　　　　B&B $$
(☑250-557-4664; www.facebook.com/caciliasbedbreakfast; 36914 Hwy 16, Tlell; r incl breakfast from $110; P❈✳🛜) Cacilia's is in a lovely spot in Tlell, a 30-minute drive north from the ferry landing. There are seven rooms, four with private bath, in a big log building, with patchy wi-fi and a friendly family atmos-

phere among guests. Cacilia prepares a tasty breakfast each morning using local produce, and the beach is a short walk away through the dunes.

All the Beach You Can Eat　　　　CABIN $$
(☑250-626-9091; www.allthebeachyoucaneat.com; Km 15, Tow Hill Rd, North Shore; cabins from $120; P) 🌊 On beautiful North Beach, five cabins are perched in the dunes, back from the wide swath of sand that runs for miles east and west. Like other properties with rental cabins out here, there is no electricity; cooking and lighting are fueled by propane. It's off the grid and out of this world.

🍴 Eating & Drinking

The best selection of restaurants is in Queen Charlotte (QCC), and there are also a few in Skidegate and Masset. There is a simple pub with food in Port Clements. Good supermarkets are found in QCC and Masset.

★**Jags Beanstalk**
Bistro & Beds　　　　CANADIAN $
(☑250-559-8826; www.jagsbeanstalk.com; 100 16 Hwy, Skidegate; mains from $10; ☺7:30am-4pm Mon-Fri, 9am-4pm Sat) Fresh, wholesome food delivered with speedy, friendly service about 1.5km north of the ferry terminal. Great coffee, pizzas, tacos and salads, with an effort to source ingredients locally. It also has cozy guest rooms above the coffee shop.

Moon Over
Naikoon Bakery　　　　BAKERY $
(☑250-626-5064; 16443 Tow Hill Rd, Masset; snacks from $3; ☺8am-5pm Jun-Aug) Embodying the spirit of its location, on a road to the end of everything, this tiny community center and bakery is housed in an old school bus in a clearing about 6km east of Masset. The baked goods and coffee are brilliant. Keep your eyes open for the sign as the bus can't be seen from the road.

Queen B's　　　　CAFE $
(☑250-559-4463; www.facebook.com/queenbscafe; 3201 Wharf St, QCC; mains from $3; ☺8am-5pm Mon-Sat) This funky place in Queen Charlotte excels at baked goods, which emerge from the oven all day long. There are tables with water views outside, and lots of local art inside.

Haida House at Tllaal　　　　SEAFOOD $$
(☑855-557-4600; www.haidahouse.com; 2087 Beitush Rd, Tlell; mains from $20; ☺5-7:30pm Tue-Sun mid-May–mid-Sep) This Haida-run restaurant

next to the river in Tlell at the end of Beitush Rd has excellent, creative seafood and other dishes with island accents, such as Haida favorites with berries. Also rents plush rooms at this magical spot in the forest.

★ **Daddy Cool's Public House at Mile Zero** PUB
(☑250-626-3210; www.daddycools.ca; Collison Ave, Masset; ⊙9am-2am, hours can vary) Can't go wrong at Daddy Cool's in Masset with a popular pub on one side and a quiet dining room specializing in pub grub on the other. The eating side is family-friendly, while the pub side usually stays open until everyone has gone home. These guys are onto it and also run a liquor store and a taxi service.

ℹ Information

Parks Canada (☑250-559-8818, reservations 877-559-8818; www.pc.gc.ca/en/pn-np/bc/gwaiihaanas; Haida Heritage Centre at Kay Llnagaay, Skidegate; ⊙office 8:30am-noon & 1-4:30pm Mon-Fri) Main Parks Canada office for Haida Gwaii. Download the Gwaii Haanas National Park trip planner from the website.
Queen Charlotte Visitor Centre (☑250-559-8316; www.queencharlottevisitorcentre.com; 3220 Wharf St, QCC; ⊙9am-7pm Mon-Sat, noon-6pm Sun May-Sep, shorter hours other times; ☎) This handy visitor center can make advance excursion bookings by phone. There's a gift shop, toilets and wi-fi.

ℹ Getting There & Away

The main airport for Haida Gwaii is at Sandspit on Moresby Island, 12km east of the ferry landing at Aliford Bay. Note that reaching the airport from Graham Island is time-consuming: eg if your flight is at 3:30pm, you'll need to line up at the car ferry at Skidegate Landing at 12:30pm (earlier in summer). **Air Canada** (www.aircanada.com) flies daily between Sandspit and Vancouver.

There's also a small airport 2km east of Masset that has daily flights from Vancouver with **Pacific Coastal Air** (www.pacificcoastal.com). Daily seaplane services between Prince Rupert and Masset are flown by **Inland Air** (www.inlandair.bc.ca).
BC Ferries (☑250-386-3431; www.bcferries.com) is the most popular way to reach the islands. Mainland ferries dock at Skidegate Landing on Graham Island, which houses 80% of residents. Services run between Prince Rupert and Skidegate Landing five times a week in summer and three times a week in winter (adult $39 to $48, children half-price, cars $139 to $169; six to seven hours). Cabins are useful for overnight schedules (from $90).

ℹ Getting Around

The main road on Graham Island is Hwy 16, the first part of the Yellowhead Hwy, which is fully paved. It links Skidegate with Masset, 101km north, passing the small towns of Tlell and Port Clements. The principal town is Queen Charlotte (previously Queen Charlotte City and still known by its old QCC acronym), 7km west of Skidegate. Off paved Hwy 16, most roads are gravel or worse. There is no public transit.

BC Ferries, with its MV Kwuna car ferry, links Graham and Moresby Islands at Skidegate Landing and Alliford Bay (adult/child $11/5.50, cars from $25, 20 minutes, from 7am to 6pm).

Eagle Transit (☑250-559-4461, 877-747-4461; www.eagletransit.net; airport shuttle adult/child $30/15) buses meet Sandspit flights and serve Skidegate and QCC.

Renting a car can cost roughly the same ($60 to $100 per day) as bringing one over on the ferry. Local companies include **Budget** (☑250-637-5688; www.budget.com; Sandspit Airport). There are several small, locally owned firms, but the number of rental cars on Haida Gwaii is limited, so think ahead.

You can rent bikes at the small **Sandspit Airport Visitor Center** (☑250-637-5362; Sandspit Airport; ⊙9:30-11:30am & 1.30-4pm) for $30 per day. **Green Coast** (☑250-637-1093; www.gck-ayaking.com; 3302 Oceanview Dr, QCC; per day $30) rents bikes in Queen Charlotte, while **Masset Bikes** (☑250-626-8939; www.massetbikes.com; 1900 Towhill Rd, Masset; per day from $30) has a good selection of rentals at Masset Airport.

Prince Rupert to Prince George

You can cover the 725km on Hwy 16 between BC's Princes in a day or a week. There's nothing that's an absolute must-see, but there's much to divert and cause you to pause if so inclined. With the notable exception of Skeena River, the scenery along much of the road won't fill your memory card, but it is a pleasing mix of mountains and rivers.

Prince Rupert to Smithers

For the first 145km out of Prince Rupert to Terrace, the Yellowhead Hwy (Hwy 16) hugs the wide and wild **Skeena River**. This is four-star scenic driving and you'll see glaciers and jagged peaks across the waters. Keep an eye out for anglers fishing for salmon on the Skeena River 10 months of the year – and also for a Kermodei or 'spirit bear', a cream-colored subspecies of black bear that is becoming increasingly imperiled by habitat loss.

The industrial timber town of **Terrace** doesn't have much to interest visitors. From there, Hwy 16 continues following the narrowing Skeena River valley 93km east to Kitwanga Junction, where the Stewart-Cassiar Hwy (Hwy 37) strikes north toward the Yukon and Alaska.

From Kitwanga Junction, the Yellowhead Hwy (Hwy 16) continues 115km to Smithers, following first the Skeena River, then the Bulkley River from where it joins the Skeena at Hazelton.

'Ksan Historical
Village & Museum   HISTORIC SITE
(☑ 250-842-5544; www.ksan.org; off Hwy 16, Hazelton; from $2; ☺ 10am-9pm Jun-Aug, shorter hours Sep-May) Just east of Kitwanga and the start of Hwy 37 is the Hazelton area, the center of some interesting indigenous sites, including this historical village. The re-created site of the Gitksan people features longhouses, a museum, various outbuildings and totem poles. The Eagle House Cafe is open 10am to 3pm daily.

Smithers

☑ 250, 778 / POP 10,600
Smithers is an appealing town with a cute old downtown area, roughly halfway between Prince Rupert and Prince George. It's the hub of the surprisingly vibrant Bulkley Valley cultural scene and makes for a good overnight stop. Make sure to get off Hwy 16 on Main St and have a wander around downtown.

Bulkley Valley Museum   MUSEUM
(☑ 250-847-5322; www.bvmuseum.org; 1425 Main St; by donation; ☺ 9am-5pm Mon-Sat) **FREE**
Sharing the lovely old Smithers Court House building of 1925 with the **Smithers Art Gallery** on the corner of Main St and Hwy 16, this museum does a great job of making local history interesting and engaging. Lots of old photos plus a number of changing exhibitions.

This is the traditional territory of the Witsuwit'en people and a permanent exhibit features artifacts, images and information about their history and culture.

Prestige Hudson
Bay Lodge   HOTEL **$$**
(☑ 250-847-4581; www.prestigehotelsandresorts.com; 3251 E Hwy 16; r from $125; P ☻ ✳ 🖤) Part of a BC-wide chain, this place has a variety of well-appointed guest rooms and suites at the southern entrance to town on Hwy 16. Two on-site restaurants cover fine dining and a sports bar and grill, while there are complimentary bicycles, laundry and fitness room.

★ **Telly's Grill**   MEDITERRANEAN **$$**
(☑ 250-847-001; www.facebook.com/tellysgrill; 3843 4 Ave; mains from $15; ☺ 4:30-9:30pm Mon-Sat) Don't let the drab exterior of the building fool you, this is one of the top places to eat in Northern BC. The Canadian-Mediterranean fusion menu offers a stunning array of mains including a Hot Chicken Caesar and Telly's mum's lasagne. Telly's comes complete with a photo of Telly Savalas sucking a lollipop and a Kojak burger on the menu.

★ **Smithers Brewing Co**   MICROBREWERY
(☑ 778-640-2739; www.smithersbrewing.com; 3832 3 Ave; ☺ 2-8pm) Try the local brews just off Main St at Smithers Brewing Co in the custom-made taproom with timber framing and stunning bar tops. Ten taps pour mainstay beers and rotating seasonal offerings, as well as cider and an in-house kombucha. Our favorite is the Scatterbrain IPA.

① Information

Smithers Visitor Centre (☑ 250-847-5072; www.tourismsmithers.com; 1411 Court St; ☺ 9am-5pm; 🖤) Can steer you to excellent mountain biking, white-water rafting and climbing.

❶ Getting There & Away

Central Mountain Air (☑ 888-865-8585; www.flycma.com) With its home base at Smithers Airport, CMA serves 16 communities across BC and Alberta, including Vancouver, Calgary and Edmonton.

VIA Rail (www.viarail.ca) trains stop in Smithers on runs between Prince Rupert and Prince George.

BC Bus North (p234) runs twice per week return connecting Prince George, Smithers and Prince Rupert.

Smithers is on Hwy 16, the Yellowhead Hwy, 371km west of Prince George and 347km east of Prince Rupert.

Smithers to Prince George

Heading south and then east from Smithers along the Yellowhead Hwy (Hwy 16) for 146km will have you passing through **Burns Lake**, the center of a popular fishing district. Continue another 128km toward **Vanderhoof**, where you can either detour north on Hwy 27 to Fort St James or carry on along Hwy 16 for 100km to Prince George.

Fort St James National Historic Site
HISTORIC SITE

(☑ 250-996-7191; www.pc.gc.ca; Kwah Rd; adult/child $7.80/free; ☺ 9am-5pm Jun-Sep) From Vanderhoof, Hwy 27 heads 66km north to Fort St James National Historic Site. The former Hudson's Bay Company trading post that's on the tranquil southeastern shore of Stuart Lake has been restored to its 1896 glory.

Prince George

☑ 250, 778 / POP 78,675

In First Nations times, before outsiders arrived, Prince George was called Lheidli T'Enneh, which means 'people of the confluence,' an appropriate name given that the Nechako and Fraser Rivers converge here. Today the name would be just as fitting, although it's the confluence of highways that matters most. A mill town since 1807, it is a vital BC crossroads, and you're unlikely to visit the north without passing through at least once.

Hwy 97 from the south cuts through the center of town on its way north to Dawson Creek (360km) and the Alaska Hwy. Hwy 16 becomes Victoria St as it runs through town westward to Prince Rupert (724km), and east to Jasper (380km) and Edmonton. The downtown, no beauty-contest winner, is compact and has some good restaurants.

◉ Sights

★ **Northern Lights Estate Winery** WINERY
(☑ 250-564-1112; www.northernlightswinery.ca; 745 Prince George Pulpmill Rd; tastings $5; ☺ 10am-9pm Mon-Thu, to 10pm Fri & Sat, to 5pm Sun) On the northern banks of the Nechako River, this is BC's northernmost winery, specializing in wines made from fruit produced on-site, including blueberry, strawberry, haskap, gooseberry, apple, cherry, raspberry, blackcurrant and rhubarb. Try Seduction, its tasty strawberry and rhubarb special. Taste four wines for $5, or better yet, savor a bottle with a meal at its popular riverside **bistro**.

Two Rivers Gallery ARTS CENTER
(☑ 250-614-7800; www.tworiversgallery.ca; 725 Canada Games Way; adult/child $7.50/3; ☺ 10am-5pm Mon-Wed, Fri & Sat, to 9pm Thu, noon-5pm Sun) PG's public art gallery is housed in the architecturally impressive Two Rivers Gallery building at the Civic Centre and has permanent collections, changing exhibitions and a lovely gift shop. The focus is on local art, encouraging local artisans, plus teaching creativity with classes for children. Admission is free on Thursdays.

Prince George Railway & Forestry Museum MUSEUM
(☑ 250-563-7351; www.pgrfm.bc.ca; 850 River Rd, Cottonwood Island Nature Park; adult/child $8/5; ☺ 10am-5pm daily Jun-Aug, 11am-4pm Tue-Sat Sep-May) This museum honors trains, the beaver and local lore. It's located in **Cottonwood Island Nature Park**, north of the train station, which has sylvan walks alongside the river.

⌨ Sleeping & Eating

Coast Inn of the North HOTEL $$
(☑ 250-563-0121; www.coasthotels.com; 770 Brunswick St; r from $100; P♿❄🐾🛜❄) One of the nicest stays in a town with few options, the Coast is a high-rise with 153 very comfy rooms, some with balcony. There's an indoor pool, which is handy during the long months of cold temperatures. It's close to the center and its nightlife.

Nancy O's PUB FOOD $$
(☑ 250-562-8066; www.nancyos.ca; 1261 3rd Ave; mains from $15; ☺ 11am-late Mon-Fri, from 10am Sat, to 3pm Sun) Locally sourced ingredients are combined to create fabulous food at Nancy O's: burgers, veggie specials, a great avocado salad and a truly amazing *steak frites*. The bottled beer selection is fab

(Belgian and BC), and there's live music and DJs many nights.

★ **Twisted Cork** CANADIAN **$$$**
(☑ 250-561-5550; www.twisted-cork.com; 1157 5 Ave; dinner mains from $25; ☺ 11am-9pm Mon-Thu, to 11pm Fri & Sat, 5-9pm Sun) As good as it gets in PG, the Twisted Cork will grab your attention with its gorgeous stone building and attractive wooden decor. The meals are superb. For dinner, mains include the elk tenderloin ($50), bison pie ($27) and wild-game burger ($27).

★ **CrossRoads Brewing** MICROBREWERY
(☑ 250-614-2337; www.crossroadscraft.com; 508 George St; ☺ 11.30am-late) PG's local microbrewery features an impressive taproom, allowing you to see into the production facility. There are nine standard brews plus seasonal favorites, a kitchen producing everything from snacks to pizzas to Kobe beef ribs and an extremely convivial atmosphere. Try the Fast Lane IPA, heavy on hops, and head outside to the patio if the weather is playing ball.

❶ Information

Prince George Visitor Centre (☑ 250-562-3700; www.tourismpg.com; 1300 1st Ave, VIA Rail station; ☺ 8am-6pm Jun-Aug, shorter hours other times; ☎) This excellent visitor center in the VIA Rail station building has info on Northern BC and can make bookings such as ferry tickets. Loans out free bikes and fishing rods.

❶ Getting There & Away

Prince George Airport (☑ 250-963-2400; www.pgairport.ca; 4141 Airport Rd) is off Hwy 97. **Air Canada** (☑ 888-247-2262; www.aircanada.com) and **Westjet** (☑ 888-937-8538; www.westjet.com) serve Vancouver.

VIA Rail (www.viarail.ca; 1300 1st Ave) trains head west three times a week to Prince Rupert (12½ hours) and east three times a week to Jasper, AB (7½ hours). Through-passengers from either direction must overnight in Prince George.

Adventure Charters (www.adventurecharters.ca) operates buses south from Prince George to Williams Lake, Kamloops, Hope and Surrey.

BC Bus North (p234) runs buses either twice or once weekly on four routes:
➡ Prince George–Smithers–Prince Rupert
➡ Prince George–Dawson Creek–Fort St John
➡ Prince George–Valemount
➡ Dawson Creek–Fort Nelson

Prince George to Alberta

Look for lots of wildlife as well as some good parks along the 375km stretch of Hwy 16 that links Prince George with Jasper, just over the Alberta border. McBride, 208km east of Prince George, is the only township of any size along the way and a good spot for food and gas. Monster Mt Robson, 3954m and highest peak in the Canadian Rockies, dominates the drive up the Yellowhead Hwy to the provincial park of the same name, while the Robson Valley is also the birthplace of the mighty Fraser River that flows all the way out to the sea at Vancouver. From the Mt Robson Visitor Centre allow an hour to get to Jasper.

◉ Sights & Activities

★ **Ancient Forest / Chun T'oh Whudujut Park** PARK
(www.env.gov.bc.ca/bcparks; off Hwy 16) About 113km east of Prince George is the site of BC's newest park, established in 2016. The Ancient Forest features two trails – a 900m boardwalk (return) and a 2.3km loop trail – both of which reveal some real behemoths of the temperate inland rainforest: old-growth red cedars and hemlocks, some reaching heights of 60m, that are more than 1000 years old.

★ **Mt Robson Provincial Park** PARK
(Map p612; ☑ 250-964-2243; www.env.gov.bc.ca/bcparks; off Hwy 16) Northern BC's major mountain attraction abuts Jasper National Park, but on the BC side of the border. Uncrowded Mt Robson Provincial Park has steep glaciers, prolific wildlife and superb hiking highlighted by the Kinney Lake & Berg Lake Trails. Mt Robson itself, highest peak in the Canadian Rockies, is a stunner. Campsites are available (from $22).

★ **Kinney Lake & Berg Lake Trails** HIKING
(Map p612; www.env.gov.bc.ca/bcparks) The trailhead for this easy 2½-hour round-trip hike into gorgeous Kinney Lake (4.5km one-way; www.valemounttrails.com/kinney-lake) is 3km north of the Mt Robson Visitor Centre. A longer hike carries on from Kinney Lake to Berg Lake (23km each way; www.env.gov.bc.ca), with seven camping areas along the way. All Berg Lake hikers must check into Mt Robson Visitor Centre before heading out.

🛏 Sleeping

**Mt Robson Lodge
& Campground** CABIN, CAMPING **$$**
(☎ 250-566-4821; www.mountrobsonlodge.com;
16895 Fransworth Rd; tent & RV sites from $30,
cabins from $139; ⊙ mid-May–Sep; 🅿 🐾) This
place, 5km west of Mt Robson Park, has
a number of comfortable cabins, all with
private bath, and lovely tent and RV sites
down by the Fraser River, each with a fire-
pit. There are stunning views of Mt Robson,
plus they also run **rafting** (from $99) and
scenic **float trips** ($59).

Mt Robson Mountain River Lodge LODGE **$$**
(☎ 250-566-9899; www.mtrobson.com; cnr Hwy 16
& Swift Current Creek Rd, Mt Robson; lodges/cabins
from $150/180; 🅿 🐾 📶) On the western bor-
der of Mt Robson Provincial Park, this lodge
commands stunning views of the eponymous giant peak. There's a main building
and a couple of cabins that share a cozy,
away-from-it-all atmosphere.

ℹ Information

Mt Robson Visitor Centre (☎ 250-566-4038;
www.env.gov.bc.ca; Hwy 16; ⊙ 8am-5pm)
Great information on the park in full view of Mt
Robson. There is also a cafe (8am to 6pm), a
gift shop a petrol station here.

Stewart-Cassiar Highway

The 724km Stewart-Cassiar Hwy (Hwy 37)
is a viable and ever-more-popular route between BC and the Yukon and Alaska. But it's
more than just a means to get from Hwy 16
in BC to the Alaska Hwy in the Yukon (west
of Watson Lake) – it's a window onto one of
the largest remaining wild and woolly parts
of the province. It's also the road to Stewart
(p242), a near-mandatory detour to glaciers
and more.

Gitanyow, a mere 15km north of Hwy
16, has an unparalleled collection of totem
poles and you can often see carvers creating
more.

🛏 Sleeping & Eating

★ **Bell 2 Lodge** LODGE **$$**
(☎ 888-499-4354; www.bell2lodge.com; 249
Hwy 37; tent/RV sites from $25/32, r from $190;
🅿 🐾 ❄ 📶) This northern oasis is at the
248km mark on the Stewart-Cassiar Hwy,
241km south of Dease Lake, where Hwy
37 crosses the Bell-Irving River. There are
tent sites, RV hook-ups, plus standard and

deluxe rooms in five log chalets. There's a
restaurant and coffee shop (8am to 8pm in
summer), a hot tub and sauna complex, and
a gas station.

★ **Ripley Creek Inn** GUESTHOUSE **$$**
(☎ 250-636-2344; www.ripleycreekinn.com; 306
5th Ave, Stewart; r from $115; 🅿 🐾 📶) The 40
rooms in various heritage buildings are decorated with new and old items; decor var-
ies greatly. The Peterson House is a former
brothel. Check out the great range of options
online.

Bus SEAFOOD **$**
(☎ 250-636-9011; 6th St, Hyder, AK; mains from
$11; ⊙ noon-8pm Tue-Sun Jun-Sep) Also known
as Seafood Express, the Bus serves the tastiest seafood ever cooked in a school bus on
6th St in tiny Hyder.

ℹ Information

Check out www.stewartcassiarhighway.com.

ℹ Getting There & Away

All major roads linking to the Stewart-Cassiar Hwy
are in excellent condition. Except for areas of construction, the highway is sealed and suitable for all
vehicles. At any point, you should not be surprised
to see bears, moose and other large mammals.

There's never a distance greater than 150km
between gas stations. BC provides **road condition reports** (☎ 800-550-4997; www.drivebc.
ca). When it's dry in summer, people drive from
Stewart to Whitehorse (1043km) or from Smithers to Watson Lake (854km) in a single day,
taking advantage of the long hours of daylight.
This a real haul, so be prepared.

Alaska Highway

Even in Prince George you can start to smell
the Alaska Hwy. As you travel north along
Hwy 97, the mountains and forests give way
to gentle rolling hills and farmland. Nearing
Dawson Creek (360km), the landscape re-
sembles the prairies of Alberta. There's no
need to dawdle.

From Chetwynd you can take Hwy 29
along the wide vistas of the Peace River valley north via Hudson's Hope to join the Alaska Hwy north of Fort St John.

Dawson Creek is *the* starting point
(Mile 0) for the Alaska Hwy and it capital-
izes on this at the **Alaska Highway House**
(☎ 250-782-4714; www.tourismdawsoncreek.com;
10201 10th St, Dawson Creek; by donation; ⊙ 8am-
4pm), an engaging museum in a vintage

WORTH A TRIP

STEWART & HYDER

Awesome. Yes, the word is almost an automatic cliché, but when you gaze upon the **Salmon Glacier**, you'll understand why it was coined in the first place. This horizon-spanning expanse of ice is more than enough reason to make the 67km detour off Hwy 37 at Meziadin Junction, 156km north of Kitwanga. In fact, your first confirmation comes when you encounter the iridescent blue expanse of the **Bear Glacier** looming over Hwy 37A.

The sibling border towns of **Stewart** and **Hyder**, AK, perch on the coast at the head of the Portland Canal. Stewart, once a boomtown of 10,000 thanks to gold and silver mines, is the much more businesslike of the pair, and has excellent places to stay and eat.

Among several campgrounds and motels, Stewart's real star is Ripley Creek Inn (p241). The 40 rooms in various heritage buildings are stylishly decorated with new and old items, and there's a huge collection of vintage toasters. For more information on Stewart see www.districtofstewart.com.

Hyder ekes out an existence as a 'ghost town.' Some 40,000 tourists come through every summer, avoiding any border hassle from US customs officers (because there aren't any), although going back to Stewart you'll pass through beady-eyed Canadian customs. It has muddy streets and two businesses of note: the **Glacier Inn** (☑250-636-9248; International St, Hyder, Alaska; ⊘noon-late), a bar you'll enjoy if you ignore the touristy 'get Hyderized' shot-swilling shtick; and the Bus (p241), which has the tastiest seafood ever cooked in a school bus. *This* is Hyder.

The enormous, horizon-filling Salmon Glacier is 37km beyond Hyder, up a winding dirt road that's OK for cars when it's dry. Some 3km into the drive, you'll pass the **Fish Creek viewpoint**, an area alive with bears and doomed salmon in late summer.

building overlooking the milepost. The nearby downtown blocks make a good stroll and have free wi-fi, and there's a **walking tour** of the old buildings. The **visitor center** (☑250-782-9595; www.tourismdawsoncreek.com; 900 Alaska Ave, Dawson Creek; ⊘7:30am-6pm mid-May–Sep, shorter hours other times; ☎) is housed in the old train station and has lots of Alaska Hwy info. Note that this corner of BC stays on Mountain Standard Time year-round. So in winter, the time is the same as Alberta, one hour later than BC. In summer, the time is the same as Vancouver.

Now begins the big drive. Heading northwest from Dawson Creek, you'll pass through Fort St John on the 430km stretch to **Fort Nelson** – it gives little hint of the wonders to come.

Fort Nelson has seen boom and bust in recent years with the fluctuation of oil prices. This is the last place of any size on the Alaska Hwy until Whitehorse in the Yukon – most 'towns' along the route are little more than a gas station and motel or two.

Around 140km west of Fort Nelson, **Stone Mountain Provincial Park** (www.env.gov.bc.ca/bcparks; Alaska Hwy) has hiking trails, with backcountry camping and a campground. The stretches of road often have dense concentrations of wildlife: moose, bears, bison, wolves, elk and much more. From here, the Alaska Hwy rewards whatever effort it took getting this far.

A further 75km brings you to **Muncho Lake Provincial Park** (www.env.gov.bc.ca/bcparks; Alaska Hwy), centered on the emerald-green lake of the same name and boasting spruce forests, vast rolling mountains and some truly breathtaking scenery. There are two campgrounds by the lake, plus a few lodges scattered along the highway.

Finally, **Liard River Hot Springs Provincial Park** (☑250-427-5452; www.env.gov.bc.ca/bcparks; 75100-81198 Alaska Hwy; adult/child $5/3) has a steamy ecosystem that allows a whopping 250 species of plants to thrive. After a long day in the car, you'll thrive, too, in the soothing waters. From here it's 220km to Watson Lake and the Yukon.

Yukon Territory

Best Places to Eat

➡ Joe's Wood-fired Pizza (p264)

➡ Klondike Kate's (p264)

➡ Klondike Rib & Salmon (p249)

➡ Antoinette's (p250)

Best Places to Stay

➡ Coast High Country Inn (p249)

➡ Moose Creek Lodge (p260)

➡ Bombay Peggy's (p264)

➡ Klondike Kate's Cabins (p264)

Why Go?

This vast and thinly populated wilderness, where most four-legged species far outnumber humans, has a grandeur and beauty only appreciated by experience. Few places in the world today have been so unchanged over the course of time. Indigenous people, having eked out survival for thousands of years, hunt and trap as they always have. The Klondike Gold Rush of 1898 was the Yukon's high point of population, yet even its heritage is ephemeral, easily erased by time.

Any visit will mean much time outdoors: Canada's five tallest mountains and the world's largest ice fields below the Arctic are all within Kluane National Park, while canoe expeditions down the Yukon River are epic. And don't forget the people: get set to appreciate the offbeat vibe of Dawson City and the bustle of Whitehorse, and join the growing numbers of people who've discovered the Yukon thanks to TV shows such as *Yukon Gold* and *Dr Oakley: Yukon Vet*.

When to Go
Dawson City

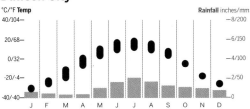

Nov–Apr Days of snowy winter solitude end when the river ice breaks up.	**Jun–Aug** Summers are short but warm, with long hours of daylight.	**Sep** You can feel the north winds coming. Trees erupt in color, crowds thin and places close.

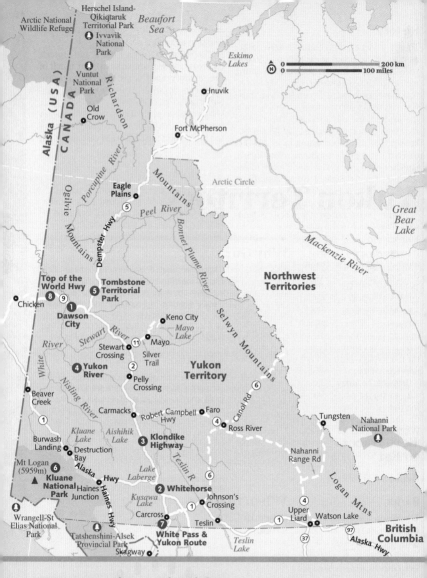

Yukon Territory Highlights

1 Dawson City (p260)
Loving the vibe of Canada's funkiest historic town.

2 Whitehorse (p245)
Spending an extra day in this surprising, culture-filled city.

3 Klondike Hwy (p258)
Spotting moose and bears along this stunning road – they may outnumber cars.

4 Yukon River (p248) Living the dream of paddlers on this legendary river.

5 Tombstone Territorial Park (p266) Losing yourself in this vast park, where the grandeur of the North envelops you.

6 Kluane National Park (p256) Naming one of the 100 unnamed glaciers in this Unesco-listed park.

7 White Pass & Yukon Route (p258) Enjoying the ride on the fabled gold rush–era railroad.

8 Top of the World Highway (p265) Marveling at the wilderness from Dawson City to Chicken, Alaska.

History

There's evidence that humans were eating animals in the Yukon some 15,000 to 30,000 years ago, depending on your carbon-dating method of choice. However, it's widely agreed that these people were descended from those who crossed over from today's Siberia while the land bridge was in place. There's little recorded history otherwise, although it's known that a volcanic eruption in AD 800 covered much of the southern Yukon in ash. Similarities to the Athapaskan people of the southwest United States have suggested that these groups may have left the Yukon after the volcano ruined hunting and fishing.

In the 1840s Robert Campbell, a Hudson's Bay Company explorer, was the first European to travel the district. Fur traders, prospectors, whalers and missionaries all followed. In 1870 the region became part of the Northwest Territories (NWT). But it was 1896 when the Yukon literally hit the map, after gold was found in a tributary of the Klondike River, near what was to become Dawson City. The ensuing gold rush attracted upward of 40,000 hopefuls from around the world. Towns sprouted overnight to support the numerous wealth seekers, who were quite unprepared for the ensuing depravities.

In 1898 the Yukon became a separate territory, with Dawson City as its capital. Building the Alaska Hwy (Hwy 1) in 1942 opened up the territory to development. In 1953 Whitehorse became the capital, because it had the railway and the highway. Mining continues to be the main industry, followed by tourism, which accounts for over 350,000 visitors a year.

Parks

The Yukon has a major Unesco World Heritage site in raw and forbidding Kluane National Park, which sits solidly within the Yukon abutting Tatshenshini-Alsek Provincial Park in British Columbia. Glacier Bay and Wrangell-St Elias National Parks are found in adjoining Alaska.

The Yukon has a dozen parks and protected areas (www.yukonparks.ca), but much of the territory itself is parklike and government campgrounds can be found throughout. Tombstone Territorial Park is remote yet accessible via the Dempster Hwy, so you can absorb the horizon-sweeping beauty of the tundra and the majesty of vast mountain ranges.

ℹ Information

There are excellent visitor information centers (VICs) covering every entry point in the Yukon: Beaver Creek, Carcross, Dawson City, Haines Junction, Watson Lake and Whitehorse.

The Yukon government produces enough literature and information to supply a holiday's worth of reading. Among the highlights are *Camping on Yukon Time*, *Art Adventures on Yukon Time*, the very useful *Yukon Wildlife Viewing Guide* and lavish walking guides to pretty much every town with a population greater than 50. Start your collection at the various visitor centers online (www.travelyukon.com). Another good internet resource is www.yukoninfo.com.

ℹ Getting There & Around

Whitehorse is served by Air Canada Jazz, WestJet and Air North (p265). There are direct flights to Vancouver and Calgary. There are even flights nonstop to Germany during summer. Air North serves Whitehorse, and Dawson City has flights to Mayo, Old Crow and to Inuvik and Yellowknife in the NWT.

There are three major ways to reach the Yukon:
➺ initially by ferry, using the **Alaska Marine Highway System** (☑ 250-627-1744, 800-642-0066; www.dot.state.ak.us) to the entry points of Skagway and Haines, AK, and then by road.
➺ by the Alaska Hwy from Dawson Creek, BC.
➺ by the Stewart-Cassiar Hwy from northwest BC, which joins the Alaska Hwy near Watson Lake.

Rental cars (and RVs) are expensive and only available in Whitehorse and Dawson City. The Alaska Hwy and Klondike Hwy are paved and have services every 100km to 200km.

To check the territory's road conditions, contact **511Yukon** (☑ 511; www.511yukon.ca).

WHITEHORSE

The capital city of the Yukon Territory (since 1953, to the continuing regret of much smaller and isolated Dawson City), Whitehorse

---

> ### YUKON TERRITORY FAST FACTS
> ➺ Population: 38,300
> ➺ Area: 482,443 sq km
> ➺ Capital: Whitehorse
> ➺ Quirky fact: twice the area of the UK, but with only 38,300 people compared to the UK's 66 million!

Whitehorse

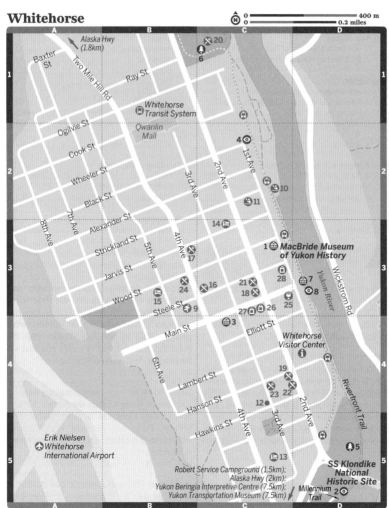

Alaska Hwy (1.8km)

Whitehorse Transit System

Qwanlin Mall

MacBride Museum of Yukon History

Whitehorse Visitor Center

Yukon River

Wickstrom Rd

Riverfront Trail

Erik Nielsen Whitehorse International Airport

Robert Service Campground (1.5km);
Alaska Hwy (2km);
Yukon Beringia Interpretive Centre (7.5km);
Yukon Transportation Museum (7.5km)

SS Klondike National Historic Site

Millennium Trail

will likely have a prominent role in your journey. The territory's two great highways, the Alaska and the Klondike, cross here, making it a hub for transportation (it was a terminus for the White Pass & Yukon Route railway from Skagway in the early 1900s, and during WWII was a major center for work on the Alaska Hwy). You'll find all manner of outfitters and services for explorations across the territory.

Not immediately appealing, Whitehorse rewards the curious. It has a well-funded arts community (with an especially vibrant visual arts community), good restaurants and a range of motels. Exploring the sights

within earshot of the rushing Yukon River can easily take a day or more. Look past the bland commercial buildings and you'll see many heritage ones awaiting discovery.

◉ Sights

You can explore Whitehorse's main sights in a day, mostly on foot.

★ MacBride Museum of Yukon History

MUSEUM

(☏867-667-2709; www.macbridemuseum.com; 1124 Front St; adult/child $10/5; ◷9:30am-5pm) This is the Yukon's pre-eminent museum, preserving and presenting the Yukon's his-

Whitehorse

YUKON TERRITORY WHITEHORSE

tory since 1952. Recently expanded, the museum offers a comprehensive view of the resilient people and groundbreaking events that have shaped the Yukon Territory's history and should not be missed.

★ **SS Klondike**
National Historic Site HISTORIC SITE
(☑ 867-667-4511; www.pc.gc.ca; cnr South Access Rd & 2nd Ave; ⊙9:30am-5pm May-Aug) FREE
Carefully restored, this was one of the largest stern-wheelers used on the Yukon River. Built in 1937, it made its final run upriver to Dawson in 1955 and is now a national historic site.

Whitehorse Waterfront AREA
One look at the surging Yukon River and you'll want to spend time strolling its bank. The beautiful **White Pass & Yukon Route Station** (1109 1st Ave) has been restored and anchors an area that's in the midst of a revitalization. **Rotary Peace Park** (off 2nd Ave) at the southern end is a great picnic spot, the **Kwanlin Dün Cultural Centre** (☑ 867-456-5322; www.kwanlindunculturalcentre.com; 1171 1st Ave; by donation; ⊙10am-6pm Mon-Sat) is a dramatic addition in the middle, and **Shipyards Park** (off 2nd Ave) at the northern end has a growing collection of historic structures moved here from other parts of the Yukon.

Whitehorse Fish Ladder LANDMARK
(☑ 867-633-5965; Nisutlin Dr; by donation; ⊙9am-9pm Jun-Aug) Stare down a salmon at the Whitehorse Fishway, a 366m wooden fish ladder (the world's longest) past the hydroelectric plant south of town. Large viewing windows let you see Chinook salmon swim past, starting in late July (before that it's grayling). The fishway is easily reached on foot via the Millennium Trail.

Arts Underground GALLERY
(☑ 867-667-4080; www.artsunderground.ca; 305 Main St, Hougen Centre lower level; ⊙10am-5pm Tue-Sat) Operated by the Yukon Arts Society. There are carefully selected and well-curated rotating exhibits of work by local Yukon artists.

Yukon Transportation Museum MUSEUM
(☑ 867-668-4792; www.goytm.ca; 30 Electra Cres; adult/child $10/5; ⊙10am-6pm mid-May–Sep) Find out what the Alaska Hwy was really like back in the day; let's just say mud was a dirty word. Exhibits cover planes, trains and dogsleds. The museum is near the airport and Beringia Centre. Look for the iconic **DC-3 weather vane** (yes, it spins!) out front.

Yukon Beringia
Interpretive Centre MUSEUM
(☑ 867-667-8855; www.beringia.com; Km 1473 Alaska Hwy; adult/child $6/4; ⊙9am-6pm) This place focuses on Beringia, a mostly ice-free area that encompassed the Yukon, Alaska and eastern Siberia during the last ice age. Engaging exhibits recreate the era, right down to the actual skeleton of a 3m-long giant ground sloth – although some prefer the giant beaver.

🏃 Activities

The visitor center can guide you to numerous local hikes and activities year-round. Otherwise, Whitehorse is a major outfitting center for adventures on Yukon waterways.

★**Takhini Hot Springs**   HOT SPRINGS
(📱867-456-8000;   www.takhinihotsprings.com; Takhini Hot Springs Rd;   adult/child $12.50/9; 🕐8am-11pm Jul-Sep, 10am-10pm Oct-Jun) These popular hot springs are 24km north of Whitehorse off the Klondike Hwy. The springs, which flow out at 47°C year-round, were used by Ta'an Kwäch'än First Nation before Europeans turned up. The first pool was built for US Army crews constructing the Alaska Hwy. These days, there are two pools, one hotter than the other, and Yukoners love them!

Canoeing & Kayaking

Whitehorse is the starting place for popular canoeing and kayaking trips from half-day trips on the Yukon River to full-on expeditions to Carmacks or on to Dawson City. It takes an average of eight days to the former and 16 days to the latter. Outfitters offer gear of all kinds (canoes and kayaks are about $40 to $50 per day), guides, tours, lessons and planning services, and can arrange transportation back to Whitehorse. Most paddlers use the map *The Yukon River: Marsh Lake to Dawson City*; available at www.yukonbooks.com.

Kanoe People   CANOEING
(📱867-668-4899; www.kanoepeople.com; cnr 1st Ave & Strickland St; half-day from $70) At the river's edge, these guys can arrange any type of trip including paddles down the Yukon, Teslin and Big Salmon Rivers. Gear, maps and guides for sale; also has bikes for rent. Lots of winter options at its wilderness facility, Fox Bay Retreat.

Up North Adventures   CANOEING
(📱867-667-7035;   www.upnorthadventures.com; 103 Strickland St; canoeing half-day from $70; 🕐9am-7pm) Offers guided tours, rentals and transportation on the major rivers. Also paddling lessons, fishing trips and winter activities such as snowmobiling, snowshoeing, ice fishing and aurora-watching.

Cycling

Whitehorse has scores of bike trails along the Yukon River and into the surrounding hills. The visitor center has maps.

Cadence Cycle   CYCLING
(📱867-633-5600; www.cadencecycle.squarespace. com; 505 Steele St; per day bike/electric bike from $35/45; 🕐10am-6pm Mon-Sat) Sells and rents good used mountain bikes. Also does repairs.

Walking & Hiking

You can walk a scenic 5km loop around Whitehorse's waters that includes a stop at the fishway. From the SS *Klondike* go south on the **Millennium Trail** until you reach the Robert Service Campground and the **Rotary Centennial Footbridge** over the river. The fishway is just south. Head north along the water and cross the Robert Campbell Bridge and you are back in the town center.

Yukon Conservation Society   HIKING
(📱867-668-5678;   www.yukonconservation.org; 302 Hawkins St; 🕐Tue-Sat Jun-Aug) **FREE** Discover the natural beauty all around Whitehorse with a free Yukon Conservation Society nature hike. There are various itineraries ranging from easy to hard.

🛏 Sleeping

Whitehorse can get almost full during the peak of summer, so book ahead. It has a lot of midrange motels that earn the sobri-

---

CANOEING 101

If the outdoors is something you've always wanted to get into but you're short on experience, consider taking a 25km, four-hour paddle in a canoe down the Yukon River. Kanoe People are right on the river in Whitehorse and you have a couple of options. For those feeling confident, you get a canoe, all the necessary safety gear, instructions and a pickup 25km downriver at the Takhini River bridge on the Klondike Hwy, all for $70 per person. Alternatively, go with a guide for $140 per person. Both options have a minimum of two people. The paddling is easy, the river serene and wildlife spotting is supreme. Expect to see eagles, a beaver or two, and if you're lucky, something on four legs. Remember, they wouldn't let you go out there by yourself if it was remotely dangerous.

quet 'veteran.' Check a room first before you commit.

★ **Robert Service Campground** CAMPGROUND **$**
(☑ 867-668-3721; www.robertservicecampground. com; 120 Robert Service Way; tent sites $20; ☺ mid-May–Sep; P 🛜) It's a pretty 15-minute walk from town on the Millennium Trail to the 70 sites at this tents-only campground on the river 1km south of town. Sites have picnic tables and fire pits. The on-site cafe has excellent coffee, baked goods and ice cream.

★ **Historical Guest House** B&B **$$**
(☑ 867-668-3907; www.historicalguesthouse.com; 5128 5th Ave; r from $105; 🖴 🛜) A classic wooden home from 1907 with three guest rooms. Top-floor options have individual bathrooms one floor down and angled ceilings. A larger unit has a huge kitchen. Rooms have high-speed internet, and there's a nice garden. A good option with character.

★ **Coast High Country Inn** HOTEL **$$**
(☑ 867-667-4471; www.highcountryinn.yk.ca; 4051 4th Ave; r from $110; P 🖴 ❄ 🛜) Towering over Whitehorse (four stories!), the High Country is popular with business travelers and groups. The 84 rooms are large – some have huge Jacuzzis right in the room. The pub is popular.

Elite Hotel HOTEL **$$**
(☑ 867-668-4567; www.elitehotel.ca; 206 Jarvis St; r from $99; 🖴 ❄ 🛜) Don't let the name have you expecting more than you're going to get. Elite Hotel probably doesn't fit in many people's 'elite' category, but it is a good cheaper option with clean, spacious rooms in a convenient location. There are restaurants and a bar in the same building and Main St is a short stroll away.

Boréale Ranch GUESTHOUSE **$$**
(☑ 888-488-8489; www.be-yukon.com; 1827 Klondike Hwy S; r from $110; P 🖴 🛜) A lodge with an emphasis on cycling, 30 minutes' drive south of Whitehorse. There are four rooms in the appealingly minimalist main building, plus detached suites. Outside there's a hot tub. Guests can use fat-tire bikes for free and there are numerous cycling programs. There are also summer-only yurts and tents with hardwood floors. The food wins plaudits.

🍴 Eating & Drinking

★ **Deli Yukon** DELI **$**
(☑ 867-667-6077; 203 Hanson St; sandwiches from $7; ☺ 9am-5:30pm Mon-Fri) The smell of smoked meat wafts out to the street; inside there's a huge selection of prepared items and custom-made sandwiches. Offers great picnic fare, or dine in the simple table area. The spicy elk sausage rolls for $3.95 are addictive. Attached to Yukon Meat & Sausage.

Fireweed Community Market MARKET **$**
(☑ 867-333-2255; www.fireweedmarket.ca; Shipyards Park; ☺ 3-7pm Thu mid-May–early Sep) The Fireweed Community Market draws vendors from the region; the berries are fabulous.

★ **Klondike Rib & Salmon** CANADIAN **$$**
(☑ 867-667-7554; www.klondikerib.com; 2116 2nd Ave; mains from $14; ☺ 11am-9pm May-Sep) The food is superb at this sprawling casual half-tent restaurant in a place originally opened as a tent-frame bakery in 1900. Besides the namesakes (the salmon skewers and smoked pork ribs are tops), there are other local faves. Great place to try bison steak ($34) or Yukon Arctic char ($28). It's half-tent, so closed when winter temperatures turn up.

Asahiya JAPANESE **$$**
(☑ 867-668-2828; www.asahiya.ca; 309 Jarvis St; dinner mains from $12; ☺ 11am-3pm & 4:30-10pm Mon-Sat, 4-10pm Sun) Top-notch Japanese prepared by Japanese chefs in downtown Whitehorse. Think sashimi, sushi and rolls, noodle dishes such as udon and soba, plus curry and meat dishes. Good bento box combinations at lunchtime, and all very reasonably priced.

Wood Street Ramen FUSION **$$**
(www.facebook.com/woodstreetramen; 302 Wood St; mains from $14; ☺ 11am-3pm & 5-9pm Tue-Sat) This colorful place is going its own way with an intriguing Yukon-Asian fusion that is proving extremely popular. While there are ramen faves such as *tonkotsu ramen* (ramen in pork bone broth), it also has dishes like crispy pork noodles ($16), Bangkok bowl ($16), and sandwiches and wraps (from $12). A top new spot in Whitehorse.

Pickapeppa CARIBBEAN **$$**
(☑ 867-456-4990; www.pickapeppayukon.com; 2074 2nd Ave; mains from $15; ☺ 11:30am-2:30pm & 5-8pm Mon-Fri, 5-9pm Sat) Nothing like a bit of Caribbean soul food to cheer you up when things are cooling down. Pickapeppa is bright, casual and vegetarian-friendly. On

READING THE YUKON

A great way to get a feel for the Yukon and its larger-than-life stories is to read some of the vast body of Yukon novels. Start with Jack London – *Call of the Wild* is free online at www.online-literature.com.

the menu you'll find dishes like jerk pork ribs ($22.95), curried goat ($22.95) and, for nonmeat eaters, chickpea curry ($14.95). The Jamaican rum balls for dessert really hit the spot.

Burnt Toast BISTRO $$
(☑ 867-393-2605; www.burnttoastcafe.ca; 2112 2nd Ave; lunch mains from $11; ☺ 7am-4pm Mon-Fri, 9:30am-2pm Sat & Sun) The food is far better than the coy name suggests! Brunch is excellent at this inviting bistro (try the French toast) and lunch specials abound. Food is local and seasonal; consult the blackboard. Good salads, sandwiches and Yukon meats. Lots of locals in here.

Sanchez Cantina MEXICAN $$
(☑ 867-668-5858; www.yukonweb.com/tourism/sanchez; 211 Hanson St; mains from $14; ☺ 11:30am-2pm & 5-9pm Mon-Sat) You'd think you would have to head south across two borders to find Mexican this authentic. Burritos here are the real thing – get them with the spicy mix of red and green sauces. Settle in for what may be a wait on the broad patio.

★ Antoinette's FUSION $$$
(☑ 867-668-3505; www.antoinettesrestaurant.com; 4121 4th Ave; dinner mains from $22; ☺ 3:30-10pm Mon-Sat) Antoinette Greenoliph runs one of the most creative kitchens in the Yukon. Her eponymous restaurant has an ever-changing, locally sourced menu. Many dishes have a Caribbean flair. There is often live bluesy, loungey music on weekends.

★ Dirty Northern Public House PUB
(☑ 867-633-3305; www.facebook.com/dirtynorthernpublichouse; 103 Main St; ☺ 3pm-late) There are hints of style at this upscale pub, which has a great draft-beer selection and makes excellent mixed drinks. Grab a booth and chase the booze with a wood-fired pizza. Top local acts perform many nights and the food comes from the sister-restaurant next door, Miner's Daughter.

Deck PUB
(☑ 867-667-4471; www.coasthotels.com; 4051 4th Ave, Coast High Country Inn; ☺ noon-midnight) The eponymous covered deck here draws crowds of locals, tourists and guides through the season. Good beer list, plus fine burgers and the like (mains from $10). How often can you have a beer at a place that stays open late and still closes before sunset?

🛍 Shopping

★ Mac's Fireweed Books BOOKS
(☑ 867-668-2434; www.macsbooks.ca; 203 Main St; ☺ 8am-9pm Mon-Sat, from 10am Sun) Mac's has an unrivaled selection of Yukon titles. It also stocks topographical maps, road maps and periodicals.

Midnight Sun Emporium ARTS & CRAFTS
(☑ 867-668-4350; www.midnightsunemporium.com; 205c Main St; ☺ 9am-6pm Mon-Sat) Has a good selection of Yukon arts, crafts and products.

North End Gallery ARTS & CRAFTS
(☑ 867-393-3590; www.yukonart.ca; 1116 Front St; ☺ 9am-6:30pm Mon-Sat, 11am-5pm Sun) High-end Canadian art featuring top Yukon artists.

ℹ Information

Whitehorse Visitor Center (☑ 867-667-3084; www.travelyukon.com; 2nd Ave & Lambert St; ☺ 8am-8pm) An essential stop with vast amounts of territory-wide information.
Whitehorse General Hospital (☑ 867-393-8700; www.yukonhospitals.ca; 5 Hospital Rd; ☺ 24hr) The top hospital in the territory.

ℹ Getting There & Away

Whitehorse is the transportation hub of the Yukon.

AIR
Erik Nielsen Whitehorse International Airport (YXY; ☑ 867-667-8440; www.hpw.gov.yk.ca/whitehorse_airport.html; off Alaska Hwy; 🛜) is five minutes west of downtown. Air Canada and WestJet serve Vancouver. Locally owned **Air North** (www.flyairnorth.com) serves Dawson City, Mayo and Old Crow, and has flights to Inuvik, NWT, plus Vancouver, Kelowna, Edmonton and Calgary. **Condor** (www.condor.com) has weekly summer flights to/from Frankfurt, Germany.

BUS

Bus services, er, come and go; check the latest with the visitor center.

Husky Bus (☑ 867-993-3821; www.klondike experience.com) Serves Dawson City ($119, thrice weekly) and makes all stops along the Klondike Hwy. Departures are from the visitor center. It will do pickups of paddlers and canoes along the Klondike Hwy with advance arrangement.

Alaska/Yukon Trails (☑ 907-479-2277; www.alaskashuttle.com) Serves Fairbanks, AK (US$385, thrice weekly June to mid-September), via Dawson City.

White Pass & Yukon Route (☑ 867-633-5710; www.wpyr.com; 1109 1st Ave; adult/child one way US$144/72; ☺ ticket office 9am-5pm Mon-Sat mid-May–mid-Sep) Offers a jaw-droppingly scenic daily 10-hour rail and bus connection to/from Skagway, AK, via Fraser, BC, in season. On some days, the bus meets the train in Carcross, which maximizes the beautiful train ride (this is the preferred option).

🛈 Getting Around

TO/FROM THE AIRPORT

A **Yellow Cab** (☑ 867-668-4811) taxi to the center (10 minutes) will cost around $22.

BUS

Whitehorse Transit System (☑ 867-668-7433; www.whitehorse.ca; $2.50; ☺ Mon-Sat) runs through the center. Route 3 serves the airport, Route 5 passes the Robert Service Campground.

CAR & RECREATIONAL VEHICLE

Check your rental rate very carefully, as it's common for a mileage charge to be added after the first 200km per day, which will not get you far in the Yukon. Also understand your insurance coverage and ask whether windscreen and tire damage from Yukon's rugged roads is included.

Budget (☑ 867-667-6200; www.budget.com; Erik Nielsen Whitehorse International Airport) The only one of the worldwide rental car companies in Whitehorse.

Driving Force (☑ 867-322-0255; www.driving force.ca; Erik Nielsen Whitehorse International Airport; ☺ 8am-6pm) These guys have cars, trucks, vans and SUVs.

Fraserway RV Rentals (☑ 867-668-3438; www.fraserway.com; 9039 Quartz Rd) Rents all shapes and sizes of RV from $200 per day depending on size (it matters) and season. Mileage extra; rates can quickly add up.

Whitehorse Subaru (☑ 867-393-6550; www.whitehorsesubaru.com; 17 Chilkoot Way) Has good rates; most cars have manual transmissions.

ALASKA HIGHWAY

It may be called the Alaska Hwy, but given that its longest stretch (958km) is in the Yukon, perhaps another name is in order...

Roughly 2224km in length from Dawson Creek, BC, to Delta Junction, far inside Alaska, the Alaska Hwy has a meaning well beyond just a road; it's also a badge, an honor, an accomplishment. Even though today it's a modern thoroughfare, the very name still evokes images of big adventure and getting away from it all.

As you drive the Alaska Hwy in the Yukon, you're on the most scenic and varied part of the road. From little villages to the city of Whitehorse, from meandering rivers to the upthrust drama of the St Elias Mountains, the scenery will overwhelm you.

British Columbia to Whitehorse

You'll never be far from an excuse to stop on this stretch of the highway. Towns, small parks and various roadside attractions appear at regular intervals. None are a massive draw, but overall it's a pretty drive made compelling by the locale.

Watson Lake

Originally named after Frank Watson, a British trapper, Watson Lake is the first town in the Yukon on the Alaska Hwy and is just over the border from British Columbia (BC). It's mostly just a good rest stop, except for the superb **Visitor Center** (☑ 867-536-7469; www.travelyukon.com; Km 980 Alaska Hwy; ☺ 8am-8pm May-Sep), which has a good museum about the highway and a passel of territory-wide info.

The town is famous for its **Sign Post Forest** just outside the VIC. The first signpost, 'Danville, Illinois,' was nailed up in 1942. Others were added and now there are over 77,000 signs, many purloined late at night from municipalities worldwide.

Some 136km west on the Alaska Hwy, past the Km 1112 marker, look for the **Rancheria Falls Recreation Site**. A boardwalk leads to powerful twin waterfalls. It's an excellent stop.

Nugget City   LODGE **$**
(☑ 867-536-2307; www.nuggetcity.com; Km 1003 Alaska Hwy; tent & RV sites $25, r from $85; P ☺ �🖤) Just west of the junction with the

Stewart-Cassiar Hwy (Hwy 37), family-run Nugget City has cabins and rooms, the Baby Nugget RV park, the Wolf It Down Restaurant and Bakery, the Northern Beaver Post gift shop and fuel. Not much going on for a while west of here.

Air Force Lodge MOTEL **$$**
(☑867-536-2890; www.airforcelodge.com; Km 978 Alaska Hwy; s/d from $89/99; ☺May-Sep; Ⓟ☺☎) The Air Force Lodge has spotless rooms with shared bathrooms in a historic 1942 barracks for pilots. While the exterior is still original, the inside has been totally refurbished.

Kathy's Kitchen CAFE **$$**
(☑867-536-2400; 805 Frank Trail; dinner mains from $14; ☺6:30am-8pm) Offering good home-style cooking with options to sit inside or out, Kathy's is popular with locals.

Teslin

Teslin, on the long, narrow lake of the same name, is 260km west of Watson Lake. It's long been a home to the Tlingits (lin-*kits*), and the Alaska Hwy brought both prosperity and rapid change to this Indigenous population.

★**Teslin Tlingit Heritage Center** CULTURAL CENTRE
(☑867-390-2532; www.ttc-teslin.com; Km 1248 Alaska Hwy; adult/child $5/3; ☺9am-5pm Jun-Aug) On the shores of beautiful Teslin Lake, 5km north of Teslin, this cultural center greets visitors with five totem poles and features exhibits of modern and traditional Tlingit arts, cultural demonstrations and a canoe exhibit by the lake. The gift shop has locally made crafts and gifts.

Yukon Motel & RV Park MOTEL **$**
(☑867-390-2575; www.yukonmotel.com; Km 1244 Alaska Hwy; r from $80; Ⓟ☺☎) Just over the bridge and on the shore of Nisutlin Bay in Teslin, the Yukon Motel offers simple motel rooms, an RV park with 70 sites, a licensed restaurant (7am to 9pm), a small shop, the Northern Wildlife Gallery (worth seeing) and a gas station (24 hours).

Johnson's Crossing

Some 50km northwest of Teslin and 127km south of Whitehorse is Johnson's Crossing, at the junction of the Alaska Hwy and Canol Rd (Hwy 6). During WWII the US Army

built the Canol pipeline at tremendous human and financial expense to pump oil from Norman Wells in the NWT to Whitehorse. It was abandoned after countless hundreds of millions of dollars (in 1943 money, no less) were spent.

The Teslin River Bridge offers sweeping views.

Johnson's Crossing Lodge MOTEL **$$**
(☑867-390-2607; www.johnsonscrossinglodge. com; Km 1295 Alaska Hwy; tent sites/RV sites/r from $27/35/95; ☺year-round; Ⓟ☺☎) Lots going on here at Johnson's Crossing Lodge, just after crossing the Teslin River on the bridge, with motel rooms, RV sites, camp-sites, restaurant and fuel.

Whitehorse to Alaska

West of Whitehorse, the Alaska Hwy is relatively flat as far as Haines Junction. From here the road parallels legendary Kluane National Park and the St Elias Mountains. The 300km to Beaver Creek is the most scenic part of the entire highway.

Haines Junction

It's goodbye flatlands when you reach Haines Junction and see the sweep of imposing peaks looming over town. You've reached the stunning Kluane National Park and this is the gateway. The town makes an excellent base for exploring the park or for staging a serious four-star mountaineering, backcountry or river adventure.

The magnificent Haines Hwy heads south from here to Alaska. The four-hour drive to Haines, traversing raw alpine splendor, is one of the North's most beautiful.

◉ Sights & Activities

Although Kluane National Park will most likely be your focus, there are some good activities locally. For a hike after hours of driving, there's a pretty 5.5km **nature walk** along Dezadeash River where Hwy 3 crosses it at the southern end of town.

Our Lady of the Way CHURCH
(Km 1578 Alaska Hwy) This much-photographed Catholic church was constructed in 1954 from an old US Army Quonset hut used during the building of the Alaska Hwy. It was split down the middle and had a height extension and windows inserted to make it

look more church-like and to allow light into the building.

Da Kų Cultural Centre
CULTURAL CENTER

(📞867-634-3300; www.cafn.ca/da-ku-cultural-centre; Km 1578 Alaska Hwy; ⊗8:30am-6pm mid-May–Aug) FREE This large and impressive facility has a variety of exhibit areas that showcase the culture and history of the Champagne and Aishihik people. It has a picnic area.

Tatshenshini Expediting
RAFTING

(📞867-633-2742; www.tatshenshiniyukon.com; rafting trip from $165, kayak rental per day $35; ⊗May-Sep) Tatshenshini Expediting leads white-water rafting trips on the nearby Tatshenshini River, which has rapids from grade II to grade IV. Trips leave from Haines Junction and Whitehorse. It also arranges custom river trips and rents gear. Based in Whitehorse and out of Village Bakery & Deli in Haines Junction.

★ Kluane Glacier Air Tours
TOURS

(📞867-634-2916; www.kluaneglacierairtours.com; off Alaska Hwy, Haines Junction Airport; tours from $270) Kluane Glacier Air Tours offers flight-seeing of Kluane and its glaciers that will leave you limp with amazement. There are four options taking in truly spectacular mountains and glaciers, beginning with a one-hour tour.

🛏 Sleeping & Eating

There's a cluster of motels and RV parks in Haines Junction. There's also a beach and shade at Pine Lake, a territorial campground 6km east of town on the Alaska Hwy.

Parkside Inn
MOTEL $$

(📞867-634-2900; www.par.sidekluaneyukon.com; 137 Haines Hwy; r from $145; P ⊝ ❄ 🌐) Five good, new self-catering units in the middle of town with fully equipped kitchens, open year-round. A good pick.

★ Village Bakery & Deli
BAKERY $

(📞867-634-2867; www.villagebakeryyukon.com; cnr Kluane & Logan Sts; mains from $8; ⊗7am-8pm May-Sep; 🌐) The bakery here turns out excellent goods all day, while the deli counter has tasty sandwiches you can enjoy on the large deck. On Friday night there's a popular barbecue with live folk music. It has milk, other very basic groceries, and even a gift shop.

ROBERT CAMPBELL HIGHWAY

To get right off the beaten path, consider this lonely gravel road (Hwy 4), which runs 585km from Watson Lake north and west to Carmacks, where you can join the Klondike Hwy (Hwy 2) for Dawson City. Along its length, the highway parallels various rivers and lakes. Wilderness campers will be thrilled.

Around 370km from Watson Lake, at the junction with Canol Rd (Hwy 6), is **Ross River**, home to the Kaska First Nation and a supply center for the local mining industry. About 62km further west is **Faro**. There is a hotel and guesthouses in Faro, as well as six campgrounds along the highway.

Guys & Dolls Bistro
FOOD TRUCK $

(📞867-634-2300; www.facebook.com/guysanddollsbistro; Steel St; mains from $12; ⊗4-9pm Tue-Sun) Stunning views from this food truck with attached outdoor seating that serves up pizzas and Greek classics. Proving very popular among locals in Haines Junction.

★ Mile 1016 Pub
PUB

(📞867-634-2093; 118 Marshall Creek Rd; ⊗noon-2am) *The* place to head to in Haines Junction for decent pub meals, drinks and a good night out. Sit outside and check out the mountains. Also check out the Facebook page.

ⓘ Information

Visitor Center (📞867-634-2345; www.travelyukon.com; Km 1578 Alaska Hwy, Da Kų Cultural Centre; ⊗8am-8pm May-Sep) Offers region-wide info.

Parks Canada Visitor Centre (📞867-634-7250; www.parkscanada.gc.ca/kluane; Km 1578 Alaska Hwy, Da Kų Cultural Centre; ⊗9am-7pm) Has park details, maps, brochures and displays; get hiking info here.

ⓘ Getting There & Away

Haines Junction is a hub of highways: the Haines Hwy (Hwy 3) and the Alaska Hwy (Hwy 1) meet here, 160km west of Whitehorse.

Who What Where Tours (📞867-333-0475; www.whitehorsetours.com) offers the only public service between Whitehorse and Haines Junction (one way $75, twice weekly June to September).

KLONDIKE

JUSTIN FOULKES/LONELY PLANET ©

Kluane National Park & Reserve (p256)
Unesco-recognized as an 'empire of mountains and ice,' this magnificent wilderness covers 22,015 sq km.

Dawson City (p260)
The center of the Klondike Gold Rush, today Dawson has a seductive and artsy vibe.

Yukon River (p248)
Hikers and canoeists are drawn to this legendary river for its beauty and wildlife-spotting opportunities.

SS Klondike National Historic Site (p247)
The SS *Klondike* was one of the largest stern-wheelers used on the Yukon River.

2

JUSTIN FOULKES/LONELY PLANET ©

Kluane National Park & Reserve

Unesco-recognized as an 'empire of mountains and ice,' Kluane National Park and Reserve looms south of the Alaska Hwy much of the way to the Alaska border. This rugged and magnificent wilderness covers 22,015 sq km of the southwest corner of the territory. Kluane (kloo-wah-nee) gets its far-too-modest name from the Southern Tutchone word for 'Lake with Many Fish.'

With British Columbia's Tatshenshini-Alsek Provincial Park to the south and Alaska's Wrangell-St Elias National Park to the west, this is one of the largest protected wilderness areas in the world. Deep beyond the mountains you see from the Alaska Hwy are over 100 named glaciers and as many unnamed ones.

Winters are long and harsh. Summers are short, making mid-June to early September the best time to visit. Note that wintery conditions can occur at any time, especially in the backcountry.

◉ Sights

The park consists primarily of the **St Elias Mountains** and the world's largest non-polar **ice fields**. Two-thirds of the park is glacier interspersed with valleys, glacial lakes, alpine forest, meadows and tundra. The **Kluane Ranges** (averaging a height of

---

EXTREME YUKON

Tough conditions spawn tough contests:

Yukon Quest (www.yukonquest.com; ☺Feb) This legendary 1600km dogsled race goes from Whitehorse to Fairbanks, AK, braving winter darkness and -50°C temperatures. Record time: eight days, 14 hours, 21 minutes, set in 2014.

Yukon River Quest (www.yukon riverquest.com; ☺late Jun) The world's premier canoe and kayak race, which covers the classic 742km run of the Yukon River from Whitehorse to Dawson City. Record times include team canoe (39 hours, 32 minutes) and solo kayak (42 hours, 49 minutes).

Klondike Trail of '98 Road Relay (www.klondikeroadrelay.com; ☺early Sep) Some 100 running teams of 10 athletes each complete the overnight course from Skagway to Whitehorse.

2500m) are seen along the western edge of the Alaska Hwy. A greenbelt wraps around the base of these mountains, where most of the animals and vegetation live. Turquoise **Kluane Lake** is the Yukon's largest. Hidden are the immense ice fields and towering peaks, including **Mt Logan** (5959m), Canada's highest mountain, and **Mt St Elias** (5489m), the second highest. Partial glimpses of the interior peaks can be found at the Km 1622 **viewpoint** on the Alaska Hwy and also around the **Donjek River Bridge**, but the best views are from the air.

In Haines Junction, Kluane Glacier Air Tours (p253) offers highly recommended flight-seeing of Kluane and its glaciers.

🏃 Activities

There's excellent hiking in the forested lands at the base of the mountains, along either marked trails or less defined routes. There are about a dozen in each category, some following old mining roads, others traditional Indigenous paths. Detailed trail guides and topographical maps are available at the information centers. Talk to the rangers before setting out. They will help select a hike and can provide updates on areas that may be closed due to bear activity. Overnight hikes require backcountry permits ($10 per person per night).

A good pause during an Alaska Hwy drive is the **Soldier's Summit Trail**, an easy 1km return hike from near the Thechàl Dhâl information center. It has views across the park and plaques commemorating the inauguration of the Alaska Hwy at this point on November 20, 1942. You can listen to the original CBC broadcast of the opening.

The Thechàl Dhâl information center is also the starting point for **Ä'äy Chù (Slim's West)**, a popular 45km round-trip trek to **Kaskawulsh Glacier** – one of the few that can be reached on foot. This is a difficult route that takes from two to four days to complete and includes sweeping views from Observation Mountain (2114m).

A moderate four- to six-hour trip is the 15km **Auriol loop**, which goes from spruce forest to subalpine barrens and includes a wilderness campground. It's 7km south of Haines Junction.

Fishing is good and wildlife-watching plentiful. Most noteworthy are the Dall sheep that can be seen on **Sheep Mountain** in June and September. There's a large and diverse population of grizzly bears, as well as black bears, moose, caribou, goats and 150 varieties of birds, among them eagles and the rare peregrine falcon.

🛌 Sleeping

⭐ **Kathleen Lake Campground** CAMPGROUND $

(www.parkscanada.gc.ca/kluane; off Haines Hwy; tent & RV sites $15.70; 🅿) Cerulean waters highlight Kathleen Lake, which has a campground and is 24km south of Haines Junction. The lake is a good stop by day and there are frequent ranger tours and programs in summer. Parks Canada also has five oTENTik, a cross between an A-frame cabin and a prospector tent mounted on a raised wooden floor, for $120 per night.

ℹ Information

Thechàl Dhâl Visitor Centre (Sheep Mountain; Km 1648 Alaska Hwy; 9am-4pm mid-May–Aug) An excellent resource with views of Sheep Mountain. Rangers have wildlife info, hiking info and binoculars set up on tripods focused on groups of sheep for visitors to peer through.

Destruction Bay

This small village on the shore of huge Kluane Lake is 106km northwest of Haines Junction. It was given its evocative name after a storm tore through the area during construction of the highway during WWII. Most of the residents are First Nations, who live off the land through the year.

Talbot Arm Motel MOTEL $$

(☎867-841-4461; www.talbotarm.com; Km 1684 Alaska Hwy; r from $90; 🅿🐾🛜) Given its monopoly on service, this motel/diner/gas station/general store is much better than it needs to be. The 32 rooms are large and comfortable; opt for one on the 2nd floor with a lake view. Meals in the restaurant (open 7am to 10pm) are straight-forward – eggs, burgers, pasta – but well prepared (mains from $10). Walk off dinner with a lakeside stroll.

Burwash Landing

Burwash Landing, 17km northwest of Destruction Bay, boasts a spectacular setting, with Kluane National Park on one side and Kluane Lake on the other. It's a good place to stretch those legs and visit the excellent museum. Next to the museum is what is said

to be the world's largest gold pan. The town was established by fur traders in 1909.

⭐ **Kluane Museum** MUSEUM

(☎867-841-5561; www.kluanemuseum.ca; Km 1700 Alaska Hwy; adult/child $5/3; 9am-6:30pm mid-May–mid-Sep) Commune with an enormous, albeit stuffed, moose at the excellent Kluane Museum. Enjoy intriguing wildlife exhibits and displays on natural and Indigenous history. It may not look like much from the outside, but this is a surprising gem in terms of museums. The gift shop features works by local Yukon artists.

Rocking Star Adventures SCENIC FLIGHTS

(☎867-841-4322; www.rockingstar.ca; Burwash Airport; per person from $160) Flying out of Burwash Airport, 2km west of Burwash Landing, these guys operate a variety of scenic flights taking in the Kaskawulsh, Donjek and Kluane Glaciers. You can also get views of Mt Logan, Canada's highest peak.

Beaver Creek

Wide-spot-in-the-road Beaver Creek, 291km northwest from Haines Junction, is a beacon for sleepy travelers or those who just want to get gas. The Canadian border checkpoint is 2km north of town; the US border checkpoint is 27km further west. Both are open 24 hours.

Beaver Creek is the most westerly community in Canada and is the spot where northbound (from Whitehorse) and southbound (from Fairbanks) construction crews met up when completing the Alaska Hwy October 20, 1942.

Church of Our Lady of Grace CHURCH

(Km 1870 Alaska Hwy) Heading into Beaver Creek from the south, you'll find this cute little Catholic church on the left. It was built using a US Army Quonset hut left over from the construction of the Alaska Hwy. If you want to go in, ask at the visitor center about the key.

1202 Motor Inn MOTEL $

(☎867-862-7600; www.1202motorinn.ca; Km 1870 Alaska Hwy; r from $90; 8am-10pm; 🅿🐾❄🛜) The 1202 Motor Inn is at the northern end of town and is reasonably appealing with basic but functional rooms. For meals, head to Buckshot Betty's just down the road. There are fuel pumps (discount if you're staying), some groceries and gifts.

**Buckshot Betty's
Restaurant and Cafe** CANADIAN **$$**
(☑867-862-7111; www.buckshotbettys.ca; Km 1870
Alaska Hwy; mains from $12; ☺7am-10pm) Your
best bet for a decent feed in Beaver Creek.
Pizzas and main dinner courses such as pork
cutlet and chicken parmesan (both $16.95).
Betty's also has a bakery, cabins (from $100)
and gifts.

Visitor Center TOURIST INFORMATION
(☑867-862-7321; www.travelyukon.com; Km 1870
Alaska Hwy; ☺8am-8pm May-Sep) Being a gate-
way town to the Yukon, the visitor center
has information on all of the territory.

HAINES HIGHWAY

If you're doing only a short loop between
Haines and Skagway in Alaska via White-
horse, this 259km road could be the high-
light of your trip. In fact, no matter what
length your Yukon adventure, the Haines
Hwy (Hwy 3) might be the high point. In a
relatively short distance you'll see glaciers,
looming snow-clad peaks, lush and wild riv-
er valleys, windswept alpine meadows and a
river delta dotted with the shadows of bald
eagles.

Heading south of Haines Junction, look
west for a close-up of the St Elias Mountains,
those glaciers glimpsed at the top stretch all
the way to the Pacific Ocean. About 80km
south, look for the Tatshenshini River
viewpoint. This white-water river flows
through protected bear country and a valley
that seems timeless.

About 10km further, you'll come to Mil-
lion Dollar Falls. For once the sight lives up
to the billing, as water thunders through a
narrow chasm. As you drive, watch for gla-
cier views.

The highway crosses into British Colum-
bia for a mere 70km, but you'll hope for
more as you traverse high and barren alpine
wilderness, where sudden snow squalls hap-
pen year-round. At the 1070m Chilkat Pass,
an ancient Indigenous route into the Yukon,
the road suddenly plunges down for a steep
descent into Alaska. The US border is 72km
north of Haines, along the wide Chilkat Riv-
er Delta.

The delta is home to scores of bald ea-
gles year-round; the handsome birds flock
like pigeons each fall when they amass in
the trees overlooking the rivers, drawn by
the comparatively mild weather and steady

supply of fish. Pullouts line the Haines Hwy
(Hwy 7 in Alaska), especially between mile-
posts 19 and 26. Take your time driving and
find a place to park. Just a few feet from the
road it's quiet, and when you see a small tree
covered with 20 pensive – and sizable – bald
eagles, you can enjoy your own raptor ver-
sion of *The Birds*.

KLONDIKE HIGHWAY

Beginning seaside in Skagway, AK, the
714km Klondike Hwy climbs high to the for-
bidding Chilkoot Pass before crossing into
stunning alpine scenery on the way to Car-
cross. For much of its length, the road gen-
erally follows the Gold Rush Trail, the route
of the Klondike prospectors. You'll have a
much easier time of it than they did.

North of Whitehorse, the road passes
through often-gentle terrain that has been
scorched by wildfires through the years.
Signs showing the dates let you chart na-
ture's recovery.

Carcross

Long a forgotten gold-rush town, cute lit-
tle Carcross (the name was shortened from
Caribou Crossing in 1902), 73km south of
Whitehorse, is an evocative stop. There's a
growing artisan community, old buildings
are being restored and the site on Lake
Bennett is superb – although Klondike pros-
pectors who had to build boats here to cross
the lake and head on to Dawson City didn't
think so. The old train station has good dis-
plays on local history.

Carcross Desert DESERT
Proudly claimed as the world's smallest de-
sert, Carcross Desert, 2km north of town, is
actually the exposed sandy bed of a glacial
lake. There are a few pine trees among the
260 hectares of sand.

★**White Pass & Yukon Route** RAIL
(☑800-343-7373; www.wpyr.com; one way from
Skagway adult/child $165/82.50; ☺mid-May–mid-
Sep) There are five trains weekly in summer
from Skagway to Carcross (and vice versa).
These five-hour rides over White Pass access
a lot of remote scenery that the shorter reg-
ular trips to Bennett don't cover. There are
packages that include bus transport in one
direction to allow Skagway-based day trips.

YUKON TERRITORY CARCROSS

ⓘ Information

Visitor Center (📞 867-821-4431; www.travel
yukon.com; 7 Austin St; ⊙ 8am-8pm May-Sep)
The VIC is in a modern complex with seasonal
shops and cafes. Get the excellent walking-tour
brochure.

Carmacks

This small village sits right on the Yukon
River and is named for one of the discov-
erers of gold in 1896, George Washington
Carmack. A rogue seaman wandering the
Yukon, it was almost by luck that Carmack
(with Robert Henderson, Tagish Charlie and
Keish – aka Skookum Jim Mason) made a
claim on Bonanza Creek. Soon he was living the high life and it wasn't long before
he abandoned his First Nations family and
headed south to the US. Given his record as
a husband and father, it's fitting that Carmack be honored by this uninspired collection of gas stations and places to stay. Like
elsewhere in the territory, residents here are
keenly attuned to the land, which supplies
them with game and fish throughout the
year. A pretty 15-minute interpretive walk
by the river provides a glimmer of insight
into this life.

⊙ Sights

Besides the interpretive center, there are
things to see on the Klondike Hwy north
and south of Carmacks.

About 25km north of Carmacks, the Five
Finger Rapids Recreation Site has excellent views of the treacherous stretch of the
rapids that once tested the wits of riverboat
captains traveling between Whitehorse and
Dawson. There's a steep 1.5km walk down to
the rapids.

South, there are a series of water features
starting with Twin Lakes, 23km from Carmacks, followed by Fox Lake. Another 24km
south, you can't miss serene Lake Laberge.
The final 40km to Whitehorse is marked by
low trees and a few cattle ranches.

Tagé Cho
Hudän Interpretive Centre   MUSEUM
(📞 867-863-5831; www.yukonmuseums.ca; off Hwy
2; by donation; ⊙ 9am-6pm May-Sep) This su-
per-friendly interpretive center has knowledgeable volunteers who explain their Indigenous life past and present.

🛏 Sleeping & Eating

Hotel & RV Park Carmacks   HOTEL **$$**
(📞 867-863-5221; www.hotelcarmacks.com; 35607
Klondike Hwy N; tent & RV sites/cabins/r from
$40/95/179; 🅿🚗❄🛜) It's all here, 177km
north of Whitehorse, with the largest ac-
commodations place on the Klondike Hwy
between Whitehorse and Dawson City. Hotel
Carmacks offers a good standard of rooms
and also features the Gold Panner Restau-
rant and Gold Dust Lounge. The RV Park of-
fers campsites, power and internet. Nothing
like this further north.

YUKON TERRITORY CARMACKS

THE KLONDIKE GOLD RUSH

The Klondike Gold Rush continues to be the defining moment for the Yukon. Certainly it
was the population high point. Around 40,000 gold seekers washed ashore (some literal-
ly) in Skagway, hoping to strike it rich in the goldfields of Dawson City, some 700km north.

To say that most were ill-prepared for the enterprise is an understatement. Although
some were veterans of other gold rushes, a high percentage were American men looking
for adventure. Clerks, lawyers and waiters were among those who thought they'd just
pop up North and get rich. The reality was different. Landing in Skagway, they were set
upon by all manner of flimflam artists, most working for the incorrigible Soapy Smith.
Next came dozens of trips hefting their 1000lb of required supplies over the frozen
Chilkoot Pass. Then they had to build boats from scratch and make their way across
lakes and the Yukon River to Dawson. Scores died trying.

Besides more scamsters, there was another harsh reality awaiting in Dawson: by the
summer of 1897 when the first ships reached the West Coast of the US with news of the
discoveries on Dawson's Bonanza Creek, the best sites had all been claimed. The Klond-
ike gold-rush mobs were mostly too late to the action by at least a year. Sick and broke,
the survivors glumly made their way back to the US. Few found any gold and most sold
their gear for pennies to merchants who in turn resold it to incoming gold seekers for top
dollar. Several family fortunes in the Yukon today can be traced to this trade.

Tatchun Centre General Store FOOD
(☑ 867-863-6171; 35607 Klondike Hwy; ⊙ 7:30am-10pm) This is the biggest store between Whitehorse and Dawson City, and offers the opportunity to purchase grocery and food items, drinks, gifts and souvenirs. There are also gas pumps outside.

❶ Information

Carmacks Visitor Centre (⊙ 9am-5pm Jun-Sep) This cute little hut at the entrance to Carmacks was built in 1903 as a telegraph station. It has no electricity or phone but is staffed during the season and has helpful maps and brochures to hand out. Pick up the Historical Building Walking Tour pamphlet.

Stewart Crossing

Another popular place to get your canoe wet, Stewart Crossing is on the Stewart River, which affords a narrow and somewhat more rugged experience before it joins the Yukon to the west for the trip to Dawson.

Little more than a petrol station and store, the village is at the junction of the Klondike Hwy (Hwy 2) and the Silver Trail (Hwy 11), which makes a 225km round-trip northeast to the nearly abandoned town of Keno City and the tiny village of Mayo.

Keno City Mining Museum MUSEUM
(☑ 867-995-3103; www.yukonmuseums.ca; Main St, Keno City; ⊙ 10am-6pm Jun-Sep) In Jackson Hall, built in the 1920s when Keno City was booming, the Mining Museum shows what life was like during silver- and gold-mining times with some superb old photographs, tools and equipment.

★ **Moose Creek Lodge** LODGE $$
(☑ 867-996-2550; www.moosecreek-lodge.com; 561 Klondike Hwy N; cabins from $125; ℗ ⊜ ☎) If you're after a bit of seclusion, head here to Moose Creek, about 24km north of Stewart Crossing. These comfy little cabins are set back in the forest with communal toilet and shower facilities nearby. The lodge restaurant uses homegrown vegetables and produce, and the gift shop offers a good selection of pieces by local artists.

❶ Information

Visitor Information Center (Klondike Hwy N, Stewart Crossing; ⊙ 9am-5pm Jun-Sep) Run by the village and small towns of Mayo and Keno on Hwy 11 to the northwest, you'll find maps, pamphlets and friendly help.

DAWSON CITY

If you didn't know its history, Dawson City would be an atmospheric place to pause for a while, with a seductive, funky vibe. That it's one of the most historic and evocative towns in Canada is like gold dust on a cake: unnecessary but damn nice.

Set on a narrow shelf at the confluence of the Yukon and Klondike Rivers, a mere 240km south of the Arctic Circle, Dawson

---

WORTH A TRIP

THE SILVER TRAIL

As prospectors found it harder and harder to become rich and stake gold claims around Bonanza Creek at Dawson City after 1898, others searched further afield and by 1920 silver had been found at Keno Hill and 600 claims staked. Shipping the heavy ore was a problem though and horse-drawn sleighs were used to haul it to the Stewart River, where it was picked up by specially designed stern-wheeler paddle steamers and shipped out, initially downriver to Dawson City, then all the way to a smelter in San Francisco. The small town of Mayo developed as a transportation center on the Stewart River where supplies were dropped off and the ore was picked up.

These days, those wanting to see these small former mining communities can take the dead-end Silver Trail (Hwy 11) northeast from Stewart Crossing. Mayo (population 450; www.villageofmayo.ca), formerly known as Mayo Landing, is 51km up paved Hwy 11. It is the largest community in the region and its airport is serviced by Air North (www.flyairnorth.com). The North Star Motel (☑ 867-996-2231; https://northstarmotel.business.site; 212 Fourth Ave, Mayo; r from $95; ℗ ⊜ ❄ ☎) is a good place to stay here.

A further 61km up the now gravel road you'll find Keno City, site of the silver mine camp, the Keno City Mining Museum and, these days, about 50 people. The only way out is back down the road you came on.

was the center of the Klondike Gold Rush. Today, you can wander the dirt streets of town, passing old buildings with dubious permafrost foundations, and discover Dawson's rich cultural life (that person passing by may be a dancer, filmmaker, painter or miner).

Dawson can be busy in the summer, especially during its festivals. But by September the days are getting short, the seasonal workers have fled south and the 1400 year-round residents are settling in for another long, dark winter.

History

In 1898 more than 30,000 prospectors milled the streets of Dawson – a few newly rich, but most without prospects and at odds with themselves and the world. Shops, bars and prostitutes relieved these hordes of what money they had, but Dawson's fortunes were tied to the gold miners and, as the boom ended, the town began a decades-long slow fade.

The territorial capital was moved to Whitehorse in 1952 and the town lingered on, surviving on the low-key but ongoing gold-mining industry. By 1970 the population was under 900. But then a funny thing happened on the way to Dawson's demise: it was rediscovered. Improvements to the Klondike Hwy and links to Alaska allowed the first major influx of summertime tourists, who found a charmingly moldering time capsule from the gold rush. Parks Canada designated much of the town as historic and began restorations.

◎ Sights

Dawson is small enough to walk around in a few hours, but you can easily fill two or more days with the many local things to see and do. If the summertime hordes get you down, head uphill for a few blocks to find timeless old houses and streets. Parks Canada operates programs and restorations with great vigor in Dawson. Check out the pass options, good for the many Parks Canada sites.

★ Klondike National Historic Sites
HISTORIC SITE
(☑ 867-993-7210; www.pc.gc.ca/dawson; Parks Canada passes adult $7-31) It's easy to relive the gold rush at myriad preserved and restored places. Parks Canada runs walking tours (p263) through the day that allow access to various examples of the 26 restored buildings. Take several tours so you can see a wide variety. Outside of tours, various buildings such as the Palace Grand Theatre are open for free on a rotating basis, usually 4:30pm to 5:30pm.

★ Bonanza Creek Discovery Site
HISTORIC SITE
(Bonanza Creek Rd) FREE Some 1.5km up the valley from Dredge No 4, this national historic site is roughly where gold was first found in 1896. It's a quiet site today with a little water burbling through the rubble. A fascinating 500m-long walk passes interpretive displays. Pick up a guide at the visitor center.

★ Dredge No 4
LANDMARK
(☑ 867-993-5023; Bonanza Creek Rd; adult/child $20/10, return transport from Dawson $10; ◎10am-4pm May-Sep, tour times vary) The scarred valleys around Dawson speak to the vast amounts of toil that went into the gold hunt. Most emblematic is Bonanza Creek, where gold was first found and which still yields some today. Dredge No 4, 13km off the Klondike Hwy, is a massive dredging machine that tore up the Klondike Valley and left the tailings, which remain as a blight on the landscape. Tours of this Parks Canada site are run by Goldbottom Tours (p263).

★ Jack London Museum
MUSEUM
(☑ 867-993-5575; www.jacklondonmuseum.ca; 600 Firth St; adult/child $5/free; ◎11am-6pm May-Aug) In 1898 Jack London lived in the Yukon, the setting for his most popular stories, including *Call of the Wild* and *White Fang*. At the writer's cabin there are excellent daily interpretive talks. A labor of love by the late historian Dick North, Dawne Mitchell and others, this place is a treasure trove of stories – including the search for the original cabin.

Crocus Bluff
VIEWPOINT
(off Mary McLeod Rd) Near Dawson's cemeteries, there's a short path out to pretty Crocus Bluff, which has excellent views of Dawson and the Klondike and Yukon Rivers. If driving, take New Dome Rd and turn at Mary McLeod Rd (ignoring the 'No Exit' signs). It is a short walk up King St from town. You can also take the 400m Crocus Bluff Connector path off the Ninth Avenue Trail,

Dawson City

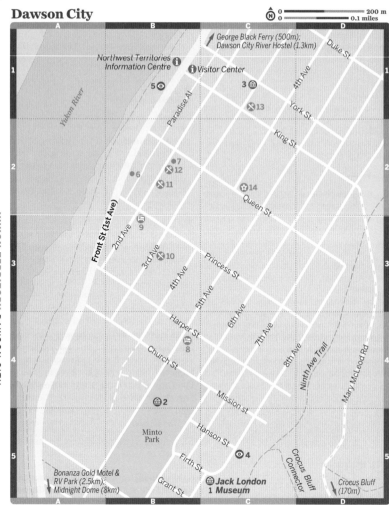

which intersects with numerous streets along its 2.5km.

Midnight Dome VIEWPOINT

(New Dome Rd) The slide-scarred face of this hill overlooks the town to the north, but to reach the top you must travel south of town about 1km, turn left off the Klondike Hwy onto New Dome Rd, and continue for about 7km. The Midnight Dome, at 880m above sea level, offers great views of the Klondike Valley, Yukon River and Dawson City. There's also a steep trail that takes 90 minutes from Judge St in town; maps are available at the visitor center.

Fortymile Gold Workshop/Studio GALLERY

(☎ 867-993-5690; www.fortymilegoldworkshop.ca; 1131 3rd Ave; ☉ 9am-6pm May-Sep) Watch as jewelry is made from local refined gold, which is silky and has a rich yellow color, as opposed to the bling you see peddled on late-night TV. Examples of gold from various local claims and locations shows how old miners could tell where gold originated.

Dawson City Museum MUSEUM

(☎ 867-993-5291; www.dawsonmuseum.ca; 595 5th Ave; adult/child $9/7; ☉ 10am-6pm May-Aug) Make your own discoveries among the 25,000 gold-rush artifacts at this museum.

Dawson City

Engaging exhibits walk you through the grim lives of the miners. The museum is housed in the landmark 1901 Old Territorial Administration building.

SS Keno — HISTORIC SITE
(☎867-993-7200; www.pc.gc.ca; cnr Front & Queen Sts; Parks Canada admission $7; ☺noon-4pm May-Aug) The SS *Keno* was one of a fleet of paddle wheelers that worked the Yukon's rivers for more than half a century. Grounded along the waterfront, the boat recreates a time before any highways.

Robert Service Cabin — HISTORIC SITE
(☎867-993-7200; www.pc.gc.ca; cnr 8th Ave & Hanson St; Parks Canada admission $7; ☺several events daily May-Aug) The 'Bard of the Yukon,' poet and writer Robert W Service, lived in this typical gold-rush cabin from 1909 to 1912. Each day in season there are dramatic readings, guided walks and tours.

🏃 Activities

Dawson City River Hostel — CANOEING
(www.yukonhostels.com; bike rental per day from $25; ☺May-Sep) Arranges all manner of canoe rentals, trips and transportation from Whitehorse and points further downstream to Dawson and from Dawson to the Alaskan towns of Eagle and Circle. Canoe rental for the 16-day trip from Whitehorse to Dawson City costs $395 plus freight; you can also rent bicycles by the day. On the far side of the Yukon River from downtown Dawson City.

★ **Parks Canada Walking Tours** — WALKING
(☎867-993-7200; www.pc.gc.ca; single tour $7, unlimited tours $31; ☺May-Aug) Parks Canada

docents, often in period garb, lead excellent walking tours. On each tour, learn about a few of the 26 restored buildings and the many characters that walked the streets (many of whom could be called 'streetwalkers'). There are also self-guided 90-minute audio tours (adult $7, 9am to 5pm).

★ **Goldbottom Tours** — HISTORY
(☎867-993-5023; www.goldbottom.com; 966 Front St; tours with/without transport from Dawson $55/45; ☺May-Sep) Run by the legendary Millar mining family. Tour the placer mine 15km up Hunker Creek Rd, which meets Hwy 2 just north of the airport. The three-hour tours include a gold-panning lesson; you get to keep what you find. You can also just pan for gold on the site for $20. The ticket office is on Front St.

Klondike Experience — TOURS
(☎867-993-3821; www.klondikeexperience.com; 954 2nd Ave; mountain bike rentals per day/week $39/150; ☺May-Sep) Runs various tours that include Midnight Dome (75 minutes; $29), the Goldfields (three hours; $59) and Tombstone Park (7½ hours; $129). It also rents mountain bikes.

🎊 Festivals & Events

★ **Discovery Days** — CULTURAL
(www.dawsoncity.ca; ☺mid-Aug) Celebrates the you-know-what of 1896, with parades and picnics. Events begin days before, including an excellent art show. It's a hoot!

Dawson City Music Festival — MUSIC
(☎867-993-5584; www.dcmf.com; ☺mid-Jul) Going for over 40 years and popular – tickets

sell out months in advance and the city fills up; reservations are essential.

Sleeping

Reservations are a good idea in July and August. Many places will pick you up at the airport; ask in advance.

Dawson City River Hostel HOTEL $
(☑867-993-6823; www.yukonhostels.com; dm $22, r from $48; ☺May-Sep; ☐☺☞) ☝ This delightfully eccentric hostel is across the river from town and five minutes up the hill from the ferry landing. It has good views, cabins, platforms for tents, and a communal bathhouse. Tent sites are $14. Owner Dieter Reinmuth is a noted Yukon author and all-around character.

★Klondike Kate's Cabins LODGE $$
(☑867-993-6527; www.klondikekates.ca; cnr King St & 3rd Ave; cabins from $175; ☺Apr-Sep; ☐☺☞) The 15 cabins behind the excellent restaurant of the same name are rustic without the rusticisms. Some units have microwaves and fridges. All have porches, perfect for decompressing.

★Bombay Peggy's INN $$
(☑867-993-6969; www.bombaypeggys.com; cnr 2nd Ave & Princess St; r from $110; ☺Mar-Nov; ☐☺☞) ☝ A renovated former brothel with alluring period furnishings and spunky attitude. Budget 'snug' rooms share bathrooms. Rooms are plush in a way that will make you want to wear a garter. The bar is a classy oasis.

★Aurora Inn INN $$
(☑867-993-6860; www.aurorainn.ca; 5th Ave; r from $120; ☐☺✻☞) All 20 rooms in this European-style inn are large and comfortable. And if there's such a thing as old-world cleanliness, it's here: the admonishments to remove your (invariably) muddy shoes start at the entrance.

**Bonanza Gold
Motel & RV Park** MOTEL $$
(☑867-993-6789; www.bonanzagold.ca; Klondike Hwy N; r from $129; ☐☺✻☞) Lots of options at this massive place out near the entrance to town on the Klondike Hwy. Motel rooms (from $119) are simple yet functional, the RV Park (from $24) packs in all those RVs racing around the Yukon, and the facilities meet the needs of travelers on the move. Think wi-fi, laundry, car wash.

Eating

★Alchemy Cafe CAFE $
(☑867-993-3831; www.alchemycafe.ca; 878 3rd Ave; mains from $8; ☺9am-4pm; ☞☝) ☝ Groovy in the best sense of the word, Alchemy combines fantastic vegetarian food with a life-affirming green ethos. The coffees are way cool (in a hot sort of way), and special events include music, talks and, yes, rap sessions. The vintage-style building has an alluring porch.

★Joe's Wood-fired Pizza PIZZA $$
(☑867-993-5326; 978 2nd Ave; pizzas from $15; ☺4-9:30pm Mon-Fri) Surprisingly authentic Italian in downtown Dawson City. Pizza options include Italian favorites and house specialties, the wine list has bottles from all over the globe, while the atmosphere is friendly, relaxed and comfortable.

★Klondike Kate's CANADIAN $$
(☑867-993-6527; www.klondikekates.ca; cnr King St & 3rd Ave; dinner mains from $14; ☺11am-10pm Mon-Fri, from 8am Sat & Sun May-Oct) Two ways to know spring has arrived: the river cracks up and Kate's reopens. Locals in the know prefer the latter. The long and inventive menu has fine sandwiches, pastas and fresh Yukon fish. Look for great specials. Excellent list of Canadian craft brews.

Drunken Goat Taverna GREEK $$
(☑867-993-5800; 2nd Ave; mains from $14; ☺5pm-late) Follow your eyes to the flowers, your ears to the Aegean music and your nose to the excellent Greek food, served year-round by the legendary Tony Dovas. A terrace out back is a fine place to while away an evening.

Drinking & Nightlife

The spirit(s) of the prospectors lives on in several saloons. On summer nights the action goes on until dawn, which would mean something if it weren't light all night.

★Bombay Peggy's PUB
(☑867-993-6969; www.bombaypeggys.com; cnr 2nd Ave & Princess St; ☺11am-11pm Mar-Nov) There's always a hint of pleasures to come swirling around the tables of Dawson's most inviting bar. Enjoy good beers, wines and mixed drinks inside or out.

Billy Goat's Pub PUB
(☑867-993-5868; www.facebook.com/billygoat pub; 950 2nd Ave; ☺5pm-late) Not a branch of

DAWSON CITY TO ALASKA

From Dawson City, the George Black (www.yukoninfo.com/dawson-city-yukon; ⊘24hr) FREE free car ferry crosses the Yukon River from the end of Front St to the scenic Top of the World Highway (Hwy 9). Only open in summer, the mostly gravel 107km-long road to the US border has superb vistas across the region.

You'll continue to feel on top of the world as you cross at the most northerly US–Canada border crossing. The land is barren alpine meadows with jutting rocks and often grazing caribou. The border crossing at Poker Creek (open 9am to 9pm Yukon time, 8am to 8pm Alaska time May 15 to September 15) has strict hours – if you're late you'll have to wait until the next day.

On the US side, Alaska shows its xenophobic side, as the first 19km connection to the intersection with the Taylor Hwy (Hwy 5) is newly sealed and gives the impression that the easy road may last forever. The old gold-mining town of Eagle on the Yukon River is 105km north from the intersection.

It's time to go back to the gravel! Some further 48km south from the intersection, over unsealed roads, you encounter Chicken, a delightful place of free thinkers happy to sell you a stupid T-shirt at one of the gas-station cafes or offer their views regarding government bureaucrats. The town was going to be called Ptarmigan, but locals didn't trust their spelling and pronunciation skills so went for Chicken instead.

Another 119km south and you reach the Alaska Hwy, where a turn east takes you to the Yukon. Just a tick west, Tok has services and motels. Alaska time is one hour earlier than the Yukon. The only place between Dawson City and the Alaska Hwy to get fuel or food is in Chicken, so prepare well.

the famed Chicago original, but a friendly lounge from Tony of Drunken Goat fame. Serves food from the Drunken Goat menu until late. Note the murals on the walls.

⭐ Diamond Tooth
Gertie's Gambling Hall   CASINO
(☏867-993-5575; www.dawsoncity.ca; cnr Queen St & 4th Ave; $15; ⊘7pm-2am) This popular recreation of an 1898 saloon is complete with small-time gambling, a honky-tonk piano and dancing girls. The casino helps promote the town and fund culture. Each night there are three different floor shows with singing and dancing, which are often surprisingly contemporary.

❶ Information

Much of Dawson is closed October to May. The biweekly, volunteer-run *Klondike Sun* (www.klondikesun.com) covers special events and activities.

Northwest Territories Information Centre
(☏867-993-6167; www.spectacularnwt.com; 1123 Front St; ⊘9am-7pm May-Sep) Maps and information on the NWT and the Dempster Hwy.

Visitor Center (☏867-993-5566; www.travelyukon.com; cnr Front & King Sts; ⊘8am-8pm May-Sep) A veritable mine of tourist and Parks Canada information (buy activity tickets and passes here). It also has essential schedules of events and activities.

❶ Getting There & Away

Dawson City is 527km from Whitehorse. Public transportation to/from Whitehorse is often in flux.

Yukon Dawson Airport (Km 694 Klondike Hwy) is 15km east of Dawson. **Air North** (☏800-661-0407; www.flyairnorth.com) serves Whitehorse and Old Crow in the Yukon, Inuvik in the NWT, and flies to Vancouver, Calgary, Edmonton and other cities.

Alaska/Yukon Trails (www.alaskashuttle.com) runs buses to Fairbanks, AK ($315, thrice weekly June to mid-September).

Husky Bus (☏867-993-3821; www.huskybus.ca) serves Whitehorse ($119, thrice weekly) and makes all stops along the Klondike Hwy. Departures are from the visitor center. Husky will do pickups of paddlers and canoes along the Klondike Hwy with advance arrangement. Also does airport transfers. Uses the Klondike Experience (p263) office.

DEMPSTER HIGHWAY

Rather than name this road for an obscure Mountie (William Dempster), it should be named the Michelin Hwy or the Goodyear Hwy for the number of tires it's sent to an explosive demise. The 736km thrill ride to Inuvik is one of North America's great adventure roads, winding through stark mountains and emerald valleys, across huge tracts of tundra, and passing through Tombstone Territorial Park. And it recently got even better, with a 144km extension north to Tuktoyaktuk on the shores of the Beaufort Sea and Arctic Ocean.

The Dempster (Hwy 5 in the Yukon, Hwy 8 in the NWT) starts 40km southeast of Dawson City, off the Klondike Hwy.

Built on a thick base of gravel to insulate the permafrost underneath (which would otherwise melt, causing the road to sink without a trace), the Dempster is open most of the year, but the best time to travel is between early June and late October, when the ferries over the Peel and Mackenzie Rivers operate. In winter, ice forms a natural bridge over the rivers, which become ice roads. The Dempster is closed during the spring thaw and the winter freeze-up; the timing of these vary by the year and can occur from mid-April to June and mid-October to December, respectively.

Check road conditions in the Yukon (p245) and the NWT (☑ 800-661-0750; www.dot.gov.nt.ca); the Northwest Territories Information Centre (p265) in Dawson City is a good resource. It takes 10 to 12 hours to drive to Inuvik without stopping for a break. (Given that William Dempster regularly made 700km dogsled journeys in subzero weather, this rugged and challenging road is properly named after all.)

Tombstone Territorial Park PARK
(☑ 867-667-5648; www.yukonparks.ca; Dempster Hwy) Tombstone Territorial Park, which lies along Dempster Hwy for about 50km, is an easy day trip from Dawson City. Shades of green and charcoal color the wide valleys here, and steep ridges are dotted with small glaciers and alpine lakes. Summer feels tentative but makes its statement with a burst of purple wildflowers in July. Clouds sweep across the tundra, bringing squalls punctuated by brilliant sun. Stand amid this and you'll know the meaning of the sound of silence.

The park's excellent interpretive centre (Dempster Hwy; ⊙ 9am-7pm Jun-early Sep), which offers walks and talks, is 71km from the start of Hwy 5.

Tombstone Mountain Campground CAMPGROUND $
(http://yukon.goingtocamp.com; Dempster Hwy; tent & RV sites $12; ℗) The park's only formal campground is at the excellent interpretive centre. There are also three backcountry

campsites at Grizzly Lake, Divide Lake and Talus Lake, with tent pads and outhouses. These require permits from June to mid-September; buy permits through the website.

Eagle Plains Hotel & Service Station MOTEL $$
(☑ 867-993-2453; www.eagleplainshotel.ca; Dempster Hwy; r from $120; ℗ ➡ ☏) The Eagle Plains Hotel, at the 370km mark and only 35km from the Arctic Circle, is open year-round and offers 32 rooms in a low-rise building in a stark setting. The next service station is 180km further north at Fort McPherson in the NWT.

ARCTIC PARKS

North of the Arctic Circle, the Yukon's population numbers a few hundred. It's a lonely land and only the hardiest venture here during the short summers.

The 300-person village of Old Crow is home to the Vuntut Gwitch'in First Nations and is unreachable by vehicle, although Air North flies there. It's at the confluence of the Crow and Porcupine Rivers and is the only village in the Yukon Territory that does not have road access. Locals subsist on caribou from the legendary 130,000-strong Porcupine herd, which migrates each year between the Arctic National Wildlife Refuge (ANWR) in Alaska and the Yukon.

A large swath of land is now protected in the adjoining Vuntut National Park and Ivvavik National Park. Information on both can be obtained from the Parks Canada office) in Inuvik, NWT. There are very limited options for organizing visits to the parks and no facilities of any kind.

Herschel Island-Qikiqtaruk Territorial Park PARK
(☑ 867-777-4058; www.yukonparks.ca) The Indigenous name of Herschel Island-Qikiqtaruk Territorial Park means 'it is island' and indeed it is. Barely rising above the waters of Mackenzie Bay on the Beaufort Sea, the park has a long tradition of human habitation. In the late 1800s, American whalers set up shop at Pauline Cove. Abandoned in 1907, the whalers left behind several surviving wooden buildings. Summer visits to Herschel Island are possible via tours from Inuvik.

Understand BC & the Canadian Rockies

BC & the Canadian Rockies Today

Despite an unprecedented 22 months when both BC and Alberta were led by left-leaning NDP governments, Canada's two westernmost provinces haven't been bosom buddies over the last couple of years. Diverging economic fortunes haven't helped. BC's economy has remained relatively prosperous, while Alberta's post-recession recovery has shown signs of slowing. Things reached a head in spring 2018 when disagreement over the much-stalled Trans Mountain pipeline deal sparked a bizarre inter-provincial trade war.

Best in Print

City of Glass (Douglas Coupland; 2000) Vancouver's most celebrated contemporary writer offers a quirky guide to his hometown.

Craft Beer Revolution (Joe Wiebe; 2015) Profiles the lip-smacking breweries of BC.

The Call of the Wild (Jack London; 1903) The story of a dog during the Klondike gold rush.

Whistle Post West: Railway Tales from British Columbia, Alberta and Yukon (various authors; 2015) Riveting stories from the region's golden age of rail.

Best in Music

Home For a Rest (Spirit of the West; 1990) Classic bar sing-along from these North Vancouver folk-rockers.

The Toronto Song (Three Dead Trolls in a Baggie; 2001) Humorous takedown of everywhere in Canada that isn't Edmonton by a popular comedy band.

Big Yellow Taxi (Joni Mitchell; 1970) Early foray into environmentally concerned songwriting from Alberta-born Mitchell.

Constant Craving (k. d. lang; 1992) Grammy-winning mega-hit by Alberta's lang.

Pipeline Politics

Arguably the biggest story in Western Canada in the late 2010s has been the controversial but still unrealized Trans Mountain project, a proposed pipeline that aims to send bitumen oil from Alberta through remote, sensitive areas of BC wilderness to a tanker terminal near Burnaby. As Canada's main oil producer, Alberta has always been the more enthusiastic proponent of the deal, often accusing the BC government of procrastinating with pedantic economic and environmental concerns. A brief impasse was reached in the spring of 2018, when Alberta's NDP government ushered in a trade war by refusing to buy BC wine and threatening to cut off its oil supply. Thankfully cooler heads prevailed, at least until the federal government bought out the pipeline in August 2018, the same day that the Federal Court of Appeal overturned the original approval citing lack of consultation with First Nations groups and concerns over the pipeline's environmental impact, particularly regarding orca habitat. As of 2019 the whole project, along with inter-provincial brotherly love (recently complicated by the election of a United Conservative government in Alberta), remains in limbo.

Adding new influence to the debate is the BC Green Party, which won three seats in the 2017 provincial election to become the first elected Green caucus in North America. The minority NDP government of John Horgan currently relies on Green support to secure a majority in parliament.

D-Day for Drugs

In a landmark law passed in October 2018, Canada became only the second country in the world (after Uruguay) to legalize recreational marijuana. In the race to promote user-friendly 420 culture to the masses, Alberta has been the quickest Canadian province out of the blocks. Seventeen licensed Albertan stores opened on the first day of legalization and, by the early spring of 2019, the traditionally conservative province could count more than 75 pot shops (the most in Canada) while BC was still in single figures. While BC supports both government and private stores, Alberta's pot shops – like its liquor stores – are purely private. The Wild Rose province also allows a lower legal age of cannabis consumption – 18 – compared to the 19 in BC and the Yukon.

New Records – for Tourists & Wildfires

A weak Canadian dollar vis-à-vis the US dollar, along with the loosening of visa requirements for some Latin American and Asian visitors, has seen tourist numbers continue their precipitous rise in Western Canada over the last two years, particularly in BC. The province logged a record six million visitors in 2018, two-thirds of them from the US, with perennial favorite destinations Whistler and Tofino performing strongly, backed up by a growing appreciation of the Okanagan wine region.

Fortunately the arriving Canada-philes weren't put off by the region's disastrous wildfires, with 2018 being the worst-ever year for wildfires in BC, narrowly usurping 2017 and coming hot on the heels of the devastating burns in Alberta in 2016. The science of why this is happening is complicated. A certain amount of blame is pointed at erstwhile firefighting policies that have allowed for the buildup of potential 'fuel' to stoke the fires, but the pressing global issue of climate change and its impact on weather patterns is never far from the equation.

Meanwhile in the Yukon

Although BC and the Yukon share a border, they share little else. The history of the Yukon has always been more closely linked to that of neighboring Alaska. The Yukon remains in many ways much as it was 200 years ago: a forbidding wilderness bursting into life during a brief summer. Its politics have traditionally leaned towards the right, an outgrowth of the area's popular image of self-reliance but, in November 2016, the Liberal party swept to power replacing the conservative Yukon Party, which had held office for 14 years. Big campaign issues included carbon taxes, the incorporation of First Nations, Inuit and Métis into government and the future of the territory's only remaining copper mine.

POPULATION: **9.1 MILLION (BC, ALBERTA & YUKON COMBINED)**

POPULATION OF BRITISH COLUMBIA: **4.7 MILLION**

GDP: **BC $282 BILLION, ALBERTA $331 BILLION, YUKON $2.8 BILLION**

....

if British Columbia were 100 people

69 would be white
23 would be Asian
2 would be Latino
6 would be Aboriginal
1 would be black

....

population per sq km

BC   CANADA   USA

👤 ≈ 1 person

History

This region's human history began at least 15,000 years ago when thriving indigenous communities emerged along the salmon-rich coastline and in the foothills of the Rockies. Everything changed rapidly, though, when Europeans arrived in the 1700s. Finding untold abundance and locals without guns, they quickly transformed the area with trade, industry and pioneer settlements. Much of this tumultuous heritage is accessible to visitors, with national historic sites – from forts to famous homes – studding British Columbia, Alberta and the Yukon.

First Peoples Kick Things Off

The ancestors of Western Canada's indigenous people were settlers who showed up in North America at least 15,000 years ago. The most prominent theory is that, after the last Ice Age, they crossed to Alaska on a land bridge over what is now the Bering Strait. Some settled along the Pacific Coast, while others found their way to the interior – Alberta, the Yukon and beyond – ultimately populating the rest of North America. This theory is not without its detractors: in recent years archaeologists have discovered the remnants of communities that appear to predate the arrival of the Bering Strait settlers.

Whatever the true story, there is little dispute over who was here first. The indigenous people of this region, thriving on abundant food and untold resources, developed sophisticated cultures and intricate trade networks over many thousands of years. Coastal people dwelled as extended families in large single-roofed cedar lodges, while inland and mountain communities generally had a tougher time, facing extremes of weather and leading nomadic subsistence lives – in the north they hungrily pursued migratory herds of animals such as moose and caribou, while in the south they chased down bison.

Europeans Poke Around

During the 18th century European explorers hungry for new sources of wealth appeared off the west coast as well as in the Rockies region after traveling through the wilderness from eastern Canada. Russian Alexsey

TIMELINE	800	1754	1774
	An ash-spewing eruption of the Yukon volcano now known as Mt Churchill causes many people to flee to southwest USA, where they may have evolved into the Navajo and Apaches.	The first European, fur trader Anthony Henday, manages to reach Alberta from eastern Canada. He spends the winter living with indigenous locals, hunting buffalo alongside them.	Spanish ships gingerly sail northwards along the Pacific Ocean coastline, nosing not very far into what would later become BC. They are the first Europeans to arrive by boat.

Chirikov is thought to have been first on the coast in 1741, followed by the Spaniards, who sent three expeditions between 1774 and 1779 in search of the fabled Northwest Passage. They ended up by the entrance to Nootka Sound on Vancouver Island, but didn't initially venture into the Strait of Georgia.

British explorer Captain James Cook also elbowed in from the South Pacific in 1778. He had a similar Northwest Passage motive, and a similar result: he hit the west coast of Vancouver Island and believed it to be the mainland. It wasn't until 1791 that the mainland-lined Strait of Georgia was properly explored. Spanish navigator José María Narváez did the honors, sailing all the way into Burrard Inlet. He named part of this area Islas de Langara.

Next up was Captain George Vancouver, a British navigator who had previously sailed with Cook. In 1792 he glided in and around Burrard Inlet and Point Roberts, briefly meeting with Spanish captains Valdez and Galiano who had already claimed the area. Then he sailed away, not thinking twice about a place that would eventually carry his name.

Despite Captain Vancouver's seeming indifference, British interest in the area grew as its abundant resources became obvious. Finally a treaty signed with the Spanish in 1794 averted war and the British assuming control.

Fur: The New Gold

The fur trade was the main lure for pioneers who followed on the heels of the first European forays, and trade grew rapidly as Western Canada's easy prey became clear. Fur trader Anthony Henday was reputedly the first European to arrive in Alberta, exploring in 1754 the outback areas now known as Edmonton and Red Deer. The region's indigenous people – inland and on the coast – soon came into contact with Europeans.

Legendary trappers such as Alexander Mackenzie, Simon Fraser and David Thompson also explored overland routes from the east during this period. At the same time the Hudson's Bay Company (HBC) rapidly became the catalyst for settler development, building fort communities and fostering trade routes throughout the region.

Of these early explorers, Mackenzie is probably the most interesting. Often compared to the Lewis and Clark expedition in the US, he traversed Canada in 1793, more than 10 years before the Americans crossed their country to the south. Exploring the Rockies, the continental divide and the Fraser River, he later produced a book on his exploits titled *Voyages from Montreal to the Frozen and Pacific Oceans in the Years 1789 and 1793*.

HISTORY FUR: THE NEW GOLD

Best Historical Sites

Klondike National Historic Sites (Yukon)

Barkerville (BC)

Fort Langley (BC)

Head-Smashed-In Buffalo Jump (Alberta)

Gulf of Georgia Cannery (BC)

1792	1793	1805	1827
Captain George Vancouver, of the British Royal Navy, sails in to the same area for one day, little knowing that the region would eventually take his name. He never returned.	Crossing the continent by land, Alexander Mackenzie almost reaches the Pacific Ocean near Bella Coola. Blocked by the Nuxalk people, he writes his name on a rock then heads back east.	The Northwest Trading Company establishes a fur-trading post at Hudson's Hope in northeast BC. It is later taken over by the Hudson's Bay Company.	The Hudson's Bay Company builds the strategically vital Fort Langley on BC's Fraser River. It's now one of the province's most popular historic attractions.

By the 1840s the US was making its own claims on the area and the HBC dispatched James Douglas to Vancouver Island, where he established Fort Victoria. A few years later the British and Americans settled their claims and the border was solidified.

Despite its relative remoteness, the Yukon was also becoming part of the action. The HBC's Robert Campbell became the first European to travel extensively in the region in the 1840s, followed by a ragtag wave of fur traders, prospectors, whalers and – as always – missionaries. Campbell established Fort Selkirk on the Yukon River as a trading post.

Gold: The New Fur

The discovery of gold along BC's Fraser River in 1858 brought a tidal wave of avaricious visitors to the region. A second wave arrived when the yellow stuff was discovered further north in the Cariboo area. Although the gold rush only lasted a few years, many of those who came remained afterwards. You can experience a sanitized version of a gold-rush town – ie without the effluent, drunkenness and prostitution – at the restored Barkerville Historic Town.

By this stage, desperate travelers were panning and scraping for gold across the region, with large imaginary nuggets forming like misshapen pupils in their eyes. For every prospector who made their fortune there were hundreds who failed to find more than a whiff of the elusive treasure.

Of course that didn't stop people trying. For years the Yukon became a byword for broken dreams and shattered fortune hunters...right up until 1896, when a discovery on a tributary of the Klondike River near what became Dawson City changed everything. The region's ensuing gold rush attracted further hopefuls from around the world – more than 99% of whom found no fortune while losing what they already had.

Rail Link Opens the West

After mainland BC and Vancouver Island were united, Victoria was named BC's new provincial capital in 1866. Meanwhile, in 1867, the UK government passed the British North American Act, creating the Dominion of Canada. The eastern provinces of Canada united under this confederation, while BC joined in 1871 and Alberta joined in 1905.

But rather than duty to the Crown, it was the train that made them sign on the dotted line. Western Canada remained a distant and forbidding frontier but the fledgling Canadian government promised to build a railway link to the rest of the country within a decade. The Canadian Pacific Railway rolled into Alberta in 1883, and nosed into BC the following year.

Best Museums

Royal BC Museum (Victoria)

Glenbow Museum (Calgary)

Whyte Museum of the Canadian Rockies (Banff)

U'mista Cultural Centre (Alert Bay)

Craigdarroch Castle (Victoria)

1846	1866	1867	1871
The US and Britain agree to the Oregon Treaty, meant to settle the border between the US and BC. However, the devil is in the details, and years of debate ensue.	Mainland BC and Vancouver Island unite, not out of any love but because mainland BC has nowhere to turn after it overspends on infrastructure.	'Gassy Jack' Deighton rows across to the southern shoreline of Burrard Inlet and opens a pub for mill workers. It triggers a ramshackle settlement that eventually becomes Vancouver.	BC joins the Canadian Confederation and is promised a rail link from eastern Canada to sweeten the deal – it eventually arrives, 16 years later.

The construction of the transcontinental railway is one of the most impressive and important chapters in the region's history. The railroad was crucial in unifying the distant east and west wings of the vast country in order to encourage immigration and develop business opportunities. But it came with a large price: the much-quoted statistic that a Chinese laborer died for every mile of track built is almost certainly true.

With the train link came a modicum of law and order. Aiming to tame the 'wild west,' the government created the North-West Mounted Police (NWMP) in 1873, which later became the Royal Canadian Mounted Police (RCMP). Nicknamed Mounties, they still serve as the country's national police force.

Also during this period, wealth from gold and revenue from the people looking for it helped the Yukon become a separate territory in 1898, with Dawson City the capital. But the northern party was short-lived – by 1920 economic decline had set in and the population dropped to just 5000, a fraction of its gold-rush heyday. And though the construction of the Alaska Hwy in 1942 opened up the territory to development and provided it with its first tangible link to BC, the glory days were over.

Big Cities Emerge...Then Burn Down

While all this nation building was going on, the region's first cities were quietly laying their foundations. And while some – Prince Rupert and New Westminster, for example – were considered as potential regional capitals (New West actually held the position in BC until Victoria took over), it was eventually Vancouver that became Western Canada's biggest metropolis. But it's worth remembering that the City of Glass almost didn't make it.

In 1867, near the middle of what's now called Maple Tree Sq, John 'Gassy Jack' Deighton opened a waterfront saloon for thirsty sawmill workers. Attracting an attendant ring of squalid shacks, the ramshackle area around the bar soon became known as Gastown. As the ad hoc settlement grew, the colonial administration decided to formalize it, creating the new town of Granville in 1870. Most people still called it Gastown, especially when Deighton opened a larger saloon nearby a few years later.

In 1886 the town's name was officially changed to Vancouver and plans were laid for a much larger city, encompassing the old Gastown/Granville area. But within a few weeks, a giant fire swept rapidly through the fledgling city, destroying around 1000 mostly wooden buildings in less than an hour.

When reconstruction began, stone replaced wood – which explains why this area of Vancouver is now packed with old brick and rock buildings that look like they were constructed to last forever. It's now home to

Inspector Constantine of the North-West Mounted Police arrived in the Yukon with a team of 20 hardy men in 1895. Their mission was to maintain law and order and uphold Canadian sovereignty, which included acting as magistrates, customs collectors and Dominion of Canada land agents.

1874	1886	1887	1896
The Mounties establish their first Alberta post at Fort Macleod. One of their first missions is to take control of the chaotic local whiskey trade.	The City of Vancouver is incorporated. Within weeks the fledgling metropolis burns to the ground in the Great Fire. A prompt rebuild ensues, with stone and brick much in evidence.	The engineering marvel of the Canadian Pacific Railway arrives in Vancouver, linking Canada's west with the east and conquering untold mountains arrayed across BC.	Sparkly stuff found in Bonanza Creek near today's Dawson City, Yukon, sets off the legendary Klondike gold rush. After three frantic years and many shattered dreams, the madness subsides.

many of Vancouver's best bars – Gassy Jack, now standing atop a whiskey barrel in statue form near the site of his first bar, would be proud.

Indigenous Turmoil

Despite the successes of colonization, the indigenous people who had thrived here for centuries were almost decimated by the arrival of the Europeans. Imported diseases. especially smallpox, wiped out huge numbers of people who had no natural immunity or medicines for dealing with them. At the same time, highly dubious land treaties were 'negotiated,' which gave the Europeans title to land that had been traditional indigenous territory. In exchange the locals were often reduced to living on small reserves.

Many of those who toiled to build the railway link across Canada came from China. But the government also lured dozens of miners from Wales to work on the Crows Nest Pass section of the project in 1897. They were offered the princely sum of $1.50 per day.

But the treatment of the indigenous people went further than a mere land grab. In what is now regarded as one of the darkest chapters in Canada's history, a process of cultural strangulation took place that ranged from attempting to indoctrinate indigenous people (especially children) with Christianity and preventing them from practicing certain age-old rites, including the potlatch (gift-giving ceremonial feast). Only in the postwar years have governments attempted to make amends, launching new treaty negotiations and finally (in 1951) repealing the anti-potlatch laws.

Moving On & Making Amends

After WWII Western Canada embraced mining and logging and a lot of money flowed into the region. Road and rail links were pushed into all manner of formerly remote places, such as those along the Stewart-Cassiar Hwy. The 1961 Columbia River Treaty with the US resulted in massive dam-building projects that flooded pristine valleys and displaced people. The Americans paid BC to hold back huge amounts of water that could be released to hydroelectric plants south of the border whenever power use demanded.

Vancouver hung out the welcome sign to the world in a big way starting in the 1980s, when Expo '86 showcased the city globally. Calgary had its own moment in the spotlight two years later when it became the first city in Canada to host the Winter Olympic Games – Vancouver joined the party in 2010 by hosting them, too.

BC has also made progress in making amends for past indigenous injustices. The first modern-day treaty, signed with the Nisga'a people in 1998, provided about $200 million and allowed some self-governance. This new process is highly controversial, however, and not everyone is on board – many non-indigenous locals do not want the claims to go too far. So far only 20% of indigenous groups have begun negotiations.

1905	1920	1941	1947
Alberta becomes a province, but it is another 25 years before the federal government allows it to control its own resources. This would prove useful quite a few years later.	Having dropped significantly since the turn of the century, the population of the Yukon falls below 5000. It doesn't increase greatly until after the Alaska Hwy is built in 1942–43.	The attack on Pearl Harbor spurs the US into working with Canada to open up the north for the countries' common defense. One of the enduring legacies is the Alaska Hwy.	Alberta makes a major oil discovery at Leduc, not far from Edmonton. As more oil and gas is discovered, the province changes forever, bringing vast wealth into the region.

Party Time & Hangovers

Alberta has always been better at making money than BC, and the region has enjoyed astonishing economic success by exploiting its oil sands. Located in northern Alberta, this is a controversial enterprise involving the labor-intensive extraction of bitumen. It has attracted the ire of environmentalists who believe it's one of the dirtiest and most ecologically damaging methods for producing oil. The companies involved – some of the world's biggest petroleum corporations – state that they operate to the highest standards and follow all government guidelines. With oil prices declining in recent years, though, the enterprise is not the lucrative license to print money it may once have seemed.

Healthy profits of a different kind were enjoyed by suppliers and developers involved with the biggest party to hit Canada in decades: the 2010 Winter Olympic and Paralympic Games, staged in Vancouver and Whistler. Maple-leaf flags and face tattoos became the norm as Vancouverites transformed the city into a wandering carnival of family-friendly bonhomie. When the flame was extinguished at the closing ceremony, the locals wiped off the red face paint and trudged back to their regular lives.

The stunning images of the region's pristine beauty that circulated around the world as a result of the Games, at the same time as international surveys proclaimed Vancouver to be one of the globe's most liveable cities, enticed more people to move to the city. Vancouver house prices rose rapidly as a result and many locals have since struggled with an increasing lack of housing affordability.

BC, Alberta and the Yukon are still relatively young enterprises at the start of their development, however, and there remains a sense that perhaps the best is yet to come for this part of the world.

Southern Alberta's ancient Siksika Nation is still renowned for its dancing prowess, especially its celebrated Chicken Dance. Inspired by the courtship moves of a chicken, it's performed by young males in the community. Check out June's World Chicken Dance Championship at the Blackfoot Crossing National Historical Park (www.blackfoot crossing.ca).

1960	1964	1998	2010
Indigenous people finally get the right to vote in BC, a key advance in a decades-long initiative to restore the rights of the province's original residents and agree to compensation.	Implementation of the Columbia River Treaty starts the construction of huge dams that forever change the Kootenays. One creates Arrow Lakes, causing Nakusp to be moved, while obliterating other towns.	BC, the federal government and the Nisga'a people agree on the first modern-day treaty, a huge settlement for the impoverished people living at Nass Camp near the Nisga'a Lava Bed.	Vancouver hosts the Olympic and Paralympic Winter Games, in front of a global TV audience estimated to be more than two billion. There's plenty of flag waving and anthem singing.

Wildlife

British Columbia, Alberta and the Yukon offer a jaw-dropping safari of wildlife-spotting opportunities. While locals may be blasé, visitors rave about the impressive animals they've seen in Canada's best critter-watching region. Expect a spine-tingling frisson when you see your first bear nonchalantly scoffing berries or a bald eagle dive-bombing a salmon-stuffed river. Then there are the whales – boat tours to see orca pods are extremely popular on the West Coast and the word 'magical' doesn't even come close to describing the experience.

Mammals

Bears

An unmissable sighting for many visitors, grizzly bears – *Ursus arctos horribilis* to all you Latin scholars – are most commonly viewed in the Rockies. Identifiable by their distinctive shoulder hump, they stand up to 3m tall and are solitary mammals with no natural enemies (except humans; try to resist the need for a selfie). While they enjoy fresh-catch meals of elk, moose and caribou, most of their noshing centers on salmon and wild berries. Black bears are also fairly common on the mainland of BC (especially in the north) as well as in the north and west regions of Vancouver Island.

Confusingly grizzlies are almost black, while their smaller and much more numerous relation, the black bear, is sometimes brown. More commonly spotted than grizzlies, black bears reside in large numbers in northern BC and in the Banff and Jasper areas, where 'wildlife jams' are a frequent issue among rubbernecking motorists. You may also see these bears as far south as Whistler and in the foothills of North Vancouver.

In 1994 coastal BC's Khutzeymateen Grizzly Bear Sanctuary (near the northern town of Prince Rupert) was officially designated for protected status. More than 50 grizzlies currently live on this 450-sq-km refuge. A few ecotour operators have permits for viewing these animals if you want to check them out face-to-face. There are also tiny bear sanctuaries in Banff, Golden and on Grouse Mountain in North Vancouver.

Kermode bears, sometimes called spirit bears, are a subspecies of the black bear, but are whitish in color. They're unique to BC and are found in the north, from Bella Coola through the Great Bear Rainforest to Stewart, mostly along the lower Skeena River Valley.

Wolves

Wolves are perhaps the most intriguing and mysterious of all Canada's wild animals. They hunt cleverly and tenaciously in packs and have no qualms about taking on prey much larger than themselves. Human attacks are extremely rare, but you'll nevertheless feel nervous excitement if you're lucky enough to spot one in the wild – typically in the distance, across the other side of a wide river.

The Rockies are your most likely spot for seeing a wolf. You may also hear them howling at the moon at night if you're camping in the bush. An intriguing and elusive subspecies of 'sea wolves' has been increasingly

E-Fauna BC (http://ibis.geog. ubc.ca/biodiversity/efauna) is a fascinating online digital atlas of the province's flora and fauna, from amphibians to mammals. It has lots of great photos of birds to look out for on your visit to the region.

BY THE NUMBERS

This region is home to more than 150 mammal species, 510 bird species, almost 500 fish species, 20 reptile species and 20 types of amphibian. About 140 species (including most of the whales, the burrowing owl, the sea otter and the Vancouver Island marmot) are considered endangered, but many more are also at risk. Ecosystems are at their most diverse in southern BC, but that's also where threats from human pressures are at their greatest.

studied in recent years. Genetically related but distinct from their inland cousins, they live primarily along the coastline of BC's Great Bear Rainforest, hunting deer as well as salmon and sea lions.

It's extremely unlikely that you'll be approached by a wolf, but they sometimes become habituated to human contact, typically through access to uncovered food in campsites. If a wolf approaches you and seems aggressive or unafraid, wave your arms in the air to make yourself appear larger, reverse slowly and do not turn your back, and make noise and throw sticks and/or stones.

Cougars

Cougars, or mountain lions, are the largest cats in North America. They thrive in the mountainous terrain of the Rocky Mountains and British Columbia and can be found throughout the region, from the Yukon down to the US border. Overall numbers aren't huge – you're far more likely to spot a bear or a moose than one of these stealthy felines. An estimated 3500 live in BC, with around a quarter of them on Vancouver Island, which has the highest concentration of cougars in North America.

Cougars are predominantly carnivorous animals hunting everything from small elk and deer to raccoons and squirrels. They are masters of the ambush, stalking their prey carefully before making a deadly leap. Although you should always be on your guard in cougar country, the cats tend to avoid human contact and attacks are rare. Due to habitat decline, however, interactions have become more common in recent decades. Children are most at risk.

Elk, Caribou & Deer

Male elk have been known on occasion to charge into vehicles in Jasper after spotting their reflection in the shiny paintwork, perhaps believing they've met a rival for their harem of eligible females. But mostly they're docile creatures. It's common to see this large deer species wandering around the edges of the town for much of the year. November's rut is the best time to observe elk, though: you'll see the bugling males at their finest, strutting around and taking on their rivals with head-smashing displays of strength.

More common in other Canadian regions, woodland caribou show up in small groups in BC and the Rockies, though the Banff population wiped itself out in 2009 by triggering an avalanche that buried a whole herd. There are still three herds active in Jasper, but numbers probably aren't sustainable in the long term.

Deer are common sights away from the cities in much of BC and beyond. Expect to spot leaping white-tailed deer and mule deer flitting among the trees and alongside the roads in the Rockies. You might also spot the Columbia black-tailed deer, a small subspecies native to Vancouver Island and BC's west coast.

If you manage to photograph one particular fabled local, you'll likely have an Instagram viral hit on your hands. Bigfoot or Sasquatch is said to roam the region's forests, avoiding cameras. Keep your eyes peeled in the BC interior and near Tofino, where 'sightings' have been reported.

This region is home to the gray wolf, also known as the timber wolf. They hunt in packs of up to a dozen, and mate for life. The females give birth to as many as 11 pups each spring.

Moose

Western Canada's postcard-hogging shrub nibbler is the largest member of the deer family, and owes its popularity to a distinctively odd appearance: skinny legs supporting a humongous body and a cartoonish head that looks inquisitive and clueless at the same time. Then there are the antlers – males grow a spectacular rack every summer, only to discard them in November.

You'll spot moose foraging for twigs and leaves – their main diet – near lakes, muskegs and streams, as well as in the mountain forests of the Rockies and the Yukon.

Moose are generally not aggressive, and will often stand stock-still for photographs. They can be unpredictable, though, so don't startle them. During mating season (September) the giant males can become belligerent, so keep your distance: great photos are not worth a sharply pronged antler charge from a massive, angry moose.

Bighorn Sheep

Often spotted clinging tenaciously to the almost-sheer cliff faces overlooking the roads around Banff and Jasper, bighorn sheep are a signature Rockies sight. They're here in large numbers, so are one of the easiest animals to spot. On the drive between Banff and Jasper, along the Icefields Parkway, you'll likely spy them looking like sculptures standing sentinel on the rocks. The best viewing season is during September and October when the rut is on and the males are smashing their heads together to prove their mate-worthy credentials.

Urban Wildlife

You don't necessarily have to travel far into the wilderness to catch sight of Western Canada's multitudinous critters. As cities have expanded outwards, the areas that once teemed with unfettered wildlife have come into direct contact with human habitation. Some animals have responded by retreating further into the wilderness, while others have adapted their way of life to co-exist with two-legged locals. It's not always an easy relationship.

In small towns such as Whistler, Dawson City and Tofino, grainy images of bears roaming around people's backyards usually light up social-media platforms around the region several times a year. But some creatures have taken it a step further. In metro Vancouver there are an estimated 3000 coyotes that live and forage in or near populated neighborhoods. It's common to see notices posted around the region during denning season (the time when pups are raised) warning local dog owners to be aware of aggressively protective coyote mothers.

In contrast the animal-human problem is mostly deer-shaped in the town of Jasper, Alberta. Here drivers are used to watching the road ahead

Resident Birds
Anna's hummingbird
Bald eagle
Northern flicker
Steller's jay
Cormorant

Other Local Critters
Coyote
Raccoon
Skunk
Marmot
Cougar
Lynx
Porcupine
Beaver
Wolverine
Douglas squirrel

TOP WILDLIFE-WATCHING SPOTS

Icefields Parkway (p76) The 230km drive between Banff and Jasper is lined with monumental mountain peaks and a regular contingent of deer, bighorn sheep and black bears.

Maligne Lake Rd (p93) Eagles, deer, elk, bighorn sheep and maybe a moose are likely sightings in this Jasper National Park area.

Khutzeymateen Grizzly Bear Sanctuary (p233) Dozens of grizzlies live in this northern BC refuge, and ecotour operators have permits for viewing.

Bella Coola Valley (p231) Boat tours along rivers are thick with sightings of grizzly bears wandering the banks.

Coyote, Jasper National Park (p91)

of them for oblivious road-crossers – they can cause massive damage (to both animals and cars) in a collision. And if you're a gardener in this region, you have to either give up your green-thumbed ways or embark on a serious fortification of your plot: a favorite deer supper here often involves flowers, vegetables and fruit trees.

Bird Life

Of the region's 500-plus bird species, the black-and-blue Steller's jay is among the most famous; it was named BC's official bird after a government-sponsored contest. Other prominent feathered locals include ravens, herons, great horned owls and peregrine falcons. You don't have to trek into the wilderness for an up-close glimpse: head to Lost Lagoon on the edge of Vancouver's Stanley Park and you'll discover a feather-fringed oasis just a few steps from the city. In fact, you don't even have to stray that far – keep your eyes peeled on Vancouver's residential streets for local and visiting hummingbirds as well as resident northern flickers, a woodpecker with a distinctive spotted plumage.

The most visually arresting birds in Western Canada are eagles, especially of the bald variety. Their wingspans can reach up to 2m and they are a spine-tingling sight for anyone lucky enough to see one in the wild. Good viewing sites include Brackendale, near Squamish in BC, where thousands nest in winter and an annual bird count lures visitors. Also train your camera lens on Vancouver Island's southern and western shorelines: it won't be long before something awesome sweeps into view.

Edited by Alison Parkinson, *Parks and Nature Places Around Vancouver* is a comprehensive guide to the top spots in and around the city where you're likely to see memorable flora and fauna. Many of the listings can be easily accessed on public transportation.

Sea Life

Divers off the BC coastline can encounter a startling and often bizarre range of aquatic life. The swimming scallop looks rather like a set of false teeth; in fact, it's a fascinating symbiotic creature able to move under

SALMON RUNS WILD

After years of depressingly declining returns, the 2010 wild Pacific sockeye salmon run on BC's Fraser River surprised and delighted scientists and local fishing operators by being the largest for almost 100 years. More than 34 million gasping salmon reportedly pushed themselves up the river to lay their eggs and die, a spectacle that turned regional rivers red with the sight of millions of crimson sockeye. However, while restaurants fell over themselves to offer wild salmon dishes for several months, scientists correctly predicted that the record run was a flash in the pan and not an indication of long-term recovery in the salmon sector. Right on cue, 2016 turned out to be a record low year for salmon, with less than one million making it up the Fraser River.

its own power, nabbing floating nutrients while a sponge attached to its shell provides protection. Giant Pacific octopuses with tentacles up to 2m in length are found on shallow, rocky ocean bottoms. The record weight of one of these creatures is 272kg. Wolf eels are known for darting out of crevices to inspect wetsuit-clad visitors and often snuggling into the crooks of their arms.

Whales

Whale-watching is a must-do activity on the West Coast and tours (typically up to three hours for around $100 per person) are justifiably popular. The waters around Vancouver Island, particularly Johnstone Strait, teem with orcas every summer, and tours frequently depart from Tofino, Telegraph Cove, Victoria, Richmond and beyond. The Inside Passage cruise ship and ferry route between Port Hardy and Prince Rupert is also a popular long-haul viewing spot.

BC author JB MacKinnon's fascinating 2013 book *The Once and Future World* illuminates the ecosystems of the past and explores the urgent need for modern society to reconnect with this natural order before it's too late.

While orcas – also known as killer whales – dominate the region's viewing, you might sight some of the 20,000 Pacific gray whales that migrate along the coastline here twice a year. If you're lucky you'll also see majestic humpbacks, which average 15m in length.

Orcas get their 'killer' moniker from the fast-paced way they pursue and attack marine life and not from attacks on humans, which are more rare than whale sightings in the Rockies. On your tour you'll likely spot the orcas' preferred nosh languishing on rocks or nosing around your boat – keep your camera primed for porpoises, dolphins, seals, Steller sea lions and sea otters.

Prime orca-viewing season is from May to mid-July. For gray whales it's mid-August to October, and for humpbacks it's August to October.

The Arts

It's easy to think Western Canada doesn't have much of an arts scene. How can mountain bikers or die-hard cowboys be interested in art, theater and literature? But in reality this region is a roiling hotbed of creativity, especially at the grassroots level. The trick is to hit the major cultural attractions first, then latch on to some artsy locals and ask for tips on the coolest off-the-beaten-path events, exhibitions and happenings. You'll likely be well rewarded for your efforts.

Visual Arts

British Columbia's Emily Carr (1871–1945) made her name by painting Indigenous villages and swirling forest landscapes on Vancouver Island. She's often referred to as an honorary member of Canada's legendary Group of Seven. But she isn't the only great painter to have come from this region. Transforming canvases a few decades later, EJ Hughes (1913–2007) created rich, stylized work that vividly depicted coastal life along the West Coast.

In recent years Vancouver has been Western Canada's contemporary art capital, with photoconceptualism especially revered here. Stan Douglas and Rodney Graham (who also works in multimedia) are celebrated, but it's Jeff Wall, a photorealist whose large works have the quality of cinematic production, who has attained global recognition, including having his work exhibited at New York's Museum of Modern Art (MoMA). Vancouver's art gallery showcases artists such as these, and the sparkling new Audain Art Museum in Whistler is dedicated to the best of BC's historic and modern-day creatives.

The region's art scene isn't just about landmark galleries. Many Vancouver locals will tell you their favorite annual art event is November's weekend-long Eastside Culture Crawl (www.culturecrawl.ca), during which about 450 East Vancouver artists open their home studios and galleries to a strolling mass of locals. Recently marking its 20th anniversary,

RIOTOUS ARTWORK

Look for the large London Drugs store in the Woodwards building on W Hastings St in Vancouver and enter the building's courtyard, which is carved from what was originally the interior of one of the city's largest department stores. The space is now dominated by the city's most evocative – and perhaps provocative – public artwork.

Measuring 15m by 9m and created by Stan Douglas, *Abbott & Cordova, 7 August 1971* is a mammoth double-sided black-and-white photo montage depicting a key moment in the history of local social protest: the night when police in full riot gear broke up a pro-marijuana smoke-in being staged in the Downtown Eastside.

The action (the image shows mounted police pushing against unarmed locals, and miscreants being stuffed into police wagons) soon spiraled out of control, with pitched battles and general chaos triggering a siege-like atmosphere on the area's streets. Later, the event became known as the 'Gastown Riot' and 'The Battle of Maple Tree Square.'

Eastside Culture Crawl is the most enjoyable way to meet the city's grass-roots artists as well as artistically inclined Vancouverites.

A strong commitment to public art across the region is apparent. Statues and installations can be found in Alberta's Calgary and Edmonton, and in BC's Victoria and Richmond. But big-city Vancouver leads the way with hundreds of camera-loving installations studding the city, many of the most dramatic appearing under its popular Vancouver Biennale initiative. And the city's most photographed public artwork? A clutch of 14 oversized bronze figures near English Bay Beach, which are laughing and smiling as if they're having a ball.

Vancouver Biennale

Operating for two-year stretches since 2005, the Vancouver Biennale installs large, sometimes challenging landmarks on the streets of the city, aiming to create an open-air art museum for locals and visitors to enjoy. While some of the works stay just for the duration of the event, others have become permanent Vancouver fixtures by utilizing sponsorship and corporate support. These include the 10m-high *Trans Am Totem,* featuring five scrapped cars stacked atop a cedar tree trunk, and *A-maze-ing Laughter,* with its chuckling bronze characters clustered near the beach at English Bay forming the city's most selfie-inviting street feature. For the location of these and other talked-about Biennale works, check out the self-guided tours at www.vancouverbiennale.com.

Literature

Perhaps due to those long Albertan winters and the month-long rain fests on the BC coast, Western Canadians are big readers. And there's no shortage of local tomes to dip into: BC has an estimated 1500 professional authors and dozens of publishers to provide material for the region's insatiable bookworms.

The bulging bookshelf of historic authors includes WP Kinsella (author of *Shoeless Joe,* the story that became the 1989 *Field of Dreams* movie), William Gibson (sci-fi creator of cyberpunk) and Malcolm Lowry, who wrote his *Under the Volcano* (1947) masterpiece here. Don't miss the writings of celebrated BC painter Emily Carr (1871–1945), especially *Klee Wyck* (1941), which evocatively recounts her experiences with local First Nations communities.

A rich vein of contemporary work exists, too. One of Canada's most revered artists and authors, Douglas Coupland lives in West Vancouver

---

Top Art Galleries

Vancouver Art Gallery (Vancouver)

Audain Art Museum (Whistler)

Art Gallery of Alberta (Edmonton)

Contemporary Calgary (Calgary)

Art Gallery of Greater Victoria (Victoria)

BEST READS

The Cremation of Sam McGee (Robert W Service; 1907) Written by the renowned Bard of the Yukon, this is a classic of regional prose about two gold miners, the cold and what men will sometimes do. It's Service at his peak.

Runaway: Diary of a Street Kid (Evelyn Lau; 1989) Tells the true story of the author's dangerous life on the streets of downtown Vancouver.

Red Dog, Red Dog (Patrick Lane; 2008) Follows two brothers trying to navigate tough times in 1950s Okanagan Valley. It's a gripping look at heartbreak, corruption and the tough lives of those who settled Canada.

Stanley Park (Timothy Taylor; 2001) Stirs together a haute-cuisine chef with a park's dark secrets. The result is a story capturing Vancouver's quirky modern ambience.

Klondike Tales (Jack London; 2001) A collection of stories drawing on the author's first-hand experiences to show the hardships, triumphs and betrayals of the Yukon gold rush in 1897. *The Call of the Wild* wins new fans every year.

ALL THE WORLD'S A STAGE

Staged every year since 1990, Vancouver's Bard on the Beach (www.bardonthebeach. org) is a quintessentially West Coast way to catch a show. The event includes a roster of three or four Shakespeare and Shakespeare-related plays performed in tents on the Kitsilano waterfront, from June to September, with the North Shore mountains in the background. It regularly sells to capacity, making it one of North America's most successful and enduring Shakespeare festivals.

and has produced genre-defining titles such as *Generation X, Girlfriend in a Coma* and the excellent 'alternative guidebook' *City of Glass,* which showcases his love for Vancouver with quirky mini-essays and evocative photography. Coupland's latest offering is *Bit Rot* (2016).

A celebrated nonfiction scene has also developed in the region in recent years, with books from local lads Charles Montgomery and JB MacKinnon winning prestigious national awards. MacKinnon's most recent title, *The Once and Future World* (2013), explores the natural abundance of the past to inspire a new way of looking at our environment today.

While Alberta falls short of the heady heights of BC for literary output, you should consider dipping into the following books before arrival for a richer understanding of the area: *The Wild Rose Anthology of Alberta Prose* (2003), edited by George Melnyk and Tamara Seiler, and *Writing the Terrain: Travelling Through Alberta with the Poets* (2005), edited by Robert Stamp.

If you make it to the Yukon, drop into Dawson City. Bookish types will love nosing around the Jack London Interpretive Centre, a cabin evoking the time when the celebrated author lived in the region. In fact, bring a book along for the trip, preferably *Sailor on Snowshoes* (2006) by Dick North, which explores London's time in the area. Alternatively dip into almost anything written by the legendary Robert W Service (1874–1958) during his pioneer-era time here; it'll exponentially increase your understanding of this rugged region.

Many BC writers live on the Southern Gulf Islands. For an introduction to their work (and the work of other BC authors), visit the annual literary festival on tranquil Galiano Island (www. galianoliterary festival.word press.com).

Theater & Dance

Local theaters can be found throughout Western Canada, with even the smallest communities providing a venue for grassroots performing troupes and visiting shows. Bigger cities such as Vancouver, Victoria, Edmonton and Calgary often have several large auditoria with their own repertory theater companies – Vancouver's Arts Club Theatre Company (www.artsclub.com) is the region's largest, staging shows at three venues around the city. The performance season usually runs from October to June, but shows frequently tread the boards outside this period. It pays to dig a little for some hidden gems as there are dozens of smaller venues with a fringe-theater approach throughout the region.

Fans of the small stage may wish to time their visits with fringe-theater events. Edmonton hosts the oldest and biggest fringe festival in North America (www.fringetheatre.ca), while there are also excellent, popular festivals in Vancouver (www.vancouverfringe.com) and Victoria (www.victoriafringe.com).

Vancouver is a major Canadian capital for dance, second only to Montréal. It hosts frequent annual events, from classical to challenging modern interpretations. If you're a true dance buff, consider picking up a copy of *Dancing Through History: In Search of the Stories that Define Canada* (2102) by Vancouver-based author and dancer Lori Henry. The fascinating book explores the nation's culture through its traditional dances.

Cinema & Television

Western Canada is a hot spot for TV producers and moviemakers looking for a handy stand-in for American locations, hence the name 'Hollywood North,' used to describe the film sector up here. Blockbusters such as *Rise of the Planet of the Apes* (2011), *50 Shades of Grey* (2015) and *Godzilla* (2014) were filmed in and around metro Vancouver, while big-budget films including *Inception* (2010) and *The Revenant* (2015) were at least partly filmed in Alberta.

But it's not all about making US-set flicks. Canada has a thriving independent filmmaking sector. Catching a couple of locally made movies before you arrive can provide some handy insights into the differences between the US and Canada. Look out for locally shot indie flicks including *Mount Pleasant* (2006) and *Carts of Darkness* (2008).

The region also has a great reputation for special effects and post-production work, with *Avatar* (2009), *Life of Pi* (2012) and the recent *Star Wars* and *Star Trek* reboots using local studios for added visual spectacle.

It's not unusual to spot movie trucks and trailers on your travels here, especially in downtown Vancouver, and you might like to try your hand at becoming an extra on your visit. See www.creativebc.com for the low-down on what's filming and which productions are looking for 'background performers.'

Popular movie, TV and media festivals throughout the year include the Calgary International Film Festival, Edmonton International Film Festival, Vancouver International Film Festival and Whistler Film Festival.

The website of the National Film Board of Canada (www.nfb.ca) is a treasure trove of north-of-the-border films available for free online viewing. Recommended is *Carts of Darkness* (2008), a riveting exploration of shopping-cart races among the homeless in North Vancouver.

Music

Ask visitors to name Canadian musicians and they'll stutter to a halt after Justin Bieber and Celine Dion. But ask the locals in BC, Alberta and the Yukon, and they'll hit you with a roster of local performers you've never heard of, plus some that you probably thought were American.

Superstars Michael Bublé, Bryan Adams, Sarah McLachlan and Diana Krall are all from BC, and their slightly less stratospheric colleagues include Nelly Furtado and Spirit of the West. For those who like their music with an indie hue, Black Mountain, Dan Mangan and CR Avery are among the area's popular grassroots performers.

Alberta has also spawned several big names: Joni Mitchell was born there for starters. Fans of indie rock are likely familiar with Feist, as well as Tegan and Sarah. Pop and country music singer-songwriter k.d. lang hails from Edmonton.

Bars are a great place to start if you want to take the pulse of the local music scene, some with free or minimal cover charges. Larger cities such as Vancouver, Calgary and Edmonton offer a wide range of dedicated venues for shows, from stadiums to cool underground spaces.

Even better, the region is bristling with great music festivals. Look out for toe-tapping options including the Vancouver International Jazz Festival and the Calgary Folk Music Festival.

Whatever your musical tastes, the best way to access the live scene on a grassroots level is to pick up local weekly newspapers and duck into small independent record stores. Cities large and small often have vinyl-selling shops staffed by musicians who know all there is to know about who's hot on the local scene.

Indigenous BC & Beyond

Western Canada's original inhabitants have called this region home for thousands of years. While first contact with Europeans ultimately had a hugely detrimental impact on these communities, many of which continue to face severe struggles in a society dominated by non-indigenous people, recent history has been characterized by attempted reconciliation and a growing respect for the area's earliest locals. On your travels you'll find fascinating indigenous museums, cultural centers and public art installations that will be highlights of your visit.

Indigenous History

Early History

The prevailing theory that the region's first human inhabitants arrived many thousands of years ago by crossing a land bridge over the Bering Strait, near what's now known as Alaska, has been challenged (and, in some quarters, discredited) in recent years. Opposing theories have suggested that the earliest residents may have arrived on the east coast via boats from Asia, Polynesia or Siberia. What is known for sure is that the current indigenous communities in this region are descendants of the people who called this area home more than 10,000 years ago.

Some of these communities settled the forested foothills of the mountains to the east, while many others stayed on the ocean coastline, reaping the seemingly endless supply of juicy salmon, deer and rich local vegetation. Inland BC didn't provide the same bounty, however, and the Salish people in places such as the Okanagan Valley had to devote much more of their time to subsistence living and surviving the long winters. In the far north, the Tagish, Gwich'in and others depended on migrating moose and caribou.

While a common perception of these people is that they lived in tipis and smoked peace pipes, there was, in fact, a huge variety of groups, each living in distinctly different ways. For example, the first Vancouverites lived in villages of wood-planked houses arranged in rows, often surrounded by a stockade. Totem poles would be set up nearby as an emblem of a particular family or clan.

The distinct communities that formed in this area at that time included the Musqueam – who mostly populated the area around English Bay, Burrard Inlet and the mouth of the Fraser River – as well as the Squamish, who had villages in the areas now called North Vancouver, West Vancouver, Jericho Beach and Stanley Park. Other groups that resided in the area included the Kwantlen, Tsawwassen and Coast Salish people.

Early Lifestyles

There is very little evidence today about exactly how these early locals went about their daily lives. Most settlements have crumbled into the ground and few have been rediscovered by archaeologists. In addition, communities mostly deployed oral records, which meant telling each

It wasn't until 1949 that BC's First Nations were given the right to vote in provincial elections. The legislation, which was highly controversial at the time, also gave the vote to Canadian residents of Chinese and Japanese origin.

other the stories and legends of their ancestors, often in song, rather than writing things down. It's important to recall that this method would have been highly successful until the Europeans arrived, at which time generations of locals were quickly wiped out by disease or military attack.

One universally accepted aspect of these early societies is that art and creativity were a key presence in many communities. Homes were often adorned with exterior carvings and totem poles, and these illustrated a reverential regard for nature. This suggests that the region's first people enjoyed a symbiotic relationship with their surroundings – in many ways they were the founders of Western Canada's current green movement.

European Contact

There are 34 indigenous languages and 61 dialects in BC alone, making the province Canada's most linguistically diverse for First Nations languages. For more on this rich linguistic heritage, see www.fpcc.ca.

Disease imported by early European visitors, such as Captain Cook, started the long slide for the indigenous people. Outright racism was rampant, as was official discrimination – perhaps the worst instance of which was the residential school system, which removed indigenous children from their families in order to strip them of their language and culture. In 1859 the governor of BC, James Douglas, declared that all the land and any wealth underneath it belonged to the Crown.

Laws enacted during much of the 20th century brutalized indigenous culture. A notorious law banned the potlatch, a vital ceremony held over many days by communities to mark special occasions and establish ranks and privileges. Dancing, feasting and elaborate gift-giving from the chief to his people are features.

In the Rockies region of Alberta similar devastating challenges were faced by the Sioux, Cree and Blackfoot people. This region is also the traditional home of the Métis, which translates from the French word for mixed blood and historically refers to the children born from Cree and French fur traders. It now refers to anyone born of mixed Cree and indigenous ancestry. Métis account for one-third of Canada's indigenous population and Edmonton is home to one of the country's largest populations.

Indigenous Land Claims

The last 60 years have seen both an effort by governments to reverse the grim course of previous decades and a resurgence of indigenous culture. A long and difficult process has begun to settle claims from the 1859 proclamation through negotiations with the various bands. Negotiations include six stages but, so far, only one treaty has been finalized, with the Nisga'a people in 2000. It provides about $200 million and allows some self-governance. Given the money involved, the treaty process is conten-

TOP 10 INDIGENOUS CULTURAL ATTRACTIONS

➡ Museum of Anthropology (p115), Vancouver

➡ Royal BC Museum (p153), Victoria

➡ Haida Heritage Centre at Kay Llnagaay (p235), Haida Gwaii

➡ U'mista Cultural Centre (p188), Alert Bay

➡ Museum of Northern BC (p233), Prince Rupert

➡ Head-Smashed-In Buffalo Jump (p101), Fort Macleod

➡ Blackfoot Crossing Historical Park (p104), Canadian Badlands

➡ Nk'mip Desert & Heritage Centre (p201), Osoyoos

➡ Squamish Lil'wat Cultural Centre (p141), Whistler

➡ Bill Reid Gallery of Northwest Coast Art (p113), Vancouver

Totem pole, Haida Gwaii (p234)

tious in Western Canada; much of the land under downtown Vancouver is subject to indigenous claims. With Justin Trudeau, a strong supporter of indigenous community, as Canada's prime minister, many are hopeful for swifter and more meaningful progress.

Haida Makes History

Hundreds of locals, visitors and dignitaries gathered in Haida Gwaii in 2013 to mark a special and highly symbolic event. In the first such ceremony in the area for more than a century, a three-story-high totem pole was manually raised (with ropes) in the Gwaii Haanas National Park Reserve. The colorful, highly intricate pole took more than a year to carve, and its symbols were chosen to show that the islands are protected from harm.

There's more to the pole than its creation: it was carved to mark the two-decade anniversary of a treaty between the Haida and the Canadian government that allows both groups to protect and co-manage this region. It was also sited on Lyell Island, where the Haida protested logging of the area in 1985. The tense standoff made national headlines and ultimately culminated in the creation of Gwaii Haanas National Park Reserve. That protest is remembered on the pole itself, with a carved area showing five men locking arms in solidarity.

Yukon First Nations

Today the Yukon region is home to 14 First Nations, which share eight languages. These First Nations include the Kluane, Teslin Tlingit and Ross River Dena communities. An estimated one-quarter of all Yukoners can trace Indigenous ancestry.

These communities often work together to share issues and raise concerns. At their annual general assembly in 2013, the Council of Yukon

BC indigenous communities have succeeded in having indigenous names officially applied to several areas. For example, the former Queen Charlotte Islands are now Haida Gwaii, an area of southern BC ocean has been designated as the Salish Sea, and some locals have called for Stanley Park to be renamed Xwayxway.

First Nations passed a resolution calling for the Yukon government to ban fracking (a controversial method of oil and gas extraction) throughout the region.

Indigenous Arts

In the past there has been little outside recognition of the art produced by Canada's Indigenous communities. But over the last several decades there's been a strong and growing appreciation of this unique creative force. For most visitors totem poles are their entry point, but the region's cultural treasures go way beyond that. Artworks such as masks, drums and paintings feature the distinctive black and red sweeping brush strokes that depict wolves, ravens and other animals from the spirit world.

Although most Indigenous groups lack formal written history as we know it, centuries of cultural traditions live on. Art has long been a method of expression, intimately linked with historical and cultural preservation, religion and social ceremony.

Today, artist Lawrence Paul Yuxweluptun explores politics, the environment and indigenous issues with his paintings that take inspiration from Coast Salish mythology. Shuswap actor and writer Darrell Dennis tackles indigenous stereotypes head-on in his thrilling one-man show *Tales of an Urban Indian.*

Tofino-based Roy Henry Vickers fuses mystical and traditional themes with contemporary approaches, while Brian Jungen has gained national and international recognition for his challenging abstract approach.

Cultural Experiences

It seems to have taken Canada many years to realize that international visitors are eager to experience indigenous culture, and to encounter and understand the country's first inhabitants – and not just by viewing a dusty diorama of an 'Indian village' in a forgotten corner of a local museum.

Large and impressive cultural centers have sprung up in BC and Alberta in recent years. These include the Blackfoot Crossing Historical Park (p104) in Alberta, where you can learn from the locals about the authentic exhibits, watch a spectacular cultural dance display (look out for the Chicken Dance, typically performed by the community's young males) and stay overnight in a woodland tipi, with the sound of coyotes howling at the moon to lull you to sleep.

The Haida Heritage Centre (p235) in Haida Gwaii, BC, offers deep immersion into the history and rich creative impulses of the fascinating Haida people. The archipelago's Gwaii Haanas National Park Reserve

INDIGENOUS TOUR OPERATORS

On your travels around BC, look out for Indigenous-themed or -led tours and excursions with the following operators. They're often a great way to gain a different perspective on the region.

Haida Style Expeditions (p236) Cultural and fishing tours.

Talaysay Tours (☑604-628-8555; www.talaysay.com; tours adult/child from $40/32) Kayaking and walking tours.

T'ashii Paddle School (p179) Interpretive canoe tours.

Spirit Eagles Experiences (www.spiriteagle.ca) Guided canoe and cultural tours.

Aboriginal Journeys (www.aboriginaljourneys.com) Wildlife-watching tours to spot everything from orcas to grizzlies.

HISTORY OF TOTEMS

The artistry of Northwest Coast native groups – Tsimshian, Haida, Tlingit, Kwakwa-ka'wakw and Nuxalk – is as intricate as it is simple. One of the most spectacular examples of this is the totem pole, which has become such a symbolic icon that it's part of popular culture.

The carving of totem poles was largely quashed after the Canadian government outlawed the potlatch (gift-giving ceremonial feast) in 1884. Most totems only last 60 to 80 years, though some on Haida Gwaii are more than 100 years old. When a totem falls, tradition says it should be left there until another is erected in its place.

Today totem carving is again widespread, though the poles are often constructed for nontraditional uses, such as public art. Modern totems commissioned for college campuses, museums and public buildings no longer recount the lineage of any one household but instead stand to honor indigenous people, their outstanding artistry and their beliefs.

(p235) also offers the chance to peruse evocative former villages on its southern shoreline, where decaying totem poles face the mist-streaked ocean as if they're telling a story. Unsurprisingly this region is viewed as one of BC's most magical and mystical, with visitors frequently citing the area as one of the unforgettable highlights of their vacation.

Vancouver itself is crammed with First Nations encounters, such as a First Nations restaurant and an indigenous-art-themed hotel, plus pertinent art in public buildings and galleries throughout the city. If you only have time for one spot, make it the University of British Columbia. It's home to the dramatic Museum of Anthropology (p115), which is teeming with astonishing art and artifacts that illustrate the rich heritage of indigenous culture and society throughout this region. The regular guided tours (free) are highly recommended.

West Coast Cuisine

Fine dining in the region used to mean choosing between doughnut varieties at a Tim Hortons outlet, but Western Canada is now sitting at the grown-ups' table when it comes to eating out. Seafood fans can stuff themselves to the gills with marine treats in British Columbia, while carnivores love Canada's steak-capital Rockies region. Throughout the area a romance with local ingredients has transformed restaurant menus, many of which offer Canada's best international dining.

Regional Flavors

Vancouver emulates Montréal and Toronto in the fine-dining field (though West Coasters don't commonly dress up much for dinner) and also rivals both those cities with its surfeit of excellent multicultural dining options. You'll be hard-pressed to find a bad Chinese or Japanese restaurant here, while its West Coast dining choices (usually fused with intriguing international influences) bring the best of the region to tables across the city.

In recent years some of the country's most innovative chefs have set up shop here, inspired by the twin influences of an abundant local larder of unique flavors and the most cosmopolitan – especially Asian – population in Canada. Fusion is the starting point here, but there's also a high level of authenticity in traditional multicultural dining: amazing sushi bars and Japanese *izakayas* jostle for attention with superb Vietnamese and Korean eateries that feel like they've been transported across the world.

Outside Vancouver, the urban areas of Vancouver Island – especially downtown Victoria – as well as the Okanagan Valley offer additional top-notch eateries. And if you're heading up to Whistler, you can expect plenty of surprisingly gourmet restaurants to restore your energy after an exhilarating day on the slopes.

Eating well is not just about fine dining, of course, and you'll find many welcoming places to nosh in more rustic areas of BC, Alberta and the Yukon, many of them delivering some taste-bud-thrilling surprises. Follow the locals to waterfront seafood diners in coastal communities such as Gibsons, Salt Spring Island and Prince Rupert for the kind of freshly caught aquatic treats that would cost several times more in the big city.

Even the smallest towns can usually rustle up a decent meal, including those ubiquitous 'Chinese and Canadian' eateries where the menu usually combines deep-fried cheeseburgers with gelatinous sweet-and-sour-pork dishes. There are also many family-oriented, mid-priced eateries and diners serving milkshakes in a metal cup for those traveling with kids. Bars are usually also just as interested in serving food as they are beer.

Food nirvana stretches across the Rockies into Alberta, Canada's cowboy country. This is the nation's beef capital, and you'll find top-notch Alberta steak on menus at leading restaurants across the country. But it's not all about steak here: look out for caribou and venison, both rising in popularity in recent years. If you're offered 'prairie oysters,' though, you might want to know (or maybe you'd prefer not to) that they're bull's testicles prepared in a variety of intriguing ways designed to take your mind off their origin.

Wherever your taste buds take you, try to score some unique local flavors with a sampling of Indigenous food. Canada's Indigenous people have some fascinating and accessible culinary traditions. Reliant on meat and seafood (try a juicy halibut stew on BC's Haida Gwaii), Indigenous tradition also includes bannock bread, imported by the Scots and appropriated by Canada's original locals. And if you think you're an expert on desserts, try some 'Indian ice cream.' Made from whipped soapberries, it's sweetened with sugar to assuage its bitter edge.

Seafood

Atlantic Canada might pretend otherwise, but the West Coast is the country's undeniable seafood capital. A trip to the region that doesn't include throwing yourself into BC's brimming marine larder is like visiting Italy without having pasta: you can do it, but what's the point?

If you're starting in Vancouver you'll find an astonishing array of innovative seafood dishes. This is the world's best sushi city outside Japan, and there are hundreds of spots to dip into, from slick joints with sake bars to cheap-and-cheerful holes-in-the-wall where you'll be rubbing shoulders with homesick overseas-language students.

You'll also find a full table of traditional and innovative dishes in the area's Chinese restaurants, from the Chinatown dim-sum dining rooms to contemporary fusion joints in Richmond, often hidden inside large Hong Kong–style shopping malls. If you're feeling adventurous look out for locally harvested geoduck (pronounced 'gooey duck'), a giant saltwater clam. It's a delicacy in Chinese dining and is shipped to chefs across the world.

It's not only multicultural menus that bring BC's seafood to local diners. Many Pacific Northwest restaurants (more typically called West Coast restaurants on this side of the border) feature seasonal fresh catches, and as you travel around the region you'll find the same amazing seafood almost everywhere you go. Juicy wild salmon is a signature here and in the autumn it dominates menus; do not miss it. Almost as popular is the early spring spot prawn season when the sweet, crunchy crustaceans turn up on tables throughout BC.

If you fancy meeting the fishers and choosing your grub straight off the back of a boat, you can also do that. The boats bobbing around the government wharf near Vancouver's Granville Island are a good spot to

---

WEST COAST CUISINE REGIONAL FLAVORS

Farmers markets are exploding across the region, bringing home-grown produce to the tables of locals and epicurious visitors. Look out for seasonal fresh-picked peaches, cherries, blueberries and apples. For BC market locations, see www.bcfarmersmarket.org; for Alberta, check www.albertafarmersmarket.com. In the Yukon, hit Whitehorse's Fireweed Community Market.

LOCAL FOOD & WINE MAGAZINES

Avenue Magazine (www.avenuecalgary.com) Lifestyle publication illuminating the Calgary restaurant scene for hungry locals. Separate Edmonton edition (www.avenueedmonton.com) also available.

City Palate (www.citypalate.ca) Covering Calgary's food and dining scene.

Eat Magazine (www.eatmagazine.ca) Free mag covering BC food and wine happenings.

Edible Vancouver (www.ediblecommunities.com/vancouver) Free quarterly with an organic and Slow Food bent, available at choice local food shops.

Growler (www.thegrowler.ca) Vancouver-based beer publication, showcasing beer producers throughout the province.

Vancouver Magazine (www.vanmag.com) City lifestyle glossy with good coverage of local restaurants and culinary happenings.

MEET YOUR MAKERS

Ask Vancouverites where the food on their tables comes from and most will point vacantly at a nearby supermarket, but others will confidently tell you about the Fraser Valley. This lush interior region starts about 50km from the city and has been studded with busy farms for decades. In recent years farmers and the people they feed have started to get to know one another on a series of five **Circle Farm Tours**. These self-guided driving tours take you around the communities of Langley, Abbotsford, Chilliwack, Agassiz and Harrison Mills, Maple Ridge and Pitt Meadows, pointing out recommended pit stops – farms, markets, wineries and eateries – along the way. To add a cool culinary adventure to your BC trip, download the free tour maps at www.circlefarmtour.ca.

try, as is the evocative boardwalk area in Steveston. The south Richmond heritage fishing village is an ideal destination for seafood fans – there are two excellent museums recalling the area's days as the center of the once-mighty regional fishing fleet, and there are several fish-and-chips joints within chip-lobbing distance of the water.

If you're lucky enough to make it to Haida Gwaii, you'll encounter some of the best seafood you've ever had in your life, typically caught that day and prepared in a simple manner that reveals the rich flavors of the sea. Keep your appetite primed for halibut, scallops and crabs, often plucked from the shallow waters just off the beach by net-wielding locals walking along the sand.

If you're buying fresh wild salmon, look for the following signs of freshness: it should not smell 'fishy'; the gills should have a red hue; and the eyes should be bright and clear. For more tips and information on the region's tasty salmon, see www.bcsalmon.ca.

Eat Streets

Some thoroughfares in the region are permanently suffused with the aroma of great cooking, as well as an attendant chorus of satisfied-looking diners rubbing their bellies and surreptitiously loosening their straining belts. If you're hungry, heading to these areas is the way to go – you'll have a great regional meal, and meet the locals into the bargain.

If you're in Vancouver there are several options to choose from. Near Stanley Park, in the West End's Denman St, you can metaphorically travel around the world in the space of four blocks. Midrange ethnic restaurants abound here, including Ethiopian, Malaysian, Ukrainian and Vietnamese. The menu is similarly diverse on Commercial Dr, Main St and Kitsilano's West 4th Ave. But if fine dining floats your boat, check out Hamilton St and Mainland St in Yaletown. Both are lined with fancy joints for that romantic, special-occasion meal.

Across the region, Richmond's 'Golden Village' area (Alexandra Rd here is also known as 'Eat St') is packed with superb Asian dining. Vancouver's other fast-growing sister city, Surrey, is known for its Indian restaurants, many of them hidden in utilitarian strip malls on arterial Scott Rd.

Victoria has its own smaller Chinatown, but also specializes in creative brunches, pub grub and afternoon tea (which can be a meal in itself in these parts). Further north on Vancouver Island, Tofino is a farm-to-table paradise where chain restaurants have yet to infringe, while back on the mainland Prince Rupert's Cow Bay Rd has fish-and-chips in abundance and some great bistro options.

Over in Alberta the Whyte Ave stretch of Edmonton's Old Strathcona neighborhood offers some excellent independent dining options, including plenty of high-end international eateries. In Calgary, where the dining scene has jumped in quality in recent years, the top dining thoroughfares are downtown's Stephen St and in the neighborhoods of Kensington, Mission and Inglewood.

Street Eats

Vancouver's sidewalk-dining revolution kicked off in mid-2010 with the introduction of 17 diverse food carts across the city. Suddenly barbecued pulled pork, organic tacos and gourmet Korean-fusion takeout were available to hungry locals. The network has since expanded to more than 100 carts. Grab delicious tacos from Tacofino and sit on the sunny steps of the Vancouver Art Gallery to watch the world go by, or dive into a creamy curry at Vij's Railway Express nearby. Visit www.streetfoodapp.com/vancouver for the latest listings and locations.

Since Vancouver kick-started the region's street-eats trend, Calgary and Edmonton have jumped on board with their own growing scenes, while trucks often pop up at smaller towns, too.

If you can't find a cart, just head to Richmond, BC. The city hosts two Asian-style night markets on weekends throughout the summer. These are stuffed with steaming food stands serving everything from spicy fish balls to 'tornado potatoes' – thin-cut spirals of fried potato served on skewers.

Vegetarians & Vegans

Traveling herbivores will find a full roster of vegetarian and vegan options in urban BC, with Vancouver especially undergoing a recent and inventive surge in meat-free dining options.

Eat heartily before you leave the city, though, as your options diminish as the towns shrink in size. In the smaller settlements of BC and the Yukon, vegetarian options can be limited to salads, sandwiches or portobello mushroom burgers, with the occasional veggie-only joint standing out like a beacon in the carnivorous darkness.

Crossing into the meat-loving Rockies, your choices will diminish faster than an ice cube on a sunny sidewalk. But it's not all doom and gloom: Calgary and Edmonton have their own dedicated veggie eateries and you can usually find some meat-free pasta options in Banff and Jasper restaurants.

In *The Boreal Gourmet: Adventures in Northern Cooking*, Whitehorse-based Michele Genest explores the Yukon's regional food specialties at the same time as offering insights into life in the region. Anyone for moose cooked in locally brewed espresso stout?

Festivals & Events

Food and drink is the foundation of having a good time in BC, Alberta and the Yukon. Languid summer barbecues, fall's feast-like Thanksgiving Day and winter family get-togethers at Christmas traditionally center on tables groaning with meat and seafood dishes, diet-eschewing fruit desserts and plentiful wine and beer.

In addition there's a full menu of annual festivals where you can dive into the flavors of the region and bond with locals over tasty treats. Recommended events include the following:

Cornucopia (p144) A bacchanalian November food and wine fest in Whistler.
Dine Out Vancouver (www.dineoutvancouver.com; ⊘mid-Jan) A three-week-long January event where local restaurants offer great-value two- or three-course tasting menus.
Feast of Fields (www.feastoffields.com) Local produce and top chefs at alfresco dinner-party days in metro Vancouver, the Okanagan Valley and on Vancouver Island.
Feast Tofino (www.feasttofino.com) A multi-week menu of Tofino events in May focused on local seafood.
Saturna Island Lamb Barbecue (p196) Pagan-esque Canada Day party in the Southern Gulf Islands.
BC Shellfish & Seafood Festival (www.bcshellfishfestival.ca; ⊘Jun) One of BC's finest seafood festivals fires up the Comox Valley on Vancouver Island in June.
Taste of Edmonton (www.tasteofedm.ca) A nine-day outdoor event in July

showcasing local eateries and producers. There's also a similar, smaller event in Calgary (www.tasteofcalgary.com) in August.

Culinary Tours

If following your nose is an unreliable method for tapping into the region's culinary scene, consider an escort: BC is especially well served by operators who can guide you through the area's flavors on a tasty tour. Slip into a pair of pants with an elasticized waist and hit the road for what may well be the highlight of your visit.

If you're attracted to Vancouver Island's cornucopia of great produce, consider a culinary exploration of Victoria with **A Taste of Victoria Food Tours** (www.atasteofvictoriafoodtours.com), starting in the public market and continuing through Chinatown and around the Inner Harbour. Of a more energetic bent are the food and craft-beer excursions offered by bike tour and rental outfit Pedaler (p158).

In Vancouver, consider a Granville Island Market tour with Vancouver Foodie Tours (p121).

Over in Alberta consider a guided tour of the Calgary Farmers Market with **Alberta Food Tours** (www.albertafoodtours.ca). The company also offers a full range of foodie tour options around the province, from Canmore to Banff to Edmonton.

When to Eat

You can get virtually anything your belly craves throughout the day in Vancouver, but outside the region's main metropolis, restaurants may shut early, even in seemingly hip places such as Victoria, Edmonton and Whistler. If it's time for dinner, be at the restaurant by 8pm outside peak summer weekends or you may find yourself out of luck.

Breakfast is usually eaten between 7am and 10am. Many hotels offer at least a continental breakfast (a hot drink, juice, toast, muffins and maybe cereal) during these hours, with higher-end joints typically serving cooked options – various varieties of eggs Benedict are very popular here (go for the smoked salmon). Most local residents eat breakfast at home on weekdays or grab a quick bite on the run with their morning coffee. But on weekends a leisurely breakfast or brunch at a cafe or restaurant is a favorite pastime. Weekend brunch service often stretches well into the afternoon at restaurants and is one of the most popular ways for locals to socialize, especially in brunch-loving Victoria and Vancouver.

Lunch is typically taken between 11am and 1pm. It can be as simple as a snack bought from a farmers market or street-food cart, or a picnic taken on your hike. Dinner is served anytime from about 5pm to 8pm, often later on weekends and in large cities as well as resort areas such as Whistler and Banff.

Dress is casual almost everywhere. For more formal restaurants the cliched 'smart casual' is perfectly acceptable.

The Yukon Gold is one of Canada's favorite premium potato varieties. With a yellow color and nugget-sized appearance, it was named after the country's gold-rush region. It is popular for boiling, baking and frying, mainly because it retains its distinctive yellow hue.

Drinking BC & Beyond

Gone are the days when drinkers were perfectly content to quaff generic fizzy beers or rocket-fuel wines made from foraged berries. Mirroring the recent rise in distinctive regional cuisine, Western Canada has developed one of the nation's most sophisticated drinking scenes. Vineyards in BC's Okanagan Valley and beyond explore the nuances of wine, while the province also leads in craft-beer production, with dozens of flavorful producers, and fosters an emerging trend towards craft cideries and distilleries.

Wine Regions

Visitors are often surprised to learn that wine is produced here, but their skepticism is usually tempered after a choice drink or two. BC's wines have gained ever-greater kudos in recent years, and while smaller-scale production and the industry dominance of wine regions such as Napa means they'll never be a global market leader, there are some surprisingly top-quality vintages.

The best way to sample any wine is to head straight to the source. Consider doing some homework and locating the nearest vineyards on your visit: they'll likely be a lot closer than you think. The Okanagan Valley (p202) and Vancouver Island are the region's main wine areas, but you'll also find wineries – alone or in mini-clusters – in BC's Fraser Valley and on the Southern Gulf Islands. And while Alberta has far fewer wineries, keep your eyes peeled while you're on the road: there are a handful of friendly (mostly fruit-wine) joints worth stopping at.

Wherever your tipple craving takes you, drink widely and deeply. And make sure you have plenty of room in your suitcase – packing materials are always available if you want to take a bottle or two home with you.

For background and further information before you arrive, peruse the Wines of British Columbia website (www.winebc.com) as well as the insightful John Schreiner on Wine blog (www.johnschreiner.blogspot.ca).

John Schreiner's Okanagan Wine Tour Guide (2014) is an in-depth tome covering the region for visiting oenophiles. It's packed with great suggestions on how to make the most of a wine-based trawl around the area.

Okanagan Valley

The rolling hills of this lakeside BC region are well worth the five-hour drive from Vancouver. Studded among the vine-striped slopes, approximately 175 wineries enjoy a diverse climate that fosters both crisp whites and bold reds. With varietals including pinot noir, pinot gris, pinot blanc, merlot and chardonnay, there's a wine here to suit almost every palate. Many visitors base themselves in Kelowna, the Okanagan's wine capital,

---

INDIGENOUS WINERY

Nk'Mip Cellars (pronounced 'in-ka-meep') became North America's first Indigenous-owned and -operated winery when it opened its doors in Osoyoos, in the heart of BC's winery-heavy Okanagan region. The swanky, state-of-the-art winery was an immediate hit with visitors for its tours and tastings. The winery, which is run by the Osoyoos Band, also has its own vineyard. Varietals produced include merlot, chardonnay, pinot noir and riesling ice wine.

before fanning out to well-known blockbuster wineries such as Mission Hill, Quails' Gate, Cedar Creek and Summerhill Pyramid Winery (yes, it has a pyramid). Many of them have excellent vista-hugging restaurants. For more information on Okanagan wines and wineries, visit www.okanaganwines.ca.

Oliver & Osoyoos

Some of BC's best Okanagan wineries are centered south of the valley between Oliver and Osoyoos, where the hot climate fosters a long, warm growing season. With gravel, clay and sandy soils, this area is ideally suited to varietals such as merlot, chardonnay, gewürztraminer and cabernet sauvignon. The 40-or-so wineries here include celebrated producers Burrowing Owl, Tinhorn Creek and Road 13 Vineyards, making this an ideal touring area. Don't miss Nk'Mip Cellars, a First Nations winery in Osoyoos that's on the edge of a desert. For more information on this region's imbibing opportunities, see www.oliverosoyoos.com.

For the lowdown on BC's burgeoning craftbeer scene, pick up a copy of *The Growler* (www.thegrowler.ca) at area breweries.

Vancouver Island & the Gulf Islands

Long-established as a farming area, Vancouver Island's verdant Cowichan Valley is home to some great little wineries. A short drive from Victoria you'll find Averill Creek, Blue Grouse, Cherry Point Vineyards and Venturi-Schulze Vineyards. Also consider the delightful Merridale Estate Cidery, which produces several celebrated ciders on its gently sloped orchard grounds.

A lesser-known winery region, the bucolic Gulf Islands are home to several small wineries, including two on Salt Spring Island that welcome visitors. If you plan to visit Salt Spring on a summer weekend, gather picnic fixings at the treat-packed Saturday Market (local-made cheese recommended) before picking up an island-made libation to accompany your alfresco feast.

For more information on Vancouver Island and Gulf Islands wineries, visit www.wineislands.ca.

Here for the Beer?

While the usual round of bland factory suds and international suspects (you know the ones we mean) are readily available, a little digging – actually, hardly any digging at all – uncovers a thriving regional microbrewing scene overflowing with distinctive craft beers.

From Tofino to Prince Rupert, BC is packed like a Friday-night pub with almost 200 breweries, many of them only established in the past decade or so. On your thirst-slaking travels, look out for taps from celebrated producers such as Four Winds (Delta), Townsite (Powell River), Driftwood (Victoria), Persephone (Gibsons), Central City (Surrey), Howe Sound (Squamish) and Powell Street (Vancouver), which crafts an utterly sublime Dive Bomb Porter.

A SIX-PACK OF TOP BEERS

On your travels around the region, look out for these taste-tested top brews:

Driftwood Brewery's Fat Tug IPA (www.driftwoodbeer.com)

Powell Street Craft Brewery's Dive Bomb Dark Ale (www.powellbeer.com)

Four Winds Brewing's IPA (www.fourwindsbrewing.ca)

Persephone Brewing's Persephone Pale Ale (www.persephonebrewing.com)

Central City Brewing's Red Racer India Red Ale (www.centralcitybrewing.com)

Howe Sound Brewing's Father John's Winter Ale (www.howesound.com)

Victoria kick-started the region's microbrewery golden age a few years back but Vancouver has seized the initiative in recent years. The reason? Breweries in Vancouver (of which there are at least three dozen) are much more likely to have tasting rooms, each operating like a de facto neighborhood pub. That means crawl-worthy brewery districts have popped up in the city, including those on Main St (don't miss Brassneck and Main Street Brewing) and another in East Vancouver (look out for Callister, Powell Street and Off the Rail).

You don't have to go thirsty in the Rockies region, either. Travelers in Alberta should hunt down local beverages from Calgary's Village Brewery and Tool Shed Brewing, Edmonton's Alley Kat Brewing, Red Deer's Blindman Brewing, and the popular Jasper Brewing Company brewpub, evocatively located in the heart of Jasper National Park. If you're way up north, it has to be Yukon Brewing (start with a pint of Yukon Gold).

The smaller the brewery the more likely it is to produce tipples that make generic fizzy beers taste like something you'd rather wash your car with. Ales, bitters, lagers, pilsners, porters, stouts, sours and even hemp beers are often available at pubs, bars and restaurants throughout the region. Some bars also host weekly cask nights, when they crack open a guest keg of something special; check ahead and find out what's available during your visit.

If you want to see how it's all done – and stoke your thirst in the process – **Granville Island Brewing** (GIB; ✆604-687-2739; www.gib.ca; 1441 Cartwright St, Granville Island; tours $11.50; ⊘tours 12:30pm, 2pm, 4pm & 5:50pm; 🚍50) in Vancouver and Big Rock Brewery in Calgary are among those offering short tours coupled with satisfyingly leisurely tastings. Cheers!

Artisan Distilling

Craft distilling has become Western Canada's latest wave of artisan booze-making. You'll find intriguing operations, most of them with inviting tasting rooms, across the region. Many are selling house-made vodka and gin that's always a delightful, aromatic surprise for those of us more used to the bland factory varieties that dominate the market. These drops are typically smooth enough to drink neat, and you can expect to pay around $40 to $50 for a savor-worthy bottle; samples are always available.

As these distillery operations mature (most of them are less than seven or eight years old), they are beginning to also sell aged whiskies – ask about this wherever you visit. Distilleries to look out for include Liberty in Vancouver, Gillespie's in Squamish, Pemberton Distillery in Pemberton, Sheringham on Vancouver Island and Eau Claire near Calgary.

Take the opportunity to try as many drops as you can handle under one roof at Vancouver's annual BC Distilled (www.bcdistilled.ca) festival, usually held in March.

Festivals

Time your visit well and you'll be sipping glasses of wine or downing pints of beer at a series of regional events. Large or small, they're a great way to hang out with the locals.

Wine lovers are well served in the Okanagan, where several events are held throughout the year. The biggest is the 10-day Fall Wine Festival, while January's Winter Okanagan Wine Festival is evocatively hosted in an icicle-draped ski resort – there's usually plenty of ice wine to go around here. For information on the region's events, see www.thewinefestivals.com.

The legal drinking age in BC and the Yukon is 19; in Alberta it's 18. If you look young you should expect to be asked for identification. Canada is very serious about curbing drink-driving, and you may encounter mandatory roadside checkpoints, especially on summer evenings or around winter holidays.

If you're in Vancouver in February, connect with the Vancouver International Wine Festiva (p121)l. It's the city's largest and oldest wine-based celebration and it focuses on one wine region each year.

Combining drinks and grub, Alberta's Rocky Mountain Wine and Food Festival (www.rockymountainwine.com) takes place on different dates in Calgary and Edmonton.

If beer floats your boat, you can sample all those BC microbrews you've been craving at the ever-popular Vancouver Craft Beer Week (p121) in late May. It's the province's biggest beer event, but it's not the only one: check out Victoria's Great Canadian Beer Festival (www.gcbf.com) as well as the five annual events staged under the Alberta Beer Festivals (www.albertabeerfestivals.com) banner.

If you're looking for something stronger, don't miss November's annual Hopscotch Festival (www.hopscotchfestival.com), staged in Vancouver and Kelowna. It covers all the boozy bases by focusing on beer, whiskey and other spirits.

Farmers markets around BC offer sales and booze samples to shoppers. Look out for wine, beer and distillery stalls wherever you go.

Where to Drink

You don't have to visit wineries, breweries or distilleries to find a good drink in the region: BC, Alberta and the Yukon are well stocked with watering holes, from traditional pubs to slick wine bars and sparkling cocktail joints, though finding a perfect Moscow Mule in smaller towns may be a tough ask. Keep in mind that most bars follow the North American table-service approach: servers come to the table for your order rather than expecting you to order your own drink at the bar. The (potential) downside is that table service means tipping is standard.

While craft booze is taking off across the region, brewpubs are still underrepresented in some areas: you'll find a handful in Vancouver and Victoria, plus single beacons of beery delight in towns such as Banff, Jasper and Kelowna. In contrast, many craft breweries in BC (with the notable exception of most in Victoria) have small, highly welcoming tasting rooms that are among the best places in the province to drink a beer with the locals. Try Persephone in Gibsons, Townsite in Powell River, Brassneck in Vancouver and Wheelhouse in Prince Rupert.

Survival Guide

Directory A–Z

Accessible Travel

➡ Guide dogs may legally be brought into restaurants, hotels and other businesses.

➡ Many public-service phone numbers and some pay phones are adapted for the hearing-impaired.

➡ Most public buildings are wheelchair accessible, and many parks feature trails that are likewise accessible.

➡ Many newer or renovated hotels have dedicated accessible rooms.

➡ Public transportation is increasingly accessible; all buses in Vancouver, for example, are fully wheelchair accessible.

➡ Start your trip planning at Access to Travel (www.accesstotravel.gc.ca), the Canadian federal government's dedicated website. It has information on air, bus, rail and ferry transportation.

➡ Download Lonely Planet's free Accessible Travel guide from http://lptravel.to/AccessibleTravel.

Other helpful resources:

CNIB (☑604-431-2121; www.cnib.ca) Support and services for the visually impaired.

Disability Alliance BC (☑604-875-0188; www.disability alliancebc.org) Programs and support for people with disabilities.

Western Institute for the Deaf & Hard of Hearing (☑604-736-7391; www.widhh.com) Interpreter services and resources for the hearing-impaired.

Accommodations

British Columbia (BC) and Alberta offer a good range of hotels, B&Bs and hostels, with reduced options in northern BC and the Yukon. Booking ahead is advisable in summer (and in winter at ski resorts), especially in Vancouver, Victoria and the main Rockies destinations.

Booking Services

Hello BC (www.hellobc.com) Official Destination British Columbia accommodations search engine.

Travel Alberta (www.travel alberta.com) Accommodations

booking engine on the province's official visitor site.

Travel Yukon (www.travelyukon.com) Online accommodations listings.

Tourism Vancouver (www.tour ismvancouver.com) Wide range of accommodations listings and package deals.

BC Bed & Breakfast Innkeepers Guild (www.bcsbestbnbs.com) Wide range of B&Bs around the province.

Camping & RV in BC (www.campingrvbc.com) Resources and site listings for the province.

Lonely Planet (www.lonely planet.com/canada/hotels) Recommendations and bookings.

B&Bs

North American B&Bs are typically more luxurious than the casual, family-style pensions found in Europe. There are thousands to choose from across the region, many of which are unique or romantic.

➡ Book ahead: B&Bs often have only one to three rooms.

➡ Check the rules: many B&Bs are adults only, while others only open seasonally and/or require a two-night minimum stay.

➡ Parking is usually free.

➡ Local visitor centers usually have good B&B listings for their areas. Also see Bed & Breakfast Online (www.bbcanada.com) for listings across the region.

BOOK YOUR STAY ONLINE

For more accommodations reviews by Lonely Planet authors, check out http://lonelyplanet.com/canada. You'll find independent reviews, as well as recommendations on the best places to stay. Best of all, you can book online.

Camping

This region is a campers' paradise with thousands of government-run and private campgrounds.

➜ Options range from basic pitches nestled in the remote wilderness to highly accessible, amenities-packed campgrounds popular with families.

➜ Campgrounds are typically open from May to September, but dates vary by location.

➜ Many popular sites are sold out months in advance: booking ahead is recommended, especially for holiday weekends and the summer peak season.

➜ Facilities vary widely. Expect little more than pit toilets and a fire ring at backcountry sites, while larger campgrounds may have shower blocks and guided interpretive programs.

➜ Camping in national or provincial parks can cost up to $45 per night, though many are around the $25 mark. Private sites may offer more facilities and charge a little more.

➜ See Parks Canada (www.pccamping.ca), BC Parks (www.discovercamping.ca) and Alberta Parks (www.reserve.albertaparks.ca) websites for information, listings and bookings for government-run sites in national and local parks.

Guest Ranches

BC and Alberta have dozens of enticing guest ranches, which is the euphemism for horse-centered dude ranches where you can join a trail ride or sit by a mountain lake. The Cariboo-Chilcotin region is a guest-ranch hotbed.

Hostels

Independent and Hostelling International (HI) hostels are easy to find in popular visitor destinations, with some areas enjoying healthy competition between several establishments.

➜ Dorms (typically $25 to $45) may be small or sleep up to 20 people, and facilities usually include shared bathrooms, a kitchen and common areas. Laundry facilities, bike storage and wi-fi are common.

➜ Private rooms in hostels are increasingly popular: they are also the most sought-after, so book far ahead.

➜ Many outdoorsy hostels offer extras such as bike or kayak rentals, while city-based hostels often have free or low-cost social programs that include guided tours or pub nights.

➜ City hostels are often open 24 hours; those in other areas may be closed during the day – check ahead.

➜ Booking ahead for hostels in popular destinations such as Tofino, Whistler and Banff is essential in summer.

➜ For locations, listings and bookings across the region, see Hostelling International (www.hihostels.ca), SameSun (www.samesun.com) and Backpackers Hostels Canada (www.backpackers.ca).

Hotels & Motels

➜ Hotel rates vary tremendously around the region. Plan to spend at least $150 for a basic double room with a private bathroom during summer peaks in Vancouver and Victoria. In less-visited areas, $100 is closer to the norm.

➜ Boutique properties and high-end hotels are readily available in Vancouver and Victoria, with chateau-like resorts common in Whistler and the Rockies.

➜ Wilderness retreats are dotted around the BC coastline and in some parts of the Rockies, offering spas and top-notch dining packages.

➜ Midrange hotel and motel rooms typically include a private bathroom, one or two large beds, a tea and coffee maker and free wi-fi.

➜ Your hotel may not include air-conditioning. If this is a deal breaker, check before you book.

➜ In distant areas such as northern BC, the Alberta outback and remote Yukon spots, you'll find hotels folksy at best.

➜ Many motels (and an increasing number of suite-style hotels) offer handy (and money-saving) kitchenettes.

➜ Children can often stay free in the same room as their parents; check to see if there's a charge for rollaway beds.

Taxes & Fees

Be aware that there will be some significant additions to most quoted room rates, including provincial taxes (up to 13% in BC) and also, in some areas, Hotel Room Tax of up to 3%. On top of this, some hotels also charge a Destination Marketing Fee of around 1.5%. Parking fees don't help either – overnight parking, especially at higher-end hotels, can be expensive, sometimes as much as $50 per night. Keep in mind that B&Bs usually include parking free of charge. Check all these potential extra charges at time of booking to avoid any unpleasant surprises.

SLEEPING PRICE RANGES

The following price ranges refer to a double room with bathroom.

$ less than $100

$$ $100–250

$$$ more than $250

Children

Family-friendly Western Canada is stuffed with activities and attractions for kids, and there's a good attitude in most restaurants and many accommodations to traveling families. For general advice on family travel, see Lonely Planet's *Travel with Children*.

Equipment Strollers, booster seats and toys can be rented from Wee Travel (www.wee travel.ca).

Resources Pick up the free *Kids' Guide Vancouver* around town and visit www.kidsvancouver. com for local tips, resources and family-focused events.

Blogs Check out www.rockies familyadventures.com for inspirational stories on how to cover the region with your family.

Parks Canada Canada's national park system offers plenty of (mostly summer) programs for visiting kids. Check individual park and historic site attractions online (www.pc.gc.ca) for detailed information.

Practicalities

Accommodations Children can often stay with parents at hotels for no extra charge. Cots may also be available. Some hostels have family rooms. Hotels can recommend trusted babysitting services.

Dining out Not all restaurants will have high chairs available; call ahead before you arrive.

Child safety seats Hire-car companies can provide these if you book head.

Breastfeeding in public This is rarely a problem for the locals in Western Canada.

Customs Regulations

➡ Check in with the **Canada Border Services Agency** (204-983-3500; www.cbsa. gc.ca) for the latest customs lowdown.

➡ Duty-free allowance coming into Canada is 1.14L (40oz) of liquor, 1.5L (or two 750mL bottles) of wine, or 24 cans or bottles of beer, as well as up to 200 cigarettes, 50 cigars or 200g of tobacco.

➡ You are allowed to bring in gifts up to a total value of $60. Gifts above $60 are subject to duty and taxes on the over-limit value.

➡ Fresh and prepared foods are the subject of myriad rules and regulations here. Just buy what you need in Canada.

Discount Cards

Parks Canada Discovery Pass (www.pc.gc.ca/en/voyage-travel/ admission) Good-value pass if you're planning to visit national parks and historic sites across the region (adult/child/family $67.70/free/136.40). Valid for 12 months.

Vancouver City Passport (www. citypassports.com) Discounts at attractions, restaurants and activities across the city for up to two adults and two children ($29.95). Redeemable by coupons.

Vanier Park ExplorePass (www. spacecentre.ca/explore-pass) Combined entry pass covering three Vancouver attractions: the Museum of Vancouver, Vancouver Maritime Museum and HR MacMillan Space Centre (adult/ child $42.50/36.50). Valid for one visit to each attraction.

Electricity

Type A
120V/60Hz

Type B
120V/60Hz

Food

The region has a fine range of eating options. Tables at the most popular restaurants in cities such as Vancouver, Victoria and Calgary need to be booked in advance.

Restaurants A full menu of options, from mom-and-pop operations to high-end spots for special occasions.

Cafes From sandwich-serving coffee shops to chatty local haunts, cafes are common and usually good value.

Bars Most bars also serve food, typically of the pub-grub variety.

Food trucks Vancouver is the food-truck capital and you'll find pockets of wheeled wonders elsewhere throughout the region.

Farmers markets Ubiquitous in summer; a great way to sample regional produce and local-made treats.

Health

A high level of hygiene in the region means most common infectious diseases will not be a major concern for travelers. No special vaccinations are required, but all travelers should be up to date with standard immunizations, such as tetanus and measles.

Before You Go
HEALTH INSURANCE

The Canadian healthcare system is one of the best in the world and excellent care is widely available. Benefits are generous for Canadian citizens, but foreigners aren't covered, which can make treatment prohibitively expensive.

Make sure you have travel insurance if your regular policy doesn't apply when you're abroad. Find out in advance if your insurance plan will make payments directly to providers or reimburse you later for overseas health expenditures.

MEDICATIONS

Bring medications in their original containers, clearly labeled. A signed, dated letter from your physician describing all medical conditions and medications, including generic names, is also a good idea. If carrying syringes or needles, be sure

to have a physician's letter documenting their medical necessity.

In BC & the Canadian Rockies
AVAILABILITY & COST OF HEALTH CARE

If you have a choice, treatment at a university hospital may be preferable to a community hospital, though you can often find superb medical care in small local hospitals and the waiting time is usually shorter. If the problem isn't urgent, you can call a nearby hospital and ask for a referral to a local physician – less expensive than a trip to the emergency room.

Pharmacies are abundantly supplied; however, you may find that some medications that are available over the counter in your home country require a prescription in Canada. In the largest cities you'll be able to find 24-hour pharmacies, though most drugstores typically keep regular store hours.

INFECTIOUS DISEASES

Be aware of the following, particularly if you're traveling in wilderness areas:

Giardiasis A parasitic infection of the small intestine. Symptoms may include nausea, bloating, cramps and diarrhea, and may last for weeks. Avoid drinking directly from lakes, ponds, streams and rivers, which may

be contaminated by animal or human feces.

Lyme Disease Transmitted by tiny deer ticks. Mostly occurs in late spring and summer in southern areas. First symptom is usually an expanding red rash. Flu-like symptoms, including fever, headache, joint pain and body aches, are also common.

West Nile Virus Recently observed in provinces including Alberta. Transmitted by Culex mosquitoes, which are active in late summer and early fall and generally bite after dusk. Most infections are mild, but the virus may infect the central nervous system, leading to fever, headache, confusion, coma and sometimes death.

MEDICAL SERVICES

For immediate medical assistance:

BC, Alberta & Whitehorse (Yukon) ☎911

Yukon (except Whitehorse) ☎867-667-5555
Generally, if you have a medical emergency, it's best to find the nearest hospital emergency room.

Insurance

Make sure you have adequate travel insurance to cover your trip. Cover for luggage theft or loss is handy, but health coverage for medical emergencies and

PRACTICALITIES

DVDs Canada is in DVD region 1.

Newspapers Most towns have a daily or weekly newspaper. The *Vancouver Sun* and *Calgary Herald* provide reasonable regional coverage.

Radio Signs at the entrances to towns provide local frequencies for CBC Radio One.

Smoking Banned in indoor public places and workplaces throughout Canada. This includes restaurants and bars.

Weights & Measures The metric system is used throughout Canada, though popular references to the imperial system (as used in the US) still survive.

treatment is vital: medical treatment for non-Canadians is expensive.

Worldwide travel insurance is available at www.lonelyplanet.com/travel-insurance. You can buy, extend and claim online anytime – even if you're already on the road.

Internet Access

➡ Free wi-fi connections are almost standard in accommodations across BC, Alberta and the Yukon.

➡ You'll find wi-fi and internet-access computers in libraries, and free wi-fi in coffee shops and other businesses.

➡ The wi-fi symbol in our listings shows where wi-fi access is available, while the @ symbol indicates where computers are available for public or guest use.

Legal Matters

➡ Cannabis has been legal in Canada since October 2018. However, it is not legal to transport it across national borders.

➡ It's illegal to consume alcohol anywhere other than at a residence or licensed premises; parks, beaches and other public spaces are (officially) off-limits.

➡ The legal drinking age is 18 in Alberta and 19 in BC and the Yukon.

➡ Stiff fines, jail time and penalties apply if you're caught driving under the influence of alcohol or any illegal substance. The blood-alcohol limit is 0.08%, which is reached after just two beers.

➡ Canada has strict regulations banning smoking in all indoor public places and workplaces. Best bet is lighting up in the middle of a big empty parking lot.

LGBT+ Travelers

In BC and Alberta, attitudes toward gays and lesbians are relaxed, especially in urban areas such as Vancouver and Calgary where there are dedicated rainbow-hued nightlife scenes. BC was one of the first places in the world to legalize same-sex marriage in 2003.

While you won't find such an open gay and lesbian culture in other parts of the region, attitudes are pretty liberal throughout the provinces and in the Yukon. That said, the lack of prominent gay and lesbian communities outside urban centers tends to mean that most people keep their orientation to themselves.

The following are useful resources for gay travelers:

Travel Gay (www.travelgay.com/destination/gay-canada) Listings for hotels, bars, clubs and saunas.

Qmunity (www.qmunity.ca) Online resources for the community throughout BC.

Daily Xtra (www.dailyxtra.com) Source for gay and lesbian news nationwide.

Gay Van (www.gayvan.com) Listings and events in Vancouver and beyond.

Maps

➡ Bookstores, gas stations and convenience stores sell a wide variety of maps, ranging from regional overviews to detailed street atlases.

➡ Topographic maps are recommended for extended hikes or multiday backcountry treks. The best are the series of 1:50,000 scale maps published by the government's Centre for Topographic Information (www.nrcan.gc.ca). These are sold around the country; check the website for vendors. You can also download and print maps from www.geobase.ca.

➡ Gem Trek Publishing (www.gemtrek.com) offers some of the best Rocky Mountains maps in scales from 1:35,000 to 1:100,000.

Money

The Canadian dollar ($) is divided into 100 cents (¢). Coins come in 5¢ (nickel), 10¢ (dime), 25¢ (quarter), $1 (loonie) and $2 (toonie) pieces. Notes come in $5, $10, $20, $50 and $100 denominations; $100 bills can prove difficult to cash. There are no 2¢ or 1¢ coins. Bills are rounded up or down to the nearest 5¢.

ATMs

ATMs are common throughout BC, Alberta and the larger towns of the Yukon. Canadian ATM fees are generally low, but your bank at home may also charge a fee.

Credit Cards

Credit and debit cards are almost universally accepted; in fact, you'll find it hard or impossible to rent a car, book a room or buy tickets online or over the phone without one.

Currency Exchange

➡ Currency-exchange counters are located at international airports such as Vancouver and Calgary. Exchange offices are common in bigger towns, cities and in tourist destinations such as Whistler and Banff.

➡ Larger banks may exchange currency, and rates are usually better.

➡ US dollars are often accepted by businesses at larger tourist towns such as Victoria and Whistler, especially in gift shops, but rates typically are not favorable.

Tipping

Tipping is expected in Canada. Typical rates:

Bar servers $1 per drink

Hotel bellhops $1 to $2 per bag

Hotel room cleaners $2 per day

Restaurant wait staff 15%

Taxi drivers 10% to 15%

Opening Hours

The following standard opening hours apply throughout the region. Note that many attractions have reduced hours in the low season.

Banks 9am or 10am–5pm Monday to Friday; some open 9am to noon Saturday

Bars 11am–midnight or later; some only open from 5pm

Post offices 9am–5pm Monday to Friday; some open on Saturday

Restaurants breakfast 7am–11am, lunch 11:30am–2pm, dinner 5pm–9:30pm (8pm in rural areas)

Shops 10am–5pm or 6pm Monday to Saturday, noon–5pm Sunday; some (especially in malls) open to 8pm or 9pm Thursday and/or Friday

Supermarkets 9am–8pm; some open 24 hours

Post

➡ Canada Post (www.canadapost.ca) is reliable and easy to use. Red storefronts around towns and cities denote main branches.

➡ Full-service Canada Post counters are ubiquitous in the back of convenience stores, drugstores and supermarkets. Look for the signs in windows. Often have longer opening hours than branches.

➡ Hotels may sell individual stamps; books of stamps available in many convenience stores.

➡ Rates for postcards and letters are $1.27 to the US, and $2.65 to the rest of the world.

Aside from the public holidays enjoyed by everyone across the region, BC, Alberta and the Yukon have their own distinctive extra days off when they spend at least a couple of hours phoning their friends across the country to brag about not having to go into work. On these days you can expect shops and businesses to be operating on reduced hours (or to be closed), so plan ahead. The region's separate public holidays:

BC Day Officially called British Columbia Day, this welcome August holiday (a trigger for many locals to take a summertime long weekend away) was introduced in 1974 and was intended to recognize the pioneers that kick-started the region.

Discovery Day The Yukon's mid-August holiday marks the 1896 gold discovery in Bonanza Creek that triggered the Klondike gold rush. It starts a week-long Dawson City festival that includes historic recreations.

Aboriginal Day Instituted in 2017 in the Yukon to celebrate Indigenous culture and traditions.

Family Day This February statutory holiday was instituted in Alberta in 1990 and in BC in 2013. It does not exist (yet) in the Yukon.

Public Holidays

National public holidays are celebrated throughout Canada. BC, Alberta and the Yukon each observe an additional statutory holiday – often called a 'stat' – at separate times of the year. Banks, schools and government offices (including post offices) close, and transportation, museums and other services may operate on a Sunday schedule.

Many stores open on Boxing Day, but some are closed.

Holidays falling on a weekend are usually observed the following Monday. Long weekends are among the busiest on the region's roads and ferry routes.

New Year's Day January 1

Family Day second Monday in February in BC; third Monday in February in Alberta

Easter (Good Friday and Easter Monday) March/April

Victoria Day Monday preceding May 25

Aboriginal Day June 21; Yukon only

Canada Day July 1

BC Day first Monday in August; BC only

Discovery Day third Monday in August; Yukon only

Labour Day first Monday in September

Thanksgiving second Monday in October

Remembrance Day November 11

Christmas Day December 25

Boxing Day December 26

Safe Travel

The region is relatively safe for visitors.

➡ Purse snatching and pickpocketing occasionally occur, especially in city areas; be vigilant with your personal possessions.

➡ Theft from unattended cars is not uncommon; never leave valuables in vehicles where they can be seen.

BEAR AWARE

Bears are rarely in the business of attacking humans but, if provoked, they'll certainly have a go. And it won't be pretty. Most bear attacks on tourists result from ignorance on the part of the visitor, so keep the following points in mind when you're on the road in bear country.

➡ When on foot, travel in groups. Consider wearing bear bells as a way to make some noise – bears will generally steer clear of you if they know where you are.

➡ Follow any notices you see about bears in the area and ask park staff about recent sightings.

➡ Keep pets on a leash and do not linger near any dead animals.

➡ Never approach a bear, and keep all food and food smells away from bears; always use bear-resistant food containers.

If the above fails and a bear attacks, do the following:

➡ Don't drop your pack – it can provide protection.

➡ Try to walk backwards slowly without looking the bear in the eye – this is seen as a challenge.

➡ Don't run – a bear will always outrun you.

➡ Try to get somewhere safe, like a car.

➡ If attacked, use bear spray. If this fails, deploy one of the following approaches, depending on the type of bear: for black bears, try to appear larger, shout a lot and fight back; for grizzlies, playing dead, curling into a ball and protecting your head is recommended.

➡ Persistent street begging can be an issue for some visitors to Vancouver; just say 'Sorry,' and pass by if you're not interested but want to be polite.

➡ A small group of hard-core scam artists works Vancouver's downtown core, singling out tourists and asking for 'help to get back home.' Do not let them engage you in conversation.

➡ Rural BC contains large tracts of wilderness. Before venturing out, wise up on avalanche dangers, recent wildlife activity and trail conditions. If traveling alone or in a small group, always let someone know your route plan.

Telephone

➡ Always dial all 10 digits even if calling a number within the same area code. To dial long distance within this region, or any other region within North America,

dial ☑1 then the 10-digit number.

➡ To call from outside North America, dial ☑011 followed by the country code and the 10-digit number. The country code for Canada is ☑1.

➡ Pay phones are increasingly rare. You'll need coins or a long-distance phone card, available from convenience stores, post offices and gas stations. Shop around for the best deal.

Cell Phones

➡ Local SIM cards can be used in unlocked European and Australian GSM cell phones. Other phones must be set to roaming – be wary of charges.

➡ SIMs generally cost less than $50, and should include some talk minutes.

➡ Much of the backcountry has no cell-phone signal.

➡ Cell phones use the GSM and CDMA systems, depending on the carrier.

Time

➡ Most of BC and the Yukon operates on Pacific Time, which is eight hours behind Greenwich Mean Time.

➡ Alberta and parts of southeast and northeast BC are on Mountain Time, which is one hour ahead of Pacific Time.

➡ Clocks are turned forward one hour on the second Sunday in March and are turned back one hour on the first Sunday in November.

➡ Canada's time zones mirror those across the border in the US.

Toilets

Compared to the rest of the world, Canadian public toilets are clean, properly stocked and relatively widespread. If you're caught short, pub-lic libraries, departments stores, shopping malls and larger public parks all have washrooms.

Tourist Information

Official websites are useful for trip planning and you'll find hundreds of visitor centers across the region. Organizations in smaller regions usually operate under the umbrella of these larger bodies:

Destination British Columbia (www.hellobc.com)

Tourism Yukon (www.travelyukon.com)

Travel Alberta (www.travelalberta.com)

Visas

Visa-exempt foreign nationals flying to Canada now require an Electronic Travel Authorization (eTA). This excludes US citizens and those who already have a valid Canadian visa. For more information on the eTA, see www.canada.ca/eta. For visa information, visit the website of **Canada Border Services Agency** (☑204-983-3500; www.cbsa.gc.ca).

Women Travelers

➡ BC, Alberta and the Yukon are generally safe places for women traveling alone, though the usual precautions apply. Just use the same commonsense you would at home.

➡ In Vancouver the Main and Hastings Sts area and Stanley Park are best avoided by solo women after dark.

➡ In more remote parts of the province, particularly in northern BC, women traveling alone will find themselves a distinct minority, though there's no shortage of feisty locals ready to assist a sister in need, especially in the Yukon.

➡ In bars and nightclubs, solo women will probably attract a lot of male attention. If you don't want company, a firm 'No, thank you' typically does the trick. If you feel threatened in an area where there are other people, protesting loudly will usually bring others to your defense.

➡ Note that carrying mace or pepper spray is illegal throughout Canada.

➡ If you are assaulted, call the police immediately. Rape crisis hotlines include those in **Calgary** (☑403-237-5888; www.calgarycasa.com) and **Vancouver** (☑604-872-8212).

Work

➡ In almost all cases, non-Canadians need a valid work permit to get a job in Canada. Obtaining one may be difficult, as employment opportunities go to Canadians first. Some jobs are exempt from the permit requirement.

➡ For full details on temporary work, check with Citizenship & Immigration Canada (www.cic.gc.ca).

➡ Don't try to work without a permit. If you're caught, that will be the end of your Canadian dream.

➡ Short-term jobs, such as restaurant and bar work, are generally plentiful in popular tourist spots such as Whistler and Banff, where the turnover is predictably high. Resort websites often have postings. Resources for potential job seekers:

International Experience Canada (www.cic.gc.ca/english/helpcentre/results-by-topic.asp?top=25)

Student Work Abroad Program (www.swap.ca)

Transportation

GETTING THERE & AWAY

British Columbia and Alberta are directly accessible from international and US destinations, while the Yukon usually requires a plane connection. Flights, cars and tours can be booked online at lonelyplanet.com/bookings.

Entering the Region

When flying into Canada you will be expected to show your passport to an immigration officer and answer a few questions about the duration and purpose of your visit. After clearing customs, you'll be on your way.

Driving across the border from the US can be more complex. Questioning is sometimes more intense and, in some cases, your car may be searched.

Air

BC-bound travelers typically fly into Vancouver. For those heading to the Rockies, arriving in Calgary or Edmonton in Alberta is more convenient; you can then travel to BC via the Rockies before departing from Vancouver. Yukon-bound travelers generally connect to Whitehorse from BC or Alberta.

Airports & Airlines

Abbotsford International Airport (www.abbotsfordairport.ca)

Calgary international Airport (www.yyc.com)

Edmonton International Airport (www.flyeia.com)

Kamloops Airport (www.kamloopsairport.com)

Vancouver International Airport (www.yvr.ca)

Victoria International Airport (www.victoriaairport.com)

Whitehorse International Airport (www.hpw.gov.yk.ca)

Air Canada (☑888-247-2262; www.aircanada.com) and **WestJet** (☑888-937-8538; http://westjet.com) are the main Canadian airlines serving this region, while many international airlines from Europe, Asia and beyond also fly in.

Land

BC is well served by major driving routes, trains and long-distance bus services from across Canada and the US.

From the USA

BORDER CROSSINGS

Many points of entry on the US–Canada border are open 24 hours. The exceptions are some minor entry points and those in the Yukon that have limited hours and/or close for the season. Entering Canada by land from the US is usually smooth at the dozens of border crossings from continental US and Alaska,

---

CLIMATE CHANGE & TRAVEL

Every form of transport that relies on carbon-based fuel generates CO_2, the main cause of human-induced climate change. Modern travel is dependent on airplanes, which might use less fuel per kilometer per person than most cars but travel much greater distances. The altitude at which aircraft emit gases (including CO_2) and particles also contributes to their climate change impact. Many websites offer 'carbon calculators' that allow people to estimate the carbon emissions generated by their journey and, for those who wish to do so, to offset the impact of the greenhouse gases emitted with contributions to portfolios of climate-friendly initiatives throughout the world. Lonely Planet offsets the carbon footprint of all staff and author travel.

but there may be a delay on weekends – especially holiday weekends – particularly at the I-5/Hwy 99 crossing south of Vancouver, where you may have to wait several hours. Either avoid crossing during these times or drive to another Lower Mainland crossing, such as Aldergrove.

See www.borderlineups.com for live cameras showing the situation at major crossings as well as stats on wait times.

Passports are required and you must comply with any necessary visas (p307) or visa-waiver requirements.

BUS

Buses travel from the US to destinations in BC and Alberta, where you can connect with Whitehorse in the Yukon.

Vehicles stop at border crossings, and passengers typically have to get off and have passports and visas processed individually.

The following services all have onboard wi-fi:

Bolt Bus (☑1-877-265-8287; www.boltbus.com) Cross-border services to Vancouver from Bellingham, Seattle and Portland. Bargain prices available if booked far enough in advance.

Greyhound (☑800-661-8747; www.greyhound.ca) The only surviving service in Western Canada is the thrice-daily bus between Vancouver and Seattle. Book tickets online in advance for best prices.

Quick Coach Lines (☑800-665-2122; www.quickcoach.com) Express buses between Seattle, Seattle's Sea-Tac International Airport and downtown Vancouver.

CAR & MOTORCYCLE

The US highway system connects directly with Canadian roads at numerous points along BC and Alberta borders. Gas (petrol) is generally cheaper in the US, so fill up before you head north: Vancouver has a reputation for having some of North America's highest pump prices.

Cars rented in the US can generally be driven over the Canadian border and back, but double-check your rental agreement. Extra charges often apply for each day you spend across the border. Make sure you have all your rental paperwork to hand when crossing the border.

The Blaine Peace Arch and Pacific Hwy border crossings near Vancouver are the region's busiest, especially on holiday weekends. Consider the quieter Lynden or Sumas crossings instead. This can sometimes save an hour or two in travel time.

TRAIN

Amtrak (☑215-856-7925; www.amtrak.com) Trundles into Vancouver from US destinations south of the border, including Bellingham, Seattle and Portland. Be aware that buses operate instead of trains on some runs; check at time of booking. You can also connect from San Francisco, Los Angeles, Chicago and beyond. Book ahead for best fares.

Rocky Mountaineer (☑604-606-7245; www.rockymountaineer.com) Luxury train operator offers some departures from Seattle to mountain hot spots north of the border. Note, this is a tourist train and way more expensive than a conventional train.

From Canada
BUS

Rider Express (☑1-833-583-3636; www.riderexpress.ca) has services from Edmonton to Saskatoon, where you can connect onto Regina.

TRAIN

VIA Rail's (☑888-842-7245; www.viarail.ca) *Canadian* service trundles into Edmonton, Jasper and Vancouver from Toronto three times a week. It's a slow but highly picturesque trip with a range of tickets, from sleeper cabins to regular seats. Book in advance for best prices.

Sea

Cruise ships arrive from south of the border on the highly popular Alaska run, typically stopping in Vancouver, Victoria or other smaller BC ports en route. Ferry services also arrive in BC from Alaska and Washington State. You'll be expected to clear Canadian customs and immigration at your first port of call in the region.

Alaska Marine Highway System (☑250-627-1744, 800-642-0066; www.dot.state.ak.us) Services arrive in Prince Rupert from Alaska.

Black Ball Ferry Line (☑250-386-2202; www.cohoferry.com) Services to Victoria from Port Angeles.

Victoria Clipper (☑250-382-8100; www.clippervacations.com) Services to Victoria from Seattle.

Washington State Ferries (☑206-464-6400; www.wsdot.wa.gov/ferries) Services run from Anacortes to Sidney on Vancouver Island.

GETTING AROUND

Air

WestJet and Air Canada are the dominant airlines servicing the region's towns and cities. An extensive network of smaller operators, often using propeller planes or floatplanes, also provides excellent, but not often cheap, quick-hop services. Reduced fares are typically available for advance booking.

Airlines with services to destinations in BC, Alberta and the Yukon include the following:

Air Canada Express (☑888-247-2262; www.aircanada.com) Regional wing of Canada's national airline, serving dozens of communities in BC, Alberta and beyond.

Air North (📞1-800-661-0407; www.flyairnorth.com) Connecting to Vancouver and serving Yukon communities from its busy Whitehorse base.

Central Mountain Air (📞1-888-865-8585; www.flycma.com) Serving Interior BC, northern BC, Vancouver Island and parts of Alberta.

Harbour Air (📞604-274-1277; www.harbourair.com) Floatplane services to Vancouver, Victoria and around BC.

Pacific Coastal Airlines (📞800-663-2872; www.pacificcoastal.com) Linking BC communities, including Powell River, Tofino and Port Hardy, to Vancouver.

WestJet (📞888-937-8538; http://westjet.com) Canada's second major airline crisscrosses BC, Alberta and beyond with dozens of routes.

Bicycle

Cycling is one of the best ways to get around and immerse yourself in the region. With their ever-increasing bike route networks, cities such as Vancouver and Victoria are especially welcoming to cyclists, and Vancouver has a public bike-share scheme.

➡ Helmets are mandatory in BC (and in Alberta for under-18s).

➡ Many forms of public transportation – the BC Ferries system and Vancouver's TransLink buses, for example – enable you to bring your bike.

➡ Off-road mountain biking is highly popular, with some ski resorts transforming into bike parks in summer.

➡ Bike-hire operators are common, even in smaller towns. You'll likely need a credit card for a deposit. Rental rates are typically from $30 per day.

Area resources:

Alberta Bicycle Association (www.albertabicycle.ab.ca)

British Columbia Cycling Coalition (www.bccc.bc.ca)

Cycling Association of Yukon (www.yukoncycling.com)

HUB (www.bikehub.ca)

Mountain Biking BC (www.mountainbikingbc.ca)

Boat

BC Ferries (📞250-386-3431; www.bcferries.com) runs 35 vessels on 24 routes around the province's coastal waters. Its extensive network includes frequent busy runs on giant 'superferries' between the mainland and Vancouver Island. Many other routes, with much smaller vessels, link shoreline communities and the Gulf Islands. The signature long-haul route is from Port Hardy to Prince Rupert, a day-long glide along the spectacular Inside Passage. The company charitably reduced its fares on many of its routes in 2018.

➡ Many of the routes are vehicle-accessible, but walk-on passengers pay much lower fares.

➡ Low-season fares are usually cheaper.

➡ Larger vessels are equipped with restaurants, shops and (sometimes patchy) wi-fi. Popular routes:

➡ **Lower Mainland to Vancouver Island** The two busiest routes are from Tsawwassen (40 minutes drive south of Vancouver) to Swartz Bay (30 minutes' drive north of Victoria), and from Horseshoe Bay (30 minutes north of downtown Vancouver) to Departure Bay near Nanaimo on central Vancouver Island. Vehicle reservations are recommended for summer and weekend travel.

➡ **Inside Passage** Among one of the most scenic boat trips in the world. Summer service (late June to mid-September) is scheduled for 15-hour daylight runs between Port Hardy (p190) and Prince Rupert (p233), in different directions on alternate days. Sailings between October and May typically include stops in tiny Indigenous villages and can take up to two days. Reserve ahead, especially in summer peak. Additional ferries connect to Haida Gwaii from Prince Rupert.

➡ **Bowen Island** An excellent and accessible day trip from Vancouver. Hop a transit bus from downtown to West Vancouver's Horseshoe Bay terminal, slide through mountain-framed waters for 20 minutes and arrive in Snug Cove for restaurants, shops and scenic walks.

Bus

In such a car-dependent country, bus choice and reach is not extensive. Transit services are most widespread in big cities such as Vancouver, Victoria, Calgary and Edmonton, but are also present in many smaller communities. Greyhound no longer operates in Western Canada (except on the Vancouver–Seattle route). Several private companies have picked up the slack.

Brewster Express (📞403-762-6700; www.banffjaspercollection.com/brewster-express) Runs regular services between Jasper, Banff, Lake Louise and Calgary.

Moose Travel Network (📞604-297-0255; www.moosenetwork.com) Backpacker bus routes across the region, linking Vancouver, Vancouver Island and the Rockies.

Snowbus (www.snowbus.com) Popular winter-only ski-bus service between Vancouver and Whistler.

Tofino Bus (📞250-725-2871; www.tofinobus.com) Operates services between every main town and city on Vancouver Island, many of them former Greyhound Canada routes.

Ebus (☑1-877-769-3287; www.myebus.ca) Connections between Calgary and Edmonton, Vancouver and Kamloops, and Vancouver and Kelowna.

Rider Express (☑1-833-583-3636; www.riderexpress.ca) Daily service between Vancouver and Calgary with stops in between.

BC Bus North (☑1-844-564-7494; www.bcbus.ca) Links half a dozen towns in northern BC.

Car & Motorcycle

Despite the huge area covered by BC, Alberta and the Yukon, driving is the best way to get around. Highways are generally excellent.

Automobile Associations

British Columbia Automobile Association (www.bcaa.com) provides its members, and the members of other auto clubs (such as the AAA in the US), with travel information, maps, travel insurance and hotel reservations. It also provides a service in the Yukon. Alberta Motor Association (www.ama.ab.ca) operates a similar service further east.

Bring Your Own Vehicle

Cars licensed to drive in North America may be driven across the border and into Canada. Make sure you have all your vehicle registration papers, driver's license and proof of insurance.

Hire

Major car-rental firms have offices at airports in BC, Alberta and Whitehorse, as well as in larger city centers. In smaller towns there may be independent firms.

➡ Clarify your insurance coverage for incidents such as gravel damage if you're going to be driving off major paved roads.

➡ Shop around for deals but watch out for offers

that don't include unlimited kilometers.

➡ Never buy the rental-car company's gas if offered when you pick up your car; it's a bad deal. Buy your own and return it full.

➡ If you are considering a one-way rental, be aware of high fees.

➡ Generally you must be over 25 to rent a car, though some companies rent to those aged between 21 and 24 for an additional premium.

➡ Regular rates for an economy-sized vehicle are typically between $45 and $75 per day.

All the usual rental companies operate in the region, including the following:

Avis (☑800-230-4898; www.avis.ca)

Budget (☑800-268-8900; www.budget.ca)

Enterprise (☑844-307-8008; www.enterprise.ca)

Hertz (☑800-654-3001; www.hertz.ca)

National (☑toll free 844-307-8014; www.nationalcar.ca)

Zipcar (☑866-494-7227; www.zipcar.ca)

RECREATIONAL VEHICLES

Recreational vehicles (RVs) are hugely popular in Western Canada, and rentals must be booked well in advance of the summer season.

One-way rentals are possible, but you'll pay a surcharge. Also budget plenty for fuel as RVs typically get miserable mileage.

Large rental companies have offices in Vancouver, Calgary, Whitehorse and bigger BC towns. Operators include the following:

CanaDream (☑888-480-9726, international calls 925-255-8383; www.canadream.com)

West Coast Mountain Campers (☑604-940-2171; https://wcm campers.com)

Driving Licences

Your home driver's license is valid for up to six months in BC. If you plan to drive here for longer, you'll need an International Drivers Permit.

Fuel

Gasoline is sold in liters in Canada, and it's typically more expensive than in the US. Gas prices are usually much higher in remote areas than in the cities. Alberta is cheaper than BC, often by around 30¢ a liter.

Road Hazards

It's best to avoid driving in areas with heavy snow, but if you do, be sure your vehicle has snow tires or tire chains as well as an emergency kit of blankets etc. If you get stuck, don't stay in the car with the engine running: every year people die of

SAMPLE DRIVING DISTANCES

ROUTE	DISTANCE (KM)	TIME (HOURS)
Banff–Fernie	360	4
Calgary–Edmonton	300	3½
Edmonton–Jasper	365	4
Jasper–Banff	290	4
Kelowna–Banff	480	6
Prince George–Prince Rupert	705	8½
Prince Rupert–Whitehorse (via Stewart-Cassiar Hwy)	1375	19
Vancouver–Kelowna	390	4
Vancouver–Prince George	790	9
Whitehorse–Dawson City	530	7

carbon monoxide poisoning. A single candle burning in the car will keep it reasonably warm.

Make sure the vehicle you're driving is in good condition and carry tools, flares, water, food and a spare tire. Rural areas usually do not have cell-phone service.

Be careful on logging roads as logging trucks always have the right of way and often pay little heed to other vehicles. It's best not to drive on logging roads at all during weekday working hours.

Gravel roads – such as those in the Yukon – can take a toll on windshields and tires. Keep a good distance from the vehicle in front. When you see an oncoming vehicle (or when a vehicle overtakes you), slow down and keep well to the right.

Wild animals are a potential hazard. Most run-ins with deer, moose and other critters occur at night when wildlife is active and visibility is poor. Many areas have roadside signs alerting drivers to possible animal crossings. Continuously scan both sides of the road and be prepared to stop or swerve. A vehicle's headlights will often mesmerize an animal, leaving it frozen in the middle of the road.

For updates on driving conditions around the region:

Alberta (www.amaroad reports.ca)

BC (www.drivebc.ca)

Yukon (www.511yukon.ca)

Road Rules

North Americans drive on the right side of the road. Speed limits, which are posted in kilometers per hour in Canada, are generally 50km/h in built-up areas and 90km/h on highways. A right turn is permitted at a red light after you have come to a complete stop, as is a left turn from a one-way street onto another one-way street. U-turns are not allowed. Traffic in both directions must stop when stationary school buses have their red lights flashing – this means that children are getting off and on. In cities with pedestrian crosswalks, cars must stop to allow pedestrians to cross.

Seat-belt use is compulsory in Canada. Children under the age of five must be in a restraining seat. Motorcyclists must use lights and wear helmets. The blood-alcohol limit when driving is 0.08% (about two drinks) and is strictly enforced with heavy fines, bans and jail terms.

Local Transportation

There is excellent, widespread public transportation in Vancouver and Victoria, BC, and in Calgary and Edmonton, Alberta. Outside these areas, service can be sparse or infrequent.

Public transit in Whitehorse will suffice for getting around town, but you'll have a hard time traveling further around the Yukon without a car.

Train

Passenger train services are limited in BC and virtually nonexistent in Alberta.

Rocky Mountaineer

A major player in the region, the luxury **Rocky**

Mountaineer (☑604-606-7245; www.rockymountaineer. com) runs multiday services from Vancouver through the Rocky Mountains into Alberta – for a hefty price (they are sold as vacation packages). Trains travel at 'Polaroid speed,' so you can get all the photos you need.

VIA Rail

Considering the time and cost that went into building Canada's railways, national carrier VIA Rail (p309)offers pretty scant services, including just one route from Vancouver. Book ahead in all cases: advance tickets offer the best deals and there are regular specials online, especially in low season.

Vancouver to Jasper The *Canadian* departs three times a week and makes a few stops in BC before reaching Jasper, Alberta. The 18½-hour trip takes in some beautiful scenery. Fares start at $220 and rise exponentially for a private sleeping cabin with gourmet meals and access to the dome car. From Jasper, connect to Prince Rupert or continue on the *Canadian* through the Prairies and on to Toronto (3½ days from Vancouver).

Jasper to Prince Rupert A daytime-only trip with an overnight stay in Prince George and stops in Terrace, New Hazelton, Smithers, Houston and Burns Lake. You must organize your own lodgings in Prince George. Fares start at $205. Deluxe service with observation car available in summer.

Vancouver Island recently lost its VIA Rail service between Victoria and Courtenay, but there is a determined effort to restore it. For updates, visit www. islandrail.ca·

Behind the Scenes

SEND US YOUR FEEDBACK

We love to hear from travelers – your comments keep us on our toes and help make our books better. Our well-traveled team reads every word on what you loved or loathed about this book. Although we cannot reply individually to your submissions, we always guarantee that your feedback goes straight to the appropriate authors, in time for the next edition. Each person who sends us information is thanked in the next edition – the most useful submissions are rewarded with a selection of digital PDF chapters.

Visit **lonelyplanet.com/contact** to submit your updates and suggestions or to ask for help. Our award-winning website also features inspirational travel stories, news and discussions.

Note: We may edit, reproduce and incorporate your comments in Lonely Planet products such as guidebooks, websites and digital products, so let us know if you don't want your comments reproduced or your name acknowledged. For a copy of our privacy policy visit lonelyplanet.com/privacy.

OUR READERS

Many thanks to the travelers who used the last edition and wrote to us with helpful hints, useful advice and interesting anecdotes: Sarah Burgess, Jenneke Ewals, Roger Farrer, Eric Hoffmann, Marie Fiona Mallon, Dawn Rothwell, Viktoria Urbanek

WRITER THANKS

John Lee

Heartfelt thanks to Maggie for joining me at all those restaurants and for keeping me calm during the brain-throbbing final write-up phase of this project. Thanks also to Max, our crazy-whiskered ginger cat, for sticking by my desk and also reminding me to chase him around the house every once in a while. Cheers also to my brother Michael for visiting from England and checking out some local breweries with me: you really know how to go the extra mile.

Ray Bartlett

Thanks first and foremost, to Buck, for the chance to work on this, and to each of the editors who will peek at it afterwards, and to the great team of co-authors. Thanks as well to my family, friends, and to the incredible collage of folks I met along the way: Kristina, Vera, Rubí, Miro, Allan & Dan, Cat and Greg, Louise and Melva, Alice H, Molly and Spencer (congrats!), Morgan, William Flenders, Josh W, Char, the Lindsays, Riya and many more.

Gregor Clark

Heartfelt thanks to all of the kind Albertans and fellow travelers who shared their love and knowledge of Banff and Jasper – especially Karina Birch, Kate Williams, Ken Wood, Paul Krywicki, Erin Wilkinson, Ed and Vanessa, Shauna and Lindsay. Thanks also to the family and friends who helped me explore Banff and Jasper's trails: Chloe, Sophie, Wes and Ted, that means you! Couldn't have asked for a more delightful research crew.

Craig McLachlan

A hearty thanks to all those who helped out on the road, but most of all, to my exceptionally beautiful wife, Yuriko, who maintained semi-control of my craft beer intake.

Brendan Sainsbury

Many thanks to all the skilled bus drivers, helpful tourist information staff, generous hotel owners, expert burger flippers, unobtrusive bears and numerous passers-by who helped me, unwittingly or otherwise, during my research trip. Special thanks to my wife Liz, my son Kieran and my mother-in-law Ammy for their company (and patience) on the road.

ACKNOWLEDGEMENTS

Climate map data adapted from Peel MC, Finlayson BL & McMahon TA (2007) 'Updated World Map of the Köppen-Geiger Climate Classification', *Hydrology and Earth System Sciences*, 11, 1633–44.

Cover photograph: Lake O'Hara, Yoho National Park, Paul Zizka/Cavan Images ©

THIS BOOK

This 8th edition of Lonely Planet's *British Columbia & the Canadian Rockies* guidebook was curated by John Lee and researched and written by John, Ray Bartlett, Gregor Clark, Craig McLachlan and Brendan Sainsbury. The 7th edition was written by John Lee, Korina Miller and Ryan Ver Berkmoes, and the 6th edition by John Lee, Brendan Sainsbury and Ryan Ver Berkmoes.

This guidebook was produced by the following:

Destination Editor
Ben Buckner

Senior Product Editors
Martine Power, Saralinda Turner

Regional Senior Cartographer Corey Hutchison

Product Editors Ross Taylor, Kate Kiely

Book Designers
Hannah Blackie, Gwen Cotter

Assisting Editors Andrew Bain, Judith Bamber, Michelle Bennett, Lucy Cowie, Emma Gibbs, Carly Hall, Victoria Harrison, Jennifer Hattam, Kellie Langdon, Lou McGregor, Jodie Martire, Christopher Pitts, Simon Williamson

Assisting Book Designer Katherine Marsh

Cover Researcher
Naomi Parker

Thanks to Sasha Drew, Bruce Evans, Andi Jones, Amy Lynch, Lauren O'Connell

BEHIND THE SCENES

Index

Map Pages **000**
Photo Pages **000**

Map Legend

Sights

- Beach
- Bird Sanctuary
- Buddhist
- Castle/Palace
- Christian
- Confucian
- Hindu
- Islamic
- Jain
- Jewish
- Monument
- Museum/Gallery/Historic Building
- Ruin
- Shinto
- Sikh
- Taoist
- Winery/Vineyard
- Zoo/Wildlife Sanctuary
- Other Sight

Activities, Courses & Tours

- Bodysurfing
- Diving
- Canoeing/Kayaking
- Course/Tour
- Sento Hot Baths/Onsen
- Skiing
- Snorkeling
- Surfing
- Swimming/Pool
- Walking
- Windsurfing
- Other Activity

Sleeping

- Sleeping
- Camping
- Hut/Shelter

Eating

- Eating

Drinking & Nightlife

- Drinking & Nightlife
- Cafe

Entertainment

- Entertainment

Shopping

- Shopping

Information

- Bank
- Embassy/Consulate
- Hospital/Medical
- Internet
- Police
- Post Office
- Telephone
- Toilet
- Tourist Information
- Other Information

Geographic

- Beach
- Gate
- Hut/Shelter
- Lighthouse
- Lookout
- Mountain/Volcano
- Oasis
- Park
- Pass
- Picnic Area
- Waterfall

Population

- Capital (National)
- Capital (State/Province)
- City/Large Town
- Town/Village

Transport

- Airport
- BART station
- Border crossing
- Boston T station
- Bus
- Cable car/Funicular
- Cycling
- Ferry
- Metro/Muni station
- Monorail
- Parking
- Petrol station
- Subway/SkyTrain station
- Taxi
- Train station/Railway
- Tram
- Underground station
- Other Transport

Routes

- Tollway
- Freeway
- Primary
- Secondary
- Tertiary
- Lane
- Unsealed road
- Road under construction
- Plaza/Mall
- Steps
- Tunnel
- Pedestrian overpass
- Walking Tour
- Walking Tour detour
- Path/Walking Trail

Boundaries

- International
- State/Province
- Disputed
- Regional/Suburb
- Marine Park
- Cliff
- Wall

Hydrography

- River, Creek
- Intermittent River
- Canal
- Water
- Dry/Salt/Intermittent Lake
- Reef

Areas

- Airport/Runway
- Beach/Desert
- Cemetery (Christian)
- Cemetery (Other)
- Glacier
- Mudflat
- Park/Forest
- Sight (Building)
- Sportsground
- Swamp/Mangrove

Note: Not all symbols displayed above appear on the maps in this book

OUR STORY

A beat-up old car, a few dollars in the pocket and a sense of adventure. In 1972 that's all Tony and Maureen Wheeler needed for the trip of a lifetime – across Europe and Asia overland to Australia. It took several months, and at the end – broke but inspired – they sat at their kitchen table writing and stapling together their first travel guide, *Across Asia on the Cheap*. Within a week they'd sold 1500 copies. Lonely Planet was born.

Today, Lonely Planet has offices in Franklin, London, Melbourne, Oakland, Dublin, Beijing and Delhi, with more than 600 staff and writers. We share Tony's belief that 'a great guidebook should do three things: inform, educate and amuse'.

OUR WRITERS

John Lee
British Columbia Born and raised in the UK, John arrived on Canada's West Coast in 1993 to study at the University of Victoria. Regular trips home to Britain ensued, along with stints living in Tokyo and Montreal, before he returned to British Columbia to become a full-time freelance writer in 1999. You can read some of his stories at www.johnleewriter.com.

Ray Bartlett
Alberta Ray has been travel writing for nearly two decades, bringing Japan, Korea, Mexico, Tanzania, Guatemala, Indonesia and many parts of the United States to life in rich detail for top publishers, newspapers and magazines. Follow him on Facebook, Twitter, Instagram, or contact him for questions or motivational speaking opportunities via www.kaisora.com.

Gregor Clark
Alberta Gregor is a US-based writer whose love of foreign languages and curiosity about what's around the next bend have taken him to dozens of countries on five continents. Since 2000, Gregor has regularly contributed to Lonely Planet guides, with a focus on Europe and the Americas.

Craig McLachlan
British Columbia; Yukon Territory Craig has covered destinations all over the globe for Lonely Planet for two decades. Based in New Zealand for half the year, he then moonlights overseas for the other half, leading tours and writing for Lonely Planet. Check out www.craigmclachlan.com.

Brendan Sainsbury
British Columbia Born and raised in the UK, Brendan didn't leave Blighty until he was 19. Making up for lost time, he's since visited 70 countries. Brendan also wrote the Plan, Understand and Survival sections.

Contributing Author
Michael Grosberg researched and wrote the Waterton Lakes National Park section of the Alberta chapter.

Published by Lonely Planet Global Limited
CRN 554153
8th edition – April 2020
ISBN 978 1 78701 365 0
© Lonely Planet 2020   Photographs © as indicated 2020
10 9 8 7 6 5 4 3 2 1
Printed in China

Although the authors and Lonely Planet have taken all reasonable care in preparing this book, we make no warranty about the accuracy or completeness of its content and, to the maximum extent permitted, disclaim all liability arising from its use.